By Irving B. Richman

CALIFORNIA UNDER SPAIN AND MEXICO, 1535–1847. With Maps, Charts, and Plans.

RHODE ISLAND. AMERICAN COMMONWEALTHS SERIES.

RHODE ISLAND, ITS MAKING AND ITS MEANING.

JOHN BROWN AMONG THE QUAKERS.

APPENZELL, A SWISS STUDY.

CALIFORNIA UNDER SPAIN
AND MEXICO

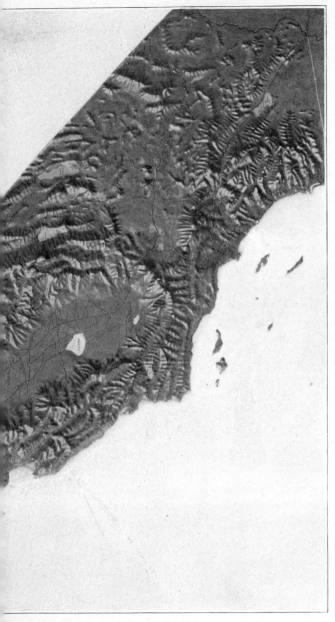

I. RELIEF MAP OF CALIFORNIA

CALIFORNIA UNDER SPAIN AND MEXICO

1535-1847

A CONTRIBUTION TOWARD THE HISTORY OF THE
PACIFIC COAST OF THE UNITED STATES, BASED
ON ORIGINAL SOURCES (CHIEFLY MANU-
SCRIPT) IN THE SPANISH AND
MEXICAN ARCHIVES AND
OTHER REPOSITORIES

BY

IRVING BERDINE RICHMAN, *1861 - 1938.*

WITH MAPS, CHARTS, AND PLANS

BOSTON AND NEW YORK
HOUGHTON MIFFLIN COMPANY
The Riverside Press Cambridge
1911

PREFACE

THE present book, fruit of two years' investigation in California and of much research elsewhere, is designed both for the general reader and for the special student. Its object, first, is to provide, from the original sources, a readable yet concise narrative of the history of California under Spain and Mexico (1535–1847), and second, to equip the narrative with a sufficient apparatus of citation and criticism.

The Atlantic Coast of North America has been dealt with in works elaborate and minute. The Pacific Coast, on the contrary, is as yet nearly a virgin field, few critical monographs having been devoted to it. The consequence is that in this field it is necessary for the historical writer to use the sources directly; and these sources are almost wholly manuscript.

They are contained in two principal repositories, — the National Archives of Spain at Madrid and Sevilla, and the Central Archives of Mexico in Mexico City. For documents pertaining to navigation and exploration, the supreme repository is the General Archives of the Indies at Sevilla, and for documents pertaining to internal administration, the Archivo General, the Museo, and the Biblioteca Nacional of Mexico. In the case of the Spanish Archives, the writer has had the benefit of a tabulation of California materials prepared at Sevilla in 1910, at the instance of Dr. Francis S. Philbrick of the University of Nebraska, and Dr. H. Morse Stephens of the University of California. In the case of the Mexican Archives, he has had the benefit of a systematic search conducted in 1907 and 1908, through the courtesy of the Carnegie Institution of Washington, by Dr. Herbert E. Bolton (now) of Leland Stanford University. Over three thousand index cards to documents bearing upon California were made by Dr. Bolton, and of the documents themselves the most important were copied in full.

Some manuscript material (copies) has been gathered from the British Archives (Public Record Office), through the courtesy of Dr. Ephraim D. Adams of Leland Stanford University, and much from national and private collections in the United States. The Library of Congress (Lowery Collection, New Mexico Documents, and Map Division) has proved rich in the extreme; and the same may be said of the Library of Harvard University (Sparks Collection), of the Lenox Library (Rich Collection), and of the Edward E. Ayer Collection in the Newberry Library in Chicago.

With regard to the collection gathered by Mr. Hubert Howe Bancroft of San Francisco, and now the property of the University of California, there is need of a special word. This unique mass of material affects not alone the history of California, but that of Louisiana, Texas, New Mexico, Arizona, Utah, Washington, Oregon, Old Mexico, Central America, and the Hawaiian Islands. For California its chief sources are: (1) Copies (largely abridged) of the early Spanish Archives of the state, in 69 volumes; (2) the Vallejo Collection of twenty thousand original letters and papers, in 36 volumes; (3) the Thomas O. Larkin private correspondence, in 9 volumes, and correspondence as United States Consul at Monterey, in 2 volumes; (4) the private papers of prominent Californians, such as José de la Guerra of Santa Bárbara, Manuel Castro of Monterey, Juan Bandini, José Ramón Pico and the Estudillos of San Diego, and others; (5) copies of Mission records and papers,

the most extensive being the records of Santa Bárbara, in
12 volumes, and of the California Archbishopric, in 5 volumes; (6) copies of diaries of northern navigation (*Viajes
al Norte*), copies of diaries and of miscellaneous documents
gathered by M. Alphonse Pinart, under the title, *Papelas
Varios*, the Mayer manuscripts (copies), and manuscript
translations of the histories and papers of the Russian-
American Company.

The serviceability of the Bancroft Collection, so far at
least as California is concerned, is in a measure impaired
by the circumstance that Mr. Bancroft and his corps of
assistants used it well-nigh to exhaustion. Within the
range of its materials, not much can be added to what
the Bancroft History itself discloses; yet, despite size and
value, the collection is limited in range and unsymmet-
rical in character. Neither by himself, nor through others,
did Mr. Bancroft make any examination of foreign
archives, — Mexican, Spanish, or British; and but little
examination of foreign private manuscript collections or of
domestic collections outside of California. For the period
of early voyages and exploration in the Pacific, and of the
occupation of California (1535–1770), the collection is very
incomplete; and for subsequent periods it lacks, in whole or
in part, many sets of documents of the first importance.
These *lacunæ*, it is but just to observe, are better known
to the curator of the collection than to any one else, and
are being rapidly overcome by the addition of transcripts
from the archives of Spain.

In the present book, the new materials for California
history — those gleaned by the writer from foreign
sources, and from home sources other than the Bancroft
Collection, and such as have been gleaned by a careful re-
examination of the Bancroft Collection itself — are in the
case of each chapter listed and cited in notes at the end

of the volume. Many of the most valuable sources used in the Bancroft History are cited in it as "MS." These sources, when cited in the notes, are assigned by volume and page to their place in the Bancroft Collection.

Attention is directed not alone to the text and notes, but to the accompanying maps, a list of which follows the table of contents. The map and the diagram ("Spanish and American Trails of the Southwest affecting California," and "Secularization in Alta California") and the chart of galleon routes in the Pacific have been prepared by special hands under the direction of the writer.

It has been said that by reason of the virgin character of the field, and of the lack therein of critical monographs, a writer upon Pacific Coast history is compelled to use his materials directly. Scattered as these are throughout the archives and collections of Europe and America, the task is not inconsiderable, for while much rewards him, much eludes his quest.

For services many and unwearied, the writer would express hearty acknowledgment to Miss Anna M. Beckley, head of the reference department of the Public Library of Los Ángeles. He is also especially indebted to Miss Nellie M. Russ, librarian of the Pasadena Public Library, and to Miss Eudora Garoutte, head of the historical department of the California State Library at Sacramento. Others who have rendered aid are Dr. James A. Robertson of the Philippines Libraries, Manila, P. I., Dr. James R. Robertson of Berea College, Kentucky (author of the as yet unprinted monograph, "From Alcalde to Mayor"), Miss Emma Helen Blair of Madison, Wisconsin (co-editor, with Dr. James A. Robertson, of the "Philippine Islands" series), Mr. Zoeth S. Eldredge of San Francisco (author of studies of the Anza routes), Fr. Zephyrin Engelhardt, O. F. M., of Santa Bárbara, Mr. A. S. Macdonald of

Oakland, Mr. Charles F. Lummis and Mr. George L. Lawson of Los Ángeles, Mr. Frederick J. Teggart, curator of the Bancroft Collection, Mr. George Parker Winship, librarian of the John Carter Brown Library, Providence, Rhode Island, Mr. Reuben G. Thwaites of the Wisconsin Historical Society, Miss Ernestina López of San Gabriel, Mr. Byron Olney Lovelace, head ranger of the San Jacinto Forest Reserve, and the librarian and staff of the Public Library of Muscatine, Iowa.

I. B. R.

Muscatine, Iowa, March 1, 1911.

CONTENTS

CONTENTS xiii

LIST OF MAPS, CHARTS, AND PLANS

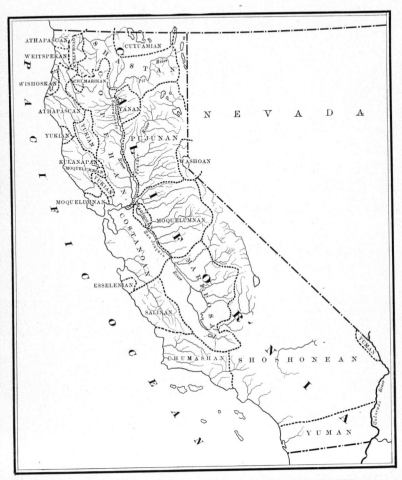

MAP II. INDIANS OF CALIFORNIA BY LINGUISTIC GROUPS

CALIFORNIA UNDER SPAIN
AND MEXICO

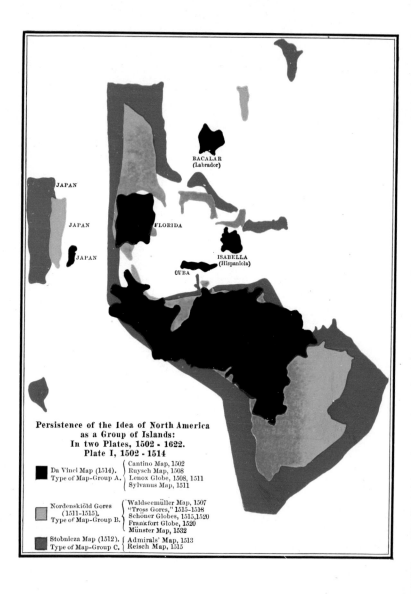

Persistence of the Idea of North America
as a Group of Islands:
In two Plates, 1502 - 1622.
Plate I, 1502 - 1514.

Da Vinci Map (1514).
Type of Map-Group A.
{ Cantino Map, 1502
Ruysch Map, 1508
Lenox Globe, 1508, 1511
Sylvanus Map, 1511 }

Nordenskiöld Gores
(1511-1515).
Type of Map-Group B.
{ Waldseemüller Map, 1507
"Tross Gores," 1515-1518
Schöner Globes, 1515,1520
Frankfort Globe, 1520
Münster Map, 1532 }

Stobnicza Map (1512).
Type of Map-Group C.
{ Admirals' Map, 1513
Reisch Map, 1515 }

BACALAR
(Labrador)

JAPAN

JAPAN

JAPAN

FLORIDA

ISABELLA
(Hispaniola)

CUBA

**Persistence of the Idea of North America
as a Group of Islands:
In two Plates, 1502 - 1622.
Plate II, 1529 - 1622**

Verrazzano Map (1529). Type of Map-Group
including Maiollo Map (1527) and Agnese Map (1536).

Gastaldi Map (1554). Type of Small Map-Group
including Lok Map of 1582.

Kaspar van Baerle (Herrera) Map (1622). Type of Map-Group
possessing many Representatives Down to 1746.

Alaska as an Island.
J. von Staehling Map, 1768.

CALIFORNIA UNDER SPAIN AND MEXICO

CHAPTER I

DISCOVERY

THE discovery of California — Lower and Upper (Baja and Alta) — was a result of the idea that North America constituted a group of islands — an archipelago — near the coast of Asia, screening the latter with its silks and porcelains from European observation and approach.[1]

Of this idea, sixteenth-century cartography from 1501 to 1520 shows in numerous instances the prevalence and persistence. In the Ruysch map of 1508, "Spagnola" is represented as off the coast of "Tebet Magni"; in the Sylvanus map of 1511, Cuba, Hayti, and Labrador not only lie off the Asiatic coast, but are near one another; in the Da Vinci map of (circa) 1514, the group of islands consists of Cuba, Labrador, and Florida; while on the Nordenskiöld Gores of 1511–15 and the Schöner globes of 1515 and 1520, Cuba forms a group with Japan. And when, for certain regions, the idea in question had to be abandoned, cartography shows that it was abandoned reluctantly. The areas that once had been islands now were joined, but by bands tentative and easily to be sundered. On the Ptolemic map of 1530 and the Ruscelli map of 1544, Labrador and Florida are united by a slender isthmus, an isthmus that in the Münster map of 1545 significantly gives place to a strait bearing the legend: *Per hoc fretu iter patet ad Molucas.* It is true that in the Castillo map of 1541, and other maps down to 1622, California is set down as peninsular, but in a whole series of maps dated between 1622 and 1746 the peninsula is replaced by an island.[2]

North America, then, while a barrier to Asia, was a barrier to be penetrated, and by the close of the first quarter of the sixteenth century various attempts to this end had been made: by John Cabot in 1497; by Gaspar and Miguel Cortereal in 1500–02; by Giovanni da Verrazzano in 1524. But the only attempt that thus far could in any wise be accounted successful was by Fernão de Magalhães (Magellan) in 1520, and it was by way, not of North America, but of the continent to the south.

The fact, however, that one strait from sea to sea had unquestionably at last been found, stimulated search for another, and among those most ardent in this search was Hernán Cortés. In his *Carta Cuarta* (Fourth Dispatch) to Charles V, dated October 15, 1524, Cortés ventures the opinion that a strait will be discovered "on the Florida [Atlantic] Coast, running into the South Sea [Pacific]"; and that "if found according to a true chart [which he has] of that part of the sea near the archipelago which Magellan discovered, it seems that it [the strait] must issue very near there [the archipelago]. . . . If," he continues, "it please our Lord that the said strait joins there, the voyage to the Spice Islands will be so convenient for these your Majesty's dominions that it will be two thirds shorter than the present course,[3] and without any hazard to the ships in going or coming; for the voyage will be entirely among states and countries [large and rich] belonging to your Majesty. Therefore," concludes Cortés, "acquainted as I am with your Majesty's desire of knowing this strait, . . . I have laid aside all other profits and advantages . . . in order to follow entirely this course." [4]

And follow it the Spanish leader did with characteristic determination. In 1526 he made ready to send a fleet from Zacatula, but was prevented by a royal order diverting the vessels to the relief of the missing navigator Jofre de Loaysa. In 1532 he did send (from Acapulco) Diego Hurtado de Mendoza and Juan de Mazuela with two ships; and in 1533 (from Tehuantepec), Diego Bezerra de Mendoza and Hernando de Grijalva with two ships. By the first expedition nothing of importance was accomplished; but by the second, — or rather by Bezerra's ship, after the latter through a mutiny had passed under the control of Fortuno Ximénes, chief pilot, — Lower California was discovered at Santa Cruz Bay.

Here was something tangible both towards "large and rich countries" (the bay was reputed rich in pearls) and towards new islands and straits (the spot was reached by sailing away from the mainland), and Cortés resolved to inspect it personally. He set forth in 1535, and on May 3 anchored at Santa Cruz (La Paz). It was while here, between 1535 and 1537, endeavoring to found a colony, that the Spanish leader, according to the historian Herrera, called the waste about him California; and that, according to Bernal Díaz, he and his island (*su isla*) were heartily cursed by his followers, — a starving band. [5]

Cortés in 1540 returned to Spain, but meanwhile (1539) one of his captains at La Paz (Francisco de Ulloa) explored the Gulf of California to the mouth of the Colorado River, proving as conclusively as ineffectually that California was not an island. [6] Meanwhile, also, Don Antonio de Mendoza, Viceroy of New Spain, and Pedro de Alvarado, Governor of Guatemala, allured by a fabulous tale of treasure to the northwest, — the tale of the Seven Cities of Cibola, — prepared, each, an expedition to fare in quest of it, — the Coronado-Alarcón expedition of Mendoza, and the so-called Navidad expedition of Alvarado. By the one, or rather the Alarcón part of it, the Gulf of California (Domingo del Castillo, *piloto*) was reëxplored and its shores charted.[7] By the other there was brought to notice the Portuguese navigator, Juan Rodríguez Cabrillo.

It is to Cabrillo that the discovery and exploration of the California of to-day — the California that forms a part of the American Union — was due. This captain had been hired by Alvarado for his projected expedition to the north, and upon the death of the latter, which occurred in 1541, Cabrillo was confirmed in employment by Mendoza. He was intrusted with two small ships, — the San Salvador and the Victoria, — and with them sailed from La Navidad on June 27, 1542. On September 28 he came to anchor in San Diego Bay, at the southwestern extremity of Upper or Alta California, and on October 18 landed at San Miguel Island. Here he had the misfortune to fall and break his arm near the shoulder. On January 3, 1543, Cabrillo died from the effects of his broken arm, at San Miguel, where his ships had temporarily returned, and the command devolved on Bartolomé Ferrelo, a native of the Levant. Before expiring, Cabrillo had given orders that the work of discovery was in nowise to be intermitted because of him; and under Ferrelo it was carried (by March 1) as far north as 42°, — the latitude of the boundary line, as later established, between California and Oregon.

It will thus be seen that by the expedition under Juan Rodríguez the entire coast line, or western boundary, of Alta California was traversed. Nor was the task inadequately performed. The ships crept warily along from point to point, anchoring at night and exploring by day. So progressing, it was noted that just below San Diego the bare, sandy land which had extended from "the extremity of Lower California [Cape San Lucas] to this place," gave way to "a country of beautiful vegetation"; that the course of the ship was closely watched by the Indians, for "great signal smokes were kindled on shore"; that, indeed, Indians could be induced to come on board, and that they spoke of "men like us traveling in the interior," — men "with beards, and armed with cross-bows and swords, and riding on horseback"; that lying off the coast were a number of large islands, — Las Islas de San Lucas, — the islands of the Santa Bárbara Channel; that near Punta de Arenas there were visible "grand sierras covered with snow," and that northward from Cape San Martín "all the coast is very bold with mountains that rise to the sky, and against which the sea beats, and which appear as if they would fall upon the ships," — La Sierra Nevada. It moreover was noted that around Cape Mendocino (not then named) the winds were boisterous and the sea high, so that, "coming from many parts and breaking over the ships," it forced the seamen as good Spaniards and devout Catholics to "commend themselves to our Lady of Guadalupe" and to "make their wills." [8]

By way of boundary for Alta California on the east, naught in the sixteenth century existed, save, to the north, mountains, and to the south, desert and the Colorado River. Of these the mountains stood in a grandeur as yet unlooked upon; while the desert and the river had been scanned, the former by Friar Marcos and the followers of Coronado, and the latter by Ulloa and Alarcón. Yet, undefined as the eastern boundary of necessity was, there lay between it (in the course that one day it was to take) and the Pacific a world of natural wonders, — wonders of topography, of climate, and of living things.

In the topographical domain came first the Coast Range, extending from the present Oregon to Point Conception, and attaining an elevation of between two thousand and eight thousand feet. Below Point Conception this range was broken by small, fertile valleys, drained seaward by slender rivers. Above the Point, the range near its centre gave way suddenly to the passage since known as the Golden Gate; [9] while north of its centre it was pierced by deep canyons conducting rivers that were turbulent and swift. Next came the Sierra Nevada Range, mingling with the Coast Range at the north, and then, after a sharp divergence to the east, extending south for some four hundred miles, to mingle again with the latter at Tehachapi and the heights of San Rafael, — a conjunction serving later to demark Northern from Southern California.

The Sierra Nevada Range, steep on its eastern face, comprehended the most imposing examples of North American scenery. Two of its peaks (Whitney and Shasta) peered sublimely down 14,522 and 14,440 feet. One of its valleys (Death Valley) crouched 200 feet below sea level. Its passes averaged 11,000 feet. One of its waterfalls (the Yosemite) plunged to a death in spray at 2600 feet. Its forests contained the largest and oldest of growing things on earth, — trees 300 feet high and over 30 feet in diameter; trees between three thousand and five thousand years old, — older than the Spanish monarchy and all Christendom; while from an altitude of 8000 feet, more than a thousand lakes mirrored the clouds and flashed back the sun.

Separating the Coast Range and that of the Sierra Nevada, lay a great plain, four hundred miles long and between thirty-five and sixty miles wide; [10] and this, from the north and south respectively, was drained by two partially navigable streams (the Sacramento and the San Joaquín), which poured their combined waters into the sheltered basin now known as San Francisco Bay. Nor was this all, for, skirting the base of the Sierra Nevada,[11] there stretched to the Colorado River miles upon miles of alkaline desert, — desert sought valiantly to be reclaimed by sentinel yucca and sprawling cactus, but everywhere white, sun-tortured, and drear.

In respect to climate, Alta California presented that diversity which might be looked for in a region extending through nearly ten degrees of latitude, and composed of seacoast, mountain, valley, and plain. A cold current washed the coast as far south as Point Conception, — a current attended by fogs and humidity; but below the Point the coast was deflected sharply to the eastward. This deflection gave to the southern part immunity from cold on the west; while the Sierra Nevada on the northeast was a great wall shielding that part from continental rigors, and husbanding its sunshine.[12] Here in summer the winds prevailed from the northwest, bringing drought; and in winter from the southeast, bringing rain; and with the rain came, first, greenness, and then, throughout all the valleys and to the summits of the hills, a riotous procession of the flowers, — golden poppies, buttercups, daisies, pinks, nemophilas, roses, violets, larkspurs, and lilies; purple pressing hard upon gold; blue upon purple; and pink and white upon blue.[13] The land, withal, at least in the coast valleys, was vexed by no violent storms of thunder and lightning, though there were not infrequent shocks of earthquake.

Last of the wonders mentioned as embraced within the limits of California at the time of the discovery were living things; and these were as varied as the topography and the climate. Along the coast might be found the whale, the sea-otter, and the seal; in the mountains, the grizzly and the brown bear, the puma, the wildcat, and the mountain sheep; in the forests and opens, the elk, the black-tailed deer, and the antelope. The thickets and streams swarmed with grouse, geese, and ducks. The air harbored the eagle, the vulture, song-birds, butterflies, and bees. On the desert, lending in a literal sense piquancy to the sands, there lurked the rattlesnake, the gila monster, the scorpion, and the tarantula.

Man alone among the sentient orders seemed inferior in his rôle. The California Indian — he of the typical eighteen small tribes of central California (and excepting always the Athapascán of the extreme northwest, the Shoshone and Yuma of the southeast, and the Chumash of the Santa Bárbara Channel coasts) [14] — was short in stature, dark of color, flat of nose, filthy in habit, a laggard in war, and a poor hunter. He dwelt near the watercourses in villages (rancherías) of dome-shaped huts of reeds, fed upon acorns and seeds, and painted his body. His female was skilled in mats and basketry; but male or female he, ethnically considered, was so far inchoate as to be without the totem, without clan organization. His religion, too (as discriminated from his philosophy), was Shamanism, — wizardism; a religion rendering him a facile dupe to the conjurations of the medicine man. In temper he was docile, and he eschewed the tomahawk, the taking of scalps, and the torture of prisoners; yet, for these very reasons, when compared on the one hand with the Iroquois or Dakota of the north, or on the other with the Apache, Navajo, Mojave, or Yuma of the south, he revealed a paucity of vigor — physical, mental, and spiritual — that was palpable.[15]

But concerning Alta California from the point of view of

its natural wonders, for the present enough. It has been the object of this chapter to show how the early Spaniards in North America, partakers of the spirit of Spain under Charles V, were led in their quest (on the course to Asia) for golden isles and treasured cities, to explore the western, and in part the eastern confines of the California region. It will be the object of the next chapter to relate how this region came to be visited with a view to its permanent occupation.

CHAPTER II

OCCUPATION OF MONTEREY

THE discovery by Magellan (1521) of an archipelago near China (the Philippine Islands) effectually disposed of the theory that North America was merely a group of outposts to Asia; but room was left for the belief that the land, though a continent, was traversed by an interoceanic strait, later called Anian,[1] connecting the Gulf of St. Lawrence with the North Pacific Ocean.

If such a strait existed, the fact was important to Spain, for by means of a passage the sea route from Spain to Asia would, as Cortés himself was to point out, be vastly shortened. Spain, however, having at last finished the work of Columbus and discovered the "Western Islands" (the Philippines), was for the moment too deeply engrossed in seeking to confirm her conquest, to bestow much thought upon Anian; a mental state which in the somewhat curious course of its working-out gave rise to a first attempt to occupy Upper California.

Magellan's expedition came to an end with the return to Spain, in 1522, of one ship, the Victoria. In 1525 García Jofre de Loaysa was sent to continue the work of Magellan, but his ships met with disaster. In 1526 Sebastian Cabot was sent on a like errand, but he got no farther than the coast of South America at the mouth of the Río de la Plata. Hereupon (1526) Cortés, who had been diligently building ships with which to discover "rich countries" (insular, Amazonian, or what not), together with that strait which he was convinced issued "very near" Magellan's archipelago, was directed by Charles V to send ships

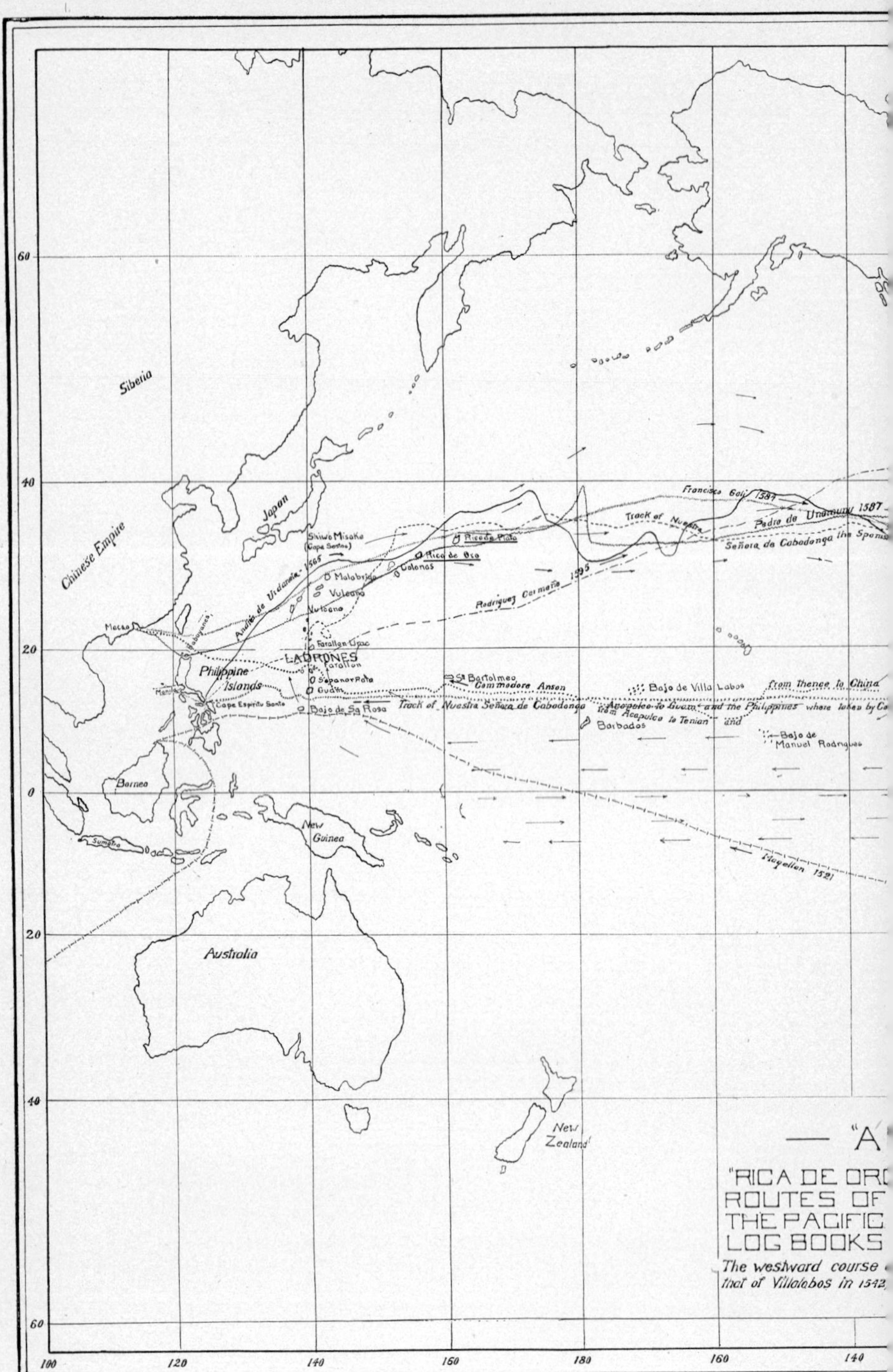
Siberia
Chinese Empire
Japan
Shiwo Misaka (Cape Sestos)
Andres de Urdaneta 1565
Rica de Plata
Rica de Oro
Colonas
Malabrigo
Vulcano
Macao
Philippine Islands
LADRONES
Farallon
Guam
Manila
Cape Espiritu Santo
Bajo de Sa Rosa
Sa Bartolmeo
Commodore Anson
Track of Nuestra Señora de Cabodonga
Acapulco to Guam and the Philippines where taken by
from Acapulco to Tenian and
Barbados
Bajo de Villa Labos
from thence to China
Bajo de Manuel Rodrigues
Rodriguez Cermeño 1595
Francisco Gali 1584
Track of Nuestra
Pedro de Unamunu 1587
Señora de Cabodonga the Spanish
Borneo
Sumatra
New Guinea
Australia
New Zealand
Magellan 1521
60
40
20
0
20
40
60
100
120
140
160
180
160
140
"A"
"RICA DE ORO
ROUTES OF
THE PACIFIC
LOG BOOKS
The westward course
that of Villalobos in 1542,

C

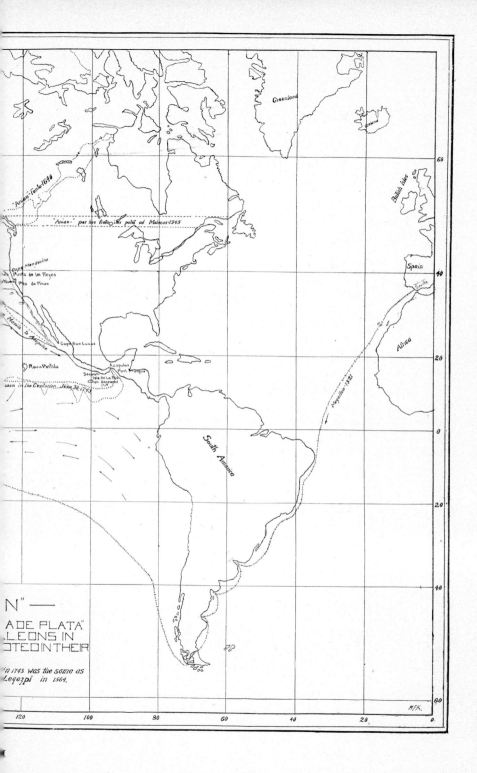

Greenland

Iceland

British Isles

"Anian" Fonte 1640

"Anian." per hoc fretu iter patet ad Malucas 1545

Spain

Cape Mendocino

Sevilla

Punta de los Reyes

Nueva Pta. de Pinos

40

Africa

Manila to Acapulco

Cape San Lucas

20

Roca Partida

Acapulco

Sacatula Isla de La Plata

Port Marques

Dian discovered 1519

ssen in the Eruption June 30, 1773

South America

Magellan 1521

0

20

N" —

A DE PLATA"
LEONS IN
OTED IN THEIR

in 1743 was the same as
Legazpi in 1564.

40

28

M.F.K.

60

120   100   80   60   40   20   0.

to glean news of Loaysa and Cabot. This expedition
(under Álvaro de Saavedra) was no more successful than
had been its predecessors, and so matters remained until
1542. By that time Coronado and Alarcón, by fruitless
journeyings northward, had destroyed Spanish faith in the
"Seven Cities," and shaken it in Anian. When, therefore,
upon Alvarado's death, it fell to the lot of Mendoza to take
entire command, he sent (under Cabrillo) only two ships
to survey the California coast; while, under Ruy López
de Villalobos, he sent six across the Pacific to "note the
products of the Western Islands." Villalobos set sail in
November, and on reaching the Western Islands, so called,
rechristened them Las Philippinas. Otherwise he effected
nothing lasting.[2]

Then came 1556. In that year Charles V abdicated his
throne, kingly and imperial, and Philip II, so far as in him
lay, succeeded to the kingly part. To this time the Moriscos (Christianized descendants of the Moors, and ever in
Spain the most valued element industrially) had carried
on in comparative peace their varied vocations. In the
Alpujarras, southeast of Granada, they cultivated the fig,
the pomegranate, and the orange, as also hemp and the
cereals. Here was grown the mulberry for its silk; and
here, in the valleys and alpine pastures, were herded great
flocks of merino sheep for their wool. Through the Moriscos, the cities of Spain (Córdova, Toledo, Segovia, Sevilla,
Valencia, Valladolid, Granada) were become centres of
manufactures and of trade. Córdova was famed for its
leather, and Toledo for its blades. As late as 1552 Segovia
employed thirteen thousand men (mostly Moriscos) in the
woolen manufacture; and after Philip's accession a like
number were employed in Sevilla in operating her sixteen
thousand looms for wool and silk.[3]

For the products named, and for others, an important

outlet was New Spain. Ever since Cortés in 1519 had established in Mexico the port of Vera Cruz, supplies of all kinds — food, wine, clothing, implements, accoutrements, arms — had annually been sent hither and exchanged for the precious metals. And the cargoes had constantly become greater. The stock of gold rifled by Spain from the Indians had not lasted long,[4] but with the discovery in 1545 of the Peruvian silver-mines of Potosí, and in 1548 of the Mexican mine of Zacatecas, — the former the *raison d'être* for the Panama town of Porto Bello, — silver bullion to the amount of 11,000,000 *pesos* per annum[5] had in considerable part been available to colonial Spaniards for the purchase of those silks, velvets, laces, ribbons, buttons, and gewgaws, which, originally the habit and fancy of the hated Moor, had now become indispensable to the Spaniard himself.

But under Philip II not alone in the Atlantic did commerce thrive between Spain and the New World. It came into existence in the Pacific. At last the Philippine Islands were beginning to pay tribute. In 1564 — twenty-two years after the fruitless expedition of Villalobos — Miguel López de Legazpi was commissioned by Luis de Velasco, successor in the viceroyalty to Mendoza, to subdue the Philippines, and in seven years he performed the task of founding Manila and of establishing trade with Mexico.[6] Little was discovered in the islands that could with advantage be sent to New Spain, but China, Molucca, and Siam were near, and soon the luxurious taste of the conquerors drew from these flowery realms a multitude of costly products: from China, raw silk and velvets, "brocades of gold and silver upon silk," "stuffs of all colors," musk, ivory, cushions, carpets, "caparisons for horses," "preserves of oranges and peaches," "very fine capons," nutmegs, ginger, nuts, "fine thread," writing-boxes, "gilt seats," "caged birds which talk and sing," beads, precious stones, and porcelain; while from Japan were derived "smart screens," cutlery, caskets of wood, and wheaten flour; from Molucca, cotton cloths, muslins, cloves, cinnamon, pepper, amber, "rich hangings and coverlets," jewels, needlework, and lace; and from Siam, ivory, rhinoceros horns, rubies, and sapphires. "Of these goods," says Antonio de Morga (secretary to the governor of the Philippines from 1595 to 1603), "the Spaniards made purchases and shipments for New Spain." In the new moon of March the islands were visited by squadrons of Chinese junks. Late in June a ship, or two ships (at first small, afterwards of galleon size), laden with wares brought by the junks, and with native cinnamon and wax, set sail for Mexico.[7] In the autumn they reached the port of Acapulco, and straightway there was held a thirty days' market.[8]

This, however, was subsequent to 1573. Prior to that year the voyages had not been distinctively commercial. The main object of them had been to find, from Manila eastward, a safe and convenient route. Passing by the north equatorial current readily westward from Acapulco, navigators down to 1565 (Saavedra and Villalobos) had not been able to reverse the process.[9]

The first to trace back a route from Asia were Alonso de Arellano (one of Legazpi's captains) and Andrés de Urdaneta, an Augustinian friar, Legazpi's pilot.[10] Their course, in order to gain a wind, was laid (June, 1565) to the northward of that of Legazpi; and therein they were followed by navigators for twenty years. But the winds upon the new course proved often baffling, and in 1584 Francisco de Gali, under orders from Viceroy Contreras to discover a better course, laid one yet farther north, thereby haply striking the great Japan current, — "a very hollow water and stream running out of the north and northwest," — which carried him "seven hundred leagues," or to within "two hundred leagues" of the coast of Alta California off Cape Mendocino: a point sighted, though not named, by Ferrelo; a point which it is possible that Urdaneta or Gali did name; one from which, in any event, Gali made his way down the California coast to Cape San Lucas and Acapulco.[11]

Gali's route was that afterwards regularly taken by galleons from the Philippines,[12] but important as it was, the voyage was of inordinate length, sometimes 204 days. It was beset by the harassments of vermin, dysentery, beriberi, and scurvy; and, near Cape Mendocino, by those of cold, fogs, and tempests,[13] — conditions which made this cape one as much to be dreaded as formerly had been Bojador on the coast of Africa. Indeed, so formidable to sixteenth-century craft was the Alta California coast along its upper stretches, that in 1595 the galleon San Augustín, pursuing explorations under Sebastián Rodríguez Cermeño, was driven behind Point Reyes into a bay called by Cermeño San Francisco, and wrecked.[14] Still the perils of the California landfall and the distresses of the Manila-Acapulco passage were not without compensation, for they prompted Philip of Spain to reflect upon Alta California as a region (because of probable bays of refuge) first to be carefully surveyed, and then permanently occupied.

But to reflection upon Alta California Philip was prompted by yet another consideration.

A revival of interest in Anian had begun. In 1542 Ferrelo had mistaken the drift from the mouth of some river (not impossibly the Columbia) for a discharge from Anian, and in 1561 Urdaneta, inditing a memorial to the King, had asked what there might be in the rumor that the French had discovered a westward route "between the land of the Baccalos [Labrador] and the land north of it."

Furthermore, in 1584 Gali had thought the deflection of the Japan current, near the California coast, an indication of a "channell or straight passage betweene the firme lande of Newe Spaine and the countreys of Asia and Tartaria." The queries of Ferrelo and Urdaneta (now that Spain was in the Philippines, — now that the East had actually been gained by sailing west) may be regarded as stimulated by the belief that, as all nature abhorred a vacuum, so equally all nature "cried aloud for a Northwest Passage"; but not so the query of Francisco de Gali. Behind it lay a fact of far-reaching import.

England, under Elizabeth, was attaining to national self-confidence upon the sea. In 1545 the tonnage of the island, according to the seventeenth-century London merchant, Sir Joshua Child, "had been inconsiderable, and the merchants very mean and few." But, after 1560, owing to the effect, in combination, of an economic dislocation of classes and of the allurements of Spanish treasure, English maritime activity had risen rapidly. In 1562 John Hawkins of Devonshire, by a slaving voyage, had "opened the road to the West Indies." In 1572 Francis Drake (Hawkins's kinsman) had surprised a Spanish caravan on its way from Panama to Nombre de Dios, and carried away gold, jewels, and silver bars. In 1578–79 the same Francis Drake had passed the Strait of Magellan, sailed up the South American coast, captured vessels little and big, including a Philippine galleon, and stowed the hold of his own ship, the Golden Hind, with silver bars "the bignes of a brick-bat eche." The adventurous Englishman had sought a route homeward by the Northwest Passage, but, failing to find it "where the north and northwest winds send abroad their frozen nimphes to the infecting the whole aire with insufferable sharpnesse," had run down the coast of California, called by him New Albion, to

Francis Drake's Bay (the San Francisco Bay of Cermeño),[15] overhauled there his ship, and reached Plymouth by way of the Cape of Good Hope in 1580.

Although Drake had not found Anian, the fact of his appearance in the Pacific at the sources of Spanish wealth (Peru and Mexico) was startling to thoughtful Spaniards. The English seaman had got safe home with half a million of treasure. What might not happen if Anian not only should be found, but be found by the English? As if to meet this reflection, Urdaneta's query of 1561 and Gali's of 1584 were revived in 1586. In that year a memorial to Philip II was prepared and signed by the members of the Royal Audiencia of the Philippine Islands, voicing, among other recommendations, this: That China be immediately occupied by Spain in order to "forestall the danger that the French and English and other heretics and northern nations will discover and navigate that strait which certainly lies opposite those regions, — that of Labrador, as those people say." [16]

Not yet, however, was Philip sufficiently roused with regard to Anian to give specific orders for the occupation of Alta California, the land (supposedly) of its western outlet. A more drastic stimulus than a memorial was required, and this was supplied by the Englishman Thomas Cavendish. He set sail with three small ships from Plymouth, in 1586, and reached the Pacific in February, 1587. Having harried the coast of Mexico, he passed with two ships to Cape San Lucas, in October, and there lay in wait for the annual Philippine galleon. The galleon of 1587 was the Santa Ana, described by Domingo de Salazar, Bishop of the Philippines, as "the richest ship to leave these islands," — a ship laden with "a thousand *marcos* of registered gold" and as much unregistered; with "twenty-two and one half *arrobas* of musk, an abundance of civet, many pearls, and the richest of silks and brocades." All this merchandise, with the ship itself, fell into Cavendish's hands after a fight of five hours. The prize was brought to shore, and, the best of the cargo having been appropriated, she was set on fire and left to her fate. Cavendish with one ship, the Desire, returned home, as had Drake, by way of the East Indies.[17]

Prior to the expedition of Drake, protection for the silver ships from Mexico had, even in the Atlantic, not been for Spain a serious problem;[18] and prior to the expedition of Cavendish, protection for the Philippine galleons had not even been thought of. It is true that after the return of Hawkins from the West Indies in 1564, the dispatches of De Silva (Spanish ambassador at London), recounting Hawkins's proceedings, had wrung from Philip startled interjections of "*Ojo! Ojo!*" But, down to 1587, so certain were the governors of the Philippines that naught of evil could befall in the Pacific, that, as Santiago de Vera wrote after the capture of the Santa Ana, "As no other ships but ours have ever been sighted on this voyage, which is through so remote regions, they have always sailed with little or no artillery and with as little fear from corsairs as if they were on the river of Sevilla."[19] Rude, therefore, was the awakening by Cavendish; so rude that surprise is hardly felt when Salazar complains to Philip that "an English youth of but twenty-two years, with a wretched little vessel and forty or fifty companions," has wrought vast damage and got away "laughing."

Cavendish's voyage performed, the culmination of the Anian question — the question of an interoceanic strait capable of seizure by the English — was rapid. Interest, between 1587 and 1592, led to the claim by various pilots (Maldonado and Juan de Fuca) of having passed through the strait. One memorial in particular invites attention.

It was prepared at Manila in 1597 by Hernando de Los
Ríos Coronel, advocated a search for Anian, and in due
time was placed in the hands of Philip.[20] But already (at
last) that procrastinating ruler had been made alive to the
reasons for the occupation of Alta California, — reasons
alike of maritime need and colonial defense, — and had
permitted to be sent northward Sebastián Vizcaino.

Of Vizcaino we hear first in 1593. In that year he, an
humble trader, applied to Viceroy Luis de Velasco for permission to engage in the pearl-fishery in the Gulf of California. Accordingly in 1594 there was revived to him, with
certain partners (Gonzalo Rodríguez Calvo, Mateo de
Solís, Melchor de las Roclas, and others), a twenty-year
merced (license) issued by the Archbishop of Mexico, on
August 7, 1585, to another company (Hernando de Santo-
tis and partners). Under the license, the company grantee
might, on payment of the usual royalties, "fish for pearls,
cod, sardines," etc., on the coast of the South Sea, "from
la Navidad to California." The company was to choose
one of its members as captain, and the latter was to take
with him two padres of the Order of Jesus. At some point
of the coast, island or mainland, a fort was to be constructed
"whereby there could be defended the whole coast where
the Englishman Don Tomás [Cavendish] had captured
and robbed the ship Santa Ana from China." By Vizcaino's contract, which was to date from March 1, the
privilege of the pearl-fishery was to continue, as originally
specified, for four years, but thereafter it was to be limited
to a district of ten leagues on the California coast to be
designated by the company. In 1595 (August) additional
concessions were sought, — the loan of a ship, and the
privilege of holding in *encomienda* all natives converted to
the Catholic faith, except one fifth to the Crown.[21] In

1595–96 ratification was obtained from the Conde de Monterey, successor to Velasco in the viceroyalty,[22] and in August, 1596, Vizcaino set sail. Owing to fierce northwest winds, he succeeded in doing little save effect a landing at the Santa Cruz of Cortés, — a spot which, from the docility of the natives, he rechristened La Paz.[23]

Vizcaino's first voyage, even as a private venture, had proved a failure; but in 1598 Philip II died, and was succeeded by his son Philip III. Searching among the papers of his late father, the third Philip came upon two documents. The first was a dispatch from the Conde de Monterey, dated the 26th of November, 1597, inclosing a memorial from Vizcaino, asking to be allowed to make a voyage with the object of exploring "the whole bight and gulf of Californias," the same to be taken possession of for the King, "turning over to the royal crown seaports, heads of departments, and cities, — all in a most quiet way, and without working any wrong to the natives." And the request was emphasized by the Viceroy, who reminded the King that with the loss of the San Agustín "the exploration of all the southern coast, which is of interest in connection with the ships from the Philippines . . . came to an end." [24] The second document was the memorial of Hernando de Los Ríos on the subject of Anian.

His imagination fired (especially by the Ríos document), the King carefully examined the latter in September, 1599, and in a fortnight a *cédula* was issued directing the Conde de Monterey to undertake yet again "a discovery and settlement in California"; a *cédula* whereof the Count took prompt advantage by commissioning Vizcaino captain-general for a second California voyage.[25]

"To-day, being Sunday the 5th of May, 1602," wrote the captain-general to the King, from Acapulco, "I sail at five o'clock, in the names of God and his Blessed Mother, for the discovery of the harbors and bays of the coast of the South Sea as far as Cape Mendocino." There were four vessels, two of them (the San Diego and the Santo Tomás) ships; the third (the Tres Reyes) a *barcolongo;* and the fourth (not named) a *lancha*. They carried two hundred picked men under Commander Toribio Gómez de Corván, Lieutenant Martín Aguilar and Chief Navigator Francisco de Bolaños. They carried also the friars (Carmelite) Andrés de la Asunción, Tomás de Aquino and Antonio de la Ascensión, and a cosmographer, Gerónimo Martín Palacios. After a severe battle of six months with northwest winds, and after passing and naming the Todos Santos and Coronados Islands, the expedition landed, November 10, in Cabrillo's harbor of San Miguel, — a harbor compared by Vizcaino to that of San Lúcar in Spain, and named by him San Diego in honor of his flagship.

Quitting this point on November 20, Santa Catalina, Santa Bárbara, and San Nicolás islands were sighted and named; the Santa Bárbara Channel (now for the first time, so called) was traversed; Point Conception, the Sierra de Santa Lucía, and Río Carmelo were named; and on December 16, Point Pinos having been rounded, anchor was cast in "a noble harbor," which in honor of the ruling Viceroy was called Monterey. Here (Mass first having been said by Ascensión under a spreading oak) Vizcaino lingered a fortnight. He took note of the region as convenient for the Philippine galleon, with its "infinite number of very large pines, straight and smooth, fit for masts and yards"; its "oaks of a prodigious size proper for building ships"; its *rosas de Castilla*, large clear lagoons, fine pastures and arable lands; and last, but by no means least, with its shellfish, its sea-fowl, its huge bears, its horned mountain sheep, and its good-natured, "well-looking and affable people."

Having dispatched the Santo Tomás to Acapulco with

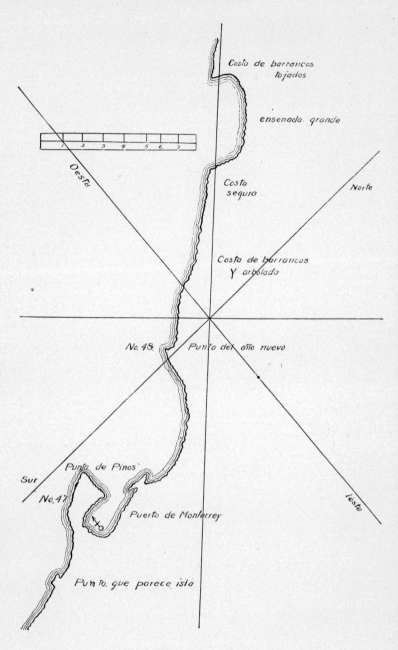

Costa de barrancos
tajados

ensenada grande

Costa
segura

Norte

Oeste

Costa de barrancos
y arbolada

No. 48. Punta del año nuevo

Ieste

Punta de Pinos

Sur

No. 47.

Puerto de Monterrey

Punta que parece isla

CHART II, PLATE 1. PORT OF MONTEREY. BY VIZCAINO, 1603
(Hitherto unreproduced)

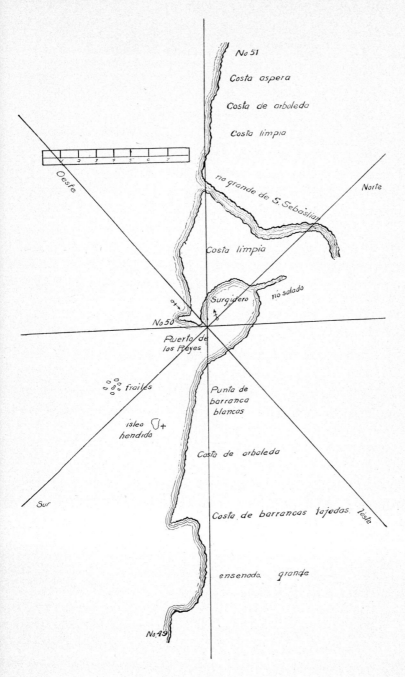

No 51

Costa aspera

Costa de arboleda

Costa limpia

Oeste

Norte

rio grande de S. Sebastian

Costa limpia

Surgidero

rio salado

No 50

Puerto de
los Reyes

frailes

Punta de
barranca
blancas

isleo
hendido

Costa de arboleda

Sur

Costa de barrancas tajadas. Teste

ensenada grande

No 49

CHART II, PLATE 2. SAN FRANCISCO BAY OF CERMEÑO (PUERTO
DE LOS REYES). BY VIZCAINO, 1603

(Hitherto unreproduced)

his sick, the captain-general on January 3, 1603, continued his voyage northward. About January 7, he, with the San Diego, passed the Farallones and reached Francis Drake's Bay (the San Francisco Bay of Cermeño), which he called the Puerto de Don Gaspar or Puerto de los Reyes. Here he looked in vain for traces of Cermeño's unfortunate San Agustín, and then, pressing further, passed Cape Mendocino on the 12th. Both the San Diego and the Tres Reyes attained the latitude of the present Cape Blanco, but about January 19 were forced by cold and illness to retrace their course to Acapulco, where, after vicissitudes many and distressing, they arrived, the Tres Reyes in February, and the San Diego in March.[26]

The second voyage of Vizcaino made it clear that there were at least two good harbors for galleons above Cape San Lucas, — San Diego and Monterey. But with respect to Anian (the inciting cause, under Hernando de los Ríos's memorial, of any voyage at all at this time) the voyage cleared up nothing. It indeed was of reactionary effect. Already in 1554 Jacobo Gastaldi and in 1582 Michael Lok, ignorant of Castillo's chart of 1541, had issued maps depicting California (Lower and Upper) as a single great peninsula, joined at its northern extremity to the American continent by a slender isthmus. Antonio de la Ascensión of Salamanca (cosmographer-assistant to Palacios) now went a step further. He asserted that not only was the mouth of the broad river, which Aguilar (like Gali) had distinguished by its drift, the outlet of Anian, but that the Gulf of California was a sea opening into this outlet. "I hold it," he said, "for certain that this sea [the Gulf of California] communicates with the Strait of Anian, and by the latter with the Sea of the North [the Atlantic Ocean]"; an assertion which, if true, abolished the Gastaldi-Lok isthmus, and left California a body purely insular.[27]

Though California might be insular, it none the less (through Anian) commanded "against those demons of English and Dutch heretics" the western littoral of North America, a fact emphasizing the need for the occupation of such a harbor as Monterey. In 1606 therefore, on the 19th of August, Philip III gave to the Viceroy of Mexico (the Marqués de Montesclaros) an urgent command to look for Vizcaino, whose whereabouts had been lost, and to intrust to his capable hands a third expedition to California; this time with the express object of "making a settlement at the said Puerto de Monterey and thus introduce the touching [of the galleons] at that port." [28]

But just here a sudden change was made in the royal plans, — a circumstance which carries us back a little in our narrative.

Sometime between September 25, 1584, and May 10, 1585, Fray Andrés de Aguirre (companion of Urdaneta in 1565) wrote to the Archbishop of Mexico, Pedro de Moya y Contreras, who lately had been made Viceroy, a letter urging upon his attention the need of a refitting station for the Philippine galleons after their long voyage across the Pacific. The idea of course was not new. Over and over had Legazpi been charged in official instructions from Valladolid not to delay among the Western Islands trading and bartering, but to return immediately to New Spain, "as the principal reason of this expedition is to ascertain the return voyage." And by sending back Urdaneta the charge had been complied with. Urdaneta's voyage, however, had been most unfortunate, for his pilot, his master, and fourteen of his men had died. Then had come the voyage of Gali. But while both voyages had served to point the need, between Manila and Acapulco, of a station for refitting, neither had accomplished anything toward finding a suitable spot. Under these conditions it was, and while contemplating sending Gali on a search for such a spot, that Contreras received the letter of Aguirre.

Aguirre told of a communication from a Portuguese captain which had been shown to him in 1565 by Urdaneta. It described two large islands, nine days to the eastward of Japan, in a port of which the captain had been forced to take refuge from a storm; islands rich in "silver, silks, and clothing," which, out of compliment to an Armenian merchant sailing with the Portuguese captain, had been named "Isles of the Armenian." [29]

Gali, as it chanced, was not sent on a voyage of search by Contreras. Instead, there was sent in 1587, in the ship Nuestra Señora de la Esperança, a navigator of Macao, Pedro de Unamunu, who on returning reported no such "isles" as those of the Armenian, or of Rica de Oro and Rica de Plata, their equivalent, to exist. [30] But Unamunu reported further: —

From the latitude of the Island of Armenio, as they call it (which is 35⅓°), we sailed on August 26 east by north and to the northeast in search of the country of Nueva España, intending to reach it at as high a latitude as we could. . . . We sailed as far as the latitude of 39°, [but] on September 3 [by reason of wind and cold and broken mainmast] we came back to the latitude 32½°. . . . Sailing on various courses . . . we succeeded in reaching the latitude of somewhat above 35½° on the 17th October. . . . On this day land was seen. . . . At the first watch we turned away from it [on account of fog]. Heading northeast . . . we encountered two little islets adjoining the mainland. . . . On Sunday the 18th at daybreak we made the shore of the land, and God, giving us the light of day, we saw toward the north a country that was elevated with only three pine trees on the highest point, which served as a landmark. . . . On the north a headland extended apparently northwest and southeast. Inside this headland appeared a bay broad toward the east, in which there seemed to be harbors. . . . When we reached it we saw toward the east a sandy beach of considerable extent and moderate breadth. We steered for that place and cast anchor . . . in twenty-seven fathoms of water. . . . We cast anchor in the said harbor on the 18th of October, the day of Saint Luke; and because it was that saint's day, the name of Puerto de San Lucas was given to the place. Here in this harbor there is an infinite number of fish of various kinds; and there are trees suitable for a ship's masts, and water and firewood, and many shell-fish, — a place where any one can, when in need, obtain supplies of all these things. . . . We took observations of the sun and found that the said harbor lies in a little more than 35½° of latitude. . . . I landed on the shore with twelve soldiers wearing their mail-coats and carrying their arquebuses. In front of us was Father Martin Ynacio de Loyola bearing a cross in his hands, with some Indians from Luçon armed with swords and bucklers. . . . On the northeast side [of a hill] we saw a river of considerable size descending through a plain below, and many well-worn roads going in various directions. . . . We tasted the water of the said river and found it very good; it flowed down the said river through sand. Thence the ascent of the river was made by way of an upward slope toward the north, where the said river formed a large lake; we concluded that some bar and harbor would be there, since the sea was so near. When we reached it we saw that it was water held back from the said river, and that its way to the sea was obstructed by a great quantity of sand. All this river, on both sides, is well shaded by willows and osiers of considerable size, with other and lofty trees which look like the ash; there are also many fragrant plants, such as camomile, pennyroyal and thyme.

. . . As a matter concerning the demarcation and crown of the King Don Felipe, our sovereign, I took possession in the said name by Diego Vazquez Mexia, one of the alcaldes appointed for this purpose. In this act he was supported, as he was a magistrate, in due legal form by planting a cross . . . and cutting branches from the trees that grew about the place.[31]

On October 21, after a conflict with Indians, Unamunu set sail for Acapulco, because "the wounded were in very bad condition," and because, "from the island of Cedros to the port of Acapulco, the whole coast had been discovered for a long time."

From the islands of Babuyanes, Unamunu observes, we sailed one thousand eight hundred and ninety leagues, on varying courses according as the weather favored us, — although a straight course would make about one thousand five hundred and fifty leagues. At that latitude and by that route there is very good navigation, better for health and shorter than it is in lower latitudes. From the said port of Saint Lucas to Cape Sanct Lucas, which has a latitude of nearly twenty-three degrees, the distance is two hundred and ninety leagues, about half of the way on a southeast course, and the other half sailing southeast by south. From this cape Sanct Lucas to the port of Acapulco it is about two hundred and sixty leagues, sailing half the way southeast, and the rest southeast by east.

Puerto de San Lucas, discovery of which is thus announced by Unamunu, was not improbably Monterey Bay. It was in a latitude "above 35½°"; its "landmark" was "three pine trees on the highest point"; on the north "a headland extended apparently northwest and southeast"; inside this headland "appeared a bay broad toward the east," and into the bay there flowed "a considerable river" (the Salinas?). But to Viceroy Contreras, bent upon the discovery, for refitting stations, of treasure islands (Isles of the Armenian or what not), Unamunu's report was little significant. It was consigned to oblivion, and the first occupation of Monterey was, and is, ascribed to Vizcaino.

It was in 1607 that the Isles of the Armenian (or rather of Rica de Oro and Rica de Plata) claimed attention again. On May 24 Viceroy Montesclaros, acknowledging receipt of the royal order of August 19, 1606, for the dispatch of Vizcaino for the settlement of Monterey, represented to Philip III that the occupation of the port in question, for a way station, would be ill advised. The most difficult part of the Manila-Acapulco passage, it was observed by Montesclaros, was not the stretch across the

North Pacific, nor yet the run down the coast of the Californias, but the devious way from Cape Espiritu Santo on the island of Manila, all along the chain of the Ladrones to the east point of Japan, called Cape Sestos (Shiwo Misaki); a way necessarily taken by the galleons, in order to gain, in the proper latitude, an offing. Galleon upon galleon, bravely cleared from Manila with music and dancing, had either been wrecked outright on the shoals and rocks of Japan, or forced reeling back to port, dismasted and forlorn. What, therefore, argued the Viceroy, was needed for the galleons was not a port-of-call in California, at the end of a voyage, but such a port off Cape Sestos at the beginning, — a need for the satisfaction of which there happily existed "two islands in latitude thirty-four or thirty-five, named Rica de Oro and Rica de Plata." [32]

Accordingly in 1608 (September 27), the King gave orders to Viceroy Luis de Velasco that Sebastián Vizcaino, instead of proceeding to occupy and settle Monterey as commanded in 1606, should go to the Philippine Islands, and "with two small and lightly laden ships" return thence for "the discovery, settlement, and opening to navigation of a harbor in one of the said islands Rica de Oro and Rica de Plata"; and that, meanwhile, "the opening to navigation and settlement of the harbor of Monterey should be suspended." [33]

Vizcaino, so far as known, did not go to the Philippines, but in 1611 he went, as admiral, in the galleon San Francisco, to Japan.[34] For Rica de Oro and Rica de Plata he sought, we are told, with extraordinary diligence throughout two hundred leagues. But the sailors having elicited from the *piloto-mayor* the statement that, in his opinion, "there were no such islands in the world" (*no había tales islas en el mundo*), a mutiny was threatened and the search abandoned. Vizcaino was yet in Japan in 1613, and, as

late as 1620, Hernando de los Ríos Coronel was urging
upon the King that a small vessel be sent from Manila to
explore the island of Rica de Plata, — an island described
by him as over one hundred leagues in circumference, and
as "placed midway the Pacific like an inn." [35]

With Monterey suspended as to settlement, attention
(1615–94) was directed to the task of gaining a foothold
at Cape San Lucas, or La Paz. In 1629 Padre Ascensión
recommended the occupation of the cape. Thus not
merely might California itself be peopled, but thus might it
be ascertained whether by the Sea of California one could
pass to the Estrecho de Anian; at what point might be
located the famous city of Quivira; where the river Tizón
entered; where lay the pearl island of Giganta, and what
parts were peopled by a white race. Ascensión's views
were approved by the royal purser, Martín de Lezama, a
son-in-law of Vizcaino, but by Henrico Martínez (royal
cosmographer) they were subjected to criticism. Great
riches and an extended population in California, Martínez
did not believe to exist. As for a lake of gold (*laguna de
oro*), described by Padre Ascensión, — a lake from which
the Indians drew vast treasure, — common sense, he declared, denied it reality. Occupation of the cape, moreover, was not necessary to afford refuge to the Philippine
galleon; for was not the latter wont to reach Acapulco
without even sighting California? As for occupation to
forestall an enemy, one could never reach the coast, so
great was the distance to be traversed; and if traverse it an
enemy should, why there could be done to him "as Pedro
Melendes did to the French in Florida, and as Fadrique de
Toledo did to the Hollanders of San Salvador and the
coast of Brazil." [36]

The views of Ascensión none the less prevailed, and by

1694 expeditions into the California gulf (most of them, like the first expedition of Vizcaino, for pearls, but with settlement as at least an ostensible object) had been undertaken by nine different adventurers: Tomás Cardona, Juan de Iturbe, Francisco de Ortega, Luis Cestín de Cañas, Porter y Casanate, Bernardo Bernal de Piñadero, Lucenilla y Torres, Isidro Otondo (under whom, April 5, 1683, the peninsula was formally named Santísima Trinidad de las Californias), and Francisco de Itamarra.

If in the seventeenth century (upon the failure of the search for Rica de Oro and Rica de Plata, and during the period of the gulf expeditions), Spain had persisted in her original plan, — the settlement of Monterey, — the opportunity so far as her enemy England was concerned was quite at hand. James I sat upon the English throne, and the spacious days of great Elizabeth — the days of the Hawkinses and the Drakes — were replaced by the petty days of the Stuarts. In 1604 the Constable of Castile had negotiated with James a treaty by which the latter had agreed "not to allow English ships to trade in the Indies"; and long thereafter the successive Spanish ambassadors at London — Zúñiga, Velasco, Gondomar — held English policy much in their own keeping.

Yet, despite favorable conditions, Spain now (1600-1700) was so broken, — the Spanish Cæsar become so utterly a simulacrum, a mere painted Jove, — that Alta California was not visited once. Its sierra slumbered in the skies, and its valleys gave subsistence to wild creatures, all amid a loneliness as profound as that before the days of Cabrillo. A single time each year, as the Philippine galleon (foul with scurvy yet towering nobly at poop and prow, and with silken cargo redolent of musk) sighted Cape Mendocino or Santa Lucía Peak, was the region glimpsed by the eye of civilized man.

CHAPTER III

THE MISSION

Siempre habían producido mejores efectos las adquisiciones que se hacían lentamente por medio de los Misioneros que las conseguidas á fuerza de armas. — Viceroy Bucarely to the King, October 27, 1772.[1]

DOWN to 1694, the year of the last expedition to the California peninsula (that of Itamarra), the means relied upon for the "reduction" of California, says the Jesuit historian Miguel Venegas, were "arms and power. . . . But," he continues, "it was the will of Heaven that the triumph when it came should be owing to the meekness and courtesy of God's ministers, to the humiliation of his cross, and the power of his word."

The singular efficacy of the Cross in the subjugation of men is a thing which historians have had occasion to remark; and it is true, as we are reminded by Venegas, that Lower California became the scene of another of its triumphs. Whether the reduction of Alta California might not have been accomplished in the time-honored secular way, by force, had it not been that in the eighteenth century the Spanish Government, though in process of rehabilitation, was extremely poor, is a question. At all events, in 1769 danger to New Spain by way of the California coast again arose; and, in the dearth of money, there was left to Spain but one tried, strong, and effective instrument of defense, — the Mission.

First, a word with regard to the danger itself; and, next, with regard to the remarkable instrument by which it was sought to be averted.

I

Under the last of her Austrian kings, Charles II (Charles the Bewitched), who died in 1700, Spain touched the lowest point of demoralization, political, industrial, and commercial, which she was destined to reach. With the accession of the Bourbons, in the person of Philip V, a slight recovery of power was to be observed; especially after the political reins, in 1714, had passed into the deft hands of Giulio Alberoni, successively priest, prime minister, and cardinal. Moreover, as the eighteenth century brought renewed activity for Spain in Europe, so, likewise, it brought for her renewed activity in the Indies.

In 1680 rumor declared that the English were to be expected soon again in the Pacific. In the words of Spanish merchants, writing to their Panama correspondents, "There would be English privateers that year in the West Indies, who would make such great discoveries as to open a door into the South Seas." The first to appear (albeit a trifle belated) was "Captain Swan." In 1686 he entered the California gulf with one ship, carrying as pilot and historiographer William Dampier, a navigator actuated by a restless ambition "to get some knowledge of the northern parts of this continent of Mexico." After Swan it was Dampier himself who, with his "knowledge," next sought to open a door into the South Seas for Englishmen. In December, 1704, he attacked with a single ship the Manila galleon of the year, below Cape San Lucas, but was beaten off. Then in 1709 came Captain Woods Rogers with two ships, piloted by the indefatigable Dampier. As a passenger in one of them was Alexander Selkirk, the true Robinson Crusoe. But though "Crusoe" joined against the galleon, the English, after a combat near the cape, were again worsted.[2]

Each of the adventurers, Swan, Dampier, and Rogers, believed in Anian (a route to the happy regions of the galleons and gold which he knew must be shorter than that around Cape Horn), and no one of them, except Rogers, was prepared to deny that California was an island. It was in 1620, by Antonio de la Ascensión, Vizcaino's assistant cosmographer, that, as noted in the last chapter, the insular hypothesis for California was revived. The hypothesis proved strong enough, be it added, to withstand distinct proof in contravention of it obtained through explorations to the Colorado River, in 1701, 1702, and 1706, by the Jesuit missionary Eusebio Francisco Kino.[3]

Some years after the Woods Rogers attack (1717), Cardinal Alberoni sought to forestall danger to New Spain from the English on the California coast. But Alberoni's tenure of power proved brief, and in 1721 Captain George Shelvocke appeared off Cape San Lucas with evil intent. He accomplished nothing, and soon departed for Canton.[4] No other Englishman of note followed him till 1740, when Captain George Anson lay long off Acapulco in wait for a galleon, finding reward at last in a richer vessel near the Philippines.[5]

After 1740 it was from a fresh quarter that danger from the English arose. The Hudson's Bay Company (organized in 1670) was operating under a charter reciting that a main consideration for the instrument was "The Discovery of a New Passage into the South Sea." Here obviously was a command to seek Anian (and hence California) from the east. But as late as 1740 it was averred by Arthur Dobbs, an enthusiastic Irishman, that no serious effort at discovery had been made by the company; wherefore in 1742 Dobbs undertook the task himself. His expedition failed to disclose an exit westward from the bay; yet so persistent was he that in 1745 he induced Parliament to vote £20,000 as a contingent reward for a further expedition. Prosecuted by the Dobbs Galley and the California, this likewise was a failure and came to an end in 1746.[6]

Meanwhile for a hundred years Russia had slowly, but with glacier-like inexorability, been moving eastward toward the only real Anian, the strait dividing Siberia from the present Alaska, and by 1706 had reached Kamtchatka. By 1728 Vitus Behring had drifted through the strait; by 1741 North America had been sighted; by 1745 a descent had been made upon the Aleutian Islands; and by 1760 a Russo-American trade in otter-skins had been opened.[7]

II

The Mission — instrument in Spanish hands (so far as the Californias were concerned) for the safeguarding of the Philippine galleon and for the control of Anian — was the result of two interacting human passions,—Religious Propagandism and Avarice. The second is the more primitive passion of the two, and it is to the credit of Spain that in the settlement of the Indies, Avarice, triumphant at the beginning, waged on the whole a losing battle with Propagandism.

The root of the Spanish propagandist passion was largely the Spanish temperament, but present and abetting were two specific influences: (1) The Bull of Pope Alexander VI, of date May 3, 1493, awarding to Spain, "in the fulness of papal apostolic power, and of the vicarship of Jesus Christ on earth," the New World, on condition that there be sent thither "worthy, God-fearing, learned, skilled, and experienced men, in order to instruct the inhabitants in the Catholic faith; [8] and (2) the personality of Queen Isabella, who so felt the responsibility of the papal injunction, that in her will (1504) leaving to Ferdinand the regency of Castile, she charged that what was commanded by the

Pope as to the Indians, "be not infringed in any respect" (*no se exceda cosa alguna*).[9]

It is with the avarice side of the account, "Spain in the Indies," that we are concerned first.

Neither Queen Isabella nor King Ferdinand saw reason why the Indians, while undergoing conversion, should not respond by the payment of reasonable tribute, provided the same were exacted from them as from other freemen and not as from slaves. But in the application of this idea (even when sought to be applied justly), there was difficulty. In 1503 Nicolás de Ovando, Governor of Hispaniola, wrote with undoubted truth that the Indians would not work even for wages, and that, indeed, they shunned the Spaniards in every relation. The reply of the monarchs was, that contact with the Indians was indispensable for ends religious as well as secular, and that Ovando, therefore, might assemble them in villages, upon lands which they could not alienate, and under a protector, and so compel them to consort with the Spaniards; he paying them such wages as he might deem fit. Nevertheless (so the monarchs insisted), what was required of the Indians should be required of them "as free persons, as they are, and not as slaves." [10] Thus enjoined, Ovando proceeded to inaugurate a system of *encomiendas* — a kind of New World feudal system. "To you," ran the deed apportioning the Indians among their *encomenderos* or protectors, " are given in trust [*se os encomiendan*], under Chief So-and-so, fifty or one hundred Indians, with the chief, for you to make use of them in your farms and mines; and you are to teach them the things of our holy Catholic faith." [11] In theory the system was not necessarily bad. What in practice it became is well known. It became slavery and robbery, and not seldom it became also murder.[12]

But what, meanwhile, of those "worthy, God-fearing,

learned, skilled, and experienced men," who, according to the Papal Bull, were to be ever present in the Indies to instruct the inhabitants in Christianity, — men wholly other than the *encomenderos* themselves, who, ninety-nine times in a hundred, were fortune-seekers of the worst type, the very incarnation of Avarice? Here there arose a fresh difficulty. The secular Catholic clergy of the day, especially the Spanish branch of it, — that is to say, the Spanish bishops and priests, — were worldly to the core. Said Cortés to Charles V in that famous *Carta Cuarta* of his, already cited: "If there be [sent to the New World] bishops and other prelates, they cannot but continue the habit, to which for our sins they are now given, of disposing of the goods of the Church, which is to waste them in pompous ceremonies and in other vices, [and] in leaving entails to their sons or relations; and should the Indians learn that such were ministers of God, and should see them given over to the vices and irreverence that are practiced in our day in those realms, it would cause them to undervalue our Faith and hold it to be a matter of jest." [13]

Seculars, however, it was who (greedy, lustful, indolent) were at first sent by Spain in fulfillment of the great proviso in the Bull of 1493. But regulars — the friars — an order of ministers armed against temptation by ample vows of poverty and chastity — soon followed, and the Pope's behest for the conversion of the Indians was given effect.

In 1510 a band of Dominican monks, under their vicar Pedro de Córdova, landed in Hispaniola. They perceived that the *encomienda* was both a fraud upon the will of the monarchs and destructive to the Indian, and forthwith they proceeded, through one of their number, Antonio de Montesino, to raise against it a vehement protest. The matter was carried to King Ferdinand, and on December 27, 1512, there was promulgated by him a series of decrees (conceived under the influence of Bishop Fonseca) called the Laws of Burgos.[14] By these laws *encomiendas* were modified and regulated, but they were not condemned. Among those who in 1512 went to Spain, because of the controversy provoked by the words of Brother Montesino, was Pedro de Córdova himself. He examined the Laws of Burgos, disapproved of them, and expressed his disapproval to the King. "Take upon yourself then, father," said the King, "the charge of remedying them; you will do me a great service therein." But the vicar, declining the task as beyond his province, took upon him work of greater moment, — the propagating in the New World of the plan of the Mission.

It was the conviction of Córdova that the Indian, so far from being dealt with for the good of his soul while in *encomienda*, — while within exploitation range of the conscienceless gold-seeking Spanish adventurer, — should be so dealt with only when in segregation, when organized apart from the lay Spaniard altogether. He, therefore, while in Spain, obtained from King Ferdinand a license to occupy with his Dominican brethren a portion of *Tierra Firme* (mainland of New Spain), there to labor with the Indians free from lay supervision and interference. Piritú de Maracapána, near Cumaná (the earthly Paradise of Columbus and Cortés),[15] was the spot chosen, and the experiment was full of promise, when suddenly it was cut short by a raid of pearl-fishers. The raiders carried away the cacique of the locality, thus rousing against the friars a suspicion of connivance, — a suspicion which brought about the death of two of the latter, though not of Córdova, who as yet had not quitted Hispaniola.

At this juncture there appeared Bartolomé de Las Casas. A bachelor of Salamanca, he had arrived in the Indies with Ovando, and, becoming an *encomendero* in Cuba, had heard, in Hispaniola, Montesino's denunciation of the *encomienda* system. By 1514 he, too, was ready to denounce it, and by the autumn of 1515 to go to Spain to try to secure a radical revision of the Laws of Burgos under which the system derived sanction. Montesino accompanied him, and by help of Cardinal Ximénez de Cisneros (regent to Ferdinand's successor, young Charles V), they succeeded in raising the whole question of Indian slavery and spoliation. Ximénez himself was a bold defender of Indian freedom, and in Council it was repeatedly proposed to abolish the *encomienda* and require of the Indians payment of a capitation tax to the Crown. This proposal was negatived by the fact, reluctantly admitted, that "the Indians had no real inclination to Christianity, and when left to themselves soon relapsed into heathen beliefs." [16] As for the Córdovan idea, — the idea of the Mission, — the idea that the way to convert the Indian was to segregate him, — it did not occur to the Council, was not suggested by Las Casas, and in any event would have been deemed too paradoxical for adoption.

With Pedro de Córdova, however, it was the Mission idea that remained uppermost, and in 1518 he sought at the hands of Charles V a grant of one hundred leagues around Cumaná, as a field for work according to the Mission plan. But in 1521 Córdova died, and there were left only Montesino and Las Casas to take resolutely a stand in behalf of the Indian. The one hundred leagues (enlarged to two hundred and fifty leagues) which had been desired by Córdova were obtained by Las Casas; but the latter, instead of organizing at Cumaná an Indian religious retreat, — a place from which the lay Spaniard was excluded, — planted the usual mixed colony, and with the usual disastrous result. [17] Depressed by failure, Las Casas in 1523 became a monk in Hispaniola, and the *encomienda* flourished.

Yet, despite all, the Córdovan idea — the idea of the Mission — the one workable idea for conserving and converting the Indian — gained gradually a wider acceptance. By 1531 one hundred friars (Dominicans and Franciscans) were in New Spain. In 1531 an *oidor* (judge) of the Audiencia for Mexico, Licenciate Quiroga, earnestly recommended to the Council of the Indies that the Indian youth of the country, reared in the various monasteries, should be settled in pueblos, "at a distance from other pueblos," and under the guardianship of "three or four religious, who [might] incessantly cultivate these young plants to the service of God." [18] What was more, Las Casas himself, now (1535) out of retirement, had advanced very nearly, if not quite, to the position of Córdova. Relying no longer on secular means for Indian conversion, he wrote a treatise in Latin (*De Unico Vocationis Modo*) in support of the thesis that men were to be brought to Christianity by persuasion.[19] Indeed, on May 2, 1537, he entered into a specific compact with Alonzo Maldonado, lieutenant to Pedro de Alvarado, Governor of Guatemala, to demonstrate by actual test that the wildest tribes of the New World could be pacified and converted without the use of force.

The people selected for the test were those of the Guatemalan province of Tuzulatlán, — a people so fierce that their land, whence thrice the Spaniards had been thrust in defeat, was a place of terror, one known as Tierra de Guerra, — Land of War. Into this land, between 1537 and 1539, Las Casas sent Fray Luis Cáncer (Alférez de la Fé), with such success that soon the province became more widely renowned as Tierra de Vera Paz (Land of True Peace) than it had been as Tierra de Guerra.[20] But, apropos of the development of the idea of the Mission, the point especially to be observed is, that when Las Casas made his compact with Lieutenant-Governor Maldonado, he insisted upon the following concessions: (1) That neither then, nor at any future time in Tuzulatlán, might Indians be given in *encomienda;* and (2) that for five years access to the province should be interdicted to every lay Spaniard, excepting only the governor, Alvarado himself.[21]

From 1539–40 to 1544 Las Casas was kept in Spain by Charles V, who was meditating his celebrated mandatory letters, "The New Laws"; and in 1543 the letters were printed. Under the Indian Code of Spain, as perfected by "The New Laws," it was provided that the Indians should dwell in civil (not distinctively religious) communities, choosing their own *alcaldes* (magistrates) and *regidores* (councilmen). But provisions useful for Mission ends were not lacking. (1) No Indian might be held as a slave; (2) no Indian might live outside his village; (3) no lay Spaniard might live in an Indian village; (4) no lay Spaniard might tarry in an Indian village overnight, unless he were ill or were a merchant, when, if a merchant, he might remain three nights; and (5) the Indian was to be faithfully instructed in religion. As for the *encomienda*, it was abolished; but in 1545, in response to colonial demands, it had to be restored to its former (1536) validity for two lives.[22]

The Spanish Indian Mission — witness to the triumph, through Córdova and Las Casas, of Propagandism over Avarice,[23] and fostered, through Charles V, by the Laws of the Indies — was to show in the course of its development some variation. As viewed by the Spanish Government, its object was the Christianizing (and that speedily) of the Indian, in order to civilize him. As viewed, on the other hand, by the friars, its object was the Christianizing of the Indian to save his soul, — a process which might be accomplished speedily, or which might require an indefinite period. A clash at times ensued with regard to the segregating of the Indian. What the government understood by "segregation" was (1) the exclusion of lay Spaniards from Indian settlements; and (2) the ministering spiritually to the natives in their own abodes.[24] What the missionaries understood by the term was not alone the exclusion from Indian settlements of lay Spaniards, and the ministering spiritually to the Indians in their own abodes, but the gathering of Indians from far and near into and about a central establishment (a mission), where they as wards or protégés might be governed in respects temporal as well as spiritual.[25]

In central Mexico, where the natives (already at the conquest not uncivilized) were mild of disposition, the clash above referred to did not occur, for segregation as understood by the government was sufficient for objects both political and religious. But in north Mexico (Upper Sonora and Nueva Vizcaya, — the borders of Apachería), a district warlike and uncivilized, necessity compelled the adoption of segregation as understood by the missionaries. This the government, amid controversy, alternately tolerated and discountenanced through the power of the *Patronato Real*.[26]

It was in Paraguay that the Spanish-Indian Mission prospered most. Introduced by the Jesuits between 1586 and 1612, it made of each village a theocratic centre — a centre civil, religious, and even military — under a missionary father.[27] In the Philippine Islands, where the Mission was introduced by the Augustinians under Legazpi in 1564, the form was less specialized. The degree of specialization attained in Alta California, where, as against the English and Russians, the Mission was employed as an instrument of state in and after 1769, will be shown in the sequel.

CHAPTER IV

CALIFORNIA NO ES YSLA

THE Mission, pending its use in 1769 as a Spanish instrument of state in Alta California, was subjected to yet a further test.

Eusebio Francisco Kino was born at Trent in the Austrian Tyrol in 1640. First a professor of mathematics at the University of Ingolstadt in Bavaria, and next a Jesuit, he crossed to Mexico in 1680. Here his labors were those equally of missionary and royal cosmographer. As missionary, his zeal spurred him to the frontier; and as cosmographer he was sent in 1683, with Isidro Otondo y Antillón, to California on the expedition which gave to the peninsula the name Santísima Trinidad de las Californias. In 1685 he was compelled to leave California because of the recall of Otondo to convoy the Philippine galleon past Dutch buccaneers to Acapulco. But so deeply had the spell of this land of Cortés been laid upon him, that ever afterwards he was eager to return and make converts of its people.[1]

"The enterprise of the conquest and conversion of California having been suspended [by royal order in 1685]," writes Kino in 1698, "I asked of the provincial (at that time Padre Luys del Canto) license to come to these Gentile people of these coasts nearest to the said California [Upper Sonora or Pimería]. . . . The fiscal of His Majesty (may God guard Him), D. Pedro de la Portilla, asserted that from these coasts there would be the greatest opportunity possible to continue . . . the conquest and conversion of

California. I set out from Mexico on the 20th of November, 1686, and arrived at Guadalaxara, whence I set out on the 16th of December [arriving at Oposura in February]." [2]

In 1687, on March 13, Kino founded the mission Nuestra Señora de los Dolores (about 120 miles south of the present Tuçón), and between 1687 and 1690, in conjunction with Padre José de Aguilar, he founded the establishments San Ignacio, San José de los Imuris, and Nuestra Señora de los Remedios. But in Mexico ill reports regarding the Pimas had been spread, and in 1690 there was sent to Sonora as *visitador* the *asistente* at Las Chínipas, Juan María de Salvatierra. Born in Milan, Italy, November 15, 1644, a sometime student at the Seminary of Parma, and since 1675 a Jesuit in Mexico, Salvatierra was an emissary strong in body, firm in resolve, prudent in judgment, and of endearing gentleness of bearing. Accompanied by Kino, he visited each of the Pimería missions in 1690 and 1691, and "in all of these journeys," writes Kino, "the Father Visitador and I talked together of suspended California, and we agreed that these so fertile lands and valleys of this Pimería would be the remedy for the scantier and more sterile lands of California." [3]

On coming to Mexico, Kino had believed California to be a peninsula. But in the account of Oñate's New Mexican expedition of 1604–05 it was intimated that the *adelantado*, proceeding westward, had reached the South Sea in 37°; moreover, most of the cosmographers now represented California as insular; and as noted by Kino himself the currents of the gulf were those rather of a strait; so he had changed his opinion. [4] As for Salvatierra, his views were those of his coadjutor. Indeed, on taking leave of the cosmographer, Salvatierra counseled him to reduce the Sobaipuris of the north and Sobas to the west, and — "in order to go [thence] to California — to build a small bark." [5] Accordingly in 1692 (August to September), Kino, with fifty beasts of burden, his servants and some Indians, went to the Sobaipuris, and at the *ranchería* of San Xavier del Bec displayed a map of the world by which he showed "how the Spaniards and the faith had come by sea to Vera Cruz and had gone to Puebla, to Mexico, to Guadalaxara, to Sinaloa, to Sonora, and now to the lands of the Pimas." And in December, 1693, still mindful of the advice of Salvatierra, he went with Padre Agustín de Campos and Captain Sebastián Romero to the Sobas. "After about eight leagues journey," he relates, "we came to a little hill which we named El Nazareno, and from its summit, on the 15th of December, we saw clearly more than twenty-five continuous leagues of the land of California, for it is not more than fifteen or eighteen leagues across to the principal *rancherías*. And . *.* . we named the spot La Concepcion de Nuestra Señora del Caborca." [6]

Nor was the building of a ship forgotten; for in July Kino went with Lieutenant Mateo Manje (*alcalde-mayor* and *capitán-á-guerra* in Sonora) to the Sobas at Sonoydag, and began the construction of "a bark twelve varas [eleven yards] long and four varas [three yards] wide, cutting the timbers and keel-beams; the rest of the framework, the flooring and the futtocks, being made here in Nuestra Señora de los Dolores, with the idea of carrying this whole bark in four parts to the sea by mules, and there to put it together, nail it, calk it, and to pass to the near-by California." [7]

But for use of the bark opportunity was delayed, and in 1694 (February) Kino, with Manje, went again to "the waters of the Sea of California." "We saw very clearly," he says, "the same California and its principal and larger hills. We named them San Marcos, San Mateo, San

Juan (for San Lucas is already the name of the Cape of California), and San Antonio, as may be seen from the map." The trip was repeated a few months later (June), resulting in the discovery of "the good port of Santa Sabina." [8]

In November, Kino visited the Casa Grande of the Gila, near which, in the *ranchería* of El Tusonimo, he said Mass, and in November, 1695, he set forth by leave of his provincial for Mexico, to discuss with the latter and with the Viceroy the "conversion of California." Arriving at the capital on January 8, 1696, whom should he meet but Salvatierra, who the same day had reached the city by another road.[9]

It was during the reign of Charles II (the Bewitched) that Kino adventured to Mexico; but for the "conversion of California" the time was inopportune, for it fell within the interval of national depression when Monterey as a port-of-call for the galleon had been abandoned in favor of the islands (one or other) Rica de Oro and Rica de Plata; an abandonment emphasized by the royal *cédula* of 1685 suspending California expeditions.

Kino was back at Dolores by the middle of May, but he had left Salvatierra in Mexico; and in 1697, on the coming of Conde de Moctezuma as viceroy, the failure of 1696 was retrieved. By Salvatierra there were won to the California cause not only the Society of Jesus, hitherto reluctant, but the Audiencia, and, last, the Viceroy himself; and on February 5 there was issued a license authorizing Kino, jointly with Salvatierra, to undertake the reduction of the Californias on two conditions: first, that reduction be at their own expense; second, that it be effected in the name of the King.[10] Salvatierra raised by subscription an endowment fund (*Fondo Piadoso*) of 47,000 *pesos*,[11] and appointed as *procurador* (financial agent) the rector of the

Jesuit College of San Gregorio, Juan Ugarte. Then, leaving Kino in Sonora, where his presence was said to be worth "a well-regulated presidio," he set sail, October 10, 1697, from Yaqui for the California coast. Comprising the expedition were a *lancha* containing six Spanish soldiers and three Indians, and a *galeota* containing six sailors, all under command of Juan María Romero de la Sierpe. Says Salvatierra, writing on Christmas Day, 1697, to the Bishop of Guadiana (Durango): —

From Hiagui [Yaqui] the currents drifted me near Sal si puedas and we took shelter at Concepcion, 25 leagues from San Bruno, the same bay where the Spaniards wintered two years, upon another attempt. . . . Having lost the launch with six men, in a storm, and not hearing anything of them for several days after, and finding ourselves in danger on account of the exposed situation of San Bruno, we drew lots, in the name of the Holy María, as to where we should go, the sailors being acquainted with some of the beaches. Our lot fell upon the Harbor of San Dionisio, and we set sail in the vessel and landed here.

The place appears to me a good one. It is a plain of some ten leagues in circumference, with good pastures and an abundance of mesquit and other trees, canebrakes, and good water. We were kindly received by the people, who begged us to continue with them. We landed our goods and provisions, and I took possession of a level piece of tableland on top of two of the highest hills on the large plain, abounding in springs of fresh water and a large reservoir of the same at the foot of the hill, for animals. We threw up our breastworks for fortifications, as best we could, having only six Spaniards, two Indians from Sonora, and another Indian. The vessel returned to Hiaqui and we few conquerors remained alone. We were in imminent risk of our lives for three whole weeks, because the cupidity of the Indians was tempted by our corn and flour, and they wished to kill us all and obtain booty. . . .

About midday, on St. Stanislaus Kostka Day, four squadrons belonging to four tribes — the Edues, Didues, Laymones, and Moquies Tapioses — charged down upon our intrenchments, with arrows, stones, and earth. They fought until the sun went down, having made several attacks, but the Virgin prevailed over the powers of Hell; the Great Madona was triumphant and victorious. Many of them fell on all sides, while I and my companions escaped unhurt. . . . The battle resulted in our favor, they humbled themselves, and we made peace with them. They are now obedient and a great many people come to learn the doctrine, and thus with a few Spaniards has this land been conquered.

We have subsequently discovered the yuca here, from the root of which the casave is made, an article of food in many of the kingdoms of America. We learned of it the day after our victory. Two days later, the launch, with the six men which were lost, appeared here. About this time also, the vessel, which it was also thought had been lost on account of accidents and getting ashore at Hiaqui, arrived, and brought me great relief from Father Francisco María Picolo, which aid, in a great measure, is due to your Reverence.

Thus on October 25, on the heights above San Dionisio, there was founded in commemoration of Our Lady of Loreto, Loreto de Concho, the first mission of Lower California.[12] Between 1697 and 1769, the year of the founding of San Diego de Alcalá, — the first Upper California mission, — there were planted in the peninsula eighteen missions,[13] all, save San Fernando de Velicatá, by the Jesuit Order. The powers conferred in the license issued by Moctezuma were to enlist, pay, and discharge soldiers for guard purposes, and to appoint proper persons for the administration of justice. In other words, the powers conferred were those which pertained to the Mission as such, whether conducted by Jesuits, Franciscans, or Dominicans; powers the outgrowth of the experience of Pedro de Córdova and Las Casas; powers sanctioned under the Laws of the Indies; powers whereby a community of Indians might be secluded from lay Spanish contact, and governed apart from lay Spanish interference, to the end that it might not be demoralized and exploited out of existence through lay Spanish avarice.[14]

For the exercise of such powers there proved to be need in California as elsewhere. Salvatierra's six recruits had all mutinied on learning that there was to be permitted no fishing for pearls, — a form of treasure-seeking wherein the earlier adventurers in the gulf had maltreated the Indians; and in 1700 the repressive attitude of Salvatierra was made matter of formal complaint by Antonio García de Mendoza, captain of the mission guard.[15]

Moreover in 1705 the vice-regal government, actuated by a belief (in which it was sustained by Madrid) that the secular authority in California was too much subordinated to the sacerdotal, proposed establishing a presidio at a point on the peninsular coast suitable for the galleon. The plan, had it been carried out, would have exposed California to the evils perpetrated in Hispaniola in the sixteenth century, — evils which the Mission had been created to forestall; and Salvatierra, now provincial of his Order, met the crisis with a successful protest.[16]

But to recur to Kino. Eager for California, he "set out," as he records, —

on the 22d of September [1698], from this pueblo of Nuestra Señora de los Dolores, with Captain Diego Carrasco, the [Indian] governor of this place, and with seven others, my servants, traveling with more than 60 sumpters toward the north and northwest to the Rio [Gila] and Casa Grande. . . . Afterwards we set out for the south and southwest and to the west about 80 leagues journey, and, arriving at the Sea of California under the lee of the estuary of the Rio Grande, we found a very good Port or Bay, in 32 degrees elevation, with fresh water and timber; and it must be the Port which ancient Geographers called the Puerto de Santa Clara; it has a southwest-northwest entrance and a sierra to the West. We came reconnoitring the whole coast from the northwest, from the Rio Grande to La Concepcion [del Caborca], which is more than 90 leagues long from north to south.[17]

Salvatierra was aroused by this *entrada*, and on March 28, 1699, he wrote to ask of the cosmographer "what sign there is on that [the Pimería] side whether this narrow sea is landlocked," and to propose a joint voyage of discovery along the inner California coast northward of 36 degrees.[18] But already Kino was on the march. On February 7 (1699), he with Padre Adamo Gilg, Lieutenant Manje, his servants, and "more than 90 sumpters," had set out for San Marcelo del Sonoydag near the port of Santa Clara. Proceeding down the Río Grande, which he and Padre Gilg now named Río de los Santos Apóstoles, the party came at San Pedro to the Cocomaricopas, from whom they learned of "the very populous Colorado, near by," where dwelt the Yumas. They, moreover, were presented by the Cocomaricopas with some curious shells of a heavenly blue (*conchas azules celestes*) which, observes Kino, "so far as I know, occur only on the opposite coast of the West of California." [19]

By the shells there was afforded Kino ground of conjecture not only that California was not an island, but that the sea dividing it from Sonora was of extent so limited that presumably the head lay not far to the west; yet at the door of discovery,— or rather rediscovery, for, from the time of the voyages of Ulloa and Alarcón to that of the voyage of Vizcaino, the limited extent of the Sea of California was known to cosmographers, — Kino was blind. That the blue shells were an indication of peninsularity was obvious, but to use his own words: —

I penetrated 170 leagues to the northwest and went beyond 35° latitude with Father Adamo Gilg and Captain Mateo Manje . . . and came almost to the confluence of the Rio Grande de Gila and the Colorado, and the natives gave us some blue shells, and still it did not occur to us that by that way there was a land passage to California, or head of its sea; and only in the Road when we were returning to Nuestra Señora de los Dolores did it occur to me that said blue shells must be from the opposite Coast of California, and the South Sea, and that by the route by which they had come from there hither we could pass thither from here, and to California; and from that time forward I ceased the building of the bark . . . which we were building at Concepcion del Caborca near the Sea of California and here at Nuestra Señora de los Dolores, to carry it all to the sea afterward.[20]

The "heavenly blue shells" of the South Sea, these now (1700) became for Kino talismanic. At San Xavier del Bec (April 26 to May 2), he catechized "the principal governors and captains from more than 40 leagues distance, to find out whether the blue shells came from any other region than the opposite coast of California." And to every inquiry the answer was the same, that the shells "came from that sea ten or twelve days' journey farther than this other Sea of California, on which there [were] shells of pearl and white and many others, but none of these blue ones which were given us among the Yumas." "I thank Your Reverence for . . . the sending of the blue shells," wrote Padre Antonio Kappus, rector at Matape. "I am very strongly of the opinion that this land in which we are is terra firma with that of California. . . . If Your Reverence accomplishes the *Entrada* by land into California, we shall celebrate with great applause so happy a journey whereby the world will be enlightened as to whether it be an Island or a Peninsula, which to this day is unknown." And the rector of Oposura (Padre Manuel Gonzáles) wrote: "A Statue Rich and Famous we must erect to you, if you do this [make a California *entrada*]; and if it [the way] be short, there will be two statues." [21]

Starting from Los Remedios on September 24, 1700, Kino descended the Gila to its junction with the Colorado, where he arrived on October 7.

I ascended [he says] a Ridge to the Westward, where we knew how to sight so as to see the Sea of California, and looking and sighting toward the West and Southwest, with a telescope and without a telescope, [we beheld] more than 30 leagues of level lands without any sea.

And on the 9th he adds: —

Having set out from San Dionisio, and from the confluence of the two rivers, we arrived in the afternoon at the Paraje de las Sandias where was our relay; and we passed on two leagues farther to a *ranchería* where they gave us much fish; and we ascended another, a higher Hill, whence at sundown we sighted plainly many lands of California, and [perceived] that the two rivers (after their confluence) ran about 10 leagues to the west, and that afterward, turning southward about 20 leagues, they emptied into the Head of the Sea of California.[22]

The problem was practically solved. California could hardly be insular. Between it and Pimería there lay but the barrier of what Kino describes as the "very full-flooded, very Populous and very fertile Rio Colorado, which without exception is the Greatest [river] that all New Spain has; is that which Ancient Cosmographers called the Rio del Norte; is very probably from La Gran Quivera." But doubters there were, and to silence them it remained to confirm the fact of peninsularity by an expedition which, starting from Los Dolores, should reach Loreto by land.

In 1701 the California establishments were in sore need of chocolate and tobacco, and about February 20, Salvatierra crossed to Pimería. He reached Dolores, from Yaqui, with ten Sonora soldiers and six California Indians, and having been joined at San Ignacio by Lieutenant Manje, and at Caborca by Kino, the entire party, on March 10, with forty loads of provisions, bent their steps California-ward along the coast of the gulf. They bore aloft a picture of Our Lady of Loreto, and before it the very trail itself broke forth into "pleasantness and beauty of roses and flowers of different colors," as, "praying and chanting praises of Our Lady in Castilian, in Latin, in Italian, and in the California language," the pilgrims made their way. On March 15, at San Marcelo del Sonoydag, letters were received from Ugarte on the way to California from Mexico, and on the 18th, at El Carrizal, there came messages, how the Quiquimas who dwelt beyond the Colorado, and who were the first objective of the expedition, were awaiting its arrival "anxiously and lovingly." [23]

But straightway the problem of the desert arose. Should the expedition pursue a course west across the sands, rounding the head of the gulf; or should it "ascend to the northwest, circling the very great sandy waste of the Head of the Sea of California, and ascending to the Rio Grande and Rio Colorado by the circuit by which [Kino] had already come in 3 other times?" Manje favored the Gila-Colorado route; but it was decided to "travel by the road shortest and most directly westward." For fifteen days men and animals pushed on over sand-dunes and lava-beds, stopping at water-holes, and making the most of the scant pasturage till they reached Pitaqui (La Petaca). "Here," says Kino, "from a little ridge which we ascended, taking with us the Picture of Our Lady of Loreto, we plainly sighted California and the great Sierra called Sierra del Mescal, and the other called Sierra Azul, and the Closing in of Both Lands of this New Spain and California." But it was declared by Indians of the locality that "to penetrate to the Quiquimas of California there lay still 30 leagues, or three days' journey, of stretches of sand so great as to be without water or pasturage; whereupon," Kino continues, "Padre Salvatierra determined that we should return, and we planned that I, on another more favorable occasion, should penetrate in higher latitude by way of the confluence of the Rivers and by San Dionisio." [24]

Kino's conviction that California was not an island was not only not fully shared by Lieutenant Juan Mateo Manje: it was not so shared even by Salvatierra. On May 16 (1701), the latter wrote to his friend, assuring him of "benedictions" for his journey and discovery "from afar" that New Spain was conjoined to New California, but stating that rejoicings at Loreto were "much greater that [his] Reverence [had] means and desires to examine at close range what on distant view might be misleading." [25] The uncertainty felt by Manje arose from the circumstance that, "from a point about 3 leagues farther to the west than the Ridge from whence we returned," there could be descried a bay of limits undefined. [26] To meet this objection, and at the same time others, there was for Kino but one way, — to pass personally into the peninsula by land. Between November 3 and December 8 he penetrated to the Gila-Colorado junction at San Dionisio, descended the east bank of the Colorado among natives amazed at the speed of the horse, — an animal never before seen by them; was ferried across the stream on a raft by the Quiquimas, and so set actual foot upon the soil of a California which, in recognition of the fact that it lay a day's journey above the head of the gulf, was given by Kino the designation of Alta. [27] The Colorado had now been crossed, but its course to the gulf had not been fully traced. This task was reserved for the year 1702. Setting out, on February 5, with Padre Visitador Manuel Gonzáles (who, ill at starting, died on the completion of the trip), Kino, in March and April, descended the river along its eastern bank to tide-water. Here, as later by the intrepid Garcés, the night was passed, and here, in Kino's words, "the full sea rose very near our beds." [28]

On this *entrada* our cosmographer was accompanied neither by Manje nor by Salvatierra, yet by it the doubts of the twain with respect to peninsularity were sensibly diminished.

I have reached and seen [Manje certified on May 15] the Arm of the Sea of California at three distant places in various altitudes of the North Pole. In that of 28 degrees I have seen and observed exactly, with mathematical Instruments, that said Arm of the Sea is no more than twenty-six leagues; and at . . . 32 degrees only twenty leagues; and at 31 degrees, where I saw it the last time, said sea has only the inconsiderable width of twelve leagues, which measures and observations testify that the nearer one approaches the said Arm of the Sea to the Northwest, the more and more does its width diminish; and in order to find out if it ended higher up to the Northwest, the said Father Euzevio Francisco Kino set out on the *Entrada* to which Reference is made. And His Reverence informed me with honesty [he has] been at the Head of the said Arm of the Sea, and saw that the land of the Pimería joined with California, and states confidently [that] it is a Peninsula. . . . I have not seen [all] to certify it here with the verisimilitude which the case requires; only I assert confidently that it is a Relation of a fervid Minister to whom has been given entire Credit, as above I stated.[29]

The testimony of Salvatierra was penned March 3, 1703, and is as follows:—

I received the [letter] of Your Reverence accompanied by the Map of the Discovery of the Landlocked Strait which is so much doubted, whereupon I have been no little weighed down. But . . . there is no reason to be discouraged, but to try well with the Superiors to make another journey, in which this truth shall be found out, this time with evidence. . . . With it, so many New Map-Makers will be silenced, for they are not going to be silenced until they see themselves confuted [*concluidos*].[30]

But be the testimony of Manje and Salvatierra what it might, Kino's faith that California was not an island was fixed, and upon it there was reared by him a great conception. To Salvatierra peninsularity meant chiefly a stable means of food-transportation to Loreto. To Kino it meant more. It meant a crossing to "the opposite coast of the Sea of California, to its Cape Mendocino, [and] to the Harbor of Monte Rey"; for the climate of California, was it not "like to that of Castilla, to that of Andalusia, to that of Italy, to that of France"? Withal, to Kino, peninsularity meant "the removing of great Errors and Falsehoods": as of "a Crowned King carried in a Litter of Gold"; of "a lake of quicksilver and of another lake of gold"; of "a walled city with Towers"; of "the Kingdom of Axa"; of "the Pearls, Amber, Corals of the Rio del Tizon," etc. Finally (so Kino argued), might not peninsularity signify that the strait of Anian itself had no more foundation than this "Arm of the Sea" which made of California an island, — the true way from Japan being by Cape Mendocino, whence "might be brought to these Provinces of Sonora the goods of the very Rich Galleon from the Philippines." [31]

But the sun of the cosmographer of Ingoldstadt was beginning to decline, and in 1711 he died among the Pimas, at the age of seventy-one years. Never after 1702 did he visit the Colorado; yet he made other journeys, and in 1706 twice penetrated to the shore of the gulf. Of these visits the first (January) resulted in the discovery of an island named by Kino Santa Inés, and of a California cape named by him San Vicente.[32] The second visit was more memorable.

General Jacinto de Fuens-Zaldaña of the *compañía volante* for Sonora was friendly to Kino, and in October sent him forth to the Sea of California attended by persons who, if California really were peninsular, could bear convincing testimony to Viceroy and King. The expedition, besides the necessary *vaqueros* and *arrieros* with pack-train and

cattle, consisted of Lieutenant Juan Mateo Ramírez,
Corporal Juan Antonio Durán, and a Franciscan padre,
Manuel de la Ojuela y Velarde, who had come north soliciting alms for the Franciscan establishment at Guadalajara.
Seemingly it was intended to round the head of the gulf,
thus completing the attempt made by Kino and Salvatierra
in 1701; for word was sent in advance to the Indian governor of Sonoydag that by that way two padres and two
soldiers would make *entrada á la California* by land. But
on reaching Sonoydag, on November 2, no Quiquima
guides had appeared, and it was decided to climb Santa
Clara Mountain and take an observation from its summit.

Santa Clara Mountain — a cluster of the Gila Range —
is described by Ojuela as "grand in the extreme." From
the midst rose three heights pyramidal in form, one to the
south, one to the east, and one to the west, forming a triangle. To look downward inspired terror, the sand-hills
so simulating the sea that the latter, though more than
nine leagues away, seemed to surge against the base. The
foot of the pile was gained on the afternoon of the 5th, and
here, at a tank in the rocks, all partook of meat and drink.
Then, with Durán in charge of the sumpters and relays,
and with the best mules as mounts, the ascent of the south
peak was begun. When the task was finished, it was sundown. "We saw," says Ojuela, "the Sea of California, its
mountains and the great sandy beach in which the said
Sea ends. . . . We could not," he adds, "discern with perfect distinctness, for straightway night fell upon us, and
here we slept." With the dawn, Ojuela hastened down the
south peak in order to ascend that to the west, which was
yet higher, and from its summit what he saw (and that
clearly) was "a port three or four leagues in circuit; . . .
a great sand beach covered, for more than sixty leagues,
with box [sage-brush], wherein the port and sea termin-

ated"; and last "the disemboguement of the full-flooded Colorado" in an estuary "great enough, perchance, to float ships of the royal navy. . . . Wherefore," affirms he, "*no es Ysla la California sino solo Peninsula*, — the truth of which the Padre Eusebio Kino, who has said and written it many times, had brought us to confirm."

The same day, concludes Ojuela, "we descended the two eminences; saddled our mules; rode to the tank where we had left our sumpters and relays; heard the padre [Kino] say Mass; ate; mounted our horses and began the return to San Marcelo [del Sonoydag]." [33]— "And Moses went up from the plains of Moab unto the mountain of Nebo, to the top of Pisgah, that is over against Jericho. And the Lord shewed him all the land of Gilead, unto Dan; and all Naphtali, and the land of Ephraim, and Manasseh, and all the land of Judah, unto the utmost sea; and the south, and the plain of the valley of Jericho, the city of palm trees, unto Zoar. And the Lord said unto him, This is the land which I sware unto Abraham, unto Isaac, and unto Jacob, saying, I will give it unto thy seed: I have caused thee to see it with thine eyes, but thou shalt not go over thither." That while Kino (a Jesuit) surveyed from afar the land of promise which he was not to enter, there should have stood beside him a Franciscan father, — one of a holy Order which later was to subdue the land and possess it even "unto Cape Mendocino and the Harbor of Monterey," — is not the least exceptional incident of this exceptional *entrada* of 1706.

Meanwhile, the California missions (there at length were two, — Loreto and San Xavier) were kept alive with difficulty. On quitting Loreto for Pimería in 1701, Salvatierra had left Piccolo as vice-rector. On returning, he found Ugarte, and by the firmness of the latter he was prevented from abandoning the peninsula in bitter tears. But, on July 17, Philip V (King of Spain since 1700) issued three *cédulas* conferring on the missions of California an annual stipend of 6000 *pesos*.[34] Piccolo at the time was in Mexico, but in 1702 he returned with the first year's stipend and with private gifts to the Pious Fund from the Marqués de Villapuente and Nicolás de Ortega and wife, of 40,000 *pesos*.[35] Moreover in 1703 this stipend of 6000 *pesos* was ordered by the King increased to 13,000.[36] At intervals between 1702 and 1711 the Crown, as represented by the Duque de Albuquerque, sought to substitute a military occupation for an occupation exclusively or dominantly sacerdotal. But the attempt was not prolonged, and California exploration and settlement were carried forward by missionaries on the Mission plan.

In 1717, on July 17, Salvatierra, while on a journey to Mexico, died at Guadalajara, at the age of seventy-three.[37] But Ugarte as yet was only fifty-seven, and in 1721, in a ship built by him at Mulegé, and named significantly El Triunfo de la Cruz, he fared to the mouth of the Colorado, testing for himself the soundness of Kino's views on the peninsular question.[38] Ugarte himself, however, died in 1730, and four years thereafter (1734) Lower California was swept by an Indian uprising provoked by a Mission order against polygamy. From this revolt, during which two padres were killed and an attack was made upon a shore party from the Philippine galleon San Cristóbal, it resulted that the Spanish Government, reverting to the idea of secular control, established at San José del Cabo a presidio for the convenience of the galleon, now regular in its stops at Cape San Lucas. The presidial commander withal was made free from missionary supervision, but the change led to disorders among the soldiery, and in 1738 the old system was restored.[39] Crowning all, there appeared in

1747, on December 4, a royal *cédula* which sanctioned for the reduction of the Californias the exact plan of Kino. Pimería Alta (the scene of Kino's labors) was to be occupied; a presidio was to be established on the Gila River; and Alta California was to be entered by way of the Arizona desert.[40]

To settle finally the question of peninsularity, Fernando Consag, a Jesuit, had in June, 1746, been sent by his provincial, Cristóbal Escobar, to the mouth of the Colorado. In due course he had made report,[41] and in the decree above cited, Ferdinand VI of Spain (successor to Philip V) pronounced that California *"no es Isla* [but] *una tierra firme,* bordering, in its upper or northern part, on New Mexico." Anian, however, was still to be reckoned with. Was there not, asked Miguel Venegas in his *Noticia de la California,* printed in 1757, a chance that the strait might be discovered by the English through the efforts of some disciple of Arthur Dobbs? As for the Russians, it was Venegas's claim that already they had taken surveys of their own coasts on the South Sea; had sailed as far as the islands of Japan, and had landed in several parts of Spanish America. Therefore, continued the Jesuit historian, emphasizing the Spanish Government's indorsement of Kino's far-reaching conception, "the missions must . . . be joined to the rest with New Mexico, [and] extended from the latter beyond the rivers Gila and Colorado to the furthest known coasts of California on the South Sea, — to Puerto de San Diego, Puerto de Monterey, the Sierras Nevadas, Cape Mendocino, Cape Blanco, or San Sebastián, and to the river discovered by Martín de Aguilar in forty-three degrees." [42]

California must be joined to Mexico not alone by way of Sonora (Pimería) but by way of New Mexico, — so declared Ferdinand VI and the historian Miguel Venegas. The idea had already been entertained by Kino.

In 1699 Kino described Pimería as extending "almost to the Province of Moqui"; and in April, 1700, when at San Xavier del Bec questioning "the principal governors and captains" about the heavenly blue shells, he said: "We also discussed what mode there might be of penetrating to the Moquis of New Mexico," a distance, as he conceived, of but sixty or seventy leagues. And in 1708 it was Kino's statement that "with these new conversions one can trade by sea and by land with . . . remote provinces and nations and kingdoms; with all Nueva Galicia, and with Nueva Vizcaya; with Moqui and with New Mexico, which shall be able to come to join hands with these Provinces of Sonora, and even with New France."

Little, however, was done for New Mexico, under Jesuit auspices, until 1743. In that year Padre Ignacio Keller was permitted to start for Moqui, and in 1744 Padre Jacobo Sedelmayr was allowed to do the same. The former, by an Apache attack, was forced to return, but the latter reached Bill Williams Fork. Sedelmayr as an explorer possessed comprehensive ideas. Like Kino he planned to make Pimería a base of operations northwestward as far as Monterey, and northward as far as Moqui.

"What of his Majesty having charged upon us the reconquest of Moqui?" asked Sedelmayr of the Viceroy from Tubutama on January 25, 1751. "Must we not first reduce the nations of the Gila and Colorado, through whose lands Moqui [and Upper California are] to be reached? . . . True is it that there are needed eleven or twelve missions to control the administration of so many nations, — Pimas, Cocomoricopas of the Gila, Cocomoricopas of the Colorado, Yumas Cuhana, Guicama, all in the valley of these rivers. . . . True is it that there will be required a presidio more numerous than the others, but by locating it on that part of the River Gila not very distant from Apachería, it

will operate, concurrently, almost to surround the Apaches; . . .
and in such case the [other] presidios will be relieved. If the
Seris be subjected, the presidio of San Miguel de Horcasitas will
be relieved, and it might be transferred to the River Gila." [43]

But while, as regards Alta California, the Mission was to
serve Spain effectively, it was not so to serve in Jesuit
hands. The Jesuits, barring a few exuberant spirits, had
never been enamoured of California. In 1686 they had
refused outright to attempt its conquest. In 1697 they
had recalled their refusal with hesitation. Later, under
Albuquerque, Salvatierra even had offered to give up the
conquest. So solitary amid rocks and thorns was Mission
life on the peninsula, and withal so fruitless, that it bred
melancholy.[44] Communication with Europe required two
and even three years, and with Mexico many months; while
as for Indian conversion (or rather "reduction"), despite
the padres it had become a process in which the disease
of syphilis,[45] spread by the presidial soldiery, had wasted
a population originally twelve thousand souls to 7149.[46]
In 1766 relinquishment was once again proposed, and,
as it chanced, with augmented reason, for the Jesuit Order
was tottering to its fall. Known throughout the world
for chastity and obedience, the Jesuits had failed to win
recognition for poverty. Neither mendicant nor lowly,
they, both in Europe and Paraguay, were deemed to have
heaped up unto themselves riches, and to have grasped at
power. Be the truth concerning them in these respects
what it may, they of a certainty had gained neither riches
nor power in California. Relief came to them in 1767. At
Loreto, on the 17th of December, they were formally notified by Gaspar de Portolá, in the name of Charles III (King
of Spain since 1759), of their expulsion from all the Spanish
dominions.[47]

CHAPTER V

REOCCUPATION OF MONTEREY, AND DISCOVERY
OF THE BAY OF SAN FRANCISCO

WITH the Mission, — Spain's sword of the Spirit, — tested and tempered by use in the Philippine Islands, in Paraguay, and, last, in Lower California, the conquest of Alta California was undertaken by Spain through the Franciscan Order of missionary friars, in the year 1769.

Of the religious Orders active in New Spain for the propagation of the Gospel, the Franciscans were by far the most popular, alike with the Spanish Government and with the Indians. The soul of their character was disinterestedness and self-abnegation. Their vows of chastity and obedience (at least since the reforms of Cardinal Ximénes) were well observed.[1] But their supreme merit was their observance of the vow of poverty, — the particular vow in respect to which the Jesuits as an Order were so signally to fail. The Franciscans at the beginning of their labors had in one point been inferior to the Dominicans. In Hispaniola they had not been unequivocally for freedom for the Indian. They had not joined with Pedro de Córdova in denunciation of the *encomienda*. But as time passed, they became so far liberalized that it was with difficulty that any inferiority to the Dominicans could be pointed out.[2]

The Order made its appearance in Mexico in 1524.[3] It came in response to royal commands and papal Bulls, issued respectively by Ferdinand (1508), by Leo X (1521), and by Adrian VI (1522); and it came in characteristic

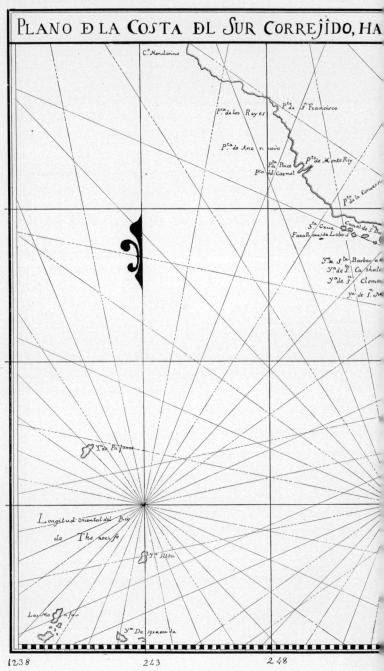

CHART III. CALIFORNIA COAST. B

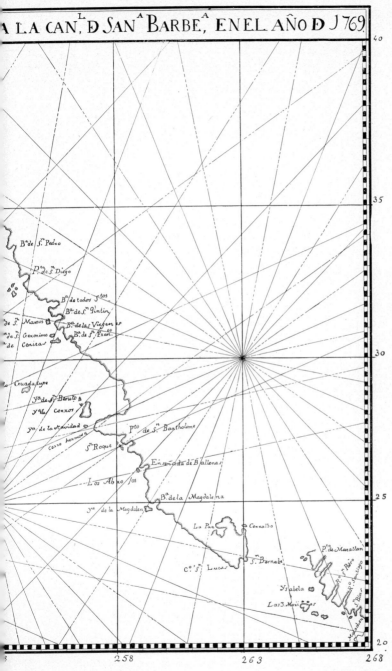

TANSÓ, 1769. (Hitherto unreproduced)

guise. Sandal-shod and in flowing gowns of sackcloth, the Franciscans, a band of twelve, the apostolic number, arrived in the capital on May 13, and were reverently greeted by Cortés, who, abasing himself at the feet of their superior, Martín de Valencia, humbly kissed his garments. Almost immediately (July 2) the *Custodia del Santo Evangelio de Propaganda Fide en la Nueva España y Tierra de Yucatán* was established, with the capital as a base; and apostolic colleges or missionary training-schools were formed at Querétaro, Zacatecas, and elsewhere, points convenient for supplying missionaries for the spirtual conquest of outlying provinces.[4]

One of the colleges so formed (1734) was that of San Fernando.[5] It was located at the capital, and in 1767 (June), on the enforcement in New Spain of the expulsion decree against the Jesuits, was assigned the duty of taking charge of the missions (soon to be vacated) of Lower California. Five of the members — among them the Mallorcans Juan Crespi and Fermín Francisco Lasuén — were in the Sierra Gorda, a district of the province of Nueva Galicia near the Gulf of Mexico. These now were recalled, and having been joined by eleven from the college, — among them the Mallorcan Francisco Palou, — the entire band was placed under the presidency of another Mallorcan, himself of distinguished service in Sierra Gorda, — Junípero Serra.[6] The band took ship from San Blas on March 13, 1768,[7] and on April 1 they reached Loreto. But the substitution by the government at Madrid of Franciscans for Jesuits as guardians in the peninsula was significant of more than at first appeared.

Charles III (successor in 1759 to Ferdinand VI) ascended the Spanish throne under favorable conditions. It was his good fortune to have had in Ferdinand a predecessor who loved peace, founded libraries and academies, encouraged the useful arts, and laid up money. To Charles there were bequeathed a National Library, an Academy of History, fifty ships of war, over fourteen thousand silk looms, and three millions in cash, — an accumulation of resources unparalleled since the days of the Moriscos. Withal under the new king there took place a revival of interest, economic and political, in New Spain, — a revival not unlike that provoked under Philip III by the memorial of Hernando de los Ríos, and under Philip V and Ferdinand VI by the ideas of Eusebio Kino. What, however, made the new revival distinctive was the confirmation thereunder of the policy of the ministers Aranda, Campomanes, and Floridablanca, who sought to curb the priesthood, — a course which in Alta California (*vide* chapter VII) was destined to be pursued by its chief lawgiver, Felipe de Neve.

In 1761 José de Gálvez of Malaga, a son of the people,[8] was sent to Mexico as *visitador* (inspector) general. In 1764 he was vested with powers well-nigh supreme, and in 1766, still further to strengthen his hands, Carlos Francisco de Croix, scion of a family illustrious in Flanders, was appointed viceroy. Shortly after the coming of Croix, war with the Indians (Apaches, Seris, Pimas) broke forth in Sinaloa and Sonora, and the Viceroy, finding his resources taxed, took earnest counsel with the *visitador*. The result (January 23, 1768) was a joint dispatch to the King, — a dispatch fundamental in the history of California, — in which it is stated that, in view of the remoteness of Sonora, Sinaloa, Nueva Vizcaya, and the peninsula of California, and of their unsettled condition, it has been decided, in council, that Gálvez shall visit these provinces, establish in them pueblos, and regulate their government. Further reasons assigned for the visit of Gálvez are: (1) Attempts for two centuries by France and England to discover the Strait of Anian; (2) the recent conquest of Canada by England, — "a nation that spares neither expense, diligence, nor fatigue in advancing her discoveries"; and (3) the efforts of Russia, by trading expeditions from Kamtchatka to the Aleutian Islands, to penetrate "our new Indies" by way of the sea of Tartary.

The joint dispatch says: —

It is known to our court by the voyages and narratives that have been published in Europe that the Russians have familiarized themselves with the navigation of the sea of Tartary, and that (according to a well-founded report) they already carry on trade in furs with a continent, or perhaps island [Alaska], distant only eight hundred leagues from the Western Coast of the Californias, which extends to the capes Mendocino and Blanco.

And again: —

It admits of no doubt that from the year 1749, [sic] when Admiral Anson came to the western coast of this kingdom, to the time of the seizure of the Port of Acapulco [by the Dutch], the English and Dutch have acquired a very particular knowledge of the ports and bays that we hold on the South coast, especially the peninsula of the Californias; so that it would be neither impossible, nor indeed very difficult, for one of these two nations, or the Muscovites, to establish, when least expected, a colony in the port of Monterey. Wherefore [the dispatch concludes], it behooves us, taking matters in time, to put in force what means are possible for warding off the dangers that threaten us. And — the peninsula of the Californias disembarrassed, and its population increased by help of the free commerce which ought to prevail between it and this kingdom — it will be easy to transport a colony to the port of Monterey by the same ships that we already have in the South Sea,—ships constructed for the purposes of the expedition to Sonora against the Indians.[9]

On this same 23d of January, 1768, the date of the above dispatch by Croix and Gálvez, it chanced that the Spanish Government itself, aroused by the voyages of the Russians eastward from Kamtchatka, was inditing a dispatch. It was addressed to the Viceroy, and commanded him to warn the newly appointed governor of the Californias — Gaspar de Portolá, occupant of the peninsula since November 30, 1767 — against Russian attempts; attempts which if possible he was to frustrate. This dispatch, received by Croix in May, was acknowledged by him on the 28th of the month, with the statement that he had communicated its contents to Gálvez, who since April 9 had been on the way to the peninsula, and that he (Gálvez) had resolved to effect a reconnoissance of the important port of Monterey for the purpose of establishing there a presidio.[10]

When the *visitador* reached Lower California (Cerralvo Inlet, near La Paz) it was the 5th of July.[11] He was met by the captain of the presidio of Loreto, Fernando Xavier Rivera y Moncada, and headquarters were assigned him at the hacienda of Manuel Osio [12] in the royal mining-camp of Santa Ana. The problems which confronted him were three: (1) The establishing of Indian pueblos; (2) the promotion of colonization by Spaniards; and (3) the expedition to Monterey. By the first problem Gálvez was not a little perplexed. He had come expecting to find a set of mission establishments well regulated and with a clientage of natives passably broken to civilization. What he in fact found was a set of establishments, — the spiritualties in charge of Serra and his Franciscans, the temporalties in charge of soldiers (*comisionados*) appointed by Portolá, — with a native clientage, if clientage it might be called, half-fed, wholly naked, devoured by syphilis, and wandering in the mountains.

The *visitador* first dismissed the *comisionados* and restored the system of the Mission, by bestowing upon the Franciscans the temporalties.[13] Next, he addressed himself to the Indians. For feeding the wretches, he brought

whole *rancherías* from the north, where population ex-
ceeded the means of subsistence, to the less burdened
south. For clothing them (a point upon which he insisted
as one indispensable to civilization), he made requisition
for bales of cloth; and for weaning them from the mountains,
he sought to establish them in *pueblos formales,* or regular
towns, "giving them houses and lands to be inherited by
their sons." [14] Finally, in order that his efforts might
be promptly seconded by the padres, he proclaimed that
Spanish honor was at stake. Very soon there were to
arrive in the peninsula six French Academicians, accompanied by two officials of the Spanish marine, to observe
the transit of Venus. What if these learned foreigners
were to behold there "the sad sights and depopulated
places that [he] had beheld four months before"? What if
they should cause it to be published in their reports that
"in the Californias the greatest and most pious monarch
of the world was lord only of the deserts, and had for vassals wandering Indians living like wild beasts"? [15] Colonization by Spaniards was also a problem of difficulty.
Solution was attempted by the *visitador* through a decree
(August 12, 1768) offering Crown lands and military
rights.[16]

But it was the expedition to Monterey (his own conception) that claimed the heart of Gálvez. It claimed also the
heart of Croix; and, straightway it was known, the heart
of Junípero Serra. An unusual group — one unusual even
for New Spain — were the three men, José de Gálvez,
visitador; Francisco de Croix, viceroy; and Junípero Serra,
president of the California missions: Gálvez, — honest,
masterful, and bluff; Croix, — honest, discerning, and
diplomatic; Serra, — a seraphic spirit, a later Salvatierra,
a New-World Francis of Assisi; post-mediæval, yet not be-

lated for his task; beholder of visions, believer in miracles, merciless wielder of the penitential scourge; [17] yet through simple purity of heart, possessed of a courage not unequal to labors the most arduous, and of a wisdom not unequal to situations the most perplexing. When, therefore, two from the group (Gálvez and Serra) met under the sanction of the third (Croix), as they did at Santa Ana on October 31, 1768, to confer regarding the exact means and course for reaching Monterey, activity was assured.[18]

There was to be an expedition, Indian auxiliaries included, of about 225 men in four divisions, — two by sea, and two by land.[19] Among the transports plying between San Blas (Spanish naval base for the Northwest), San José del Cabo, and Guaymas, were the Lauretana, the Sinaloa, the Concepción, the San Carlos, and the San Antonio or Príncipe. Of these the first three were used by Gálvez to bring supplies to La Paz, while the other two (brigantines) were appointed by him to take, each, from that point a division of the expedition. Northwestern navigation in 1768 was no less formidable than in the days of Vizcaino, and from the moment that the *visitador* charged himself with the fate of these vessels he scarcely slept. "Both the San Carlos and Príncipe may reach La Paz between the 20th and 25th of this month," he writes to Serra on September 15, "but if retarded, the months of October and November will be suitable for sailing, as then, according to a Filippine pilot, there prevail winds favorable for Monterey." [20] On October 7, he writes: "I long with eagerness for the coming of the packet-boats, and, as I am persuaded that at San Blas the Equinox is passed, I conceive them as already this hour on the sea. God grant that they come soon to La Paz!" [21] Four days later he has heard that in a tempest on the 29th of September the Lauretana and Sinaloa were driven aground but have

escaped damage. "Implore our patroness Lady of Loreto," he adjures Serra, "that she bring safely the packet-
boats, for without them everything will be undone." [22] At
length (November 12) word comes of the arrival at Cape
San Lucas of the San Carlos, and the vessel is impatiently
ordered by Gálvez to hasten to La Paz.[23]

From the elaborate and somewhat costly vestments
and silver utensils (censers, candlesticks, chalices) with
which the Jesuits had provided the peninsular churches
of La Pasión, San Luis, and Todos Santos, the *visitador*
has been making requisitions for the north. "I think,"
he writes to Serra on October 11, "that we shall not be
able to establish more than three missions right away, and
to each of these we can assign six sets of vestments; while
as for the utensils, they are being cleaned and repaired by
the official silversmith." [24] Names for the new establishments had been considered on September 15. The ancient
discoverers had given the name San Diego to a port
where one of the new missions was to be placed. There
should be no change. To another famous port they had
given the name of the glorious patriarch San Francisco.
Here especially no change should be made, as by the intercession of so great a father there would be facilitated
the founding of a mission at Monterey. As for the intermediate mission, let it, in order to share the intercession,
be called San Buenaventura; while as for the fort and
pueblo to be erected at Monterey, no name should be considered but San Carlos, — name at once of "our beloved
sovereign, of the Prince of Asturias, and of the Viceroy of
New Spain." [25] Then there were other matters: bells
(three of five belonging to La Pasión and San Luis) to be
unhung and packed, and a supply of sour fruits ("precious
against scurvy in latitude 30° and beyond") and of oil,
dates, wine, brandy and vinegar, to be collected. "So

infinite is my business, so many are the things to be seen to by me at one time," exclaims Gálvez in distraction, "that even though my ardor rises with my difficulties, my days not merely are consumed, but in great part my nights!" [26]

Meanwhile the San Carlos (brigantine of eleven sails), on arriving at La Paz, had been found unseaworthy, had been careened, and was being thoroughly overhauled both as to her keel and sides. The work, closely supervised by the *visitador*, was finished on December 27, and although performed with scant resources, was pronounced excellent in character.[27] The day fixed upon for sailing — whether the Príncipe (San Antonio) should be come or not — was January 8, 1769. Besides the church furniture, the oil, the dates, the wine, etc., already mentioned, there were on board meat, fish, maize, lard, wood, coal, sugar (white and brown), figs, raisins, salt, red pepper, garlic, flour, bread, rice, chick-peas, water, cheese, chocolate, hams, smoked tongue, lentils, candles, bran, beans, hens, a few live cattle, and 1000 *pesos* in money. There also was on board a carefully chosen company: Captain Vicente Vila (Andalusian) of the royal navy, with a mate (Jorge Estorace) and crew of twenty-three sailors and two boys; Cosmographer Miguel Costansó, — an engineer already distinguished, and destined to become yet more so in connection with notable undertakings in Mexico; Surgeon Pedro Prat of the royal navy; Lieutenant Pedro Fages, with twenty-five volunteers from the Catalan company serving in Sonora; four cooks; two blacksmiths; and last a chaplain, Hernando Parrón, one of Serra's Franciscans.[28] Serra himself, as well as Gálvez, was present at the departure.[29] "*Oratio brevis*," the latter writes to Palou, on January 9, from La Paz, "the San Carlos is just sailing from this port for the Sacred Expedition. . . . The twelve

[Indian] boys whom you sent have pleased me much. I turned them over to the priest here to aid in the confessions and to assist at the ceremony of blessing the packet-boat and banners, — a ceremony performed by the Father-President. Then *I* preached, the worst of all."

Gálvez in the Concepción accompanied the brigantine as far as Cape San Lucas, alike to observe her behavior and to intercept, near the cape, the San Antonio (unable, it was thought, to reach La Paz), and to send her forward as division two of the Sacred Expedition. Solicitous at first, as he watched the San Carlos, his own handiwork, meet the seas, the *visitador* quickly gained a joyous confidence.

We cast anchor on the 14th [he wrote to Serra, from the cape, on January 26] and in truth might have come in two days, had I put myself in the San Carlos; for, to keep in convoy the Concepción, which carried full sail during the voyage, the blessed packet-boat carried only her fore-topsail and her main-topsail half lowered. In short, the San Carlos, with a moderate wind, growing fresh as on the second day we left the island of Cerralvo, went six knots an hour. It may be imagined how she would have sped if she had been free to use but half her sails. Your Reverence may offset with this truth (which all have noted with admiration) the infamous lies which are spoken of the packet-boat, — a vessel, without exaggeration, one of the best possessed by the King in his armadas.

And he adds: —

Joachín Robles, and all the old sailors who came in the Concepción, exclaimed constantly in benedictions and praises of the San Carlos, and say that she is worthy to be enchased in gold. Your Reverence may conceive the satisfaction of those sailing in her, and my satisfaction to see falsified all the coward prognostications of the distrustful, and my own projects realized, which, undertaken with constant faith and a pure heart, God has willed should find complete fulfillment in this voyage to the cape.[30]

But concerning the voyage of the San Carlos, let us be advised by the log of her commanding officer: —

Noon of Monday, January 9, to noon of Tuesday, January 10, 1769. — At midnight, with a shore breeze (cat's paw) south-southwest, hove anchor [from La Paz], and with everything set and launch at prow prepared to sail. Tide contrary and so strong as scarcely to be stemmed. At one o'clock (wind seaward northwest) anchored in mid-channel in three fathoms of water, mud and sand. At midday, hoisted jib, fore-topsail and spanker; the launch with a kedge doing all possible, by way of towing, to give us an offing.

Tuesday, 10, *to Wednesday,* 11. Continued kedging till half-past four in the afternoon, when cast anchor almost in the mouth of channel, for already the tide was rising. At half-past six in the morning set topsails, wind brisk from the southwest. At this hour descried the packet-boat standing out with flag at main-mast, the Most Illustrious Señor Visitador-General on board, bound for Cape San Lucas and the Bay of San Bernabé. At half-past seven, passing [the packet-boat] to starboard, lowered topsails and saluted by hail and by the six guns which were mounted, keeping in convoy. At midday saw Cerralvo Island to southeast six or seven leagues, finding myself still in channel be-tween Point San Lorenzo and the island of Espiritu Santo. . . . The bottom of the channel, which sounds four, five, or six fathoms, is clear, consisting of sandbanks and stone, with some mud. And it is said by coast pilots that these banks bear pearl-produc-ing shells.

Wednesday, 11, *to Thursday,* 12. . . . , Sunrise: the coast and smoky horizon gave no sign of the Concepción or Comandante till nine o'clock, when boat was sighted in-shore to starboard, and I shortened sail to wait for her. . . . Made out the island of Cerralvo to the northwest and Cape Pulmo to the southeast.

Thursday, 12, *to Friday,* 13. Followed, with moderate wind, on lookout for Pulmo, topsails lowered, to avoid passing the Con-cepción, till four in the afternoon, when, coming within hail, his Excellency ordered me to press sail, as he wished to see the packet-boat [San Carlos] show her speed. At sunset, being about a league from the Comandante, furled all light sail and lowered the great sails, continuing with the topsails. . . . At Angelus, two huge fires seen on Pulmo. At midnight, hove to off Cape Porfía to await Comandante, and at four in the morning pro-ceeded in convoy.

Friday, 13, *to Saturday*, 14. Continued in convoy of Comandante, wind contrary with moderate sea, etc. At eleven o'clock, Comandante passed. Kept in wake on lookout for Cape San Lucas.

Saturday, 14, *to Sunday*, 15. Followed Comandante, wind moderate, sea calm, to within a league of the coast, all sail set. At four o'clock in the afternoon, a league and a half from the bay of San Bernabé, wind almost calm, the Comandante lowered and sent ashore a boat. At Angelus, Comandante, with our ship alongside, anchored in twenty fathoms. At eight o'clock, went to kiss the hand of his Excellency, and at nine returned on board. Night passed in calm, and at half-past seven in the morning his Excellency came on board with his suite and the crew of the Concepción. Mass over, his Excellency said farewell to all, giving orders in particular that without loss of time I should sail for my destination, governing myself exactly by the instructions already given me.[31]

Stopping at San Lucas only long enough to take fresh water, and hay for the cattle, the San Carlos, on the night of January 15 stood for the South Sea. And here occurred a thing not unmixed with pathos. For four days there prevailed light and contrary winds, with opposing currents of the ocean, and on each of the four days the *visitador*, from a high hill (*cerro eminente*), watched with anxious gaze the far-off and baffled ship. But on the 20th good breezes sprang "from the east and southeast," and "straightway the San Carlos disappeared." The founding of Alta California was indeed begun. The first division of the expedition to that end had been dispatched. "The Lord conduct it prosperously, the undertaking is all his!" prayed Gálvez.[32]

The San Antonio (which on January 15 had reached La Paz, despite efforts by Gálvez to intercept her off Cape San Lucas) dropped anchor at the cape on the 25th, and at once was beached and overhauled "from keel to pennant." More heavily provisioned even than the San

Carlos, and with a crew of twenty-eight men, she was got to sea, under Juan Pérez (Manila *piloto*), Miguel del Pino (master's mate), and Chaplains Juan Vizcaino and Francisco Gómez, on February 15. The day was further made memorable by the arrival at the cape of the San José, a new packet-boat especially built at San Blas for Monterey uses. "We blessed the ships and standards," facetiously writes the *visitador* on February 20, "by the help of four friars, two cannon, and a homily by me *á la burlesca*, as at La Paz. . . . It will be said that in the Californias there is verified *la comedia del Diablo Predicador*, and I shall laugh that so they call me, if only we gain the blessed object of our enterprise. . . . But," he continues, "the tongue, in my preachments, but spoke the feelings of my heart, which had gone in the ships, I not being able myself to go with them."

Thus was dispatched the second division of the expedition to Monterey. And all the while the heart of Gálvez grew lighter, for the winds continued to set from the south and southeast. "We have not had a day of northwest," writes the *visitador* (February 20), "since the sailing of the Príncipe (San Antonio); the winds have been so favorable that we all deem the ships as already at the doors of San Diego, and even as at anchor in that port. Both sail like birds." And two days later: "I have no doubt that the San Antonio is in San Diego, as the south and southeast winds have continued." [33]

There remained the two divisions by land to be dispatched, — divisions three and four of the expedition.

In these Gálvez put not the same trust as in the divisions by sea, as in his opinion they had not been undertaken with the same *viva fé*. But he wrought valiantly by exhortation to set them in motion. Of the first division Rivera y Moncada was commander, and by him, from and after

September, 1768, there were gathered (originally at Santa María, the most northerly of the peninsular missions, but afterwards at a point of good pasturage eighteen leagues further north) supplies of cattle (200 head), horses (38 head), mules (144 head), pack-saddles, leather bags, sides of leather, bottles, wheat, flour, dried meat, lard, sugar, figs, raisins, and wine.[34] And now that the San Carlos and San Antonio both had sailed, there was need that camp be broken by the land force. On February 20, therefore, Gálvez sent to Rivera a peremptory order to advance, expressing the wish that "God might lend wings to the bearer"; for was not news soon expected that "the packet-boats were lording it in that *famoso puerto* which had cost so many expeditions and anxieties"?[35] The division having on March 22 been joined at Velicatá by Padres Crespi and Lasuén (the former to accompany it and the latter to bless its departure), the captain, at four o'clock of the afternoon of the 24th, guided by the cosmographer, José Cañizares,[36] and at the head of 25 cuirassed men from the garrison of Loreto, 42 Christianized Indians, and three muleteers with 188 mules and horses, took up his march.

The fourth division (second of the two by land) had been mustered at San Juan de Dios, a spot some six leagues to the north of Velicatá, and on May 21 it followed Rivera. It was led by Governor Portolá himself (Catalan officer of dragoons, forty-seven years old),[37] a man laconic to the point of dropping his *h*'s, but honest withal and circumspect. Comprised in it were 10 soldiers (cuirassiers) of the presidio of Loreto, under a stout sergeant, José Francisco Ortega; 44 Christianized Indians; four muleteers with 170 mules; and two servants.[38] The division was accompanied by Junípero Serra, president of the new establishment, who had joined it on May 5, and one of the servants was for him. In the winter of 1749–50, the year of his arrival in Mexico, Serra, alive to the observance of Franciscan austerities, had insisted on proceeding from Vera Cruz to the capital on foot. A part of the way was infested with mosquitoes, and, sleeping one night in the open air, one of his ankles had been cruelly stung. The wound, envenomed by scratching and neglect, had developed into an ulcer, and but for his servant's help the Father-President would have been unable to mount his mule.[39] "Although it is an act of temerity," Gálvez had written him on March 28, "for you to set forth on a journey so great and laborious with your foot inflamed, I have no doubt that midway the fatigue it will grow better, and even well; for so the Lord rewards the *viva fé* of his followers who look to him as physician sovereign and unique."[40] For some weary leagues Serra proceeded under the inspiration of the words of the *visitador*. Then he had recourse to muleteer's ointment, a remedy by which speedily he found relief.

On May 1, the *visitador* himself had sailed for Sonora. The things upon which, when leaving, he had insisted were (barring the Monterey expedition) those upon which he had insisted when he came: Indian pueblos and colonization by Spaniards. As the site for a pueblo, Loreto had been designated. Hither were to be brought from the other peninsular missions one hundred families to dwell in whitened adobes, on tree-shaded streets, about a plaza. The youth were to be instructed in the propagation of the cochineal; while pearl-fishing, which, as sought to be practiced by the Spanish soldiery, had so plagued Salvatierra, was now to be conducted humanely under missionary superintendence.[41] But ever present to the mind of Gálvez, as prerequisite for the civilization of the California Indian, was that he be clothed, — "the men and boys in jackets and trousers, and the women and girls in chemisettes and skirts"; and this, too, before the spectacle of their nakedness should, to the scandal of Church and State, be revealed to the French Academicians shortly to arrive at Cape San Lucas. To this end, therefore, and to forward supplies by the San José, Francisco Palou was delegated by Serra to remain at Loreto as peninsular mission president *pro tempore*.[42]

Spanish colonization had received from Gálvez an impulse through a decree for a Spanish settlement; [43] but it was not until May 14 that a final matter of importance was carried out. For the support of the three establishments to be planted in the north (San Diego, San Buenaventura, and San Carlos), it had early been decided by the *visitador* to plant three between Santa María and San Diego. Of these the first (and, as it proved, also the last) was founded with appropriate ceremonies, on the date named, at Velicatá, — the mission of San Fernando.[44]

The objective of the Gálvez expedition was Monterey (Vizcaino's haven), but the four divisions had been ordered to rendezvous at San Diego, and here, by favor of the spouse of Our Lady of Loreto (St. Joseph, patron of the undertaking),[45] and by virtue of propitiatory litanies and Masses, the San Carlos, the San Antonio, Rivera, and Portolá were all arrived by July 1.

The division first to arrive had been the San Antonio. Keeping an inside course, the vessel had proceeded north to 34°. Thence turning southward she had sighted Vizcaino's Isla de Gente Barbada, which she had renamed Santa Cruz, and with two dead from scurvy had cast anchor on April 11.

As for the San Carlos, she had not only been behind the San Antonio, but far behind. By February 15 she had reached Guadalupe Island in 29°. By the 17th she had passed northward, encountering northwest winds with fog, rain, and heavy seas, and on the 26th had sighted the California mainland. For nearly a fortnight she had surveyed the coast for a watering-place, but without success; and on March 7 had stopped at the island of Cerros (Cedros). On the 26th (the northwest winds becoming "northwesters"), a sheltered course had been sought between Cerros Island and that of Natividad, and for the first time scurvy had appeared. By the 18th of April, twenty-two seamen and ten of Fages' squad were incapacitated, and the coxswain, Fernando Álvarez, had died. On the 24th, all the sick, even those not reconciled with the Church, had confessed and received the Sacrament, and there had died the coast pilot, Manuel Reyes. On the 26th, the San Carlos being within sight of Point Conception, Vila had decided to change his course to the southward. Inland rose "lofty sierras all covered with snow, like the Sierras Nevadas of Granada as seen along the Mediterranean on the coast of Motril and Salobreña," — an indication of the Santa Lucía Range at which the Philippine galleons were wont to alter direction for Acapulco. From Point Conception, down through San Pedro Bay (where anchor was dropped) to the Coronados Islands, the San Carlos under press of canvas, but with what were indeed "a ghastly crew," had reached San Diego near sundown on April 29.[46]

But what meanwhile of the divisions by land? On May 28, Serra records: "Until now we had not seen any woman among the Indians; and I desired for the present not to see them, fearing that they went naked as the men. When amid the *fiestas* two women appeared, talking as rapidly and vivaciously as this sex knows how and is accustomed to do; and when I saw them so honestly covered that we could take it in good part if greater nudities were never seen among the Christian women of the missions, I was not sorry for their arrival." And on June 24: "We slept under a very corpulent oak, and here we lacked the privilege of Lower California of the exemption from fleas, for we were covered with them and some ticks." On July 3 the Father-President records further: "About midway from Velicatá the valleys and rivers began to be delightful. We found vines of a large size and in some cases quite loaded with grapes. We also found [and here a touch that endears Serra to all lovers of California] in water-courses along the way . . . besides grapes, *varias rosas de Castilla.*" Already on June 2 he had noted: "Flowers many and beautiful, . . . and to-day we have met the queen of them all [*Reyna de ellas*], the rose of Castile. As I write, I have a branch before me with three full-blown roses, others in bud, and six unpetaled." [47]

The first land division (Rivera's) had made camp on May 14, and the second (Portolá's) on June 28; and in point of spirits and health both were unexceptionable. Serra, even, was cured of his lameness. Camp made, however, the scene beheld by the newcomers was most piteous.[48] Addressing the guardian of San Fernando on June 22, Crespi says that twenty-three persons (two of them Catalan volunteers) have died.[49] Portolá's account, sent July 4, is even more discouraging. Of the sea divisions, "all without exception," he declares, "seamen, soldiers, and officers, are stricken with scurvy, — some wholly prostrated, some half disabled, others on foot without strength, until the total number of dead is thirty-one." [50]

Vila, under orders issued by the *visitador* on January 5, was to proceed with the San Carlos, Fages and his men on board, at once from San Diego to Monterey. But this was conditioned upon the presence of the land division under Rivera. Should Rivera be anticipated by the San Carlos in arriving, the vessel was to wait for him twenty days and then proceed to Monterey, the San Antonio accompanying her if at that time in port.[51]

As we know, the San Antonio in fact reached San Diego before the San Carlos, but this was of little moment. What was of moment was the prevalence of the scurvy. By it the whole expedition was deranged. Seamen there virtually were none, and if Monterey was to be occupied at all, it must be by a force by land. Word (July 9) was sent to the Viceroy; the San Antonio, with five men and such of the sick as were able to be transported, was dispatched to San Blas for fresh crews for herself and the San Carlos; and, on July 14, the expedition — Portolá, Rivera, Fages, Ortega, Costansó, Crespi, and Gómez, 27 cuirassiers, 8 volunteers, 15 Christianized Indians, 7 muleteers, and 2 body-servants, 67 persons — again set out for the north.[52]

At San Diego — to found the mission of San Diego de Alcalá and to speed to Monterey the San José — there were left Vila, Serra, Vizcaino, Parrón, Cañizares, Prat, a blacksmith, a carpenter, and forty-five or fifty sailors and soldiers, mostly ill. The founding, the principal ceremony of which was a Mass by Serra under a great cross, was effected on July 16;[53] but as for the San José, she never came. Dismasted in the gulf in the year 1769, she, in May, 1770, sailed for the north and was lost.[54]

All the way from Velicatá the natives had been docile, but San Diego was in a Yuma district, a district of robbers, and in resisting depredations from certain of these on August 15, a fight was precipitated by the guard. Three Yumas and one Spaniard were killed, — the latter by an arrow in the throat; while Fray Vizcaino was disabled by an arrow in the hand.[55]

The Monterey party (to recur now to the expedition)

depended chiefly for guidance on two books in the hands of Miguel Costansó: the *Noticia de la California* of Venegas, which contained the account, from Torquemada, of Vizcaino's voyage of 1602–03, and a manual of navigation by the celebrated galleon pilot, Cabrera Bueno, printed at Manila in 1734.[56] The manual placed the far-famed port in 37°, and to the attainment of this latitude the party looked forward with eagerness. Their route lay by the seashore past San Clemente and Santa Catalina Islands to the site of the present city of Los Ángeles; thence through the San Fernando Valley to the headwaters of the Santa Clara River; thence, by the river valley, to the sea again; thence past Points Conception and Sal to the extremity of the Santa Bárbara Channel; thence inland to the site of the mission of San Luis Obispo; thence through the Cañada de los Osos to the sea at Morro Bay, and up the coast till progress was barred by the Sierra de Santa Lucía at Mount Mars. The sierra crossed (*camino penoso*), the route lay by the Salinas River Valley to the sea; and so to Point Pinos, which, according to Cabrera Bueno, was the index of Monterey.[57]

At the head of the party [writes Costansó] went Portolá with most of the officers, the six [eight] men of the Catalonian Volunteers, and some friendly Indians with spades, mattocks, crowbars, axes, and other pioneering implements, to chop and open a passage wherever necessary. Then came the pack-train in four divisions, each with muleteers and an escort of soldiers. The rear was closed by the remainder of the troops under Rivera y Moncada, who convoyed the horse-drove and the mule-drove for relays. By the necessity of regulating marches with reference to watering-places [Costansó continues], camp was pitched early each afternoon, so that the land might be explored one day for the next; and at four-day intervals more or less general fatigue, or the recovering of animals stampeded by a coyote or the wind, compelled a halt more protracted.[58]

Adventures were few. The party culled roses, — troops of them; fed on antelope; felt, near the present Los Ángeles, — a spot described by Crespi as "possessed of all the resources required for a large town,"[59] — *horrorosos temblores*, or frightful shocks of earthquake; noted springs and streams of sweet water; saw Indians, — the males "totally naked (*totalmente desnudos*) like Adam in Paradise before the fall"; remarked the number, stature, intelligence, and skill in canoe-building of the tribes along the Santa Bárbara Channel coasts; killed bears (*brutos ferocísimos*) in the Cañada de los Osos; gazed in discouragement from Santa Lucía Peak, 3000 feet high, on a foreground and background billowy with mountains; suffered from scurvy; and on October 1 (1769) gazed joyfully from a hilltop out over the bay of their search, indicated, as the histories said, by a beautiful point of pines.[60] But where was the harbor, the *puerto?* What was to be seen was simply an open roadstead. *Ni Puerto de Carmelo, ni de Monterei*, sorrowfully records Portolá.[61]

There remained, however, a point to be considered. The party as yet had not quite reached latitude 37°. So, after a council of officers and padres, at which it was agreed to find (by God's aid) Monterey with the San José there in waiting, or perish in the attempt, they on October 8 started again northward. Food ran short; scurvy reappeared; men had to be borne in litters; three cuirassiers received extreme unction; Portolá and Rivera themselves fell ill.[62] But at length rains came and all the sick recovered. Amid trials Crespi notes: "We came (October 10) on some tall trees of reddish-colored wood of a species unknown to us, having leaves very unlike those of the Cedar, and without a cedar odor; and as we knew not the names of the trees, we gave them that of the color of the wood, *palo colorado* (red wood)."[63] By the 1st of November the party reached

Point San Pedro, and from a hill (first of a series which barred further passage) saw before them in the distance Point Reyes, and at its base, extending toward the northeast, — six or seven *farallones* in its mouth, — the San Francisco Bay of Cermeño, — in a word, the present Bay of Francis Drake.[64]

Costansó, with his Cabrera Bueno, found little trouble in identifying the bay; but, to make fully certain, Ortega was sent by Portolá to examine Point Reyes, and during his absence (November 2) a thing occurred which caused perplexity. Some soldiers, climbing the hills to the northeast in pursuit of deer, came suddenly in sight of a new Mediterranean, the great inland sea now known as San Francisco Bay. How so extensive a body of water had hitherto escaped observation — the observation of Unamunu, of Cermeño, of Bueno, and of other northern navigators — was the question.[65] It was not answered, for Ortega, cut off from Point Reyes by the channel of the Golden Gate,[66] soon returned with a report by Indians of a ship anchored at the head of the newly discovered sea, — a ship which might be the long-expected San José. Upon search, however, no ship was found, and on November 11 Portolá, convinced that Monterey either had been passed in the fog, or long since had been obliterated by sand, started with his command, short of rations, back to Point Pinos, where he arrived on November 28.[67]

Monterey, not recognized by the explorers on the way north in October, was not recognized by them on the way south in November; and, having on December 10 erected as declaratory of their visit two great crosses, — one on the shore of Carmelo Bay, and the other on that of the very bay of which they were in quest, — they on December 11 pressed forward, reaching San Diego on the 24th of January, 1770.

For a little time the fate of the Gálvez expedition, and with it that of Alta California, trembled in the balance. At San Diego there had been many deaths, — fifty up to February 11, 1770; thirteen of them from Fages's band of Catalans alone.[68] Moreover, there was great scarcity of food. On January 28, Portolá calculated that the quantity on hand (maize, flour, etc.) would last fifty-four persons and fourteen Christianized Indians (his entire land force) twelve and one half weeks. Accordingly, March 20 was fixed upon as the latest date to which, with safety, a return of the expedition to Velicatá might be deferred. The gloom was general and it was deep. On February 11, Rivera with twenty-two men was sent to Velicatá to fetch north the cattle gathered there, and a sharp lookout was kept for the San Antonio, the return of which with supplies and a crew for the San Carlos was hoped for rather than expected.[69] Summing up, on February 9 and 11, to the *visitador* and Viceroy, respectively, the results of the Monterey adventure, Crespi and Portolá put stress upon the bright side. "I am not at all chagrined," writes the former, "that we failed to hit upon the port of Monte Rey; . . . and if in time we still fail of it, we possess of a certainty and as an actuality the Port of San Francisco." "To me," writes Portolá, "there remains the consolation that by this expedition there has been lost nothing but our great labor in the six months and a half that it has consumed. Exploration has been carried to the very precincts of San Francisco. The spirit of the *gentilidad* has been tested. The infinity of the population of the Channel of Santa Bárbara has been made known. The illusion that Monterey exists has been dispelled." [70]

But though Portolá might be convinced that Monterey no longer existed, and though Crespi might entertain as to its existence some doubt, Serra, who had remained at San

Diego, was firm in faith to the contrary, and made, according to Palou, a compact with Vila of the San Carlos to go in search of the port by sea, on the coming of the San Antonio, even though Portolá should on March 20 abandon the country. All day long on March 19 (St. Joseph's own day), the Father-President and his coadjutors prayerfully strained their eyes seaward for a sail. One appeared toward evening, but vanished with the fall of night. It nevertheless brought hope. Portolá deferred his departure, and five days later the San Antonio, under Pérez, sailed into port. When sighted she had been on her way with supplies to Monterey, under the belief that San Diego had already been visited by the San José. Landing near Point Conception for water and to regain a lost anchor, it was gleaned from the natives that the Monterey party had withdrawn, and course was at once changed to the southward.

The coming of the San Antonio, falling as it did on the day of St. Joseph, was taken for a strong omen by Portolá. It in fact quite roused his mind. Persuaded now that to fail in his undertaking would be disloyalty á Dios, al Rey, á mi 'onor, and remembering that on leaving the peninsula he had resolved "to perform his commission or to die," he took counsel with Pérez, with the result that on April 16 the San Antonio, carrying Pérez, Serra, Costansó, and Prat, was dispatched up the coast; while on the day following, Portolá with seven cuirassiers, Fages with twelve volunteers, and Crespi with five Christianized Indians, followed by land. Pérez was to proceed first to the estuary seen of the deer-hunters on the second of the preceding November (the present San Francisco Bay), where exploration was to be made by Costansó for a port and for a mission site. Next, the San Antonio was to go in search of the port of Monterey, — a spot which, although not found by land, might, as Gálvez had intended, be found by sea.

As a common rendezvous Point Pinos was selected. Thus, in the discovery of Monterey (if the port existed), the land force might participate with the ships. If, however, Monterey no longer did exist, a mission and presidio were to be established in whatever good port might be chanced upon, — perhaps the port of San Francisco; for the farther north such outposts were established, the farther north would be extended the dominions of the King.[71]

The land party reached Monterey Bay on May 24, and Crespi and Fages, attended by a soldier, at once hastened to the cross which had been erected. At its foot they found arrows, feathers and offerings of meat and fish. They then turned to the beach. The day was clear; the great bay lay like a lagoon between Points Pinos and Año Nuevo; and within it, at play, were to be seen numberless seals and two great whales. A few steps more, and the bay assumed the form of a vast O. With one voice the three men exclaimed: "This is the port of Monterey which we seek, in form exactly as described by Sebastián Vizcaino and Cabrera Bueno!" On the 31st, Monterey was reached by the San Antonio, which, although having attained the latitude of the estuary, had not stopped to explore it; and on June 1, Portolá received the embraces and congratulations of Fages and Crespi.[72]

With the occupation (under Gálvez) of Monterey by Serra and Portolá, — an occupation destined to be permanent, — there were brought to an end two hundred and thirty-five years of effort on the part of Spain to possess herself of California; effort at no time designedly relinquished, save during the years 1607 to 1612, when interest in Anian lay dormant, and when, as a substitute for Monterey as a port-of-call, the islands Rica de Oro and Rica de Plata were vainly sought, amid storm and stress, by Sebastián Vizcaino off the coasts of Japan.

But occupation as a feat was not permitted to over-
shadow occupation as an event. Recognizing with respect
to California a vital nexus between the days of Philip III
(1606) and those of Charles III (1770), Gálvez had enjoined occupation under penalty (in case of failure) of
offense "to God, the King, and the country"; and under
requirement (in case of success) of suitable and stately observances. The latter, participated in by the chief functionaries of Church and State, were now (June 3) duly
celebrated.

On the beach, near Vizcaino's oak, there was erected an
altar equipped with bells and surmounted with an image
of Our Lady. Before it (President Serra in alb and stole
representing the Church) the assembled company chanted
in unison, upon their knees, the beautiful *Veni Creator
Spiritus*. The President then, amid din of exploding arms
on land and ship, blessed a great cross and the royal
standards of Castile and León. He next sprinkled with
holy water the beach and adjoining fields, "to put to flight
all infernal enemies," recited the Mass, and preached.
With a *Salve* to the image of Our Lady, and with the
singing by the company of *Te Deum Laudamus*, the religious ceremony was brought to a close. It was followed by
a ceremony on the part of the State. Here as representative, the governor, Gaspar de Portolá, officiated. In his
presence the royal standards were again unfurled, grass
and stones were wrenched from the earth and scattered
to the four winds, and the varied proceedings of the day
were made matter of record.

It had been the express order of Gálvez that *Te Deum* be
sung at Monterey. And, in order that the hymn might be
repeated in Lower California and in Mexico, proclaiming
there the glad northern tidings, he had directed that word
of the occupation be dispatched southward as rapidly as

possible. Intrusted to a cuirassier (Joseph Velásquez), who left Monterey on June 15, it reached Todos Santos on August 2. Meanwhile, on July 9, the mission and presidio San Carlos Borromeo de Monterey having been founded as described, and duly christened, Portolá turned over to Fages the military command, and with Costansó and Pérez sailed in the San Antonio for San Blas. Arriving August 1, he at once sent a courier to the Viceroy, announcing his intention to rest at Tepic and then personally to present himself at the capital. This news, anticipating that borne by Velásquez, was received by Viceroy Croix on August 10.[73] It was heralded, first, by the bells of the city cathedral,[74] and then, responsively, by those of the churches. A solemn Mass in thanksgiving was attended by the government dignitaries, and on the 16th the news was spread throughout New Spain by an official proclamation.

In these rejoicings the *visitador*, who, victim of vast exertions, had for the greater part of the year 1769 lain prostrate of fever at Álamos,[75] was happily able to take part. At the viceregal palace, in company with Croix, he was made the recipient of hearty congratulations.

The Sacred Expedition was ended. Its fruits were yet to be gleaned. By the letters of Crespi, written in 1769 and 1770 from San Diego to his superior and to Gálvez, it became evident that six new California missions — three for the peninsula north of Santa María and three for Northern California — would not meet the needs of the dense population which had been encountered: ten thousand souls, it was estimated, along the coasts of the Santa Bárbara Channel alone. Indeed, as early as March 28, 1769, Gálvez had expressed to Serra the hope that the fleet which had sailed from Cádiz on November 4, 1768, would bring at least part of an expected reinforcement of Franciscans.[76] On June 8, 1769, the *visitador* had written from Álamos to Guardian Fray Juan Andrés, to send to the Californias all the *operarios* possible; [77] and two days later he had expressed to Croix the hope that, "of the forty-five friars levied from Spain, some had come in the present fleet." Forty-five, under Fray Rafael Verger as superior, ultimately did come, and on November 12, 1770, Gálvez and the Viceroy signified to Serra and Palou: (1) That five new establishments (San Gabriel Arcángel, San Luis Obispo, San Antonio de Padua, Santa Clara and San Francisco de Asis) were to be planted in the upper land under ten of the forty-five friars; and (2) that five other new establishments were to be planted in the peninsula, north of Santa María, under twenty of the same band.[78] They stated also that henceforth in California, as Gálvez had confided to Serra, missions would be founded and missionaries paid from the proceeds of the Pious Fund; the Indians themselves not being required, as by the Jesuits, to contribute.[79] For founding a mission, the allowance would be 1000 *pesos;* and for the salary of a missionary, 275 *pesos.*[80] In conclusion, attention was called to two sets of vestments contributed by the Viceroy, — one set, "very rich," for Loreto; and the other, "sumptuous" and "complete," for Monterey.

By the Monterey contingent of friars, after the arrival, May 21, 1771, of the ten from Spain, the missions San Antonio de Padua and San Gabriel Arcángel were established on July 14 and September 8, respectively. In 1772 (September 1) the mission San Luis Obispo de Tolosa was founded. San Carlos itself was not permitted to retain its original site, but, church, storehouses, and magazine, was reërected before the end of December, 1771, in an attractive spot in the Carmelo Valley.[81]

CHAPTER VI

SAN FRANCISCO FOUNDED

Á la que estoy del Río Colorado no hávia pasado hasta hoy la tropa de
S. M. — Juan Bautista de Anza to Viceroy Bucarely, February 9, 1774.[1]

IN 1771, both Viceroy Croix and Visitador Gálvez were
recalled to Spain.[2] Each had deserved well of his country, and each was to be suitably rewarded. Croix was made
viceroy and captain-general of the kingdom of Valencia,
and Gálvez was made *ministro universal* (general minister)
of the Indies. Serra, alone of the remarkable trio, remained
in Alta California to face in the field the problems to which
the occupation was fast giving rise. To sustain him in his
task there was the tradition of Croix-Gálvez pro-mission
methods, but this might be little regarded by a viceroy
personally or officially hostile.

Serra's presidency of the missions of Alta California
(terminated only by his death in 1784) outlasted the
natural life of Croix's immediate successor, Antonio María
Bucarely y Ursúa, and the official life of the first governor
and comandante of the soon-to-be-created Provincias
Internas, — Teodoro de Croix.[3] It was marked, moreover,
by events of the highest importance: The transfer, in 1772,
of Lower California to the Dominicans; the establishment,
in 1773, of a *modus vivendi* or working arrangement between
the mission authorities (the padres) and the comandante
and his subordinates; the overland expeditions, between
1774 and 1777, of Captain Juan Bautista de Anza, resulting
in the founding of the presidio and mission of San Francisco; the dispatch northward, between 1774 and 1779, of

three maritime parties in search of the Russians; the establishment, in 1777 and 1781, respectively, of the pueblos San José and Los Ángeles; and the attempted founding, between 1780 and 1782, of "pueblo missions" on the River Colorado. Of these events the present chapter will deal with the first three.

The transfer of the peninsular missions to the Dominicans was the outcome, first, of a plea by the Order itself, made in 1768 to Charles III, for a license to found establishments on the west coast of California; and, second, of a suggestion to the Viceroy, made in December, 1771, by the guardian of the College of San Fernando, that the Dominicans, or some other Order, take in charge seven of the establishments already controlled by the Franciscans.[4] The project, from fear of a clash between the Orders, was opposed by Croix and Gálvez;[5] but in 1770, by a royal *cédula* of date April 8,[6] a division of territory was commanded, and on April 7, 1772, there was signed a *concordato* fixing at fifteen leagues below San Diego the line of apostolical demarcation between the two Californias.[7] This act was followed in 1773 (August 19) by the erection on a high rock, by Palou, of a wooden cross bearing the inscription: *División de las Misiones de nuestro Padre Santo Domingo y de nuestro Padre San Francisco, Año 1773.*[8]

It will be remembered that on receipt of the news of the founding of San Carlos, five new missions for Alta California were planned by Gálvez and Croix. One was to be located between San Buenaventura and San Diego; two were to be located between San Buenaventura and Monterey; and two north of Monterey. This requirement, so far as the interval between San Buenaventura and Monterey was concerned, had by 1772 been met by San Antonio de Padua

and San Luis Obispo; and, with respect to the interval between San Buenaventura and San Diego, by San Gabriel
Arcángel; but as yet San Buenaventura itself had not been
founded. The cause was scarcity of soldiers for guard purposes. As early as August, 1770, Serra had been advised by
Matías de Armona (successor to Portolá as governor of the
Californias)[9] that the "vehement desire" of his Reverence
to establish missions additional to those of San Diego and
Monterey was, in the dearth of troops, nothing less than a
tentación del demonio.[10] But orders from the Viceroy (November 12, 1770), not only to found San Buenaventura,
but to survey the port of San Francisco and found there
at least one mission, as an outpost against the Russians,
were urgent; [11] and to the time of the founding of San
Gabriel (September 8, 1771) Comandante Fages had
sought diligently to execute them. To replace the twelve
volunteers lost by scurvy, Viceroy Croix had sent to the
comandante twelve men from Guaymas, and there had
been transferred to him by Felipe Barri (successor to
Armona) twenty cuirassiers of the peninsular force under
Rivera.[12] Thus encouraged, he, on July 18, 1771, had
made known to Croix from San Diego, whither, with Serra,
he had come from San Antonio, his determination to found
San Buenaventura immediately after San Gabriel.[13] What
had prevented was a conflict with the Indians just after
the San Gabriel founding; an affair which more than ever
impressed Fages with the need of strong guard detachments for the missions.[14]

By the failure to found San Buenaventura in 1771,
Serra, who deemed the caution of Fages unnecessary, was
much exasperated.[15] But something was to arise by which
he was to be exasperated still more. In 1770, in Lower
California, Palou, through Padre Dionisio Basterra, had
complained to Visitador Gálvez of a disposition on the part

of the governors of the peninsula to assert control of the
temporalties and to treat the padres as subalterns.[16] In
1771–72 a like disposition became manifest in Fages. He
meddled in the discipline of neophytes; he withheld and
opened letters; he appropriated the mission mules; he
diverted mission supplies; and he refused to retire soldiers
for bad conduct. The last act perhaps gave most serious
offense, for by reason of it the men were more or less protected in their illicit relations with Indian women, — relations which, aside from the effect in neutralizing the moral
teaching of the padres, were laying the basis for a wide
infection of the northern Indians with the same disease
which had wrought havoc in the south.

By the course of Fages, there was raised for Alta California the whole question of the Mission. Was State Sacerdotal to control State Secular, or to be by it controlled?
As developed by Córdova and Las Casas (1518–43), the
Mission involved for the Indian, during tutelage, segregation under missionary supervision. As further developed
by Kino and Salvatierra (1697), the Mission involved for
the missionary the right to "enlist, pay and discharge soldiers of the guard." Before 1697 the Mission in Paraguay
had assumed to control secular agencies, including the
military; but despite this fact, and the fact of such control
in Lower California by the Jesuits, Serra and Palou had not
come to Monterey advised by a consistent practice on the
part of the Spanish Government. What they could aver
was, that in 1747, in the Sierra Gorda, under Lieutenant-
General José de Escandón, it had been found necessary,
after five or six years of secular control of temporalties, to
intrust to the Franciscans both temporalties and spiritualties, — a course which in twenty-three years had brought
about secularization; and that in the peninsula the same
thing, after the expulsion of the Jesuits, had been found

necessary by José de Gálvez.[17] This accordingly Serra did aver; and, to make his words the more effective, he set out in September, 1772, for Mexico, to wait personally upon Viceroy Bucarely.

Antonio María Bucarely was a lieutenant-general of the royal forces, a knight commander in the Order of St. John of Malta, and a great viceroy. He was descended, on both the paternal and maternal sides, from Italian and Spanish families illustrious through popes, cardinals, and dukes; and before coming to Mexico had been governor of Cuba. When, therefore, Serra arrived in Mexico in February, 1773, he met a chief capable of understanding and appreciating the Croix-Gálvez tradition. The President's grievances were heard, and he was asked to digest them in a memorial. He prepared two papers, March 13 and April 22, embodying in all thirty-three representations. Of these the most important were the complaints against Fages.[18] But there were two others of much importance: first, that the method of sending northward mission supplies by sea from San Blas (the Gálvez method) be not discontinued, as was proposed, in favor of a system of mule caravans from Lower California; and, second, that, looking to the future, supply routes be explored, first, from Sonora, and then from New Mexico; routes to be secured by a chain of missions past the head of the California gulf, as designed by Kino.[19]

Over Fages the triumph of Serra (and hence of the Mission idea) was speedy and complete. His representations were reviewed by the Board of War and Finance (*Junta de Guerra y Real Hacienda*), and by this body it was decided that mission guards should be retired for irregular conduct, at the instance of the padres, without specification by the latter of the irregularity prompting the request. Furthermore (and herein lay a distinct recognition of the idea of the Mission), the missionaries might manage their establishments as *in loco parentis*, to wit, as a father would manage his family, — a procedure sanctioned by Spanish law since the conquest.[20] Finally, mission letters were not to be intercepted by the comandante, nor the mission supplies withheld. The action of the board was approved by Bucarely on May 12, and in August Fages was recalled.

Nor was Serra less fortunate with regard to San Blas as a supply station. Delay, suffering, and peril pertained to the sea. Not only had the San Carlos lost practically her whole crew by scurvy on the voyage to San Diego in 1769, but in February, 1771, she had been driven by fierce " north-westers " from San Blas nearly to Panama. Her rudder dangling by a single bolt, her casks drained, her decks blistered by a torrid sun, saved only by a timely flood of rain, she, as buffeted as the barque in "The Ancient Mariner," had reached Loreto on the 23d of August. Yet the Father-President was able to show that, to supply the new missions overland from the south, there would be required fifteen hundred mules and one hundred guards and muleteers, — an argument so forcible for San Blas and the sea, that it was approved by the Viceroy without a reference.[21]

In respect to details, — details both politico-military and financial, — Alta California was left to an expert, Juan José de Echeveste, forwarder of supplies. By him there was drafted a plan providing, in the case of the united Californias, for a governor at a salary of 4000 *pesos* with residence at Loreto; and, in the case of the non-peninsular division, for a captain, three sergeants, eighty soldiers, eight mechanics, two storekeepers, and four muleteers.[22]

The annual cost was to be 42,985 *pesos*. San Blas, with

a small transport fleet, was to be kept as a naval base, at a cost per annum of 63,907 *pesos*. The grand expenditure (Lower California at 12,450) was to be 119,342 *pesos*. To meet this total there were declared available (counting the proceeds of the Pious Fund, the yield of salt works near San Blas, and an annual subsidy of 33,000 *pesos* promised by the King in 1772) about 63,808 *pesos*. The deficit (nominally some 55,534 *pesos*) was to be made good by the royal treasury.[23]

Echeveste's plan, or *Reglamento* as it was called, went into effect January 1, 1774, and on May 25 of the same year Captain Rivera y Moncada succeeded Fages as northern comandante. Meanwhile Palou, having erected the cross of apostolical demarcation between Baja and Alta California, had by permission of his college made his way northward to Monterey, arriving in November, 1773. On May 11, 1774, the same point was reached by Serra. He came overland from San Diego, where he had arrived on the Santiago, a new ship commanded by Pérez, and brought, among other news, that of an increase, at the instance of Echeveste, of the annual stipend for each padre to 400 *pesos*.

But what of Serra's representation in favor of explorations for supply routes to Alta California by way of the present Arizona and New Mexico?

Here likewise his views were sanctioned. Whatever might be true of the California Indian as a being comparatively docile and inactive, the Apache — occupant, settled or nomadic, of the region east of the tributaries of the Gila to Moqui — had never been docile, and rarely inactive; and Christianity with him had made headway haltingly.[24] As late as 1773, the year of Serra's visit to Mexico, Kino's and Sedelmayr's dream of permanent missions on the Gila and Colorado — links in a chain, Sonora to Moqui, and Sonora to the two Californias — remained to be fulfilled.

But to go back a little.

In 1737 the presidio of Santa Rosa de Cordeguachi, or Fronteras, a presidio of northern Sonora, was in charge of Captain Juan Bautista de Anza, an officer in whom there glowed something of the ardor of the *conquistadores* of old. In 1732 it had been the duty of Anza to escort bands of Jesuit padres to exposed points northward toward the Gila, where missions were to be established. Later (1736) it became his duty to report upon the discovery, then recent, of the Bolas de Plata mines. Unsettled still in 1737 was the query, — Is California insular? And to this query there was added by the mine discovery a further one: After all, might not the Seven Cities of Coronado's time — with the great Teguaio or Quivira at the head, and with the Strait of Anian as a connecting highway — be more than a myth? At all events, Spain had ever responded to the lure of souls to be converted and of gold, silver, and pearls to be won. Wherefore, on January 14, 1737, Anza urged upon Viceroy Juan Antonio that it were well that he (Anza) — with a volunteer force of fifty or sixty men-at-arms, some Pimas, two Jesuit padres, a train of horses, mules, and cattle, carpenters for constructing canoes to cross the Gila and Colorado Rivers, and gifts for the Indians — be commissioned to penetrate toward Quivira, and to establish a *villa* on the Colorado.[25]

The plea was considered, and on June 13, 1738, was referred by the King to a *junta*, which (Anza falling by the Apaches in 1739) was the last of it for thirty-four years.[26] But the doughty commander of Santa Rosa had left a son, — Juan Bautista. In what year Anza junior was born is not known, but he grew to manhood imbued with the ardor and ambition of his sire, and in 1772 commanded the presidio of Tubac.[27] By this time the traditions of Quivira and Anian were a good deal faded, but between the desert and the sea there still slept much of enticing mystery; and what was more, the expedition of Gálvez to Monterey had invested that mystery with a practical aspect. Could the desert be crossed with a view to succoring the new establishments?

A request of Anza junior to be permitted to open communication between Sonora and Monterey was referred to Viceroy Bucarely on May 2, 1772. It was based largely upon an *entrada* made in 1771 to a point near the mouth of the Colorado, by Francisco Garcés,[28] a missionary of the College of Querétaro, who in June, 1768, had been appointed to San Xavier del Bec. "Padre Garcés and I are persuaded," wrote Anza, "that the distance from Tubac to Monterey is not so great as formerly was thought, and that it may not be impossible to overcome it; . . . wherefore I hope that your Excellency will instruct the president of these [the Querétaro] missions to permit the said padre to accompany me. I consider October [1773] an opportune time for an expedition, as then there can be spared from my company 20 or 25 soldiers, a force which in my opinion will be sufficient." [29]

As a skilled engineer, and as one of the party which had just made the journey to Monterey, Miguel Costansó was consulted by Bucarely, and his advice (the distance from Tubac to San Diego being estimated at 180 "common Spanish leagues," 473.4 miles) was that the request of Anza be granted. Costansó, however, advised that two soldiers from the Loreto garrison, who had been at San Diego, be detailed to accompany Anza as guides.[30] And by the governor of Sonora, who also was consulted, it was suggested that, in order to avoid exciting the Indians,

Anza proceed to San Diego escorted only by Padre Garcés.[31]

It was with the Anza project at this stage that (February–March, 1773) Bucarely was waited upon by Serra. Garcés's diary of the *entrada* of 1771 was examined, and on September 17, the captain of Tubac was authorized to make a military reconnoissance to the establishments of Monterey.[32]

A start was effected on January 8, 1774. It was made from Tubac, at one o'clock of the afternoon after solemn Mass, and with the following troop: Captain Juan Bautista de Anza; two padres from Querétaro, — Francisco Garcés and Juan Díaz; twenty volunteer soldiers from Tubac presidio; one soldier versed in California routes; one interpreter of the Pima dialect; one Indian from Tubac presidio; five muleteers, and two servants. Good horses and pack animals were important for the expedition, and 130 of the former had been collected at Tubac. But just before the start they were stolen by Apaches, and it became necessary to proceed to the presidio of Altar, and make from that point, with other animals, very ill-conditioned, a start anew. At Altar, Anza added to his troop a useful member, Sebastián Tarabel, a neophyte of Lower California who had accompanied Portolá to San Diego, but who, later, attaching himself to the mission of San Gabriel, had deserted thence across the desert to Sonora.[33]

From Caborca Mission, district of Altar, Anza set forth on January 22 with 65 head of cattle, and with his saddle and pack animals recruited to 140. His course to the coast was to involve three well-defined stages: the first (January 22 to February 8), Altar northwest to the Gila-Colorado junction; the second (February 9 to March 10), the Gila-Colorado junction west to the foot of the San Jacinto Mountains; the third (March 11 to April 18), the San

Jacinto Mountains northwest to San Gabriel Mission, and north to Monterey. Stage one lay over desert, lava-bed and mountain, but it had been traversed by Kino in 1700 and by Garcés in 1771, to say naught of the crossing in 1540 by Coronado's hapless lieutenant, Melchior Díaz. At the Gila-Colorado junction the Yuma nation of Indians centred, and here Anza was met and welcomed by the Yuma chief Salvador Palma, with whom he had become acquainted at Altar, and whom he now, by a medal and an *alcalde's* staff, invested with authority under the King.[34]

It was stage two of the progress that developed a crisis, and proved the mettle of both leader and men. "Where I am," wrote Anza to Bucarely on February 9, "no troop of the King has ever passed the Colorado." [35] From the stream in question, which above its junction with the Gila was easily crossed by fording, there stretch to the Sierra Madre of Southern California hills of sand. Unstable as sea-billows, albeit often as gracefully curled, they harbor for the traveler bewilderment and death. To avoid these, Anza kept by the river-margin to Santa Olaya,[36] the last watering-place within the jurisdiction of the Yumas. Here Palma, who had been attending him, turned tearfully back, and he found himself in the country of the Cojats or Cajuenches.[37] By them he was welcomed, but he still was confronted with the sand-hills. Making into these on February 15, and soon deserted by the few Cojats who had proffered guidance, he was first compelled by the exhaustion of his mules to leave half of his baggage under guard at a place of brackish water (*La Poza de las Angustias* — Well of the Afflictions), and then to face the advisability of returning to the Yumas, of leaving with them half of his baggage and half of his men, and with the remainder pushing rapidly forward to California. To this plan Padre Díaz agreed, but Garcés was opposed, and the expedition held its course until, encountering a sand-hill too high to be surmounted, it became necessary to change direction to the south, where at no great distance rose a sierra.[38]

The mountains were gained at sundown, and the night was spent by Garcés in anxious quest for an Indian *ranchería* (San Jacome), which he was sure that he had visited hereabouts in 1771. Naught came of the search, and, as now many of the soldiers were on foot leading their jaded beasts, Anza gave orders for a return to Santa Olaya. This point, after the loss of a number of cattle and other animals, but with recovered baggage, was reached by the expedition in detachments between February 19 and 23. Palma cheerfully charged himself with the care of surplus articles and of seven of the men. With the remainder, all of whom expressed readiness to proceed *pie á tierras* if necessary, Anza on March 1 resumed his advance. On the 7th he came to a watering-place (Yuha Springs) recognized by Tarabel as one of the camping-spots of Portolá, and on the 8th reached the base of the mountains of San Jacinto.[39]

If stage one of the Anza progress may be called "Purgatorio," and stage two, "Inferno," stage three was indubitably "Paradiso." Entering, on March 11, the dry bed of the San Felipe River, the troop was cheered by news of a sea three days to the westward (*Océano de Filipinas*), and of people "like ours," — the dwellers at San Diego. On the 13th, amid the steeps of Coyote and Horse Canyons, grass and trees began to appear, and on the 15th running water. At 4700 feet a pass disclosed itself, named by Anza *El Real de San Carlos*,[40] and from it, as by a *coup de théâtre*, it was possible to descry beautiful, flower-decked plains and a white-capped sierra spiked with pines, oaks, and other trees native to cold lands. Here (just west of

Vandeventer Flat) the waters divided, running some toward the Gulf of California, and others toward the "Philippine Ocean"; a demonstration that the ridge in question was a continuation of that of California Baja. From San Carlos Pass the route led through Hemet Valley past Hemet Reservoir and along the San Jacinto River to San Jacinto Lake; thence to the Santa Ana River; and finally (on the 22d) to the mission of San Gabriel, which was reached at sundown, and where the sturdy captain of Tubac — worthy fulfiller of the ambition of a worthy parent — was received with rejoicing, with pealing of bells, and chanting of *Te Deum*.[41]

During a stop at the mission of eighteen days, Anza obtained supplies from the vessel Santiago, then at San Diego, and sent back to the Yumas, at the Gila-Colorado junction, Padre Garcés and all of his troop but six.[42] With the latter he took on April 10 the road (Portolá's) for Monterey, where, despite great scarcity, he was entertained at the presidio by Fages, and at the mission by the padres. He left Monterey on April 22, accompanied by six of Fages's men, to whom the way across the desert was to be shown, and on the 27th, below San Luis Obispo, met Serra, the Father-President, recently landed from the Santiago. With him he tarried the night to relate the story of his journey, and on May 1 was once again at San Gabriel. Thence his course, save a stretch through the sands to Santa Olaya, was that by which he had come. At the Gila-Colorado junction he dismissed Fages's men, received from Palma his own troop and baggage, and, having on the 21st left Garcés on the Gila, seeking communication by letter with Moqui, reached Tuçón on the 25th, and Tubac on the 27th.[43]

By the success of Anza (a success due in part to the presence of Serra in Mexico, in the spring of 1773) the work of Portolá was made sure of completion.

As yet no presidio and mission had been established at San Francisco. "Our father, St. Francis, is he to have no mission?" had anxiously been asked of Gálvez, by Serra, at La Paz. "Let him show us his port," the *visitador* had replied, "and he shall have a mission." [44] On November 21, 1770, Fages, with six soldiers (event hitherto unchronicled), had obtained a distant prospect of the present San Francisco Bay. This survey had been followed in 1772 (March-April) by one under Fages and Crespi, — a survey planned to include Point Reyes, in order to determine whether the estuary first seen by the deer-hunters in 1769, and again in 1770 by Fages's men, was a part of the Cermeño bay. But the Fages-Crespi party had reached only the mouth of the San Joaquín River, having been turned back by the waters and by news of starvation at San Diego. [45]

The truth is that until 1774, year of the Anza expedition, it had not so much as been settled where (strictly) lay that port of St. Francis at which there were ultimately to be planted two missions and a presidio, and at which the planting of at least one mission was deemed by Bucarely a present need. What, however, was presumed was, that the estuary of 1769 and 1770 (the present San Francisco Bay) was appurtenant to the old San Francisco Bay of Cermeño. Said Costansó in 1772, in a letter to the Viceroy: "On the fourth day of November [1769], following the eastern Shore or Branch of the Bay [*Estero*] (which we already called that of San Francisco), [46] we entered into a Sierra," etc. And on a map, with which the diary of the Portolá journey, as kept by Costansó, was supplemented, the present San Francisco Bay is called *Estero de S. Francisco.* [47]

To found San Francisco on the estuary,[48] therefore, would, it was adjudged, be admissible; and, in view of the fact that as yet Fages had not been furnished with soldiers sufficient for the founding even of San Buenaventura, there arose (apropos of the coming of Anza) the question: Could not men for the founding of San Francisco — and this, moreover, as suggested by Costansó accompanied by their families — be brought overland from Sonora? Furthermore, could not Kino's long-dreamed-of missions now be established on the Gila and Colorado Rivers? In a word, could not the views of Kino, Salvatierra, Sedelmayr, Anza (father and son), Serra, Costansó, and Bucarely be now, by what the secretary to the Viceroy happily called "a Sonora-Monterey hand-clasp," brought to a common fruition? [49]

Anza himself so believed. At Monterey he had proposed to Palou a chain of establishments "from these of California to the last of those of Querétaro in Sonora." He also (because of an Indian report that the estuary of San Francisco was connected by a branch of the Colorado River with the Gulf of California) had proposed that the annual Philippine galleon, stopping either at Monterey or at San Francisco, should there discharge Chinese goods for the benefit of Sonora and New Mexico.[50] But the determining consideration in favor of founding San Francisco on the estuary by men from Sonora, and of establishing missions on the Colorado to secure the Sonora connection, was the experience at Monterey of the new comandante, Rivera y Moncada.

Appointed successor to Fages on August 14, 1773, he had been instructed by Bucarely to explore the port of San Francisco for a mission site. Later (September) he had been notified of the expedition of Anza, for the guidance of which he was to furnish two soldiers. With fifty-one

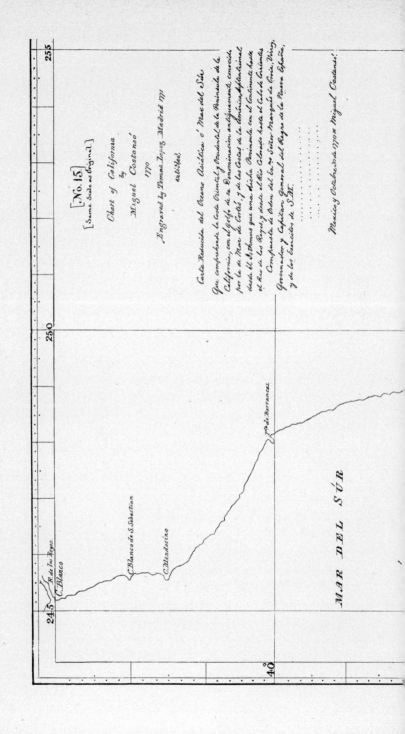

[No. 15]
[Same Scale as Original.]

Chart of California
by
Miguel Costansó
1770

Engraved by Tomas Lopez Madrid 1771
subtitled.

Carta Reducida del Oceano Asiatico, ó Mar del Sur
Que comprehende la costa Oriental y Occidental de la Peninsula de la
California, con el golfo de su Denominacion antiguamente, conocido
por la de Mar de Cortés, y de las Costas de la America Septentrional
desde el Isthmus que una dicha. Peninsula con el Continente hasta
el Rio de los Reyes y costa al Rio Colorado hasta el Cabo de Corriente.
Compuesta de Orden del S.r Señor Marqués de Croix, Virrey,
Governador y Capitan General del Reyno de la Nueva España,
y de los Exercitos de S.M.

Mexico y Octubre 30 de 1770. Miguel Costansó.

C. Blanco
R. de los Reyes.
C. Blanco de S. Sebastian
C. Mendocino
P.ta de Barrancas.

MAR DEL SÚR

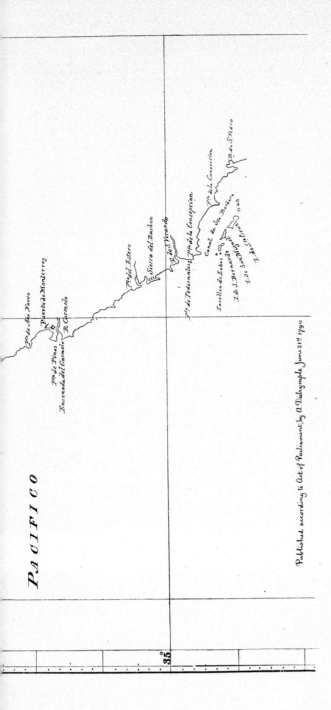

CHART IV. CALIFORNIA COAST. BY COSTANSÓ, 1770

Published according to Act of Parliament by A. Dalrymple, June 21st. 1790

persons (soldiers and their families) recruited in Sinaloa, Rivera reached the peninsula in March, 1774, but too late to furnish guides to Anza, or to join him. His assumption of duty at Monterey took place, as has been seen, on May 25, and in June there began to issue to Mexico a stream of plaintive dispatches: Supplies were scarce; arms were lacking or defective; Indians were vicious; desertions occurred. Regarding a San Francisco mission, he wrote to Bucarely on October 8, "Most excellent Señor, for founding a mission at San Francisco the number of soldiers is too small." [51]

Anza's project, in the broad view of it taken by Costansó, had been approved by the King on March 9,[52] and now (December) that communication with Alta California was actually open, a *junta* was called by the Viceroy. By this body it was determined: (1) That the port of San Francisco should be occupied by Anza with forty soldiers and their families, — soldiers chosen from the *Alcaldías* (alcalde districts) of Culiacán, Sinaloa, and Fuerte, where "most of the inhabitants were submerged in the greatest poverty and misery"; (2) that twenty-eight of the soldiers, under a lieutenant and sergeant, should be volunteers, and ten should be veterans of the reconnoissance; (3) that there should be chosen as lieutenant, either Joseph Joachim Moraga of Cordeguachi, or Cayetano Simón of Buenavista; and as sergeant, either Joseph Espinosa or Pablo Grijalva, both of Terrente, or Antonio Bravo of Buenavista; (4) that of the total cost of the expedition (computed at 21,927 *pesos* and 2 *reales*) the Pious Fund, "this one time only," should be called upon for 10,000 *pesos;* (5) that Padre Garcés should attend the expedition as far as the banks of the Colorado, there to await its return, and that Fray Pedro Font should attend it throughout; (6) that on his arrival at Monterey, Anza should turn over to Rivera y Moncada the volunteers, and, having with his own ten men aided in a survey of the *Río de San Francisco*, should return with them to Tubac.[53]

A start from Tubac was effected on October 23, 1775, with a large company: forty soldiers under Anza as lieutenant-colonel,[54] Moraga as lieutenant, and Grijalva as sergeant; ninety-six soldiers' families and four other families; three padres, — Garcés, Font, and Tomás Eixarch; one purveyor, Mariano Vidal; fifteen muleteers; three herdsmen; three servants to the padres; four servants to the comandante; five interpreters of the Pima, Yuma, Cajuenche, and Nifora idioms; 165 mules, 340 horses, and 302 cattle. Our Lady of Guadalupe, Saint Michael, and Saint Francis of Assisi figured as patrons of the expedition, and there was observed the following order on the march: four scouts; Anza with a vanguard; Font with the settlers; a rear-guard under Moraga; and last, in a long train, the mules heavily packed, the horses, and the cattle. Each morning the *Alabado* (Praise of the Sacrament) was sung by the company, and it was sung by them again each evening on reciting their beads.

The route as at first taken (*via* San Xavier del Bec and Tuçon) was more direct than that of the year 1774, but it merged into the latter at Yuma, and thence so continued to San Gabriel. On the present occasion, sand-hills were not to give so much perplexity, and the watering-places were known, but tribulations were not to be lacking. Between Anza and Font bickerings arose. The comandante, so Font declared, wished him to receive no credit for taking altitudes; nor would he permit him to use a musical instrument with which, for the edification of the Yumas, he had provided himself. It was the rainy season, — November, December, January, — and in the mountains the rain became snow, and strong winds blew. On December 17,

Moraga was stricken with deafness in both ears. On the 20th, when ascending the Baja-Alta California Cordillera, such cold prevailed that at night roaring fires were maintained at the cost of all sleep. At San Carlos Pass (the 26th) it rained, the storm culminating in a peal of thunder; and on issuing from the pass the sierra was beheld so covered with snow that its summits seemed the crested billows of the South Sea. To the women of the company, reared in a warm land, the sight though grand was disheartening, and they sorely wept. Moreover, cattle constantly perished, and there took place the last of eight childbirths, few of which had been achieved without *dolor violento*.[55]

The most significant incidents of the journey were a meeting with Palma on November 27, and an involvement in January (1776) occasioned by an uprising of the Indians at San Diego. As for Palma, he was the embodiment of cordiality, tendering his people as Spanish vassals, and his lands for missions. Informed by Anza that establishments on the Colorado could not at once be planted, he declared that on the return of the comandante he would accompany him to Mexico, there personally to make solicitation of the Viceroy.[56] Unable himself to stop with the Yumas, Anza left with them Garcés and Eixarch, commissioned to investigate what Dr. Elliott Coues characteristically renders "the animus and adaptability of the natives for the catechism and vassalage of the King"; and with the padres he left three interpreters, three servants, and supplies for four months. To Palma, to insure his goodwill, Anza presented a gift from the Viceroy, — a costume consisting of a shirt, a pair of trousers, a waistcoat yellow in front, a laced blue-cloth coat, and a gemmed and plumed black-velvet cap. This attention Palma reciprocated by a feast (served under a bower) of cakes, calabashes, corn, and watermelons.

San Gabriel was reached on January 4,[57] but the approach had awakened solicitude, for on January 1, it had been learned from three soldiers sent to the mission with dispatches for Rivera, that on the night of November 5, 1775, the mission at San Diego had been attacked and burned by conspiring bands of neophytes and Gentiles, and that Fray Luis Jayme had been killed.[58] The outbreak, as it proved, was an incident significant in two ways: the founding of San Juan Capistrano (an establishment authorized by the Viceroy in May, 1775, and begun by Lasuén and Lieutenant Ortega, of San Diego, in October) was suspended;[59] and the founding of San Francisco — that founding which, now that the estuary was deemed a part of the bay of Cermeño, was being more and more urged from Madrid — was deferred.

Anza, prevailed upon by Rivera (by whom he was met at San Gabriel)[60] to lend aid at San Diego, arrived with seventeen of his own men on January 11, and, between that date and February, supported the comandante in dispatching search-parties to the various *rancherías*. With Rivera, however, punishment of the Diegueños was but a secondary object. Opposed to any foundation at San Francisco, he yet was afraid that a foundation would be effected by Anza, and sought by dilatory action to detain the latter at San Diego in the hope that he would relinquish command of his soldier colony there, instead of at Monterey, and return to Sonora.

Every day [records Font] we talked a great deal about Monterey, and more yet of the San Francisco Port; the Señor Rivera ever saying that we could omit this trip, as we would not attain the object of it. . . . "What is your object in going there?" he would say. "To get tired out? I have told you that I have examined everything well, and have informed the Viceroy that there is nothing there suitable for that which he has planned." . . . "Friend," replied Señor Anza, ending the discussion, "I am going there, and if we find that river [of San Francisco], I shall draw a phial [*limeta*] of water, cork it well, have its genuineness certified by Fray Pedro here, and present it to the Viceroy." The Viceroy, Señor Anza declared, had ordered that if he did not find a fit site at the mouth of the port, the settlement should be established where it seemed best, even if that were some leagues away, — just so the port could be taken possession of by Spain.[61]

On February 3, word came from Moraga and Vidal, at San Gabriel, that the mission food-supply was becoming exhausted, and on the 9th, Anza, leaving at the mission ten of his men under Grijalva, set out with the remainder for San Gabriel, where he arrived on the 12th. From this point (Moraga with ten men first having been dispatched after some deserting muleteers) he on the 21st, with seventeen men, their families and his trains, started northward. On March 7, at San Antonio, he was rejoined by Moraga who had overtaken the deserters, and he reached Monterey on the 10th.[62]

At San Carlos Mission, Anza lay ill for a week of what seems to have been pleurisy; but on the 17th he was able to send to Rivera eight men from the presidio to relieve the ten left at San Gabriel under Grijalva; and on the 23d, with Moraga, Font, and eleven soldiers, started for the estuary, — henceforth by common consent called the Bay of San Francisco. In 1774 (November-December), Rivera with Palou and a guard — a fact adverted to by Rivera in the conversation with Anza — had skirted the estuary to Point Lobos, where Palou had erected a cross.[63] In 1775, night of August 5, Lieutenant Juan Manuel de Ayala of the royal navy, instructed to discover what connection there might be between the estuary and the bay of Cermeño,[64] had in the San Carlos passed the Golden Gate,[65] opposite which he had cast anchor at an island called by him

Isla de Los Ángeles.[66] Moreover, in September, the naval officer Bruno Heceta, likewise under orders for Anza's benefit, had with Palou penetrated by land to Point Lobos.[67] The advent of Anza to the bay, therefore, was to a water by no means uncharted,[68] and on March 28 he chose on a *cantil blanco* (white cliff), "where nobody had been," a site for a *fuerte* (Fort Point) and *nueva población;* and the next day, at a spot called by him from the calendar Los Dolores (Mission Bay), he chose a site for a mission.[69]

Regarding Fort Point, Font writes: —

The comandante decided to fix the holy cross, which I blessed after Mass, on the extreme end of the steep rock at the interior point of the mouth of the port; and at eight o'clock he and I went there with four soldiers, and the cross was fixed at a suitable height to be seen from the entire entrance of the port and from some distance. At the foot, under some rocks, the comandante left a report of his coming, and a plan of the port. On departing we ascended a short hill to a very green flowery tableland abounding in wild violets and sloping somewhat toward the port. From it the view is *deliciocisima*. There may be seen [not only] a good part of the port with its islands [but] the mouth of the port and the sea, whence the prospect ranges even beyond the *Farallones*. I judged that if this site could be well populated, as in Europe, there would be nothing finer in the world, as it was in every way fitted for a most beautiful city, — one of equal advantages by land or water, with that port so remarkable and capacious, wherein could be built ship-yards, quays and whatever might be desired. . . . I examined the mouth of the port, and its configuration, with the graphometer, and I tried to sketch it, and here I place the sketch.[70]

The squad sent south by Anza on the 17th had carried a letter to Rivera, requesting him to make known at once his intention with regard to the founding of San Francisco; but on Anza's return to Monterey on April 8 (a return effected by way of the present San José, Berkeley, and Monte Diablo), no reply had been received. Ill-con-

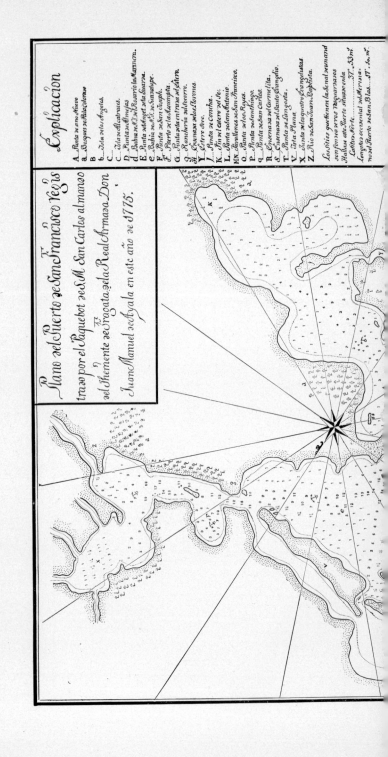

Plano del Puerto de San Francisco Regis trazado por el Paquebot de S.M. San Carlos al mando del Theniente de Fragata de la Real Armada Don Juan Manuel de Ayala en este año de 1775.

Explicacion

A. Punta de... Pino
a. Bosques de Palo Colorado
B. Isla de los Angeles
C. Isla de Alcatraces
C. Isla de Alcatraces
D. Punta de Almejas
d. Bahia del Rosario de la Matanza
E. Punta de Angel de la Guarra
e. Bahia del N.tra S.ra de Saralupe
F. Punta de San Joseph
f. Puerto de la de Saneapla
G. Punta de la entrada del Estero
g. Rancheria del desorre
h. Ensenada de los Florones
Y. Cerro d.e
I. Punta de Concha
K. Fin del Estero del d.e
L. Punta de San Antonio
MN. Cavallones de San Francisco
O. Punta de los Reyes
P. Punta de San Diego
q. Punta de San Carlos
R. Ensenada del Carmelita
S. Ensenada del Santo Evangelio
T. Punta de la Angosta
V. Isla Plana
X. Punta de los quatro Evangelistas
Z. Rio de San Juan Baptista

Los Sitios que tienen la letra el demand son forma... no los Resguardados
Hallase este Puerto situado en la Latitud Norte........ 37...53.m.
Longitud occidental del Merridia-
no del Puerto de San Blas... N.º...10.m.

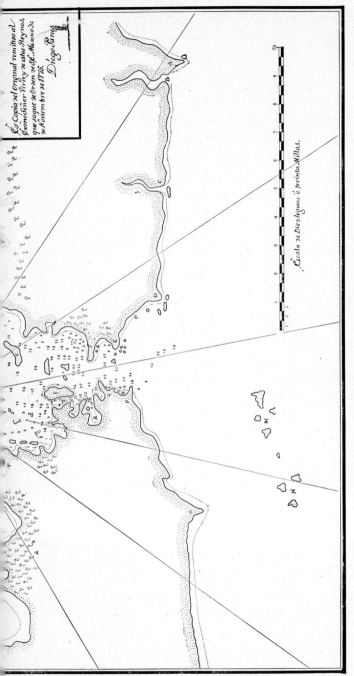

La Copia del Original remitido al
Exmo. Señor Virrey de estos Reynos,
que sague de Orden de el Mismo 3e
de Noviembre de 1775.

Diego James

Escala de Diez leguas ó treinta Millas.

CHART V. PORT OF SAN FRANCISCO. BY AYALA, 1775

tent at the situation, and weak from his pleuritic attack,
Anza now sent word to Rivera by a sergeant (José María
Góngora) that he would meet him at San Diego on April
25 or 26, for consultation; and having turned over the
command of the colony to Moraga, set out on the 14th for
Sonora, — a day, by reason of the tears and farewells of

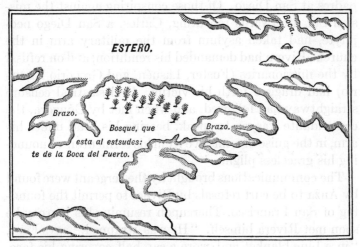

ESTERO.

Brazo.

Bosque, que
esta al estsudes:
te de la Boca del Puerto.

Brazo.

Boca.

CHART VI. SAN FRANCISCO BAY, BY PEDRO FONT, 1776

the settlers, pronounced by the sturdy soldier the saddest
ever known at Monterey.

On the 15th, Anza, to his surprise, met Góngora returning with news that Rivera was just behind him. He had
come upon the comandante near San Antonio, and had
tendered him the letters in his charge. These Rivera had
declined to receive, bidding the sergeant retire. Afterwards he had consented to take the letters, and, thrusting
them unopened into his pouch, had, in exchange, handed
Góngora two communications for Anza, bidding him go in
advance and deliver them. "Señor," said Góngora (drawing Anza to one side), "my captain is either fatuous or

mad, and those with him say that he comes from San Diego
Presidio excommunicated because of having taken from
the church the Indian Carlos." [71]

Rivera was not mad, but he undeniably was fatuous; and
the reason was twofold. He was envious of Anza; and he
had involved himself in an uncomfortable tangle with the
padres at San Diego. Of those conspiring against the mission but afterwards repenting, Carlos, a San Diego neophyte, had taken asylum from the military arm in the
church. Rivera had demanded his rendition, and on refusal
by the missionaries (Fuster, Lasuén, and Gregorio Amurrio) had dragged forth his victim. Ecclesiastical censure
straightway had followed, and when met by Góngora, the
comandante was, so to speak, bearing his head under his
arm, in the guise of a missive from his tormentors announcing his graceless plight.

The communications brought by the sergeant were found
by Anza to be curt refusals by Rivera to permit the founding of San Francisco. Thereupon resuming his journey he
soon met Rivera himself. "He was wrapped," says Font,
"in a blue blanket and wore a cap half covering his face,
leaving visible no more than the right eye and a little of
the beard, which he wore very long." Rivera complained
of his health. "I am sorry you are ill," said Anza. "While
at San Gabriel," replied the former, "I contracted a pain
in this leg," pointing to the right one. He then took Don
Juan's left hand, drew it over his right arm, said "Á Dios,"
put spurs to his mule, and passed on. "You may reply to
me at Mexico or wherever it pleases you," called Anza.
"So be it," answered Rivera, and the colloquy ended.

Toward the comandante there now was assumed by
Anza a punctilious reserve. The former proceeded to
Monterey, was refused absolution by Serra until Carlos
should be restored to his asylum, and on April 19, started

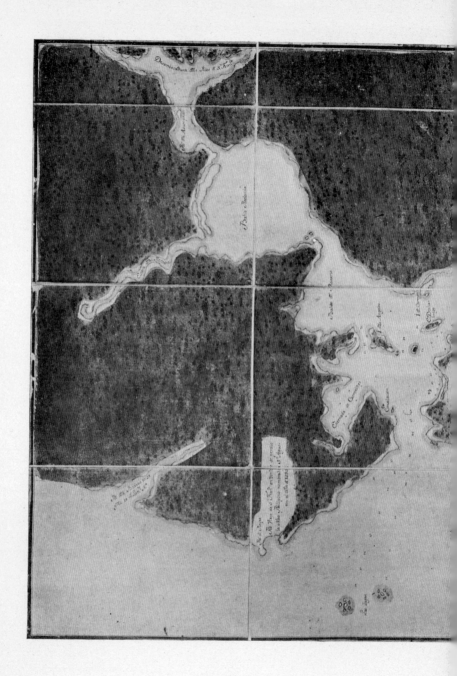

CHART VII. SAN FRANCISCO BAY SUBSEQUENT TO FOUNDING OF SAN FRANCISCO PRESIDIO AND MISSION. BY SAN BLAS NAVAL OFFICERS. (Hitherto unreproduced)

for San Diego. At San Luis Obispo a letter of formal apology from him was delivered to Anza, and a meeting solicited; but the Sonora leader declined intercourse except in writing, and on May 2 set out for the Colorado; while, the next day, the way southward was resumed by Rivera. At Yuma (May 11), Anza was joined by Eixarch and by Palma, — the latter still resolute in his determination to go to Mexico to make in person submission to the Viceroy. As for Garcés, he was thought to be on the Colorado, three days to the northward of Yuma, among the Galchedunes. Dispatching him a letter, Anza on the 14th left by way of Sonora, Caborca, and Altar for San Miguel de Horcasitas, where he arrived June 1, and where at once he began preparations for a journey to the capital.[72]

The retreat of Garcés is presumed by Dr. Elliott Coues to have been near the present Needles. But what had been the course of this indefatigable man since December 4, 1775, — the date of the departure of Anza from the Gila-Colorado junction? And what was to be his course to September 17, 1776, the date of his return to his mission of San Xavier del Bec?

Provided with a banner, on one side of which was portrayed the Holy Mary, and on the other a lost soul, Garcés, by May 11, 1776, had penetrated to the mouth of the Colorado,[73] had revisited San Gabriel, and (near Bakersfield) had entered the Tulare, or great central valley of California, — the first Spaniard so to do save Pedro Fages, who in 1772 had pursued thither a party of deserters.[74] Thus much in fulfillment of the Viceroy's commission "to investigate the animus and adaptability of the natives on the Colorado for the catechism and vassalage of the King." But another commission of the Viceroy's demanded fulfillment, and by it the course of Garcés was determined to the time of his return to his mission.

Serra, in his memorial to Bucarely, March 13, 1773, had revived an idea broached by Kino and emphasized by Sedelmayr. He had not only recommended that communication be opened between Alta California and Sonora, but also between Alta California and New Mexico, — Santa Fé. "Let an order be given," the Father-President had said, "to some *jefe* (officer) of New Mexico"; and by the War Board it had been declared advisable that an expedition from New Mexico be conducted separately from that from Sonora.[75]

To the idea of a Santa Fé expedition to the coast, impetus had been given by the return of Garcés and Díaz from the first Monterey expedition of Anza, for it was undeniable that the Anza route was fraught with peril by its sands and lack of water. Even in Sonora, officials — notably the governor of that province, Francisco Antonio Crespo — were of the opinion that a route to Monterey, by way of Santa Fé, Moqui, and the Galchedunes, would be found preferable to Anza's route: first, because the region was more fertile, and second, because such a route would rend Apachería and bring about the reduction of Moqui, — a district defiantly independent. It was indeed the suggestion of Crespo, that until the route in question could be explored (by himself), it might be well to suspend the founding of San Francisco.[76] No exploration by Crespo, however, was authorized, and in 1775 the matter was taken in hand at Santa Fé. Here were two zealous Franciscans, Silvestre Vélez de Escalante and Francisco Atanasio Domínguez, — the former resident padre at Zuñi. After an *entrada* in June, the two padres, July 29, 1776, set forth northwestward, with eight men, for Monterey, and actually reached the vicinity of Great Salt Lake; but, provisions failing, they were forced to return, arriving at Zuñi on November 24.[77]

The viceregal commission to open communication with
Alta California by way of Santa Fé — a commission intrusted by Bucarely neither to Crespo nor yet to "some
jefe of New Mexico"; one, moreover, unsuccessful in the
hands of Escalante and Domíngue — was accomplished
by Garcés. Quitting the Tulare Valley on May 11–17, 1776,
he went east to the site of Fort Mojave on the Colorado
River, and thence again east by way of the Grand Canyon
(which he named *Puerto de Bucarely*) to Moqui.[78] Here,
despite the allurements of his banner, he (July 2) was but
coldly received, being given shift in a court-yard; and on
July 4, chagrined, he withdrew southward. Approaching
San Xavier del Bec, where, as stated, he arrived on September 17, his heart was cheered by greetings from the
Pimas (Kino's nation), who in affectionate drunkenness
assured him that they were "well," were "happy, knew
about God, and were the right sort of men to fight the
Apaches." [79]

San Francisco, meanwhile, had been founded at last.
On May 8, Rivera at San Diego, repentant (upon thought
of the Viceroy) of his peremptoriness in refusing to permit the founding, sent to Moraga instructions to establish
a presidio on the site chosen by Anza, but to defer the
establishing of a mission. The lieutenant, accompanied
by Padres Palou and Benito Cambón, at once went with
the Sonora colonists to the San Francisco peninsula, and
on June 27 camped near the spot called by Anza Dolores,
— a spot within easy reach of the presidio site. By help
of Cañizares and others of the crew of the San Carlos,
which came from Monterey in August with supplies, presidial quarters — chapel, comandante's dwelling, and warehouse, all of palisades with roofs of earth — were soon
ready; and on the 17th of September, day of the coming

of Garcés to San Xavier, the foundation was dedicated
with a Mass, a *Te Deum*, and with salvos of artillery.
At Dolores a settlement had grown up under Palou.
Moraga, regardless of Rivera's injunctions, now added a
church and a priest's dwelling; and on October 9 the whole
was formally dedicated as the mission (sixth in the Alta
California list) of San Francisco de Asís.[80]

Rivera himself was advised in July of a transfer of
Barri's successor, Felipe de Neve, to Monterey, and of his
own transfer to the peninsula as lieutenant-governor.[81]
In November, he paid to San Francisco an official visit
of inspection, and approved all that Moraga had done.
The spot, in April, 1777, was visited by Neve; and, on
October 10, the venerable Junípero Serra, gazing from
the *castillo*, beheld within the Golden Gate that which, in
measure more than sufficient, was a response to Gálvez's
demand that St. Francis disclose his port.[82]

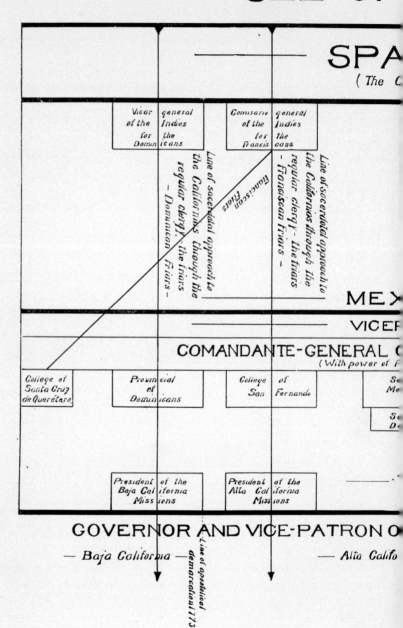

SEE OF

SPA
(The C

Vicar general
of the Indies
for the
Domin icans

Comisarie general
of the Indies
for the
Francis cans

Line of sacerdotal approach to
the Californias through the
regular clergy - the friars
- Franciscan Friars -

Line of sacerdotal approach to
the Californias through the
regular clergy - the friars
- Dominican Friars -

Franciscan Friars

MEX

VICER

COMANDANTE-GENERAL (
(With power of F

College of
Santa Cruz
de Querétaro

Provincial
of
Dominicans

College of
San Fernando

Sc
Me

Se
D

President of the
Baja California
Missions

President of the
Alta California
Missions

GOVERNOR AND VICE-PATRON O

— Baja California —

Line of apostolical
demarcation 1773

— Alta Califo

ROME ——————

IN ——————

(own)

Line of political approach to the Californias from crown through viceroy, comandante-general and governor

Line of ecclesiastical approach to the Californias from Papacy through the secular clergy - Archbishops, bishops and curates

ICO ——————

OY ——————

F THE PROVINCIAS INTERNAS

ronato Real)

of
ico

of
ango

he *Californias* ——————

T THE CALIFORNIAS

ia ——.

Spanish System of Government, Sacerdotal-secular, as Exemplified by The Californias, 1781 ——

Under the plan of Gastadios, 1782 (see text Chapter VIII), the colleges and presidencies would have been suppressed, leaving the direct control in the Comisario or vicar - general

CHAPTER VII

THE PROVINCIAS INTERNAS

L AST in the catalogue of Alta California notable events which took place in the lifetime of Junípero Serra, were the three anti-Russian maritime expeditions, 1774–1779; the founding (1777 and 1781) of San José and Los Ángeles; and the attempted founding (1780–1782) of pueblo missions.

On March 24, 1773, the Marqués de Grimaldi wrote to Viceroy Bucarely that the King had news that it was designed by the celebrated English navigator "Bings" to sail, in May, straight for the Pole, to ascertain if it might not be practicable to pass thence to the west, and so reach California. In case the design was carried out, and Monterey or other ports were visited, the ships were to be detained and their papers, maps, etc., seized under the Laws of the Indies. But this for the present aside.[1]

In 1773, on April 11, — San Francisco being yet unfounded, — there was received at Madrid, from the Conde de Lacy, Spanish minister at St. Petersburg, a hurried dispatch. It stated that in 1769 an official of the Russian navy, named Tscherikow, had, from Kamtchatka, undertaken for his country the task of exploration toward America; that in 1771 he had returned from his voyage, and that, leaving his crew in Siberia, he, early in 1772, had with his secretary reached St. Petersburg, where his papers had been deposited by the government in an archive sealed with three seals, and where he and his secretary had both been sworn to profound silence regarding his discoveries.[2]

On September 25, two other dispatches from Lacy were

received, — one stating that Russia was about to force the Great Wall of China with 25,000 men, and then assail Japan from Kamtchatka; the other, that the famous Albrecht von Haller, professor in the Royal Academy at St. Petersburg, had advised the sending of a Russian squadron by way of the Cape of Good Hope to Kamtchatka, there to continue the Russian advance toward America, — a land belonging to Russia more than to any other power by reason of having originally been peopled from Siberia.[3]

Upon the Lacy dispatches, the first of which reached Mexico in July, and the last in December, action by Bucarely was promptly taken. Juan Pérez, the naval officer first with his ship at San Diego in 1769, was communicated with; and by January 24, 1774, he, furnished with maps of the routes of Behring and Tscherikow, with a ship's company of eighty-eight men, and with a ship itself of his own selection (the Santiago), had set sail from San Blas. He was required to follow the coast northward to latitude 60°, the limit, according to Lacy, of exploration by Behring and Tscherikow,[4] and everywhere, by religious ceremonies and the planting of great crosses, to take possession in the name of Charles III. Pérez, in fact, — first stopping at San Diego to put ashore Serra (*vide* chapter VI), and then (May 23–June 11) at Monterey to receive as chaplains and diarists Padres Crespi and Tomás de la Peña, — surveyed the coast, including Nootka Sound, from Mendocino to the extremity of Queen Charlotte Island in latitude 55°, and returned to Monterey on August 27.[5]

With the voyage of the Santiago (60 degrees not having been attained, nor anywhere a landing effected) dissatisfaction was felt in Mexico, and on November 26, 1774, the Viceroy advised the King of a second expedition, one designed to reach 65 degrees. Available for it were six naval officers of ability from Cádiz and Ferrol, whose coming had been announced the preceding August; among them Lieutenants Bruno Heceta and Juan Francisco Bodega y Quadra.[6] Under the former, with Pérez as *piloto*, the Santiago in 1775 (March 16) sailed from San Blas. She reached latitude 49° on August 11, and anchored at Monterey on the 29th, having discovered the port of Trinidad and, probably, the mouth of the Columbia River.[7] As for Bodega y Quadra, assigned as second officer to the Sonora (a schooner requisitioned by Heceta for the exploration of ports and bays), and unexpectedly given first place by the transfer of his superior Juan de Ayala to the San Carlos, he in his cockle-shell, thirty-six feet "over all," reached 58 degrees, discovered Bodega Bay, and anchored at Monterey on October 7.[8]

A deal of coast had been laid bare, but naught of the Russians had been found, save, by Pérez, a bayonet and part of a sword in the hands of Indians on Prince of Wales or Queen Charlotte Island. In 1776, therefore, a third expedition to the north, with Heceta and Bodega y Quadra in command, was ordered by the King.[9] It was to take place in 1777, and this for a specific reason. The rumor of 1773 — that the English under Admiral Byng were about to seek California by way of the Pole — had proved false; but in March (1776) it had come to the knowledge of Spain that Captain James Cook — fulfilling Venegas's forecast of a further search for Anian by a successor to Arthur Dobbs [10] — was preparing with two ships, the Resolution and the Discovery, to sail for the South Sea and the Northwest Coast. That Anian, whether as an outlet to the bay of James, of Baffin, or of Hudson, was a myth, had been proved to the satisfaction of Bucarely by the exploration of 1775; yet in quest of it, and of possessory rights over the territory about it, Cook evidently was coming; that, too, stimulated by a Parliamentary grant of twenty thousand pounds contingent upon success; and it behooved Spain to be represented in northern waters when he arrived.[11]

This project was prevented by lack at San Blas of a vessel that could be spared for the purpose, the Santiago being destined to Peru; and it was not until 1779, the year of Bucarely's death, that the expedition (two *fragatas*, the Princesa and the Favorita, built respectively at San Blas and Lima, and commanded, the one by Lieutenant Ignacio Arteaga, and the other by Lieutenant Bodega y Quadra) was able to set sail.[12] It quitted San Blas on February 11 under orders to reach latitude 70°; but having on July 1 attained about 60 degrees, was forced back by scurvy, making on the way an examination of Drake's Bay (the bay of Cermeño), and anchoring at San Francisco the middle of September.[13] Meanwhile (1778) Captain Cook, unchallenged, had visited the Northwest Coast, stopped long in Nootka Sound, and, striking across the Pacific to the southwest, had met death in the Sandwich Islands.

By the three expeditions of Pérez, Heceta, and Arteaga and Quadra, it became evident that the Russians, whatever their ultimate designs, were as yet making no southward encroachments. For delayed projects of a domestic nature, therefore, the time was opportune.

In 1768, in that dispatch, basic for the history of Alta California, wherein Gálvez and Croix had pointed out to the King the necessity, as against both the English and the Russians, of the occupation of the port of Monterey, something had been pointed out besides, to wit: the advisability (so assumed) of the creation in New Spain of a new territorial and administrative unit. As in the sixteenth, seventeenth, and eighteenth centuries, Spaniards of central Mexico — soldiers, priests, and miners — had fared constantly farther to the north, divers provinces had become delimited: Sinaloa, Nueva Vizcaya, Sonora, New Mexico, the Californias, Coahuila, and Texas. Because of remoteness from the capital, these provinces had early been called the Provincias Internas (Interior Provinces).[14] The meeting-ground of two of them — northeastern Sonora or southeastern Arizona, and southwestern New Mexico — had long been the roaming district of the Apaches; and here by 1768 two presidial groups were in existence: one, coastwise and linear from Guaymas to Pitic, including Horcasitas; the other, inland and wedge-shaped with Fronteras at the apex, including, besides Fronteras, Altar, Terrente, and Tubac. As for Nueva Vizcaya (Chihuahua) and New Mexico (central portion), a line, including Janos and Paso del Norte, connected San Buenaventura with Santa Fé; while in the Californias, to say nothing of posts in Coahuila and distant Texas, there was the presidio of Loreto.[15]

Control, from the capital, of military groups such as these was a task the difficulty of which had in 1768 been impressed upon *visitador* and viceroy alike by the war in Sonora.

If [so the dispatch recommending the formation of outlying provinces into a unit of separate administration had averred] from the glorious conquest, as achieved by Hernan Cortés, of these dominions that fall under the name of New Spain, it had been the practice of successors in the government to follow up and prosecute the high designs of that hero, there would have supervened the light of the Gospel and the dominion of the august kings of Spain to the ultimate bounds of this immense and unexplored continent. But as the spirit of activity and of conquest was quenched with the life of that inimitable man, so (with his death) there ceased the rapid progress made, until of late no one has sustained or conserved the possession of those rich territories on the frontiers of Sonora and Nueva Vizcaya. Of the decadence and veritable destruction which the unfortunate inhabitants of these provinces have suffered (with grave prejudice to the State) the exact causes are, in reality, the total neglect with which the provinces in these last years have been regarded from Mexico, by reason of the distance of more than six hundred leagues from this capital at which they are situated; and the great mass of occupations and cares, near at hand, which weigh upon the attention of a viceroy of New Spain; since, destitute of subaltern aids, it is impossible that either his active dispositions or the influence of his authority should reach to the remote confines of an empire almost illimitable.[16]

The new administrative unit was to be a *comandancia-general*, or military department, and not a second viceroyalty. Thus would be avoided " odious embarrassments " sure to arise "between adjacent *jefes* when equal." It furthermore was to embrace only Sonora, Sinaloa, Nueva Vizcaya, and the peninsula of the Californias. Justice was to be dispensed from Guadalajara, and it was suggested that the capital be fixed either at Caborca Mission, or at the confluence of the Gila and Colorado Rivers, so that, from a point almost equidistant from the Californias and Nueva Vizcaya, the governor might with facility pass to one or the other. In respect to power, the *comandancia* was to be invested with all that was required for keeping itself free of the barbarians and for extending its territorial limits. With reference to the viceroyalty, its subordination was to be that only of making reports and of asking aid when necessary.[17]

In 1776, on August 22, five years after Gálvez's return to Spain, the Provincias Internas — in essential respects as recommended in the dispatch of 1768, but including Coahuila and Texas as well as the Californias — were created by royal decree an administrative unit, with capital fixed at Arizpe in Sonora.[18] Of the department in question — one where, if anywhere, it were needful "for the man with the crucifix to be backed by the man with the musket " — there was appointed as governor and comandante-general, with power of the *Patronato Real*,[19] Teodoro de Croix

(Caballero), native of Flanders and nephew of the Marqués de Croix, the predecessor of Bucarely. Croix reached Mexico in December, 1776, and Durango in Nueva Vizcaya (his provisional capital), in September, 1777. Fond of parade, he was disposed to claim as much equality with the Viceroy as possible, and forthwith contrived it that at low Mass his confession was received standing, and that at solemn Mass salutation was made to him by priest and deacons from the altar, — ceremonies permitted by the laws to none but the viceroys of Mexico and Peru.[20] With regard, however, to Alta California, the significant fact in connection with Comandante-General Croix is that he valued personally and supported officially the new governor, Felipe de Neve.

Neve, a major at Querétaro (originally from Sevilla), had on September 27, 1774, been sent as governor to Loreto, to compose bitter differences which had arisen in the peninsula between State Secular and State Sacerdotal, — the one as represented by Governor Barri, and the other by the Father-President of the Dominicans, Vicente Mora.[21] But in 1776 the Viceroy, in view of the outbreak at San Diego, was ordered by the King to transfer Neve to Monterey. Northern California was not an alluring field, and it was only after a second order from Madrid that Neve, on November 3, was constrained to manifest his submission to the royal will.[22]

Reaching Monterey on February 3, 1777, he was soon put in possession of two communications, the contents of which, as assimilated and carried into effect by his own strong intelligence, materially changed for Alta California the status civil and religious. The first, dated December 25, 1776, was a letter of instructions from the Viceroy. In it Neve was directed to give attention to four things: first, the strengthening of connection between Loreto, San Diego, and San Francisco by the erection of various missions, two, as Serra had long prayed, on the Santa Bárbara Channel, — Concepción and San Buenaventura, — and one to the north of San Carlos, — Santa Clara; second, the determining of the practicability of a connection with Mexico by way of San Gabriel through missions to be erected on the Gila and Colorado Rivers; third, a distribution of lands to colonists and soldiers with a view to rendering the province independent of the royal treasury; and fourth, the gaining of the Indians "by attention, love, and gifts, and not by rigor." [23] As for the second communication, which also was from the Viceroy, it notified Neve of the arrival in Mexico of Croix to take command in the Provincias Internas, — a *jefe* with whom, thereafter, he was to conduct all correspondence, except regarding supplies; [24] while as for the third (dated August 15, 1777), it was from Croix himself. It advised the Governor that by a royal order of March 21, 1775, the *Reglamento* of Echeveste was to be remodeled, and asked Neve to suggest what he could for its improvement. [25]

Hitherto in the Californias the subordination of State Secular to State Sacerdotal had been marked. It had been with comparative ease that Palou in the case of Barri, and Serra in that of Fages, had triumphed as to Mission control of the soldiery and Indians; and that Serra and his colleagues in the case of Rivera y Moncada had triumphed as to a mission at San Francisco and a course of mildness toward the revolted neophytes of San Diego, of whom the culprit Carlos was an example.

Neve, however, impressed with the injunction to render the province of Alta California self-supporting, resolved first to found two pueblos of Spaniards, — two communities for the exclusive support of the presidios; namely, San José on the Río Guadalupe near Santa Clara, and La

Reina de los Ángeles on the Río Porciúncula near San Gabriel.

Gathering fourteen heads of families, — nine of them presidial soldiers of Monterey and San Francisco, and five of them men from Anza's party (sixty-six persons), — the Governor, on the 29th of November, 1777, through his representative Moraga, laid the foundations of San José.[26] The town — a few houses of plastered palisades with flat roofs of earth — was constructed facing a plaza, and to each family there was assigned a *suerte*, or field, for the irrigation of which the waters of the Guadalupe were restrained by a dam. And for the present this was all that was attempted. If pueblos were to be founded, settlers of Spanish blood must be provided in numbers sufficient for the purpose. Anza had succeeded in transferring by the Colorado route a considerable company from Sonora to the north. But so far as Los Ángeles was concerned, the site selected lay far to the south, and might be reached either from Loreto or from the Colorado. Accordingly, in 1779 Lieutenant-Governor Rivera y Moncada was sent by Neve to Arizpe, to receive from Croix, as comandante-general of the Provincias Internas, instructions to escort to California from Sinaloa and Sonora a second body of Spanish colonists, — a body specifically for the founding of the pueblo Los Ángeles.[27]

This body was to consist of twenty-four families, each family to receive ten *pesos* a month and regular rations for three years, together with an advance of clothing, livestock, seed and implements, to be repaid from the yield of the soil. The quota must include a mason, a carpenter, and a blacksmith. With the whole there were to go as an escort, and for service in California, fifty-nine soldiers; and all, settlers and soldiers alike, were to be bound to remain at least ten years. By December, 1780, Rivera had secured fourteen families of settlers, and these, escorted by seventeen soldiers, he dispatched to San Gabriel by way of Loreto and San Diego.[28] He himself, with forty-two soldiers under Lieutenants Cayetano Limón and José Dario Argüello, and a train of 960 horses and mules, set out for the same point in the spring of 1781, by way of the Colorado River.[29]

It was August 18 when the settlers with their soldier escort reached San Gabriel, and on the 26th instructions for the founding of the new pueblo were issued, prepared by Neve, after a law for the Indies by Philip II.[30] It was to be located on high ground near the Porciúncula, from which, as from the Guadalupe at San José, irrigation was to be provided for a wide area. It was to centre in a plaza 200 by 300 feet, so quartered that the corners faced the cardinal points, and with each of the four sides intersected perpendicularly by three streets. The east side of the plaza was to be reserved for a church and royal buildings, and all house-lots were to be twenty *varas* in width by forty in depth.[31] As early as March 8, 1781, Neve had issued a *bando* (edict) specifying in minute detail the course to be pursued in the assignment of lands, and the conditions upon which they were to be held.[32]

The classes of lands recognized by Spanish law and custom were four: *solares* (house-lots), *suertes* (planting-lots, or fields, 550 feet square), *ejidos* (commons), and *propios* (income-producing lots for public uses).[33] Of these each settler was to be assigned (by lot) one *solar* and four *suertes;* two of the *suertes* being irrigable and two dry. No settler might sell any portion of his assignment, for "the lands, all and each, must be indivisible and inalienable forever"; nor might any portion be mortgaged, but it might by testamentary disposition be given to one child in preference to another. For five years settlers were to be exempt from all tithes and taxes; but within one year their houses must be wholly finished and provided with six hens and a rooster. Irrigating ditches must be opened within one year; within three years a public granary must be built, and within four years the royal buildings must be erected. Each settler must be provided with two horses, a saddle complete, a firelock and other arms. Animals must be marked and branded, and the brands placed of record. Patents of title to lands were to be issued, and of these also a record was to be made. Finally, the pueblo Los Ángeles, as likewise San José, "was to be given *alcaldes* (magistrates) of the first instance, and other officials of the *cabildo* (council), yearly," — officials who for the first two years were to be appointed by the Governor, but thereafter were to be nominated by the people and approved by the Governor.[34]

Los Ángeles was founded on September 4, 1781, with eleven families, — forty-six persons, — of whom only two even claimed to be of pure Spanish blood, the remainder being confessedly Indian and mulatto.[35] In the case of San José, the five-year probationary period expired in 1782, and in May, 1783, Moraga, as *comisionado* for the Governor, placed of record a plat of the town. The same service for Los Ángeles was performed in 1786 (September), by José Argüello as *comisionado*. Thus the plan of Neve for succoring the presidios was carried into effect.[36]

But from the point of view of the Mission, Spanish pueblos in a province like that of Alta California were an anomaly, and not unfraught with peril. If, as colonists, Spaniards were to be permitted to form themselves into communities autonomous and apart from the missions, to trade with the Indian (a being as yet nomadic or merely neophyte), and to exploit him, as Spaniards (laymen) in the New World were wont to do, what was to become of the great Mission idea, — the idea of Córdova and Las Casas? This query, between 1778 and 1782, had given pause to Serra, and had pointed his pen in an animated correspondence with Governor Neve.[37]

Nor as between State Sacerdotal and State Secular, under the *comandancia-general* in California, was this all. The College of San Fernando had early applied to Rome for a grant to Junípero Serra of the power to administer confirmation, — a power which had been granted to Jesuit superiors by a Bull of Pope Benedict XIV. The request had met with favor, and on July 16, 1774, the *comisario-prefecto* of the Franciscans in America (Juan Domingo de Arricivita of Querétaro) had been authorized to delegate the power in question to one friar in each Franciscan college. Delegation in the case of Serra — after approval by the Council of the Indies, the Audiencia of Mexico, and the Viceroy — had been made on October 17, 1777, and by the end of 1779 he had confirmed no less than 2431 souls. But about the middle of 1779, he had suddenly been required by Neve to cease confirming and to surrender his patent to Croix, as wielder of the *Patronato Real*, for inspection. In Serra's opinion, an ecclesiastical patent was something with which a comandante-general had no concern, and he continued to practice confirmation throughout the year 1780. The result had been that, after correspondence between the College of San Fernando and the Viceroy, Serra himself had sent the instrument to Croix, who, finding it regular, had returned it with orders to Neve to permit the Father-President to continue his administration.[38]

The course of Governor Neve with regard to San José and Los Ángeles was sanctioned by the King in the autumn of 1779;[39] but bearing in mind the need, according to royal behest, of a post and missions on the Santa Bárbara

Channel, — and not forgetting the request of the coman-dante-general for a new *Reglamento* for the Californias, — Neve, on June 1, 1779, had submitted to Croix a paper of high significance; a paper, which, approved by the latter in September, was approved by the King, under the hand of José de Gálvez, on October 24, 1781. As Article Fourteen, the *bando* on land-distribution was used. As Article Fifteen, five sections appeared, which fixed the number of Santa Bárbara Channel mission establishments at three, and directed that there be established, at from fourteen to twenty leagues to the eastward of the existing Alta California mission-chain, a second chain so contrived as to cover with its units the interstices of the first. Guards for the establishments of this second chain were to be provided by diminishing the escorts in the older establishments; padres, by gradually reducing the quota at each of the older establishments from two to one; and funds, by the saving effected in missionary salaries.[40]

Article Fifteen of the *Reglamento* of Neve was adverse to the plan of the Mission, and in that part of the Californias between San Diego and San Francisco it was nullified by the determined opposition of the College of San Fernando. But, for the present, to the Colorado.

Returning from the second Anza expedition, Garcés (January 3, 1777) prepared his diary for submission to the Viceroy. He indicated fourteen or fifteen points on the Gila and Colorado Rivers, as suitable for missions, but, assuming that the government would not care to found more than four, — two on the Gila, and two on the Colorado, — he advised suppressing the presidios, now disused, of San Miguel de Horcasitas and Buenavista and the founding of two new presidios of fifty men each, — posts whence a guard of ten men could be detailed for each of the river missions, "the surrounding nations being numerous, powerful, and warlike"; and in this advice Anza concurred.[41]

The question of Gila-Colorado missions at this time (1776–77) was one of extreme interest both to the Viceroy and to the King. But connected with it were at least three problems: Should establishments be placed on the Gila exclusively? Should they be placed at the confluence of the streams, to wit, in Palma's country? And if placed at the confluence, should they be manned by Dominicans from the peninsula, or by Franciscans from Querétaro?[42]

It was the opinion of Padre Juan Díaz, who had been Garcés's companion to San Gabriel in 1774, that missions should be placed mainly if not exclusively on the Gila, because of aid often extended by the Gileño Pimas "to our arms against the Apaches"; because of the greater directness of the Pima-New Mexico route to Monterey; and because of the greater fertility of the Pima lands.[43] Governor Crespo of Sonora, Governor Mendinueta of New Mexico, and Comandante-Inspector Hugh Oconor were of a like opinion. Crespo recommended one mission "in Palma's country," but he laid much greater stress on the "reduction of the district between the junction of the rivers Gila and San Pedro and the presidio of Terrente."[44] As for Oconor, he ignored altogether the claims of Palma, but thought that by "three or four missionaries, picked and known for their talent and apostolic zeal," Sonora and Monterey might be conjoined through the medium of the hitherto intractable Moquis.[45]

On suppressing the presidios of San Miguel and Buenavista, Díaz and Crespo were in accord with Garcés and Anza.[46] They recognized the need of a presidio on the Colorado, but it should be placed some thirty leagues to the northeast of the confluence with the Gila; hence not in Palma's country (that of the Yumas), but above the entrance of Bill Williams Fork — the country of the Galchedunes.[47]

To Croix, however, the idea of Gila-Colorado missions was distinctly unattractive. Not so much that the comandante-general was opposed to occupation of the two rivers, — or of the Colorado, — but that, like Neve, unsympathetic with priests and beset by need of economy in administration, he was resolved to put in practice on the river boundary of Alta California a scheme of "reduction" still more emasculated than that which in Article Fifteen of the *Reglamento* Neve had outlined as for the future to be practiced on the coast boundary, — a scheme adumbrative of the plan of the *Custodia*, about to be tried in Sonora, an account of which will be given in chapter VIII.

Strange moreover to say, the attitude of Croix received countenance from within the cloisters of Querétaro itself. In 1777, Fray Juan Agustín Morfi, a *lector* (professor) of the college, to whom the Viceroy had submitted the diary of Escalante and Domínguez, condemned unsparingly the Escalante *entrada*, declaring that the padres had gone far astray, not knowing that Santa Fé and Monterey were in the same latitude. He even assailed missionary *entradas* in general. The object of them was to convert as many heathen as possible. They were made without instruments for taking altitudes, and in such haste that no sooner was one mission founded than it was quitted to found another deeper in the wilderness. The padres as they moved along depicted to the Indians the riches of the King of Spain in colors so brilliant that never afterwards was the government able, by its gifts, to meet the expectations so created. Instead of *entradas*, he advocated soldiers and war. Not even among the Yumas would he, for the present, establish missions. If war was to be waged, the best of the Yuma nation, as allies of the Spaniards against the

Apaches, would be absent on campaigns; so let the founding of missions be postponed until a general pacification, to wit, for two or three years.[48]

But if on the Colorado sham establishments only were to be erected, and these not for some years to come, the fault was not to be Palma's. He and his people had beheld too distinctly "the riches of the King of Spain" lightly to forego a bounty (beads, blankets, and tobacco) conditioned upon so simple a thing as baptism. The Yuma chief, a brother, and two others of his family, escorted by Anza as governor-elect of New Mexico, reached Mexico City on October 27, 1776. Palma on November 11 made, for his nation, submission both political and religious, and on February 13, 1777, after a season of catechism and regalement, was duly baptized under the name of Don Salvador.[49]

News of the submission having been received in Spain, the King on February 10, 1777, sent an order to the Viceroy and to Croix, that, in response to Palma's desire for "a presidio and mission in the heart of his country, there be given to these Indians missionaries and a guard of presidial troops."[50] The royal order was officially indorsed by Bucarely on May 16, and Palma, gratified, proud, and confident of speedy action, returned to the Yumas.

Months now passed, but from Croix, absent in Nueva Vizcaya, nothing was heard, and in March, 1778, Palma, a little anxious, made a visit of inquiry to Altar. Pacified with the excuse of Croix's absence, he returned home. More time elapsed, and the prestige of Palma, as the good friend of the rich king who evermore was to supply the Yumas with unlimited commodities, began seriously to decline. A second visit to Altar was essayed by Palma, and one to Horcasitas, the seat of military government for Sonora. Informed of these visits, and apprehensive of the effect of continued delay, Croix wrote from Chihuahua, in

February, 1779, to the Guardian of the College of Querétaro to ask that Garcés, with a companion, be sent to the Colorado; and to the Governor of Sonora, to direct that soldiers and supplies be furnished.[51]

With an escort of twelve men and a sergeant, all that could be spared from the presidios of Altar and Tuçón (Tuçón in 1776 having taken the place of Tubac), Garcés, accompanied by Juan Díaz, started, August 1, 1779, for the Gila-Colorado junction. Díaz and ten of the escort were forced by lack of water to return to Sonoita to await rains, but Garcés, in order not further to disappoint Palma, pressed forward with two soldiers, reaching his destination the last of the month. Palma's immediate followers he found "jovial," but the others "restless and surly." Yet remembering that "this was the first undertaking of the comandante-general"; that, as a thing especially charged upon him by the Court, it involved his honor; and that "with God all is possible," he resolved to establish a mission. Success might not have been wanting had Croix been sufficiently instructed, or prescient, to send with the padres a supply of gifts. Palma in Mexico had been laden with promises. With the coming of Spaniards to the Colorado, there was to begin for him, he was told, an era of splendor and power hitherto unconceived. Accordingly, when, on October 2, Garcés was rejoined by Díaz with his ten men, expectation on the part of the Yumas was intense, and the little band of white men was surrounded and clamorously besought for trinkets, stuffs, and tobacco.

Unable to respond, yet alive to the dangers of refusal, Díaz in November was sent to Arizpe to lay the matter before Croix. The latter, forestalling the plan of the *Custodia*, met the case, March 20, 1780, by an order providing for two settlements (pueblo missions) on the west bank of the Colorado River, — La Purísima Concepción and San

Pedro y San Pablo de Bicuñer. Twenty families and twelve laborers were to be distributed, and lands were to be assigned as afterwards at San José and Los Ángeles. In each settlement two padres were to be stationed, — Garcés and Juan Antonio Barreneche at Concepción, and Díaz and Matías Moreno at San Pedro, — and their duties were to be twofold. To the Spaniards they were to minister as curates; but to the Indians they were to be missionaries, visiting them in their *rancherías* and effecting there their conversion. The converted, as neophytes, were to dwell in the settlements, and, stimulated by Spanish example, assume the ways of industry and civil life. No presidio was to be erected, but for the protection of the new pueblos a guard of ten soldiers was to be allotted to each.[52]

It was not until the autumn of 1780 that, escorted by Lieutenant Santiago de Islas, the aforesaid company of settlers, laborers, and soldiers actually arrived, and that Concepción and San Pedro y San Pablo were in fact founded. The settlers brought 192 head of cows and horses and 200 sheep, and the soldiers 42 riding animals. These, ranging along the river margin, were suffered, despite protests, to trample the corn-fields of the Indians. Then in June, 1781, Rivera y Moncada came with his 42 soldiers and 960 head of horses under Limón and Argüello. Most of the men, with the lieutenants, were sent forward to San Gabriel, but Rivera himself with a detachment of a dozen recrossed to the east bank of the Colorado to pasture his emaciated beasts. And here, as on the west bank, the animals wrought damage, destroying the mesquite plants. Finally, stocks and a whipping-post were set up, and while Ignacio Palma, brother to Salvador, was put by Santiago in the one for insolence, certain of Palma's compatriots were publicly castigated at the other for theft.

Deluded and bitterly disappointed, there lay before the Yumas the choice either of losing utterly their Colorado heritage or of smiting the dispossessor; and, led by Salvador Palma, the worst deluded yet most long-suffering of them all, they smote without relenting. San Pedro y San Pablo was attacked on the morning of July 17. Díaz and Moreno, the soldiers, and some of the settlers were killed. Others of the settlers were made prisoners, the church and adjacent buildings were burned, the sacred vestments stolen, and the images and ornaments hurled into the river. On the same day, at the same hour, an attack was made on Concepción. The soldiers and a few settlers were killed, but the padres were not molested, and at midday the Indians withdrew. This, however, was but to enable them to cross the Colorado and attack Rivera. The captain dug hurriedly a trench about his camp, and when on the next morning he was set upon by a "tumultuous throng," he and his few men with their firelocks fought to the end.[53] At Concepción, meanwhile, the survivors were disposed to congratulate themselves on a happy escape, but on the afternoon of the 18th the settlement was again assailed. The buildings were burned and many were killed, including Garcés and Barreneche, although there is evidence that death for the padres, especially Garcés, was contrary to the wish of Palma.

In the massacre on the Colorado, the Yumas, it is worthy of remark, glutted their vengeance exclusively on the male element of the population. There was no destruction of women and children. In the case even of the men, cruelty of a wanton sort was not practiced. The victims were dispatched as promptly as possible with the club.[54] As for the principal victims, — Rivera y Moncada and Garcés, — each met a death honorable to his calling. But while in the calling of the soldier Rivera was commonplace, in that of the priest Garcés was, exceptional. Compared with his prototype Kino, he was, if not so original a mind, fully as valiant an explorer. In him was the cardinal virtue of sincerity, and by Pedro Font, his colleague on the second Anza expedition, a spirited portrait of him has been sketched.

Padre Garces is so fit to get along with Indians, and go about among them, that he seems just like an Indian himself. He shows in everything the coolness of the Indian; he squats cross-legged in a circle with them; or at night around the fire, for two or three hours or even longer, all absorbed, forgetting aught else, discourses to them with great serenity and deliberation; and though the food of the Indians is as nasty and disgusting as their dirty selves, the padre eats it with great gusto, and says that it is appetizing and very nice. In fine, God has created him, I am sure, totally on purpose to hunt up these unhappy, ignorant, and boorish people." [55]

But what of the massacre on the Colorado as determining the practicability of Kino's design of uniting Sonora with California by a chain of missions northwestward past the head of the Gulf?

Here again an interesting contrast is afforded between Rivera y Moncada and Garcés. Rivera had ever been averse to communication between the Colorado River and the coast, — so averse that when Garcés, faring westward in 1776 from the Needles to San Gabriel, sought at the mission to obtain an escort wherewith to pass to San Luis Obispo as a starting-point for New Mexico, he was refused. The ground of the refusal was danger from the Yumas; and the massacre of 1781 would, had Rivera survived it, no doubt have been regarded by him as a confirmation of his fears. Still the establishments Concepción and San Pedro y San Pablo were not missions. With the plan of the Mission they stood at variance. There was no segregation of the Indians; the padres administered no temporalties; respect was inspired by no presidio. If, as recommended by Garcés and Anza, two garrisons, strong and mutually supporting, had been placed by Croix on the Gila and Colorado, and if, under cover of these, there had been placed on each stream two missions, — establishments to which the natives were solicited, or even compelled, to repair, and at which rewards and punishments were meted out to them, — there seems reason to believe, whatever the view as to the ultimate effect of the Mission upon native character, that the design of Kino might have been accomplished.[56]

"Drooped the willows; pale the poplars; sad the birds; fled the fish; shrouded the sun; horror-stricken all nature, the day that saw the dusk waters of the Colorado crimsoned by the innocent blood of our four beloved brothers," wrote Padre Francisco Antonio Barbastro of the College of Querétaro to Guardian Agustín Morfi, on September 25, 1781. "Yesterday a messenger sent by Palma came to this presidio [Altar] with a letter for the captain, asking pardon for what had been done. To-morrow there go from here troops destined for the Colorado."[57]

News of the massacre had reached Croix in August, at Arizpe, by way both of Tuçón and of Altar. A council of war had been held on September 9, and by its decision a force under Pedro Fages (lieutenant-colonel) was to be sent against the Yumas to chastize them as rebels and apostates. The expedition, 90 strong, started from Pitic on the 16th, passed by way of Altar, where it was reinforced to 110, and reached the Colorado on the 19th of October. Here, the ransom of 64 captives, mostly women, was effected by means of blankets, beads and tobacco. The expedition returned to Sonoita, whence the ransomed were dispatched to Altar. By November 30 Fages was at the Colorado again. At Concepción and San Pedro y San Pablo he

recovered ten more captives, and secured certain church
vestments and the bodies of the four missionaries and of the
dead soldiers and settlers. But upon the Yumas, elusive as
the wind, no distinct harm was inflicted, and early in 1782
Fages found himself back at Pitic with exhausted horses.[58]

Hope of chastisements nevertheless was not abandoned.
On January 3, Governor Neve at Monterey was notified
by Croix that Fages with 40 men would proceed to San
Gabriel, and that Pedro Tueros, captain at Altar, would
march to the Colorado. At the river, Tueros was to be
joined by Neve with all the troops in California. Fages was
met by Neve at San Gabriel on March 26, but, it being
decided that the high water of the Colorado would be a
hindrance, Tueros was informed of a postponement of
action until September. On the new basis, which Croix
approved, Captain José Antonio Romeu with 108 men
reached the Colorado by September 16, and was there
joined by Neve with 60 men, but unaccompanied by Fages.
The latter had been turned back by orders received on
the way; orders which directed that Neve proceed to
Sonora to assume the office of inspector-general of the
Provincias Internas, and that Fages proceed to Monterey
to be installed as governor. As for Romeu, he conducted
against the Yumas a campaign which resulted in 108 natives being killed, 85 taken prisoner, five Christians freed
from captivity, and 1048 horses recovered. Otherwise the
result was naught. "Neither then nor afterwards," declares the chronicle of Arricivita, "was subjection secured.
Hope of reëstablishing the pueblos, or of reducing the
Indians, none remained; and the expenditures incurred for
communication between Sonora and Monterey by the
Colorado River were wasted."[59]

As far back as June, 1777, Felipe de Neve had written to
Viceroy Bucarely that, mindful of the ease with which the

eight or ten thousand Indians along the Santa Bárbara Channel might, if so disposed, interrupt transit to the north, he had decided to found, in addition to the terminal establishments San Buenaventura and Purísima Concepción, a central establishment to be called Santa Bárbara.[60] Until the coming, in the summer of 1781, of the 42 soldiers recruited by Rivera in Sonora, this had been impracticable. Meanwhile Croix had issued his decree for pueblo missions on the Colorado.

The provisions of this instrument, consonant as they were with the views of Neve, and to be carried out, as they were, within Neve's own province, may have suggested to the latter imitation with respect to the establishments for the Channel; especially as the Colorado Yumas and Channel Chumash were alike in being numerous and so located as to derive a regular subsistence from their trade of fishing. At all events, in 1782, on March 6, Neve issued to Lieutenant Ortega instructions that the establishments about to be erected as missions were to be operated as *hospicios*. The Canaleños were not to be withdrawn from their *rancherías* and put to agricultural and mechanical tasks, but to be converted by pastoral visitations.[61] On March 31, San Buenaventura — the mission beloved of Gálvez — was founded by Ortega in conjunction with Serra, and on April 21, Neve and Serra founded the presidio of Santa Bárbara.[62]

But, on August 23, 1779, the great Viceroy, Bucarely (deceased, April 9), had been succeeded by Martín de Mayorga, — a man imbued with the spirit of Neve and Croix. A field-marshal in Spain, Mayorga in America had been governor, president, and captain-general of Guatemala. Under him (December, 1780) the College of San Fernando, warned by the recent decree of Croix denying temporalties to Garcés and his companions, had consented to send six friars to the Channel, provided they were assigned two to a mission, and were allowed the usual vestments, bells, live-stock, implements, and funds for foundations. This offer Mayorga, on April 5, 1781, had rejected. Between College and Viceroy a deadlock thereupon had ensued, but news of it had not reached the Channel at the time of the founding of San Buenaventura Mission and Santa Bárbara Presidio.

With the creation of the district of Santa Bárbara, short by two establishments though it was, the organization of Alta California, secular and sacerdotal, became complete. Secularly there now were the four military districts, — San Diego, Santa Bárbara, Monterey, and San Francisco;[63] and the two pueblo districts, — San José and Los Ángeles. Sacerdotally there were the missions, — San Diego, San Juan Capistrano, and San Gabriel; Santa Bárbara and San Buenaventura; San Carlos Borromeo de Monterey, San Antonio de Padua, and San Luis Obispo; San Francisco and Santa Clara, — establishments where nineteen friars, charged with the care of 4000 neophytes, 4900 head of mules and horned cattle, and 7000 head of sheep, goats, and swine, were able to grow wheat, maize, and barley to the amount of a predictable annual yield of 22,500 bushels.

In Alta California, prior to 1781, the secular head was the *jefe militar*, or *comandante de armas*, to whom appeal might be taken from the presidio comandantes, and from the *cabos* (corporals) of the mission guards. Civil rule began with the introduction of the pueblo, with its *alcalde* and *regidores*,[64] — functionaries of great antiquity, especially the *alcalde*, who, an outgrowth of the Roman municipality, derived his designation from the *cadi* of the Moors.[65] Neve, the first Alta California political head (*jefe político*, or *gobernador*), was such not so much by his position as by the fact that he founded two pueblos, from the *alcaldes* and *cabildos* [66] of which (as also from his own *co-misionados*) appeal to him might be taken; he in turn being subject to be appealed from to the comandante-general or Audiencia (Supreme Court) of Guadalajara.

As for the sacerdotal head, he was, prior to 1781, as afterwards, the president of missions. From him appeal might be taken to the College of San Fernando, and thence to the *comisario-general* of the Franciscans in Spain. Withal, down to 1781, when the Californias became part of the diocese of Sonora, they had been part of that of Durango; but this fact signified naught, for not only were there no curacies in the province, but, from regular to secular, from monk to bishop, there was no appeal; save, perchance, in cases like that of the neophyte Carlos, who by taking refuge in the mission church of San Diego had raised the question of right of asylum.

Under the organization described, advantage lay (as ever in the Spanish dominions) with State Secular; for while, as between State Secular and State Sacerdotal, the former was free from authoritative intervention by the latter, the reverse did not obtain. In criminal causes, the missions, as has been seen, were subject to the governor; and in so far as by a choice of Indian *alcaldes* and *regidores* the missions became pueblos, they were thus subject to the extent of the governor's approval of the choice made. By virtue, moreover, of the *Patronato Real* the entire Spanish clergy, regular as well as secular, could (*vide* chapter III) be controlled in everything save the internal regulation of their own corporations. [67] Advantage lay with State Secular, too, from the broad circumstance, noted in chapter v, that Charles III was king, and that during his reign Madrid, influenced by rationalized France, had set out to curb the priesthood.

CHAPTER VIII

STATE SECULAR *vs.* STATE SACERDOTAL

BY the promotion of Neve on July 12, 1782, to the position of *comandante-inspector* in the Provincias Internas, Pedro Fages had become governor of the Californias. It now was thirteen years since, from his "high hill," near Cape San Lucas, José de Gálvez had watched the San Carlos vanish below the horizon of the South Sea; and the pioneers of the Sacred Expedition were beginning to pass away. On January 1, 1782, the diligent Juan Crespi had died at the age of sixty-one; and on August 28, 1784, he was followed, at the age of seventy-one, by Junípero Serra.

On the 18th of August, Palou (recalled to Monterey from San Francisco) found Serra, who lately had completed an arduous round of mission calls, suffering from trouble of the chest, and from a recurrence of his old trouble of the leg. He found him distressed also by rumors of an impending displacement of the Franciscans in Alta California by the Dominicans.[1] On the 27th, fever supervened, and at the church, attended by Indians and cuirassed men, the Father-President received the last Sacrament. On the 28th, the fever increasing, he was visited in the morning by Captain José Cañizares, whose ship lay at anchor in the bay; and between one and two o'clock in the afternoon, having drawn about him his cloak and composed himself on his bed of planks, he resigned his spirit. His funeral, which took place on the 29th in the presence of mariners, soldiers, and neophytes, was conducted with solemn pomp. The body, covered with *rosas de Castilla* (token of 1769–70) and attended by guardsmen with lighted tapers, was borne amid chanting about the plaza to the church, where, in the presbytery on the epistle side, it was interred near that of Crespi.

> One sees the pulpit o' the epistle-side,
> And somewhat of the choir, those silent seats,
> And up in the aëry dome where live
> The angels, and a sunbeam's sure to lurk.

On September 4, Serra's garments were distributed as amulets, and on the 6th, Palou, writing to José de Gálvez in behalf of the nine missions of northern California, — "daughters of the fervid zeal of your Excellency," — set forth the incidents of which use has been made in the above account.[2]

It has been said in chapter v that Junípero Serra was seraphic in spirit, simple in faith, and pure in heart. That he was not unpossessed of shrewdness has there also been intimated. In 1781, in view of his course on the confirmation question, Neve, writing to Croix, charged upon him "unspeakable artifice," — a "pretended obedience to an authority [the government] which he in fact eludes." And in 1783, Fages found him "despotic" and opposed "to every government undertaking." In the larger sense, which also is the truer, Serra is not so much to be regarded as a person as a force, — a representative, less astute than Salvatierra, less even than Palou, of the idea of the Mission: in personal concernments, tractable to the point of humility; in concernments of faith, steadfast to the point of aggression.

Crespi and Serra were dead. Palou yet survived but was becoming infirm. Before the death of Serra he had applied to the King for leave to retire to San Fernando; but, pending the arrival at Monterey of Fermín Francisco Lasuén, who meanwhile had been named as Serra's successor, he was kept at the head of the Alta California establishments.[3]

On reaching his college (1786) he was made guardian, and in 1787 he published his *Relación Histórica de la Vida . . . del venerable Padre Fray Junípero Serra*, a book of nearly three hundred and fifty pages. It is agreeably written, and bears as a frontispiece a portrait of its subject. The original picture (a painting) was secured through the liberality of former Guardian Verger, now Bishop of Linares.[4]

The Gálvez-Croix dispatch of 1768 declared, that

if from the glorious conquest (as achieved by Hernan Cortés) of those vast dominions that fall under the name of New Spain, it had been the practice of successors in the government to follow up and prosecute the high designs of that hero, there would have supervened the light of the Gospel and the dominion of the august King of Spain to the ultimate bounds of this immense and unexplored continent.

But the "high designs" of Cortés had not been followed up, and by way of remedy there was proposed a *comandancia-general* for the Provincias Internas. A system of *intendencias* was also proposed. Durango, Sonora, and the Californias were to be placed, each, in charge of a *gobernador-intendente,* — an official who, with entire independence of initiative as to government, police, justice, treasury and war, was to be subject to the Viceroy, or comandante-general, and Audiencia, and to the *Superintendente de Hacienda* (Secretary of the Treasury) on appeal.[5]

The problem which confronted Gálvez and Croix, however, was not alone one of administration. It was the problem, early noted by Gálvez,[6] of reduction of the natives to civilized life. In the days of Cortés "reduction" had given no serious trouble. It had been an incident of conquest. Between 1530 and 1540, conversions in the City of Mexico, in Texcuco, in Michoacán, and elsewhere — all, too, at the hands of but sixty missionaries, — had amounted to millions; and, upon conversion as a base, civil organization had straightway been engrafted. To-day in Sonora and Nueva Vizcaya conversions were not only few, but the converted remained civilly as "unreduced" as when they were infidels. Evidently something was required to meet the problem other than *comandancias-generales* and *intendencias*. Gálvez and Croix did not disclose this something, but by recalling the methods of Cortés, political and religious, they indicated it.

In 1772 (July 13), Fiscal Areche observed, that

to check decadence a new method of government, spiritual and temporal, was necessary. [In it] there should be digested all the rules of experience for erecting the missions in regular towns, and not in *rancherías* as most of them were; rules that would be useful for the good domestic government of the Indians, — for introducing among them family order, obedience to superiors, the practice of agriculture and commerce; rules that in the days of Cortés had been observed in Michoacán with a success such as to render its pastor and bishop, Don Vasco de Quiroga, worthy of a foremost place in the history of America.[7]

The same year, on November 15, Guardian Verger said: —

When Hernan Cortés entered these kingdoms, he found villages, towns, and pueblos already formed, civilized, and improved with everything necessary, as the histories say, excepting only the knowledge of the true God and of his Holy Law, by which they were to serve, love, adore, and reverence Him. But as for the Gentiles whom we are striving to conquer, they lack all of this, insomuch that for the most part they go naked, wandering in their intricate mountains and extended valleys.

Still, if it were desired to profit by Cortés's example, let it be remembered how, upon the coming of the first friars, he went forth to receive them in the Avenue of Tepayac (now called that of Guadalupe), and, kneeling in the dust, kissed the hand of each, and by his interpreter said to the Indians: —

Although I, in the name of the Emperor, govern the bodies of men, these fathers are come in the name of the head of the Church, which governs their souls, with authority from the same God whom we adore, to guide them to his glory. What the fathers command, obey even as ye have seen me obedient first.

By some *jefes* (so Verger affirmed) it was made their first business to tell the Indians that they need ask permission of the fathers in nothing; that "the fathers were not allowed to inflict punishments; that their authority extended only to the hearing of confessions and the saying of Mass."[8]

But on the question of the attainment of civil status for the Indian by a "new method of reduction," it was deemed well to obtain the opinion of Padre Antonio de los Reyes. His college (Querétaro) had in 1773 been emphatic in support of the plan of the Mission, but in 1776, Reyes, about to become Bishop of Sonora, had rejected this in favor of the plan of the *Custodia*, — the plan of "reduction" so successful under Cortés; one, withal, expressly sanctioned in 1686 by a Bull of Pope Innocent XI. Let the Provincias, said Reyes, be divided into *custodia* districts. In the head town of each district let there be established an *hospicio*, or "home," of six or more padres under a director responsible to the *comisario-general* of his order. From such *hospicio* — or, where desirable, from a sub-*hospicio* of three padres under a president — let the inmates go forth as missionaries to Spanish pueblos and mining-camps and to Indian *rancherías*. As for support, let it be obtained somewhat by royal donation, but chiefly by "the charity of the faithful." Only two *custodias* were contemplated for the entire Provincias: one, — including the missions of Parra nearest the Sierra Madre, of Toranmora Alta and Baja, of

Sonora and of the Californias, — with seat at Arizpe; the other,— including the missions of New Mexico, Chihuahua, Coahuila, and Texas, — with seat near the centre of the territory. To the general plan of Reyes assent had been expressed by the Franciscan *comisario-general*, Manuel de la Vega, in November, but Vega had suggested four *custodias* instead of two: one for New Mexico (La Concepción), one for Nueva Vizcaya (San Antonio), one for Sonora (San Carlos), and one for Alta California (San Gabriel).[9] Thus the matter stood on the advent of Fages to power, at Monterey, in 1782.

In 1783 (February 11), the three Franciscan missionary colleges — Guadalupe de Zacatecas for Durango, Santa Cruz de Querétaro for Sonora, and San Fernando de Méjico for Alta California — united in a determined protest against the whole *Custodia* scheme. The royal *cédula* enjoining it bore date May 20, 1782, and with the *cédula* there had come a Bull of sanction by Pope Pius VI and elaborate *estatutos* (ordinances) drafted by Manuel de la Vega. "The colleges," the protest confessed, "are overwhelmed with weight of authority, Pontifical, Royal, and Prelatical." But *custodias* — successful under Cortés among the semi-civilized nations of the South— could, it was averred, never be aught but a failure in the North. Success for the *Custodia* required clergy, convents, churches, money, — the incidents and appurtenances of a settled condition, — and it was notorious that a settled condition in the North did not obtain, but one of robbery and murder, as witness the four padres of Querétaro lately put to death on the banks of the Colorado River.[10] By Bishop Reyes the protest was pronounced full of *falsas suposiciones y expresiones injuriosas*, and on January 14, 1784, it was disallowed by the King. Yet it so far served its purpose that, whereas the *custodia* of San Carlos in Sonora was erected

without delay, the erecting of the *custodia* of San Gabriel
in Alta California was postponed; a postponement that
proved a nullification, for in 1792 (August 17) the King
decreed that even in Sonora the plan of the Mission should
be resumed.[11]

But the *Custodia* was not the only means of "reduction,"
civilly, for the Indian to which, between 1776 and 1791,
the government of the Provincias was to have recourse.
By a Law of the Indies called the *alcalde* law (*vide* chapter
III), Indians were required to dwell in pueblos, choosing
for themselves *alcaldes* and *regidores*. As early as December, 1778, Neve instructed the San Diego and San Carlos
padres to put neophytes through the form of choosing two
alcaldes and two *regidores;* and the padres at San Antonio,
San Luis, and San Gabriel to contrive an election of *alcaldes*
and *regidores* in number proportioned to population.[12] In
1781, Comandante-General Croix revived viceregal decrees
which required the furnishing of inventories and statistics
to the Governor, and invoked the *Patronato Real* to the
effect that, except for urgent cause, no padre might be
transferred from one mission to another. By order of Neve
in 1782 padres were forbidden military escort save when
visiting a presidio or *ranchería* to hear confessions; and the
same year, apropos of a *cédula* of 1776 directing the landing of the Philippine galleon at Monterey, it had been
ordered that no priest should pass on shipboard.[13] The
privilege, too, of franking letters had been abridged;[14] and
not alone this, but padres wishing to retire to their college,
or to Spain, were obliged to obtain a government permit.[15]
Finally, there was the question of the employment by
the padres of Indians as messengers and *vaqueros*, — of
teaching the neophytes to ride. To control the military, as
had been permitted the Jesuits in Paraguay, and the Fran-

ciscans in Lower California and in Texas, this was to
wield temporal power indeed; and Neve, by his virtual in-
terdiction of escorts, had, in the interest of State Secular,
seen to it that such power was not wielded in Alta California.[16]

Promulgated by Neve and Croix, it was upon Fages that
for the most part it devolved to put the foregoing laws and
decrees into effect. And Fages, loyal to the government,
yet mindful of his rustication in 1773 at the instance of
Serra, found himself between two fires.

In vain did he protest to Palou that in the business of
governing he had a partner, a veritable Jorkins. With the
best intentions he dared not too much disregard orders, for
his adjutant (Soler), animated by a keen desire to be governor himself, was "deadly at intermeddling." In vain
did he modify a rule of Neve's that absconding neophytes
were never to be brought back by the military.[17] His concessions — so, Hamlet-like, he averred to Father Cambón
— were requited only by insult. Did he go half a league
from San Carlos Presidio to greet Father Palou — he was
rebuffed by scowls and taciturnity. Did he furnish the
padre three attendants and three of his best horses, and
direct in his honor a salute of two guns — Palou would not
even break bread with him. Did he pay a visit to San Carlos Mission — Father Matías, in Palou's presence and by
him abetted, stamped roundly his foot, and cried out upon
him. Did he, at San Luis, ask from Father Caballer (Catalan like himself) an inventory, saying that inventories had
been rendered at the other missions of the South — he was
told to his beard that he would be believed when the documents were produced. His love for the padres had been
such that it had gained for him the nickname of *frailero*
(panderer to friars), yet the padres, even in their letters,
denied him the courtesy of the usual forms of address, —

Muy Señor mio (My very respected Sir), and *Beso á Vd. su mano* (I respectfully kiss your hand). At such disrespect, he ("not as Fages but as governor") stood fairly aghast. Because he obeyed orders, he was said by the populace to be "persecuting the *frailes*," when, in truth, he had endured so to be dragooned by them that, looking within, he had been obliged to say to himself, "I am governor, not Fages." Distraught, however, though he was, and with the feet of their reverences the padres upon his very head, he was resolved to depart no jot from duty. So comporting himself he could not be put to blush, and would have his reward from conscience.[18]

The Governor by 1785 had determined upon a course of action, — an appeal to the Viceroy. Under date of September 26, the chief immediate grievances, — failure of the padres to perform chaplain duty at the presidios,[19] disregard of the *Patronato Real*, unwarranted charges for mission produce, refusal to render inventories, failure to solicit permission when quitting the province, — all had been formulated. The document was sent by the Viceroy (through the Audiencia) to the College of San Fernando, where Palou on his arrival in 1786 was intrusted with the task of reply.

Chaplain duty, said Palou, was by favor and not by requirement, and should be paid for. As for the *Patronato Real*, Fages, ignorant of its scope, made of it a cloak for despotism. As for the tariff of prices for produce (an attempt to regulate what should be left to demand and supply), it never had been sanctioned by the King. As for permission to retire, padres, by order of Viceroy Mayorga, were so permitted on exhibiting a license from their prelate. Palou said nothing as to inventories, but on the point (not raised by Fages) that under the new *Reglamento* but one padre was to be allowed at a mission, he pleaded an abrogation of the requirement by the King in his *cédula* of May 20, 1782.[20] By way of general counter-charge upon the Governor, Palou submitted that the *Reglamento* had not been published in the Californias until September, 1784,[21] when Fages's bill of grievances bore date, and that escorts had been withheld, to the crippling of the business of the Mission, temporal as well as spiritual.[22]

"State Secular *vs.* State Sacerdotal in Alta California" was thus ready for adjudication. But the points involved were delicate, and the Audiencia, glad of a chance to shift the responsibility of deciding them, referred the case to the comandante-general of the Provincias Internas, — Jacobo Ugarte y Loyola. On the appointment, in 1783, of Caballero de Croix to be Viceroy of Peru, Felipe de Neve, his comandante-inspector had been given the place of comandante-general. But Neve had died in 1784, and as no officer with adequate knowledge was available as a successor, a compromise was effected in 1785 by restoring to the Viceroy of Mexico (Conde de Gálvez) supreme authority as possessed by Bucarely, and by creating Ugarte y Loyola his subordinate. When, therefore, the Alta California case was received by Loyola, it was received reluctantly as by one without authority. In the emergency the Comandante-General applied for light to Lasuén, the new mission president at Monterey.[23]

The points which Lasuén emphasized were three which Fages did not make. "What I oppose and resist with my whole strength," he declared, "is being left alone in a mission. I offer myself for every kind of hardship (even unto death in these parts) at the order of my superior, but no man is able to convince me that I ought to subject myself to solitude in this ministry." The use of Indians as messengers and *vaqueros* he upheld as necessary, but the instituting of Indian *alcaldes*, — "lazy, overbearing, and conniving in dereliction," — he pronounced a legal formality, farcical, mischievous, and unseasonable.[24]

By Ugarte y Loyola the Alta California case was vouchsafed a determination no more definite than by the Audiencia. By both Audiencia and Comandante-General the finding was, that Mission and Government in Alta California — State Sacerdotal and State Secular — were to keep each within its own sphere and jurisdiction, observing *armonía y correspondencia*. If either litigant triumphed, it was the Mission rather than the Government, for the Audiencia explicitly recommended that the padres at San Francisco be paid for saying Mass at the presidio, and that on "indispensable journeys" the padres be furnished by the Government with escorts.

Regarding San José and Los Ángeles, as civic institutions under Fages, they were as uncomfortable a Neve heritage as the *Reglamento* itself. Both towns were fretted by disorders from three causes: gambling on the part of the settlers; immorality on the part of the settlers with the Indians; and horse-stealing on the part of the Indians. At San José, Ignacio Vallejo was *comisionado*, and at Los Ángeles, Vicente Félix; and in 1787 Fages found it necessary to furnish to the latter minute instructions as to police.[25] Through the pueblos, indeed, there was taking place the very thing which the Laws of the Indies, by strict prohibition of miscellaneous intercourse between Indians and whites, had sought to preclude, to wit, demoralization of the Indians by whites demoralized already. Lasuén, therefore, was justified when, alluding to San José, he said in his plea to Ugarte y Loyola that Gentile Indians (male and female), employed at the pueblo in tasks of house and field, were by their "scandals and libertinism" fast neutralizing the good done by the adjoining mission of Santa Clara.

Hurt by the projected *Custodia;* hurt by the enforced toleration of Indian *alcaldes* and *regidores;* hurt by fear of the *Reglamento;* hurt by need of interposing at Mexico and Arizpe defense against charges of insubordination; and hurt, lastly, by the presence, aggressive and unsavory, of the pueblos, there yet remained to State Sacerdotal a consolation. The missions of Santa Bárbara and La Purísima Concepción — desired by Serra and planned by Neve, but suspended in their founding by the refusal of the College of San Fernando to assign to them padres — both at length were to be erected. "You will oppose all innovation, and will refuse to supply priests on the Río Colorado method," wrote the Guardian of San Fernando to Lasuén on April 1, 1786; and the terms, perforce, had been accepted.[26] The day of founding for Santa Bárbara was December 4, 1786; for Purísima, December 8, 1787.[27] Nor were these foundings the only consolation of the time. To a recommendation made in November, 1787, by Nicolás Soler, who, besides being "deadly at intermeddling," was dominated by Neve ideas, that the missions straightway be dissolved and their lands granted in severalty, Fages interposed the pertinent comment, that as yet the Indians had not been weaned from their Gentile state, nor could they be addressed without an interpreter.[28]

By 1789, strife between the secular and sacerdotal elements in Alta California had, in obedience to the Audiencia, been suffered to become appeased. Not that bitterness was easily laid aside by Palou. Writing on January 28, 1781, to Comisario-General Manuel María Truxillo, the Guardian said: —

Little have the missions grown spiritually since my departure, — a backwardness due to the contrary attitude of that Señor Gobernador Don Pedro Fages, who in everything has set himself to impede the apostolical zeal of the missionaries; due also to the scandals committed upon the poor neophytes by subaltern officers; and due, finally, to the bad example of the soldiers. The said Don Pedro (always governor in fact) ruled at the beginning under the title of comandante, but the Venerable Father Junípero Serra, perceiving that the conquest was in nothing advanced but rather hindered, felt himself obliged to perform the task of coming to this court and making representations to the Most Excellent Señor Viceroy Don Antonio María Bucarely; whence it resulted that the said Fages was recalled and that straightway the conquest, spiritual and temporal, was advanced notably. But with the transfer, after a few years, of the Provincias Internas to the command of a comandante-general, separate and apart from the captaincy-general and viceroyalty of New Spain, there supervened the return of Don Pedro with more honor and with the title of governor. And, coming thus, he, as all the padres feel, has acted much according to his whim; either because of his nature, resentful of dependence, or by way of avenging himself for what, during his first incumbency, was accomplished by the report of the Venerable Father Junípero.[29]

But *pace* Palou. Fages, on May 18, 1790, was relieved of the office of governor at his own request. He was fifty-six years old, and for seven and a half years had faithfully served the King at Monterey. He left behind him nine missions in four presidial districts (an addition of two establishments, — Santa Bárbara and Purísima) and the two pueblos. Of San José, the population now was about 80, and of Los Ángeles about 140. In the latter were 29 adobe dwellings, an adobe town-hall, barracks, guard-house, and granary, all inclosed by a wall of adobes.

The new governor, a client of Viceroy Revilla Gigedo, was José Antonio Romeu. Fages was required to yield office to him at Loreto, and then proceed to Mexico to be invested with a colonelcy. The transfer was made, however, by José Joaquín de Arrillaga (lieutenant-governor) on April 16, 1791.[30] Romeu reached Monterey on October 13, and soon thereafter Fages set sail for San Blas. He had already dispatched south his wife, Doña Eulalia de Callis, with his children, and had brought to conclusion a series of intimate notes to his successor.

September 14, 1790. You will find in this *casa real,* which is sufficiently capacious, the necessary furniture; a sufficient stock of goats and sheep which I have raised; and, near by, a garden which I have made at my own expense, from which you will have fine vegetables all the year. *February* 26, 1791. Half a league from this post I made a garden in the year 1783. It is 308 *varas* long and 80 wide. There are in it grapes and about six hundred fruit trees, — pear, apple, peach, apricot, quince, etc. *May* 24, 1791. With the Dominicans I have had no serious trouble, but with the Fernandinos quarrels have arisen. They are opposed in the highest degree to the *Reglamento* and Government. That you will be able to endure their independent ways, I much doubt.[31]

But to partake of the fruits and vegetables of Fages's garden, or to match diplomacy with the friars, Romeu had little opportunity. He died on the 9th of April, 1792, and was buried at San Carlos Mission, — a spot, by its hallowed dust of saints and rulers, fast becoming a Santa Croce of the wild. Romeu's successor *ad interim* was Lieutenant-Governor Arrillaga, who held office until 1794, when he was replaced by a governor *proprietario,* — Diego de Borica.

The governors and comandantes of the Californias whom thus far in the course of narration we have met, have been seven: Portolá, Armona, Barri, Rivera y Moncada, Neve, Fages, and Romeu. Portolá was kindly but negative; while as for Armona and Barri, neither had passed north of the peninsula. It may be said of the one that, accomplished, and approved by Palou, he shrank before difficulties; and of the other, that, arbitrary in temper, a conspicuous trait was violence. In Rivera y Moncada hauteur was made grotesque by envy, but personality lacked interest through mediocrity. Neve and Fages remain, each a man of character, but, strange to say, only one (Fages) a man of personality. Neve, indeed, possessed so much character, was so imperturbable, kept so well his temper, wrought with an inexorability so final, as to be personally of scant account. Neve was the *Reglamento* and the *Reglamento* was Neve — little besides. Among early California rulers, therefore, it is upon Fages that personally the emphasis falls, for, to cite from New Netherland a parallel, Fages in whatever relation viewed was a veritable Peter the Headstrong.

According to Serra, with whom he had had trouble, he often had trouble with his men. Then there was his adjutant, Soler. With him, whom Neve had not found insupportable, he could do nothing. "The caviling spirit of our Don Nicolás disturbs me much," he writes in 1787. "He persists in transacting affairs, and in ventilating here and there his chimerical schemes, to the disquietude of all."

Last (and hereby a tale) there was the *gobernadora*, Fages's wife Doña Eulalia. We get a glimpse of her first in a letter from Fages to Father Morfi from Pitic, dated February 12, 1782: —

On June 10 last, I informed you of my arrival at Arizpe accompanied by my wife, Catalan servants, and soldiers. At the same time there was given me the satisfaction of an increase in my command, with whom God was pleased to rejoice us the night of the 30th of last May, and who was baptized on the 4th of June, the Señor Intendente, Governor Don Pedro Carbalon, being godfather. The child was named Pedro José Fernando, and I trust that your Reverence will be pleased to add him to the number of your children.

We get another glimpse on September 13, 1784: —

In the mission of San Francisco [writes Palou to Guardian Juan Sancho], we remained with the Governor more than four weeks.

Being on a visit to the presidio with his wife, he there awaited the birth to her of a child whom we baptized. The *señora* was pleased with our behavior, and was a notable example to the neophytes and soldiers. Much was accomplished by her bearing and presence.

But Doña Eulalia, delicately bred, was fearsome of the frontier. Her presence at Monterey had only been secured by repeated urgings from Fages, in which Neve and Romeu joined; and no sooner had she arrived (escorted by her husband, amid rejoicings, from Loreto) than she was eager for the latter to resign his governorship and return with her to Mexico. Means for accomplishing her will were few, but among them was one upon which she relied with confidence, — rigid exclusion of her consort from the conjugal couch. For three months, October, 1784, to February, 1785, this means was tried, but at the end of the term, the Governor's steadfastness continuing, Doña Eulalia was constrained to affect jealousy, — jealousy toward a servant of the house, a Yuma maid, Indizuela. Vowing divorce, she fled tempestuously her abode; and although dealt with by the padres, who enjoined seclusion and forbade the bruiting abroad of scandals against the governor, she became so violent as to provoke threats of castigation and handcuffs.[32]

Eulalia began divorce proceedings in April, 1785, before the Acting Comandante-General José Antonio Rengel, at Chihuahua, but Asesor (Solicitor-General) Galindo Navarro decided that, the case being one of divorce, its proper forum was the ecclesiastical court of the Bishop of Sonora. By advice of the *asesor*, however, an order was entertained for the removal of both Doña Eulalia and the maid Indizuela to "some house of honest matrons" in Sonora, and for a writ upon a third part of the salary of Fages, to enable the complainant to prosecute her suit. The Bishop, before whom the case came in November, spurned the interlocutory findings of the *asesor* — "eager to thrust his sickle in the grain" — as beyond the secular jurisdiction, and as, therefore, a reprehensible affront. But here censure and, as well, the suit were stayed; for in December it became known to Rengel that Fages and Eulalia had been reconciled in September.[33]

My family are well [writes Fages to Palou, on January 2,1787]. Suddenly one morning Eulalia with a thousand protests summoned me, and amid tears humbly sought pardon for all the past. She confessed that all had been pure illusion and falsity, and that she herself had suborned Indizuela to ensnare me. Afterwards she summoned Don Hermenegildo Sal [the paymaster], Vargas [the sergeant], and other persons, and told them the truth, that they might make it public in discharge of her conscience. *Gracias á Dios* that now we dwell in union and harmony![34]

What Fages did not write was that it was largely due to Nicolás Soler, "deadly at intermeddling," that the reconciliation had been brought about.

But, reconciled or no, Doña Eulalia did not abate her activity. Determined to exchange the barbarism and fogs of Monterey for the refinement and salubrity of Mexico, she in 1785 came near to proving a factor as fatal to her husband's governorship as Serra in 1773 had proved to his *comandancia*. In the year named, on October 25, Fages was compelled to notify the authorities at Chihuahua that his wife had petitioned the Audiencia for his transfer for health reasons, and to beg of them that the petition be disregarded.

CHAPTER IX

DOMESTIC EQUILIBRIUM

DIEGO DE BORICA — native of the Basque town of Vitoria, and Knight of the Order of Santiago — was the most sagacious and chivalric of the men sent by Spain to represent the King at Monterey. Under him old things in Alta California passed away, and many (if not all) things became new, — new, that is, by a reversion of conditions to what they were under Viceroy Bucarely. But this making of the province new, by causing it to revert to the old, signifies not that the early forces were controlled by the early minds. In 1794 Lasuén, a figure venerable and benign, still lived and wrought, but the grave had closed upon Crespi, Serra, and Palou, and (1787) upon José de Gálvez, and (1788) upon King Charles III himself. In part, the newness mentioned is to be ascribed to the withdrawal, in 1793, of the Californias from the jurisdiction of the Provincias Internas.[1] In part, also, it was due to the accession of Charles IV to the throne, representative in Spain of a European reaction (guillotine-bred) toward Absolutism and the Church.

But whatever its source, the newness prevailed, and its manifestations were dual: (1) a revival of interest in Anian, the English, and the Russians, — a revival involving undertakings which set Alta California before the world as an entity, a something with boundaries political as well as natural; a something, withal, through guns and fortifications, with power; (2) a culmination of the Mission dynamically, — a culmination marked on the one hand by

additional Mission foundations, and on the other by a growing severity of attitude (reflex of Indian incorrigibility) by
padres toward neophytes.

I

In 1778, men of Captain Cook's command, when at
Nootka, obtained from the natives a number of skins of
the sea-otter. These, while in the hands of the natives, had
been used as garments, and had become infested with lice;
nor was their condition improved by Cook's men, who used
them in high latitudes as bed-coverings. But at Canton, in
December, 1779, they fetched, the best of them, $120 each.[2]
The Russians had for thirty years been selling otter-skins,
obtained from the Aleutian Islands, to Chinese merchants
at Kiakhta, and the English had for a like period been ex-
porting to St. Petersburg, for Kiakhta delivery, skins of the
otter and beaver from Hudson's Bay, — facts made known
to the world in 1780 by William Coxe in a book entitled
"Russian Discoveries."[3] Yet it remained for Cook's
"Voyage," published in 1784, to create a world-interest in
the Northwest fur-trade.

In August, 1785, Nootka was visited for furs by Captain
James Hanna from Macao. In September of the same
year, the Nootka region was sighted by two captains from
England, both of whom had served with Cook, Nathaniel
Portlock and George Dixon. Between June and September,
1786, the Northwest Coast, from Alaska down past Nootka
to Monterey, was surveyed by the French navigator Jean
François Galaup, Comte de la Pérouse; and in September,
1788, Nootka was made a rendezvous by two fur-trading
vessels from Boston, the Lady Washington and the Columbia Rediviva.[4] Spain herself (in government circles
at least) was roused to an interest in furs by the voyages
of Cook; and in August, 1786, Vicente Basadre y Vega ar-

rived at Monterey, as royal commissioner, to begin collecting skins of the otter and seal. He was met in Monterey by Pérouse, who records an anticipation by Spain of brilliant results from a trade in California furs with China by way of Manila. But the scheme, a government monopoly, lacked in enterprise, and in 1790 was abandoned.[5]

Just after the northern expedition of Arteaga and Cuadra, in 1780, Spain, satisfied that the Russians were making no dangerous approaches toward California, had ordered northern explorations to cease. But with the coming in 1786 of Pérouse, — co-religionist, accomplished scientist, and gallant gentleman, — fresh alarm was created. On December 18, Esteván José Martínez, who had just returned to San Blas from a supply trip to Monterey, wrote to Viceroy Gálvez: —

On the 14th of September last, while at anchor in the port of Monterey, two *fragatas* were seen, distant about five leagues and making as though to enter the port. I observed that their flags were French, and concluded that the vessels must be those destined by His Most Christian Majesty for the work of discovery. . . . Said *fragatas* were the Brujula and Astrolabe, under command of the Conde de la Pérouse, etc. The Señor Conde assured me as a fixed fact that the Russian nation was in possession of the island of Oonalaska. . . . Not only were they in possession of the said island, but of portions of the coast that extends from 61° southwest; and their furthest establishment was in latitude 56°: 30'. The business of the Russians with the Indians, the Count assured me, was to exchange manufactured iron for otter-skins.[6]

Martínez in the Princesa, and López de Haro in the San Carlos, were sent in 1788 by Viceroy Manuel Antonio Flórez to make an investigation. They found the Russians on Kadiak and Unalaska Islands, the latter the largest of the Aleutian group, and heard of them on Cook's River. Martínez wrote to Flórez on December 5, 1788: —

Eustrate Delarof [Russian factor at Kadiak] told me that as a result of his having informed his sovereign of the commerce which the English from Canton are carrying on at Nootka, he was expecting four *fragatas* from Siberia to sail next year for the purpose of making an establishment at Nootka. He assured me that his sovereign had a better right to that coast than any other power, on account of its having been discovered by the Russian commanders Behring and Tscherkow, under orders from the Russian Court, in the year 1741. It therefore seems to me advisable that an attempt should be made next year, 1789, with such forces as you may have at hand, to occupy the said port and establish a garrison in it. . . . By accomplishing this we shall gain possession of the coast from Nootka to the port of San Francisco. I say this, at the same time offering myself to carry out the project; and to prove the feasibility of it, I will sacrifice my last breath in the service of God and the King, if you approve.[7]

Here, bodily made manifest at last, were the Russians, for whom since 1774 Spain had been probing with such diligence the North; and, despite the decree of 1780, Flórez felt warranted in heeding the request of Martínez and in sending him, together with Haro, back to Nootka, in 1789, to occupy the spot and to protect it with fortifications. Martínez arrived in the sound on May 5, and discovered there an American vessel, the Columbia, and an English brig under Portuguese colors, the Iphigenia. The American craft was not molested, but between May 6 and July 14 the Iphigenia, her consort the Northwest America, and the Argonaut (the latter under Captain James Colnett), — all British vessels, — were seized by Martínez as poachers on Spanish preserves. Spain afterwards made restitution, but the matter was dwelt upon by Great Britain, and, after much warlike demonstration, the two powers, on October 28, 1790, ratified the Nootka Convention. By this treaty Spain yielded claim of exclusive sovereignty to the Northwest Coast, but obtained from her adversary an agreement "not to navigate or fish within ten leagues of any part of this coast which Spain already occupied." [8]

But the treaty was not without ambiguity. It provided for a restoration of "buildings and tracts of land" to owners. The provision was a sequel to the fact (as claimed) that in 1788, — the year preceding that of the Spanish occupation of Nootka, — John Meares, instigator of the voyage of the Iphigenia, had built there a house and breastwork; acts which the British Government was not disinclined to regard as acts of occupation by the English. [9] On the part of Spain, it was not admitted that Nootka had been occupied in a jurisdictional sense by any power other than herself; and under Conde de Revilla Gigedo, appointed Viceroy in 1789, Nootka, abandoned for some unknown cause by Flórez, was reoccupied and refortified. [10]

Furthermore, through the gradual development of the fact that the Northwest Coast was skirted and masked by a narrow but complex archipelago, Spain saw fit between 1789 and 1793 to renew a search for Anian by way of the Straits of Juan de Fuca and Maldonado. In 1790, she sent out Salvador Fidalgo, Francisco Elisa, and Manuel Quimper; in 1789–91, Alejandro Malaspina; in 1792, Jacinto Caamaño; and in 1793, Dionisio Galiano and Cayetano Valdéz in the schooners Sutil and Mexicana. By the latter expedition — the last to the north of California undertaken by Spain — that government was able to confirm a growing conviction of the non-existence of an interoceanic passage below the Arctic regions, and to give to Anian its quietus. [11]

The situation, barring the Sutil and Mexicana expedition, was as described, when, in November, 1792, Captain George Vancouver arrived at Monterey. He came from Nootka, where he and Bodega y Cuadra, as commissioners for Great Britain and Spain respectively, had been trying

to agree as to the meaning of the restoration clause of the
Nootka Convention.[12] Vancouver had demanded a transfer
of the port to Great Britain jurisdictionally. Cuadra, refusing, had nevertheless proposed, under instructions from
Spain and the Viceroy, that Nootka be abandoned by both
Spain and Great Britain, and that the northern boundary of California be fixed at the Strait of Fuca.[13] Nothing
was effected, but ultimately (January 11, 1794) Great
Britain and Spain entered into a convention, which was
executed, that Nootka be transferred to the former, but
that immediately the port be abandoned, and that thenceforth neither of the two powers claim therein any right of
sovereignty or territorial dominion to the exclusion of the
other.[14]

By the struggle for Nootka, — a struggle in which Spanish power to the northward in America met its term, not,
as might have been expected, in the presence of Russia, but
of England, — there was foreshadowed for Alta California
its first political boundary.

The earlier incidents of the Nootka affair took place
during the governorship of Pedro Fages and that of José
Antonio Romeu. It was while Fages was governor (1786)
that Monterey was visited by Comte de la Pérouse.

On the 18th of September [wrote Basadre y Vega], the Conde
with all the scientists and people of both *fragatas* went to the
mission of San Carlos, where they were received by the Reverend
Father Fermín Francisco Lasuén, and three other religious, with
choir-cape, cross, and candle-bearers, who ushered them into the
church where *Te Deum* was sung. A repast followed, simple and
frugal, as befitted the character of those who gave it. All these
expressions of religion and affection were received by the French
with demonstrations so extraordinary that I lack words for a
sufficient account. The final acknowledgment proffered by the
strangers was that they had gained the satisfaction of knowing

and meeting men truly apostolical, followers of Peter and Paul in the life evangelical and in the work of reducing the Gentiles.[15]

But the attitude of Pérouse toward the California Mission as part of a system was that of José de Gálvez, of Neve, and of Fages.

I confess [he says], that, more a friend of human rights than a theologian, I could have wished in the case of the Indian that to the principles of Christianity there had been joined a legislation that by degrees should make citizens of men the condition of whom differs scarcely at all from that of the negroes of our own colonies. . . . I know that upon the Indian reasoning has no effect, that it is necessary to impress the senses, and that corporal punishments, with rewards of double rations, has up to the present been the only means adopted by his legislators. But would it be impossible for an ardent zeal and an extreme patience to make known to a small number of families the advantages of a society based upon human rights; to establish among them the right of property so attractive to all men; and, by this new order of things, to induce each one to cultivate his field with emulation, or else to devote himself to work of some other kind?[16]

Later, Monterey was visited by the Malaspina expedition. The visit took place during the term of Romeu (1791) but before Fages's departure; and to Lasuén, — of whom Pérouse had spoken as one whose *douceur*, whose *charité*, whose *amour pour les Indians*, are inexpressible, — Malaspina made a gift of cloth, of wine, of chocolate, and of wax.

As noticed in chapter VIII, José Joaquín de Arrillaga became acting governor of California on April 9, 1792. Under him therefore it was, though prior to his arrival from the south, that Monterey (as also San Francisco) was visited by Vancouver. The English captain was regaled with feast and frolic by Sal, the senior comandante, and at San Francisco was permitted with seven of his officers to penetrate inland to Santa Clara, and at Monterey to San

Carlos. But Spain, though disposed to be courteous because of the Nootka affair, desired to keep from the world, and especially from the English, knowledge of the weakness of the California defenses. Indeed, at the very moment of Vancouver's visit, Viceroy Revilla Gigedo (November 24) was cautioning Arrillaga to be on the watch for English vessels, so as to prevent the true state of the province from becoming known. Sal was accordingly rebuked for his hospitality, and right ruefully did he confess: "I had at San Francisco but one cannon, and it was out of commission." [17]

To be armed against the future, the Viceroy in 1793 resolved to fortify the port of San Francisco, to erect works at Monterey and San Diego, and to occupy Bodega Bay.[18] At Monterey there were "eight guns and three swivels, all in good condition"; at Santa Bárbara, "two guns and one swivel"; at San Diego, "three guns." But at Santa Bárbara and San Diego the guns were "dismounted and without artillerists." As for troops, Arrillaga could n't vouch for it, but he thought there might be thirty-five in each presidio. From these must be deducted the *habilitados* (paymasters), the surgeon, invalids, blacksmiths, masons, etc. He recommended a force of 264 men, to be allotted, 75 at San Diego and Monterey; 63 at Santa Bárbara; and 51 at San Francisco.[19]

The occupation of Bodega was designed to forestall England in any attempt to fix the northern boundary of California as far south as the mouth of the Bay of San Francisco. Herein Revilla Gigedo was governed by the motive which the year before had led him to favor Fuca Strait as a northern limit. But Fuca Strait was not Anian, and now (April 12) the Viceroy, narrowing his pretensions, urged that Spain cease straining toward the Pole and be content with a boundary at the Columbia River or Bodega Bay, either of which, assuming Anian to exist, might be its outlet. The Columbia was far to reach, so effort was concentrated upon Bodega. Lieutenant Juan Matute reached the bay with the Sutil in July; and on August 5 Lieutenant Felipe Goycoechea of Santa Bárbara was dispatched with a sergeant and ten men to open a road thither from San Francisco.

During the sixty-four days consumed in my voyage [wrote Matute to Francisco de Elisa, comandante at San Blas], I encountered no ship or foreign settlement. It is my conclusion that this was due to there being at Bodega no port deep enough for boats larger than the Sutil, and to there being, near the anchorage, neither timber nor firewood. For this cause, indeed, it was impossible for me to build there a house or to subsist myself. Signs of prior occupation of the bay there were none, save some sawed trees left by the Englishman Colner [Colnett], who was driven there in a tempest, and whose chart of the port (1790) has served all vessels commissioned to that destination up to the present. . . . I undertook an expedition, with the small boat of the schooner, to the southeast, to see whether there might not be disclosed the mouth of some river or estuary in the same roadstead exterior to Bodega. After three days of rather perilous search I came upon a *puerto nuevo* very good for boats of a draught of not to exceed fifteen feet, but, with the northwest winds, subject to be barred by sand.

On July 16, the *fragata* Aranzazu reached Bodega from San Blas, with soldiers, artisans, supplies, and tools. But as it was impossible to bring the vessel to a point near the *puerto nuevo*, she, together with her men and stores, was sent to San Francisco on the 24th. On August 8, Goycoechea arrived. He was shown the difficulties of the situation, and, a chart of the locality having been made, Matute on the 11th withdrew to San Francisco, where, falling ill, he contented himself, in view of the cost of other arrangements, with recommending that a *lancha* be constructed wherewith to reach the *puerto nuevo*, or Bodega, and that the points named be occupied by one or two missions. Bodega,

suffice it to say, never again was sought to be made an
ultimate outpost for California. In 1794, on June 9, the
Viceroy informed Arrillaga that its occupation had been
indefinitely postponed.[20] As for San Francisco, — the exposure of the innocuous condition of which had been the
undoing of Sal, — the Governor on December 8 dedicated
at Fort Point the Castillo of San Joaquín.

But the year 1794 was that of the advent of Borica. His
appointment was of early date, and, setting out overland
from Loreto on July 24, he arrived at Monterey on November 9. A lover of "Don Quixote," we find him, as
we should expect, urbane and cultured, a man fond of
society, of badinage, and of good Rhenish, port, and ma-
deira. Should it be said of him that more than any of his
predecessors he suggests Bucarely, — himself a master of
urbanity and a connoisseur of vintages, — no injustice will
be done to either. His family (by whom he was accompanied) consisted of his wife, Doña María Magdalena de
Urquides, and a daughter of sixteen, Josefita, who was
accounted beautiful. He brought with him a valet, a maid,
a cook, and a negro page. From Loreto he had written
on May 15: —

Monday at 3 P. M. we arrived in the Peninsula. María Magdalena and my daughter were quite seasick. They disgorged,
among other things, ire. Narcisco [his valet] and Juan José [the
cook] did not lift their heads till they went ashore. The little
negro was quite seasick, but he was the only one able to prepare
for the rest a little chocolate, garlic soup, and some stew. Don
Andrés and myself kept firm. The trip to Monterey will be by
land, as the Señoritas are horror-stricken at the mere thought of
the sea.[21]

But now that Monterey had been reached, whom should
Borica meet but Vancouver? In 1793 the English captain
had visited San Francisco and Monterey a second time,

but Arrillaga himself had been at the capital, and the privileges conceded had been few. "With the Señores Vancouver, Peter Puget, and others," writes the new Governor on November 13, "I am waging a contest. None of them can beat me over a dozen of wine. . . . This is a great country, neither hot nor cold. One finds good bread, the finest of meats, dainty fish, and (best of all) *bon* [*sic*] *humeur*." In other letters, Borica describes California as a land where the general fecundity extends even to the people. " We are all beginning to look like Englishmen. . . . To live long and without care, one must come to Monterey." Vancouver sailed for England on December 2. "We did not give him time," wrote the Governor, "to observe again certain things of which it were well that he remain ignorant."[22]

That, prior to Borica, Alta California should practically have been without defenses is upon the whole little surprising. Down to 1769 there had in the local sense been no California north of the peninsula. The predatory visits of Drake and Cavendish, of Swan, Dampier, and Woods Rogers (1578–1709), and of Shelvocke and Anson (1721–1740), were to Alta California — the California of 1794 — as though they had never occurred. In 1780 and 1781 excitement had risen at Monterey upon a warning to beware of English war-ships; and like excitement had risen at San Francisco in 1789, upon the receipt of orders to seize the American ship Columbia, "belonging to General Washington."[23] In other respects quiet had ruled until 1793, when war (offspring of the French Revolution) had been declared by Spain against France.

Borica assumed office with hostilities as something seriously to be reckoned with; nor throughout his incumbency did foreign relations improve.[24] In 1796 war was declared by Spain against England. In 1799 Spain became em-

broiled with Russia, and Alta California was admonished
to be prepared for invasion by way of Kamtchatka; while,
between 1797 and 1800, a rumor, pronounced by Borica
purely Platonic [speculative], became rife that all New
Spain was about to be invaded from the United States.[25]

The Conde de Branciforte, successor to Revilla Gigedo
in 1794, referred the question of fortifications for Alta California to Miguel Costansó. In the opinion of the veteran
engineer, to fortify would be to entail an expense altogether
insupportable. The English were a people skilled, intrepid,
audacious; their acumen in things relative to navigation
was consummate; they were successful, and how? By
colonies and commerce. Therefore instead of forts, let
Spain place at San Diego and Monterey groups of settlers,
and establish with Alta California relations that were commercial. Thus only could the province be retained.[26]

But in 1795 war with France made armament indispensable, and by a war board, of which Costansó was a member, batteries and cruisers were authorized. During 1796
and 1797 there arrived at Monterey and San Francisco a
company of Catalan volunteers, seventy-five strong, under
Lieutenant-Colonel Pedro Alberni, an artillery detachment of eighteen under Sergeant José Roca, and (with the
artillerists) the engineer Alberto de Córdoba. The latter
inspected the fortifications and found them all worthless,
not excepting the new Castillo of San Joaquín. He nevertheless established at San Francisco (Black Point) the
supplementary battery of Yerba Buena. Having constructed a battery at San Diego and made a map of the
country, Córdoba in 1798 was recalled.[27]

The views of Costansó as to the need in Alta California
of Spanish colonists, while of necessity deferred, were not
disregarded. Were not his the views of Gálvez, of Anza, of
Neve? It was proposed to erect a settlement, which, though

a municipality, should at the same time be a fortress, — in other words, a *villa*, a town palatine. In 1780–81 there had, in the case of the Indians, been tried upon the Colorado the pueblo mission. In 1789 there had, in the same case, been tried in Sonora, at Pitic, the *villa*. Now, therefore, — not in the case of the Indians, who had given no trouble, but in that of whites upon the coast, who had, — it was designed to try the *villa* in Alta California. Organized as a presidio under a comandante subject to the Audiencia of the district, the *villa* was designed to become as rapidly as possible a pueblo; armed, it is true, but ruled by *alcaldes* and *regidores*.[28] Preparations for the California *villa*, called Branciforte, were made by Borica and Córdoba with enthusiasm.

But could the province endure another pueblo? Already there were San José and Los Ángeles; and their condition, — what was it? At neither did the settlers do aught but gamble, strum the guitar, and trifle with the Indian women. Said Father Isidro Alonso Salazar to Viceroy Branciforte in May, 1796: —

The two towns founded twenty years ago have made no advancement. The people are a set of idlers. For them the Indian is errand-boy, *vaquero*, and digger of ditches, — in short, general factotum. Confident that the Gentiles are working, the settlers pass the day singing. The young men wander on horseback through the *rancherías* soliciting the women to immorality.[29]

And the same month José Señán declared: —

In Alta California the pueblos hardly deserve the name, so formless and embryonic is their state. The cause is scant relish for work on the part of the settlers. One is more likely to find in their hands a deck of cards than the spade or the plow. For them the Gentile sows, ploughs, reaps and gathers the harvest. Debased, moreover, by the bad example of his white associates, the Gentile continues in the darkness of heathenism, when from distant *rancherías* many are won to the fold of Holy Church.[30]

That Branciforte might ever come to the condition of San José and Los Ángeles, — Branciforte, the pride of the Viceroy, — was a thought not to be entertained. "Don Alberto Córdoba" (so, on November 18, 1795, it was ordered) "was to proceed to the port of San Francisco and locate the *villa* so as to give it connection with the battery, and make it defensive of the coast, — a sally-port against disembarkations; the engineer availing himself of the rules of fortification wherein he [was] well versed."[31] The environs of San Francisco were decided to be unfit for the new establishment, but between San Francisco and Monterey on the Río San Lorenzo, at a spot accessible from the sea, — a spot where the mission of Santa Cruz had been founded on September 25, 1791, — conditions were excellent.[32] "This locality," Palou had written in 1769, "is not only sufficient for a village but for a city. Not a single necessary thing is lacking. Fine lands, water, pastures, firewood, timber, — all are close at hand in abundance. The bay of Monterey is at a short distance, and the town could be located . . . not more than one fourth of a league away."

So by the river, opposite the mission, on the site of the present town of Santa Cruz, the *villa* Branciforte, with plazas, streets, churches, and government buildings, — all as at Pitic, — was to be founded. Its garrison was to be the Catalan company under Alberni, and Alberni himself might be made lieutenant-governor. Its citizens, "Christian in conduct," were to be recruited chiefly in Mexico. Among its officers and officials (who were to dwell in flat-roofed houses), Indians who were captains of *rancherías* were to be invited to dwell in like houses, — a Pitic custom. Such was the dream.[33]

The first colonists (nine families — seventeen persons — from Guadalajara) arrived at Monterey in 1797 on May 12. On May 26, Corporal Gabriel Moraga, son of the

founder of San Francisco, was ordered by Borica to build
for their accommodation wooden structures each capable
of holding fifteen or twenty families, and the colonists were
sent to their destination. Instructions, wherein doubt
as to the Christianity of the *villa* founders may be dis-
cerned, were issued on July 17. There was to be neither
gambling, drunkenness, nor concubinage. On days of
obligation, all were to attend Mass under penalty of three
hours in the stocks. Returning from work, the men were
to recite the rosary of the Blessed Virgin in the guard-
room. Lent was to be rightly observed, and of such right
observance a certificate was required. With the Indian
rancherías there was to be no communication by day or
night. On Sundays a general inspection of trappings,
arms, and implements was to be held, and stolen articles
were then to be returned to their owners.[34]

A few years, and the Christianity of the Branciforteans was in doubt no longer. In 1798–99 the colonists
were rebuked for laziness; some were threatened with irons
for desertion, and all were forbidden trips to San José —
the Monte Carlo of the province. By 1800 they had so far
degenerated as to be arraigned before the Viceroy as not
alone a scandal for immorality, but as would-be assassins
in the bargain, for one had attempted the life of the
lieutenant at Monterey, and another that of Borica himself.[35] But long ere 1800 the *villa* as such had disappeared.
On staking it out in the summer of 1797, Córdoba had
estimated its cost at 23,405 *pesos*, an estimate so disheartening that straightway (October 24) the Governor
had issued an order for the suspension of all work.[36]

Gone was the *villa*, but not the Branciforteans. To provide such of them as were unmarried with wives, Borica in
1797 asked the Viceroy for women "young and healthy,"
each provided with "a woolen skirt, a coarse *rebozo*, a

bodice, two sets of muslin underwear, a pair of coarse stockings, and a pair of heavy shoes." But for bachelor maids the allurements of California in the eighteenth century were not great, and none responded to the appeal.[37] In 1800, when San José boasted of a population of perhaps 170, and Los Ángeles of perhaps 315, Branciforte (any comparison of which with the two pueblos would in 1795 have been regarded by Borica as presumption) could claim in all — guard, retired soldiers, and original colonists — 66 souls.

II

Of Mission progress under Borica, — a progress so considerable as to mark in Alta California the culmination (dynamically) of the institution of the Mission, — the beginnings are to be sought under Romeu. In 1791, on September 25, there was founded, as already noted, the mission of Santa Cruz. But the same year yet another mission was founded, — Nuestra Señora de la Soledad, — Our Lady of Solitude. La Soledad, though circumscribed by the Coast Range, was designed as the first of the second or interior chain of establishments planned by Neve in his *Reglamento*. It covered the interval between San Carlos and San Antonio; and the early padres, Mariano Rubí and Bartolomé Gili, were priests of the Order of Friar Tuck.

In this asylum of San Fernando, where, upon reaching New Spain, these padres withdrew themselves [records Guardian Tomás de Pangua on September 13, 1793], they passed the day in sleep and idleness and the night in outrages, disturbing the repose of those that having spent the day in work must needs sleep at night. They behaved, indeed, like sons of darkness, forcing bolts to rob the supply-room, breaking the jars where the chocolate of the community was kept, stealing the chocolate-pots to beat them for drums; and, appropriating the balls which were kept by the community for the recreation of the religious, bowled them through the dormitories at unseasonable hours of night, with result to the religious of terror and confusion.[38]

Besides La Soledad, the establishments of the second mission chain were San José, covering the interval between San Carlos and San Francisco; San Juan Bautista, covering that between San José and San Carlos; San Miguel Arcángel, that between San Antonio and San Luis Obispo; and San Fernando Rey de España, that between San Buenaventura and San Gabriel. But San José, San Juan Bautista, San Miguel, and San Fernando (Borica foundations of the year 1797) were as little free of the Coast Range as was La Soledad.[39] A final Borica establishment — a mission for closing the gap between San Juan Capistrano and San Diego — was San Luis Rey de Francia, founded in 1798.

The total number of Alta California missions was now eighteen, and the disposal of them was varied. Above the sea and dominating it stood San Diego and Santa Bárbara; beside the sea and greeting it, San Juan Capistrano, San Buenaventura, and Santa Cruz; aloof from the sea yet with observant eye upon it, San Luis Rey, La Purísima Concepción, San José, San Carlos, and San Francisco. As for San Gabriel, San Fernando, San Luis Obispo, San Antonio, San Juan Bautista, Santa Clara, — they were inland, but pleasantly accessible amid spaces purple-girt and parked with liveoaks. Only two establishments were gloomy and remote. These — situated in the throat of a valley long, level, windy, and arid; often hot, ever alone — were La Soledad and San Miguel. Special interest attaches to one mission — La Purísima. Placed at the mouth of an *arroyo* leading to the clustered heights of San Rafael, it served to mark that line of cleavage which, as noted in chapter i, Nature in Alta California had traced between the northern and southern portions.

In 1798 the problems of Mission management in Alta California were many. Neophyte population was mounting past the thirteen-thousand mark; [40] and of artisans to give instruction in blacksmithing, carpentering, bricklaying, mill-making, tanning, shoemaking, weaving, and saddlery, the need was urgent. So far as this need had existed in 1787, Fages had sought to supply it by the introduction of convict artisans; and the idea being approved by Borica, some twenty-two such were obtained. But respectable craftsmen were preferred, and, as early as 1795, twenty had been brought from Mexico. Thenceforth, at the principal missions, the wool of the province was woven into coarse cloth, and the hides were converted into rude shoes and saddles. [41] Soap and pottery were made, and water-power and horse-power mills erected. Moreover, in 1795 at San José the cultivation of flax and hemp was undertaken.

Then there were the old problems. Padres still clamored for escorts, and the rigid rule of Neve, forbidding guards at a mission to sleep outside the mission walls, was in a degree modified. [42] As for the election of Indian *alcaldes* and *regidores* under the Laws of the Indies, — a practice which the padres had avoided since 1792, — it was ordered by Borica in 1796 to be resumed, but with the proviso that these functionaries were to be under missionary supervision, except in causes of blood, wherein they were to be under the supervision of the mission corporal. [43] Apropos of one instead of two padres at a mission, it was conclusively demonstrated in 1797 by Pedro Callejas, Guardian of San Fernando, that the two-padre plan was sanctioned alike by precedent and by royal order. "To the profound speculative wisdom of the Señor Don Felipe de Neve," exclaimed Callejas, "this apostolical college opposes the profound practical knowledge of all the missionaries who in all times have protested against solitude."[44]

But of all problems under Borica, that of most importance was the problem of disciplining the neophytes.

As early as 1771, Guardian Verger (vexed at Gálvez) had declared, with regard to the missions of the peninsula, that "they never had been, were not, and never would be complete pueblos";[45] and in 1796 Borica had averred, with regard to those of Monterey, that "at the rate they were then moving, not in ten centuries would they be out of tutelage."[46] It was twenty-five years since the first establishments had been planted in Alta California, and according to what had been achieved in the Sierra Gorda in twenty years, to say naught of what had earlier come to pass under Cortés in ten, civilization on the part of the California native was something the Spanish Government had reason to expect. That the expectation was not being met was proof that it was likely never to be met; but so to admit would be to confess the Mission in Alta California a failure.[47] What the padres did, therefore, was to strive to stimulate the native in religious observances, and in the performance of tasks of house and field, by the hobble, the stocks, shackles, and the lash.[48]

On the right to flog, provided the punishment was moderate, State Sacerdotal and State Secular were agreed. On that memorable day in 1524 when Cortés had abased himself in the dust before Martín de Valencia, the great *conquistador* had also submitted his back to the lash. In 1772 and 1780 Verger and Serra had mentioned the conduct of Cortés, and an act of the Lima Council whereby it had been determined that, "for the Indian, correction by words was not sufficient."[49] For Alta California the question had been settled by the *junta* of 1773, which had decided that it belonged to the padres to "educate and correct" the natives, just as to a natural parent it belonged to educate and correct his sons, — a decision the obligation of which had been recognized even by Neve. Nor did Borica dispute it. Twenty-five lashes he pronounced to be a moderate punishment.[50] But in 1795 neophytes in large number (280) deserted the mission of San Francisco, and the question presented itself: Was the general treatment of the Indians there that of a parent or of an exacting task-master ?

At San Francisco, in 1796, Father Antonio Dantí was succeeded by Father José María Fernández; and the latter, convinced that the desertions of 1795 had been due to harshness by Dantí, so informed Borica. Upon investigation the charge of Fernández was substantiated, and the Governor admonished Lasuén to effect a reform. Almost at once, however, the chivalric spirit of Borica asserted itself, for, on receipt of word from the Father-President that reform would be attempted, he wrote: "If I use strong language, it is but to inspire those who have the power to do good. I am a soldier, and thou a holy father. It is natural that the one, full of fire, should desire the other to imitate him in zeal that may be precipitate."[51] The charge by Fernández proved to be but the prelude to charges more vigorous and sustained.

When in 1795, Esteván José Martínez, hero (or culprit) of the Nootka affair, was returning from Spain to Mexico, there came with him to Vera Cruz a friar, — Antonio de la Concepción. In 1797, Concepción was sent to Alta California, where in company with Buenaventura Sitjar, a missionary of long service at San Antonio de Padua, he was assigned by Lasuén to the new establishment of San Miguel Arcángel. He reached his post in July, but hardly was he settled ere he began to manifest the mental disorder called megalomania. On arriving at the College of

San Fernando, he had laid claim to the position of *maestro de ceremonias*, an office unknown to apostolical colleges; and on arriving at San Miguel he assumed the air and port of a dictator. Having ostentatiously made his hard Franciscan couch comfortable with blankets, his first act was to compose himself for a prolonged siesta. The same day he boisterously indulged in criticism of Mission management, and the day following, during a walk with Sitjar, wrought himself to such frenzy over the "tyranny" of certain padres that with shaking body, hands smiting the breast, face discolored, and froth covering the lips, he declared: "Little lacked it last night that I took a course with the Father-President that would have resounded in the land."

His foremost grievance was that padres did not compel neophytes to speak Castilian; and, as Sitjar was of those who connived at the use of the native idiom, he took occasion in his first sermon to proclaim to the Miguelinos that they must discard it, and that the Spaniards "as lords and judges" had come to see that discard it they did. For twenty-seven days Concepción girded at the mission servants, issued orders to the guard, anon fell silent, and anon broke into peals of witless mirth, when, a general horror of him seizing upon neophytes and guard alike, it became necessary to appeal to Lasuén.

The latter, upon whom Sitjar waited at Santa Bárbara, ordered Concepción taken to Monterey to be dispatched (with Borica's consent) to Mexico, as one demented. The padre's chest, containing various *cédulas* on the use of Castilian, and a brace of pistols, was sent in advance, and on September 13 the Governor wrote to the Viceroy that having found the padre a "braggart" and of "imperfect judgment, qualities prejudicial to his calling," and having *con arte* secured his pistols, he had sanctioned Lasuén's order.

Back at his college, Concepción, on July 12, 1798, sent a memorial to the Viceroy. The document embraced five charges; to wit: that the Indians of Alta California, contrary to royal order, were taught the *Doctrina* in their own tongue; that they were baptized without previous instruction; that they were permitted to return to the mountains, and sometimes, after several years, were baptized a second time; that the missionaries, though possessing more or less wealth, and spending hundreds for liquor, were unwilling to give wine for the Mass; that in business they disregarded the tariff of prices fixed by the *Reglamento;* and finally, that they treated neophytes in ways "the most cruel that history records," visiting the slightest delinquencies with shackles, with the stocks, and with stripes. It was because of exposure of practices such as these, Concepción explained, that he had been accused of dementia, and he asked that he might finish his ten years of required missionary service in the province of Michoacán, model "reduction" under the conquest. The plea for a transfer was not granted, but early in 1799 Concepción was sent to Querétaro. As for his charges, they were submitted by the Viceroy to Borica for serious investigation on August 31, 1798.

Borica's report, accompanied by special reports from Argüello, Sal, and Goycoechea,[52] — comandantes at San Francisco, Monterey, and Santa Bárbara, — was ready by December 31. It stated that while Concepción's charges as to the neglect of Castilian, as to baptism without instruction, and as to permission to wander in the mountains, were not to be seriously taken, the charge of illtreatment was in the main well-founded. At the same time, it must not be forgotten that reform could not be effected through the Governor, as his authority over Mission affairs was little or nothing. Even in respect to temporalties he might not intervene. At a year's end he knew nothing as to the condition of the Mission exchequer. It probably was richer than was supposed.

The King — so Borica thought — should issue an *instrucción breve*, prescribing in the case of Mission establishments rules for the construction of lodgings and infirmaries; for the assignment of tasks and the fixing of hours of performance; for the selection of work to be undertaken; for the choosing of pastimes; and for fixing the punishments which the padres might inflict for delinquencies outside the royal jurisdiction. Furthermore, presidents of missions should be made subject to local prelates, as were priors or guardians in their convents.

The cause of Concepción against the Order of St. Francis in Alta California had made thus far no small progress. Indeed, so much progress thus far had it made that the Viceroy, suspecting the matter might be becoming one-sided (Concepción, moreover, having returned from Querétaro, where, in the archiepiscopal palace, he had been denied a claim to the high privileges of preacher and confessor), appealed on September 12, 1799, to the Guardian of San Fernando — Miguel Lull. The honor, *fama y estimación pública* of an entire college, Lull replied, were at stake. Concepción's *denuncia* was full of "grave deceptions," "manifest falsehoods," and of "accusations blackening, opprobrious, offensive, and defamatory." Nor did the chivalric Borica himself escape defiance. He was taunted by the Guardian with "bloodying his pen" and "voiding his venom" against the Alta California missionaries in respect to their entire "conduct, management, and procedure."

It was resented in particular by Lull that Borica should have intimated that the exchequer of San Fernando was in some wise rich. The books of the college, certified by the *aviador* and *síndico*, showed, he said, that as late as July 7,

1799, there stood to the credit of the Alta California establishments a total of only 12,279 *pesos*, as against liabilities of over 14,000; the annual cost of maintenance being about 26,000 to 27,000. "I pray and entreat," exclaimed the Guardian with indignation,

that the Señor Gobernador abstain (as commanded by Law 73 of Book i of Title 14 of the *Recopilación*) from prosecution of the missionaries on idle grounds, as otherwise padres cannot be kept in the Alta California field. And I supplicate that your Excellency be pleased either to intrust the reductions there to other hands, or else that before the King our sovereign, the public his vassals, and all the world, the honor, credit, and good name of the individuals of this college, and the fame and reputation of our sacred habit, be wholly cleared and vindicated, — a right which we cannot forego, and one that before all tribunals we shall ever maintain.

Henceforth the cause of Concepción waned. On June 19, 1801, Lasuén (who next was consulted by the Viceroy) defended the missionaries in a plea eloquent and extended. As for flogging, said the Father-President, the Indians were flogged, — and wherefore not? They were "a people without education, without government, without religion, and without shame. . . . Accustomed to avenge injuries with death, they were addicted also to lasciviousness and theft. Men of this quality we are commanded "to correct and punish." Yet the watchword was ever "patience." Only twenty-five lashes were permitted, and these "with an instrument that caused no blood or noticeable contusion"; while as for the women, they were beaten apart from the men, and by one of their own sex. The desertions from San Francisco complained of by Fernández had been from fear of contagion, not from fear of the lash. All missionaries, it was true, were not alike. Some had more virtue than others, more prudence, more gentleness, more zeal, more knowledge; but the Father-President had known none that "could be called hard, much less cruel." Let it not be forgotten by the government that "with the aid of but six soldiers the padres had reared amid the *gentilidad* a Christian pueblo [Loreto]. They had sustained, nurtured, and brought it to a condition so flourishing that, as a fruit of their labors, the happy stability and useful blessings of human society, of the Christian religion, and of *el vasallaje Español* were assured."

The charges of Concepción were reviewed in 1804 by Borica's successor Arrillaga. Not in an experience of seven years, averred the new Governor, had a single complaint of cruelty come to him. Padres he thought likely to err toward the Indians in indulgence rather than in rigor, even though occasionally excessive rigor might be practiced. Father Concepción ought to remember that what he considered cruelty and tyranny had been the way in the peninsula since its reduction, — more than a hundred years, — and that of all the California governors, presidents, and missionaries in that time, he only had been censorious.

Upon Arrillaga's verdict the *odiosa causa* was brought to an end. In 1805, on April 15, the fiscal certified that the representations of Concepción were false, and that naught remained but to restore the missionaries to their good name and credit, a restoration which was declared effected. As for Concepción himself, he in 1801 had been pronounced by the physician of San Fernando a hypochondriac who ought to be sent to Spain; and in 1804, with the consent of the Viceroy and the Council of the Indies, he was placed on shipboard. When last seen he was being conducted to his province from Madrid, after a season at Aranjuez, where in the royal audience chambers he had sought to attract notice by ringing a hand-bell and uttering pious ejaculations. "Such," wrote the Guardian to the Viceroy in 1805, "is he who denounced us." [53]

It was on January 16, 1800, that Borica, after six years of service as governor of the Californias, was permitted by Viceroy Azanza to retire. Of his wife, Doña María Magdalena de Urquides, and of his daughter Josefita, nothing, after their arrival at Monterey, has been recorded. What Borica himself accomplished for the defense of his province, and what for the advancement therein of the Mission, has in the main been told. As comandante, he sought to revive the old projects of direct communication with New Mexico and Sonora;[54] and as *jefe político* he wrought hard for secular education, establishing primary schools at the presidios and pueblos, and making attendance compulsory.[55] Of the revenues secular and ecclesiastical, — derived from a poll-tax, a tax on tobacco, postal charges, sales of indulgences, and tithes, — Borica was a faithful guardian. An important change which he advocated was the separation of the Californias into distinct provinces.[56] Through the Nootka affair, a political boundary for Alta California had been foreshadowed on the north. Separation from the peninsula would determine a like boundary on the south. Under Borica, Alta California, founded by priests for the glory of God, and organized by Neve for the glory of the King, became so far unified in its elements as to settle measurably into equilibrium.

CHAPTER X

THE PROBLEM OF SUBSISTENCE

ON June 26, 1803, there died Fermín Francisco Lasuén. He was buried in the mission church of San Carlos, near Crespi and Serra. In March, 1769, Lasuén had pronounced the blessing upon Rivera's men as they broke camp for the journey to Monterey. By 1786 he had attained the dignity of president of the Alta California establishments, and of *vicario* with power to confer all the sacraments, including that of confirmation. His successor was Estev023n Tapis, who held office until 1813. From 1804 to 1814 the governor of Alta California was José Joaquín de Arrillaga. The period of Tapis and Arrillaga, as between State Sacerdotal and State Secular, was one of substantial equilibrium; but outwardly it partook of the fear of England and Russia incident to Borica's rule.

In west and northwest America, at this time, the problem was one of subsistence. From San Diego to Monterey there was for the Spaniard need of manufactured goods, especially clothing; and at Kadiak, Behring's Bay, and Sitka there was for the Russian need of food-stuffs. A determined effort on the part of Spaniard and Russian alike to supply his respective needs, gave to the period its character. But, first, a word with respect to the problem of subsistence in Alta California from the beginning.

For four years the first missions were almost wholly dependent for supplies (grain included) upon Mexico. The transports, of which annually there were two, brought maize, wheat, beans, lentils, hams, sugar, chocolate, olive oil, wine, and brandy. In 1772, however, the San Antonio and San Carlos were unable to reach San Diego until late, and failed of Monterey altogether, and both points were threatened with famine. At Monterey, indeed, Fages in desperation formed a party for a bear hunt in the Cañada de los Osos.[1] And about the same time, at San Diego, Crespi wrote to Palou: —

Though his Majesty has put his hand to so much new Christianity as is here, what are we to do if there is not wherewith we can maintain ourselves? If the escort for a long time is maintaining itself with the sole ration of half a pint of corn, and of only twenty ounces of flour, daily; and the Fathers the same with a little milk — how are they able to endure? . . . God grant that Father Dumetz arrive promptly with the succor for these missions, and that the Barque bring it to us. For otherwise we are lost.[2]

It was Monterey that in the prevailing scarcity suffered longest, for, as Palou wrote to Guardian Verger in November, 1773, the *pilotos*, after making San Diego against fierce head-winds, were loath to protract the voyage, against still fiercer head-winds, to the north.[3] As late as April, 1774, when Anza on his reconnoissance reached Monterey, padres and soldiers were weak from hunger, a condition relieved only by the coming of the Santiago in May. After 1774 famine no longer threatened, but the founding of San Francisco was the more readily conceded by Bucarely to Serra, in view of the practicability (assumed to have been demonstrated by Anza) of provisioning the post overland from Sonora.

Trade as a means of succor was an idea scarcely entertained.[4] To private ships, trade was forbidden; and to private persons it was permitted only under heavy restrictions through the medium of the San Blas transports. Respecting the Manila galleon, which, in the days when California consisted of the peninsula, had been wont to touch for fresh provisions at Cape San Lucas, Viceroy

Bucarely in 1774 reminded the' King that "continually from the date of the conquest of the Philippine Islands, there had been sought on the north coast of California a port that might serve as a refuge to the galleons that came to this New Spain." And on May 16, 1776, the King ordered that henceforth these vessels ascend to the latitude of Gali's course, for the purpose of making port at either San Francisco or Monterey.[5] But while in 1782 the order was enforced by a penalty of 4000 *pesos*, trade with the galleon was as much interdicted as it had been when the port-of-call was Cape San Lucas.[6]

In 1786 trade by the transports was freed from restrictions for five years, and in 1794 this concession was renewed for a decade; but it is significant that in 1791 Fages condemned the freedom as conducive to luxury,[7] and that in 1797 pleas for commerce by Borica and Manuel Cárcaba, — the latter paymaster-general at San Blas, — met with no response.[8]

José Joaquín de Arrillaga (born in 1750 at Aya, Spain, in the province of Guipúzcoa) became governor *proprietario* of the Californias on November 16, 1804. The problem of subsistence had already asserted itself in a revival of two projects which had given solicitude to Borica, — a division of the Californias, and a route overland from Santa Fé. The division project was the result of a general desire for simplified administration. Delay incident to the approval at Monterey of *memorias* exclusively for Loreto, could no longer be endured, and, as elsewhere pointed out, division was effected in 1804 on August 29.[9] As for the project of a Santa Fé route, there was not the unanimity of approval of earlier years. In 1796 Borica had urged the dispatch of a party of Indian explorers to Santa Fé from Santa Bárbara. He had learned from Fernando de la Concha, retiring governor of New Mexico, that there were in New Mexico some fifteen hundred *gente de razón* useless from lack of employment. Why might they not be transferred to the coast? But Lasuén feared evil from contact between the neophytes and the Indians of the Tulares, and Pedro de Nava, comandante-general of the Provincias Internas, deprecated any attempt to withdraw population from a land where, as he maintained, abandoned settlements were about to be reëstablished.[10]

Divided Californias and a Santa Fé route were means for solving the subsistence problem which may be classed as direct. Further direct means were certain proposed community colonies and certain actual royal farms or *Ranchos del Rey*, the chief of which was located at the present Salinas City near Monterey, with a flourishing branch at San Francisco.[11]

The first colony to be mentioned is one that in 1788 was proposed for the island of "Owyhee" (Hawaii). When seeking Russian settlements near Nootka Sound, Martínez met in Cook's River a Scotch navigator, William Douglas, who had had in his ship an Hawaiian, — King Tayana, — whom he had afterwards restored to his country. The Indian had spoken much of the fruitfulness of Hawaii in cassava, sugar-cane, and watermelons, and had said that foreign vessels on their way to Nootka always supplied themselves with these foods. "I conclude from this," Martínez wrote to Viceroy Revilla Gigedo, "that it would be useful to form in Hawaii an establishment of our nation, in order that the Indians there may be 'reduced,' and that foreigners may be deprived of a port of refuge, where their commerce is nourished, and their passage to our 'coasts of Californias' facilitated." For meeting the cost of an Hawaiian establishment, Martínez suggested the formation of a commercial company in Mexico, with exclusive right for fifty years to deal in otter-skins, and to export tropical woods to Canton. But the Viceroy, though impressed with the usefulness of Hawaii as a port-of-call for the Philippine galleon, had not deemed its exploitation practicable.[12] Then, in 1797, Padres Mugártegui and Peña (retired) had proposed founding a Carmelite convent of twelve priests at San Francisco "for the cultivation of the soil" and the rendering of "great service to God, the King, and the Public," — a convent that "by its domes and towers should give a favorable impression to foreign navigators."[13]

But the most pretentious colony of a community kind projected for Alta California was one for which Luis Pérez de Tagle of Manila solicited permission in 1801. The plan, Tagle said, of compelling the Manila galleon to stop at Monterey, in order to lure the Indian to the coast, had notoriously failed. He (Tagle) would therefore beg, if haply the King might so far condescend, that the government of the port and coast of Monterey be conferred upon him. In return, he would engage to bring from Manila his family and others, including artisans, for the improvement of the country. Thus by a colony of "culture and commerce" the Indian would be led to know his King and to eschew fraudulent commerce with the English. Tagle's scheme found favor with Arrillaga, but it came to naught under the scrutiny of the Viceroy and the Crown.[14]

As between the two classes of means, direct and indirect, for meeting the problem of subsistence for Alta California, the indirect means were most in evidence; and of these smuggling was the chief.

Few trading craft of any nationality touched upon the coast prior to the arrival at Monterey, on October 29, 1796, of the Otter of Boston, commanded by Ebenezer Dorr. The publication of Cook's "Voyage" in 1784 had led to the

sending to Nootka from Boston, in 1788, of the Lady
Washington and Columbia Rediviva. Throughout the remainder of the eighteenth century, and down to the year
1812, Boston fur-trading vessels flocked to the Northwest.
Outnumbering by many to one the vessels of other nations,
they extended their operations above and below Nootka,
gathering from the Indians rich cargoes of furs, which
were taken to China and exchanged for teas, nankeen,
and lacquers. The Russians, who claimed sovereignty
southward of Kadiak, met the American intruders with
protests; but the Spaniards, who but yesterday had
yielded claim to sovereignty over the whole South Sea,
met them with artillery. For a time, knowledge of the
strict non-intercourse trade regulations of the Spanish
Government, coupled with a plentiful supply of the best
otter in northern waters, deterred Bostonians from smuggling operations below San Francisco. But as the northern
and better otter became scarce, and knowledge of the
ineffective nature of the California defenses became more
definite, the Americans grew bolder.[15]

The Otter (despite her name) does not seem to have
visited California with intent of unlawful trade, but of
American vessels between 1801 and 1810 — the Lelia Byrd,
the Alexander, the Hazard, the Enterprise and the O'Cain
— as much may not be said. Spanish comandantes, therefore, whether at San Francisco, Monterey, Santa Bárbara,
or San Diego; and Spanish padres, whether at the points
named or at others, found themselves beset with temptation and behaved each according to his cloth. If comandante, he frequently, though not always, accepted a bribe;
if padre, he usually — in pursuance of a custom which
made of him a general importing agent — sold otter-skins
to the foreigner.[16]

Ventures by American craft were many, but the boldest

was one made in March, 1803, by the Lelia Byrd under command of William Shaler, with Richard J. Cleveland as mate. Hearing at San Blas — where, on a voyage round the Horn, they had contrived to purchase a quantity of sea-otter skins — that a further quantity might be obtained at San Diego, Shaler and Cleveland, on March 17, brought the Lelia Byrd to anchor there on the regulation plea of need of supplies. The comandante, Manuel Rodríguez, was approached but proved non-corruptible, and placed on board the ship a guard of five men. Don Manuel, more-over, was resourceful. He set decoys, and certain of the crew of the Lelia Byrd, who while bartering were en-trapped, were thrust by him in bonds and paraded on the beach. They were liberated by Cleveland under cover of pistols, and the Lelia Byrd, shipping her port battery of three 3-pounders to the support of the 3-pounders of her starboard side, put to sea past the Spanish defenses, — a battery (relict of Alberto de Córdoba) of some six or eight 9-pounders. Between shore and ship a fiery inter-change took place, the ship receiving damage aloft and a shot between wind and water; and the Spaniards, during the hottest of the engagement, fleeing nimbly to cover. It is related that so terror-stricken were Rodríguez's guard on board the absconding vessel, first from flying iron, and next from thought of expatriation, that being set on shore (once the vessel was well past Point Guijarros), they cele-brated their deliverance by falling on their knees, crossing themselves, and shouting, *Vivan, vivan, los Americanos!* [17]

But what, meanwhile, of the problem of subsistence, as at Kadiak, Behring's Bay, and Sitka it confronted the Russians? A potent figure in Russian America — an elemental man, one prodigious for energy, wondrous for fidelity — was Alexander Baránoff. In 1790, Gigor Ivanovich Shelikof, projector of the principal Russian-American trading company of the time, made Baránoff his agent, and when in 1799 the Russian-American Company itself was chartered, Baránoff became administrator. His abiding care was the providing of food. Each year in March there occurred a run of herring announced by the presence of sea-gulls; and from this time to the end of November edible fish of divers sorts were more or less to be obtained. But in the winter, eagles, crows, devilfish, mussels, seals, and sea-lions, with for tidbit an occasional halibut, were what the larder must welcome.[18]

Baránoff had sought to bring food from Chile, the Sandwich Islands (Owyhee), and even Manila, and was still sorely perplexed for it, when in October, 1803, he met at Kadiak Captain Joseph O'Cain. Of the captain's vessel (called by him the O'Cain, and by the Russians the Boston) Abel and Jonathan Winship of Boston were owners. The first American "trader" to visit Kadiak had been the Enterprise (April 24, 1799), with O'Cain as mate; and Baránoff, reviving acquaintance with the latter through a purchase of goods, entered into a compact by which the captain, seconded by a company of Aleutian Islanders, was to go southward and take otter for himself and Baránoff.[19] Under O'Cain, the Winships, and others, Russo-American otter-hunting expeditions along the California coast, from Trinidad Bay to Todos Santos Islands and into the very estuary of San Francisco, — expeditions in which the Russians furnished the hunters, and the Americans the equipment, — remained a feature of California annals down to 1815.

It, however, was not so much the coast of California as California itself, — land of flocks, of herds and yellow grain, — to which instinctively the Russians turned. In 1794, on the conclusion between Spain and Great Britain of the treaty for the abandonment of Nootka, Baránoff had urged that the spot be seized by Russia. But now (1805) a plea affecting California was to be preferred by a dignitary much higher.

Nikolai Petrovich Rezánoff (erstwhile protégé of Catherine II) was chamberlain to the Czar. His wife, a daughter of Shelikof, had but recently died, and, as a resource in bereavement, the chamberlain, with an ardor that recked neither of scruple nor self, had espoused patriotism. His most cherished plan was the securing for Russia of trade concessions from Japan, and in 1803–04 he was sent as ambassador extraordinary to the Mikado. Meeting with no better success for Russia than Sebastián Vizcaino had met with for Spain, he was eager

to destroy settlements, to drive the Japanese from Sakhalin Island, to frighten them away from the whole coast, and break up their fisheries, and to deprive 200,000 people of food, which will force them all the more to open their ports. . . . It may [he proceeded] be your pleasure, most gracious Sire, to punish me as a criminal for proceeding to active measures without waiting for orders, but I would be guilty of the greater offense of neglecting your interest if I hesitated at a decisive moment to sacrifice myself to your glory. I would be ashamed to limit my undertaking to a simple voyage around the world, a feat which is accomplished every year by merchant vessels.[20]

Besides credentials to Japan, the Chamberlain bore commission as royal inspector of Northwestern establishments and plenipotentiary of the Russian-American Company, and, after the failure of his diplomatic enterprise he was brought by the ship Nadeshda (A. J. von Krusenstern, commander) to Kamtchatka. Thence, with a suite comprising the naturalist G. H. von Langsdorff, two naval lieutenants, Nicholas A. Schwostoff and Gavril I. Davidoff, and others, he crossed to the Aleutian Islands, reaching Unalaska in July, 1805.

Rezánoff was at New Archangel by September, and here the first thing to confront him was Baránoff's problem, — food for the Russian settlements. Purchasing from J. De Wolf (slave-merchant of Bristol, Rhode Island) the Juno, copper-bottomed, fast, and laden with a cargo of Yankee merchandise, he at the same time gave orders for the construction of a vessel to be called the Awos. "In order to get provisions for this country," he wrote to the directors of the Russian-American Company on February 15, 1806, "it is necessary that I should go to California, and I hope to weigh anchor in the Juno on the 20th of this month. The equinoctials threaten us with gales, but to stay here will be to risk starvation." He would go first to Prince of Wales or Queen Charlotte Island to purchase sea-otter; but this only in passing, for "both time and circumstances compel us to hurry to California." In May he would return to Sitka, and go with the Juno and the Awos to Alexander Island for astronomical observations. Thence he would send the Awos to Russia with dispatches. The Juno he would send back to New Archangel, preparatory to taking her "to California for the winter, where I intend to remain and go to Manila on a Spanish vessel, and from there to Batavia and Bengal, in order to make a first experiment in trading with the Indies through Okhotsk." [21]

Impatient of rivalry, Rezánoff counseled the building of a war-brig to drive the Bostonians from California waters. From the latter, he said, Spaniards in California bought surreptitiously every trifle, and, having neither factories nor trade, paid for them in otter-skins. What was sold to the Spaniards by the Bostonians, — cloth, linen, iron-ware, — ought to be supplied by the Russians from factories in Siberia, in exchange for breadstuffs. Yet, if the Bostonians were to be tolerated, it should be on condition of their dealing with the Russians exclusively, bringing them flour, groats, butter, oil, tallow, vinegar, pitch, and rum. Besides, it might be practicable to found a settlement on the Columbia

from which we could gradually advance toward the south to the port of San Francisco, which forms the boundary line of California. If we could but obtain the means for the beginning of this plan, I think I may say that at the Columbia we could assemble population from various localities, and in the course of ten years become strong enough to make use of any favorable turn in European politics to include the coast of California in the Russian possessions. The Spaniards are very weak in this country, and if in 1798, when war was declared by the Spanish Court, our company had possessed adequate means, it would have been easy to seize a part of California north from the 34th degree (latitude of the mission of Santa Bárbara) and to appropriate this part forever, since the geographical position of Mexico would have prevented her from sending any assistance overland. The Spaniards, on account of their shiftlessness, make hardly any use of their lands, and have advanced toward the north only to secure the boundary.[22]

As already stated, patriotism with Rezánoff had become a passion. He disclosed his heart to the acting chamberlain (A. A. Vitovoff) on February 16, 1806.

No personal considerations have entered into my unrestrained revelations, but only the thought of glory and of the common welfare. . . . A man robbed of his tranquillity of soul by a merciless fate does not care for himself, and much less for honors and praise, as they are all insufficient to fill the void in his being which only death can bridge by uniting him again with the one whom he has lost. . . . The moral sufferings, the voyage, and troubles have undermined my physical strength; various diseases have developed themselves; my children in the meantime tell me that I have abandoned them. In my thoughts I am often at St. Petersburg, embracing them and the dust of my friend who lies buried there. The welfare of my fellow beings alone causes me to brave the seas and intrust my orphans to Providence, and I have often shed bitter tears when Nature awakened in me the parental yearnings.[23]

Quitting Sitka on March 8, but driven from the mouth of the Columbia River by the surge of its discharging waters, the Juno on the morning of April 5 — harassed by scurvy but with Rezánoff, Langsdorff, and Lieutenant Davidoff on board — swept in defiance of challenge past San Joaquín Battery, through the Golden Gate, into the Bay of San Francisco. "With pale and emaciated faces," Rezánoff afterwards wrote to the Russian Minister of Commerce, "we reached San Francisco Bay, and anchored outside because of the fog. . . . As a refusal of permission to enter meant to perish at sea, I resolved, at the risk of two or three cannon-balls, to run straight for the fort at the entrance."

The Nadeshda and consort, the Neva, had, under advices from Madrid, long been expected at San Francisco, and, the fact once established that the Juno was Russian, Rezánoff and his party were "overwhelmed with civilities." Comandante José Argüello was absent from home, and to an inquiry regarding the ships, politely put by Luis Argüello, his son, the adroit reply was made that they had returned to Russia, but that Rezánoff "had been intrusted by the Czar with command over all his American possessions, and in this capacity had resolved to visit the Governor of New California to consult him with regard to mutual interests." Monterey was his destination, but he had stopped at San Francisco because of contrary winds. Rezánoff would write to Governor Arrillaga of his purpose to visit him. A letter was sent, but the Governor, wary of the Chamberlain's object, replied that he would do himself the honor of meeting so distinguished a guest at the port of his arrival.

"While awaiting the Governor," Rezánoff explained to the Minister of Commerce, "we visited every day at the house of the hospitable Argüello, and soon became intimate there. Among the beautiful sisters of Luis Argüello, Doña Concepción has the name of being the beauty of California, and your Excellency will agree with me when I say that we were sufficiently rewarded for our sufferings, and passed our time very pleasantly." Arrillaga, a gray-haired man of fifty-six, reached San Francisco on April 17, and on the 18th there arrived the comandante, José Argüello, who at once invited Rezánoff to meet the Governor at his house at dinner. The meeting took place, and as Arrillaga spoke French the Chamberlain made known the true object of his presence. "I frankly tell you," he said, "that we need bread, which we can get from Canton; but as California is nearer to us, and has produce which it cannot sell, I have come here to negotiate with you a preliminary agreement to be sent to our respective courts." This proposal the Governor asked time to consider.[24]

As for Doña Concepción (about to enter our narrative), her mother was niece to José Joaquín Moraga, Anza's lieutenant in the founding of San Francisco. She herself was fourteen years old, and, as described by the intelligent Langsdorff, "was lively and animated, had sparkling, love-inspiring eyes, beautiful teeth, pleasing and expressive features, a fine form and a thousand other charms, yet was perfectly simple and artless, —

the heavenly dawn into one drop of dew, —

a beauty of a type to be found, though not frequently, in Italy, Spain, and Portugal."[25] What California had been to Doña Eulalia de Callis, that it was to Doña Concepción, — and she pined for adventure.

"The day following my interview with Governor Arrillaga," Rezánoff observed in his communication to the Minister of Commerce, "I learned from a devoted friend in the house of Argüello, word for word what had been said after

my departure. . . . From day to day, though by means
imperceptible to the Governor, my relations with the house
of Argüello became more intimate. . . . 'You have accustomed us to your company,' said Don José de Arrillaga,
'and I can assure you that the good family of my friend
Argüello prize highly the satisfaction of seeing you at their
house, and sincerely admire you.'"

But what regarding a sale to the Russians of breadstuffs? Here the Governor kept silence. Rezánoff had been
invited to dine with the padres, whose "desire for trade was
very noticeable"; presents, judiciously distributed, had
attracted padres from distant missions;[26] beyond these
things nothing had been gained.

Seeing [wrote the Chamberlain to his minister] that my situation was not improving, expecting every day that some mis-
understanding would arise, and having but little confidence in
my own [ship's] people, I resolved to change my politeness for
a serious tone. Finally, I imperceptibly created in Doña Concepcion an impatience to hear something serious from me
. . . which caused me to ask for her hand, to which she
consented. My proposal created consternation in her parents,
who had been reared in fanaticism. The difference in religion
and the prospective separation from their daughter made it a
terrible blow for them. They ran to the missionaries, who did
not know what to do; they hustled poor Concepcion to church,
confessed her, and urged her to refuse me, but her resolution
finally overcame them all. The holy fathers appealed to the decision of the throne of Rome, and if I could not accomplish my
nuptials, I had at least the preliminary act performed, the marriage contract drawn up, and forced them to betroth us.[27]

Heedless of designs upon India, Rezánoff now conceived
the project of going to Madrid as Russian envoy; of effecting a treaty of amity and commerce with Spain; and
(having returned to San Francisco by way of Mexico) of
marrying his betrothed. But this for the future. For the

present, the cause of the Chamberlain was won. On May 21 the Juno, laden with flour, peas, beans, and maize, and with Rezánoff on board, sailed for Sitka amid the thunders in farewell of the battery of San Joaquín.[28]

But the Chamberlain, — did he return to wed the *Señorita?* In September, 1806, he crossed to Kamtchatka, whence the same month he set forth overland for St. Petersburg. Ill when starting, he was attacked by fever, met a fall from his horse, and on March 1, 1807, died at Krasnoyarsk, where his tomb, fashioned like an altar but void of inscription, was visited by Langsdorff in 1807. It is the opinion of the latter that to gain the vital object of his visit to California, Rezánoff would unhesitatingly have "sacrificed himself" in marriage to the daughter of Argüello.[29] Whether later he would have performed with her his nuptial contract (with naught for Russia to be gained thereby) is open to question. Concepción, be it said, doubted her suitor never. For her the Chamberlain's death, the circumstances of which she learned from Sir George Simpson at Santa Bárbara in 1842, explained all. She remained unwedded, passing the earlier years of her bereavement partly in Mexico and partly at La Soledad Mission as a member of the Third Order of Franciscans. In 1851, she, as Sister María Dominica, entered the Dominican Convent of Santa Catarina at Monterey, and in 1854 followed the convent to Benicia. Here, on December 23, 1857, at the age of sixty-six years, she died. She was buried in the convent cemetery under a brown stone cross bearing the inscription: "Sister María Dominica O. S. D. [Order of Sant Dominic]." The subjoined is from the records of the institution: —

In the convent of Sta. Catarina of Siena at Benicia, California, died Sister María Dominica Argüello, December 23, 1857. She was buried on Christmas Eve, dressed in her white habit as a nun.

She was carried on a bier into the chapel of the convent. First came the cross-bearers bearing the cross; then the young girls of the convent dressed in black; then the novices in white, with white veils, carrying lighted tapers; then the professed nuns, with black veils and lighted tapers, signifying that she had gone from darkness up to light and life. After the solemn requiem service was ended, the last Benediction of the Catholic Church, *Requiescat in Pace*, was pronounced over her mortal remains, and a tired soul was dismissed out of all the storms of life into the divine tranquillity of death. The next morning was Christmas Day. *"Glory be to God on high, and on earth Peace to men of good will."* [30]

Rezánoff's sojourn at San Francisco involved more than the obtaining of a single shipload of provisions. There came of it the founding, within California limits as at present defined, of the Russian fort and settlement of Ross. "Russia would not take California as a gift. It would cost too much to maintain it. Besides, Russia has an inexhaustible treasure in furs." Thus with facile tongue had the Chamberlain addressed Arrillaga at their first interview. "But," observed the former afterwards, "he [Arrillaga] frankly confessed to me that his court feared Russia above all other powers." And well it might. From Sitka the Chamberlain thus exhorted his government: —

Our American possessions will know no more of famine; Kamtchatka and Okhotsk can be supplied with bread. . . . When our trade with California is fully organized, we can settle Chinese laborers there, etc. They [the Spaniards] only turned their attention to California after 1760, and by the enterprise of the missionaries alone this fine body of land was incorporated. Even now there is still an unoccupied interval fully as rich and very necessary to us, and if we let it escape us, what will posterity say? I at least shall not be arraigned before it in judgment. [31]

In the autumn of 1808, Ivan Alexándrovich Kuskof was sent by Baránoff to "New Albion" for otter, and to select a site for a Russian settlement. The expedition consisted of two ships, the Nikolai, destined for the Columbia River but wrecked in passage, and the Kadiak, which with Kuskof on board touched at Trinidad Bay, but in January, 1809, entered Bodega Bay, and there tarried until late in August of the same year. A favorable report was made by Kuskof concerning Bodega, and the Russian-American Company solicited from the Czar a treaty with Spain permitting trade with California. At the same time the Czar was asked to afford "highest protection" against opposition by Americans to any settlement that might be made on the Columbia. The " gradual advance southward to the port of San Francisco as the boundary line of California," which Rezánoff had advocated in 1806, was thus put in course of execution.[32]

"Highest protection," when needed as against opposition by Americans, was promised by the Czar, but the projected Columbia River settlement was never made. As for the post on Bodega Bay, it was forecast by order of the company in a proclamation announcing to "our friends and neighbors, the noble and brave Spaniards, inhabitants of the Californias," the sending of a ship for trade. But attempts to move southward from Sitka were unsuccessful till March 4, 1811, when Kuskof again reached Bodega. The voyage was repeated early in 1812 (this time in force), and on September 10, at a point 18 miles north of Bodega, on a bluff 100 feet above the sea, Ross, a fortification of ten guns, was dedicated by ninety-five Russians assisted by a party of Aleutian Islanders in forty bidarkas.[33]

As already seen, American craft, lured to Northwest waters by the fur-trade, found it their best course to secure skins either by exchanging for them contraband goods with the California padres, or by hunting sea-otter, on shares with the Russians, off the California coast. But more. When Louisiana was purchased by the United States from France in 1803, overtures were made to Spain for the purchase of the Floridas. The overtures were rejected, but Americans had begun to hover upon the Florida-Texas-New-Mexico border, and by 1805 a United States Government expedition — that of Lewis and Clarke — had actually penetrated to the Pacific at the mouth of the Columbia River, a point, according to Spanish claims, within the limits of California. Encroached upon by Americans landward, the encroachments seaward became yet more significant, and the royal and viceregal decrees of 1776–1800 were vigorously reaffirmed.

In 1802 Charles IV notified the American Government that vessels caught smuggling on the California coast would be confiscated.[34] In 1806 Felipe de Goycoechea, as Governor of Baja California, urged that the naval station at San Blas be transferred to the peninsula, the better to check American designs "in the Gulfs of California and of Spain"; and the same year Viceroy Iturrigaray warned Arrillaga of possible warlike demonstrations by the United States because of the failure of the negotiations for Florida.[35] But it was Arrillaga himself who depicted the situation most forcibly. The United States, he said to Rezánoff in 1806, already possessed New Orleans; and Pensacola being near New Mexico, even Santa Fé was beginning to use American goods.

Having [he observed] personally witnessed in our own waters the enterprise of this Republic, I do not wonder at their success. They flourish in trade and know its value. And who at present does not, except ourselves, who pay for our neglect with our purses? . . . The American States sometimes send out ten or fifteen regular robbers, who, on account of our small force, are able to disturb our peace and corrupt our honesty.[36]

Among American ships active in partnership with Baránoff between 1809 and 1813 there were, besides the O'Cain
and Albatross, owned by the Winships, the Mercury, the
Catherine, and the Amethyst, owned by Benjamin W. Lamb
and others of Boston. The Mercury was navigated by
the Bostonian George Washington Eayrs, and her story
(from documents here first used) illustrates the times.
In February, 1806, at Tepic, José Sevilla, a saddler of
Monterey seeking government employment, petitioned
Viceroy Iturrigaray to be made coast-guard in California.
It was, he alleged, the practice of English [American] vessels
to anchor at the Santa Catarina Islands ten leagues from
the coast, and there exchange China and East India goods
for otter-skins and cattle. The trade, he said, was one at
which even the officials themselves connived, and, should
he be appointed coast-guard, he asked that the military
and naval commanders be instructed not to injure him.

Whether Don José was granted an appointment, we are
not told, but between 1808 and 1813 the Mercury appeared on the California coast, bearing Mr. George Washington Eayrs.

Writing on February 7, 1814, Eayrs said:—

I left China in the year 1808, with the small Amt of Cargo
about five thousand Dolls, my first Business was Hunting Furs,
This Business I entered into with the Russian Governor & continued several years, in which time I was in the Winter season as
far South as California for supplies and the purpose of taking
Seal Skins, I received several Letters, from the head People &
Pardres of California intreating me to bring them many Articles
that they was in distress for & could not obtain from the Continent [!] . . . The Hunting and Sealing Business, I continued in
untill two Years since when I obtained a large Amount of Furs of
the Russian Governor. . . . I entered into a Contract with the
Russian Governor, to continue in the Hunting Business; while
imployed in this Business, I received Letters from Cape Sⁿ Lucas,

intreating me to bring them many Articles, that they was Naked, & was in great want.

As specimens of the letters mentioned above as received from the "Pardres of California," the Eayrs papers supply the following: —

FRIEND DON JORGE: It is necessary that early in the morning a boat be landed to enable me to embark and purchase that of which I have spoken to you. So, as soon as a fire on shore is seen, despatch the boat; since thus I must manage in order to act with safety.

FR. PEDRO MARÍA DE ZARATE.

SÑO. ROSARIO [Lower California], April 19, 1812.

SEÑOR COM^{dte} AND FRIEND DON JORGE: To-day there goes to you the padre of San Fernando who was unable to go last week because of illness. Trade with him, and to-morrow (God willing) I will come to your *Fragata* to dine, and we two will trade on our own account. I am now sending the corporal with a little vege-table stuff for you and the other two comandantes, and also some eggs, the whole a present, I wishing only the honor of serving them. There will be sent likewise the otter-skins which on my coming we will examine. Also be pleased to receive a small pig for yourself, and another for the two comandantes, — a present. *Á Dios* till to-morrow (Monday) at noon.

I remain your friend,

FR. JOSÉ CAULAS.

FRIEND DON JORGE: Greeting. I expect you to dine with me at the *casa del rancho*. Come with this *vaquero* and we will talk of what is interesting in the news from Europe and the whole world. We will also trade, unless you bring things as dear as usual. The boy says that you asked him why I was out of humor with you, and I say I am out of humor with nobody. *Á Dios;* since I do not know what you bring, I ask nothing; and since you say nothing, I get nothing.

Thy friend Q. B. T. M.

FR. LUIS [MARTÍNEZ?]

Just what the commodities were for which the California padres were thus willing to become smugglers, it would be interesting to know, and here again the Eayrs papers prove serviceable. We find mentioned: hardware, crockery, fishhooks, gunpowder, cotton cloth and blankets for covering the prevalent "nakedness," shoes, etc.; and besides these things others, to wit: camel's-hair shawls; Chinese silk, *color de rosa;* white ladies' cloth with embroidered edge; large towels (*perfiladas*) for women; fine men's kerchiefs of different colors; fine white thread; blue twisted silk; twisted white silk; cochineal floss; black floss; black handkerchiefs; decorated water-jars; gilded crystal stands, each with twelve small crystal bottles decorated with *flores de oro;* flowered cups for broth; porcelain plates; platters flowered in green and red, with tureens to match; shaving-basins; black mantillas; Brittany linens; peppers; nutmegs.

But the interesting transactions between Mr. Eayrs and the "Pardres of California" were destined to come to an end. The smuggling points of the coast, from Cape San Lucas to Monterey, included San Quentín, San Juan Capistrano, San Pedro, San Luis Obispo, and Santa Cruz; but the chief of them was El Refugio, about fifteen miles below Santa Bárbara, a rancho owned by the descendants of José Francisco Ortega, whom Serra had wished Bucarely to make governor. Here on June 3, 1813, the Mercury, as she lay at anchor about a mile from shore, was surprised by a boat from the Lima coast-guard ship La Flora, under Captain Don Nicolás Noe, and seized as a prize. Eayrs himself was on board with a crew of fifteen men, an Indian boy, "bought in Oregon," and "a young female which he had had several years and whom he esteemed equal the same as if lawfully marryed to him, and a Daughter only twenty-five days old when the Ship was taken." All were made prisoners, and the comandante at Santa

Bárbara, José Argüello (Eayrs spells it Arwayus), took possession of Eayrs's papers, and of the ship and cargo subject to condemnation proceedings in Mexico.

The period was that of war between the United States and England, and, to lessen chance of trouble from the seizure, orders were given that Eayrs and his family should be well treated. So far as the family were concerned, José de la Guerra certified in 1816 that he had taken charge of them in 1814; that the young woman (known in her Gentile state as Pequi [Peggy]) had been baptized as María Antonia de la Ascensión Stuard, he acting as godfather; and that she had been one of his family, till at length she had gone to San Blas. Eayrs himself was sent first to San Diego, and then to Tepic. In 1814 and 1815 he addressed letters to the Viceroy, to the comandante-general of Nueva Galicia, and to the comandante at San Blas, lamenting eloquently in bad English a poverty due to delay in the sale of the Mercury, which, though appraised by the government at 23,310 *pesos*, had been allowed to depreciate to a fraction of her value.

But in the entire case of the Mercury the significant point is the open recognition by California officials of the fact that the province, denied subsistence under Spanish commercial regulations, must countenance smuggling or perish.

In general all the officials resident on this coast [said Eayrs in a letter translated for him into Spanish] have encouraged my trade, and at their request I have given them agricultural tools and other things that they needed. I have provided the priests with what they required for instructing the natives and for the ceremonies of religion. . . . They have paid me with provisions and some few otter-skins. I have clothed many naked, and they have given me in return products of the soil, as the officers of this district can inform your Excellency. . . .

My dealings have not been clandestine, but with the full and tacit consent of the governors. Let Fray Marcos Amistoy at Santa Bárbara be questioned in *verbo sacerdotis, tacto pectore,* concerning these transactions.

And on November 12, 1819, Argüello wrote to Viceroy Calleja: —

The padres are concerned in illicit trade from a grave and general necessity of clothing and other materials which they have experienced in the past, and experience more and more from day to day in the jurisdiction of this government. A rule of the canonical law says: *Hace lícito la necesidad lo que no es lícito por la ley* [Necessity makes lawful that which by the law is illicit].[37]

The case of the Mercury was not disposed of until after 1819. Meanwhile, on July 13, 1812, Tapis had been succeeded as Father-President by José Señán, and, on July 24, 1814, Governor Arrillaga (sixty-four years old) had died at La Soledad. Under Arrillaga the private rancho — a species of holding instituted in 1784 by Fages, and approved in 1793 by Don José himself — assumed importance. No grants had as yet been made in the districts of San Diego and San Francisco; and of six or seven made within the Monterey district, at least five had been abandoned. But in the district of Santa Bárbara (especially near Los Ángeles) former grants — San Rafael, Los Nietos, San Pedro, Portezuelo, Encino, and possibly El Refugio — were supplemented by Rancho de Félix, Las Vírgenes, El Conejo, and Santiago de Santa Ana.[38]

Multiplication of ranchos and increase of horses led to the expedient of killing the surplus animals. As early as 1784 it had been found necessary to reduce by slaughter surplus cattle at the San Francisco presidio.[39] But horses (mares more especially) were less valuable than cattle, and having increased to vast herds which consumed the mission pasture, and in the San Joaquín Valley roamed hither and yon in squadrons devastating though picturesque, it was ordered in 1805, at the instance of President Tapis, that their number be reduced; and between 1805 and 1810 they were slaughtered by tens of thousands.[40] Nor was the livestock of the province reduced alone by voluntary means. In 1805, in the single district of Monterey, over four hundred head were destroyed by wolves and bears, and by the accident of miring at the lagoons.[41]

But the harm wrought by wild beasts was as naught to that wrought by *temblores*, or earthquakes. In 1808 San Francisco was rudely shaken, and between December, 1812, and February, 1813, a series of violent shocks devastated Southern California.

These quakes [President Señán wrote on April 9] will form an epoch in history for their great destructiveness. . . . There must be built anew the churches of San Fernando and Santa Bárbara. . . . The San Gabriel Mission suffered somewhat, as did that of San Buena Ventura. At the latter the tower is ready to fall and the chancel front is cracked from the ceiling to the ground. . . . At Purísima the quake was so violent that it caused the bells to swing till they gave forth their chimes. In a few brief moments the building was reduced to fragments and ruins, presenting the spectacle of Jerusalem destroyed. At San Juan Capistrano, California's most famous temple was ruined and forty neophytes killed. Had the catastrophe occurred at High Mass and not when it did (at early Mass), scarcely a neophyte would be left. As it was, six only escaped. No whites were injured. The *celebrador* [priest] saved himself by fleeing through the private door leading to the sacristy.[42]

Arrillaga was, as intimated, a conserver of the equilibrium between State Secular and State Sacerdotal attained under Borica. So pronounced, indeed, was his conserving, that it amounted almost to sacerdotalism. Through him, in 1802, Lasuén successfully withstood a belated attempt from Mexico to introduce into the Californias the Neve-Croix type of Mission discredited on the Colorado.[43] Nor in opposing secular designs was the Governor merely passive. In 1800 a band of twenty foundlings, ten boys and ten girls, reached Monterey, and the girls, though "fond of cigars," turned out well.[44] But toward colonists of any kind the Governor was little favorable. For such as were of the convict class, he deemed California too good; and for such as were of the respectable class, it was, he deemed, not good enough.[45] Padres, in his opinion, should be treated with consideration. If they rode abroad attended by mounted Indians, it was because the soldiers had grown negligent of their comfort. Let the padres be waited upon by the soldiers. "It would be an attention, an act of civility, of good breeding and of respect." If padres chose for religious ends to remain at Gentile *rancherías* overnight, let the escort remain with them.[46]

Indeed, the standard of military subordination under Salvatierra and Serra was now somewhat restored; for when at San Antonio de Padua a corporal (José Castro) and soldier misconducted themselves, they on complaint of Padre Marcelino Cipres were transferred.[47] Concerning manufactures, Arrillaga was pessimistic, and education he neglected.[48] His incumbency was marked on September 17, 1804, by the founding, at the base of the Santa Inés Mountains, of a new mission, — companion to La Purísima, and nineteenth of the list, — the mission of Santa Inés or Saint Agnes.[49]

CHAPTER XI

THE PROBLEM OF SUBSISTENCE (*continued*)

FOR nearly three hundred years prior to 1810 semi-tropical North America and all of South America, with the exception of Brazil, had been under the dominion of Spain. The principal South American districts on the Pacific Coast were Peru and Chile, and on the Atlantic the valley of the Río de la Plata, where, since 1535, there had risen near the sea a city of forty thousand inhabitants, called, because of its grateful breezes, the city of Buenos Ayres. Throughout Spanish South America discontent with colonial methods (exclusion from official station of all natives even though of Spanish parentage, and restrictions on trade) had been augmenting; and when, in June, 1808, the legitimate sovereign of Spain, Ferdinand VII (son of Charles IV), was displaced by Joseph Bonaparte, the act was made by the colonies occasion for revolt. Of this revolt one of the most active centres was Buenos Ayres. The city was not unlike a city of the ancient Levant, cosmopolitan, commercial, intensely independent, — a resort for freebooters, French, English, and American, — and among its insurgent activities was the commissioning, between 1816 and 1819, of privateering craft to seize the ports of Peru and Chile, and to foment revolution in New Spain itself.

On August 30, 1815, José Argüello (Acting Governor of Alta California) was succeeded by Lieutenant-Colonel Pablo Vicente de Sola of Mondragón, Guipúzcoa. California was loyal to Ferdinand VII, — that ruler having been acclaimed at each presidio as late as March, 1809, — but it was loyal more especially to Spain. Mexico since 1810 had been agitated from causes the same as those affecting Peru and Buenos Ayres, but California had remained tranquil even to monotony. For Sola, therefore, military problems, should they arise, would be extraneous in character.

In April, 1816, word reached Mazatlán of the capture of Spanish vessels by the privateers of Buenos Ayres, and of a blockade by the latter of the ports of Valparaíso, Callao, and Guayaquil.[1] This word was promptly communicated to José Argüello, at Loreto, and by him to Sola, who received it in June. Presidial comandantes were exhorted to gather bows and arrows, and, if they knew the art, to prepare against the enemy *balsas rosas* (red-hot balls); while padres were instructed to hold themselves alert to furnish *vaqueros* armed with *reatas* (lassoes), to pack and conceal Mission silver, and to drive Mission livestock to the interior.[2]

It was not until 1818 that the dreaded insurgents actually appeared. As early as October 6, warning of their approach was given at Santa Bárbara by the Clarion, an American brig, and on November 20 the Argentina, of perhaps thirty-eight guns (Captain Hippolyte Bouchard), and the Santa Rosa of perhaps twenty-six guns (Lieutenant Pedro Covale), were sighted from Point Pinos. What ensued is worthy the recording genius of the authors of the "Pirates of Penzance."

On the morning of the 21st, the Santa Rosa, which had been denied permission to land, sought to force a landing by opening fire. The fire was promptly returned by a shore battery of eight guns under Manuel Gómez and José Estrada. After some time, during which the Spaniards, at least in imagination, wrought upon the enemy havoc with their shot, the Santa Rosa struck her flag, sent ashore an officer and two men, and the conflict subsided. Soon, however, the Argentina approached and dropped anchor. Bouchard, commander of the expedition, thus being arrived, he made known his presence and authority by sending to Sola a flag of truce demanding a surrender of the province. The demand was rejected with hauteur, and hereupon, as though the stage lacked a prompter, again ensued a pause. It lasted until the next morning at eight o'clock, when Bouchard sent ashore nine boats carrying a body of men and four field-guns. Against this force (some three hundred) the presidial troops available to contest a landing (twenty-five men) could effect nothing, and a retreat was executed, first to the presidio and then to the *Rancho del Rey*. From Monterey, where the presidio was set on fire, and where the fort and *casa real*, with its vegetable garden and orchard, were partially destroyed, the invaders set sail on November 27 for the south.

It was presumed that Santa Bárbara, where José de la Guerra held command, would be the next point of attack, and families and goods were dispatched inland to Santa Inés. But near by lay the rancho of Refugio, — rich, it was rumored, through smuggling, — and here the insurgents,

trying their hand at a burglaree,

landed on December 2. Against them — from Santa Inés, Purísima, and San Luis Obispo—the padres, inflamed by prayers, fastings, and flagellations, mustered with their neophytes the Canaleños.[3] But, although supported by a detachment of troops from Santa Bárbara under Sergeant Carlos Antonio Carrillo, naught was accomplished save the capture of three of the enemy who had ventured apart from the main body; and the rancho having been burned and plundered, the vessels quitted Refugio, and on December 6 cast anchor before Santa Bárbara itself.

To Guerra, Bouchard offered terms. He would leave the coast upon an exchange of prisoners. And now of a surety, facts conspired in aid of some composer of *opéra comique;* for when, as a sequel to Bouchard's offer, Guerra assembled his captives (Lieutenant William Taylor of Boston, Martín Romero of Paraguay, and Mateo José Pascual, negro without domicile), the insurgents brought forward in counterpoise a drunken settler of Monterey by name Molina. The exchange effected, — whereat Governor Sola was much scandalized, — the Argentina and Santa Rosa duly sailed away. On December 14 and 15, the vessels stopped at San Juan Capistrano, but were guilty of no serious depredations; and although at San Diego the comandante awaited them with the "red hot balls" recommended by Sola in 1816, they inconsiderately passed him by, fading in mystery out of sight in the direction of Acapulco.[4]

Manuel Gómez and José Estrada were both made lieutenants for gallantry, while Sola himself was made a colonel. But what of the padres? Had they not mustered their lariated *vaqueros* and archered neophytes, and stood ready themselves at the sound of the *Kyrie Eleïson* to fall fiercely upon the invader, — a foe formidable enough to be stigmatized by Señán as "heretic, schismatic, excommunicate, heathen, and Moor"? Yet was it not true that no mention at all of these things had been made by Sola? The affront was one not meekly to be borne, and on June 19, 1819, Fray Antonio Ripoll of Santa Bárbara appealed to Sola, a course which elicited from that officer, and from the Viceroy, thanks grateful though belated.[5]

The Mexican revolt, by depleting the viceregal resources and barring routes of exit from the country, had stopped

the annual supplies for the missions. Writing to President
Tapis in February, 1811, the Guardian of San Fernando
observed: —

The insurrection began last September in the pueblos of Dolores and San Miguel el Grande. The story would be long were I
to relate each event, but the newspapers, which I suppose you
read, as they are sent to the various missions, will instruct you
fully, etc. . . . We have recovered [from the insurgents] the
port of San Blas and the *fragata* Princesa, but it has been impossible to send either the supplies or five or six padres whom I
had meant to send this year. We must see how . . . the spirit
of agitation [*vertigo*] that the devil has awakened in this unfortunate kingdom will end. We must see what his Excellency [the
Viceroy] will resolve, for he will necessarily take some step, either
through Acapulco (also cut off) or through San Blas. . . . I have
not sent this letter because of the roads. . . . The supplies for
this year have not yet left Mexico, nor can the padres be sent
while the roads are obstructed.[6]

Hemp, important as an article of California produce,
could no longer be taken to San Blas to be bartered for
manufactured goods; and, by the seizure of the Peruvian
ports in 1816 by the Buenos Ayres privateers, the exchange of tallow for cloth — an exchange effected annually through carriers from Lima — was brought to an end.[7]
Comandantes complained loudly to Arrillaga of lack of
shirts and of food for their men; and Comandante Luis
Argüello at San Francisco begged of Sola clothing for
his own family. Sola himself in 1816 pictured the state
of the province as deplorable through "ruined fortifications, crumbling esplanades, and dismounted guns." He
pointed out how worse than death for him it would be
to fail in this remote land after he had given to the world
proofs of his quality in conflicts from the beginning of
the revolutionary movement. "To see," he said, "the
good troops of California going through their evolutions

entirely naked, and their families in like case, pierced him to the heart."

So unremitting was the distress, that in 1817 Sola parted with needed clothing of his own to cover the nakedness of troops compelled to "pursue Gentile Indians in their wild retreats"; [8] and the same year a Yankee trader, James Smith Wilcox, — lean, lank, hatted in beaver and coated in swallow-tails, yet (*pace* Rezánoff) aspirant for the hand of Doña Concepción, — made it an excuse for smuggling that he had thereby served "to clothe the naked soldiers of the King of Spain," when, for lack of raiment, they could not attend Mass, and when the most revered fathers had neither vestments nor vessels fit for the churches, nor implements wherewith to till the soil.[9]

A climax was reached in 1819, the year following the attack by Bouchard. In January, Guardian López of San Fernando, lamenting the failure of *memorias*, told the Viceroy that the missionaries of Alta California had been forced to celebrate the *tremendo sacrificio* of the Mass with candles of mere tallow; and that so great was the discontent among neophytes, settlers, and soldiers, that it was only in default of a single insurgent spirit that the province had not become revolutionary along with the others.[10] Thanks to López, supplies to the value of 36,000 *pesos* were soon consigned to José de la Guerra, agent for California in Mexico.

After 1812, want to a great extent was relieved from Ross. In raising grain the Russians proved little adept, but resorting for it, as they did, to San Francisco, they left in exchange valuable merchandise. Occasionally (as in 1818) a Manila ship, driven into Monterey by scurvy, furnished supplies; or an American smuggler, like the Mercury, was laid under tribute; but the principal dependence was Ross. Brought by the diplomacy of Rezánoff to one sale of breadstuffs to the Russians, Arrillaga had found

it easy to consent to further transactions; and although
Lieutenant Gabriel Moraga had kept upon Ross a close
watch, visiting it on the eve of its dedication and again in
1813, it was with undoubted warrant that Tikhemeneff
wrote in his "Historical Review of the Russian American
Company": "The Russian colonies lost a true friend by
the death of Arrillaga."

Nor at first did traffic with the Russians provoke censure
from Madrid. The reaction in Spain under Charles IV
(reflected in Alta California by Borica and Arrillaga) continued under Ferdinand VII to the time of the displacement of the latter by Joseph Bonaparte, when — the
leaven of the American and French Revolutions asserting
itself — there developed a counter-reaction entailing a
regency. "The kingdoms, provinces, and islands of the
dominions of America," so it was resolved in 1809, "shall
have national representation, and, through deputies sent
to the Spanish peninsula,[11] shall constitute part of the supreme council of the monarchy." And on March 12, 1812, at
Cádiz, there was adopted for the entire *Monarquía Español*
a constitution redolent of fraternalism, anti-clericalism,
and popular sovereignty. News of the founding of Ross,
therefore, reached the regency at a juncture singularly
favorable for the Russians, as witness a dispatch to the
Viceroy of date, February 4, 1814: —

I [Secretary José Lurando] have informed the *Regencia del
Reyno* of your Excellency's secret dispatch No. 7, wherein I am
notified that the Russians have formed an establishment near
the port of Bodega on the coast of Alta California. By the report
which your Excellency incloses from Don Francisco Xavier [*sic*]
de Arrillaga, it cannot be absolutely determined that the establishment is one formed with design. It is formed perhaps from
necessity. That is to say, if the Russian vessel be in bad condition
as reported, it is not strange that they should seek to repair it;
or, if totally useless, that it should have put them under the neces-

sity of remaining in the locality to which they have come. The circumstance that the aforesaid Russians are in a very necessitous condition indicates perhaps the best method of getting rid of the establishment, — withholding provisions except upon their coming to the presidio; in which case they may be deprived of their arms, munitions, and artillery, in order that these things may be kept on deposit and be restored to them when they embark to return to their country.

But this ministry has information that the Russians desire to open traffic between the establishments which they have in Unalaska and the Spanish presidios of Alta California. There are certain claims so absolutely just and mutually convenient as not to be denied when based upon intimate relations of friendship. Considered from a true point of view, it will be found that said establishments, both Russian and Spanish, separated as they are from the commerce of the rest of mortal kind, are almost compelled to help each other; that the traffic which they would conduct *inter se* is the perfectly spontaneous kind which a common humanity points out to men even less civilized; that to attempt to prohibit this entirely is not only impossible but highly inhuman; and, finally, that, limited to what may be called a natural exchange, and one exclusively with the presidios of Alta California, it may be considered that the prohibition of the laws is not violated thereby.

Thus regarded, and with the noble object of diverting the Russians from projects of settlements which they have conceived, it seems to S. A. very fitting that your Excellency direct that the *vista gorda* [broad view] be taken; but that the respective authorities be very alert not to permit traffic to be extended to any point other than the missions of Alta California, — not to those of la Baja; and that it be limited to the exchange of effects adapted to the agriculture and industry of both the Spanish and Russian settlements; since, in other respects, S. A. can enjoin upon your Excellency nothing less than this, that what the laws determine in the particular case be observed and carried out. The zeal, prudence, and shrewd judgment of your Excellency are relied upon to conduct this affair with the delicacy required, in order to secure the removal of the Russian settlement without compromising the friendship of the two nations,[12] etc.

But in March, 1814, Ferdinand (restored) repudiated Liberalism and all its works, including the Constitution of 1812; and although in 1816 he directed Viceroy Calleja to take what course he chose with the Russians in California, provided no harm were suffered to befall "the territory of the Crown,"[13] Calleja deemed it wise to be cautious. Early in 1815, José Argüello notified Kuskof that orders from Mexico required that the Russian post be abandoned.[14]

Kuskof came personally to San Francisco in August, 1815, to assure Argüello that Russia made no claim to territory south of Fuca Strait; and in 1816, in October, a conference concerning Ross was held at San Francisco between Kuskof and Sola on board the Russian exploring vessel Rurik, under Lieutenant Otto von Kotzebue.[15] Yet Calleja not only directed Sola to discontinue relations with Kuskof, but to "eject the Russians from the port of Bodega."[16] Henceforth the Governor was insistent that there be an abandonment of Ross. To Lieutenant Padushkin (emissary from Baránoff), to Baránoff's successor Hagemeister, to Lieutenant Golovnin, and to other emissaries, his answer was ever the same: ground of complaint could only be removed by a withdrawal of the Bodega establishment beyond the Spanish boundaries, — to wit, beyond the Strait of Fuca. Otherwise the King of Spain could not consent to a proposal for placing the products of California at the disposal of the Russians.[17] And to these terms the Russian-American Company at length was constrained to yield. In 1820 it announced to the Czar that it "would willingly abandon its settlement, which fills the Spaniards with fear, and nevermore think of choosing another site on the coast of Albion, if it could by this sacrifice but gain the privilege of permanent trade with New California."[18]

The Bodega Bay controversy, now, in its acute phase, at

an end, served colorably to reëstablish the northern line of
Alta California (limited to San Francisco Bay by the
Nootka Convention) at Fuca Strait. The Spanish claim
to jurisdiction north of the bay had been strengthened
by the founding on December 14, 1817, of the *asistencia*
of San Rafael Arcángel, a retreat to which Indians from
San Francisco Mission might be assigned for reasons of
health.[19] And in 1819 there arrived from Mexico, for use,
if need were, against the Russians, a reinforcement of two
hundred men. Half of them (cavalry from Mazatlán under
Captain Pablo de la Portilla) were excellent material; but
the other half (infantry recruited at San Blas) were a gang
of wretches, mixed in race, short in stature, venomous in
temper, *sin disciplina y sin religión*, drunkards, gamblers,
and thieves, — in a word, the Cholos.[20]

As early as the time of Borica and Lasuén, a tendency
to flee the missions began to be manifested on the part of
neophytes; a tendency that led to the charges of cruelty
preferred by Father Fernández. Dissatisfaction, however,
did not fail of expression more drastic. At San Miguel, in
1801, Padres Baltasar Carnicier, Andriano Martínez, and
Francisco Pujol were each seized by violent illness, of which
Pujol died; and afterwards certain of the Miguelinos
boasted of having administered poison.[21] The same year,
at Santa Bárbara, a female *shaman* (wizard) declared that
it had been revealed to her that a pulmonary disease fatal
among the neophytes was a penalty inflicted by *Chupu*,
the god of the Channel coast, vengeful at the defection of
his worshipers.[22] In 1805 President Tapis ascribed neophyte restiveness to the withdrawal to Mexico in 1803 of
the Catalan Volunteers, a body of seventy men of whom
the Indians stood much in awe. He said: "At San Gabriel
forty neophytes have fled toward the Colorado; at Santa

Bárbara two hundred; and at all the missions there are neophytes mal-inclined, uneasy, and disposed to fight, — evils which can only be corrected and prevented by an increase of troops and by repeated expeditions."[23]

The resort of the fugitives was the great valley or plain of the Tulares between the Coast Range and that of the Sierra Nevada, — a spot of intricate marsh covered with tall reeds, home of the Mariposa tribes, and a way-station to the Colorado. Into this valley, "where the sun rose and set as on the high sea," Fages, it will be remembered, had penetrated in 1772, and Garcés and a portion of Moraga's force in 1776. Throughout 1806 local troops in search of fugitives, under Moraga and other commanders, ranged the Tulare region from Tejón Pass to the latitude of San Francisco. Incidentally the object was exploration, the selection of sites for missions, and the effecting of baptisms. Kings' River (Río de los Santos Reyes) had been discovered and named in 1805, and now the Merced and the Mariposa were discovered.[24] Several mission sites were chosen, and a few Gentiles (192 out of an estimated total of 5300) were baptized.[25]

But neophyte restiveness did not abate. In 1811, at San Diego, a neophyte cook sought to poison Padre José Pedro Panto;[26] and in 1812 Andrés Quintana, padre at Santa Cruz, was murdered by neophytes, who lured him from his room at night on the pretext that his ministrations were required for a dying man.[27] Fear, too, of the Gentile Indians as corrupters of neophytes prevailed, and as early as 1810 Moraga fought a spirited engagement with bands opposite San Francisco.

Señán, as president of missions, was succeeded in 1815 by Mariano Payéras, and it was the opinion of the latter that the time had come for heeding the *Reglamento* provision for founding establishments east of the Coast Range,

— missions not merely, but strong presidios. Said Payéras in his biennial report for 1817–18: —

The object of our ministry being the propagation of the Faith among the Gentiles, and [Gentiles] no longer existing among the coast mountains, the padres of various missions have attempted to baptize those living in the district called the Tulares. They, however, have never succeeded. The Tulare Indians are inconstant. To-day they come, to-morrow they are gone, — not on foot, as they came, but on horseback. With such guests, no horse is safe in the northern valley. And the worst of it is that having crossed the Tulare Valley and the mountains that surround it, they kill the horses and eat them. The government has not been neglectful in pursuing such deadly enemies, but little has been effected, because great lagoons surrounded by green tules furnish them shelter from our horsemen. For this reason, the padres and more intelligent officers think it needful to form in the valley of the Tulares a new chain of missions with presidios. . . . If this be not done, the time will come when the existence of the province will be threatened, and a region that up to a recent time has been the centre of tranquillity will be changed into an Apachería.[28]

And in July, 1819, Payéras wrote to the padres: —

The Governor of this province, Don Pablo Vicente de Sola, advises me that he has been informed from the South of the scandalous abuse at certain missions [San Fernando and San Gabriel] of neophyte equestrianism. Neophytes take with brazenness, and in broad daylight, horses even though tied. They load them with women in the public roads. I am reminded by the Governor of the many royal *cédulas* forbidding Indians to ride, and that even your reverences cannot give them permission to own or use a horse, if Law 33 of Book vi, Title 1, of the *Recopilación* is observed. . . . In the Tulares (I am told by the Governor) both Christians and Gentiles make their journeys on horseback. Even the women are learning to ride. Fairs are held at which horses stolen from the missions are put up for sale.[29]

Neophytes, Payéras avowed, were losing respect for the padres. The Tulare *rancherías* of Telame (east of Tulare

Lake), some four thousand strong, were "a republic of hell and a diabolical union of apostates." If something were not done, the occupation of the missionaries in California would be at an end.[30] By Sola, therefore, the work of beating the Tulares was prosecuted as vigorously as it had been by Arrillaga.

But it was not alone among neophytes that respect for the padres was declining; it was declining among Mexicans themselves. As early as 1808, Viceroy Marino, reviving the idea (emphasized by Gálvez, by Caballero de Croix, by Neve, and by Fages) of reduction of the Indian to civil status, had informed the Guardian of San Fernando that neophytes must be instructed in the principles of social living; must be transformed from barbarians to men. Later (1810) there had come the Mexican revolt against Spain, with stoppage of missionary stipends and traveling expenses, and still later (1817) an impost on Mission goods levied by Sola despite hints of excommunication from the *comisario-prefecto*, Vicente Francisco de Sarría.[31] But it was the Spanish Constitution of 1812 that was most disturbing. By the principles of this instrument men everywhere were politically equal and entitled to a voice in the government. Accordingly, in 1813 (September 13) the Spanish Cortes had issued a decree requiring the immediate secularization of all missions of ten years' standing.[32]

It was believed, both in Spain and Mexico, that "reduction" in Alta California was impeded because of gain to the padres personally by the Mission system. Padre Concepción had pronounced the Alta California establishments richer than they would acknowledge; and though it had been disproved that they had riches at all, the charge had not been quieted.

Your Reverences [Guardian José Gasol wrote in warning to his California flock in 1806], the office that you exercise does not excuse you from the extreme poverty that we profess. Consequently, the use of silver watches and other valuable jewelry is prohibited. . . . I advise that those who have silver watches, or other jewelry of value for personal use, send them immediately to the Father-President, and he to the *síndico* of Tepic or of Guadalajara, so that, having been sold, the money may be used to aid the respective missions.[33]

And in 1817, Prefect Sarría wrote: —

You should realize that it is edifying for a missionary to appear in the greatest simplicity. *Así se tapa la boca al mundo* [so is the mouth of the world stopped], and so it [the world] is caused to understand that the interest we take in the things of the Mission is not personal, but that of Our Saviour Jesus Christ in the poverty-stricken, as are the neophytes. It sounded ill to me, as to others, to learn that carriages [*volantas*] had arrived (that is, if they are for us), and I wish that you would abstain absolutely from taking them. I might go into detail concerning fine hats, costly chests, etc., but enough.[34]

Discouraged by what was deemed recreancy to sacerdotal vows in Alta California, but more by lack there of padres to take the places of such as had retired or were become superannuated, the College of San Fernando, on December 19, 1816, formally petitioned Viceroy Apodaca to be permitted to cede to the recently founded College of San José de García of the Villa de Orizaba the nine establishments southward of and including La Purísima. The Guardian recalled the services of the Fernandinos against the Buenos Ayres privateers, and the desired permission was obtained, but it was not acted upon. The nine southern missions were the flower of the entire California sisterhood, and Payéras, who became prefect in 1819, opposed with success the cession of them to a new college with a name to win.[35]

Meanwhile, in California, the decree by the Spanish Cortes of 1813 was suffered to remain inoperative. On

May 20, 1814, Naval Lieutenant Pablo de Paula Tamariz submitted to the Viceroy a report characterizing the Alta California Mission as a sacerdotal monopoly; and, to consider this report, the King on July 5 ordered the assembling in Mexico City of a *junta* "composed of five or seven persons of prominence versed in business and familiar with the country." This body, which was known as the *Primera Junta de California,* and which met on July 5, 1817, advised the King to be circumspect, but he was to demand of the Alta California padres, "why, after forty years, the establishments in their charge had not been consigned to the ordinary ecclesiastical jurisdiction, according to the Laws of the Indies."[36] In 1820, on April 21, the decree of 1813 was confirmed by Ferdinand, and it was officially proclaimed in New Spain by Viceroy Benadito on January 20, 1821.

Spain and Mexico were urgent for Secularization, and in 1818 Payéras had written to the Bishop of Sonora that as president of the Alta California missions he was ready for the change. "We, Señor," he said, "do not seek our own welfare in this world, being men dead to it. We live herein only because of necessity. Our one desire is to obtain souls for Jesus Christ. The day these missions are lawfully declared civil communities, we shall welcome dismissal from charge of them to a new apostolic field."[37] And in 1821, on July 7, Payéras as prefect wrote thus to Sola: —

Through my Holy College of San Fernando I have just received a proclamation [from the Viceroy] in which the King, our master, reaffirms the decree of the General and Extraordinary Cortes issued in Cádiz, September 13, 1813 — a decree providing in Article 6 the following: "The missionary priests will retire immediately from the government and administration of the haciendas of the Indians. Upon the Indians it will devolve to arrange, by means of their *ayuntamientos* [town councils], with the aid of the *jefe superior político* [superior political officer], that there be named among them such as are the best fitted for administration, and by these the Indian lands will be reduced to private property and distributed. . . . We desire to carry out exactly the said royal order," etc.[38]

But while Payéras spoke thus to bishop and governor, it was far from his meaning that the Alta California neophyte was ripe for citizenship, or the Alta California missions for a pueblo status. Nor did he fear that citizenship or a pueblo status were things in fact impending. There were no curates with whom the Bishop of Sonora might replace the missionaries, and the latter could not be compelled to serve as curates against their will. On July 8, 1821, the day following his declaration of submission to the secularization decree, Payéras addressed to the padres a cordillera letter inclosing a confidential note, in cryptic phrase of Spanish and Latin, which the recipients were bidden either not to read or, having read, to keep secret. Indignation was expressed toward such in Mexico as had wrought evil for the missionaries. At the same time the padres were exhorted to keep everything in such order that, at the first summons of the leaders clerical and political, they in *vox sonora* could respond: "*Domine, ecce adsum*"; — all, of course, provided the Señor Bishop should be found to have *clérigos* (curates) with whom to replace the padres, — "*grande cosa*"![39]

Be it added that in December the Bishop of Sonora, Sinaloa, and the Californias "took satisfaction" in notifying the prefect that the decree of 1813 had not been enforced in America, and that Payéras and his colleagues in Alta California might therefore continue to develop their "pious and most Christian desires."[40]

Last of the governors of Alta California under Spain, Sola was the first of its governors under Mexico. In his

Hispanic character he belonged rather to the secularists — Neve and Fages — than to the sacerdotalists — Borica and Arrillaga. Under him, State Secular, which in 1779 could claim a white population of about 500 persons, and in 1783 of not over 1000, could in 1820 claim 3270, of whom about 700 were soldiers. He realized the need of Spanish colonists, and urged strongly their introduction to the number of one thousand. With him, as with Borica, education was important, and he not only reëstablished primary schools at the presidios and pueblos, but advocated for Monterey a school for neophyte boys, like the *Colegio de Indio* in Mexico, and at each mission a girls' school where Indian girls might be placed at the age of three for tuition in domestic work, and for the preservation of their chastity. He interested himself in promoting blanket-weaving and tanning, — industries which, with blacksmithing, were nearly all that survived from the Borica period. Mining, which Arrillaga had pronounced delusive, "even though one went thirty, forty, or fifty leagues inland," he thought possibly worth while in view of the fact that "the greater part of the mountains gave indications of various metals," and that "eight or nine *marcos* of silver" had already been obtained.[41]

To Sola, as to Neve, the Mission in Alta California was little else than an expensive failure. True it was that by the founding of San Rafael, the number of establishments had been advanced to twenty; that by baptisms the number of neophytes had been increased to 20,500 — a gain since 1800 of 7000; that livestock (cattle, horses, mules and sheep) had reached the total of 349,882 head, — a gain of 162,882; and the agricultural products (wheat, barley, corn, beans, and peas) a total of 113,625 bushels, — a gain annually of 57,625. Yet, whereas at the end of 1800 the death-rate had been 50 per cent of baptisms, in 1810 it had been 72 per cent, and now it was 86 per cent. In 1810, President Payéras had declared that at Purísima nearly all Indian mothers gave birth to dead infants; and in 1815 it had been reported that throughout the province the proportion of deaths to births had for many years been as three to two.[42] Sola pronounced the Indian "lazy, indolent, and disregardful of all authority, costing for half a century millions of *pesos*, without having made in that time any recompense to the body politic." "Settling at the missions," said the Governor, "the Indians become spoiled. Instructed in agriculture and other branches, they are able but half to cover their bodies."[43]

But Spanish rule for California was at an end. In February, 1821, Agustín de Iturbide, a dashing royalist cavalry officer (seduced from his allegiance) proclaimed independence for Mexico; and in August and September he received the submission of the Viceroy (Juan O'Donojú) and his capital.

CHAPTER XII

THE RIGHTS OF MAN

DOWN to 1821 Alta California had been a world-factor. Cortés groping toward Anian in 1535 had touched California at the nether verge. Searching for Anian in 1542 (but more especially for the Seven Cities that lined its course), Cabrillo and Ferrelo had fared from San Diego to Cape Mendocino. In 1602 Vizcaino, searching for Anian, but now (the age of fable waning) with intent of forestalling France and England, and of providing a station for galleons, had taken possession of the Puerto de Monterey. And in 1769, after a quest long and fruitless for Rica de Oro and Rica de Plata, José de Gálvez, under a discerning policy at Madrid, had availed himself of the instrumentality of the Mission to dot the coast of the Pacific from San Diego to San Francisco with establishments, centres of propaganda for Spanish fealty and the Catholic faith.

But if down to 1821 Alta California had been a world-factor, what of change was wrought by the Revolution?

There are two forces to the appeal of which the man of Latin extraction may be expected to respond, — Tradition and Personality. When, therefore, as in the case of the separation of Mexico from Spain, Tradition is broken (Tradition as ample as ancient) and there arises no figure strong enough to replace it by Personality, that which ensues is that which since the Independencia has ensued in Latin America everywhere — derangement and vertigo. This it was that from 1821 to 1846 ensued in Alta California. This of change it was that the Revolution wrought.

The Mexican governors of Alta California were eleven: Pablo Vicente de Sola (holding over), Luis Antonio Argüello, José María de Echeandía, Manuel Victoria, Pío Pico (twice), José Figueroa, José Castro, Mariano Chico, Nicolás Gutiérrez (twice), Juan Bautista Alvarado, and Manuel Micheltorena. These men, by birth, training, and the conditions locally of the time, failed of equality with their predecessors the Spanish governors, and this despite the circumstance that the prestige and dignity of the latter were kept from becoming in any wise Homeric by incidents such as the quarrel between Rivera y Moncada and Anza, the domestic embroilment of Fages, and the operations against Bouchard.

From José María de Echeandía to Pío Pico in his second term (1825–45) there was no governorship, save Castro's, three months in duration, and the first of Gutiérrez's, four months, not beset by conspiracy and revolt. Against Echeandía the revolt was by the soldiers for lack of pay. Against Victoria, — a miniature Charles I seeking to rule without a parliament,—it was by the people. Against Pico it was double: by Echeandía and by Captain Agustín V. Zamorano, — each on his own account and each against the other. Against Figueroa it was by Los Ángeles. Against Chico it was by Monterey. Against Gutiérrez it was by Alvarado in opposition to military rule. Against Alvarado (himself a local Díaz) it was chronic and complex, to wit: by the South against the North; by the North (at Monterey) in favor of Mexican placemen; by the South in behalf of a "pretender" — Carlos Carrillo. Finally, against Micheltorena it was by the people over a Cholo soldiery; and against Pico (second occasion), it was by José Castro, a rival patriot.

On the capitulation of Viceroy O'Donojú in the summer of 1821, a *junta gubernativa* was assembled in Mexico. Ac-

cording to a plan promulgated by Iturbide in February at
Iguala, New Spain was to be an empire, with Ferdinand
VII of Old Spain, or one of his family, as emperor; but
executive power might temporarily be lodged in a regency
of five members, and soon a regency was installed with
Iturbide as president.[1] José Manuel Herrera was made
Secretary of Relations, and José Antonio de Andrade
political and military governor of Guadalajara. As for the
intendencias, they already had been resolved into five
captaincies-general, one (Nueva Galicia) under Pedro
Celestino Negrete, and another (the Provincias Internas de
Oriente y Occidente, embracing the two Californias) under
Anastasio de Bustamente.

But in naught of this had the Californias been consulted.
What would be their attitude toward Mexican independence? The people (soldiers and colonists) would, it was
assumed, be favorable; the padres as stanch Spaniards
would, it was known, be unfavorable; while as for the
Governor, Pablo Vicente de Sola, all was conjecture. The
matter for Mexico was one of disquietude and anxious
interest. As early as October, 1821, Andrade informed
Iturbide that "to demarcate, organize, and consolidate
the *nuevo imperio* would be a task arduous and difficult."
He had noted with apprehension the danger that menaced
"our new possessions of Alta California." The military
force there was weak and for eleven years had gone
unsuccored, and this despite the fact that the Russians
had established themselves at Bodega, and that trading-
stations on the Pacific were coveted by the North Americans.[2] Andrade thought that, pursuant to an understanding of the period of the Buenos Ayres privateers, there
was grave chance that Spain, impotent otherwise against
Mexico, would cede the Californias to Russia.[3]

In January, 1822, the San Blas comandante addressed to

General Negrete the query, whether it were not the part of wisdom to send north in the San Carlos a force of 150 men.[4] The views of the comandante were approved, and on February 8, Iturbide, in the name of the Regency, gave orders that a division of troops be sent to the Californias, "to occupy the country, administer the oath of independence, raise the flag of the empire, depose Sola, and disavow any treaties made by him with the Russians." But Iturbide had failed to count the cost, and having been advised by Negrete that instead of an armed force an agent with dispatches might be sufficient, the suggestion was adopted, and Negrete was asked to name for the undertaking some one *á propósito*.

Choice fell upon a canon of the Cathedral of Durango, a man jovial, bibulous, and addicted to cards, — Agustín Fernández de San Vicente. His appointment bore date April 10, 1822, and his instructions — drawn with the approval of the four secretaries of state, the captains-general of Nueva Galicia and the Provincias Internas, the padre provincial of the Dominicans, and the guardian of the College of San Fernando — were as follows: He was to go to Loreto with dispatches for the governor of the peninsula (José Argüello) and with pastoral letters for the padres, and not depart until fully informed as to the trend of opinion regarding Mexican independence. At Monterey (whither he was to go next) he was to do as he had done at Loreto. At both Loreto and Monterey he was to inquire concerning the prosperity or decadence of the Californias, and with regard to peril from the Russian and American establishments. He was to ascertain in particular whether Americans had descended the Columbia River and "located themselves on the borders of San Francisco," and whether the Russian force at Bodega was of respectable size. As for the United States, it was to be borne in mind that by treaty her limits were to transcend 42 degrees.[6] On April 2 the above instructions were enlarged. San Vicente was authorized to name, for Baja and Alta California respectively, an acting governor; care being exercised to select an individual well disposed to "our system of independence," and beloved and esteemed by the inhabitants of his province.[7]

With copies of twenty-five government decrees in his pocket, the genial San Vicente prepared to set sail. On May 19, however, Iturbide, by action of the soldiery and rabble, was himself raised to the position of Emperor of Mexico. His agent, therefore, when on June 12 he embarked for the Californias, did so under orders of June 9 (issued to Naval Lieutenant José María Narváez) to make known everywhere the accession to the Mexican throne of his imperial majesty Don Agustín I.[8]

Meanwhile, in March, Sola, advised of the installation of the regency, had convened in council the *comisario-prefecto*, the president of missions, the comandantes of the presidios, and the captains of the Mazatlán and San Blas companies, by whom on April 11 allegiance was sworn to the Mexican Empire.[9] Alta California, moreover, being one of the Provincias Internas, and as such entitled to representation in the Cortes of the Empire, it was decided on April 12 to hold, under the forms of the Spanish Constitution of 1812, an election for *diputado* (delegate).

The province, so Sola directed, was to be divided into five *partidos*, — the first to consist of the presidial district of San Francisco, together with the pueblo San José and the *villa* Branciforte; the second, of the presidial district of Monterey; the third, of that of Santa Bárbara; the fourth, of the pueblo of Los Ángeles and the missions of San Gabriel and San Juan Capistrano; and the fifth, of the presidial district of San Diego. By each mission and pueblo and by the *villa* Branciforte there was to be chosen an elector *de partido*, the mission electors to consist of the neophyte *alcaldes* and *regidores*. Men favorable to the Independencia alone were to be accepted as candidates, and priests and soldiers were excluded from candidacy by their cloth. On a day to be fixed by the *jefes de partido*, the electors *de partido* were to meet at the respective *partido* capitals and cast their votes for electors *de provincia* (provincial electors); and by the latter (convened at Monterey) the *diputado* was to be chosen. Sola proved to be the individual upon whom the honor fell, and on May 21, his election was duly certified by José M. Estudillo, secretary of the Council of State.[10]

San Vicente reached Monterey on September 26. He came from Loreto, where, in the absence of the regular comandante, José María Ruiz, he on June 27 had replaced Governor José Argüello (who voluntarily had resigned) by Fernando de la Torba, and where on July 9 news had been received of the acceptance of Mexican independence in Alta California.

The impact of republican ideas had been too widely and sensibly felt for San Vicente to be other than a discreet envoy. At Monterey he substituted the eagle of the Mexican Empire for the lion of Castile, and he proclaimed with ardor Iturbide as Agustín I; but otherwise imperially he did little. In November he saw to it that the Council of State named as *jefe político* (civil governor) the comandante at San Francisco, Luis Argüello. Under the old régime, the position would have gone to the senior comandante, José de la Guerra of Santa Bárbara; but that it did not go to him now was one proof more that the old régime had passed. Argüello, unlike Guerra, was not a Spaniard. Liberalism with him, moreover, was an incident of birth. His sister Doña Concepción had been affianced to Rezánoff, and his father, Don José, had connived at Russian trade.

But San Vicente did more than select a governor. He established, under the Spanish Constitution of 1812, — an instrument recognized in the plan of Iguala, — a *diputación* or legislative body of six *vocales* (members) and a president, — one *vocal* for each presidio and pueblo district. He withdrew, by abolition of the office of *comisionado*, control by the governor over *alcaldes* and *ayuntamientos* in the pueblos of Los Ángeles and San José. Lastly he relaxed the bonds of neophytes. They were declared possessed of citizenship, and, where capable, might live apart from a mission, subject to the judge of the vicinage. Stocks, fetters, and imprisonment were permitted as formerly,[11] but lashes on the bare back were forbidden. Under Luis Argüello, inhibition of commerce straightway ceased. A contract (January 1, 1823) was put in effect whereby the English house of McCulloch, Hartnell & Company was to take for a term of three years, at a stipulated price, all the hides and tallow of the province;[12] and on December 1 an agreement was made with the Russian-American Company for the hunting of otter on shares.[13]

So very widely and sensibly, however, had the impact of republican ideas been felt, that the imperial name and trappings even were become distasteful. In Mexico on April 8, 1823, a National Congress was assembled and Iturbide was proclaimed an exile. Federalism *versus* Centralism now was the dominant thought, and on November 19, 1823, and January 31, 1824, there were passed in Mexico provisional acts which, on October 4 of the same year, were followed by the adoption of a federal instrument based on the Constitution of the United States and designed to be permanent.[14] The National Congress had been recognized by Argüello's government in November, 1823, and, pending the arrival from Mexico of news of some plan of federation including Alta California, a local plan of government had been adopted on January 17, 1824.[15] In 1825 (March) the news awaited from Mexico was received, and in May the federal instrument — whereby Alta and Baja California were created territories entitled severally or jointly to a governor, and severally to a legislature and delegate [16] — was ratified at the presidios and pueblos. This instrument, on August 18, 1824, and April 14, 1828, was supplemented by decrees favorable to colonization and naturalization,[17] and as thus supplemented remained to 1836 the most significant expression of the spirit of the Mexican people as newly enfranchised.

Argüello's rule — the succession having been declined by General Juan José Miñón — was terminated by the arrival at San Diego in October, 1825, of Colonel José María Echeandía, a man of scholastic bent and training and of Castilian lisp.

Under Echeandía complications arose from two causes: the appointment by the Mexican Government of José María Herrera as *comisario* or financial agent in the Californias, subordinate to a *comisario-general* of the West at Arizpe; and the arrival at Monterey along with Herrera in July, 1825, of a company of eighteen Mexican convicts. Herrera as *comisario* was independent of Echeandía as governor. In 1825 he renewed for five years the contract with the Russians for hunting otter from Cape San Lucas to the port of San Francisco; and in 1827 he addressed to the *comisario-general* a sweeping indictment of the Spanish padres, of José de la Guerra, and finally of Echeandía himself. His suspension from office was soon effected by the Governor on the charge of peculation.[18] As for the convicts, they by nature were intractable. When therefore in 1829 a revolt of the troops (induced by destitution) occurred, it was opportunity for Herrera and for the convicts alike. The latter, through one of their number, Joaquín Solís, took the initiative, but the ending was farcical, for the rebels, after running from the foe on every field, — Santa Bárbara, Cieneguita, and Dos Pueblos, — were all graciously pardoned except the leaders. These (Herrera and Solís among them) were sent to Mexico, where they too, Solís no less than Herrera, were promptly set at liberty.[19]

Noteworthy, also, under Echeandía, were the occurrences following: The surrender to Argüello at Monterey in May, 1825, of the Spanish warships Asia and Constante; the visit the same month to Santa Bárbara of the revolted Spanish warship Aquiles; the completion in December, 1825, or January, 1826, by Captain José Romero, of a trip from Tuçón to San Diego and back over the Anza route; the visit to San Francisco and Monterey, in 1826 and 1827, of the English ship Blossom, under Captain Frederick William Beechey;[20] the convening at Monterey in 1827 of the first territorial *diputación* of six *vocales* under the Federal Constitution — a *diputación* which voted ineffectually to change the name of California to Montezuma;[21] the visit in 1827 and 1828 of the French ship Le Héros under Auguste Duhaut-Cilly;[22] the arrival from Mexico, in 1828 and 1829, of copies of laws ordering the expulsion of Spaniards from Mexican territory; the receipt in 1827 and 1829 of orders to establish a fort and military colony on "Carmelite" (Richardson's) Bay against the Russians; and the arrival in 1830, despite protests, of 130 Mexican convicts.

The journey of Romero coastward from Tuçón, and the orders from Mexico to establish a fort and military colony on Carmelite Bay, bespeak attention.

In October, 1822, San Vicente, accompanied by Payéras, had made a visit to Ross, and, impressed with the need of an overland route from Sonora, had directed that the course of Anza be reopened.[23] On June 8, 1823, Captain Romero, with ten men and Padre Félix Caballero (a Dominican of the peninsula), set forth down the Gila from Tuçón, reaching the Colorado on the 29th. The Cajuenches, whom Anza had used as guides, conducted the party to the mouth of the stream. Here rafts were constructed, and the men with their arms, baggage, and clothing were embarked under the guidance of the Indians. But mid-stream the wily natives deftly overturned the rafts, and Romero, Padre Félix, and the ten men with their effects were thrown into the water. "We extricated ourselves," Romero wrote to Governor Narbona of Sonora, on July 6, "with a thousand labors, and on foot, without accoutrements, clothing, or shoes, have managed to reach Santa Catalina Mártir."

From Santa Catalina, Romero with his escort proceeded to San Diego, to seek from Portilla, stationed there with the Mazatlán Company, help against the Cajuenches; but, wrote the comandante at Loreto, such a move is to be deprecated as "we seem to be menaced by the Russians on the north." The result was that in December, 1825, Romero, under orders from José Figueroa, and escorted by Lieutenant Romualdo Pacheco, reached the Colorado without having been able to reopen the route of Anza, and that from the river in question he made his way back to Tuçón.[24]

In regard to the fort and military colony against the Russians, nothing was done by Echeandía, although his orders were explicit.

The Mexican Government [he was assured] could not view with indifference the way in which the Russians, having possessed themselves of the port of Bodega, were encroaching by way of the interior upon San Francisco, manifesting an intention to appropriate the Río de San Juan Bautista, alias del Sacramento, and to plant themselves at the point called on the old maps La Junta de Evengelistas. . . . Wherefore he was to select two or three men to choose a site for a fort to command the principal river emptying into the Puerto de Sanfrancisco. This fort he was to construct without loss of an instant, and, near it, gather a population for a military colony, — not less than five hundred persons. For four years military discipline was to be maintained there; the President of the Republic during that interval suspending elections, as, by his extraordinary powers under the Constitution, he might lawfully do. The settlement was to be protected by a moat and counter-moat, and the *entradas* with drawbridge and other works.[25]

But the most important occurrence under Echeandía was in the domain sacerdotal, namely, the formulation in 1828 of a plan of Secularization for the missions, and the publication on January 6, 1831, of a *bando* for putting the plan into effect.

The Spanish Government had long made it plain that instruction of the Indians in civil polity, with a view to a conversion of the missions into pueblos, was of the first importance. For Mexico, therefore, the question of the maintenance of the Mission arose at once; and, with the adoption in 1823 of a Mexican law forecasting Federalism, it became insistent. Said Lucas Alamán, Mexican Secretary of Relations, in a report to Congress, dated November 8, 1823: —

It is necessary to consider other interests than those of the missionaries in the vast and fertile peninsula of Californias. . . . If the Mission system is that best suited to draw savages from barbarism, it can do no more than establish the first principles of society; it cannot lead men to their highest perfection. Nothing is better to accomplish this than to bind individuals to society by the powerful bond of property. The government believes that the distribution of lands to the converted Indians, lending them from the Mission fund the means for cultivation, and the establishment of foreign colonies, which perhaps might be Asiatic, would give a great impulse to that important province.[26]

But in this connection, what of the report of Tamariz, upon which in 1817 Viceroy Apodaca had convened a *Junta de California*? This report the Mexican Government now set itself to examine. "I wish," wrote General Juan José Minión to the Secretary of War and Marine, "to inform myself regarding an *expediente* in the office of the Secretary of Relations that treats of a reform in the government of the peninsula of California, and that contains a memorial by Comisario-General Don Francisco de Paula Tamariz," etc. The request was followed by the creation in 1824 or 1825 of a California promotion committee (*Junta de Fomento de Californias*) of which Tamariz himself was a member and leading spirit. To the first President of the Mexican Republic, Guadalupe Victoria, the *Junta de Fomento* said: —

The *junta* is not ignorant that from the Spanish system of discoveries and spiritual conquests has resulted all the progress made in the Jesuit missions of Old California and in those founded later in New California by the Fernandinos. . . . Still, the *junta* has not been able to reconcile the principles of such a system with those of our independence and political constitution, nor with the true spirit of the Gospel. Religion under that system could not advance beyond domination. It could be promoted only under the protection of guards and presidios. The gentiles must renounce all the rights of their natural independence to be catechumens from the moment of baptism; they must be subject to laws almost monastic, while their teachers deemed themselves freed from the laws which forbade their engaging in temporal business; and the neophytes must continue this without hope of ever possessing fully the civil rights of society. . . . The present condition of the missions does not correspond to the great progress which they made in the beginning.[27]

Such were the views of republican Mexico. In Alta California, however, there was an element — the Spanish friars — which, because of the dependent condition of the Indian, was not favorable to Secularization; and which, because of the pleas for Secularization above set forth, was not favorable to the Republic. In 1823, on April 28 and August 24, respectively, Prefect Payéras and ex-President Señán, both men of poise, had died; and Señán had been succeeded as prefect and president by Vicente Sarría, a prelate of energetic qualities. But in April, 1825, Sarría resigned the presidency of missions to Narciso Durán, from whom in 1827 it was transferred to José Sánchez, who held it, contemporaneously with Sarría's prefecture, to the advent of Governor Victoria. It accordingly was with Payéras, Señán, Sarría, Durán, and Sánchez that Echeandía, in the matter of Secularization, was called upon to deal.

The political phase presented itself first.

Since 1810, the year of the Mexican revolt, the padres in Alta California had submitted to exactions for the support of the state, — exactions which though inevitable were contrary to precedent. These exactions, so long as the Spanish royalist régime lasted, had been so made as not to compromise the dignity of the priestly office; but now that the Mexican or republican régime prevailed, the dignity of the priestly office was well-nigh sacrificed. The state was poor, — poorer than ever, — and to support it the padres were not only compelled to pay the usual trade duties and forced loans, but a secular tithe besides; and when they complained that the pueblos paid nothing, they were charged with insolence and presumption.

One day Padre José Barona of San Juan Capistrano, on setting out for San Diego, was assailed by the mission guard and so treated that his horse was caused to throw him, — an affront characterized by Padre Gerónimo Boscana as "the most scandalous ever perpetrated in California."[28] Nor was the situation without effect upon the neophyte. Indian labor at the presidios was no longer recompensed by bountiful *memorias* from San Blas. The soldiers in consequence were disliked, and on February 21, 1824, a revolt of neophytes broke forth at Santa Inés. Spreading rapidly to Purísima and Santa Bárbara, it resulted in the death of several white men and a number of Indians, and, after an expedition to the Tulares, was only quieted by a general pardon secured from Argüello by Padre Antonio Ripoll.[29]

But where the Mexican Republic came most sorely in conflict with the Spanish element — the padres — was with regard to an oath of allegiance. In 1822, Payéras, Señán, and Sarría had sworn to the Independencia, under promise by the Regency to summon to the throne of Mexico Ferdinand VII, or one of his brothers. Nor when the summons failed had any difficulty been made by Payéras over words of fealty to Iturbide as Agustín I. Orders to swear to the Federal Constitution of October 4, 1824, however, were for the most part disregarded. Early in 1825, Sarría and Durán each refused to take the oath, and in October Sarría, by command of the Mexican Government, was put under constructive arrest preparatory to being sent to Mexico, — a step never carried out.[30]

At one time or another in Alta California there were Franciscans — Serra, Lasuén, Tapis, Payéras, Señán — conspicuous for virtue and capacity; but there were others more conspicuous still for idiosyncrasy. Of the latter (stirred by the question of allegiance to the Republic) were Antonio Ripoll of Santa Bárbara and Luis Martínez of San Luis Obispo. In 1818, during the invasion of Bouchard, padres of the type of Payéras and Señán had yielded to excitement, the former (Patrick Henry-like) exclaiming: *"Viva Dios, viva la religión, viva el Rey, viva la patria, y ó vencer ó morir en tan preciosa defensa!"* Not surprising, therefore, is it that Ripoll and Martínez had donned garb of war and proffered advice in tactics. But ardor once roused was not easily repressed. Ripoll, rather than swear allegiance, took with him José Altimíra (founder of San Francisco Solano), stole on board an American brig, the Harbinger, lying at Santa Bárbara, and sailed for Spain.

As for Martínez, his fate was exile. Having exhibited sympathy for the rebel cause in the Solís-Herrera revolt of 1829, he was arrested in February, 1830, by order of Echeandía, tried by court martial, found guilty of conspiracy, and on March 20 sent to Spain by the English ship Thomas Nowlan.[31] Short in stature, swarthy of countenance, knowing in trade, generous of larder, fancier of cattle, horses, and mules, prone to vanity in respect of bebraceleted and beribboned neophyte attendants, yet in naught a scandal to St. Francis, — it is with reluctance, Padre Martínez, that thou art dismissed from our pages to Briebes in Asturias, thy native town.[32]

In 1829 the number of padres in Alta California who remained incorrigible was fourteen. Among those who had taken the oath the one most compliant, and hence highest in favor in Mexico and with Echeandía, was Antonio Peyri. With him, together with three others of the compliant, the Governor in 1826 took counsel and matured a plan of emancipation for deserving neophytes. All not minors, nor likely to become a public charge, might, by consent of their presidial comandante, have the liberty of *gente de razón.* Corporal punishment, moreover, might be exercised only upon males who were minors and unmarried, and was to be limited to fifteen lashes a week.[33]

Emancipation, it is needless to say, was but preliminary to Secularization. In the summer of 1830, a secularization plan was submitted by Echeandía to the territorial *diputación*, and after slight amendment was approved. The various missions one by one (beginning with those nearest the four presidios, two pueblos and one *villa*) were to be converted into pueblos. Each pueblo was to consist of the neophytes who had belonged to it as a mission, and of such Mexicans as it might attract. Land to the extent of a house-lot (*solar*) and a field (*suerte*) was to be assigned to each family (neophyte or immigrant) in severalty, and land to the extent of one square league for each 500 head of livestock was to be assigned in common. The livestock of each family was to be made up by an allotment in severalty of sheep, swine, cows, bulls, horses and stallions from the flocks and herds of the former mission; but of the land assigned in severalty none was to be sold within five years, nor was it to be mortgaged by a holder or by his heirs. The former missionaries might remain as curates of the newly formed pueblos, or they might form mission establishments in the Tulares. For the use of the curates the mission church with its appurtenances was to be assigned, but the rest of the mission buildings were to be converted into prisons, barracks, school-houses, hospitals, and quarters for the *ayuntamientos*, — the whole scheme of public improvement to be supported by the income from mission property not otherwise employed.[34]

Secularization for the missions of Alta California was also forecast by the virtual dissolution of the Franciscan College of San Fernando. This ancient institution — mother of Alta California missionaries, and so in an important sense mother of Alta California itself — was described in 1824 by José Gasol, the guardian, as on the verge of extinction; and in 1828 it had passed into the hands of a *vicario de casa,* under whom the inmates were three padres, two invalid Spaniards, and a few servants.

Meanwhile, as for Echeandía's plan, it was thwarted by a change of political equilibrium in Mexico. The first president, Guadalupe Victoria, had been succeeded in 1829 by Vicente Guerrero. Both Victoria and Guerrero were representatives of Liberalism, as opposed to Conservatism in the guise of Centralism; but Conservatism had for some time been gaining, and in 1830, under Anastasio Bustamente, it triumphed. The result for Alta California was that on March 8, 1830, Echeandía was supplanted by Lieutenant-Colonel Manuel Victoria, half Indian, friend of the padres (especially of Sarría whom he openly praised), and foe to Secularization. To take office, Victoria was compelled to proceed first to Santa Bárbara and then to Monterey, reaching the capital on January 29, 1831. But on January 6, a decree of Secularization (instigated, it was thought, by José María Padrés, newly come from Loreto as adjutant-inspector) was issued, to take immediate effect.[35] The response of Victoria to this *coup* was a sharp order interdicting all action; and interdicted Secularization accordingly remained throughout Victoria's term. In yet another way, during 1831, was Secularization given pause. Alta California's *diputado* in the Mexican Congress, Carlos Carrillo, secured by the old arguments in favor of the maintenance of the Mission the rejection of a plan for confiscating the estates of the Pious Fund.

The rule of Victoria was destined to be brief. Acquainted only with military methods, and arbitrary by nature, his course begat opposition on every hand. He refused to convene the *diputación,* or legislative body, because of its known bias toward Liberalism, including Secularization; and his administration of justice, though marked by the un-Mexican virtue of promptitude, was startling in its employment of the penalties of death and exile. Victims of the latter penalty were José Antonio Carrillo, Abel Stearns (from Massachusetts), and J. M. Padrés, the republican adjutant.[36] The inevitable revolt, heralded by manifesto on November 29, was directed politically by Echeandía, Pío Pico, senior *vocal* of the *diputación,* Juan Bandini, alternate delegate to Congress, José Carrillo, and Abel Stearns; while Pablo de Portilla, comandante at San Diego, was induced to lead in the field.[37]

Warned of trouble, Victoria started south almost alone; but finding at Santa Bárbara a squad under Captain Romualdo Pacheco, he put himself at their head, and with, in all, about thirty men advanced toward Los Ángeles. Between the pueblo and the mission of San Fernando, he, on December 5, came upon Portilla with about 150 men posted on an acclivity. A short parley ensued, at the end of which Pacheco, incensed at a gibe by the Governor at his valor, charged toward the enemy. The latter promptly fled — all save a party headed by José María Ávila, ex-*alcalde* of Los Ángeles, who in turn charged upon Pacheco. Like two jousting knights, though with deadlier intent, Pacheco and Ávila were carried past each other in the lists, delivering cut and thrust with sword and lance. Turning in his saddle, Ávila drew a pistol, shot Pacheco through the heart, and rushed upon Victoria. A *mêlée* ensued, and the Governor was hurled from his horse by a thrust of Ávila's lance. As for Ávila, he was seized by the fallen Victoria, who unhorsed him and transfixed him with his sword.[38]

Between men of Spanish extraction in Alta California, actual warfare had taken place for the first time; — fighting in which red blood had been shed. The field was circumscribed and the combatants were few, but the *gaudium certaminis*, the joy of battle, had been there, and the ridiculous fiascos — the *opéra bouffe* sallies — of other years were atoned for. Honors too had not been unequal, for if Ávila had fallen on the side of Portilla and civil rule, Pacheco had fallen on the side of Victoria and militarism. The wounded governor was carried to San Gabriel Mission, where, under the hands of Dr. Charles Anderson, he gained strength, but only to yield himself to Echeandía with a request to be sent to Mexico, a destination whither on January 17, 1832, he was dispatched in the American ship Pocahontas.[39]

Secularization in Alta California was destined to come ere long. The fact was made evident in connection with the founding in 1832, under Argüello, of the twenty-first and last California establishment — the mission of San Francisco Solano. At a conference in 1822 between San Vicente (the *canónigo*), Argüello and Payéras, it had been decided to transfer the mission of San Francisco, with its erstwhile *asistencia* San Rafael, to the Gentile country north of San Pablo Bay. Argüello having secured from the *diputación*, through José Altimíra, padre at San Francisco, approval for the transfer, submitted the matter to the authorities in Mexico, and sent a party to choose a mission site. Sonoma was selected, and dedicatory ceremonies were held in 1823 on July 4. But neither Señán nor Sarría could be induced to sanction the suppression of San Rafael. To the prelate alone, they contended, and in no sense to the *diputación*, pertained the right "to recommend the founding, suppressing, or moving of establishments." Argüello's reply — a reply itself declaratory of Secularization — was that, State Sacerdotal having in fifty years failed to do aught in the north for the Gentiles, the task now would be undertaken by State Secular. A compromise was effected. Neither San Francisco nor San Rafael was suppressed, but San Francisco Solano, with Altimíra in charge, was given existence as an independent mission.[40]

CHAPTER XIII

FEDERALISM AND CENTRALISM

I

Figueroa

THE manifesto against Governor Victoria — drafted by Juan Bandini and known as the Plan of San Diego — sought two objects: (1) The removal of the Governor, and (2) the separation of the political and military commands.[1]

By a Mexican law of May 6, 1822, it was provided that in case of the death, absence, or disability of a *jefe político*, the position should be assumed by the senior *vocal* of the *diputación*. Accordingly, on January 11, 1832, Pío Pico, as senior *vocal*, was chosen by the *diputación, jefe político* for Alta California, and Echeandía was so notified. But the ex-Governor, after some wavering, refused to recognize Pico, preferring to keep in his own hands what of political power had been placed there by the Revolution.

On January 24, the comandante at Monterey, Agustín V. Zamorano, began a movement against both Pico and Echeandía, — a movement culminating, on February 1, in a manifesto at the hands of a *junta*, prominent in which was William E. P. Hartnell of McCulloch, Hartnell & Company, against the Plan of San Diego as the work of plotters and rebels.[2] Echeandía's course on Secularization had won for him the friendship of the neophytes, and in March and April they in great force mustered to his aid near San Gabriel. Zamorano thereupon consented to a conference, and on May 9 it was agreed between the rival comandantes that, pending the appointment of a governor by Mexico, Alta California should remain divided into two parts, — one from San Gabriel southward under Echeandía; the other from San Fernando northward under Zamorano. The district between these points (that of the pueblo of Los Ángeles) was left in a condition of guaranteed neutrality. Echeandía was to advance no armed force to the northward of San Juan Capistrano, and Zamorano none to the southward of San Buenaventura. As in other Alta California revolutionary movements, so in this, no blood was shed, but zest was imparted by the sending of a band of convicts south from Monterey against Echeandía — a band that, soon dispersing, excited terror until captured.

A strong hand was needed, and it was possessed by Brigadier-General José Figueroa. The Californias were not unknown to Figueroa, for in 1824, he, as comandante in Sonora, had been sent to the Colorado to meet the Mazatlán Company, then (supposedly) on the way home from San Diego under Romero.[3] The General was of Aztec blood, hence swarthy in color; and besides being a man of courage, was of popular address. Made *jefe político* on May 9, 1832, he set sail from San Blas on July 7, in the brig Catalina, with a force of seventy-two Cholos of the Acapulco convict class, and reached Cape San Lucas on the 30th. Here, on a return trip of the brig, he was joined by ten Zacatecan friars and by Lieutenant Nicolás Gutiérrez, bearer of 20,000 *pesos* in coin. But the Cholos, tempted beyond endurance by the money, mutinied and put back to San Blas. It was not until December 17 that Figueroa, with some thirty soldiers and his band of friars, was able to quit the peninsula for Monterey, where he arrived on January 14, 1833.[4]

The duties of the new Governor, as signified in his in-

structions, were the fortification and colonization of Alta
California northward toward the Russians; precautionary
measures against Anglo-Americans; and a cautious Mission policy.[5] Between April, 1833, and January, 1834,
Lieutenant Mariano Guadalupe Vallejo, with a few settlers,
and a few neophytes from the mission of San Francisco
Solano, occupied the sites Petaluma and Santa Rosa;[6]
but attention was diverted by news of the approach from
Mexico of a large colony — 204 individuals led by José
María Padrés and José María Híjar. The object of the
colony was to realize the instructions, given to Echeandía
in 1828, to plant on Carmelite Bay a strong barrier against
the Russians. But under the changes in Mexico there
was involved with this object much that was personal.

Bandini had prayed that in Alta California the political
and military commands might be separated, and to this
end, in the spring of 1833, two sets of occurrences took
place in remarkable conjunction: (1) Padrés became
friends with Bandini (now California congressman), and
with Gómez Farías, Vice-President under Bustamente's
successor, Antonio López de Santa Anna. (2) Figueroa,
because of ill health, resigned; Padrés on July 12 was
dispatched to Alta California to assume the *comandancia;*
and on July 15 Híjar was created *jefe político.*[7]

Already two organizations had been effected: a colonization company, of which Híjar was made director on
July 16, and a mercantile company (*compañía cosmopoli-
tana*), of which Bandini was chosen vice-president. Withal,
on November 26, by a decree of the Mexican Congress,
the governmental side of the Padrés-Bandini-Híjar combination was empowered "to adopt all measures to insure
the colonization and make effective the secularization of
the missions of Alta and Baja California, . . . using for
that purpose in the most convenient manner the estates

of the Pious Fund of these territories, in order to furnish
resources to the commission and families now in this capital and intending to go there." [8] And on April 23, 1834,
Híjar, as *jefe político* and director of colonization, was
instructed to take possession of all the property belonging
to the missions of both Californias.[9]

It was early in 1834 that Figueroa heard of the coming
of Híjar and Padrés. Nor was he pleased. The separation
of the commands was to his distaste as a move by Californians toward "home rule"; [10] and on July 18, he wrote
to Mexico that his health, upon the precariousness of
which his resignation had been predicated, was improved.
This news, adverse to the interests of the combination,
was soon followed by other news. Santa Anna, who, with
a view to studying the probable next leap of that lithe
lion the Mexican populace, had withheld himself from the
presidential seat, now, perceiving that Federalism under
Farías was verging on Radicalism, assumed office on
July 25. A first step was to dispatch across the desert to
Figueroa orders to continue administering the *jefatura*.
When, therefore, the colony, half under Padrés, and half
under Híjar and Bandini, reached Monterey, — the Padrés division by sea on September 25, and the Híjar-Ban-
dini division overland from San Diego on October 14, —
they were met by the Governor with the instructions from
Santa Anna.

Colonization for Alta California (occupation by substantial settlers — farmers, tailors, carpenters, shoemakers,
blacksmiths, saddlers, and teachers — such as the Híjar
colony contained) was a thing the need of which had
been proclaimed from the days of Neve to those of Sola.
Accordingly in the winter of 1835 the colonists for the
most part were gathered under an *alcalde* at and near San
Francisco Solano (Sonoma), the point where settlers were

required as against the Russians. Híjar himself was permitted by the *diputación* to retain of his varied titles that only of director of colonization; while as for Padrés, he was forced to choose between his military office of adjutant-inspector and the civil office (which was his) of sub-director of colonization under Híjar, — a dilemma which he resolved in favor of the civil post.[11]

But Padrés, Híjar, and their associates were not to be shaken off so easily. The Solís revolt against Echeandía, although perhaps not instigated by José María Herrera, was an opportune occurrence for him. In March, 1835, a revolt at Los Ángeles came opportunely for Padrés and Híjar. In 1834, Santa Anna, who for a year had been dallying with the Centralists, had convoked a new Congress. The elections had gone for the Centralists (the clergy and army) overwhelmingly, and the Los Ángeles movement was probably little other than a reflection of Mexican conditions. Be that as it may, the promoters of the revolt were two men — Antonio Apalátegui, a Spaniard from Sonora, and Francisco Torres, a Híjar colonist. A *pronunciamiento* was issued by Apalátegui, declaring it to be the purpose of the rebellionists to restore to the very reverend missionary fathers exclusive charge of temporalities, and to separate the military and political commands, — a separation which was not to affect Híjar in his position as director of colonization. The *pronunciamiento* contained a sop to Herrera in the declaration that Figueroa (like Echeandía) "disposed of the soldiers' pay at his own will, without knowledge of the chief of revenue." [12]

For the conspirators, however, Figueroa was prepared. Híjar and Padrés were in arrest, by March 26; and by May 8, they had been joined at San Pedro by Apalátegui and Torres, — all bound as exiles for San Blas.[13]

The overthrow of Governor Victoria had given Echeandía opportunity to proceed so far with Secularization as
to appoint *comisionados*, or receivers, at certain southern
missions, — missions beyond Zamorano's jurisdiction,
namely, San Luis Rey, San Juan Capistrano, San Gabriel,
and San Diego.[14] The government's instructions to Figueroa counseled caution, but were yet sufficiently radical.
Article 4 recommended a distribution of lands to deserving
neophytes, in order that "the influence of the missionaries [might] be lessened until only the spiritual administration was retained by them." Furthermore, it was
decreed on August 17: (1) That Secularization in Alta
California should take place at once; (2) that the secularized missions should be made each a parish under a
secular priest; and (3) that the cost of the change should
be met by the income of the Pious Fund.

The task of Secularization was assumed by Figueroa
under rules issued on July 15, 1833, called *Prevenciones
de Emancipación;* rules not differing materially from the
Plan of Echeandía. *Comisionados*, aided by the padres,
were to gather into pueblos along the *camino real*
(king's highway) such Indians as had been Christianized for more than twelve years; such as were married or
were widowers with children; and such as knew how to cultivate the soil or ply a trade and were "addicted" to work.
The pueblos, for the present, were to be attached to the
nearest municipality or presidio, but were to be initiated
in self-government through officers appointed annually
from among themselves. For the support of churches,
schools, etc., landed estates (*propios y arbitrios*) were to be
formed. Finally, neophytes who should prove neglectful of their new opportunities were to be returned to the
establishment of which they formerly had been inmates.[15]

Of the success of the *Prevenciones*, we know chiefly

that in 1833 San Juan Capistrano was converted into a pueblo, and that pueblo beginnings were made at San Diego and San Luis Rey.[16] Criticism, however, was not lacking. Said President Durán: "The free Gentile Indians of the pueblo of Los Ángeles are more wretched in estate and more severely chastised for offenses than are the Indians of the missions." Said President Diego, of the Zacatecans: "The Spanish Government that framed the law of 1813, what could it know of California conditions? Under emancipation the Indian will revert to nakedness and barbarism. It is only by force that he can be made to perform religious duties." Said Durán again: "The Indian by nature is apathetic and indolent, so much so that the Spanish rule of a ten years' *neofitia* is for him wholly inadequate." But by this time (October) the law of August 17, 1833, was in force, and Secularization was pressed forward as fast as possible.

On August 9, 1834, it was provided by a *Reglamento Provisional* that house-lots, pasture-lands, and livestock should be assigned to heads of families, and to all males over twenty years of age, much upon the basis of the Plan of Echeandía and of the *Prevenciones*. But it also was provided, that in addition to a *comisionado* or general superintendent of Secularization, a major-domo, or head steward, should be appointed in each mission for the care of all undistributed Mission property; that henceforth the missionaries should be prohibited from slaughtering cattle for hides and tallow; that " nunneries," where for the good of their morals neophyte children were kept apart from their parents, should be abolished; and that isolated *rancherías* having twenty-five families should be permitted to form, if they wished, separate pueblos.[17]

The *diputación* had reckoned that before the end of

October, 1834, every Alta California mission would have become a civil community. In fact, only nine missions had been secularized by the end of the year: San Luis Rey, San Juan Capistrano, San Gabriel, San Fernando, Santa Bárbara, Purísima, Santa Cruz, San Francisco, and San Rafael. By the end of 1835 there were added: San Diego, San Luis Obispo, San Antonio, Soledad, San Juan Bautista, and San Francisco Solano — a grand total of fifteen. As for San Buenaventura, Santa Inés, San Miguel, Santa Clara, and San José, the records for 1834–35 show no change.

Figueroa, a victim of vertigo and of the fogs of Monterey, died on September 29, 1835, and his funeral was celebrated to the noise of cannon. Against his own judgment, but in deference to California opinion as voiced by Bandini, he, at the last, had separated the political and military commands, conferring on José Castro, senior *vocal* of the *diputación*, the *ad-interim jefatura*, and on Lieutenant-Colonel Nicolás Gutiérrez the *ad-interim comandancia*. In January, 1836, however, in obedience to an order from Mexico dated a year before, the two offices were again combined through a transfer of the *jefatura* by Castro.

The only occurrence of note under Gutiérrez was the formal recognition, on January 4, of Los Ángeles as capital of Alta California. In 1825, Echeandía, as governor of both Californias, had fixed upon San Diego as a place of residence, and the South ever since had contended with the North for the seat of government. In 1835 (May 23) the efforts of southern politicians — the Bandinis and Carrillos — had been rewarded by a decree of the Mexican Congress declaring that "the pueblo of Los Ángeles in Alta California, hereby created a city, shall be the capital of that territory." This decree Gutiérrez as governor made public by proclamation.[18]

But what meanwhile of Mexico? First, Liberal or Federalist, — the views of Presidents Victoria and Guerrero reflected in Alta California by Echeandía; next, Conservative or Centralist, — the views of Vice-President Bustamente reflected by Governor Victoria; again Liberal (this time Federalist radically), — the views of Vice-President Farías moderately reflected by Figueroa, and emphatically by Padrés and Bandini, — Mexico now (the autumn of 1835) repudiated Federalism altogether, and repealed the Constitution of 1824.

As governor of Alta California, Colonel Mariano Chico, a Mexican congressman, was chosen, and he received his commission on December 16, 1835, the day following the promulgation by the Mexican Congress of certain "Bases" preliminary to a new constitution. Chico was a second Victoria, captious, tactless, and void of balance, and his administration, like that of his prototype, was incisive and short. He began it in May with addresses eulogistic of Centralism, and by exacting an oath to the "Bases." He continued it by reviving Victoria's quarrel with Abel Stearns, whom he ordered to quit the country.[19] He further continued it by repairing to Los Ángeles and arresting a number of citizens for participation in the lynching of a murderer and his paramour. Again he continued it by ordering the arrest of President Durán for refusing as a Spaniard to swear to the "Bases." On July 31 he brought it to a close by fleeing to Mexico, — an act the sequel to a complicated politico-social imbroglio at Monterey, due to the parading by Chico of his mistress, Doña Cruz, and her friend (even less savory of reputation) Doña Ildefonsa, wife of Herrera, at a public entertainment.

II

Alvarado

Mexico from the first had made Alta California an asylum for Mexican officials, and the fact was resented. Those by whom it was resented most were the young Californians, — the "young Italy" of the land, — and chief among such was Juan Bautista Alvarado.

Born at Monterey on February 14, 1809, Alvarado in 1836 was twenty-seven years old, having held the position of customs-inspector and secretary of the *diputación*, and being now *diputación* president. A protégé of Sola, he had been taught penmanship and arithmetic, and his school companions had been his uncle Mariano Guadalupe Vallejo and José Castro. The few books accessible to him — "Don Quixote," the "Laws of the Indies," a dictionary of geography, "Lives of Celebrated Spaniards," and Venegas's "California" — perchance, despite clerical vigilance, *Gil Blas* and the *Julie* of Jean Jacques — he had read with zest, but his principal study had been life and the ways of men. His acquirements were to be tested against Gutiérrez, to whom the fleeing Chico had confided the *ad-interim jefatura* and *comandancia*.

That once again the political and military commands were combined in the same individual, and he not only a Mexican but a Mexican of Spanish birth, was more than young California was able to bear, and it straightway proceeded to rebel. Alvarado — aided by his friend Castro, and watched sympathetically at a distance by his uncle Guadalupe — led. He gathered recruits, formidable among whom were a hired band of sailors and American backwoodsmen under a Tennesseean, Isaac Graham; and on November 3, 1836, the castillo of Monterey was taken without resistance. Designs were then matured against the presidio,

which capitulated on November 5. The capitulation was
followed by the deportation to Cape San Lucas of Gutiérrez and others, among them José María Herrera, who as sub-
comisario had returned to old scenes along with Padrés.[20]

Through its diputación, headed by José Castro, Alta
California, on November 6, had set up an independent
government, — one with the motto Federación ó Muerte;
one based on the declaration that the land "was free and
would hold aloof from Mexico until no longer oppressed
by the present dominant faction called central government." [21] On November 7 Vallejo was made comandante-
general of the newly created state, and on December 7
Alvarado was made governor, or, more accurately,
autocratic president. On December 9 the diputación, or
State Congress, passed a decree dividing the land into
two cantons, that of Monterey and that of Los Ángeles.
In each there was to be a jefe político, — at Monterey
the Governor himself, and at Los Ángeles some one to be
appointed by the Governor from a terna (trio) elected by
the Angelinos.[22]

A political chief for the South was a confession of peril
to the supremacy of Alvarado from southern discontent
at the persistent refusal of the North to recognize Los
Ángeles as the territorial capital; and no sooner was
Alvarado installed than the South, through Los Ángeles,
published a determined caveat to the proceeding.[23] It
was admitted that Alvarado had delivered the land from
Mexican placemen (a thing laudable enough), but he had
also separated it from Mexico, styling it an Estado libre
y soberano. Moreover, he had been aided by Anglo-
Americans, at whose hands might be expected for California the fate of Texas. Finally, he had so far impugned
the national religious faith as to promise to molest no
one in his private religious opinions.[24]

Backed by a force of eighty men, — native sons under José Castro and Americans under Isaac Graham, — Alvarado on January 23, 1837, appeared in Los Ángeles. He dictated a compact extolling Federalism, but insisting henceforth on none but natives (*hijos del país*) for California rulers, and providing for summoning a new *diputación*. The latter, which met at Santa Bárbara on April 11, approved Alvarado's programme, so modified as to embody stipulations for the maintenance of the full supremacy of the Catholic faith, for an undivided *jefatura*, and for the preservation of California as an integral part of the Mexican Republic;[25] and on May 1 the approval by the *diputación* was in turn, though reluctantly, accepted by the *Ayuntamiento* of Los Ángeles.

The South having been placated, Alvarado returned to Monterey. Here, on May 30, he found himself confronted by three new demonstrations against his authority, — the first at Los Ángeles under Juan Bandini; the second at San Diego and San Luis Rey under Captain Andrés Castillero; and the third at Monterey itself, under Ángel Ramírez and Cosme Peña. The Ramírez-Peña revolt proved trifling. With the Bandini-Castillero affair (for the two movements speedily become one) it was otherwise.

On the night of May 26, 1837, Juan Bandini had made himself master of Los Ángeles. On June 12, Andrés Castillero, one of Gutiérrez's companions at the fall of Monterey, had appeared at San Diego with the Mexican Laws of 1836 (the so-called Seven Laws, sequel to the "Bases" of 1835), and having received thereto, despite the Centralism which they established, the enthusiastic subscription of the Diegueños and Angelinos, had joined Bandini, who, with the South in arms under Pablo de Portilla, had taken post at San Fernando. Alvarado was foiled, but stooped to conquer. He induced Castillero to become his representative to Mexico, once again under Bustamente as president, and on July 9, pronounced for the Centralist system: *"Viva la Nación! Viva la Constitución del año de '36! Viva el Congreso que la sancionó! Viva la Libertad! Viva la Unión!"* [26]

The South of a surety was circumvented now, and from the sorrow of campaigning the soul of Alvarado might find surcease. Not so. Forestalling Castillero, Congressman José Antonio Carrillo secured from the Mexican Government the appointment of his brother Carlos as Acting Governor of Alta California, an appointment carrying with it the power to fix the capital provisionally where circumstances might require. It was fixed on December 1 at Los Ángeles, and there on the 6th Carrillo was duly inaugurated. But Alvarado refused to recognize Carrillo's claim, and the latter, sustained by the South, resolved in February, 1838, to fight. He mustered a force under Juan Castañada, and to oppose it Alvarado sent a force under Castro. The two armies, about one hundred men each, met near San Buenaventura, and on March 27–28 fought the kind of action that Carrillo had intended — one loud with cannon, thick with smoke, and devoid of casualties. Castañada none the less was worsted, for his force was dispersed and he himself taken prisoner. A further hostile demonstration by Carrillo at Las Flores in April was followed by a conference between Carrillo and Alvarado at San Fernando.[27] But on May 20 the Governor, suspecting treachery, arrested José Antonio Carrillo, Pío Pico, and other Southerners, and sent them to Sonoma to be watched by Vallejo. Don Carlos himself was arrested, but was permitted to depart on parole to his home in Santa Bárbara.

A third time was Alvarado greeted by the hope that the hour of respite had come.[28] But in August word was received that Don Carlos had violated his parole and fled by boat to Lower California. Deliverance, nevertheless, was at hand. On August 13, a vessel from Mexico brought news that Castillero's mission had succeeded, and that both Alvarado and Vallejo were to be provisionally confirmed in the respective positions which they had held so long.

Alvarado, his right to rule recognized, and his heart blessed in 1839 by a suitable marriage, gave attention to what was the most important phase of the Mexican régime in Alta California — Secularization. But, first, there was to be put into effect the new system of Centralism, which the arms of Santa Anna and the policy of Bustamente had established.

By the Constitution of 1836 — the Constitution of the Seven Laws — the Constitution to which Alvarado with *vivas* had bidden Californians subscribe — the two Californias, Alta and Baja, were converted from two territories into a single department, entitled to a governor, an assembly, and one congressional delegate. The department was required to be subdivided into districts and *partidos* under prefects and sub-prefects, the former to be appointed by the Governor and approved in Mexico; and the latter to be appointed by the prefects and approved by the Governor. On February 27, 1839, three prefectures were designated, — two for Alta, and one for Baja California; the respective capitals being at San Juan de Castro (late mission of San Juan Bautista), Los Ángeles, and La Paz. The two Alta California prefectures were divided each into two *partidos*, with head towns (*cabeceras*) at San Juan de Castro, San Francisco, Los Ángeles, and Santa Bárbara. No *partido* division was as yet attempted for Baja California.[29]

So far as *ayuntamientos* were concerned, they were permitted by the new laws only to the larger towns, the smaller being placed under the authority of justices of the peace.[30] Centralist in design, the new laws wrought a triumph for that Federalist principle of home rule through the assertion of which Alvarado had gained power, for henceforth the Alta California governors were to be appointed from a *terna* of names to be submitted by the assembly to the Mexican Government. And on August 7, 1839, Alvarado himself was chosen governor by President Bustamente from a *terna* embracing the names of Juan B. Alvarado, José Castro, and Pío Pico.

The conditions of Secularization, as they presented themselves to Alvarado, may be summarized thus: Sixteen establishments in the hands of *comisionados;* further Secularization forbidden by law in 1835 pending the appointment of curates; three missions — Santa Inés, San Buenaventura, and San Miguel — delivered to *comisionados* by Chico, despite the law; and two — San José and Santa Clara — so delivered by the *diputación* under Alvarado. The Mission property, by virtue of the curacy law and of civil strife, was being neglected, wasted, stolen, and destroyed. To stop spoliation was the first and paramount duty of a governor, and Alvarado promptly addressed his efforts to the task. It was in his favor that, Spain having recognized the independence of Mexico in 1836, President Durán and the Fernandinos had in 1837 taken the long-deferred oath to support the Mexican Government.

On January 17, 1839, the Governor issued a *Reglamento Provisional* requiring *comisionados* to present accounts in full to December 31, 1838; to submit a statement of Mission debts and credits; to take a classified census of inhabitants; to make monthly reports of expenditures; to pay no claims except upon government order; to prevent the unnecessary slaughter of cattle and the barter of horses and mules, with New Mexicans, for woolens.[31] At the same time the appointment of an inspector of Mission administration was announced — William E. P. Hartnell. The duties and powers of the latter, which Durán approved, included the enforcement of accounting and economy, and the suspending of *comisionados* from office.[32] By October 12, 1839, Hartnell had visited every mission from San Diego to Sonoma; and on March 1, 1840, Alvarado issued a *Reglamento de Misiones*, a feature of which was the substitution of moderately paid major-domos or stewards for excessively paid *comisionados*.[33] Hartnell made a second inspection tour under the *Reglamento* in 1840, but at Sonoma his authority was defied by Vallejo, and at San Luis Rey he was resisted by Pío Pico, and on September 7, he resigned.

The situation, as disclosed by Hartnell's tours, was one of ruin at nearly every mission. At San Luis Rey, San Juan Capistrano, and San Gabriel — establishments which in 1833 were yet the abode of thousands of neophytes, and where crops and livestock were yet abundant — there were left in 1839 and 1840 but a few hundred neophytes, neither well cared for nor well treated; and crops and stock were given over to peculation or neglect. But the most significant fact disclosed was, that in order to control the neophytes yet remaining, the old method of the padres, the method of the Mission of Córdova, of Las Casas, and of Junípero Serra alone was practicable. Despite the humanitarianism of republican Mexico, — a humanitarianism which, harking back to Borica and Neve, shrank from the flogging of recalcitrant neophytes, — it was found by Alvarado imperative to provide in his *Reglamentos* that the neophyte be made to work for the community and be "chastised moderately for his faults"; that there be enforced upon him morality and an attendance on religious duties; finally, that no *gente de razón* be allowed to settle among neophytes gathered in community. As for separate pueblos of Indians, such as had been set up by Figueroa at San Diego (Dieguito and San Pascual) and at San Luis Rey (Las Flores), they were already disintegrating. Even San Juan Capistrano, the most promising of them all, a pueblo with which special pains had been taken by both Figueroa and Alvarado, had been a failure, and as a distinctively Indian town was dissolved.[34]

The rule of Alvarado, a rule noteworthy for many things, was brought to an end by the appointment as governor on January 22, 1842, of Manuel Micheltorena.

CHAPTER XIV

ANGLO-AMERICANS

THE retirement of Alvarado from the Alta California governorship was effected chiefly by his kinsman and schoolmate Mariano Guadalupe Vallejo, the *comandante-militar*. First, however, with regard to those Anglo-Americans against whom Figueroa had been warned.

Under Spain, English and American residents in Alta California had been few; but in 1822 and the years immediately following, the number of residents English and American (English especially) fast increased. In June, 1822, there came the Englishmen Hugh McCulloch and William E. P. Hartnell (McCulloch, Hartnell & Company), and, the same year, William A. Richardson; while in 1824 came the highly influential Scotsman, David Spence. The men named were of substantial character, mercantile in their aims, and interested in the maintenance of a stable Mexican government. Of like qualities and pursuits were certain Americans, prominent among whom were John R. Cooper who came in 1823, W. G. Dana and Henry O. Fitch who came in 1826, John C. Jones and Alfred Robinson in 1829, Abel Stearns in 1830, John Warner in 1831, Thomas O. Larkin (afterwards United States Consul at Monterey) in 1832, and Jacob P. Leese in 1833.

But between 1830 and 1840 Anglo-Americans of a different type presented themselves. To the southwest of the Missouri River lay the ancient Mexican town of Santa Fé. Here trappers and traders — Yankee, English, and

French-Canadian — met to effect exchanges and to
organize expeditions; and hither adventurers and refugees
repaired, some of them finding their way into California.
Of such was Isaac Graham, who in 1836 had led an effective contingent for Alvarado against Gutiérrez. Graham's
vocation in 1840 was that of distiller near Monterey,
and his cabin was headquarters for men of roistering temper, — woodsawyers, ex-sailors, and the like; men without passports, yet who were not permitted to forget that
Mexico was a land where foreigners were required by law
to give an account of themselves. In April, 1840, a Gra-
hamite who thought himself in extremity, confessed to
Padre Suárez del Real of San Carlos that an uprising of
American settlers was in contemplation. Suárez notified
Alvarado, who in turn notified José Castro, prefect of the
northern district.[1]

The alarm was great. In a total population of two thousand adult males, the number of foreigners was between
four and five hundred.[2] Texas had achieved independence through its American element in 1836. If the Grahamites were tolerated further, might not independence
be the destiny of Alta California? Such evidently was the
conclusion, for Castro having by threats secured from one
of Graham's associates, William R. Garner, a declaration
that an uprising was imminent, and that Graham and
an Englishman, Albert Morris, were its promoters, laid
plans with secrecy, and between April 7 and May 8 arrested in the North, and at Santa Bárbara and Los
Ángeles, not less than one hundred and twenty men.
None were molested who had passports, or who were
married to native women, or who were honest and regular in their mode of life.[3]

Forty-six of the prisoners, shackled, and guarded by
Castro, were sent to San Blas, to be dealt with by the

Mexican Government.[4] On April 18, however, Thomas
J. Farnham — an American traveler from the Hawaiian
Islands — had reached Monterey. Warmly espousing the
cause of the prisoners, he gave them all possible aid and
followed them to Tepic, their ultimate destination. Here
he enlisted in their behalf the services of the British Consul, Mr. Eustace Barron. An earnest correspondence was
begun with the Mexican officials and with the British and
American ministers,[5] and though some twenty-six of the
accused were banished from Mexican territory, about
twenty (Graham and Morris among them) were purged
of conspiracy, awarded compensation, and in July, 1841,
restored to Alta California. As for Castro, he was tried
for cruelty, but was acquitted, and reached Monterey in
September.[6]

But there were Anglo-Americans other than those led
by Graham. On July 3, 1839, Johann August Sutter, a
native of Baden who had acquired citizenship in Switzer-
land, arrived at Monterey. His journey had involved a
trip to Santa Fé, a trip by the Oregon Trail to Vancouver,
and a voyage to Honolulu. Sutter was magnetic and tact-
ful, spoke (besides German) English, French, and Spanish,
and bore letters of introduction from officials of the Hudson's Bay and Russian-American companies, and from
Honolulu merchants. At Monterey, David Spence presented him to Alvarado, who, charmed with his bearing,
urged him to announce an intention of becoming a Mexican
citizen, and to select in the interior a tract of land, title
to which under Mexican law might be perfected within a
year. He was furnished with letters to Vallejo, upon whom
he called at Sonoma, and he paid a visit to Ross, the rock-
bound site of which, "dashed upon by the sea," impressed
him. Early in August he set out with a pinnace and two
hired schooners for the Sacramento River, landing after

eight days on the south bank of its tributary, the American. He had with him eight Kanakas, three white men, an Indian, and a bull-dog. Two temporary structures of poles and grass were built on high ground, and the settlement thus begun he christened New Helvetia.[7]

Sutter, by the summer of 1840, had ingratiated himself with the Western trappers, and shown resourcefulness with the Indians. In August, therefore, on completing his citizenship, he was made by Alvarado a Mexican official, a representative of the government on the frontiers of the Río Sacramento. Meanwhile Ross, — the settlement which Sutter had visited and admired, the settlement which as a Rezánoff legacy had disquieted Sola, and against which Echeandía had been ordered to plant a *villa*, — this settlement the Russian-American Company had definitely decided to abandon.[8] Between 1830 and 1839, Baron Wrangell, as Governor of Russian America, had made a resolute effort to secure from Mexico land southward of Ross to San Francisco, and eastward to the Sacramento, but without avail, and Ross by itself was not worth keeping. An offer of the buildings and livestock of the establishment was made to Vallejo in 1840 for 30,000 *pesos*. It was declined, and on December 13 the same offer was made to Sutter and accepted. And not only did Sutter buy the Russian movables, — he obtained a quitclaim to such title (or lack of title) as the Russians possessed to the land.[9]

Enriched by his Russian purchase, which included wooden buildings and some brass ordnance, Sutter in 1841 began the erection at New Helvetia of a fort of his own, a structure embracing an area of 150 by 500 feet. The fort in its finished condition, in 1845, is described as protected by adobe walls, eighteen feet high, with bastioned corners. As early as 1842 it boasted an armament of twelve guns. Indeed, by the year named, Sutter at New Helvetia was a veritable lord of the marches. His domains were eleven square leagues in extent. He owned 4200 cattle, 2000 horses, and 1900 sheep, and he trafficked profitably in beaver-skins. He commanded the routes westward from the United States and southward from Oregon. His trappers, ever welcome and quartered without price, were his willing retainers; while his Indians, taught blanket-weaving and hat-making, and organized in military companies, obeyed him like slaves. It is worthy of note that at the time of the Graham affair no question was raised regarding the strangers without passports — the sojourners at New Helvetia.

Grahamites and Sutterites combined, however, were not the only Anglo-Americans. There were others still, and by the autumn of 1841 they began to appear near Sonoma. In 1805, on November 7, Lewis and Clark had reached the mouth of the Columbia.[10] In 1811, Astoria had been founded. Taken by the British during the War of 1812, the post had been restored to the United States in 1818. In 1822, the Ashley Fur Company had been organized, and in 1826, Jedediah S. Smith had reached Alta California (at San Diego) from Salt Lake by a route to the Colorado and through the Mojave country. Smith in 1828 had been followed by Sylvester and James O. Pattie, whose destination had also proved to be San Diego, and in 1833, Joseph Walker, commissioned by Captain Bonneville, had reached Monterey.[11]

As for Jedediah Smith, the Patties, and others, they had either been banished eastward over the Rockies by Echeandía, or imprisoned. But could such a course be taken with the Americans who were approaching in 1841? It was the Bartleson-Bidwell Company — first overland emigrants from the Missouri — who were in question.

Sixty-nine strong, they on May 19 had quitted camp on
the Kansas River, — part of them for Oregon, the remainder for California. Sixty-nine strong, they had reached
the vicinity of Great Salt Lake by way of the Platte, —
South and North Forks, — South Pass, Green River, and
Bear Valley. Thence, by way of the desert, Mary [Hum-
boldt] River, Walker River, Sonora Pass, the Stanislaus
River, they on November 4, to the number of thirty-
two, had arrived at the rancho of Dr. John Marsh, near
the foot of Monte Diablo.[12]

The retirement of Alvarado from the Alta California
governorship in 1842 was due, it has been said, to Vallejo.
Soldier-bred, a disciplinarian and a warm patriot, the
presence of foreigners in Alta California — of Americans
especially — was distasteful to the latter as a menace to
the country. Graham at Monterey, Sutter on the Sacramento, the Bartleson emigrants at Marsh's rancho, what
did they one and all portend but evil?[13]

Complicating the situation was Alvarado himself.
Wearied by his wars with the South, he for the most part
had declined into sloth. In the words of Sir George Simpson, "from a spare Cassius-like conspirator, the Governor
had become a plump and paunchy lover of singing, dancing, and feasting." In December, 1841, the apprehensions
of Vallejo were suddenly confirmed. Northwest America,
including what is now Washington, Oregon, and Montana,
was the field of the Hudson's Bay Company. Relations
between the latter and Alta California were friendly, even
cordial. The Company never encroached, and early in
1841 an agreement was made with Alvarado whereby its
trappers might operate along the Sacramento. To this
agreement Sutter objected, on November 8, in an angry
letter which early came to the hands of Vallejo.

Very curious Rapports [wrote the lord of New Helvetia] come to me from belaw, but the poor wretches don't know what they do. I explained now Mr. Spence to explain these ignorant people, what would be the consequence if they do injure me, the first french freggate who came here will do me justice. The people don't know me yet, but soon they will find out what I am able to do. It is to late now to drive me aut of the country the first step they do against me is that I will make a Declaration of Independence and proclaim California for a Republique independent from Mexico. I am strong now, one of my best friends a German Gentleman came from the Columbia River with plenty people, another party is close by from Missouri. One of the party arrived here, some of my friends and acquaintances are among them, they are about 40 or 50 men of Respectability and property, they came in the intention to settle here. I am strong enough to hold me till the courriers go to the Waillamet for raise about 60 a 70 good men, an another party I would dispatche to the mountains and call the Hunters and Shawnees and Delawares with which I am very well acquainted, the same party have to go to Missouri and raise about 2 or 300 men more. That is my intention sir, if they lete me not alone, if they will give me satisfaction, and pay the expenses what I had to do for my security here, I will be a faithful Mexican, but when this Rascle of Castro should come here, a very warm and hearty welcome is prepared for him. 10 guns are well mounted for protect the fortress, and two field pieces, I have also about 50 faithful Indians which shot their musquet very quick. The whole day and night, we are under arms and you know that foreigners are very expensive, and for this trouble, I will be payed when a french Fregatte come here. I wish you tell the Comandante General Vallejo that I wish to be his friend, and that I am very much obliged for his kindness when my people passed Sonoma. But all is out question so long they let me alone and trouble me not, but I want security from the Government for that.[14]

Sutter, as Vallejo explained to Mexico, assumed the title of *Gobernador de Fortaleza de Nueva Helvecia*, made war on the neighboring Indians, and sold to service such of the Indian children as his wars reduced to orphanage. "I inclose his original letter," he concluded, "*cuerpo de delito infragable."* [15] But on December 9 the comandante was called upon to face the Bartleson Company. Informed by Marsh of the indispensability of passports, they had repaired to San José, where Vallejo met them, and from necessity issued to them temporary papers. "If," wrote the latter on the 11th, " there be realized the invasion that on all sides is threatened, the only certainty is that the Californians will die. I dare not assure myself that California will be saved." [16]

On December 11, 1841, it devolved upon Vallejo to report to Mexico the survey of San Francisco Bay and of the Sacramento and San Joaquín Rivers by a North American squadron under Captain Charles Wilkes, [17] and on the 12th to announce the sale to Sutter of Ross. The sale, he said, was a matter of no great satisfaction, for the Mexican flag had not been raised; and was there not fair chance that "the Russian eagle would be replaced by the Cruz Britanica"? He pointed out that the Hudson's Bay Company already "had foot" in California. They had established a house in the port of San Francisco, and they had secured territory on the Sacramento for the purposes of a colony.

What was needed, Vallejo urged, was two hundred soldiers assured of their pay; fewer civil officials; a reliable mail-service; reconstruction of the fort at San Francisco; the erection there of a wharf and custom-house; and colonization by Mexicans. Was not the land capable of every product, and yet did not the Californians purchase brandy from Catalonia, tobacco from Virginia, vinegar from Marseilles, cloth from Boston, manufactured goods from everywhere; even things the most common and trivial, as, for example, brooms from the Sandwich Islands? But above all else what was needed was a *jefe,* free from the bonds of consanguinity, to rule freely, firmly, and impartially, —

an end easily to be attained, provided such *jefe* were invested with both civil and military authority.[18]

These representations were emphasized by the arrival in the South of a party of twenty-five Americans from Santa Fé, — the Workman-Rowland party, so called; and on February 22, the Mexican Government notified Vallejo that there had been appointed to succeed Alvarado as *jefe político*, and himself as *comandante-militar*, a governor in whom the two offices were combined, namely, Manuel Micheltorena, general of brigade.[19]

The new Governor reached Los Ángeles late in September, 1842, attended by a force of about three hundred recruits, largely convicts. Setting out after a short interval for Monterey, he was met on the night of October 24, at his stopping-place near San Fernando Mission, by a letter from Alvarado, dated midnight of the 19th, stating that Monterey had just been surrendered to a squadron of United States ships, commanded by Commodore Thomas ap Catesby Jones. It had been Jones's surmise, first, that war had been declared between the United States and Mexico over Texas; and, second, that England had sent a squadron to seize California. On October 20, therefore, he had landed 150 marines, and raised over Monterey the American flag; but having on the 21st learned from Mexican newspapers that war had not been declared, he the same day had restored the Mexican colors, withdrawn his men, and fired a salute in apology.[20]

So far as Monterey was concerned, the incident was at an end; but Micheltorena invited Jones to meet him in personal conference at Los Ángeles, and on January 17, 1843, the commodore arrived at San Pedro Harbor. He was met by a squad of twenty-five lancers, and after a champagne dinner at the port, was conveyed in an "oak ark-barouche" to the southern capital. The party were entertained at the house of Abel Stearns. Here Jones met the beautiful Mexican wife of his host, and was presented to Micheltorena, who, with fifteen or twenty richly uniformed aides, awaited his coming. For an hour all was nod of plume and shimmer of gold and silver braid, when, the reception over and a ball arranged for the next evening, Jones, intrusted with the password, was ushered to his quarters.[21]

The business of Micheltorena, as it proved, was to present to the American commodore demands for indemnity — demands which it was known could not be entertained, but which later might not be without a tactical value.

But to recur to Mexico. As early as January 9, 1842, F. de Arrángoiz, the Mexican Consul at New Orleans, wrote to the Minister of Relations that the American Government had expressed a determination to acquire territory for a naval station between the Columbia River and Guayaquil. The consul advised that Americans be denied admission to California, and that all such as were domiciled without passports be expelled. On May 7, the same official announced that it was stated in the New Orleans papers that thirty American emigrants (the Bartleson Company), who had reached California without passports, had at first been put under arrest, but later had been liberated by order of the Governor and had had passports given them. Finally, on June 24, he wrote that at the end of May there had left Independence (Missouri) about one hundred individuals who said they were going to settle in Oregon, but who probably were destined for California.[22]

Arrángoiz's advice to deny to Americans admission to California could no longer be disregarded. Accordingly, on July 4, President Santa Anna issued instructions to Micheltorena, that from and after a date to be fixed by him "no individuals belonging to the United States were to be admitted to his department." [23]

The news from Arrángoiz had been disquieting enough, but on October 2, news more disquieting still was received from Juan N. Almonte, Mexican representative at Washington.

There can be no doubt [Almonte asserted], that of the thousand families that this year have emigrated from the States of Arkansas and Missouri, and the Territories of Tova [Iowa?] and Wisconseis in the direction of Oregon, more than a third part have gone with the intention of establishing themselves in Alta California. . . . I infer that the objects of these emigrants are not pure, and that there is involved a project that time will disclose. This I communicate to the end that the comandante-general of the department may be forewarned, not losing sight of the fact that this scheme of emigration may be in consonance with plans that the Texans some time since entertained concerning that beautiful land.

As a result of Almonte's letter, the order excluding Americans from California was reinforced by a second order, dated October 7, which was directed to be communicated to Micheltorena. [24]

A rumor that exclusion measures had been adopted reached the American Minister in Mexico, Waddy S. Thompson, on December 23; but although Thompson made a peremptory demand for revocation, no reply was elicited other than that the measures complained of were not directed against Americans *pacíficos y honrados*, but against those *inicuos*, *turbulentos*, and "unworthy the generous hospitality of the Mexican nation." [25] It is probable that Thompson's protest came early enough to enable the Mexican Government to recall the obnoxious instructions before Micheltorena received them. [26]

At all events, emigration to the Northwest flowed on unchecked. In 1843, it amounted to eight hundred persons. Of these the Hastings company (some thirty-six strong) and the Chiles-Walker company (about fifty) entered California, the first in one division, from Oregon, and the second in two divisions, one by way of Fort Boisé and New Helvetia,[27] and the other, by way of Owens River and Lake, the Tulares, and Gilroy's rancho.[28] In 1844, three companies came: one (twenty-five strong) under Lieutenant John C. Frémont by way of the Carson River;[29] a Kelsey contingent (thirty-six strong) by a route not definitely known; and the Stevens party (over fifty strong) by way of Truckee and Bear Rivers — line of the modern railway.[30] The companies of 1845 were six or seven in number, and their total membership was perhaps two hundred and fifty. One of them under Green McMahon — a party of which James W. Marshall, the discoverer of gold in California, was a member — came from Oregon. Of the others the best known were the Sublette, the Grigsby (wherein William B. Ide was enrolled), the Frémont-Walker party, and that of Lansford W. Hastings. Aside from the Oregon party, all entered California by the routes of the Sacramento or lower San Joaquín Valley, except the Walker party, which came by Owens River and Lake.

The Oregon Trail had now become a highway. From Independence (suburb of the present Kansas City) to the South Fork of the Platte River (Leroy, Nebraska, — 296 miles) the course was over undulous or rolling prairie sown with wild flowers, well supplied with game — elk, antelope, wild turkeys — and with wood, water, and grass. Its drawbacks were sultry heat, rattling thunder-storms, an occasional cyclone, a cattle stampede, and possible Indians. Along the South Fork — a stream broad and sluggish — the country was sandy, but it was the country of the buffalo, — buffalo by tens of thousands, buffalo as far as the eye could reach, buffalo for days together, buffalo in a herd which, pressing headlong, must at times be split by rifle volleys to save caravans from being trampled out of existence. To the North Fork of the Platte transition was made by Ash Hollow, and here the course increased in ruggedness, disclosing Court-House Rock, Chimney Rock, Scott's Bluffs, and, at a distance from Independence of 616 miles, the low walls of Fort Laramie. Thence the course led to Fort Bridger (southern Wyoming, 1070 miles), a stretch full of the picturesque — Independence Rock and Sweetwater Gap, South Pass marking the summit of the Rocky Mountains, and (beyond the divide) Green River, with anon in the distance the snow-capped peaks of the Wind River Range. Soda Springs on Bear River (1206 miles) came next, and here, or at Fort Hall, eighty miles distant, there disengaged itself from the Oregon Trail the trail for California.[31]

Of the California Trail the first and second stages — Fort Hall southwest to the head of Humboldt River (300 miles) and Humboldt River to its sink (about 350 miles) — were well defined. The first stage, skirting as it did the Salt Lake Desert, was arid, alkaline, and visited by thirst; while the second stage, semi-arid and short of game, was fatiguing from its monotony. As for the third stage, — the sink of the Humboldt to the Sacramento Valley, — it was the worst of the entire journey from Independence. At Humboldt Sink, the emigrant, as a test of his faith, found confronting him a stupendous barrier, that of the Sierra Nevada. Over it, starving and dogged by peril of snow-storms, he might struggle by Walker and Stanislaus Rivers, as did the Bartleson-Bidwell party of 1841; or by Owens River and Walker Pass, as did the Walker-Chiles

party of 1843; or by the route, harder than any other, of
Carson River, as did the Frémont party of 1844. It was
not until the arrival of the Elisha Stevens company in 1844,
late in December, that it was demonstrated that the route
the most practicable was that of the Truckee and Bear
Rivers.[32]

It will be remembered that in 1794 the northern boundary
of Alta California had been forced by the British southward to Fuca Strait, and that in 1812 the Russians had
sought to establish it at Bodega Bay. Now, by the American occupation of Oregon (coupled with the evacuation of
Ross), it was projected again northward to a point below
the valley of the Willamette.

Micheltorena, saved by the timely course of Waddy
Thompson from collision with intruding Americans, was
yet full of trouble. On June 12, 1843, Mexico had adopted
a Centralist Constitution more radical than the instrument of 1836. On November 1, Alta California cast a
unanimous vote for Santa Anna as president, and on
February 10, 1844, submitted a *terna* of names (the name
of Micheltorena first) for governor. But the old question of headship between Monterey and Los Ángeles remained undetermined, and Pío Pico, emulative of Bandini, plotted industriously to secure from the departmental assembly recognition for Los Ángeles. So menacing,
moreover, was deemed to be the attitude of the United
States, as shown by the seizure of Monterey by Jones, that
despair became enthroned in the Governor's heart. "The
latter country," he declared, was "extremely desirous of
an accession of eight hundred and more leagues of coast
of the highest fertility, of every climate, and of every
product. To be sure there was no gold, but there were
silver-quartz, limestone, salt, sulphur, and fur-bearing

animals." If clothing and money for his troops were not supplied, he could die, but that would not restore a province worth four times Texas, the most precious part of the Mexican Republic.[33]

Awaiting him, however, was trouble more immediate. His soldiers — ex-convicts at the best, and unpaid and unclothed — filled Monterey (as already they had filled Los Ángeles) with consternation by their thievery. Like the classic rogues in "Erminie," whom in respect to rags and tatters they resembled, they stole not alone from hunger, but from constitutional inability to withstand temptation. Pots, kettles, shirts, kerchiefs, chickens entangled by hook and line, — there was nothing that they did not steal. From the house of Mrs. Ord, daughter of José de la Guerra, they once, during a few moments' absence of the cook, filched an entire meal. Valuables they stole when possible. At a dance given in Los Ángeles by Don Vicente Sánchez, twelve Cholos employed as guards carried off a chest of jewelry; and it was by no means unusual for them to force pedestrians to stand and deliver at the point of the sword.[34]

The result of this insubordination was a revolt, led by Alvarado and José Castro. On November 22, 1844, Micheltorena left Monterey with 150 men, and within a few days was met by the rebellionists, 220 strong, near San José. After the feints and flourishes inevitable upon such occasions, there was concluded, on December 1, the treaty of Santa Terésa, whereby cause of complaint was removed through an agreement by the Governor to send his Cholos to San Blas.[35]

But the end was not yet. On the appointment of Micheltorena as governor, Vallejo had been made comandante of the northern frontier from Sonoma to Santa Inés, a district including the Sacramento. This had been galling

to Sutter, richer and prouder than ever; but (from desire
of more land) he had taken pains to cultivate the new
Governor and to become to him *persona grata* from the
start. While on a trip to Monterey with John Bidwell,
in October, 1844, Sutter had heard of the conspiracy on
the part of Castro and Alvarado against Micheltorena,
and had promised to aid the latter with a force of backwoodsmen and Indians. The campaign of Santa Terésa
had put the Governor at a disadvantage, but the treaty
could be violated. The signal was to be the appearance
of the New Helvetian in the field, backed by his Indians
and an American rifle corps.[36]

On January 1, 1845, Sutter, with Indians to the number
of about one hundred, with Dr. John Marsh, and with one
hundred riflemen under Captains John Gantt and Isaac
Graham, — the latter lusting for the blood of Alvarado,
— marched southward. Micheltorena — his treaty with
Alvarado and Castro canceled by proclamation — joined
Sutter at Salinas on the 9th. Meanwhile, the conspirators,
surprised, but with a small force, started for Los Ángeles.
Here Alvarado put Micheltorena in the wrong by a well-
worded appeal to the assembly,[37] and on February 14
and 15, after a refusal by the Governor (then with Sutter
at Santa Bárbara) to listen to argument, he declared him
deprived of office and superseded, provisionally, by the
senior *vocal*, Pío Pico.[38]

The opposing armies, each four hundred strong, met,
February 20, at Cahuenga, and artillery shots were exchanged at long range. The next day, at the Verdugo
Rancho, the armies met again, and at a range equally
long exchanged more shots. But on the side of Alvarado
there was a contingent of American backwoodsmen under
William Workman and B. D. Wilson, and these, commun-
icating with the Gantt-Graham contingent on the side of

Micheltorena and Sutter, resolved not to contend against one another. Shorn of his principal strength, Micheltorena promptly capitulated. Late in March, in accordance with a treaty signed on the 22d of February at San Fernando, whereby Pío Pico was recognized as governor and José Castro as comandante-general, the Governor and his troops were deported from Monterey to San Blas. As for Sutter, not only had his prestige suffered a hard blow, but he was in personal peril. "Sutter," wrote John C. Jones to Thomas Larkin, "has fallen, and I think, like Lucifer, never to rise again." [39]

Micheltorena was a Centralist and pro-Cleric, a brother in spirit to Victoria and Chico, — in brief, a reactionary; and Manuel Castañares, the representative of Alta California in the Mexican Congress, was of the same faith. Fervently had the latter set forth the needs of his department: the danger from Americans, the wretched plight of the Governor with his poverty-stricken force, the likelihood of revolution. [40] When, therefore, Micheltorena was overthrown, and news of the fact reached Mexico, it was deemed prudent to dispatch north a *comisionado* to placate sentiment, and at the same time, in view of possible complications with the United States, to occupy the country with a military force of six hundred picked men. For *comisionado*, there was chosen our acquaintance of other days, José María Híjar, and for military commander the accomplished soldier (fated never to reach his destination), Colonel Ignacio Iniestra. [41]

Híjar reached Santa Bárbara on June 8. Thence he proceeded to Los Ángeles, where, in December, after some mild official deliverances, he died. As a result of Híjar's coming, the Alta California assembly submitted to Mexico, on June 27, a *quinterna* of candidates for governor, Pío Pico being named first and Juan Bandini second; and on August 1 the department cast its vote for José Joaquín de Herrera as President of the Mexican Republic, — Santa Anna having on June 3 been forced into exile through a Federalist revolt provoked by heavy taxation.

"Ye gods," John C. Jones wrote to Larkin on March 21, 1845, "the idea of Pío Pico with the title of 'Excellency'!" But Pío Pico — a man of moderation — it now was; and with him (and with the selection by him of Juan Bandini as secretary) power came to the South, for at length Los Ángeles was recognized by the North as the departmental capital.[43]

The first thing of importance under Pío Pico was to complete the secularization of the missions. In 1836, on September 19, the Californias had been made by Mexico an independent diocese, to the bishop whereof the Pious Fund was to be intrusted.[44] On April 27, 1840, Fray Francisco García Diego, president of the Zacatecans in Alta California, was approved as bishop, and by January 11, 1842, he had established his episcopal residence at Santa Bárbara, where, for nominal pay but from a throne canopied in crimson and gold, he was prepared to dispense ecclesiastical justice.[45]

With the Pious Fund of the Californias controlled by a California ecclesiastic, the opportunity for a pro-clerical governor to oust the wasteful *comisionados* from the missions was too valuable to be lost, and on March 29, 1843, Micheltorena issued a decree restoring to Mission management (temporal as well as spiritual) the twelve establishments — San Diego, San Fernando, San Luis Rey, San Juan Capistrano, San Gabriel, San Buenaventura, Santa Bárbara, Purísima, Santa Inés, Santa Clara, San Antonio, and San José. The restoration was on condition that one eighth of the total annual produce of each mission be paid into the public treasury, and was carried out (in so far as carried out at all) under Joaquín Jimeno and Narciso Durán, respectively, president and prefect of the Fernandinos, and under José María de Jesús Gonzales, president of the Zacatecans.[46]

It was not long that Bishop Francisco was able to maintain himself by virtue of the Pious Fund. On February 8, 1842, at the behest of Santa Anna, the Mexican Congress passed a decree restoring the administration of the fund to the supreme government; and this decree, on October 24, was followed by one directing a sale of the Pious Fund estates, and the covering of the entire proceeds into the national treasury as a loan.[47] Thus practically had come to an end a fund which, established by Salvatierra in 1697, had under Ugarte and his successors supplied the missions, first of Baja and then of Alta California, with money for stipends, foundations, and subsistence down to 1810, — a fund which, though since 1810 diverted in Mexico as to its proceeds, had until 1842 been kept well intact as to its principal.[48]

In February, 1844, the missions subject to the Franciscans were thus described by Durán: "Three (San Miguel, San Luis Obispo, and San Diego) as *in toto* abandoned; two (Santa Inés and San Buenaventura) as moderately equipped"; and the remaining nine as "destroyed, and their neophytes demoralized." It no doubt was the condition of the missions as thus described that led the departmental assembly in August to pass a vote ordering a sale, an hypothecation, or a leasing of the mission properties, to provide means for defense, in case of aggression by the United States.[49]

No action under the vote of the assembly proved to be necessary in 1844, but in 1845 (October 28) there was issued by Pío Pico a *Reglamento* (based on a departmental decree of May 28 framed largely in accordance with the views of Prefect Durán) under which the then abandoned establishments (Zacatecan and Fernandino) San Rafael, Dolores(San Francisco), Soledad, San Miguel, and Purísima were to be sold at public auction. The establishments yet occupied (mission pueblos), San Luis Obispo, Carmelo (San Carlos), San Juan Bautista, and San Juan Capistrano, were also to be sold, but with a reservation in each instance of church and parsonage. The ten other establishments were to be rented to the highest bidder for a term of nine years. Where there were Indians (ex-neophytes), they were to be free to go or remain as they listed, and if remaining to receive title to their lands. Each mission pueblo was to be self-governed under four Indian *celadores* (watchmen) chosen monthly and subject to the justices of the peace of the locality. In case of sale, the proceeds after payment of debts were to be for the support of public worship.[50]

By July 7, 1846, — date of the formal cessation of Mexican rule in Alta California, — there had been sold by Pío Pico, under the decree of May 28, 1845, and a further decree of March 30, 1846, all of the missions save San Francisco, San Carlos, Santa Cruz, San Antonio, and San Francisco Solano. The sales were to individual purchasers, and for the most part were in contravention of an order by the Mexican Government (reflecting Centralism) that Micheltorena's re-transfer to the padres should not be disturbed.[51]

With the Pious Fund virtually confiscated in Mexico, and with the mission establishments sold and their neophytes dispersed in Alta California, both Bishop Francisco García Diego and Prefect Narciso Durán — chagrined, disappointed, and disheartened — laid down the burden of existence, the one in May, and the other in June, 1846. The Alta California Mission, the work of Córdova and Las Casas, the work of Kino, of Salvatierra, and of Ugarte, the work of Junípero Serra and of Francisco Palou, was dead.

The object of the Mission, under the Laws of the Indies, was everywhere to secularize the Indian; to municipalize him by reducing him to a condition of pueblo life, of civic autonomy. But no pueblo the result of Secularization long survived. The shortest lived were the pueblos purely Indian, — San Dieguito, San Pascual, and Las Flores. In the mission pueblos, ex-neophytes were not as such permitted to vote; local officers (*alcalde, regidores*, and *síndico*) being chosen by the *gente de razón* and *emancipados ;* yet even so, none lasted.[52] Vallejo at Sonoma, by availing himself of the municipal organization of the Híjar colonists, did succeed in replacing a mission (San Francisco Solano) by an enduring pueblo, but the instance is unique.

Nor may surprise be felt. Even with the *gente de razón*, it was by the slowest degrees that pueblo life in Alta California was established. Felipe de Neve founded San José and Los Ángeles, and Borica the *villa* Branciforte, yet throughout the Spanish régime civil rule in these communities was merely nominal. The rule actually exercised was that of the Governor's *comisionado* — military rule. Arrillaga, it will be remembered, deemed it farcical and supererogatory for him to qualify as *jefe político*. Under Mexico the *comisionados* were withdrawn, but the pueblos did not improve. As late as 1846, San José was described as "a village of 600 to 800 inhabitants in a fine valley [Santa Clara] of adobe buildings and very irregular streets, with thousands of ground squirrels burrowing in the plaza, and

men and women of all classes engaged in gambling";
while Los Ángeles, with a population of perhaps 1250, and
not without indication of public improvements, was nevertheless (for its gambling, murders, and lewdness) of repute
so evil as to be portrayed to Sir George Simpson as a "den
of thieves, — the noted abode of the lowest drunkards
and gamblers of the country." It was no better with Branciforte. Its *comisionado* was gone, and by union with the
ex-mission of San José it had risen in population to 470
souls; but morally it was profligate, and politically it
remained subject to Monterey, where it had been placed
in 1835.

The establishments best fitted for municipalization
were the presidios. As fortresses they had fallen to de-
cay, but otherwise they were improved. They were seaports, and as such gathered to themselves inhabitants and
developed activity. San Diego, which in 1827 is described
by the traveler Duhaut-Cilly as "without doubt the best
port geographically in all California," had in 1835 been
made a municipality by the introduction of an *ayuntamiento*, and in 1840 consisted of fifty adobe structures.
Santa Bárbara, which in 1827 had been "a closed square
surrounded with houses of a single story," — some "sixty
to eighty of them, each with its little garden," — had
become a municipality in 1834, and in 1842 consisted
of perhaps 900 inhabitants — their houses "whitewashed
adobes with painted balconies and verandas." Monterey,
which in 1825 had been a presidial quadrangle with forty
houses outside the walls, had in 1826 been made a municipality by the election of a full *ayuntamiento*, and in 1841
consisted of a population of about 500, housed, except
when on horseback, which was "almost always," in the
usual adobes. Finally, San Francisco, which in 1825 had
as a presidio consisted of "120 houses and a church,"

had become a municipality in 1835, and by 1846 — counting the fifty souls of the new village of Yerba Buena, added in 1840 — possessed a total of about 300.[53]

In promoting municipalization, Governor Figueroa was foremost. He introduced *ayuntamientos* at San Diego and San Francisco, and perfected them at Santa Bárbara and Monterey.[54] Under Alvarado the movement, though progressive, was conducted on lines less liberal. In 1837, under the Centralist Constitution of 1836, prefectures, *partidos,* and justices of the peace were introduced. *Ayuntamientos* were restricted to the capital, to communities where they had existed prescriptively, to seaports of a population of 4000, and to pueblos of a population of 8000. Places deprived of *ayuntamientos* were to be governed by justices of the peace, who were to be proposed by the sub-prefects, nominated by the prefects, and approved by the governor. The first effect of this system, so far as Alta California was concerned, was to abolish *ayuntamientos* at all points except Los Ángeles (the capital), and San José, Monterey, and Branciforte, — places entitled to them by prescription. Its second effect was to systematize the judiciary.

Judicial recourse under Spain (*vide* chapter VII) was first to the presidial comandante, or pueblo *comisionado,* and then to the governor. It remained unchanged under Mexico save as change was effected by the removal of the *comisionados.* California by 1828 had been brought within the jurisdiction of a circuit court for Sinaloa and Sonora; and by 1830 in that of a district court nominally within Alta California borders.[55] In 1831 the President of the Mexican Republic advised that the system of *alcalde* rule, which on the removal of the *comisionados* had become completely established, should be superseded by that of *jueces de letras* or district judges; but Victoria declared that the distances were such that one judge would be insufficient.

He furthermore declared that so ignorant and seditious was the Alta California population, that they could be ruled only by a system purely military; the Governor himself having been compelled to suspend the territorial *diputación*.[56]

A supreme court for the territory was prescribed by law in 1837 (a tribunal of four members with a *fiscal* and *procurador*), but it could not be organized until 1842.[57] Even then it was little in session, owing to the disinclination of the Southerners, who controlled it, to meet at Monterey. Micheltorena, who abolished the prefectures to save expense, reorganized this court; but under Pío Pico, by whom the prefectures were restored, it was superseded by a court to consist of two justices and a *fiscal*, — a body which came into existence not at all.[58]

American emigration to Alta California came for the most part by the Oregon Trail, but in some part it came by way of Santa Fé, New Mexico. This fact now assumes a degree of importance in connection with measures taken by Pío Pico against New Mexican horse-thieves.

Aside from John A. Sutter, the Alta Californian most successful in managing the Indians was Mariano Guadalupe Vallejo. The tribes of the North were less docile than those of the central region, and an officer like Vallejo — one regardful of ceremony and the high proprieties, yet upon occasion willing and able to strike home — appealed to the Indian heart. But if between 1834 and 1846 order among the Indians was preserved near Sonoma, such was not the case to the southward. How, under the Mission, Indians, both neophyte and Gentile, had learned to ride, and how, by a diminution of military force, coupled with a failure to plant a presidio in the Tulares, the thing feared by Rivera y Moncada had resulted, and the southern neophyte, seduced by the Colorado tribes, had waxed insolent, — all this we have seen in chapter xi. But with regard to the particular phase assumed by the insolence of the Indians, it remains to be said that it was horse-stealing. "Crossing the Tulare Valley and the mountains that surround it," Payéras wrote in 1818, "they [the Indians] kill the horses and eat them." And Payéras's testimony is confirmed by that of John Bidwell. "We came," he says (recalling the days of 1841), "to a place in the Sierra Nevada where there was a great quantity of horse-bones, and we did not know what it meant; we thought that an army must have perished there. They were of course horses that the Indians had driven in there and slaughtered."

But horse-stealing was not practiced by Indians alone; it was resorted to by Mexican traders. Since 1824 cara-vans of wagons had made annual trips from Independence, Missouri, to Santa Fé, with stocks of cottons and calicoes, and the route pursued had become famous as the Santa Fé Trail.[59] The trail, however, did not altogether terminate at Santa Fé. As early as 1828 an American trapper of that town — Sylvester Pattie — had worked his way, by the course of the Gila River and Colorado Desert, into Baja and Alta California; and between 1829 and 1833 the trap-pers William Wolfskill, David E. Jackson, and Ewing Young had reached Alta California, the first by way of Taos and the Mojave River to Los Ángeles, and the others more directly by way of the Gila. Wolfskill was accom-panied by a few New Mexicans, and it being discovered that in exchange for *serapes* and blankets large, well-formed, serviceable mules could be obtained, a brisk trade was begun between Santa Fé and Los Ángeles.[60] In this trade the caravans were composed of pack-animals, and during the thirteen or fourteen years, 1833–1846, that the trade flourished, those engaged in it (including bands of Canadians and Americans) proved to be even more expert as horse- and mule-thieves than as merchants.

A favorite field of operations between 1838 and 1841 was the line of ranchos from San José pueblo to San Juan Bautista Mission, and another favorite field the Los Ángeles-Santa Bárbara district as far north as San Luis Obispo.[61] Raids were now at times attended by arson, by ravishing, and by killing, and culprits when taken were given short shrift. Knowing their peril, a band of thieves — Indians, Mexicans, Americans — would descend upon a Tulare rancho, stampede its horses, and push thundering across the valley for the Puerto del Cajón, beyond which they were comparatively safe. Pursuit was a task not coveted, and men were secured for it only at good wages, and then with difficulty. Especially was this true at Los Ángeles, for in the South the marauders were often Americans expert with the rifle.

In April, 1840, a daring theft of horses was made from San Luis Obispo Mission, and on May 30 Juan B. Leandro, informing the prefect of the results of a pursuit, stated that the thieves, though overtaken on the 25th at the Wells of Ramón, about one hundred leagues distant in the desert, had fled, leaving some baggage, a few horses tied, and about 1500 slaughtered. The pursuers had seen other bands of thieves with more than 1000 horses that had been stolen in small lots. "The robbers composing the rear-guard," Leandro naïvely observed, "were about twenty citizens of the United States."[62]

Resolving to put a stop to depredations, Pío Pico, on the surrender of Micheltorena in 1845, made a compact with Captain John Gantt and Dr. John Marsh to attack the *rancherías* of the lower San Joaquín and of the Merced Rivers, and deliver the captives to "Señor Sutter."[63] On his own part he organized (with what result does not appear) a movement in the South.

As already intimated, the Santa Fé Trail west of Santa Fé was but a trail of the footman and pack-mule.[64] There were two branches, — a southern branch (the general course of Anza) and a northern one, the course in part of Garcés; a course exploited in opposition to that of Anza by Governor Antonio Crespo of Sonora. In 1845, as in all the years from Anza's expedition to the expedition of José Romero, the desert awaited its master.

CHAPTER XV

WAR WITH THE UNITED STATES

"As military men, the Californians have been underrated." Lieutenant
J. B. Montgomery to Lieutenant-Colonel P. St. George Cook, January 18,
1847.

I

WHALING and the port of San Francisco were
what first drew to California the attention of the
United States Government. But a word with regard to
"hides and tallow."

Under Spain the hide and tallow trade had been confined
to government vessels like the Flora, the ship that brought
such disaster to Mr. George Washington Eayrs. But
under Mexico, with its policy of open ports, the trade became extended to the Bostonians John R. Cooper, William A. Gale, Nathan Spear, and Bryant & Sturgis, and to
the Englishmen David Spence, and McCulloch, Hartnell
& Company. In 1826 there were in California not less than
200,000 head of cattle. At the private ranchos, slaughter
(*matanza*) took place yearly, and at the missions weekly.
The hides, when not sold green, were staked out to dry;
while the tallow was "tried" and run into bags of bullock-
skin (*botas*), each with a capacity of an *arroba*, — twenty-
five pounds. An agent or supercargo (we are told by
Thomas O. Larkin) would fit up a store on board ship
with shelves, show-cases and drawers, and from it dispense
tea or shot, from a pound to a box or bag; and silk or calico,
from a yard to a bale. Men, however, like William H.
Davis (agent for Nathan Spear), or Alfred Robinson

(agent for Bryant & Sturgis), were too energetic to wait the coming of buyers to the ship. They either brought them in the ship's boats, or personally visited the ranchos and missions, penetrating to the remotest establishments around the bays of San Francisco and San Pedro.[1]

The ports of California were "open," but the term was relative. At first it applied to all ports, and the duties were moderate, averaging about 25 per cent. Later, foreign vessels were permitted to trade at presidial ports only, the way-places Santa Cruz, San Luis, Refugio, San Juan Capistrano, being closed, except to such as might enter them by favor; and the duties were increased to an average of 42.5 per cent. Still later (January, 1828) all way-ports were closed to foreign vessels, except San Pedro, and in July it also was closed. This was followed by the closing to foreigners of every port of Lower and Upper California, except Loreto and Monterey; although in Upper California San Diego was kept open by special license. Monterey itself was not granted a customs building till 1837.

As a result of the conditions named, smuggling recurred, and the Sandwich Islands were built up at California's expense. Martínez had pointed out to the Viceroy as early as 1788 that foreigners, by using Hawaii as a haven of refuge and a source of food, were to menace Spanish supremacy, and his words were significant. In 1820, seven American missionaries from New England had landed at the Islands. They, who of course were Protestant, were followed in 1827 by two Catholic padres, Alexis Bachelot and Patrick Short. In 1831, the padres were banished by order of the Hawaiian native government; and in 1843, "Mr. Coan," pastor of the Protestant congregation at Honolulu, wrote: "The power and grace of our God have hitherto preserved us from these 'ravening wolves.' Adored be his name!"[2]

But be the attitude of the New Englanders what it might, prosperity grew under their sway. A whaler (the Mary) arrived the first year. In 1827 the ship-yard and wharf of Robinson & Company were built. In 1836 a newspaper in English, the "Sandwich Island Gazette," was established, with an American editor. Indeed, so far as trade and ideas were concerned, Honolulu by 1836 was a distant suburb of Boston. People after siesta read the "Transcript" and Dr. Lyman Beecher's lectures. At Monterey whalers were allowed to purchase provisions by selling a limited quantity (four hundred dollars worth) of manufactures. At Honolulu they might purchase provisions by selling any quantities of manufactures. It was estimated in 1844 that the annual whaling-trade at the Islands was worth at least two hundred and fifty thousand dollars. Said the "California Star" in 1848, "If we allow a fair proportion of the trade with whalers, merchantmen, and men-of-war to be transferred [from Honolulu] to the coast, it will make an immediate change of about half a million a year."

But what of smuggling? By the more timid it was conducted through the method, time-honored and genteel, of the *douceur* or "gratification." The bolder traders — those with a taste for adventure — preferred to "transship" the valuable part of a cargo at one of the Santa Bárbara Channel Islands or at some retired nook of the mainland coast, and, having paid duties on the remainder, to return to the rendezvous, reship, and proceed with the voyage. The Sandwich Island traders, Master John Lawler of the Karimoko, and Captain John Bradshaw of the Franklin, were guilty of transshipment practices in more than an ordinary degree. Lawler made his rendezvous at the Island of Catalina, while Bradshaw's favorite resorts were in Lower California. The latter was arrested in 1828 at San Diego, but, like his predecessor of the Lelia Byrd, managed to get aboard his vessel and run the gauntlet of the defenses, the whole ship's company deriding the Mexican flag, as, pursued by forty cannon-shot, they sped past it seaward.

We are indebted to the trade in hides and tallow for "Two Years Before the Mast," by Richard H. Dana, Jr., of Boston, who first in the Pilgrim and then in the Alert traversed the California coast in 1834–36. Of San Juan Capistrano, Dana says: —

The country here for several miles is high table-land running boldly to the shore and breaking off in a steep cliff at the foot of which the waters of the Pacific are constantly dashing. . . . The rocks were as large as those of Nahant or Newport, but to my eye more grand and broken. Besides, there was a grandeur in everything around, which gave a solemnity to the scene, a silence and solitariness which affected every part! Not a human being but ourselves for miles, and no sound heard but the pulsations of the great Pacific. . . . Reaching the brow of the hill . . . we found several piles of hides, and Indians sitting around them. One or two carts were coming slowly from the Mission, and the Captain told us to begin and throw the hides down. This, then, was the way they were to be got down, — thrown down one at a time, a distance of four hundred feet. . . . Standing on the edge of the hill and looking down the perpendicular height, the sailors

> That walked upon the beach,
> Appeared like mice; and our tall anchoring bark
> Diminished to her cock; her cock a buoy
> Almost too small for sight.

But it is not alone "Two Years Before the Mast" that we owe to the hide and tallow trade. Indirectly we owe to it Alfred Robinson's "Life in California." Dana's book, though charming, lacked in appreciation of the Californians; and to present in this respect a truer picture, Robinson, in 1846, wrote his book, — one hardly less charming than its predecessor.

II

As has been remarked in chapter xiv, San Francisco in 1846 contained about three hundred *gente de razón*.[3] Of this population by far the most active portion was that identified with Yerba Buena, the anchorage to the south of Telegraph Hill. In 1842 the settlement consisted of but ten or a dozen houses, all near the waterside (Montgomery Street);[4] and the principal residents were William A. Richardson, William Hinckley, Nathan Spear, Jacob P. Leese, Jean Jacques Vioget, and William G. Rae. Rae was local factor of the Hudson's Bay Company. Alvarado had conceded a franchise for the Company to Chief Factor James Douglas in 1841, and its actual presence in 1842 gave rise to a solicitude regarding California that was general. The feeling was entertained not only by Californians, but by England, France, and the United States.

Sir George Simpson, governor-in-chief of the Hudson's Bay Company, and John McLoughlin, the company's chief factor on the Pacific Coast, visited San Francisco, Monterey, and Santa Bárbara in January, 1842. Lord Palmerston, British Foreign Secretary, had just quitted office, and officials everywhere were under the influence of his assertive temper. In 1841 James Douglas had noted in his journal: "We have . . . objects [in entering California] of a political nature."[5] It appears that such objects were not alien to the mind of Sir George Simpson. Addressing Sir John Petty, governor of the Hudson's Bay Company, on March 10, 1842, the former said: —

This sale [of Ross to Sutter] was effected previously to my arrival, otherwise it is probable I should have made a purchase of the establishment for the Hudson's Bay Company with a view to the possibility of some claim being based thereon by Great Britain at a future period. . . . The Governor [Alvarado], who seven years ago was appraiser of custom-house goods, is an ignorant, dissipated man, quite devoid of respectability and character; and the commander of the forces [Vallejo], the next in rank and standing, who was a few years back a lieutenant in the army, has no pretension to character or respectability, and, like most others in the country, betrays a gross want of honesty and veracity, while much jealousy and ill-will exists between these great men, who are total strangers to every feeling of honor, honesty or patriotism, and, I believe, are ready to sell themselves and their country at a moment's notice, to the highest bidder. . . . Many of the British residents are much respected, and the feeling of the different classes of the natives is favorable to Great Britain, while they look upon the United States, and her citizens, with much jealousy and alarm. . . . I have reason to believe they would require very little encouragement to declare their independence of Mexico, and place themselves under the protection of Great Britain.[6]

A circumstance tending at this time to invoke Palmerstonian methods was the Graham affair. Barron, the British vice-consul at Tepic (instigated by the American Thomas J. Farnham), had been active in behalf of the Grahamites through representations to Minister Pakenham in Mexico; and on August 30, 1841, the latter had written to Palmerston that it was by "all means desirable, in a political point of view, that California, once ceasing to belong to Mexico should not fall into the hands of any power but England." It was to be regretted, he said, that "advantage should not be taken of the arrangement some time since concluded by the Mexican Government with their creditors in Europe, to establish an English population in the magnificent Territory of Upper California." Especially was this to be regretted, as there was "reason to believe that daring and adventurous speculators in the United States had already turned their thoughts in that direction [i. e., control of California]."[7]

But Palmerston could no longer be approached, and the

pacific Lord Aberdeen, his successor, dismissed the Pakenham suggestions with promptness. In 1842, however, the
British Minister appointed a vice-consul at Monterey,
James A. Forbes, and it soon became evident that the
opinion of Simpson and Barron that California was inclined toward a British protectorate was not without
foundation. In September, Forbes was waited upon by
a body of native Californians, and the question was put to
him: "Whether this country can be received under the
protection of Great Britain, in a similar manner to that
of the Ionian Isles, but to remain for the present under the
direct government of one of its natives, though under
the same form as the government of that Republic."[8]

To this question, submitted by Forbes through Barron,
the British Secretary replied, on December 31, 1844, that
while Great Britain could not interfere as between California and Mexico, still she "would view with much dissatisfaction the establishment of a protectoral power over
California by any other foreign state."[9] Aberdeen's change
of attitude had been caused by fear of expansion of the
United States through the annexation of Texas.[10] What
Great Britain now looked forward to with satisfaction
was a Texas and a California both independent of Mexico,
and both at the same time independent of the United
States.

So far as France was concerned, solicitude for California was that rather of the reflective observer than the
politician. Pérouse in 1786 and Duhaut-Cilly in 1827 had
each reported intelligently upon the country; and in
August, 1839, Captain Cyrille Pierre Théodore Laplace
had visited Ross, San Francisco, and Monterey, in the
Artémise. His description of the California women —
*jolies, gracieuses, bien faites, de grands yeux noirs au
regard expressif, de belles dents bien blanches, une longue*

*chevelure couleur de jais digne de leur descendance anda-
louse* — recalls the word-portrait of Doña Concepción
by Langsdorff. What political element the French position involved was emphasized by the visit of M. Eugène
Duflot de Mofras in 1841. He came from Mexico, where
he was attaché, by way of the coast states, and, having
stopped at Monterey and San Francisco, passed to Fort
Vancouver, whence he returned to San Francisco in the
same ship with Sir George Simpson and John McLoughlin.
In Mofras's opinion, it was the fate of California "to be
conquered by Great Britain or the United States, unless it
placed itself under the protection of some European monarchy — preferably France. . . . All the people," he said,
"were by religion, manners, language, and origin naturally
antipathetic to the English and to the Americans." [11]

Between Mofras and Vallejo (precisians and martinets)
no love was lost, and the anxieties of the latter regarding the Anglo-Americans, the Hudson's Bay Company, and
Sutter were increased by anxiety regarding the possible
intentions of His Majesty, Louis Philippe. "There is no
doubt," wrote Vallejo to Alvarado in July, "that France
is intriguing to become mistress of California"; [12] and,
to confirm the suspicion, the French Government, on
November 18, 1847, appointed a vice-consul of its own
at Monterey, M. Louis Gasquet.

It was the United States, however, as Sir George Simpson pointed out, toward which California had come to feel
alarm genuine and immediate. So long as the country was
known at a distance, — known, that is, through a few serviceable representatives like Stearns, Robinson, and Larkin,
and (be it said) like Mr. George Washington Eayrs, — she
was respected and even admired. Tired of Mexico, — her
Victorias, her Chicos, her Cholos, and her tariff, — and

eager for a rule of "native sons," the American theory of government appealed to the California leaders, padres no less than politicians. "When will your government come and take possession of this country?" asked the padres of Alfred Robinson; while as for the politicians, one at least (Alvarado) exalted Washington. During the contest with Gutiérrez, Don Juan Bautista had thought of qualified independence for the land under some protectorate foreign yet benign, — possibly that of the United States.

But the United States was a power whereof the Californians were destined to gain a nearer view. In 1826 and 1827 Captain Frederick William Beechey (H. M. S. Blossom) had visited California while awaiting the arrival of Sir John Franklin from the Arctic regions, and in 1831 had published an account of his voyage. It was evident, Beechey wrote, that California must awaken from the lethargy by which it was possessed "under the present authorities or fall into other hands. . . ." It was of "too much importance to be permitted to remain longer in its present neglected state."[13] But before the coming of Beechey, California had been visited by an American skipper, Captain Benjamin Morrell, Jr., of the Tartar, and in 1832 Morrell likewise had published a book. "These beautiful regions [were they but the property of the United States] would not," he said, "be permitted to remain neglected." "The eastern and middle states would pour into them their thousands of emigrants, until magnificent cities would rise on the shores of every inlet along the coast, while the wilderness of the interior would be made to blossom like the rose."[14]

The observations of Morrell show that even thus early the United States was not indifferent to California's future; and in 1835 President Andrew Jackson, mindful of whaling interests on the Northwest Coast, authorized the American chargé in Mexico, an old comrade in arms, Colonel Anthony Butler, to purchase "the whole bay of San Francisco." It was suggested that a line be run northward along the east bank of the Río Bravo del Norte to the thirty-seventh parallel, and then west to the Pacific. Monterey might be excluded from the purchase, as it was not the desire of the United States "to interfere with the actual settlements of Mexico on the Pacific Coast."

But the inception of the movement for the acquisition of California lies further back. In 1819 Spain had ceded to the United States all her North American territory west of the Mississippi River to the northward of the forty-second parallel, — to the northward, that is, of Texas, New Mexico, and California. President John Quincy Adams contemplated acquiring Texas in 1825, but quitted office without actual overtures, and in 1829 Adams was succeeded by Jackson, who offered five million dollars. The offer was made through Butler, but failed, and in 1835 the chargé came to Washington. While there he submitted a new plan of operations. Texas was to be secured by bribing Hernández, Santa Anna's confessor. "Five hundred thousand, judiciously applied," Hernández had assured Butler, "would conclude the matter." The treaty, Butler said, "would be the first of a series which must at last give us dominion over the whole of that tract of territory known as New Mexico, and the higher and lower California, an empire in itself, a paradise in climate, . . . rich in minerals, and affording a water route to the Pacific through the Arkansas and Colorado Rivers."[15]

Naught came of the plan, and in 1841 John Tyler became President, with Daniel Webster as Secretary of State, and Waddy Thompson as Minister to Mexico. In 1842, on April 29, Thompson informed Webster that he was convinced that Mexico would cede Texas and the Californias in payment of claims by American merchants.

As to Texas [he said], I regard it as of but little value compared with California, the richest, the most beautiful, and the healthiest country in the world. Our Atlantic border secures us a commercial ascendency on the Pacific. The harbor of San Francisco is capacious enough to receive the navies of the world. In addition to which California is destined to be the granary of the Pacific. It is a country in which slavery is not necessary, and therefore, if that is made an objection, let there be another compromise. France and England both have had their eyes upon it. The latter has yet. I am profoundly satisfied that in its bearing upon all the interests of our country, the importance of the acquisition of California cannot be over-estimated.[16]

The proposition of Thompson was accepted by Webster to the extent of authorizing negotiations for "a good harbor on the Pacific." Great Britain was consulted, and Lord Aberdeen (his original attitude as yet unchanged) gave assurance that "the Queen's Government . . . had not the slightest objection to an acquisition of territory [by the United States] in that direction."[17] Then (October, 1842) came the seizure of Monterey by Commodore Jones and negotiations ceased.

They were resumed in 1845 under James K. Polk. Texas had been annexed on March 1, and it now was intended (so Polk himself declared[18]) to enter if possible into diplomatic relations with Mexico, and secure California by purchase. The Mexican Government was responsible in various amounts to American merchants; let these amounts be liquidated by a cession of territory. To manage the affair, representatives were required at two points, — Mexico City and Monterey. John Slidell accordingly was dispatched as plenipotentiary to the one, while at the other Thomas O. Larkin, who had served as

United States Consul since April 2, 1844, was made "confidential agent." On July 10, 1845, Larkin had warned the American Government of the maintenance by France and England of consulates in California, and of the fact (so believed) that Mr. Rae had in 1844 furnished the Californians with arms and money to enable them to expel the Mexicans from the country; and it was because of this warning that the confidential agency was created.

You should exert the greatest vigilance [the consul was instructed on October 17] in discovering and defeating any attempts which may be made by foreign governments to acquire a control over that country. In the contest between Mexico and California we can take no part, unless the former should commence hostilities against the United States ; but should California assert and maintain her independence, we shall render her all the kind offices in our power as a Sister Republic. . . . The President could not view with indifference the transfer of California to Great Britain or any other European power. . . . On all proper occasions you should not fail prudently to warn the government and people of California of the danger of such an interference [by Great Britain or France] to their peace and prosperity, — to inspire them with a jealousy of European dominion, and to arouse in their bosoms that love of liberty and independence so natural to the American Continent. . . . If the people should desire to unite their destiny with ours, they would be received as brethren. . . . The President has thought proper to appoint you a confidential agent in California; and you may consider the present dispatch as your authority for acting in that character.[19]

Thus in 1845 the United States placed herself toward California in the exact position in which Great Britain had placed herself in 1844. That is to say, she would welcome independence with a view to acquisition. Further than this there was to be a difference. Great Britain as a suitor was to be observant and passive. The United States was to be observant and active.

But to complicate matters for the latter, there arose just here the fact of the "nearer view." Graham and his followers had ridiculed California officials and defied California laws. The land, moreover, was fast filling with American settlers of whom the greater part, though not like the Grahamites, were yet little tolerant of what to them were institutions paternal and antiquated. For Larkin, therefore, to inspire among Californians a wish to "unite their destiny" with that of his countrymen was a task not without difficulty. Leading men (José Castro, more especially) gave the new agent to understand that they might not object to the United States, provided, in the event of a transfer of allegiance, they could be assured of their positions and salaries.[20] On April 27, Larkin wrote to Jacob P. Leese at Sonoma, Abel Stearns at Los Ángeles, and John Warner at San Diego (all Mexican citizens, but all former Americans and all friendly to the United States), urging them to foster pro-American opinion in their respective localities. He then procured a translation of his official instructions into Spanish, and, adroitly modifying the document, showed it as "my opinion" to "different Californians in authority." And not only so, but at a General Council of Pueblos called to meet at Santa Bárbara on June 15, 1846, to consider the state of the country, he used every effort to secure the attendance of Leese, Vallejo, and Stearns. It was Larkin's opinion at this time that one thousand emigrants would arrive at New Helvetia in October. Should this prove true, and should the number for 1847 be commensurate with that for 1846 the destinies of California would, he declared, be decided by 1848.[21]

James K. Polk had planned to obtain California by purchase, but in the event that Mexico would not sell, what had he planned to do then? Did he purpose to force

Mexico into war, or were his concentration of troops on the Texas border and his increase of naval force in the Pacific (both effected in 1845) merely precautionary measures against hostilities by Mexico; hostilities which Mexico had threatened should the United States annex Texas? To these questions conflicting answers were (and are) possible; [22] but what concerns us here is the fact of the arrival in California of John C. Frémont.

III

Thirty-two years old, son of a French father and Virginia mother, Frémont was son-in-law to Thomas H. Benton (United States Senator from Missouri) and brevet-captain of topographical engineers in the United States Army. [23] He had entered California in 1844, performing the feat of crossing the Sierra Nevada, amid cold and snow, by way of Carson River and Johnson's Pass. The expedition of 1844 was his second to the West, the first (1842) having taken him to the summit of the Wind River Chain of the Rocky Mountains, at a point known since as Frémont's Peak. With twenty-five men our explorer had gone from the Dalles (Oregon) south to Klamath Lake, thence southeast past Pyramid Lake (Nevada), which he named, to Salmon Trout (Truckee) River, and thence to Carson River, whence he had turned west. The objects of his search had been, first, Mary's (Humboldt) Lake, and next, " the San Buenaventura River, reputed to flow from the Rocky Mountains to the bay of San Francisco." After a fortnight at New Helvetia, the party, reduced to nineteen, had ascended the San Joaquín to Kings River, traversed Tehachapi Pass, found the Santa Fé Trail, and passed by it to Utah Lake.

The tours of 1842 and 1844, described in a lucid report to the government, [24] brought to Frémont reputation at home and abroad; but the present tour, that of 1845–46, was to bring him notoriety. Entering California by way of Walker Lake and the Truckee, he reached Sutter's Fort on December 10, 1845, and turned southward to meet a division of his party under Joseph Walker, who had entered by way of Owens River and Lake, and were encamped at "the forks of the main river flowing into Tulares Lake." But by the expression, "forks of the main river," Walker understood the Kern River Forks, and Frémont those of Kings River; and the two divisions (in all about sixty men) remained separated until February 15, when they were united at the Laguna Farm, some twelve miles south of San José.[25]

In 1844 the California authorities had been curious to know Frémont's business, for hardly had he gone south ere an officer had appeared at Sutter's Fort. Now, January 29, 1846, Prefect Manuel Castro sent to Consul Larkin, whom the captain had visited on the 27th at Monterey, a note of inquiry. With what object, he asked, had United States troops entered the department? Frémont's reply, addressed to José Castro as comandante-general, was that the party had come by order of the United States Government to survey a route to the Pacific; that the men (fifty in number) were not soldiers, — that they had been left on the departmental frontier; and that when recruited from their journey they would proceed thence northward to Oregon.[26] But in February, after the reunion of his command, our captain started for the coast by way of Los Gatos and the Santa Cruz Mountains. His appearance with his men in the Santa Clara Valley roused apprehension, and on making camp in the Salinas Valley, at Hartnell's Rancho, he was met, March 5, by an order from José Castro "to retire beyond the limits of the department," as he had "entered the settlements, a thing

prohibited by law." Later a similar order was received
from Prefect Manuel Castro,[27] and Frémont, orally refusing compliance, retired to Gavilán (Hawk) Peak, where
he erected fortifications and raised the United States flag.

Whatever Frémont's motive in approaching the coast
(and there is no indication that he meant to provoke
enmity),[28] his withdrawal within fortifications, without
explanation, was a blunder. Castro menaced him with a
force of two hundred men, and Larkin warned him against
"treachery" and "the vengeance of the common people."
Accordingly, on the 9th, having written to the consul that
he was preparing in the case of attack "to fight to extremity and accept no quarter," he quitted his defenses, proceeded by slow marches to Sutter's Fort, thence to Lassen's
Rancho, and by May was at the north end of Klamath
Lake on the way to Oregon. While here (May 8) he was
overtaken by couriers with the news that behind him was
a United States naval officer with "dispatches" — Lieutenant Archibald H. Gillespie. Hastening south, attended
by the pick of his followers (Kit Carson, Richard Owens,
Alexis Godey, Basil Lajeunesse and four Delaware braves),
— men, their leader said, worthy to be made marshals for
cool courage, — Frémont, after a ride of twenty-five miles,
met the lieutenant, obtained his "dispatches," and went
to bed. That night his camp was surprised by Indians,
who killed Lajeunesse and one of the Delawares; but by
May 24 the party were again in the Sacramento Valley.

Americans, as would-be settlers in California, were
without status. Passports, it is true, had been given them
by Vallejo, Castro, or Sutter (the latter upon his own responsibility), but the holders, not being Mexican citizens,
were disqualified from owning or occupying land. Aware
of the situation, the Mexican Government on July 10,

1845, had instructed the Governor of Alta California "to prevent the introduction of families from the Missouri and Columbia Rivers, as otherwise the general order of the department would be subverted, foreign relations complicated, and embarrassment created."[29] These instructions it was that had pointed the pens of the two Castros in their curt missives to Frémont. "The undersigned," wrote Manuel Castro to Larkin, on March 8, 1846, "when he ordered Captain Frémont to withdraw, based his action on repeated orders and decrees of the supreme government of the Mexican Republic, which prohibit the introduction not only of troops belonging to any power, but even of foreigners who do not come provided with passports."[30] And on April 30, Sub-Prefect Francisco Guerrero sent word to Larkin that "a multitude of foreigners [having] come into California and bought fixed property [land], a right of naturalized foreigners only, he was under necessity of notifying the authorities in each town to inform such purchasers that the transactions were invalid and they themselves subject to be expelled whenever the government might find it convenient."[31]

But noticeable as was the effect of the instructions from Mexico upon the California officials, the effect upon the settlers themselves was more noticeable still. Warnings such as those from Castro and Guerrero recalled the summary eviction of the Grahamites, and alarm became widespread. It was reported, and everywhere believed, that José Castro had threatened to drive all foreigners from the country. Larkin, in April, wrote of "rumors that Castro was collecting people to force settlers from the Sacramento." As early, indeed, as November 4, 1845, the consul had officially declared: "There is a strong jealousy springing up in this country against Americans. . . . I shall be in continual expectation of hearing of some outbreak from one or the other, in one or two years, perhaps in less time." [32]

Frémont (a United States Army officer), returning from the borders of Oregon with Gillespie (an officer of the Navy), was to the fears of the settlers as a spark to powder. Had he not withdrawn to avoid a conflict? Had not Gillespie followed him with dispatches, and had he not, on being overtaken, returned? What could it mean but that the cause of the settlers was to be championed from Washington? That Frémont was in fact directed, or authorized, to incite, encourage, or countenance disorder in California is not, I think, to be believed. The statement almost refutes itself. Gillespie, at the same time that he brought dispatches to Frémont, brought to Larkin the instructions creating the confidential agency, instructions which forbade interference in California affairs. Is it likely that what was forbidden to the agent was permitted to the officer? [33] But concerning the instructions, the settlers knew as little as concerning the "dispatches," and they were controlled by their imaginings.

About June 5, 1846, General José Castro obtained from Vallejo, comandante of the northern frontier, 170 horses. They were put in charge of Lieutenants Francisco Arce and José María Alviso, who were to conduct them across the Sacramento, by way of Knight's Landing, to the general at Santa Clara. Rumor declared that the horses were to be used in operations to free the land of foreigners and to establish a fort on Bear River. This rumor Knight carried to Frémont's camp at the junction of the rivers Bear and Feather, and on June 9 some dozen men from near the camp started in pursuit of Arce. The band, commanded by Ezekiel Merritt (phenomenal as a tobacco-chewer), surprised Arce at dawn of the 10th, seized the horses, and telling the lieutenant that if Castro wanted them he might come and take them, rejoined Frémont, now on Bear River, on the morning of the 11th.[34] The same day it was decided to capture Sonoma, where, under Vallejo, nine small cannon and two hundred muskets constituted a kind of presidio. Twenty in number, the band at once set forth (Merritt in command), and having passed through Napa Valley, where by help of Dr. Robert Semple and John Grigsby its number was recruited to thirty-two or thirty-three, appeared on June 14 at dawn before Vallejo's house.

Merritt and Semple, with perhaps others, entered, and Jacob P. Leese (Vallejo's son-in-law) was chosen interpreter. Leese was surprised at the "rough looks" of the Americans. Semple he describes as "six feet six inches tall and about fifteen inches in diameter, dressed in greasy buckskin from neck to foot, and with a fox-skin cap." The object of the revolt, Semple said, was "to make California a free and independent government; arms and horses were needed, and these Vallejo could supply." A capitulation, embracing Vallejo, his brother Don Salvador, and his secretary Victor Prudon, was drafted and signed, and, stimulated by liberal refreshment, the Americans withdrew. In so doing, however, they insisted on sending the capitulators to Frémont as prisoners.

Merritt by this time had been superseded in command by Grigsby, but the latter resigning, William B. Ide was chosen in his stead. By him the prisoners were dispatched inland, under Merritt, Semple, Grigsby, and others. No vigilance was exercised, and rescue would in all probability have been effected at the stopping-place for the night, Vaca's rancho, had not Vallejo refused to coöperate. Frémont, after some search, was found (June 15) on American River, and, though disclaiming any part in the Sonoma affair, gave orders for the arrest of Leese, who still was in attendance as interpreter, and for the confinement of all the prisoners in Sutter's Fort. "We pass[d] the next day," writes Leese, "in the most aughful manner a reflecting on the cituation of our familys and property in the hands of such a desperate set of men."[35]

But the news had spread. On the 15th, José J. Estudillo wrote from San Leandro to José Dolores Pacheco, justice of the peace, at San José: —

Just this moment [eleven o'clock at night] I have learned from the citizen Rafael Feliz, who was sent post haste by Don Jesus Vallejo on behalf of his brother Don Guadalupe, that yesterday Don Guadalupe and Don Salvador Vallejo, Don Victor Prudon, and Don Luis Leis [Leese] were surprised in their houses by the American foreigners, and were taken prisoners toward Feather River, the same Feliz having seen them pass the rancho of Cayetano Suarez, guarded by twelve foreigners including Merritt as Captain.[36]

At Sonoma, meanwhile, quiet prevailed. A flag (the "Bear Flag") had been raised, and Ide was inditing a proclamation.[37]

From the capture of Sonoma two things resulted: (1) The plan of Larkin — that of the Polk administration, that of securing California by quiet and unobtrusive means, a plan the consummation of which would have brought to Larkin personally much distinction — was shattered;[38] (2) Englishmen in California were stirred with renewed expectation of a British protectorate. The Vallejo circle, personal and political, had been favorable to the United States. The effect upon it of the harsh treatment of Vallejo himself (Frémont consenting) may be surmised. At the time of the activities on Gavilán, Larkin, apprehensive of bloodshed, had sent to United States Consul John Parrott, at Mazatlán, for a warship, and on

April 22 the Portsmouth, John B. Montgomery commander, had cast anchor at Monterey. Just before leaving Sonoma, Vallejo had contrived to send to Montgomery, then at Sauzalito, a messenger, José de la Rosa, asking protection for his family. Lieutenant John Misroon was commissioned to visit Sonoma, where, on June 16–17, he found the Bear Flag flying, Ide's proclamation ready, and Vallejo's household alarmed and indignant.

But alarm and indignation in the Vallejo circle were not confined to the Vallejo family. On the 17th of June, — the day of Misroon's departure, — José Castro, in a proclamation from Santa Clara, spoke of the children of Don Guadalupe as "snatched from the bosom of their father, who is prisoner among foreigners"; and adjured his "fellow countrymen" to "rise *en masse*, irresistible and just." His own force he recruited to 160 men under J. A. Carrillo, Joaquín de la Torre, and Manuel Castro, and on the 23d sent Torre with fifty or sixty men across from San Pablo to Point Quentín, to reconnoitre the position of Ide, which within a day or two he meant to attack with his entire command. It so happened that on June 18 or 19 two men, Cowie and Fowler, had been sent by Ide to the Fitch Rancho on Russian River for powder. The men were captured by a band of Californians under Juan Padilla (a Mexican barber) and Ramón Carrillo, and put to death with torture and mutilation. William L. Todd and other Americans were captured about this time, and on the 23d, the day that Torre crossed to the Sonoma side of the bay, Lieutenant Henry L. Ford of the Bear party, with some eighteen volunteers, set forth to effect a rescue. At Olompali, between San Rafael and Petaluma, he came upon Torre's men, with those of Padilla, breakfasting at the Camilo Rancho. The Americans were attacked by the enemy, but having posted themselves behind trees, so handled their rifles as to kill one Californian (Lieutenant Manuel Cantua) and wound several others.

The Bear party had anticipated a demonstration by Castro north of the bay, and, on the same 23d of June, Frémont (regardless of circumspection[39]) left American River with ninety men for Sonoma. From this point, which he reached on the 25th, he set out with 130 men for San Rafael Mission. While here (June 28) a boat with four strangers was seen approaching from San Pablo. This boat Kit Carson with a squad was sent to intercept. It landed at Point San Pedro, and, three of the strangers having debarked, Carson and his men left their horses, advanced, took careful aim, and shot them down. The victims proved to be Francisco and Ramón de Haro of San Francisco, and José de los Reyes Berreyesa, an aged ranchero of Santa Clara. An eye-witness of the affair, Jasper O'Farrell, stated in 1856 that Carson asked Frémont whether he should make prisoners of the strangers, and that the lieutenant, waving his hand, replied, "I have no room for prisoners." The tragedy is explained by Senator Benton in a letter. "In return," he says, "for the murder of Cowie and Fowler, three of De la Torre's men, being taken, were instantly shot." It was Joaquín de la Torre whom Frémont and the "Bears" in reality sought, but the former was wily, and by dispatches written to be intercepted sent his adversaries, alarmed, to their base; while he, with seventy-five or eighty Californians, made good a retreat to the south of the bay by way of Sauzalito. Frémont thereupon (July 1) crossed, by help of Captain W. D. Phelps of the Moscow, to the Castillo of San Joaquín, and spiked each of its unresisting ten guns.

Expectations of a British protectorate as a result of the capture of Sonoma rested upon three facts: First, that on

January 28, 1846, Consul Forbes had formally protested against the presence of Frémont in California; second, that the same year, early in June, H. M. S. Juno, under Captain Blake (Pacific fleet of Admiral Sir George Seymour), had arrived at Monterey, conveying the Irish priest and missionary Eugene McNamara; and third, that on June 17 the Juno, with McNamara and Consul Forbes both on board, sailed for Santa Bárbara. "It is the duty of the undersigned," so Forbes's protest ran, "to state clearly and distinctly to this Departmental Government that while Great Britain does not pretend to interfere in the political affairs of California, she would view with much dissatisfaction the establishment of a protectorate power over this country by any other foreign nation."[40]

The visit of the Juno to Santa Bárbara — a visit to obtain from Governor Pico approval of a grant to McNamara of land for a colony [41] — served to give emphasis to this protest, for both Blake and Forbes warned Pico against a protectorate.[42] Whether the protest and warning were warranted, depended on whether Aberdeen intended to abide by his instructions to Forbes of December 31, 1844. As it chanced, circumstances for Great Britain had changed; and the Foreign Office, reverting to the position assumed when it had assured Webster that, so far as California was concerned, "the Queen's Government . . . had not the slightest objection to an acquisition by the United States of territory in that direction," dismissed Forbes with the curt observation, "Her Majesty's Government do not approve of his late proceeding."

IV

Embarrassment from the Sonoma affair was forestalled by an event long looked for: war between the United States and Mexico.

The American force at this time in the Pacific — two ships (the Savannah and Congress), four sloops (the Warren, Portsmouth, Cyane, and Levant) and a schooner (the Shark) — was commanded by Commodore John D. Sloat. Under instructions from Secretary George Bancroft, issued June 24, 1845, and reiterated at intervals to May 13, 1846, Sloat in the event of war was to "possess himself of the port of San Francisco" and of such other California ports as might be open to seizure, "preserving if possible the most friendly relations with the inhabitants." News of war reached Sloat at Mazatlán in 1846 on May 17, but the commodore, though sending the sloop Cyane under Captain William Mervine to Monterey with a confidential message for Larkin, was disposed to await a formal declaration of hostilities before proceeding north himself. On June 7, however, word was received of an attack upon General Taylor and of a blockade of Vera Cruz, and on the 8th Sloat set sail, reaching Monterey with his flagship (the Savannah) on July 2. Here under the influence of Larkin (loath to resign the old plan) the commodore delayed five days, but at length, on the 7th, he disembarked 250 men, who raised over the custom-house the American flag, fired a salute, and posted a proclamation declaring California annexed to the United States.[43] On July 9, by order of Lieutenant Montgomery of the Portsmouth, the flag was raised by Lieutenant Joseph W. Revere over San Francisco and Sonoma, and on the 11th, by Revere's messenger, Edward M. Kern, over Sutter's Fort.

Under the treaty of February 22, 1845, with Micheltorena, the civil and military commands in California were disjoined, and, as of yore, the disadvantages of the arrangement were manifest. Pico was governor, but José

Castro was comandante-general. The one, moreover, represented the South and the other the North. Trouble with the United States (a military matter) was apprehended, wherefore Castro, arrogating supreme authority, refused to divide with Pico — a mere civil functionary — the departmental revenues in the proportion (lately decreed in Mexico) of two to one in favor of the latter.

By the date of the seizure of Monterey, the situation between Pico and Castro was Brutus and Cassius-like in the extreme. On March 17, the comandante-general had reported to the assembly the affair with Frémont, announcing an intention to defend the country alone, if the Governor, in a rôle suitably subordinate, should not come to his aid; moreover, that the defense might be the more effective, Castro early in April had sent Andrés Castillero (discoverer of the Almadén quicksilver mine) to Mexico for munitions, and had summoned a military *junta* at Monterey. This *junta*, which had met in April, had on April 30 been violently assailed by Pico, who on May 13 had summoned the General Council of Pueblos, already mentioned, for "determining all that [might] be deemed best [in order] to avoid the fatal events impending at home and abroad." To Castro a General Council was "abominable"; was the "product of the insane hydra of discord"; was "execrable profanation"; was "unheard-of disloyalty"; was "perjury"; and on June 8 he had proclaimed martial law. Thereupon (June 16) the Governor had quitted Los Ángeles with a military force, and by the 21st had been at Santa Bárbara on his way north to exact submission. Here on June 23 he had heard of the capture of Sonoma, and from here, after much parley with Manuel Castro, he had consented to march to Santa Margarita Rancho, near San Luis Obispo, to meet the comandante-general, not to exact of him submission, but to concert with him measures for defense against the Americans. At the rancho (reached July 11) Pico, through a message from Castro, had first learned of the action of Sloat.

Operations by the United States for the reduction of California present an earlier and a later phase, — the earlier (July 7 to September 24, 1846), when American dominion was acknowledged, and the later (September 24, 1846, to January 13, 1847) when such dominion was disputed. It is to the later phase more especially that significance attaches, for the occurrences constituting it inspired in the conquerors what before they had little possessed, to wit, respect for the conquered.

Possessed of Monterey, Commodore Sloat invited Comandante-General Castro to meet him at the port and sign articles of capitulation. Two days later the commodore wrote to Frémont, asking him to hasten to Monterey with at least one hundred men. Castro, who was at San Juan Bautista, promptly notified Sloat that the Governor and assembly were the proper authorities to whom to apply for a capitulation, it being his duty to defend the country at all sacrifice. About July 10, Castro withdrew southward, and on the 17th, Frémont, from New Helvetia, took possession of San Juan, which he occupied jointly with a party of dragoons sent by Sloat under Purser Daingerfield Fauntleroy to hoist at that point the American flag. Meanwhile as for Ide and the Bear party, their importance had vastly diminished. "I presume," wrote Larkin to Ide on the historic 7th, "you will be inclined to desist from any contemplated movements against the natives, and remain passive for the present." Indeed, on the 4th, the Ide party, with Ide a private member, had resolved itself into an organization of three companies under John Grigsby, Henry L. Ford, and Granville P. Swift, an organization which, for the most part joining

Frémont at Sutter's Fort, had come with him to San Juan Bautista as the California Battalion — 160 men.

The battalion entered Monterey on July 19, and here, legitimately, we obtain that element of the picturesque, a desire for which, in connection with Frémont, possesses the minds of the most sedate. "They were a curious set," wrote Lieutenant Frederick Walpole of Admiral Seymour's flagship, the Collingwood [44] —

A vast cloud of dust appeared at first, and thence in long file emerged this wildest wild party. Frémont rode ahead, a spare, active-looking man, with such an eye! He was dressed in a blouse and leggings, and wore a felt hat. After him came five Delaware Indians, who were his body guard; they had charge of two baggage horses. The rest, many of them blacker than the Indians, rode two and two, the rifle held by one hand across the pommel of the saddle. . . . The dress of these men was principally a long, loose coat of deer-skin, tied with thongs, in front; trousers of the same. The saddles were of various fashions, though these and a large drove of horses and a brass field-gun were things they had picked up in California. . . . They are allowed no liquor . . . and the discipline is very strict. . . . One man, a doctor [Semple], was six feet six high, and an odd-looking fellow. May I never come under his hands.

William Peel, a son of Sir Robert, was an officer of the Collingwood, and it is related by W. F. Swasey that Dr. Semple astonished him by his familiarity with English politics and history. Peel was yet more astonished, Swasey relates, by the accuracy with which Frémont's men were able to bring down with their rifles, at 160 yards, Mexican silver dollars provided by the Englishmen as targets.

At Monterey Frémont met Sloat. Apprehensive lest his course, like that of Jones in 1842, had been precipitate, the commodore could be induced to go in the way of conquest no further than he had gone already. On July 23, however, Commodore Robert F. Stockton, who had

arrived from Norfolk on the 15th, was made by Sloat
commander-in-chief of all forces and operations on land.
By Stockton (a militant character) Frémont's contingent
was accepted as a battalion of volunteers, with Frémont
himself as major and Gillespie as captain. On the 29th,
Sloat sailed for home, and Stockton, now in supreme
command, issued a proclamation. It announced that the
commodore

could not confine [his] operations to the quiet and undisturbed
possession of the defenseless ports of Monterey and San Francisco, . . . but [would] immediately march against [the] boast-
ing and abusive chiefs who had not only violated every principle
of national hospitality and good faith toward Captain Frémont
and his surveying party, but who unless driven out [would], with
the aid of the hostile Indians, keep this beautiful country in a
constant state of revolution and blood.[45]

By July 24, Pico and Castro (reconciled) were at Los
Ángeles, the capital of the department; Castro making
headquarters at Campo de la Mesa. Frémont with his
battalion reached San Diego by sea on the 29th, raising
there the American flag; and on August 6, Stockton, accompanied by Larkin as conciliator, but with 360 men,
reached San Pedro. Here the commodore was met by
messengers from Castro (Pablo de la Guerra and José M.
Flóres) empowered to arrange for "a suspension of hostilities." This proposition Stockton declined. "I cannot,"
he wrote, "check any operations to negotiate on any other
principle than that California will declare her independence, under the protection of the flag of the United States.
If, therefore, you will agree to hoist the American flag in
California, I will stop my forces and negotiate the treaty."

Castro on August 9 notified Pico that, being unable to
muster more than "one hundred men, badly armed and
worse supplied," he was resolved to quit the country. On

the 10th, Pico reported Castro's message to the assembly, which adjourned without date, and Castro and Pico together (each the author of a farewell address) took the road for Sonora. The former reached Altar by way of the Colorado in September, and in 1848 returned to California. The latter for a time secreted himself near his rancho, but in September escaped into Lower California, whence he passed to the mainland, returning to California the same year with Castro.

Stockton, joined by Frémont, entered Los Ángeles on August 13. The flag was raised; Juan Bandini and Santiago Argüello declared themselves for the new régime; and the conquest of California was deemed complete. So complete, indeed, was it deemed, that the commodore, having on the 17th proclaimed the country a territory of the United States, and having on September 2 created Frémont military commandant (news whereof he dispatched to Washington by Kit Carson), reëmbarked his men and sailed for the North. Frémont himself left Los Ángeles on September 8, reached Santa Bárbara on the 13th, where he garrisoned the presidio with nine men under Lieutenant Theodore Talbot, and by the end of the month was in the Sacramento Valley. News awaited him: The Vallejos, Prudon, and Leese had been liberated from durance at Sutter's Fort; Dr. Robert Semple, seconded by Rev. Walter Colton, chaplain of the Congress, had on August 15 issued the "Californian," the first American Pacific Coast newspaper; and the Walla Wallas (baseless tale) were menacing the northern frontier with 900 warriors.

California was conquered, but refused to be so regarded. On leaving Los Ángeles, Stockton had appointed Lieutenant Archibald Gillespie, a man of Frémont ideas, southern commandant, with fifty men, and with orders to maintain martial law, but to exercise discretion in granting permits to proper persons to be out before sunrise and carry weapons. Gillespie, whose opinion of Californians was not favorable, made the error of construing his orders strictly, and of harassing, by acts of interference and exaction, the Angelinos, among whom, as in the days of Figueroa, there was a turbulent Mexican element. The result was that on September 24 certain demonstrations by Sérbulo Varela became magnified into an insurrection. Castro's old officers, José María Flóres, José Antonio Carrillo, and Andrés Pico, took command, the town was invested, and Gillespie was powerless.[46]

Once ignited, the spirit of revolt leaped wildly throughout the South. The struggle was one not so much of cavalry against infantry, of lance against musket, as of lightness and mobility against weight and mass; of the dynamics of war against the statics. And what was more, neither combatant at first comprehended the military efficiency of the other. To the Californians Frémont's "Bears" were bears indeed; and Stockton's sailors and marines clowns; while, to the Americans, Carrillo's and Torre's horsemen, ubiquitous on the hills, were guerillas who never could be brought to bay.

The first fight occurred at the Chino Rancho, a point about twenty-five miles to the eastward of Los Ángeles. Benjamin D. Wilson, an early resident, had been given command of twenty Americans (flouters of Californian courage) with whom to guard the frontier along the Colorado against Castro. Satisfied that for the present Castro was harmless, Wilson went hunting. On returning, he was told of the rising at Los Ángeles, and was invited to establish himself at the Chino Rancho owned by Isaac Williams, where he was assured there was a supply of powder. No sooner was the rancho gained (September 26) than two bodies of Californians, one under Varela, Diego Sepúlveda, and Ramón Carrillo, and the other under José del Carmen Lugo, — in all some sixty-five or seventy men, — appeared and demanded a surrender. The house — an adobe of three sides, with but few openings, and with an asphaltum roof — was shielded by a ditch and some adobe corrals. On the morning of the 27th, Varela's and Lugo's horsemen charged these obstructions, losing in the movement one killed (Carlos Ballesteros) and two or three wounded. But the building now furnished cover, and the assailants were enabled to fire the roof with dried grass. Williams, who was brother-in-law to Lugo, presented himself amid the smoke, with his children, and begged for quarter. Varela repeated the demand for surrender, but promised the inmates protection as prisoners of war. The terms were accepted, the garrison, some of whom had suffered wounds, marched forth, and despite the wish of Sepúlveda to shoot them in revenge for the death of Ballesteros, were taken to Los Ángeles and given in charge of Flóres.[47]

Back from Chino, Valera and Lugo found the tricolor afloat over the plaza, and Gillespie surrounded on Fort Hill. Flóres, however, at the intercession of Eulogio Celis and Francisco Figueroa of Los Ángeles, offered, through Wilson, to permit the American commander to march with the honors of war to San Pedro, there to take passage for Monterey by the transport Vandalia. Gillespie departed on September 30, but did not embark till October 4. By the articles of capitulation, which bore date the 29th, and are here first used,[48] he was to consume at the port "only so much time as was indispensable to embarkation"; and, for observing the stipulation, he was placed "on his word of honor." " Devoid of shame, good faith, and word of honor" (records Flóres), Gillespie "prolonged his stay to give time for the arrival of a warship."

But what of events at Santa Bárbara and San Diego? At the former, Talbot and his squad avoided capture by flight to the mountains. The chaparral was set on fire to drive them out; but they made their way northward and reached Monterey in November. At San Diego it was much the same. Gillespie had garrisoned the port with a dozen men under Ezekiel Merritt, and these, on the approach from Los Ángeles of fifty men under Manuel Garfías, betook themselves, not to the mountains but to a whale-ship, a cover whence they dared not emerge for twenty days.

That Gillespie protracted his embarkation in expectation of a warship is more than probable. On September 24 he had dispatched to Stockton by an expert rider (Juan Flaco, "Lean John"), a plea for help. The messenger was instructed to make desperate speed, and he obeyed. Provided with cigarettes concealed in his hair, the wrappers inscribed "Believe the bearer," he set out, pursued by Mexicans, who shot his horse. He reached successively Santa Bárbara and Monterey, where he was aided, at the one place by Talbot, and at the other by Larkin, and arrived at Yerba Buena on the evening of the 29th, — five hundred miles in five days, — a feat paralleled in earlier times by Santa Anna's messenger to Figueroa, and in later by Frémont personally.[49] On receipt of "Lean John's" message, Mervine was at once sent south in the Savannah with 350 men, and Frémont in a transport, the Sterling, with 160 men; Stockton following in the Congress.[50] These vessels met the Vandalia, with Gillespie on board, and Frémont, ascertaining that no horses could be obtained at Santa Bárbara, debarked at Monterey to proceed by land; while Mervine with Gillespie in his wake made all haste for San Pedro, where he arrived on October 6. The day following, the two commands started together for Los Ángeles. The night was passed at Domínguez Rancho, and on the 8th Mervine resumed the advance; his centre composed of seamen and marines in hollow formation, and his flanks covered by Gillespie's squad as skirmishers.

The Californian force consisted of some sixty horsemen, with a field-piece, under José Antonio Carrillo. The Americans once within range, the gun was discharged (by a cigarette, it is said) then dragged by *reatas* to a safe distance and reloaded. Four of Mervine's force had in this way been killed and six wounded, when at the end of an hour the captain withdrew to San Pedro and reëmbarked, leaving to the enemy some baggage and a flag.

Within thirty days two considerable actions had been fought, and in both the Americans had been worsted. The unsuccessful combatants were settlers, sailors, and marines. It remained to be proved what would be the fate of an American force more regularly constituted for military, or at least land, operations.

By the Californians the interval was utilized in reëstablishing civil government, and by Stockton in occupying San Diego. On October 20, the departmental assembly elected José María Flóres acting governor and comandante-general, and named Manuel Castro northern comandante, with Francisco Rico as subordinate.

I have resolved [wrote Flóres to Mexico on October 24] either to oppose the enemy in guerilla warfare, or to risk all on a single battle as may seem best, since up to to-day the land forces of Captain Frémont have not arrived, and there are in view only those which, since the action of the 8th, have remained on board the warships at San Pedro and San Diego, with the hope of the arrival of Frémont, who on the 10th of this month was on the Sacramento, 150 leagues from this capital. . . . The army of invasion is composed of 400 riflemen (hunters), under Captain

Frémont, and three warships capable of landing 1200 men. Besides, there are thirty whale-ships the crews of which are volunteers for the United States. Furthermore, I have reliable news of the impending arrival at the Sacramento River of 3000 male immigrants. . . . From the port of San Diego to the point of San Luis Obispo there are 400 or 500 natives poorly armed; a third part without firearms, and the remainder with four or five rounds each. Even meat for subsistence can no longer be obtained. The skeleton of the missions, the one resource upon which we ought to be able to count, these [sic] the Governor of the department sold for his own benefit on the eve of his flight from this capital.

It was October 23 when Stockton himself reached San Pedro, and he was at San Diego by November. Both points he found closely invested, the hills being "horse-covered," and he was planning with Gillespie an attack toward the north when an important letter was handed to him. It was from an officer of the United States Army, — General Stephen W. Kearny.

Whether Polk's military and naval activity in 1845 was or was not purely precautionary, one thing is certain: if war with Mexico was to ensue, it was Polk's resolve that the acquisition of California should be its principal fruit. When, therefore, Kearny, in August, 1846, had subjugated New Mexico, the successful general was ordered to proceed from Santa Fé to California. He set out on September 25 with 300 men of the First Dragoons, and on October 6, just below Socorro, met Kit Carson. Learning that California was already subdued, he took charge of Stockton's dispatches and compelled Carson to return as scout to his own command, a force which he now reduced to 100 men by sending 200 back to Santa Fé. With him he kept Captain Henry S. Turner, Captain Abraham R. Johnston, Major Thomas Swords, Lieutenant William H. Emory, Lieutenant Davidson with

two mountain howitzers, William H. Warner (topograph-
ist), Assistant Surgeon John R. Griffin, and Antonio
Robidoux (guide). Mules served both as pack-animals
and mounts, and the route was by the Gila to the Colorado junction, which was reached November 22. The
Colorado Desert, pronounced by Emory the worst stage of
the journey, was crossed southward of the Anza Trail, and
on December 2 the command was at Warner's Rancho.
From here Kearny, as already seen, apprised Stockton
of his presence.

To meet the general and conduct him to San Diego, the
commodore on December 3 sent Gillespie with thirty-
nine men, among them ten carbineers from the Congress,
with Acting Lieutenant Beale and Passed Midshipman
Duncan, and twenty-five of the California Battalion under
Captain Samuel Gibson. Andrés Pico had for some time
been watching the Americans from near San Luis Rey
Mission, and by the 5th (when Gillespie met Kearny) was
encamped at the Indian pueblo of San Pascual. At
Stockton's suggestion and with the strong approval of Kit
Carson, it was decided by Kearny and Gillespie to attack
him. The night of the 5th was cold and rainy, and a
reconnoissance proved the Californians to be unsuspect-
ing. In the early dawn of the 6th, Captain Johnston of the
vanguard charged with twenty men down hill upon the
village. The onset was met by Pico's force with pistol and
lance, and Johnston fell, shot through the head. Kearny
and Gillespie now approached, and the Californians, re-
treating, drew after them the Americans in hot pursuit
but much scattered. Suddenly the fleeing squadron — some
eighty men — stopped, turned, closed its ranks and rushed
upon the foe. Poorly mounted and with empty weapons,
the Americans were entrapped. The lance deftly wielded
made sabre and clubbed musket vain things, and the con-

flict though short was deadly. Ere the rear guard could arrive with the howitzers, Moore with sixteen others was killed, and Kearny, Warner, Gillespie, — the latter resisting dexterously with his sword, — Gibson, and Robidoux, with fourteen others, were badly wounded. For the Californians San Pascual was the fight *par excellence* of the war. In no other were their peculiar tactics so advantageously exercised, — the retreat, the pause, the *volte-face*, the couched lance, the rattling spur, the rush, the shock, the carnage, and again the retreat.

On the night of the 6th, Alexis Godey with one or two companions was sent to Stockton for help, and on the 7th Kearny (able to be in the saddle) camped on a hill near the rancho of San Bernardo. But Godey did not return, and on the night of the 8th Kit Carson, Lieutenant Beale, and an Indian set out to find Stockton. On the 11th a reinforcement of 200 marines appeared, and by the 12th the entire Kearny-Gillespie force was at San Diego.[51]

Under Governor Flóres, fortune favored the insurrectionists, but revolt was brewing. The Governor was unpopular for divers acts, but his crowning error was a decision to send the Chino captives to Mexico. So considerable (as the husbands of native women) was the influence of the captives, that Flóres himself was put under arrest by connivance of his subordinate Francisco Rico. Tried by the assembly, he was acquitted of intentional wrong and reinstated in authority, Rico being imprisoned in his stead. But mention of Rico carries us to the North, whence the latter had just returned, and where, early in October, we left Frémont preparing to move south to coöperate with Stockton.

At Monterey, between October 28 and November 17, Frémont recruited by help of Edwin Bryant and W. F.

Swasey 428 men, some of them Walla Walla and California Indians. Horses he took wherever they could be found, giving receipts to be honored by the United States after the war. On the 29th he started south by way of the Salinas Valley, and on December 14 reached San Luis Obispo. Here Jesús Pico lived. He was cousin to Don Pío, the self-expatriated governor, and to Andrés Pico, the hero of San Pascual, but had broken his parole, and feeling was strong against him. When discovered (at Wilson's rancho), he was tried by court martial and sentenced to be shot.

On the morning appointed for the execution [writes Swasey, who was present] the battalion was ordered to parade. I, accompanied by Owens and some few other officers, entering Frémont's room, found him surrounded by Pico's family bathed in tears, the little hands of the children outstretched toward him, beseeching mercy. Captain Owens, myself, and some others immediately added our intercessions . . . alleging Pico's crime to have been committed more through ignorance of the laws of war than from deliberate dishonor. After a moment of hesitation, Frémont turned toward the prisoner. "I had," he said, "rather meet a thousand in the field to-morrow. I pardon you. You are free!"

Frémont himself writes: —

I pointed through the window to the troops paraded in the square. . . . You were about to die, but your wife has saved you. Go thank her! He fell on his knees, made on his fingers the sign of the cross, and said: "I was to die — I had lost the life God gave me — you have given me another life. I devote the new life to you"; a pledge not broken.[52]

From San Luis the battalion, amid fierce winds and torrential rains, crossed the Santa Inés Mountains to Santa Bárbara, where it remained a week. On January 3, 1847, it resumed its march, and, closely surveyed by horsemen from the hills, entered the plain of San Fernando on the 11th. But again our attention must revert to the North.

Early in November, near San Luis Obispo, Manuel Castro, together with Rico, Joaquín de la Torre, and José Antonio Chavez, raised a force of 100 men. On the 15th, Chavez captured Thomas O. Larkin at Joaquín Gómez's rancho of Los Verjeles, where the consul had stopped for the night on his way to Yerba Buena; and on the 16th, an American force under Captains Charles Burroughs and Bluford K. Thompson (newly arrived immigrants) was repulsed with spirit. The fight was begun by Torre, who attacked a scouting party of eight or ten men sent by Burroughs from San Juan Bautista. Driven to the shelter of a grove on the Natividad Rancho, the party wounded a number of their assailants but lost their leader, George Foster. News of the plight of the scouts was brought to Burroughs by Walla Wallas, and the whole American force, about fifty mounted men, advanced. They encountered Castro's force, the main body of which had come to Torre's support, exchanged shots with them, and delivered a charge. The foe feigned flight (tactics of San Pascual),[53] then turned and in a short *mêlée* killed five Americans, including Burroughs, and wounded as many more. The conflict at Natividad and a brush with a combative ranchero (Francisco Sánchez) by Captain Ward Marston of the marines, near Santa Clara, on January 2, 1847, — a brush followed by Sánchez's capitulation, — were the last acts of the war with the United States, north of Tehachapi.

In the South, Stockton had begun a movement for the recovery of Los Ángeles. Accompanied by Kearny and Gillespie, he left San Bernardo on January 1, 1847, with 600 men, and near San Luis Rey was met by a proposal from General Flóres for a truce, pending confirmation of rumors of peace between the United States and Mexico. The proposal was rejected, but at San Juan Capistrano the commodore issued to all Californians, except Flóres, who, like Jesús Pico, had broken his parole, a proclamation of amnesty. It had been intended to intercept Stockton at La Jabonería near the first ford of the San Gabriel River, — a spot covered with willows and adapted to ambuscade, — but the plan being revealed, the American force was directed to Paso de Bartolo, a ford higher up. Here Flóres confronted it with nearly 500 men: the main body — 200 men with two pieces of artillery — being posted opposite the ford, on a bluff fifty feet high and back from the stream some six hundred yards; and the flanks being protected by squadrons of cavalry under Andrés Pico and José Antonio Carrillo.

Stockton's advance through the water was contested by Flóres with round-shot and grape; but, owing to worthless powder, the guns wrought no execution, and a cavalry charge was ordered. The order was not vigorously obeyed, and the Americans having now passed the river, a shot from a field gun aimed by the commodore himself shattered the best gun of the Californians, who, retiring forthwith, pitched their camp on the circumjacent hills. On January 9, the march for Los Ángeles was resumed. It was contested, near the Cañada de los Alisos, by artillery and cavalry, but was not checked; and on the 10th, the Americans entered the town with flags displayed and bands playing. Gillespie raised again the banner which four months before he had lowered in capitulation.[54]

Frémont at San Fernando learned of the fall of Los Ángeles on January 10, and the same day sent his faithful adherent, Jesús Pico, to counsel general submission. The counsel was heeded, and on the 13th commissioners from both sides signed a treaty at Cahuenga. The Californians "surrendered their artillery and public arms," and promised "not again to serve during the war." In return, they were "guaranteed life and property," were acquitted of obligation to take an oath of allegiance, might "leave the country without let or hindrance," and were granted "equal rights and privileges as enjoyed by the citizens of the United States of America." On the 14th, Frémont with his battalion entered the city, and on the 15th, Stockton reported to Washington that he had approved Frémont's course.

It remains to be observed that Flóres had already liberated from confinement Thomas O. Larkin, who had been brought by his captors to Los Ángeles for safe-keeping; [55] had transferred the command to Andrés Pico; and, emulous of the example of his predecessor Don Pío, had figuratively fallen upon his sword by quitting California for Sonora in company with Manuel Castro.

CHAPTER XVI

MISSION, PRESIDIO, PUEBLO, AND PRIVATE RANCHO

Mission

MISSION, presidio, pueblo, and private rancho, each was characterized by its own architecture, its own domestic routine, its own traffic, and its own social life. In the case of the Mission, architecture has proved the most enduring memorial.

The Mission style [writes Mr. Hector Alliot] is first cousin to the Spanish Colonial in Mexico, young, powerful, and distinctive if somewhat unpolished. According to all recognized canons, it embraces essential features of novelty. . . . The thick walls with restraining buttresses, the construction about a court, the arched corridors, the patio, tiled roofs, domed towers, and pierced belfries should alone be sufficient to establish a style; but there are besides two features entirely original, — the terraced bell-tower and the serrated ascent of the curved arch surmounted by the cross.

It has been observed in chapter V that the principal buildings of San Carlos Mission in 1771 were a church, a priest's dwelling, a storehouse and a guard-house, all of wood; all, that is, of posts of pine or cypress set close together and plastered within and without with clay. These "buildings," the guard-house excepted, were but sections of a low earth-roofed structure, fifty yards long and seven wide, constituting one side of a quadrangle (70 by 43 yards) inclosed by a stockade with a single entrance secured by a strong gate.

Down to 1780, California mission buildings everywhere

much resembled those at San Carlos, excepting that where wood was scarce, as at San Diego, adobes or sun-dried brick were used. Indeed from 1778, adobes — a material widely accessible and entirely non-combustible — came into use more and more. By 1780, there was an adobe church at San Diego; and by 1783 there were two priests' dwellings, a guard-house, granary, storehouse, infirmary, nunnery, wood-shed, larder, kitchen and oven; the whole forming three sides of a quadrangle, the fourth side of which was protected to a height of three *varas* (nearly three yards) by an adobe wall. By 1782 an adobe church had been built at San Francisco, and by 1784 one at Santa Clara. But it was soon learned that adobe walls and earth roofs crumbled, and that roofs of tules succumbed to fire; and by 1790 the wood-adobe type of construction — a type involving an earth or tule roof — began to yield to an adobe-brick or adobe-stone type with roof of tiles. At Santa Cruz, in 1793–94, a church was built the front and walls of which, to a height of three feet, were of stone; and at San Juan Capistrano, in 1797, there was begun a stone edifice (arched and towered), the noblest to be built in Alta California, one the ruined fragments of which —

the chapter-room, the cloister-porch —

impart to-day to a quiet landscape an incomparable melancholy.

Church building had either reached or was fast approaching finality, when, in 1812–13, the earthquake shocks occurred which are described in chapter X; shocks so destructive at the South that nearly every establishment (San Gabriel, San Juan Capistrano, Santa Bárbara, San Buenaventura, Purísima, and Santa Inés) was required to be reared anew. As late as 1818 and 1820, — as late as the end of the Spanish régime, — dedications

were taking place. But how at any period Indians super-
intended by a few guardsmen, the latter in turn superin-
tended by two padres, could have achieved the beauty of
bell-accentuated San Gabriel, the strength of domed Santa
Bárbara, the grace (flowing yet varied) of San Luis, and
the stateliness, wide-flung, of Capistrano, has remained
a mystery.

So far as artisans were concerned, they were few from
the first. San Carlos was reared by four Indians and three
sailors. San Diego de Alcalá (second structure) was undertaken by neophytes and twenty sailors. Rivera's recruits
for Los Ángeles numbered one mason, one carpenter, and
one blacksmith. Borica, even, brought to Alta California
but six masons, two carpenters, and three blacksmiths;
and of these nearly all returned to Mexico in five years;
wherefore in 1797 it became necessary to import a
master-mason from Culiacán to superintend the stone-
work of San Juan Capistrano.

For San Gabriel, Santa Bárbara, San Luis, and San Juan
it must be that we are indebted to the padres themselves.
Santa Clara (best of the earlier structures) was designed,
we know, by one of its priests, Joseph Antonio de Jesús
María de Murguía of Domaiquía, Álava, a priest who as
a layman had in 1748 laid the first masonry in Serra's old
district of Sierra Gorda. As for San Luis Rey, twin edifice with Santa Bárbara in features distinctively Mission,
its designer was its priest Antonio Peyri of Parrera, Catalonia. To what extent Muraguía and Peyri worked from
plans or pictured representations, Spanish or Mexican, we
do not know; but whatever their models they were not
slavish in imitation. Alta California was a land of out-of-
doors, — a land of earthquakes and of peril from primitive
men; and by these facts Mission architecture was conditioned. Spaces generous and unpreëmpted, coupled with

lack of connoisseurs, dictated dependence on mass and line. Peril from primitive men prescribed a construction fort-like and corridored about a fountain; while, as against the earthquake, walls were made thick, and the buttressing was heavy.[1]

But, in the case of the Mission, domestic routine concerns us even more than architecture. Within the mission quadrangle, or partly within it and partly without, were huts for the neophytes, huts originally of reeds, but since 1790 (notably at Santa Bárbara) of whitewashed and tiled adobes. At sunrise a bell was struck, and from their huts the neophyte population gathered to hear morning prayers (*oraciones*), and to be instructed in Christian doctrine. Then came breakfast (*desayuno*) — a meal of maize-gruel called *atole;* the married partaking of it in their own abodes, and the unmarried in a common quarter, the *pozolera.* Tasks, which came next, were assigned with regard to individual capacity. The males were sent, some to the mountains to hunt; some to the fields to sow or reap grain; some to the shops where the trades — masonry, carpentry, shoemaking, blacksmithing, tanning, soap-boiling, etc. — were taught; and some, mayhap, to the neighboring presidio, to work under contract on the walls or fortifications. The duties of the females were cooking, spinning, knitting, and embroidering. A second meal (*comida*) consisting of *pozole* — meat cooked with corn or beans — was served at midday. In the afternoon, boys and catechumens were instructed in Christianity, and *cena* (a meal of *atole*) was served at seven in the evening. On festival days, attendance upon Mass and religious instruction was exacted with rigor, each catechumen, as his name was called, being required to advance and kiss the hand of the father missionary.[2] Whatever the exercise, — religious, agricultural, or industrial, — the padres were assisted by an overseer, nominally an *alcalde* elected by the Indians, but in fact and of necessity an appointee, more or less trustworthy, of the padres themselves. The nunnery, wherein widows and unmarried girls were restrained at night (and for bachelors there was a like institution), was guarded jealously by a native duenna, vigilant and grim, who kept the key.

The life of a neophyte was one of regular labor (a new thing), but it was not without its recreations. There were games of hoop and ball, and there were dances. For the latter a fire was built, and about it the participants, stripped to the loins, streaked with paint and crowned with feathers, executed to the sound of a drum, horn, and rude castanets a slow movement at once rhythmic and weird.[3] Music, in the rationalized sense, was a means much relied upon by Catholic missionaries everywhere to promote the faith, and it was so in California. At San Gabriel, Indian boys with passable voices chanted at the celebration of the Mass, while such as were apt in the use of instruments essayed the flute, guitar, violin, drum, triangle, or cymbals.[4]

The *gente de razón* who dwelt at the missions were few, and social life for the padres came largely through traffic. How exultantly the visits of Mr. George Washington Eayrs were received has been told already. But dinners aboard ship and at the "ranch house" — dinners seasoned no less by gossip than by wine — present the social side of traffic in its initial stage. After the bargain had been struck, after the goods had been secured, then came forward the rancheros, eager to possess themselves of the wares and merchandise of the luxurious East. A trader of the Eayrs type was Captain William Heath Davis of

Boston. He carried to China sandal-wood from the Sandwich Islands, taking in return silks, teas, and lacquered articles; and his favorite California port was El Refugio, near Santa Bárbara. Here in 1816 he was officially waited upon by Comandante Don Ignacio Martínez, with an aide and two soldiers; but so royal was his treatment of his guest, so artfully did he ply him with wine and gifts, that not a single embarrassing question was propounded. Martínez's daughter — she who became Señora Estudillo — was then but eleven years old, and it is related by her that when, on returning from his visit, her father displayed *serapes*, shawls, fancy silk handkerchiefs, satin shoes, sewing-silk of all colors, and gleaming lacquers, the family were captivated. Never in all their lives had they seen anything so beautiful and so rich.

But in the social intercourse of the padres, large as was the element contributed by traffic, there was another element still. It was that which arose from the part performed by the missions as houses of entertainment for the traveler. Up and down the coast went the horseman, nor ever was he anxious as against the night. Each day at sunrise he quitted one consecrated portal, to be enfolded beneath another at sunset. From San Diego to San Luis, from San Luis to San Juan Capistrano, from San Juan Capistrano to San Gabriel, the sea was his guide. From San Fernando the mountains led him to San Buenaventura. Here, sea and mountain at feud, San Buenaventura confided him to Santa Bárbara, Santa Bárbara to Santa Inés, and Santa Inés to La Purísima, whence, under escort of wide valleys, his course was sure. Nor anywhere for lodging, for meat or drink, for peaches or pomegranates, for relays of horses or for *vaqueros*, was there cost to him of aught. The traveler brought to the padres news, which was life, and news acquitted him.

Presidio and Pueblo

The architecture of the California presidios displayed itself in the barracks of quadrangles and in the walls of certain outlying defenses. At San Diego and Monterey in 1769 the presidial inclosure was also the inclosure of the mission. At San Francisco (1776), where mission and presidio were separate, the space for the latter was 92 yards square, and the walls were of palisades. At Santa Bárbara in 1782 the walls were of palisades, and the inclosure was a square of 60 *varas*. By the energy of Neve, in 1778, the palisades of San Francisco were replaced by adobes, and Monterey was provided with barracks 136 by 18 feet, and with a wall of stone 537 yards in girth, 12 feet high and 4 feet thick.[5] In 1793, Vancouver deemed Santa Bárbara Presidio, with its red tiles, the best of the Spanish establishments, and that of San Diego the worst.

Defenses proper — batteries — were erected, one of logs, in 1793, at Monterey, with eleven guns; one of adobes, in 1794, at San Francisco (battery of San Joaquín), with eight guns; one of adobes, in 1797, at San Diego on Point Guijarros, with eight guns; and one of fascines, in 1797, at Yerba Buena (Black Point), with five guns. In 1816, San Joaquín was rebuilt, and in 1820, it mounted twenty guns, three of them 24-pounders; while at Monterey in 1830 the armament consisted of twenty guns behind a breastwork of adobes. By 1835, the presidio and fort at San Diego had both been abandoned.

In respect to dwellings, presidio and pueblo were architecturally alike: single-story adobes, with whitewashed walls and roofs of asphaltum, or red tiles, but with small barred windows and without gardens. A few dwellings (notably the Guerra house at Santa Bárbara) were more pretentious. They were built after the Moorish fashion,

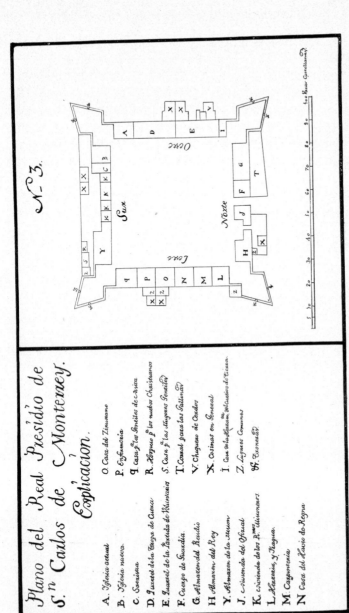

Plano del Real Presidio de S.ⁿ Carlos de Monterrey.

Explicacion.

A. Yglesia actual
B. Yglesia nueva.
C. Sacristia
D. Quartel de la Tropa de Cuera
E. Quartel de la Escolta de Voluntarios
F. Cuerpo de Guardia.
G. Almazen del Presidio
H. Almazen del Rey
Y. Almazen de la Mission
J. Crivienda del Oficial
K. Crivienda de los R.ᵐᵒˢ Misioneros
L. Herreria y Fragua.
M. Carpinteria
N Casa del Navio de Regoa

O. Casa del Zirujano
P. Enfermeria
q. Casa p.ᵃ las Gentiles de servir
R. Rogpeso p.ᵃ los nuebos Christianos
S. Casa p.ᵃ las Mugeres Gentiles
T. Corral para las Gallinas
V. Chiquero de Cerdos
X. Cosinas en General
I. Casa de la Mission, del Cuidado de Tierras.
Z. Lugares Comunes
H. Escorsaos

N.º 3.

MONTEREY PRESIDIO AS PLANNED, APPROXIMATELY 1771. (Hitherto unreproduced)

round a court containing a garden and fountain, and were
furnished with tables and mirrors from the United States,
Mexico, and China.

The men of California were tall and vigorous, and withal
they were picturesque. They wore dark-colored, low-
browed, broad-brimmed hat; short jacket; open-necked
shirt; rich waistcoat, knee-breeches and white stockings,
or trousers slashed below the knee and gilt-laced; deer-skin
leggings and shoes; a red sash, and a *serape*. The women
were not tall, but, as we know, they had glossy black hair,
lustrous black eyes, and the whitest of teeth. Their habit
was a gown of silk, crêpe, or calico, loose and short-sleeved;
bright-colored belt; satin or kid shoes; necklace and ear-
rings; with hair, if unmarried, in long braids, and if married, on a high comb. Within doors the head-drape was
the *rebozo;* out of doors it was the mantilla. Beef, red beans,
and tortillas constituted the food of the humbler class,
a fare to which folk of greater means added chocolate, milk
or coffee, but not usually wine, as it was costly. Moreover,
at meals, families, except at the best houses, remained
standing.

Children were numerous, — thirteen to twenty per wedded
pair, — and the deference paid to parents was profound.
No son, even if fifty or sixty years old, dared to smoke or
wear his hat in his father's presence, and fathers not infrequently chastised a grown son with the lash.[6] At the
Guerra home the régime was patriarchal. Rising at dawn,
the household repaired to the dining-room, where they
partook of coffee, the father at the head of the board
(standing), with sons and daughters on either hand.
Breakfast, a hearty meal, was taken at eight or nine o'clock.
At noon luncheon was served; at four o'clock, tea; and at
eight or nine, supper. After supper there were prayers.

These concluded, the sons and daughters withdrew, each bending the knee to the father and kissing his hand.[7]

Objects of pride with the California housewife were the family garments stitched and embroidered to a nicety; but objects of supreme pride were the beds. Not less than luxurious must they be, with ticks filled with down, silken counterpanes, and satin pillow-covers edged with lace or embroidery.

Society at the presidio was dependent somewhat upon traffic, but at the pueblo it was so dependent scarcely at all. The supply-ships with officers from San Blas came annually to San Diego and Monterey; and after 1806, the Russian ships (also with officers) came from New Archangel and Ross to San Francisco. But it was the vessels of the exploring expeditions sent out by England, Spain, and France — the vessels of Vancouver, Pérouse, Malaspina, Duhaut-Cilly, Beechey, Petit-Thouars, and Laplace — that, with their lighthearted midshipmen, their bands of stirring music, and their hospitality, contributed to society most.

Nor were the Californians insensible to amenities on the part of vessels from the United States. At Monterey, in 1842, Commodore Jones emphasized apologies for untimely calls by an entertainment. At San Francisco, in 1846, on the evening of September 8, the American vice-consul, William A. Leidesdorff, gave a grand ball in the large hall of his residence, one hundred Californian and American ladies attending. And, at Monterey, in 1847, on April 9, the United States naval officers gave in the barracks a ball still grander. Present were Commodore Biddle and suite, General Kearny and staff, ex-Governor J. B. Alvarado, ex-Comandante-General M. G. Vallejo, the French Vice-Consul (Gasquet), the English Vice-Consul

(Forbes), and many besides. "The ladies," observes the "Californian," "turned out *en masse*, and if we can judge from the evidence of our eyes, the ladies of California are fairly determined to conquer the conquerors of their country, and then of course *to the victors belong the spoils*." "For a month," the same journal remarks, "the question among the ladies has been: 'Shall they or shall they not adopt the use of bonnets?' From present indications the ayes have it. Who will supply them?"

The presidio was more sedate than the pueblo, a condition which its social life, as a rule, reflected. Once, however, the presidio of San Diego was startled by a flagrant breach of decorum, — an international elopement. Henry D. Fitch was a New Bedford sailor, young, and in command of the Maria Esther. Stopping at San Diego in 1826, he fell a victim to the charms of Doña Josefa, daughter of Joaquín Carrillo. He was Protestant, she Catholic, and again there arose the dilemma which in other years had embarrassed Rezánoff. "Why don't you carry me off, Don Enrique?" the lady is said to have finally inquired. And carry her off Don Enrique did; or rather Pío Pico, cousin to the lady, did for him; for at night the latter bore her a-gallop on his best steed to the seashore, where she was met by a boat, taken on board the Vulture, — a ship navigated by Fitch's friend, Captain Richard Barry, — and on July 3, 1829, was married at Valparaíso. In 1830, at Monterey, Padre Sánchez procured Fitch's arrest, and for a time there was danger that the marriage might be pronounced a nullity. So radical a step was not taken; but in December Sánchez condemned the culprit "to give as a penance, and as a reparation, a bell of at least fifty pounds in weight for the church at Los Ángeles, which barely has a borrowed one."

Many were the forms of social pleasure prized in California (picnics among them), but the form prized most was the dance — the folk-dance. For the scene, a hall within doors or a bower without; for participants, cavaliers with braided hair, and ladies with hair flowing; for instruments, the violin and guitar; for figures, *la jota* (performed by four to sixteen couples, singly or in chain), *la zorrita* (couples), *el caballo, el jarabe,* and *el fandango.* Says Alfred Robinson of a dance which he witnessed at the Bandini home in San Diego: —

The female was erect with her head a little inclined to the right shoulder, as she modestly cast her eyes to the floor, whilst her hands gracefully held the skirts of her dress, suspending it above the ankle to expose to the company the execution of her feet. Her partner . . . was under full speed of locomotion, and rattled away with his feet with wonderful dexterity. His arms were thrown carelessly behind his back, and secured, as they crossed, the points of his serape, that still held its place upon his shoulders. Neither had he doffed his sombrero, but just as he stood when gazing from the crowd he had placed himself upon the floor.

A popular *jota* began: —

A mouse I had, with thirty mice.

Extremely popular was *la zorrita* (the little fox), nor is it forgotten at San Gabriel to this day.

The little fox went to the hills,
And because she went on a lark, a lark,
She came back shorn.

It is related by Thomas Savage that, conversing with Doña Eulalia Pérez, a famous Californian dancer of old days, she thus apostrophized him in farewell: —

O Thomas dear, would I explain
To thee my pain!
.   .   .   .   .   .
With greatest gladness,
And sweetest calmness,
To give to thee my soul and love,
Is my intent.

As for *el caballo*, —

Cuando el caballo entró en Cádiz,

— it was performed by couples with gestures significant of the gallop. *El fandango*, too, was performed by couples, the features being a flourish of castanets, songs, and amorous compliments.

> Do not say to me " Nay "!
> . . . .
> Do not kill me with harshness;
> Do not treat me with cruelty;
> Do not deny me your lealty;
> Do not despise my love,
> No, for I 'm yours alone;
> Do not say to me " Nay "!

When a lady danced with unusual spirit and grace, male spectators were wont to show appreciation by throwing coins at her feet and piling their sombreros one after another upon her head.[8]

Then there was Carnival: —

> Follow me, follow me, nobody ask;
> Crazy is Carnival under the mask.

Throughout this season, at the dance or frolic, it was customary for friends to break upon each other's heads egg-shells (*cascarones*) filled with spangles or scented water. The cavalier who could oftenest thus cause a lady to "float in lavender and cologne" was accounted best; and *vice versa*. William H. Davis relates that calling one day upon Doña Encarnación Briones at North Beach, he failed to catch her off guard, he being so caught by her several times. As he was leaving, she archly remarked: "*Usted vinó á trasquilar, pero fué trasquilado*" (You came to shear, but you were shorn).[9] "The wit of a Californian lady," Davis perhaps was reminded, "glances here and there like the sun-rays through the fluttering leaves of a wind-stirred forest."

Nor was the drama a pastime unknown to Californians.

In the church on Christmas Eve [writes Walter Colton] the
Virgin Mother bends before the altar over her new-born babe.
A company of shepherds enter. In their wake follows a hermit
with long white beard, tattered missal, and sin-chastening lash.
Near him figures a wild hunter in the skins of the forest. Last
of all comes the Evil One with horned frontlet, disguised hoof
and robe of crimson flame. Approaching the manger, the shepherds, led by Gabriel, kneel and to the notes of the harp chant
a hymn of praise. The hermit and hunter are not among them;
they have been beguiled by the Tempter and are lingering at a
game of dice. The Tempter, emboldened, shows himself among
the shepherds; but here he encounters Gabriel, who knows him
of old. He quails under the eye of the angel and flees his presence. Hermit and hunter, disenthralled, make their homage
penitential.[10]

A masque, *El Diablo en la Pastorela*, composed by Padre
Florencio of La Soledad, was rendered on Christmas
Night, 1837, with much *éclat* at the house of Pío Pico in
San Diego; and the year before, at Monterey, Governor
Chico was regaled by the feats of a troupe of Mexican
acrobats.

Probably the most elaborate function, ceremonial and
social, ever celebrated in Hispanic California was the in-
auguration of Governor Pablo Vicente de Sola at Monterey in 1816. It opened in the plaza with a military display under the flag of Castile. Next came a reception at
the *casa real*. Twenty beautiful *señoritas* advanced, and,
kissing the hand of the Governor in the name of their respective families, —Estudillo, Vallejo, Estrada, and others,
—received in return boxes of sweetmeats from Mexico.
A collation followed, the tables graced with roses, and
laden with oranges, pomegranates, figs, olives, dates, cor-
dials and wines. After a feast in the plaza by the populace,
space was cleared, and bulls and grizzly bears were set upon

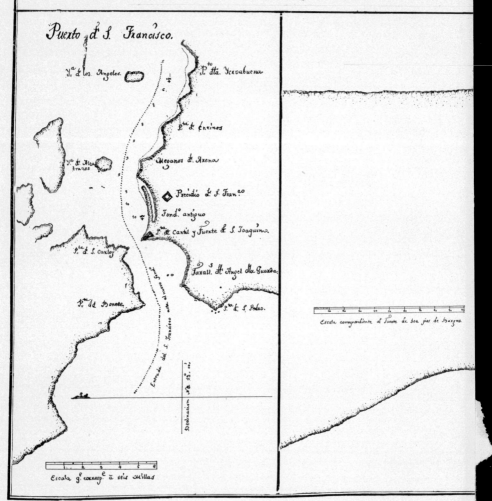

Plano que manifiesta el Puerto de San Francisco situado en la Costa Septentrional de Californias en 37° 4'...
do de San Joaquin colocado en la punta del cantil del mismo Puerto construido por el Señor Gobernador interin...
Conde de Revilla Gigedo Virrey de N.E. advirtiéndose que los trozos de muralla q.e lleva el color de carmín indica ser...

Nota que desde la superficie del agua en la punta del cantil asta el canto alto de la muralla tiene de Elevación 120. pies

Puerto d.e S. Francisco.

Y.a d.e los Angeles.

P.to d.ta Yervabuena

P.ta d.e Encinos

Mesanos d.e Arena

Presidio d.e S. Fran.co

Fond.o antiguo

P.ta d.e Cantil y Fuerte d.e S. Joaquin.

Y.a d.e Alcatrazes

Taxall. H.t Angel d.la Guarda.

Y.a d.e S. Carlos

P.ta d.e S. Pedro.

P.ta d.el Bonete

Entrada del S. Francisco con el Rumbo...

Declinacion N.E. 15°. ...

Escala q.e corresp.e a seis Millas

Escala correspondiente al Fuerte de los pies de Burgos.

PORT OF SAN FRANCISCO, AND BATTERY O

Altura de Polo N° y en 55°. 33′ al O.te del Meridiano de San Blas como hasi mismo el Fuerte nombra-
de la Peninsula de californias D. Jose Joaquin de Arrillaga en el presente año de 1794 por Orden de Exma Señor
al y canto y lo restante que hace frente àla entrada del Puerto es de peña viva.

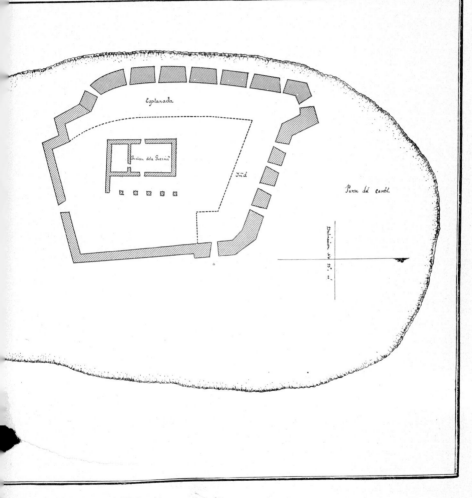

Esplanada

Quartes dela Guarni.

Smd

Punta del Cantil

F SAN JOAQUIN, 1794.   (Hitherto unreproduced)

one another. Two days later, Sola and his suite — cuirassed cavaliers with shields and lances, and ladies on palfreys, a cavalcade out of the "Faery Queen" itself — set forth to San Carlos Mission. The way led through a wood past stations of the Cross. Suddenly there appeared a band of monks attended by Indian acolytes. Behind came padres from all California, bearing upon a platform an effigy of Christ crucified, and followed by Indians to the number of many hundred. Sola and his officers alighted, kissed the feet of the Christ, and, amid the odor of incense from censers swung by the acolytes, entered the mission. To crown all, Padre Amorós of San Carlos preached, and the Indians presented a sham battle.[11]

Fights between bulls and bears were not uncommon at presidios, and they occasionally were tolerated at a mission; but the audience to whom they appealed with peculiar force was that of one of the two pueblos, San José or Los Ángeles. Around the sides of the plaza a strong wooden barrier was erected, and behind it a high platform for spectators. Bull and bear were then introduced, a hind foot of the bear attached by a long *reata* to a fore foot of the bull. After a vain attempt to escape on the part of the bull, there was a close struggle, the bear it is said usually proving victor. Bulls sometimes were baited by *toreadors*; but more popular at the pueblos than such sport were cockfighting, horse-racing, and gambling; the latter pursued at the very doors of the sanctuary, and not seldom culminating in a duel with swords.

With regard to education, it proverbially was the thing about which the Californian, priest or layman, troubled himself least. For girls it was said to consist of dancing, music, religion, and amiability. "In 1840," observes Prudencia Higuera, "I went to school in an adobe near where the town of San Pablo now stands. A Spanish gentleman was the teacher, and he told us many new things, for which we remember him with great respect. But when he said the earth was round, we all laughed out loud, and were much ashamed." The more enlightened Californians, when possible, sent their children abroad. Sons of Hartnell, Pacheco, and Spence were educated in the Sandwich Islands. The Suñols sent sons to Paris. Vallejo sent a son to Valparaíso, and other children to the United States.[12]

Private Rancho

By the Laws of the Indies, the settlement of new countries was to be effected by companies of not less than thirty under an *impresario*, or by private companies of not less than ten. Such companies were to establish pueblos, and it was in accordance with the laws in question that Neve founded San José in 1777 and Los Ángeles in 1781. The ultimate conversion of missions into pueblos was assumed. Indeed, the governmental or secular idea of "reduction" involved no segregation of neophytes apart from their abodes. For the native, the pueblo form of organization was to be both first and final. Presidios, too, it was assumed, would become towns by attracting around them a population which sooner or later could be subjected to the laws governing the pueblo.

The first specific legislation affecting California pueblos and presidios was Bucarely's Instructions of August 17, 1773, to Rivera y Moncada. By these not only might the comandante-general designate common lands (*tierras de comunidad*), he might distribute lands in private to such Indians as would dedicate themselves to agriculture and stock-raising, and he might distribute lands among the other *pobladores* according to merit. But in each instance all recipients of lands in private must live "in the town (pueblo) and not dispersed."[13] On October 22, 1791, Pedro de Nava, comandante of the Provincias Internas de Occidente, specifically authorized presidial comandantes to grant house-lots and lands to soldiers and citizens, but only within a district (pueblo limit) of four common leagues, measured from the centre of the presidio square; and only to such soldiers and citizens as should desire fixed places of residence.[14] For California, then, the private rancho — land to be owned and occupied by an individual apart from the community — was at first not contemplated. It was an estate not readily subjected to supervision. In a word, it was alien to the paternalistic spirit of Spanish rule.

Still, circumstances arose under which the private rancho was deemed a necessity, and in 1775 Rivera made such a grant to Manuel Butrón. The land was soon abandoned, and in 1784 Fages, who had been making grants of the kind provisionally, sought counsel of Comandante-General Ugarte. By advice of Asesor Navarro, Ugarte empowered Fages in 1786 to make non-pueblo grants, provided they did not exceed three leagues in extent, were beyond the limits of existing pueblos, did not conflict with missions or *rancherías*, were equipped by the grantee with a stone house, and were stocked by him with at least two thousand head of animals. It was under this authorization that the private ranchos enumerated in chapter x — San Rafael, Los Nietos, San Pedro, and others near Los Ángeles — derived quasi-validity. But though countenanced by the secular power, the private rancho met determined opposition from the missionaries. They regarded it as territorially an infringement upon the Mission, and they deemed it conducive to neophyte insubordination. Under the Spanish régime the number of such holdings was small, not more than twenty.[15] With the coming of Secularization, and the enactment of the naturalization and colonization laws of 1824 and 1828, whereby a single colonist might own not to exceed eleven square leagues, but might own that amount absolutely in fee, the number rapidly increased. By 1830 it was fifty, and by 1840 it was approximately six hundred.

That under Nava's order many (or any) California ranchos were dignified with stone houses is not probable. The houses were of palisades, or adobes, with roofs of tules or tiles, and with ox-hide or wooden doors. They might be of two rooms, one for living and one for sleeping, with a few *vaqueros* and Indian servants; or they might be of many rooms about a court, with *vaqueros* and Indian servants by the score.[16] In either case, the exterior — save for corrals and a vegetable patch — was absolutely bare, there being neither barns, stables, nor gardens.

Prior to 1824, a Californian wishing to become a ranchero, would apply to the *alcalde* of his district for land. The latter, taking with him two witnesses, would erect a mound or pile of stones as a point of starting, then with a *reata* fifty feet in length would measure the tract — five to twenty or even thirty leagues — at a smart gallop. In a few years the owner, or (prior to 1821) royal tenant, could boast of 2000 to 10,000 head of cattle, 1500 to 2000 horses and mules, and 10,000 to 20,000 sheep. Of these the cattle and mules were the most readily exchanged for commodities, although the horses were indispensable. During the period of the fur-trade (1771–1816), and before that of the tallow-trade with Lima (1813–18), the ranchero possessed almost no exchangeable or convertible property; his cattle and sheep were of use merely to subsist and clothe himself and retainers. The period of his prosperity was from 1828 to 1846. Then, as noted in chapter xv, he found a ready American and English market for hides and tallow.

The *matanza*, or slaughter, involved as a preliminary the grand *rodeo* or "round-up," and the *rodeo* involved trained horses, and men skilled as wielders of the *reata*, and not unused to the trick of throwing an unruly bull by a twist of the tail. Previous to the grand *rodeo* (held in March or April), *rodeos* were held for the purpose of accustoming cattle to rendezvous at a particular spot. At the grand *rodeo*, stock was counted, or rather estimated; the portion belonging to the ranchero was separated from that belonging to his neighbors; and calves (500 to 3000 head) were branded. It was thus determined what proportion of a herd might properly be slaughtered. The slaughtering itself came later. A band of *vaqueros* armed with knives rode over the fields, selected each an animal, deftly severed a nerve in the nape of the neck, and it fell dead. Or — a more common procedure — the cattle were dispatched after having been corralled and bound with *reatas*. In either event *peladores* (flayers) stripped off the hides, and the meat was cut up by *tasajeros*, or butchers. The *matanza* necessarily caused much offal, and scores of dogs were kept for consuming it. A ranchero riding to town was, it is averred, not infrequently attended by a train of dogs half a mile long. Horses when in excess were destroyed by being driven over a precipice; or by being thrust into corrals, whence, as they were liberated one at a time, they were pierced with the lance. Moreover, as the pueblo possessed its *alcalde*, so the country possessed its high functionary, the *juez de campo*, or judge of the plain, an officer supreme at the *rodeo*.[17]

In agriculture the ranchero was neither interested nor versed. He raised grain (barley and wheat) in quantity barely sufficient for his own need, cultivating it with ludicrous plow and harrow, reaping it with the sickle, threshing it under the feet of mares, and winnowing it in the wind.

Save for the block-wheeled ox-cart, low, crude, and creaking, and the *volanta* of the padre, there were no vehicles; nor was the ranchero, though a cattle-owner, enough of a domesticator of cattle to provide himself to any extent with milk, butter, and cheese.

The better-class ranchero was wont to awaken early, partake of chocolate, rise, order a favorite horse, and ride over his land. Between eight and nine o'clock he breakfasted on *carne asada* (broiled meat), eggs, beans, tortillas, and (occasionally) coffee. Dinner, which was like breakfast, was served at noon or at one o'clock. Then the ranchero rode forth again; this time perchance to the estate of a neighbor; and at eight o'clock he went to bed. His dress differed not materially from that of his fellow countryman of the presidio or pueblo. Both were cavaliers, but the ranchero was cavalier *par excellence*. His pride was his horse, his saddle, his bridle, and his spurs. The horse (of Andalusian descent) was beautiful and strong. White, dapple-gray, or chestnut in color, he was full-chested, thin-flanked, round in the barrel, clean-limbed, with unusually small head, feet, and ears, large full eyes, expanded nostrils, and full flowing mane and tail.[18] The saddle — huge and apparently clumsy — consisted of a "tree," high fore and aft, beneath which were spread two or three broad and low-hanging aprons of leather, the outer one (or two) stamped in figures and embroidered in red, green, gold, or silver. The bridle was of horse-hair and was adorned with silver buckles and buttons; the stirrups were of oak shielded in front with long leather coverings; and the spurs bore rowels of four or six points.

To promote good-fellowship or greet his lady, the ranchero while mounted would sing and play the guitar, his steed stepping in time to the tune: [19] —

Ah for the red spring rose,
 Down in the garden growing,
Fading as fast as it blows,
 Who shall arrest its going?
Peep from thy window and tell,
 Fairest of flowers, Isabel.

Or for a wager, he would pick up at full dash a coin or a kerchief from the ground; nor was a pause needful even to light a cigarette. It was, however, in throwing the lasso (instrument of twisted hide or horse-hair) that the ranchero found the diversion most congenial to him. Sometimes his quarry was the grizzly bear, an animal which, despite its great strength, could be reduced by the *reata* to helplessness.

Our leader [says Colton, describing a hunt in which he had participated] dashed up to [a] tree, which was instantly surrounded by the whole troop. "Give us pistols," exclaimed the *señoritas*, as bravely in for the sport as the rest. Click, crack! and a storm of balls went through the tree-top. Down came old Bruin with one bound into the midst, full of wrath and revenge. The horses instinctively wheeled into a circle, and as Bruin sprung for a death-grapple, the lasso of our *baccaros*, thrown with unerring aim, brought him up all standing. He now turned upon the horse of his new assailant; but that sagacious animal evaded each plunge, and seemed to play in transport about his antagonist. The pistols were out again, and a fresh volley fell thick as hail around the bear. In the smoke and confusion no one could tell where his next spring might be; but the horse of the *baccaro* knew his duty and kept the lasso taut. Bruin was wounded, but resolute and undaunted; the fire rolled from his red eyes like a flash of lightning out of a forked cloud. Foiled in his plunges at the horse, he seized the lasso in his paws, and in a moment more would have been at his side, but the horse sprang and tripped him, rolling him over and over till he lost his desperate hold on the lasso. The pistols were reloaded, and *señoritas* and *caballeros* all dashed up for another shower of fire and lead. As the smoke cleared, Bruin was found with the lasso slack, a sure evidence that the horse who managed it knew his antagonist was dead.

Instead of the bear it might be the elk that the hunter sought, an animal not deficient in prowess, yet capable of being dragged alive into a settlement by the *reatas* of two rancheros. Or the object of pursuit might be a wild horse of the Tulares. In this event, the saddle would be discarded, and a section of lasso be wound loosely about the ranchero's horse, just behind the forelegs. To the rope the rider would attach his *reata;* beneath it he would slip his knees; and thus disencumbered yet secured, would brave the dangers of trampling or a stampede.

Cattle on a rancho were virtually wild, and to proceed among them on foot (a thing which the ranchero or *vaquero* himself never did) was fraught with peril. Parties from vessels at times had narrow escapes from bulls "clothed with all the terrors of the Apocalyptic beast"; and John Bidwell, who deemed bulls more to be dreaded by the footman than grizzly bears, tells of dodging into gulches and behind trees, to avoid them, in 1841. To none, however, it is safe to say, did there befall adventure more remarkable than to J. Ross Browne in the Salinas River Valley, some thirty miles north of Soledad Mission.

Thrown from his mule, Browne was proceeding wearily on foot, when he discovered that a large band of Spanish cattle was beginning to close in toward the line of his route.

A fierce-looking bull [he writes] led the way, followed by a lowing regiment of stags, steers and cows, crowding one upon the other in their furious charge. As they advanced, the leader occasionally stopped to tear up the earth and shake his horns; but the mass kept crowding on, their tails switching high in the air, and uttering the most fearful bellowing, while they tossed their horns and stared wildly, as if in mingled rage and astonishment. . . . The nearest tree was half a mile to the left, on the margin of a dry creek. . . . Scarcely conscious of the act, I ran [for it] with all my might. . . . The thundering of heavy hoofs after me, and the furious bellowing that resounded over the plain, spread a contagion among the grazing herds on the way, and with one accord they joined in the chase. It is in no spirit of boastfulness that I assert the fact, but I certainly made that half-mile in as few minutes as ever the same distance was made by mortal man. When I reached the trees, I looked back. The advance body of the cattle were within a hundred yards, bearing down in a whirlwind of dust. I lost no time in making my retreat secure. As the enemy rushed in, tearing up the earth and glaring at me with their fierce, wild eyes, I had gained the fork of the tree, about six feet from the ground, and felt very thankful that I was beyond their reach. . . .

While in this position, with the prospect of a dreary night before me, and suffering [from thirst] the keenest physical anguish, a very singular circumstance occurred to relieve me of further apprehension respecting the cattle, though it suggested a new danger for which I was equally unprepared. A fine young bull had descended the bed of the creek in search of a waterhole. While pushing his way through the bushes he was suddenly attacked by a grizzly bear. The struggle was terrific. I could see the tops of the bushes sway violently to and fro, and hear the heavy crash of drift-wood as the two powerful animals writhed in their fierce embrace. A cloud of dust rose from the spot. It was not distant over a hundred yards from the tree in which I had taken refuge. Scarcely two minutes elapsed before the bull broke through the bushes. His head was covered with blood, and great flakes of flesh hung from his fore-shoulders; but, instead of manifesting signs of defeat, he seemed literally to glow with defiant rage. Instinct had taught him to seek an open space. . . . But scarcely had I time to glance at him when a huge bear, the largest and most formidable I ever saw in a wild state, broke through the opening.

A trial of brute force that baffles description now ensued. Badly as I had been treated by the cattle, my sympathies were greatly in favor of the bull, which seemed to me to be much the nobler animal of the two. He did not wait to meet the charge, but, lowering his head, boldly rushed upon his savage adversary. The grizzly was active and wary. He no sooner got within reach of the bull's horns than he seized them in his powerful grasp, keeping the head to the ground by main strength and the tremendous weight of his body, while he bit at the nose with his teeth, and raked strips of flesh from the shoulders with his hind paws. The two animals must have been of very nearly equal weight. On the one side there was the advantage of superior agility and two sets of weapons — the teeth and claws; but on the other, greater powers of endurance and more inflexible courage. . . .

In the death-struggle that ensued [Browne continues] both animals seemed animated by a supernatural strength. The grizzly struck out wildly, but with such destructive energy that the bull, upon drawing back his head, presented a horrible and ghastly spectacle; his tongue, a mangled mass of shreds, hanging from his mouth, his eyes torn completely from their sockets, and his whole face stripped to the bone. On the other hand, the bear was ripped completely open, and writhing in his last agonies. Here it was that indomitable courage prevailed; for, blinded and maimed as he was, the bull, after a momentary pause to regain his wind, dashed wildly at his adversary again, determined to be victorious even in death. A terrific roar escaped from the dying grizzly. With a last frantic effort he sought to make his escape, scrambling over and over in the dust. But his strength was gone. A few more thrusts from the savage victor, and he lay stretched upon the sand, his muscles quivering convulsively, his huge body a resistless mass. A clutching motion of the claws — a groan — a gurgle of the throat, and he was dead.

The bull now raised his bloody crest, uttered a deep bellowing sound, shook his horns triumphantly, and slowly walked off, not, however, without turning every few steps to renew the struggle if necessary. But his last battle was fought. As the blood streamed from his wounds a death-chill came over him. He stood for some time, unyielding to the last, bracing himself up, his legs apart, his head gradually drooping; then dropped on his fore-knees and lay down; soon his head rested on the ground; his body became motionless; a groan, a few convulsive respirations, and he too, the noble victor, was dead.[20]

As has been said, the private rancho was an object of dislike to the padres, because of its effect upon the Indian. President José Señán wrote to Viceroy Branciforte in 1796:

Under no pretext, it seems to me, should retired soldiers or others be permitted to establish themselves in places solitary and withdrawn from men. The evils to which those thus dwelling in solitude are subject cannot easily be computed. They live exposed to the ridicule of the Gentiles; exposed to the committing of many excesses without correction or punishment, without King to command, or Pope to excommunicate. . . . It is no small part of the task of the padres to keep their neophytes congregated in the missions, and to subdue in them their instinct for the wild. But if *gente de razón* adopt the same mode of life, to what purpose their efforts? [21]

Rancheros deserving of censure, civil and ecclesiastical, there undoubtedly were, but there also were those who were ornaments to their class. One of the stateliest men of his time (1775–1860) was a ranchero, Antonio María Lugo. Tall, proud, the owner of countless acres, he might have been seen upon the Los Ángeles streets, shoulder draped in Saltillo *serape*, and sword beneath his arm.

In the style of their dwellings, presidio and pueblo were alike. In respect to birth, bridal, and burial, the likeness extended to the private rancho. Scarcely was a child born ere it was hurried to the priest for christening and baptism. When eight or ten, it often was betrothed; and when thirteen or fourteen, if a girl, married. Fathers made the contract, and the wedding festivities were elaborate. Says Colton: —

The bridegroom must present [the bride] with at least six entire changes of raiment, nor forget, through any sentiment of delicacy, even the chemise. Such an oversight might frustrate all his hopes, as it would be construed into a personal indifference, — the last kind of indifference which a California lady will forgive. He therefore hunts this article with as much solicitude as the Peri the gift that was to unlock Paradise. Having found six which are neither too full nor too slender, he packs them in rose-leaves which seem to flutter like his own heart, and sends them to the lady as his last bridal present. . . .

Two fine horses procured for the occasion are led to the door, saddled, bridled, and pillioned. The bridegroom takes up before him the godmother, and the godfather the bride, and thus they gallop away to church. The priest, in his rich robes, receives them at the altar, where they kneel, partake of the sacrament, and are married. This over, they start on their return, — but now the gentlemen change partners. The bridegroom, still on the pillion, takes up before him his bride. With his right arm he steadies her on the saddle, and in his left hand holds the reins. They return to the house of the parents of the bride, where they are generally received with a discharge of musketry. Two persons, stationed at some convenient place, now rush out and seize him by his legs, and, before he has time to dismount, deprive him of his spurs, which he is obliged to redeem with a bottle of brandy.

The married couple then enter the house, where the near relatives are all waiting in tears to receive them. They kneel down before the parents of the lady, and crave a blessing, which is bestowed with patriarchal solemnity. On rising, the bridegroom makes a signal for the guests to come in, and another for the guitar and harp to strike up. Then commences the dancing, which continues often for three days, with only brief intervals for refreshment, but none for slumber; the wedded pair must be on their feet; their dilemma furnishes food for good-humored gibes and merriment.[22]

Nor was burial itself always a scene entirely sad. If the dead were a little child, it was deemed to have passed in angelic form straight to Abraham's bosom. "Its coffin, draped in white and garlanded with flowers, was borne amid voices of gladness. The untimely blight and the darkness of the grave were all forgotten."

With the American occupation of California, Hispanic institutions fell at a blow. In 1849 the people adopted an American constitution. By this instrument it was provided that all laws in force should remain in force until altered or repealed by the legislature. The first legislature

(1850) passed on April 20 an act repealing every Spanish
law but one, and that, it is interesting to note, a law
pertaining to the private rancho, — the law providing for
a *juez de campo*, a judge of the plain.[23] As for California
life, — the life led under Serra and Fages, and their
successors, — it has declined rapidly. Something of it
lingers in San Diego and San Gabriel, in Guahome and
Camulos Ranchos, in Los Ángeles, Santa Bárbara, and San
Luis Obispo, and most of all in Monterey; but it lingers
in nooks and corners only.

One day in Venice Mr. William D. Howells saw from
a balcony on the Grand Canal a boat bearing a strange
figure. It was a man clad *cap-à-pie* in a suit of gleaming
mail, with visor down and shoulders swept by heavy raven
plumes. What Mr. Howells saw was ancient Venice come
back. One day in Monterey the writer saw from the
street a figure not so strange as the armored Venetian, but
yet strange. It was a man in jacket, slashed trousers, and
sombrero. He bestrode with Spanish grace a steed that for
mettle and trappings might well have been Andalusian.
The day was not a festival. The rider seemingly was without intent. He was simply old California — California
under Spain and Mexico — come back.

NOTES

WITH LISTS OF SOURCES

ABBREVIATIONS USED IN NOTES

M. A. = Mexican Archives; S. A. = Spanish Archives; B. A. = British Archives; A. A. = American Archives; B. C. = Bancroft Collection. Under M. A., "Cor. de Virreyes, ser. II, t. 2/12, No. 376, f. 74," would signify: Correspondence of the Viceroys, second series, serial volume 2, volume 12, document No. 376, page 74. In making the card index to California material in the Mexican Archives, Dr. Bolton was compelled to create his own system of designation, there being none in existence. With regard, therefore, to the correspondence of the Viceroys he numbered the volumes both consecutively from first to last, and by series. Under S. A., Est. (*estante*) = section; caj. (*cajón*) = shelf; and leg. (*legajo*) = bundle or package. Under B. C., designations such as "Prov. [or Dept.] St. Pap. [or Rec.]" = Provincial [or Departmental] State Papers [or Records]. The abbreviation Mil. = Military; and Leg. Rec. = Legislative Records. Under B. A., F. O. = Foreign Office.

NOTES

CHAPTER I

DISCOVERY

NEW CHAPTER SOURCES. — *Application of the name California:* — Letter, Marqués del Valle to Cristóbal Oñate, Santa Cruz, May 14, 1535; Depositions relative to the discoveries of Francisco de Ulloa, Mexico, May 29, 1540; Map of the World, by Alonzo de Santz Cruz, 1542, — E. W. Dahlgren, Stockholm, 1892 (S. A.); *Informe de Gonzalo de Francia*, boatswain Vizcaino expedition, 1629; Tattonus Map of California, Benjamin Wright, 1600 (Library of Congress). *Derivation of name:* — " M. L." of Fresno, San Francisco *Chronicle*, June, 1893; *The Origin and Meaning of the Name California*, by Dr. George Davidson, Geographical Society of the Pacific, San Francisco, 1910. (Specific citations below.)

1. By *Marco Polo's Book* (A. D. 1477) it became known that the Asiatic coast was heavily fringed with islands. There was " Chipango [Japan], an island toward the east in the high seas 1500 [!] miles distant from the continent — a very great island." And " the sea in which lay the islands of those parts was called the sea of Chin [China]." And " with regard to that eastern sea of Chin, according to what was said by the experienced pilots and mariners of those parts, there were 7459 islands [Philippines and Moluccas] in the waters frequented by the said mariners." — " In those islands grew pepper as white as snow, as well as the black in great quantities. In fact the riches of those islands was something wonderful, whether in gold or precious stones, or in all manner of spicery; but they lay so far off from the mainland that it was hard to get to them." — " Moreover, Messer Marco Polo never was there." (*The Book of Ser Marco Polo* (Yule), 3d ed., 2 vols., 1903, vol. ii, pp. 253, 264.) See also map of Toscanelli (thought to have been used by Columbus) as reproduced in Sir A. Helps's *The Spanish Conquest in America*, London, 4 vols., 1900, vol. i, p. 58.

In Spain, for over two hundred and fifty years, North America (Asiatic Archipelago that it was presumed to be) was known rather as " the Indies " (Columbus's own designation) than as America. With South America the case was different. Looking, as the post-Columbian navigators were, for an Asiatic continent to the westward and southward of the islands, they deemed the conditions fulfilled by South America (described by Amerigo Vespucci in 1504), and this region was charted as continental from as early a date as 1507. Indeed, where the early navigators erred was not in their hypothesis as to the Asiatic coast-line, which was singularly correct, but in their confounding of North America — insular and peninsular — with insular Asia.

2. Map III (two plates, head of chapter I) portrays North America as a group of islands. The earliest maps representing California as apart from the continent are the "Herrera" (Kaspar van Baerle) map of 1622, the "Purchas" (Briggs) map of 1625, the "Prospect" (Speed) map of 1626, and the "World Encompassed" (Drake) map of 1628. (See chap. II of text, n. 27.) It moreover is in connection with insularity that there arises the question of the name California.

THE NAME CALIFORNIA

Bestowing of the name. — By "California" (a name first used in a book published in Spain in 1510 — *Las Sergas de Esplandián*) there was implied insularity coupled with riches. " 'Know,' the *Sergas* says, 'that on the right hand of the Indies there is an island called California, very close to the side of the Terrestrial Paradise; and it was peopled by black women, without any man among them, for they lived in the fashion of Amazons. They were of strong and hardy bodies, of ardent courage and great force. Their island was the strongest in all the world, with its steep cliffs and rock shores. Their arms were of gold, and so was the harness of the wild beasts they tamed to ride; for in the whole island there was no metal but gold.' " (Edward Everett Hale, *Proceedings American Antiquarian Society*, April 30, 1862, p. 45; *Atlantic Monthly*, vol. xiii, p. 265.)

With the *Sergas*, moreover, Cortés and his followers (the discoverers of Lower California, 1533–1535) had ample opportunity to be acquainted. Hardly less than the *Amadis de Gaul* was it a favorite in sixteenth-century Spain. Cervantes, writing in 1605, brands the *Sergas* as among the tales which had turned the head of Don Quixote. And in the Indies so much were books of its class prized, that in 1543 Charles V forbade their importation, describing them as *libros de romance que traten de materias profanas y fabulosas y historias fingidas.* (*Recopilación de Leyes de las Indias*, lib. i, tit. xxiv, ley 4.)

But Cortés and his followers — discoverers of California though they were, and familiar with the *Sergas* though they may have been — did not, it would seem, give to the land its name. Having sighted California on May 1, "day of the two apostles," says Cortés, and "because in the part sighted there were the highest sierras of this land, there was given to them the name 'Sierras de San Felipe.' . . . This same day," he continues, "we discovered an island near the land, and we called it Isla de Santiago [Cerralvo]. And soon we saw two others, one of which was called Isla de San

Miguel, and the other, Isla de San Cristóval [*Perlas* of Cortés's map, *post*, IV]. And reaching this port and bay of Santa Cruz, the day of Santa Cruz, May 3, it therefore was given that name." (Marqués del Valle to Cristóbal de Oñate at Compostela, from the port and bay of Santa Cruz, 14th of May, 1535, — S. A., Madrid, Academia de la Historia, Colección de Muñoz, tom. 80, fol. 137; *Congreso Internacional de Americanistas* (" Actas 4ª Reunión," Madrid, 1881), Madrid, 1883; vol. ii, p. 332.)

Furthermore, in 1537 [?] Cortés deposited with the government a map bearing at the point of his landing the name Santa Cruz (*post*, IV), and in 1540 Lower California was repeatedly referred to by him as *la tierra de Santa Cruz*. "I arrived," he says, "at the land of Santa Cruz and was in it . . . and being in the said land of Santa Cruz, I had complete knowledge of the land." (Memorial que dió al Rey el Marqués del Valle en Madrid, *Documentos Inéditos de las Indias*, vol. iv, p. 211.) And the companions of Cortés, when officially catechized as to the country, its name, etc., testified: one, that it was called Tarsis; another, that it had no name, but that the bay was called Santa Cruz; and some, that they could remember no name. (" Probanza," Pacheco y Cárdenas, *Docs.*, vol. xvi, pp. 12, 22, 27.)

The first time (so far as known) that the name of California was applied to any actual body of land was in 1539. In that year Francisco de Ulloa, one of the lieutenants of Cortés (a man who had been with the Spanish leader to Santa Cruz in 1535), made, under orders from his superior, a second voyage thither, taking with him as diarist Francisco Preciado. The latter employs the name California at various times and each time in the same sense. He says: (1) " On November 10 we found ourselves 54 leagues distant from California a little more or less always in the southwest, seeing in the night three or four fires "; (2) and (3): " In the meanwhile our Chichimeco interpreter, borne in the isle of California, was come unto us," etc. "The captain commanded the Indian our Chichimeco to speake unto them [Indians of the northeast coast of Lower California], but they could not understand him, so that we assuredly believe that they understand not the language of the isle of California." (Ramusio, *Viaggi*, 1565, vol. iii, pp. 343, 347; Hakluyt, *Voyages*, 1600, vol. iii, pp. 406, 412.)

In 1539, therefore (and to Preciado), "California " was an island; one so situated that on November 10, Ulloa was distant therefrom some 54 leagues. That at this time California signified Cortés's "land of Santa Cruz " (Lower California) may well seem improbable, for the allusions by Preciado to California as to it as insular unequivocally and *per se*, whereas his allusions to Lower California are to it, first, as almost certainly non-insular, and, second (whether insular or not), as not California, but " Santa Cruz." "Wee began," says Preciado, "to be of divers opinions, some thinking that this coast of Santa Cruz was a firme land . . . others the contrary," etc. (Hakluyt, 1600, vol. iii, p. 399.) And (after rounding the head of the gulf): " Here from this day forward wee began to bee afraid, considering that we were to return to the port of Santa Cruz; for it was supposed, that all along this mighty gulfe from the entrance in at Culiacan until the returning backe unto the said haven was all firme land, and also because wee had the firme land alwayes on our right hand and it goeth round circle-wise unto the sayd haven." (*Ibid.*, p. 402.)

But if California was not the Lower California of to-day, but so distinct and apart from it as to be an actual island, — an island so actual as to have supplied Ulloa with his interpreter, — what island was it?

It may have been Cerralvo (the Santiago of Cortés), or Espiritu Santo (so named by Francisco de Ortega in 1632), both at the mouth of the Bay of Santa Cruz, now La Paz. Cerralvo Island especially is so situated as to answer to that "California" from which on November 10, 1539, Ulloa was distant 54 leagues, — a California placed even by Bancroft (*History of California*, vol. i, p. 65, n. 2) "at or near Santa Cruz." But not only by their situation do these islands to-day answer to Preciado's California of 1539; they in 1539 — by their real pearls (maps, *post*, IV, V, VI) and reputed Amazons — answered to the California of the *Sergas de Esplandián* of 1510. Said Cortés, writing to the Emperor Charles V, on October 15, 1524: "He [one of my captains] brought me an account of the chiefs of the province of Ceguatán, who affirm that there is an island inhabited only by women without any men, and that at given times men from the mainland visit them. . . . This island is ten days' journey from the province, and many of them went thither and saw it, and told me also that it is very rich in pearls and gold." (H. Cortés, *Historia de Nueva España*, Lorenzana, 1770, p. 349.) Again (a bit of evidence quite new), Gonzalo de Francia, boatswain of the ship which, under Sebastián Vizcaino, visited Santa Cruz Bay in 1597, wrote to the King on May 27, 1629: "We came upon *un puerto grande* which was called *el puerto de la Paz* . . . and an island at the mouth which was called Island of Women, who were without men, none passing over to them except in summer on rafts made of reeds." (S. A., Madrid, Dirección de Hidrografía, Colección Navarrete, t. 19, no. 15.) Finally (a bit of evidence quite as new as the last), Pedro de Valencia, *escribano público* of Ulloa's armada, submitted to Cortés in 1540 (May 29) a report which described the Indian interpreter with the armada, who could not be understood by the natives of northeastern Lower California, "as from the port and bay of Santa Cruz" [*el yndio que llevábamos del puerto y baya de Santa Cruz*], an indication that Preciado's "isle of California" was within Santa Cruz (La Paz) Bay limits. (*Testimonio de los descubrimientos que hizó el Capitán Francisco de Ulloa, por orden de Hernán Cortés en la costa Norte de Nueva España, con una relación de su viaje desde Acapulco hasta la Isla de los Cedros, Méjico, 29 de Mayo, 1540*, S. A. (Sevilla), Arch. Genl. de Indias, est. i, caj. i, leg. 1–20.)

When and by whom, on the foregoing hypothesis, the name California was transferred from Cerralvo, or Espiritu Santo Island, to the mainland, is a question to which no definite answer is possible. It may have been in 1541 by Hernando de Alarcón, who in that year made thither an expedition, for on Alarcón's map, drawn by Castillo (*post*, v), the mainland is for the first time shown under the designation California.

But the hypothesis presented is not without a competing one. Preciado (Ulloa's diarist) discriminates between the "isle of California " and the "land of Santa Cruz." Yet it is not impossible that by California he means a portion of Lower California itself, to wit, the portion below Santa Cruz Bay — a portion which, though not charted as insular by Cortés, may in the mind of the lay Spaniard have been identified with the famed Amazonian isle "ten days' journey from Ceguatán." At any rate, as early as 1542 the cosmographer royal of Charles V (Alonzo de Santa Cruz) published a map (*post*, VII) which shows California as in the lower part insular, and in the upper part peninsular. The lower part bears the legend: *Ysla que descubrió el Marqués del Valle;* and the upper, *Tierra que enbió á descubrir Don Antonio de Mendoça* ("Map of the World by Alonzo de Santa Cruz, 1542," E. W. Dahlgren, Stockholm, 1892). "This map," says Dahlgren, "is almost identical with the great official Spanish Map (now lost) by Alonzo de Chaves, royal cosmographer to Charles V, issued in 1536 to correct the cartography of the world to date. It may be taken as embodying geographical ideas to 1539."

Derivation of the name. — M. Venegas (*Noticia de la California*, tom. i, pte. i, sec. 1, p. 3) mentions as a derivation for the name California, *calida fornax*, hot furnace, from the heat of California, but does not think the Spanish adventurers "could boast of so much literature." His own suggestion is that the derivation is from some Indian word misunderstood by the Spaniards. This suggestion gains weight from the contention of Upper Californians (Vallejo, Alvarado, and others) that the derivation is *kali forno*, an Indian phrase of Lower California signifying " high hill," " sandy coast," or "native land." The suggestion is countenanced by Bancroft (H. H.), who states that an old Indian of Sinaloa (Mexico) called the peninsula (A. D. 1878) *Tchalifalni-al* — "the sandy land beyond the water." On the other hand, the *calida fornax* derivation (rejected by Venegas because too "literary " for the *conquistadores*, and by Bancroft because the peninsula though hot was not so compared with other regions to which the *conquistadores* were accustomed) emerges rehabilitated at the hands of Jules Marcou, who ascribes it to Cortés, "to whom [he says] is due the appropriate classification of the Mexican regions into *tierra fria, tierra templada, tierra caliente,* and *tierra california.*" To such as find Marcou's derivation faulty, yet cling to the phrase *calida fornax*, there is left the chance that the phrase relates not to the climate, but to the hot baths (*temescales*) which were wont to be taken by the Indians. (J. Marcou, *Notes;* Washington, 1878.) For derivations almost certainly fanciful, see J. Archibald, "Why California? " in *Overland Monthly*, vol. ii, p. 437.

In 1910 (the year just past), Dr. George Davidson, President of the Geographical Society of the Pacific, published a monograph entitled *The Origin and Meaning of the Name California*. The publication mentions the first uses of the name California, and gives a list of the early maps on which the name appears. The *Sergas de Esplandián* is accepted as the source of the name, and the etymology is dealt with as follows: California; from κάλλος, beauty (or κάλλι-, beautiful), and ὄρνις (ornis), a bird. "In this island are many griffins . . . which can be found in no other part of the world. The queen took five hundred of these griffins to assist in the capture of Constantinople."

Professor Davidson alludes to a derivation by "M. L." of Fresno, printed in the San Francisco *Chronicle* for June, 1893. He says: "A late writer, M. L. of Fresno, who appears to be well posted on the subject, and who has evidently examined the geology of Lower California, expresses the opinion that the name came from the Indians. In approaching Loreto (on the eastern coast of the peninsula in latitude 26° 10') he saw snow-white heaps upon a knoll, and asked the guide, ' *Qué cosa es?* ' ' *Cal y forno,*' answered the Indian; when he knew at once he had the true meaning and origin of the name California, because these white heaps were lime-kilns; *cal* meaning lime, and *forno* an oven or kiln. He believed that Ulloa, remembering Montalvo's California, accepted the name for the country. (*Transactions and Proceedings of the Geographical Society of the Pacific*, 1910, vol. vi, part 1, pp. 34, 38.)

3. See chart I (head of chapter II) showing "Anian" and route of Magellan.

4. H. Cortés, *Historia de Nueva España*, Lorenzana, 1770, p. 382. Translations: M. Venegas, *History of California*, 2 vols., vol. i, p. 127; G. Folsom, *Dispatches of Hernando Cortés*, 1834, pp. 417–18; F. A. MacNutt, *The Letters of Cortes to Charles V*, 1908, 2 vols., vol. ii, pp. 207–209; H. H. Bancroft, *North Mexican States and Texas*, vol. i, p. 5, n. 4. In June, 1523, Cortés had been ordered by the King to hasten the search for a strait (Pacheco y Cárdenas, *Docs.*, vol. xxiii, p. 366); and in 1525 Estevǎn Gómez actually made a search, coasting from Nova Scotia to Florida. (W. Lowery, *The Spanish Settlements in the United States*, 1901, p. 169, notes.)

5. *Y adelante la California adonde llegó el primer Marqués del Valle que le pusó este nombre.* (Antonio de Herrera, *Historia General*, 1601, dec. viii, lib. 6, cap. 14; B. Díaz, *Historia Verdadera de la Conquista de la Nueva España*, 1632, cap. 200.)

6. Hitherto the only available account of Ulloa's voyage has been that of Preciado. The account submitted by Pedro de Valencia agrees generally with Preciado's, but it is worthy of note that, although Preciado is mentioned therein as a Franciscan padre, and the name Santa Cruz is used to designate Lower California, the name California is not used at all.

7. "But because your Lordship comanded mee that I should bring you

the secret of that gulfe [California], I resolved that although I had knowen I should have lost the shippes, I would not have ceased for anything to have seen the head thereof. . . . And it pleased God that after this sort we came to the very bottom of the Bay; where wee found a very mightie river [Colorado], which ranne with so great fury of a streame, that we could hardly saile against it." (Hakluyt, 1600, vol. iii, p. 425.)

— 8. Diary of Cabrillo and Ferrelo, Pacheco y Cárdenas, *Docs.*, vol. xiv, p. 165; *Florida Coll. Docs.*, vol. i, p. 173. Translation, R. S. Evans, *Report of U. S. Geological Survey* (Wheeler), vol. vii, p. 293.

9. According to physiographists, the Golden Gate originally was the outlet for the combined waters of the Sacramento and San Joaquín Rivers. By a subsidence of the bed of these streams, the sea was admitted through the Golden Gate, thus forming San Francisco Bay.

10. See map I (relief map of California), head of chapter I.

11. "It is held by geologists that the Sierra Nevada originated at the close of the Jurassic period, and that through the Cretaceous, Eocene, and Neocene periods it was worn down to a region of low relief. There may have been disturbances, but during this long period the range was certainly much lower than now, and the Great Valley of the San Joaquín occupied by a body of brackish or salt water. At the close of the Neocene, which was the time of the accumulation of the great deposits of auriferous gravels, there was a removal of faulting along the eastern side of the range, and this disturbance was accompanied by volcanic outbursts. The mountain range began to rise toward its present position, and these movements with relation to the depressed areas of the Great Basin have not yet ceased. With reference to the depressed valley known as Owens Valley, the crest of the Sierra is probably higher now than it has been; but during the glacial period it is likely that this region as a whole was higher than now." (H. W. Fairbanks, 1910, University of California.)

12. "The prevailing easterly drift of the atmosphere in temperate latitudes, causing the well-known winds from the west, is one of the prime factors in modifying the climate of the coast of California. This coast-line, stretching for 10 degrees of latitude, is subjected to a steady indraft from the west. In this movement, together with the fact that to the west is the Pacific Ocean, lies the secret of the difference in temperature between the Atlantic and the Pacific coasts at places of like latitude. For some years there has been an impression that the milder climate of the Pacific Coast was due to a warming influence of the Kuro Siwo, or Japan Current. No reliable data exist to support such a belief, and it is quite unlikely that the Japan Current plays any important part in modifying the climate of the Pacific Coast. The active factors are, as said above, the prevailing easterly drift of the atmosphere and the proximity of the mass of water, a great natural conservator of heat. One of the most noticeable differences between the climate of the Atlantic and Pacific seaboards is found in the trend of

the isotherms, those of the Atlantic Coast corresponding more or less with the parallels of latitude, while on the Pacific Coast the isotherms run more nearly like meridians. Too much emphasis cannot be laid upon the effect of these two factors, the easterly drift of the air and the proximity of the ocean in modifying climate. It is probable that if one of these conditions could be reversed, and the general movement of the air in these latitudes be from east to west, marked differences in climate conditions would result, and the Pacific Coast might then have a rigorous climate." ("Climatology of California," U. S. Dept. of Agriculture, *Bulletin L*, 1903, p. 15.)

13. John Muir, *The Mountains of California*, 1903 ; C. F. Lummis, *Encyclopedia Americana*, 1903, article " California."

14. See map II (Indian Linguistic Families), head of chapter I.

15. "From the time of the first settlement of California, its Indians have been described as both more primitive and more peaceful than the majority of the natives of North America. On the whole this opinion is undoubtedly true." "The picturesqueness and dignity of other Indians are lacking." — "Throughout the greater part of the State the civilization of the Indians is very much alike." — "The exceptions are Southern California and the northwesternmost part of the State." — "More than two thirds of the State, including all the central part, show a fundamental ethnical similarity, whose distinguishing characteristics furthermore are not found outside of the State." — "Structures of brush or tule were common." — "The shape of the houses was conical or domed." — "Basketry alone [among the arts] had reached a considerable development. Pottery was virtually unknown." — "Beyond the family, the only bases of organization were the village and the language." Religion was manifested not as symbolism and ritualism but as "individual shamanistic effort." The above characteristics of culture "pertain to all the Indians between Point Conception and Cape Mendocino, and between this stretch of coast and the Sierra Nevada, extending from north to south, from Mount Shasta to the Tehachapi Range." (A. L. Kroeber, *Types of Indian Culture in California*, 1904, University of California Pubs., vol. ii, no. 3; F. W. Hodge, *Handbook of American Indians North of Mexico*, Washington, 1907, part i, p. 190.)

The Indian substitute for the deity is the culture hero. But among the California Indians "the conception of a culture hero is wanting. Instead of a human divinity there is almost everywhere a true creator, a god who makes. Sometimes he is a person, sometimes an animal. . . . Often he makes the world from primitive water. Generally he makes also mountains and rivers. Usually he creates food. Almost always he creates men, and frequently divides them by languages and localities." But "the exceptional tendency of the California Indian to form real creation myths is seemingly not the result of a higher intellectuality which seeks and finds explanations, and to which other Indians have not attained. The tendency is probably due rather to a lack on the part of the Californian of the mythological specialization which characterizes other American Indians." (Kroeber, *supra*.)

Sta. Bárbara Channel Tribes, University of California Pubs., vol. iv, no. 3, p. 152. *California Tribes as Differentiated by Basketry, Ibid.*, vol. ii, no. 4, p. 151. Minute descriptions of the California Indians are to be found in B. C., *Arch. of Sta. Bárbara*, vol. vii, pp. 150–214. Extracts have been published under the title *A Mission Record of the California Indians*, A. L. Kroeber, University of California Pubs. in American Archæology and Ethnology, 1908, vol. viii, no. 1. For further description of the California Indians, see Powers, *Tribes of California;* Fages, *Noticias del Puerto de Monterey y Diario Histórico de los Viages Hechos al Norte de California*, 1775 (M. A., *Misiones*, vol. iv).

CHAPTER II

OCCUPATION OF MONTEREY

MATERIAL for the present chapter hitherto unused has been found in portions of the correspondence of Philip II and Philip III with Miguel López de Legazpi, Viceroy Luis de Velasco, the Audiencia of Manila, Andrés de Urdaneta, Santiago de Vera, Hernando de los Ríos Coronel, Viceroy Marqués de Montesclaros, Viceroy Pedro de Moya y Contreras, and others, as printed in *The Philippine Islands*, edited by Blair and Robertson. Much also, especially as relating to the islands of Rica de Oro and Rica de Plata, and to the voyage of Pedro de Unamunu (neglected subjects in their bearing upon the history of California), has been found in the Spanish Archives at Sevilla. The same archives have proved rich in material on Sebastián Vizcaino. Some of it is in print in *Documentos Referentes al Reconocimiento de las Costas de las Californias desde el Cabo de San Lucas al de Mendocino, Recopilados en el Archivo de Indias*, por D. Francisco Carrasco y Guisasola, coronel y capitán de fragata, Madrid, Dirección de Hidrografía, 1882. Other printed material of value for the chapter is the *Sucesos* of Antonio de Morga, 1609; *Transactions of the Royal Society*, London, 1674; *En Studie i Historisk Geografi*, by E. W. Dahlgren, Stockholm, 1893 and 1900; *Tasman's Journal* (Heeres), Amsterdam, 1898; and *Ein Unentdecktes Goldland*, by O. Nachod, Tokyo, 1899. (Specific citations below.)

1. In *Periplus*, Nordenskiöld states that the first dated map bearing the name Anian is the Zalterius map, Venice, 1566. It possibly (he says) is on an older map in the Correr Collection, Venice, Museo Civico.

2. Blair and Robertson, "Life and Voyage of Magellan" (*The Philippine Islands*, 55 vols., 1903–1909, vol. i, p. 250). "Expedition of García de Loaysa," "Voyage of Alvaro de Saavedra," and "Expedition of Ruy López de Villalobos," *Ibid.*, vol. ii, pp. 25–73.

3. H. C. Lea, *The Moriscos of Spain*, 1901, pp. 6, 394; M. A. S. Hume, *The Spanish People*, 1901, ch. xi.

4. A. Helps, *The Spanish Conquest* (Oppenheim, 1902, vol. i, p. 334, n. 3; vol. ii, p. 44, n.). Las Casas points out that between 1514 and 1519 a million of gold (£300,000, or £3,000,000 present value) had been taken from the Indians, but that only 3000 *castellanos* had been sent to the King in that time.

5. W. Cunningham, *Western Civilization in its Economic Aspects*, 1900, vol. ii, p. 192.

6. B. and R., "Expedition of Miguel López de Legazpi" (*Philippine Islands*, vol. ii, p. 77, vol. iii, p. 44); J. A. Robertson, *Legazpi and Philippine Colonization*, 1909.

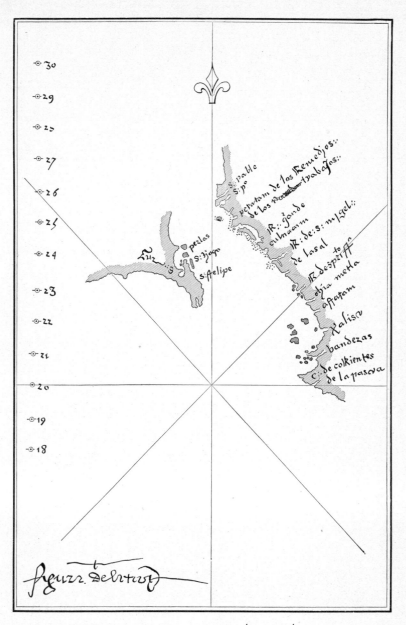

MAP IV. CALIFORNIA. BY HERNÁN CORTÉS, 1535

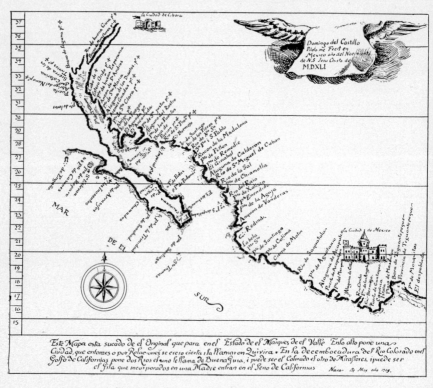

MAP V. CALIFORNIA. BY DOMINGO DEL CASTILLO, 1541

MAP VI. TATTONUS MAP OF CALIF

MAP VII. CALIFORNIA. BY ALONZO DE SANTA CRUZ, 1542

Y[sl]a que descubrió el marqués del Valle.
Tierra que enbió á descubrir don Antonio de Mendoça

7. Antonio de Morga, *Sucesos de las Islas Filipinas*, 1609 (Hon. H. E. J. Stanley, 1868), p. 336; B. and R., *Philippine Islands*, vol. ii, pp. 142, 198, 223, 236, vol. iii, pp. 57, 76, vol. vi, p. 150.

8. La Navidad (latitude 19° 13′ N.) was at first the principal port on the Pacific, but after 1550 Acapulco rapidly took precedence.

9. Felipe II to Viceroy Luis de Velasco, September 24, 1559: Two ships to be sent for the discovery of the western islands toward the Moluccas; these ships to return to Nueva España, " so that it may be known whether the return voyage is assured " (B. and R., *Philippine Islands*, vol. ii, p. 78); Legazpi, report of ship sent to discover return route (*Ibid.*, pp. 175, 239). Bancroft (*North Mexican States and Texas*, vol. i, p. 139, n. 10) notes that Burney (*Chronological History of the Discoveries in the South Sea*, London, 1803, vol. i, p. 271) mentions a voyage to the Philippine Islands in 1566 by the San Gerónimo and return voyages to New Spain in 1567 by the San Juan and two other ships. In B. and R., *Philippine Islands* (vol. iii, p. 129), may be found a document noting in detail the voyages immediately following that of Legazpi. On June 1, 1565, Urdaneta sailed for New Spain, reaching Acapulco early in October. A return vessel reached the Philippines, October 15, 1566. On November 16, 1567, a Philippine ship reached New Spain, etc. Perhaps the earliest date of regular systematic trade was 1573, for on December 5 Viceroy Martín Enríquez wrote to Philip of the arrangement for that year as " an initial attempt " (*Ibid.*, p. 214). See also Bancroft, *History of Mexico*, vol. ii, p. 600, and notes.

10. The San Lucas (under Alonso de Arellano) deserted her consorts, and, returning to New Spain by the course of the Japan Current, actually anticipated the arrival of Urdaneta at Acapulco by three months. The object was reward for the discovery of a return route. But Arellano was sent back from Spain to Mexico to be punished for disobedience. (Morga, *Sucesos*, B. and R., *Philippine Islands*, vol. xv, p. 47; Bancroft, *North Mexican States and Texas*, vol. i, p. 139, n. 9.)

11. F. Gali (Ramusio, *Viaggi*, 1565, vol. iii, p. 343; Hakluyt, vol. iii, pp. 446–447). For the orders to Gali, see B. and R., *Philippine Islands*, vol. vi, pp. 69, 307. Between 1580 and 1583 Gonzalo Ronquillo, Governor of the Philippine Islands, tried to find a southern route to Nueva España, but his captain Juan Ronquillo de Castillo only succeeded in reaching Nueva Guinea (Morga, *Sucesos*, B. and R., *Philippine Islands*, vol. xv, p. 56). As to the naming of Cape Mendocino, all is conjecture. Torquemada (*Monarquía Indiana*, vol. i, p. 693) ascribes it to Urdaneta (or Arellano). Hittell (*History of California*, vol. i, p. 76) ascribes it to Cabrillo. Bancroft discusses the subject: *North Mexican States and Texas*, vol. i, p. 139, n. 9; *History of California*, vol. i, p. 94.

12. See chart I (head of chapter II). A description of the Acapulco-Manila and Manila-Acapulco routes is given in detail in Morga's *Sucesos* (B. and R. *Philippine Islands*, vol. xvi, pp. 200–209). From Acapulco, galleons began

their voyages between February 28 and March 20, and from Manila, on or after June 20. The route from Acapulco was invariable: southwest to 13° or 14°, then straight west to Guam in the Ladrones, where from the year 1668 Spain maintained a beacon station; but from Manila the route varied with conditions of wind and weather. According to Morga (1609), the California landfall was (then) usually made just below Cape Mendocino, between 40° and 36°. According to a Spanish chart of 1742 (chart I, head of chapter II), it (then) was made below 36°. Urdaneta (*Documentos Inéditos de Ultramar*, tom. ii, pp. 427–456) reached latitude 39° 30', Arellano 43° (*Ibid.*, tom. iii, pp. 1–76), and Gali, by his own reckoning (Hakluyt, *Voyages*, vol. iii, pp. 442–447), sighted California in 37° 30'. The route down the coast of New Spain to Acapulco is described by Cabrera Bueno (native of the island of Teneriffe and *piloto-mayor* of the Philippine voyages) in *Navegación Especulativa y Práctica*, Manila, 1734. See F. Palou, *Noticias de California* (J. T. Doyle, 1874), vol. ii, pp. 201–203, n.

13. G. Careri, "A Voyage Round the World," 1693–1699 (Churchill, *Voyages*, 1704, vol. iv, p. 486); Dr. P. C. Sebastián, *Peregrinación del Mundo*, 1688, p. 268; E. G. Bourne, Introduction to Blair and Robertson, *Philippine Islands*, vol. i, p. 65. Storms off Cape Mendocino in 1603 vividly described by Morga in the *Sucesos* (B. and R., *Philippine Islands*, vol. xvi, p. 28).

CERMEÑO'S SAN FRANCISCO BAY

14. Cermeño's *piloto-mayor*, Francisco Bolaños, afterwards served under Vizcaino. Some of the crew of the San Agustín, therefore, were saved. But no writer down to a date subsequent to the publication of the Bancroft Pacific Coast histories seems to have been possessed of any details of the matter. Bancroft (*North Mexican States and Texas*, vol. i, p. 147) says: "Whether the ship escaped after being lightened of her cargo, or was accompanied by a tender on which the crew escaped, is not recorded. . . . It is not impossible that some additional results of the expedition were intentionally kept secret by the government; at any rate no record has ever come to light in the archives." Again (*History of California*, vol. i, p. 96): "It is possible that the San Augustin was accompanied by another vessel on which the officers and men escaped; but much more probable, I think, that the expression 'was lost' in the record is an error, and that the ship escaped with a loss of her cargo."

The following are the facts: On May 31, 1591, Viceroy Luis de Velasco wrote to Philip II that the frequent disasters befalling the Philippine ships made it very necessary to discover *los puertos de la tierra firme*, and to survey them and know their locations. Accordingly, on January 17, 1593, Philip gave orders to Velasco to institute " a survey of the harbors to be found on the voyage to and from the Philippine Islands." On April 6, 1594, Velasco reported to the King that he had directed a survey to be made by Sebastián Rodríguez Cermeño, " a man of experience in his calling, one who could be depended upon and who had means of his own — although he was a Portuguese, there being no Spaniards of his profession whose services were available." On February 1, 1596, the royal officers at Acapulco wrote to Viceroy Conde de Monterey that on Wednesday, January 31, there had entered the port a *viroco* (a small open vessel propelled by square sails and by sweeps) having on board Juan de Morgana, navigating officer, four Spanish sailors, five Indians, and a negro. These reported the loss of the San Agustín "on a coast where she struck and went to pieces," and the drowning of a barefooted friar and one other. Some seventy men had escaped in the *viroco*, all but themselves having landed at La Navidad. The La Navidad party in due time reached Mexico City. The story of their journey became exaggerated, and when, on October 9, 1772, Miguel Costansó wrote to the royal secretary a letter describing the re-discovery of the San Francisco Bay of Cermeño (Francis Drake's Bay), he said: "Some mariners of its [the San Agustín's] crew with the pilot saved themselves, who, traversing the immense country which intervenes between said port [Drake's Bay] and New Biscay, arrived at the end of many days at Sombrerete [near Zacatecas], a mining-camp of that government bordering upon New Galicia." (*Documentos*, por D. Francisco Carrasco y Guisasola, Madrid, Dirección de Hidrografía, 1882, nos. 3, 6, 10; Publications of the Historical Society of Southern California, *Documents from the Sutro Collection*, 1891, nos. 3, 4, 5; *Out West*, Jan., 1902, p. 58.)

Cermeño's *Derrotero y Relación*, dated Mexico, April 24, 1596, is in the Archivo de Indias at Sevilla (Simancas, Secular, Aud. de Méjico, est. lviii, caj. iii, leg. 16). Cermeño says: "We left the port of Cavite, Philippine Islands, on July 5, . . . and sighted New Spain at Cape Mendocino on November 4. . . . We left the bay and port of San Francisco, which is called by another name, a large bay where we were wrecked the morning of Friday, December 8. The bay is in 38 2/3°, and the islets in the mouth are in 38½°, the distance between the two points of the bay being 25 leagues. . . . On Sunday we discovered a very large bay and we named it San Pedro. It is 15 leagues from point to point and the latitude is 37°." (Very probably Monterey Bay.)

15. G. Davidson, *Identification of Sir Francis Drake's Anchorage in 1579* (California Historical Society Publication); *The Discovery of San Francisco Bay*, 1907, pp. 13–23.

16. Memorial by citizens of the Philippine Islands, B. and R., *Philippine Islands*, vol. vi, p. 226.

17. Letter, Manila Audiencia to Felipe II, June 25, 1588, B. and R., *Philippine Islands*, vol. vi, p. 311; Vera to Felipe II, June 26, 1588, *Ibid.*, vol. vii, p. 52; Salazar to Felipe II, June 27, 1588, *Ibid.*, vol. vii, pp. 66, 68; "Viceroy of India," a letter, *Ibid.*, vol. vii, p. 81.

18. As early as 1556, Spanish-American treasure was carried to Spain by

a fleet of fourteen vessels; but the fleet system in the Atlantic was not legally established until 1561. (*Recopilación de Leyes*, lib. ix, tit. 30, ley 1. See Bourne, *Spain in America*, 1904, p. 284.)

19. Letter, Vera to Felipe II, June 26, 1588, B. and R., *Philippine Islands*, vol. vii, p. 53.

20. B. and R., *Philippine Islands*, vol. ix, p. 307.

21. S. A., Madrid, Dirección de Hidrografía, Navarrete, t. xix, nos. 4, 5.

22. Monterey hesitated to confirm his predecessor's contract because, first, the instrument "had reference to the pearl-fishery only, and not at all to the entry and pacification of the land"; and to the circumstance, second, that Vizcaino, "as leader and chief," was "obscure," and apparently not possessed of the "resolution and capacity necessary for so great an enterprise" as entry and pacification would involve. (Monterey to Felipe II, February 29, 1596, Pub. Hist. Soc. of South. Calif., *Sutro Collection*, no. 8.) There was much vacillation on the part of the Viceroy and of the Spanish Government (docs. 8 and 11), but Vizcaino finally was allowed to proceed. (Cf. *Documentos*, por Carrasco y Guisasola, *supra*, 14.)

23. Sutro, 9 and 10. On the bestowing of the name La Paz the testimony is direct. Says Gonzalo de Francia, *contramaestre* (boatswain) of Vizcaino's flagship, May 27, 1629: . . . *Un puerto grande que el pusieron el puerto de la Paz porque allí nos salieron los indios de paz.* (S. A., Madrid, Dir. de Hid., Navarrete, tom. xix, no. 15.)

24. Letter, Vizcaino to Felipe II, 1597; Letter, Monterey to Felipe II, November 26, 1597, in Pub. Hist. Soc. of South. Calif., Sutro, 10 and 12.

25. M. Venegas, *Noticia de la California*, 1757, 3 vols., vol. i, p. 189; Translation, 1759, 2 vols., vol. i, p. 168; *Cédula*, August 19, 1606, B. and R., *Philippine Islands*, vol. xiv, pp. 182–183.

On May 31, 1602, Viceroy Monterey wrote to the King that he had not been able, as ordered on September 7, 1599, to send an expedition to survey the ports and bays of the South Sea. It had been ascertained that there would be needed two vessels and a *lancha* and sixty mariners. As there was at Acapulco no vessel fit for the voyage, he had ordered that the ports of Guatemala be searched, and for this task he had named Captain Toribio Gómez, lately from Castile, a seaman of sixteen years' service in the royal armadas. Gómez, with another captain of distinction, had sailed in July of the past year, intending to be back by November, when the *lancha* was to be ready. Meantime he had chosen for the chief command Sebastián Vizcaino, as more familiar with that coast than any other man in the kingdom, — a person of diligence and reliability and of moderate talent. He had chosen as officers Captain Peguero and Lieutenant Alarcón, who had served in Flanders and Brittany, and as cosmographer Gerónimo Martín (Palacios), who bore the title " cosmographer" from the Casa de Contratación at Sevilla, and who had served twenty years in the royal fleets and armadas. But Toribio had been delayed, etc. The expedition had sailed from Acapulco about

May 5. It was hoped that there would be discovered "some good port and harbor where the ships from China might recruit." Vizcaino, on penalty of his life, was to make no stop in the Enseñada de las Californias. Instructions in detail, dated March 18, were annexed. (Carrasco y Guisasola, *Docs.*, nos. 18, 19, 20.) From Tezcuco, on March 26, 1603, Monterey wrote to the King that Vizcaino had returned. He had discovered "three very good ports, — San Diego in 33°, another adjacent to it of less consequence [San Pedro?], and a third, greater and better adapted to the ships from China, called Monterey, in 37°." The Viceroy wrote again, on May 28, transmitting *relaciones* of the voyage and a map and table of reckonings. On November 22 (from Otumba) he wrote, stating that in view of the great services performed by Vizcaino he had made him "general of the ships this year making the voyage to the Philippines," so that on returning he might examine more closely the port or ports he had discovered, and entering them might procure wood and water and whatever else the ships required. The various captains also were recommended for honors. On July 10, 1604, Viceroy Montesclaros was charged by the King to put the recommendations into effect. (Carrasco y Guisasola, *Docs.*, nos. 23, 25, 26.)

26. Letters by Vizcaino: Acapulco, May 5, 1602, Monterey, December 28, 1602, Mexico, May 22, 1603, Sutro, 13, 14, 15. (Cf. Carrasco y Guisasola, *Docs.*) *Viage y Derrotero* [with 34 charts] *de las naos que fueron al Descubrimiento del Puerto de Acapulco á cargo del G^{rl} Sebastián Vizcaino Año de 1602*, by Martín Palacios, cosmógrafo-mayor, S. A., Sevilla, Arch. Genl. de Indias, Simancas, Sec., Aud. de Méjico, Año de 1602, est. lx, caj. 4, leg. 37; copy, Acad. de la Hist., Madrid, Col. Muñoz, tom. xxxiv, fols. 139–190; copy, S. A., Madrid, Direc. de Hid., Navarrete, tom. xix, no. 9; copy in part (10 maps), Library of Congress, Washington, Lowery Coll., Calif., 1588–1800, Am. S. 1517, Ac. 854. Palacios's *Derrotero*, accompanied by an anonymous *relación*, is printed in Carrasco y Guisasola, *Docs.*, as no. 28. *Derrotero cierto y verdadero desde el Cavo Mendosino hasta el Puerto de Acapulco. . . . Hecho por el P. Fr. Antonio de la Ascensión . . . que fué por Segundo Cosmógrafo del dicho descubrimiento;* copy, S. A., Salamanca, Colegio Mayor de Cuentas, MSS., no. 354; copy, British Museum, Add. MSS. 17583, ff. 206–217v. *Relación* by Ascensión (early copy), with appendix in Ascensión's own hand, 16 chapters, Ayer Coll., Newberry Library, Chicago. See J. Torquemada, *Monarquía Indiana*, lib. v (embodying Ascensión's *Relación*); and for translation of Torquemada, Venegas, London, 1759, vol. ii, p. 229. *Derrotero cierto y verdadero, etc., hecho por Francisco Bolaños piloto, y reformado por Fr. Antonio de la Ascención*, 1603 (S. A., Madrid, Bib. Nac. MSS. 3203).

On Palacios's chart, sections 49–50 (chart II, two plates, pp. 22–23 of text), the concave trend of the coast-line called *enseñada grande* (at the bottom of which lies the "Golden Gate") is unbroken, showing the failure of Vizcaino to suspect the existence of the present Bay of San Francisco. Chart-sections 37–53 show the following present-day nomenclature: Islas de Todos Santos, Puerto Bueno de San Diego, Islas de Santa Catalina, Santa Bárbara y San Nicolás, Punta de Limpia Concepción, Punta de Pinos, Puerto de Monterey, Puerto de Año Nuevo, Puerto de Los Reyes, Cabo de Mendocino. Under a nomenclature different from the present are shown: Enseñada de San Andrés (San Pedro Bay), Islas Gente Barbada, San Ambrosio y San Cleto(Islands Santa Cruz, Santa Rosa, and San Miguel), Enseñada del Roque (Carmelo Bay), Los Frailes (Farallones). As for the name Puerto de Don Gaspar (mentioned in Palacios's *Derrotero* as an *alias* for the name Puerto de los Reyes), it was a further tribute to the Viceroy, Don Gaspar de Zúñiga y Azevedo. In *relaciones* of dates October 12, 1620, and March 22, 1632, Ascensión mentions Santa Catalina Island and Carmelo River as having received their present names under Vizcaino.

27. Torquemada (*Monarquía Indiana*, vol. i, p. 725) observes: "Had only fourteen persons been able to do duty at Cape Blanco, the General intended to have entered the strait called Anian . . . and thence if possible to have reached the North Sea, and after visiting Newfoundland to sail directly for Old Spain. This," he naïvely continues, "would have been making the tour of the world, Cape Mendocino being the antipodes to old Castile and particularly to the cities of Salamanca, Valladolid, and Burgos." In allusion to Aguilar's river, Torquemada (vol. i, pp. 719, 725) says: "It is understood that this river is the one that leads to a great city discovered by the Dutch, and that this is the strait of Anian, etc., and that it is of this place that the relation treats which His Majesty read and by which he was moved to the exploration." (See also Bancroft, *Northwest Coast*, vol. i, p. 88.)

One of Ascensión's accounts, dated October 12, 1620, was sent to the King (Philip III) in December (*Documentos*, Pacheco y Cárdenas, vol. viii, p. 539). Another account (dated at the Carmelite Convent of Valladolid de Michoacán, May 20, 1629) is that from which quotation is made in the text. It is preserved in S. A., Madrid, Direc. de Hid., Navarrete Col., tom. xix, no. 12, and was prepared in response to an order of Philip IV, August 2, 1628. In it Ascensión mentions his *Relación* of the Vizcaino voyage of 1602, and a *Breve Relación* for the King,—the latter document evidently that of October 12, 1620. On June 8, 1629, and March 22, 1632, Ascensión made further reports: that of 1629, emphasizing the points of the report of May 20 of the same year, and that of 1632 recommending the port of Monterey because of its nearness to the Strait of Anian, *en que puerto y paraje está el gran ciudad de Quivira* (Navarrete Col., tom. xix, nos. 16, 21). Between 1629 and 1636 the *relaciones* of Ascensión were subjected to much critical comment by royal officials (Navarrete Col., tom. xix, nos. 17, 19, 20, etc.), and in 1636 (Sept. 17), the question of the insularity of California was elaborately argued by Alonso Botello y Serrano, and Pedro Porter y Casanate. *Unos* (it was declared) *hacen Ysla la California; otros, tierra firme. Unos ponen Estrecho de Anian, otros no*, etc., etc.

It is worthy of note that the German cosmographer Eusebio Francisco Kino, in his long-lost and newly discovered (1908) manuscript on California and Pimería (see chapter IV of Notes), ascribes the prevalence of the conception of California as insular not to Ascensión but to Francis Drake. "The said Drake," he writes, "on his return to his country misled all Europe, — almost all the cosmographers and geographers of Italy, Germany, and France, etc. He delineated California as an Island " (M. A., *Favores Celestiales*, part ii, book iv, chap. 1). The Drake voyage, from what we know of it through the cartography of the years 1582–1593, is chargeable with no such revolution as that stated by Kino; but its influence was toward insularity for California, as is shown not only by the Lok map of 1582, but by the Molineaux globe of 1592, on which the course of Drake is indicated (J. Winsor, *The Kohl Collection of Maps*, reëdited by Phillips, Wash., 1904, sec. 281. See also Mercator-Hondius Atlas, 1613, *Ibid.*, sec. 284). Kino's idea of the effect of the Drake voyage may have been derived from the Herrera map of 1622, or the Briggs map of 1625, or the Hondius map of 1628 (*post*, VIII, IX, X), all of which represent California as insular (*Ibid.*, secs. 91, 284). The *Arcano del Mare* of Robert Dudley, 1630 (a work executed under the influence of Drake's voyage), says in its last paragraph: "The Vermilion Sea begins at the Cape Santa Clara of California [*Cabo Santa Clara della California*], as shown elsewhere, and passes by the island which is named de' Giganti, and is in the Northern Sea, in 43° of latitude, through the kingdom of Coromedo; and this determines that California may be an island off Western America, and not *terra firma* as Giovanni Jansonio states on his chart."

28. *Cédula*, Venegas, *Noticia*, vol. i, p. 200; Translation, vol. i, p. 178; newly translated, B. and R., *Philippine Islands*, vol. xiv, p. 182.

29. Letter, Aguirre, Pub. Hist. Soc. South. Calif. (Sutro, 1); Letter, Viceroy Marqués de Villamanrique to Felipe II, May 10, 1585 (*Ibid.* 2); S. A., Sevilla, Arch. Genl. de Indias, Audiencia de Méjico, Años 1607 á 1609, est. lviii, caj. 3, leg. 16. It is the shrewd surmise of the Swedish writer E. W. Dahlgren (*En Studie i Historisk Geografi*, vol. xiii, Ymer. Tidskrift Utgifven af Svenska Sällskapet för Antropologi och Geografi, 1893) that Aguirre's " isles of the Armenian" were no other than Los Dos Hermanos named by Mercator, map of 1569.

30. Viceroy Marqués de Villamanrique to King, Dec. 10, 1587: Gali had been sent by the Archbishop, Governor of the Philippines, to make discoveries, but Doctor Santiago de Vera, President of the Philippine Audiencia, had intervened, and Pedro de Unamunu had been sent instead. (S. A., Sevilla, Arch. Genl. de Indias, Sim., Sec., Aud. de Méj., est. lviii, caj. 3, leg. 10.) On November 29, 1588, Villamanrique to the King: Gali, returning from an expedition to survey *la tierra firme* of Japan and los Yslas de Armenico, on which he had been sent by the Archbishop, had died, and Unamunu had made the voyage to Acapulco in his stead. (*Ibid.*)

31. Unamunu's account is of such interest that the whole deserves to be reproduced in translation.

32. *Cédula*, Sept. 27, 1608, recites the substance of the letter by Montesclaros (B. and R., *Philippine Islands*, vol. xiv, p. 270; S. A., Sevilla, Arch. Genl. de Indias, Sim., Sec., Aud. de Méj., est. lviii, caj. 3, leg. 16). On tempests off the coast of Japan and loss of Spanish vessels in 1576 and 1609, see letter by Antonio de Morga to Felipe II, June 30, 1597, and *Relación*, 1609–10, by Padre Gregorio López (B. and R., *Philippine Islands*, vol. x, p. 26, and vol. xvii, p. 132).

33. *Cédula*, Sept. 18, 1607, directs that 20,000 ducats appropriated for settlement of Monterey be used in promoting colonization of Rica de Plata. *Cédula*, May 3, 1609: this supplementary document directs that unless Vizcaino has undertaken his voyage, the matter be withdrawn from his hands and placed in those of the Governor of the Philippines (B. and R., *Philippine Islands*, vol. xiv, pp. 270, 275). The cause of the change of plan was a series of letters from Hernando de los Ríos Coronel, contending that an expedition from Manila would be less expensive, could be made at a better season, and above all could be so made as to use Japan, where conditions were now favorable to foreigners, as a base of operations. (Coronel letters, *Consulta del Consejo de Indias*, and *Cédula*, A. D. 1610, Sevilla, Arch. Genl. de Indias, Secretaría de N. E., Secular., Aud. de Filipinas, est. lxix, caj. 1, leg. 6.) In 1602, Feb. 16, the King had approved and sent to Pedro de Acuña, Governor of the Philippines, a letter written by Hernando de los Ríos Coronel, counseling that for the discovery of the Straits of Anian it would be well to "take possession of la Isla de Armino, in order to make of it a station for the galleon." (S. A., Madrid, Direc. Filipinas, tom. iii, p. 62–d2a.)

34. On April 7, 1611, Viceroy Velasco informed the King that according to royal order, Sebastián Vizcaino had set out on an embassy to Japan. He was not to touch at the Philippines. His ship's company comprised 50 persons, 40 *arcabuses* and *moxquetes*, two pieces of artillery, and some little merchandise, the whole voyage to cost not to exceed 20,000 ducats (S. A., Sevilla, Arch. Genl. de Indias, Sim., Sec., Aud. de Méj., Años 1610 á 1617, est. lviii, caj. 3, leg. 17). On Dec. 2, 1613, the King issued a decree stating that Don Juan de Silva, Governor of the Philippines, had written that certain religious had declared that Vizcaino had taken to Japan a cargo of merchandise, and that he had engaged in trade and given the Japanese license to build ships for New Spain, etc., — all contrary to his instructions; wherefore let the said matter be investigated. (S. A., Sevilla, Arch. Genl. de Indias, Aud. de Méj., Registros de Oficio, tom. vi, fol. 91 vto, est. lxxxvii, caj. 5, leg. 2.)

35. Vizcaino, *Relación del Viage hecho para el Descubrimiento de las Islas llamadas Ricas de Oro y Plata*, 1611–14 (Pacheco y Cárdenas, *Docs.*, vol. viii, pp. 101–199); "Reforms needed in the Philippines," Hernando de los Ríos Coronel (B. and R., *Philippine Islands*, vol. xviii, p. 326). Says Ríos: "I

believe that a decree [the decree of Feb. 16, 1602, cited above] was sent to the Governor in a former year to explore it [Rica de Plata]; but that must be ordered again. A man of experience should be sent, so that he may display the prudence and make the exploration requisite, in accordance with the art and science of hydrography." Vizcaino is reported by Venegas and others to have died at the end of his second voyage to California; but the *Relación* cited above negatives this statement.

Apropos of the Rica de Oro and Rica de Plata expedition, Bancroft (*North Mexican States and Texas*, vol. i, p. 162), following the *Relación*, says: " Vizcaino actually sailed from Acapulco in March, 1611, on the San Francisco. But meanwhile reports of certain Islas Ricas de Oro y Plata in the far west seem to have rendered the occupation of the northwest coast for the time a secondary consideration; and the General went as ambassador to Japan to seek license for further explorations in that region. Probably it was still intended to take steps on his return for the occupation of Monterey; but his experience in Japan was so disastrous, the complicated details having no bearing on the present subject, that Vizcaino was obliged in poor health to give up all his projects and to return as a passenger on his own ship in 1613. The return was by the usual northern route, the California coast was sighted in December, and finally the San Francisco arrived at Zacatula in January, 1614. This seems to have been the end of Vizcaino's career as an explorer." There is here a failure to perceive that the Rica de Oro and Rica de Plata expedition was planned by Spain, not in temporary suspension of the Monterey project while search was made for fabulous isles of treasure near Japan, but with a view to finding a port which should render occupation of Monterey, and hence of Alta California, unnecessary.

GOLD AND SILVER ISLANDS

The actual existence of North Pacific islands which served to suggest to early Spanish navigators the mythical " Isles of the Armenian " is a question not without interest. Such islands were mentioned first by Villalobos in 1543. (Gastaldi maps, 1550, and Mercator map, 1569; latter containing Los Dos Hermanos.) As for Rica de Oro and Rica de Plata, into which the Isles of the Armenian seem early to have been resolved, they appear first in 1586, when Pedro de Unamunu was sent to search for them together with the Isles of the Armenian. Unamunu knew the Orient, and according to the folklore of Japan there lay east-northwest from the province of Osui, between 37° and 39° N. L., two islands, Kinsima (Gold) and Ginsima (Silver). (E. de Kaempfer, *De Beschryving van Japan*, Amsterdam, 1729, p. 49.) At no time was the location of these islands precise, the variation in respect to latitude being from 29° 30' (Delisle, 1723) to 31° 10' (Stockholmskartan); and in respect to longitude from 152° 20' (John Meares, 1788) to 158° 10' (Stockholmskartan). By an error of reckoning, Meares placed the actual island Lot's Wife in longitude 154° 44', a position nearly the same as that in which he placed Rica de Oro, and it has ensued that the two ever since have been regarded as one and the same.

The failure of Vizcaino to discover Rica de Oro and Rica de Plata in 1611 quieted the Spanish mind until 1729. In that year it was reported that a Jesuit padre on the way from China to New Spain had actually seen these islands, and in 1730 the Spanish Government sought earnestly to discover whether anything about them were known by navigators; the idea still being entertained that in one or other a port of refuge for the galleon might be found. Satisfactory information was not obtained, and on December 12, 1741, it was ordered by the King that no galleon should depart from its course to search for them. (Burney, *Chron. Hist.*, vol. ii; S. A., Sevilla, Arch. Genl. de Indias, Secretaría de N. E., Secular., Aud. de Filipinas, Años 1740–1742, est. lxviii, caj. 3, leg. 31.) In 1639 and 1643 search for the gold and silver islands of the Pacific was made by the Dutch under Abel Tasman (*Tasman's Journal*, Amsterdam, 1898), and Mattys Quast (*Transactions of the Royal Society*, London, Dec. 14, 1674). In 1798 the French commander Comte de la Pérouse made a like search (*Voyage autour du Monde*, vol. iii, p. 210). And all this while a group of islands convenient for the purposes of the Spanish galleon actually did exist, as was pointed out in 1777 by Captain James Cook. " If," he said, " the Sandwich Islands had been discovered at an early period by the Spaniards, they would doubtless have availed themselves of so excellent a station, and have made use of Atooi, or some other of the islands, as a place of refreshment for the ships that sail annually between Manila and Acapulco. They lie almost midway between the last mentioned place and Guam, one of the Ladrones, which is at present their only port in traversing this vast ocean; and it would not have been a week's sail out of their ordinary route to have touched at them." (*Voyage*, vol. ii, p. 192.) On the whole subject see O. Nachod, *Ein Unentdecktes Goldland*, Tokyo, 1899.

36. S. A., Madrid, Dirección de Hidrografía, Navarrete Coll., tom. xix, nos. 12, 17, 19.

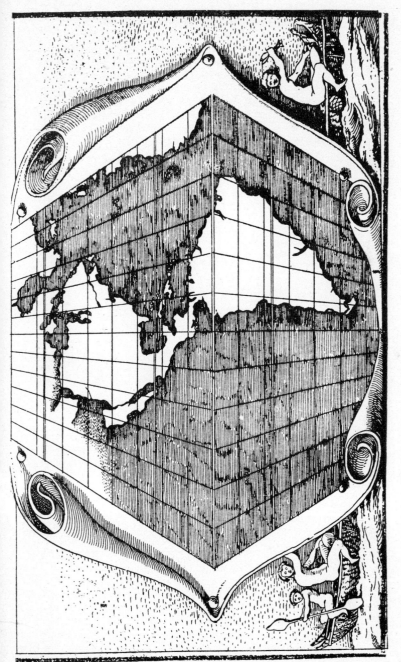

MAP VIII. THE WORLD. BY KASPAR VAN BAERLE, 1622

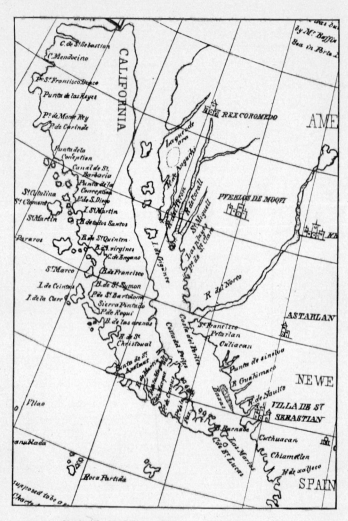

MAP IX. NORTH AMERICA. BY BRIGGS, 1625

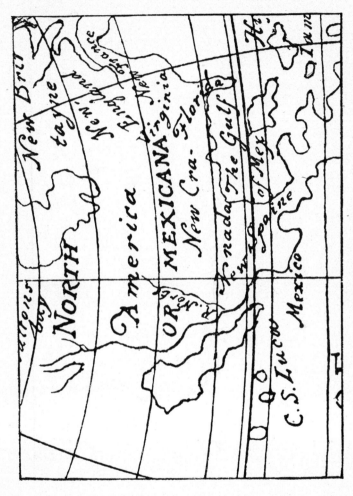

MAP X. DRAKE "WORLD ENCOMPASSED" MAP. BY HONDIUS, 1628

CHAPTER III

THE MISSION

NEW CHAPTER SOURCES: — Indian segregation (Mission and *Custodia* plans), letters of Antonio de los Reyes, Rafael Verger (Guardian of the College of San Fernando) and " A Minister of St. Francis." (M. A.) (Specific citations below.)

1. " The acquisitions which have been made slowly by means of the missionaries have always resulted better than those secured by force of arms."

2. W. Dampier, *New Voyage round the World*, 1699–1709; W. Rogers, *Cruising Voyage round the World*, 1718. Alexander Selkirk, the original of Defoe's Robinson Crusoe, was rescued from the island of Juan Fernández, three hundred miles off the coast of Chile, by Captain Woods Rogers on February 1, 1709. He is described as " a man in goat-skins who looked wilder than the first owners of them."

3. The Kino explorations are treated in chapter IV.

4. G. Shelvocke, *Voyage round the World*, 1719–1722, 1726. In October, 1719, Simon Hatley, mate of Captain Shelvocke's ship the Speedwell, observing " in one of his melancholy fits " that the ship was followed by an albatross, imagined from its color that it might be of ill omen, and so shot it, — an incident developed by Samuel Taylor Coleridge into the poem " The Rime of the Ancient Mariner."

> " And a good south wind sprung up behind;
>   The Albatross did follow,
>
> .   .   .   .
>
> — all averred I had killed the bird
>   That made the breeze to blow."

5. R. Walter, *Voyage round the World* [George Anson], 1748.

6. A. Dobbs, *An Account of the Countries adjoining to Hudson's Bay*, etc., 1744; H. Ellis, *Voyage to Hudson's Bay*, 1748; J. Winsor, *Narrative and Critical History of America*, vol. viii, p. 1, *et seq.*; G. Bryce, *The Remarkable History of the Hudson's Bay Company*, 1900, ch. 8: " Dream of a Northwest Passage."

7. B. C., P. Tikhmeneff, *Report on Colonies*, part i; W. Coxe, *Account of the Russian Discoveries between Asia and America*, 1780. Authorities summarized by Bancroft: *History of Alaska*, chaps. I–VIII; p. 217, n. 43; *History of the Northwest Coast*, vol. i, pp. 149–150, n. 20; *History of California*, vol. i, p. 112; vol. ii, p. 58; G. Davidson, *Tracks and Landfalls of Bering and Chirikof on the Northwest Coast of North America, June to October, 1741*, 1901.

8. B. and R., *Philippine Islands*, vol. i, pp. 100–101. As late as 1546 it was resolved by a synod of prelates in Mexico that " the final and only reason why the Apostolic See had given supreme jurisdiction in the Indies to the kings of Castile and León was that the Gospel might be preached and the Indians converted. It was not to make those kings greater lords and richer princes than they were." (Sir A. Helps, *The Spanish Conquest in America*, vol. iv, p. 209; F. A. MacNutt, *Bartholomew de Las Casas*, 1909, p. 273.)

9. *Recopilación de Leyes de los Reynos de las Indias*, 1681, lib. vi, tit. x, ley 1. The original will is kept in the monastery of La Rabida. It was displayed at the Columbian Exposition in Chicago in 1893. The text in Spanish and English may be found printed in *The American Anthropologist*, 1894, p. 194.

10. Sir A. Helps, *The Spanish Conquest*, vol. i, pp. 138–139, and notes; E. G. Bourne, *Spain in America*, 1904, pp. 207–210, and citations.

11. B. Las Casas, *Historia General de las Indias*, 1875, vol. iii, p. 71.

12. The *encomienda* of Ovando was an amplification of the *repartimiento* of Columbus. By the former a given plantation with its cacique and band was assigned to a given Spaniard as overlord. By the latter it was not so much the plantation that was assigned as the cacique and band upon it. In the *encomienda*, in other words, the emphasis was placed upon persons, and its tendency therefore was toward slavery. (Sir A. Helps, *The Spanish Conquest*, vol. i, pp. 103, 123, 139, vol. iii, pp. 79, 92, vol. iv, p. 237; W. Lowery, *Spanish Settlements in the United States*, 1901, p. 109; E. Armstrong, *The Emperor Charles V*, 1902, vol. ii, p. 99; E. G. Bourne, *Spain in America*, 1904, p. 255. See also Bancroft, *History of Central America*, vol. i, p. 262, n. 7; F. A. MacNutt, *The Letters of Cortés to Charles V*, 1908, 2 vols., vol. ii, appendix to fourth letter.)

13. F. A. Lorenzana, *Historia de Nueva España por Hernan Cortés*, 1770. Translations of passage: Helps, vol. iii, p. 20; Lowery, p. 86. On morals of the secular clergy, H. C. Lea, *Sacerdotal Celibacy in the Christian Church*, p. 564; — says Mr. Lea: "A majority of the ecclesiastics seeking the colonies of Spanish America were of the worst description "; Lowery, p. 87 ; MacNutt, *Letters of Cortés*, vol. ii, pp. 214–215.

14. Sir A. Helps, vol. i, p. 185.

15. "By night sweet odors, varying with every hour of the watch, were wafted from the shore . . . and the forest trees, brought together by the serpent tracery of myriads of strange parasitical plants, might well seem to the fancy like some great design of building, over which the lofty palms, a forest upon a forest, appeared to present a new order of architecture. In the background rose the mist, like incense. These, however, were but the evening fancies of the mariner who had before him fondly in his mind the wreathed pillars of the Cathedral of Burgos, or the thousand-columned Christian mosque of Córdova, or the perfect fane of Seville; and when the moon rose, or the innumerable swarms of luminous insects swept across the

picture, it was but a tangled forest after all, wherein the shaping hand of man had made no memorial to his Creator." (Sir A. Helps, vol. ii, p. 95.)

16. Sir A. Helps, vol. i, p. 356, note by editor.

17. MacNutt, *Bartholomew de Las Casas*, chaps. 11, 12.

18. S. A., Madrid, *Muñoz MSS.*, tom. 79; cited by Helps.

19. MacNutt, *Bartholomew de Las Casas*, p. 191. By a law of the Indies, promulgated in 1523, and again in 1618, it was forbidden to convert the Indians to Christianity by force. (W. Roscher, *The Spanish Colonial System* (Bourne), p. 9; *Recopilación*, lib. vi.)

20. A. Remesal, *Historia de Chiapa y Guatemala*, 1619, lib. iii, cap. 2, par. 3; Sir A. Helps, *The Spanish Conquest*, vol. iii, book xv, chaps. 6, 7.

It is related by Remesal (lib. iii, cap. 2, par. 1, p. 124) that a potent means for the conversion of the people of the Tierra de Guerra was found in music. The great doctrines of salvation were translated in Quichi verse; the verse was then set to simple music and sung to the accompaniment of Indian wind-instruments. Upon this story in some of its details Bancroft (*History of Central America*, vol. ii, p. 350, n.) casts not unreasonable doubt. It, however, is probable that music played a part in the subjugation of Tuzulatlán. Remesal states (lib. iv, cap. x, p. 190) that Luis Cáncer, having returned in 1542 to Vera Paz, procured for the delectation of converts some Mexican Indians who knew how to sing and play church music (Lowery, *Spanish Settlements*, p. 414). It was even commanded by the King (Remesal, lib. iii, cap. 21, p. 155) that "some Indians who knew how to play loud wind-instruments, clarions, sackbuts, flutes, and also some singers of church music out of those in the monasteries of the Franciscans in New Spain," be permitted to be taken by Las Casas into the province (Helps, vol. iii, p. 255). Indeed, wherever the Spanish missionary went, music, with its proverbial power to soothe the breast of the savage, was a means of conversion not neglected. It was made use of in Mexico, in the Philippines (A. de Morga, *Sucesos*, B. and R., *Philippine Islands*, vol. xvi, p. 152), and (as related in the text, chapter XVI) it was employed in California.

21. (I) "For which I say and promise you and give my word in the name and on behalf of his Majesty, in virtue of the royal powers delegated to me, that you or any of your monks, being at present Father Bartholomew de Las Casas, Rodrigo de la Drada, and Pedro de Angulo, bringing and securing by your teaching and persuasion whatsoever provinces with the Indians within them (all or in part I hold from his Majesty) into conditions of peace, so that they recognize the lordship of his Majesty and agree to pay him a moderate tribute, according to their possibility of personal service and poor possessions, such as they can conveniently give, whether in gold, if there be any in the land, or in cotton, maize, or in whatsoever other things they possess or are accustomed to cultivate or traffic with among themselves, — that I, in virtue of the powers I hold from his Majesty and in his royal name, will place all those provinces and the Indians in them so agreeing under his

Majesty in chief that they may serve him as his vassals, and will not give them to any Spaniard in *encomienda*, now or at any future time." (Remesal, lib. iii, cap. 9, p. 122; translated, Helps, vol. iii, p. 233.)

(II) "And I shall order that no Spaniard molest them, nor approach them, nor their lands, under serious penalty for five years. As for myself, I shall go when you think it convenient [fitting], and when you can go with me." (*Ibid.*, p. 123; F. A. MacNutt, *Bartholomew de Las Casas*, chap. xiv.)

22. The first of the two letters constituting "The New Laws" (a letter signed jointly by Charles V and his mother Doña Joanna, daughter of the venerated Isabella) was dated from Barcelona, November 20, 1542. The second was dated from Valladolid, June 4, 1543. They were printed together at Alcalá de Henares, July 8, 1543, and were sold at the price of 4 *maravedis* for each sheet. A translation of the Laws into English was made in 1893 by the late Henry Stevens (of Vermont) and Fred W. Lucas (of London), and the same year the translation (together with a facsimile of the originals and an historical introduction by Mr. Lucas) was issued (privately) from the Chiswick Press in an edition of 88 copies. One copy is owned by the University of California.

"The New Laws" were distinctly an advance upon any which had preceded them, in two clauses: (I) that "after the death of the conquerors of the Indies, the *repartimientos* of Indians which had been given to them in *encomienda*, in the name of his Majesty, should not pass in succession to their wives or children, but, as in stipulation 1 between Las Casas and the lieutenant-governor of Guatemala, should be placed immediately under the King, the said wives and children receiving a certain portion of the usufruct for their sustenance"; (II) that "the bishops, monastic bodies, governors, presidents, auditors, corregidors, and other officers of his Majesty, both past and present, who held *repartimientos*, should be obliged to renounce them." (Helps, *The Spanish Conquest*, vol. iv, p. 104; MacNutt, *Bartholomew de Las Casas*, p. 204.) On the enforced partial abrogation of "The New Laws," see Helps, vol. iv, pp. 237, 253; E. G. Bourne, *Spain in America*, p. 255.

For the laws cited in the text other than "The New Laws," see *Recopilación de Leyes*, as follows: Indians to live under own magistrates (lib. vi, tit. iii, ley 15); Indians not to be slaves, — text of decree by Ferdinand and Isabella (lib. vi, tit. ii, ley 1); Indians not to live outside village (lib. vi, tit. iii, ley 19); no lay Spaniard, negro, *mestizo*, or mulatto to live in an Indian village (lib. vi, tit. iii, ley 22); no Spaniard to tarry more than a night (lib. vi, tit. iii, ley 23); but Spaniards who were ill or who were merchants might tarry not more than three days (lib. vi, tit. iii, ley 24). Infraction of original act forbidden under penalty of fine of 50 *pesos* in gold. An *encomendero*, even, was not permitted to own a house in an Indian village, or to remain there more than one night. His relatives and slaves might not enter at all (lib. vi, tit. ix, ley 14). Indians to be instructed in the Catholic faith (lib. vi, tit. iii, ley 1). Useful summaries of Spanish legislation for protection of the Indians: J. G. Bourke, Capt. U. S. A., "The Laws of Spain in their Application to the American Indians," *American Anthropologist*, 1894, vol. vii, p. 193; W. Roscher, *The Spanish Colonial System* (Bourne), 1904.

23. Says Mr. Edward Armstrong, apropos of the fierce struggle in New Spain between the passions of Avarice and religious Propagandism — that struggle whereby the system of the Mission was evolved (*The Emperor Charles V*, 2 vols., 1902, vol. ii, pp. 101, 105): "The Spanish missionary was pitted against the Spanish conqueror and proved a foeman worthy of his steel. . . . Charles [the Emperor] it must be admitted was on the side of the missionary." The steps by which, through Charles, the essential idea of the Mission (Indian segregation under sacerdotal protection) came to be embodied in law were the following: (1) Laws of Burgos (1512, Ferdinand), sanctioning enforced association of Indians with Spaniards (Las Casas, *Historia*, tom. i, lib. iii, cap. 7, 9); (2) Laws of Las Casas (1515, Ximénes Regent for Charles V), providing for settlements of Indians in villages under a *clérigo* (secular priest) or *religioso* (friar), and, for civil ends, under a cacique and Spanish administrator, the latter to be married and not to live in the settlement (*Docs. Inéd. de Ultramar*, vol. iv, pp. 109–128); 3 *cédulas* (1526, Charles V), ordering resumption of plan for settling Indians "in villages by themselves with their own priests," the first village, 1517, having been broken up by smallpox (R. de la Sagra, *Historia . . . de la Isla de Cuba*, vol. ii, *apéndice; Docs. Inéd. de Ultramar*, vol. iv, pp. 109–128). In a report on village settlements by Governor Guzmán (Sagra, vol. ii, *apéndice*), the Governor calls such settlements the King's "project for peaceful colonization."

24. Segregation, according to the governmental or secular conception, was known as the *Custodia* plan, operations being conducted from an *hospicio* or "home," whence the missionaries issued, and whither they returned. On June 20, 1783, it was pointed out by Antonio de los Reyes, Bishop of Sonora, a secular minister, that in 1538 and 1618 (laws 19 and 20 of the *Recopilación*, lib. vi, tit. i) it was provided that the Indians were to be " *puestos en policia* and taught to apply themselves to useful and profitable work." Earlier (Sept. 16, 1776) the Bishop had cited a Bull of Innocent XI, of date Oct. 16, 1686, directing the reduction of mission Indians to *pueblos formales*. The same bishop cited the course of Cortés as demonstrating the sufficiency of the *Custodia* plan of segregation. (M. A., Arch. Genl., *Misiones*, xiv.)

25. On the part of the missionaries of upper Sonora (Pimería) and of the Californias, 1771, 1772, pleas were urgent for segregation, according to the Mission plan, as a present and pressing necessity; yet what was asked was recognized as contravening old customs and opinion. Said Rafael Verger, Guardian of the missionary college of San Fernando, to his superior on Nov. 15, 1772: " It is true, most excellent Señor, that law 6 of book i, title 13 of the *Recopilación*, prohibits these and other things [temporal control] to *curas*,

doctrineros, clérigos y religiosos. But such are pastors of civilized Indians and lack the title of tutors and guardians." Much reliance was placed by the missionaries upon decrees issued in 1719 by Baltasar de Zúñiga, Marqués de Valero, and in 1740 by Pedro de Castro y Figueroa Salazar. (M. A., Museo, *Trasuntos.* Cf. chapter VI of text, n. 15, 16; chapter VIII of text, n. 24.) It is stated by a "minister of St. Francis" (cited chapter VIII of text, n. 9) that the first Mexican mission, in the missionary sense of the term, was the *villa* of Sinaloa, founded in 1611.

26. The *Patronato Real* was the right of church regulation, on the part of the Crown, under Bulls by Alexander VI, 1493 (*Docs. Inéd. de las Indias,* vol. xxxiv, p. 14, — translated, J. Fiske, *Discovery of America,* app. B), and Julius II, 1508 (A. J. de Ribadeneyra, *Regio Patronato,* pp. 408–409); and under a *cédula,* 1574, by Philip II (translated, B. Moses, *South America on the Eve of Emancipation,* 1908, p. 123). The Crown might nominate and license bishops and all subordinate ecclesiastics; reprimand and remove the same, fix the salaries of benefices; collect tithes; take cognizance of ecclesiastical causes; inspect papal Bulls; grant permission for erecting churches and hospitals. Finally, the Crown might license friars; permit the erection of monasteries; and pass upon all patents, or general orders to religious houses by their superiors, naught being exempt from review save rules of such houses for their internal government. (J. C. Icazbalceta, *Zumárraga,* p. 127; Montemayor, *Sumarios,* pp. 36–38; A. J. de Ribadeneyra, *Manual Compendio de el Regio Patronato,* pp. 51–68; Sarsfield, *Derecho Público Eclesiástico,* 1889.) Subject discussed: Bancroft, *History of Mexico,* vol. iii, p. 684; W. Lowery, *Spanish Settlements,* p. 381; B. Moses, *South America on the Eve of Emancipation,* ch. 6.

27. Helps, vol. iv, pp. 272, *et seq.,* "The Missions of Paraguay"; W. Roscher, *The Spanish Colonial System* (Bourne), p. 15. It may be observed that the great Jesuit establishment in Canada — the mission to the Hurons — was much less specialized than the Paraguayan or Mexican establishment. The proud, intractable character of the northern Indian nations made Mission control more difficult. Still, with the Hurons, had it not been for the struggle forced upon them by the Iroquois, the Mission might have succeeded. If so, the model, we are told, would have been that of Paraguay. "Que si celuy qui a escrit cette lettre a leu la Relation de ce qui se passe au Paraguais, qu'il a veu ce qui se fera un jour en la Nouvelle France." (Le Jeune, *Relation,* 1637.) Regarding the *Patronato Real,* and the Spanish Mission in Paraguay and in California, see R. Altamíra y Crevea, *Historia de España,* 1906, tom. iii, pp. 417, 346.

CHAPTER IV

CALIFORNIA NO ES YSLA

THE principal authority for the present chapter is an unpublished manuscript, the *Favores Celestiales* of Eusebio Francisco Kino. This book (lost since 1767, the year of the composition by Alegre of the *Historia de la Compañía de Jesús en Nueva España*) was found in 1908 by Dr. Herbert E. Bolton of the University of Texas (now of Leland Stanford Jr. University), in the Archives of Mexico. As described by Dr. Bolton, the book in the original manuscript contains 433 folio pages (about 150,000 words) and covers the period of Kino's entire service as rector of Jesuit missions in Pimería Alta, 1687–1710. Not all of the record is new. The *Apostólicos Afanes*, by Padre José Ortega, 1754, is based upon it and constitutes a summary of it. Portions more or less complete are to be found in various MS. collections and in print, — the Boturini Collection (Real Academia de la Historia, Madrid); *Documentos para la Historia de Méjico*, etc.

The Peabody Museum (Hemenway Collection), Harvard, contains a volume of transcripts (426 pages) from the Biblioteca Nacional of Mexico, which includes the *Luz de Tierra Yncógnita* (1720) of Kino's friend and companion Manje, and the latter's *Relación diaria de la entrada al noroeste* . . . *de Septiembre hasta 18 de Octubre* [1698], *y Descubrimiento del desemboque del río grande á la mar de la California y del Puerto de Sta. Clara* — dated Nuestra Señora de los Dolores, Dec. 8, 1698. A further source is the manuscript volume: *Establecimiento y progresos de las Misiones de la Antigua California y Memorias piadosas de la Nación Indiana por un Religioso de la Provincia del Santo Evangelio de México, Años 1790, 1791* (Edward E. Ayer Collection, Newberry Library, Chicago). The *Establecimiento* sustains to the history of Lower California a relation equivalent to that of the *Noticias* of Palou to the history of California Alta. (Specific citations below.)

1. Kino, sketch of life, *Favores Celestiales*, part i, book iv, chap. 1; *Apostólicos Afanes*, 1754, par. 230, 328. The more important *entradas* by Kino are delineated on general map of the Southwest (pocket).

2. *Favores Celestiales*, part i, book i, chaps. 1–3.

3. Salvatierra, sketch of life, Alegre, *Historia de la Compañía de Jesús*, vol. iii, 96; *Favores Celestiales*, part i, book ii, chaps. 1–3.

4. *Favores Celestiales*, part ii, book iv, chap. 1.

5. *Ibid.*, part i, book ii, chap. 3.

6. *Ibid.*, part i, book ii, chap. 5. Bancroft, following Manje's *Informe*, dates this *entrada* February, 1694.

7. *Favores Celestiales*, part i, book ii, chap. 6. Bancroft dates this *entrada* also 1694. For dimensions of the boat, *Favores Celestiales*, part ii, book i, chap. 2. Description of boat by Manje, *Docs. para la Historia de Méjico*, série iv, tom. i, p. 243.

8. *Favores Celestiales*, part i, book ii, chap. 7.

9. *Ibid.*, part i, book ii, chap. 8. Kino here says nothing about Mass in the Casa Grande itself. His words are: " The First Ranchería of El Tusonim we named La Encarnación, as we arrived there to say Mass on the First Sunday in Advent." Manje states that Mass was said *dentro de las cuales (casas grandes)*. He may have had reference to the locality in general. (Cf. E. Coues, *The Trail of a Spanish Pioneer*, 1900, vol. ii, pp. 537–538.) To Kino the *casas grandes* were " certainly the seven cities mentioned by the holy man, Fray Marcos de Niza." Regarding the visit to Mexico, *Favores Celestiales*, part i, book v, chap. 1.

10. M. Venegas, *Noticia de la California*, Mexico, 1757, 3 vols., vol. ii, p. 14; Translation (London, 1759, 2 vols.), vol. i, p. 224. Decree translated in full, *Proceedings Mexican and American Claims Commission*, Claim no. 493, transcript, Washington, 1902, p. 401.

11. See note 35 *post*.

12. Translated, *Proceedings Mexican and American Claims Commission*, Claim no. 493, transcript, p. 405. See also Salvatierra to Ugarte, Nov. 27, 1697, S. A., Madrid, Real Acad. Historia, Boturini Coll., tom. i; *Docs. para la Historia de Méjico*, série ii, tom. i, p. 103.

13. *Proceedings Mexican and American Claims Commission*, Claim no. 493, transcript, p. 418.

14. Cf. chapter vi.

15. Venegas, *Noticia*, vol. ii, p. 69; Translation, vol. i, p. 277. See also *Noticia*, vol. ii, pp. 264, 274, 278, 281; Translation (here incomplete and weak), vol. i, pp. 452, 455.

16. J. M. Salvatierra, " Informe Sobre puntos de las Cédulas Reales, 25 de Mayo, 1705," Venegas, *Noticia*, vol. ii, p. 153; Bancroft, *North Mexican States and Texas*, vol. i, pp. 418, 437.

17. Letter, Kino to Visitador Horacio Polici, Oct. 18, 1698 (M. A., Arch. Genl., *Historia*, 16; *Favores Celestiales*, part i, book vi, chap. 4). Bancroft is perhaps correct in his statement (*North Mexican States*, vol. i, p. 266, n. 53) that as yet Kino had discovered no convergence of the Pimería and peninsular coasts at the mouth of the Colorado; for in the *diario* none such is mentioned. It was later, in retrospect, that Kino stated: " In the year 1698, on a very high Hill [Santa Clara], I descried most plainly the juncture of these lands of New Spain and of California."

18. *Favores Celestiales*, part i, book vi, chap. 5.

19. *Ibid.*, part i, book vi, chap. 6.

20. In 1699 (November) " the Señor lieutenant [Manje] and I passed on to San Raphael of the other Actum and to San Marzelo del Sonoydag, 20 leagues journey, to inform ourselves better in regard to the passage by land to California . . . and we informed ourselves very well in regard to the blue shells of the opposite coast, and to the passage by land to California." (*Favores Celestiales*, part i, book vii, chap. 4.)

21. *Ibid.*, part ii, book i, chaps. 4, 6.

22. *Favores Celestiales*, part ii, book i, chaps. 9, 10.

23. *Ibid.*, part ii, book i, chaps. 12–14; book ii, chaps. 1–6.

24. *Ibid.*, part ii, book ii, chaps. 7, 8. The view from the ridge had not satisfied Manje. He states: "We remained in the same doubt as when on the beach." (*Docs. para la Historia de Méjico*, série iv, vol. i, p. 334.)

25. *Favores Celestiales*, part ii, book ii, chap. 11.

26. *Ibid.*, part ii, book ii, chap. 12. Manje himself states that, although the sea seemed to narrow, it might turn and widen again as that of Gibraltar in Spain into the Mediterranean. There might be a connection with the South Sea on the westward, for the sea extended also in that direction (*Ibid.*, p. 332). A letter for Piccolo was intrusted to the Indians, but it never reached him (*Ibid.*, p. 333).

27. *Favores Celestiales*, part ii, book iii, chaps. 2–5. It is of interest to note that Kino fixes the south line of Alta California at the Meridian, "because its Meridian passes through the midst of its Head of the Sea of California." (*Ibid.*, part ii, book iv, chap. 3.)

28. *Ibid.*, part ii, book iv, chaps. 2–5.

29. *Ibid.*, part ii, book iv, chap. 12.

30. *Ibid.*, chap. 13.

31. *Ibid.*, chap. 11.

32. If, as is probable, Kino was at La Libertad, or between it and Tepoca, he might have been looking southwest between the islands Angel de la Guarda and Tiburón. His companion was Padre Gerónimo Minutuli, and on June 7 the latter wrote that a passage into California by the newly found island and cape ought not to be very difficult. On Nov. 4, Kino, replying to an appeal for help from Ugarte at Loreto, wrote that the bark which he (Kino) had partially constructed at Dolores and at Caborca was yet available. All that was needed (now that the passage by way of the island and cape was known) was a couple of ship's boys or Chinamen *para la dirección del barquillo, ó lancha, ó canoa grande.* (*Favores Celestiales*, part iv, book iii, chap. 3; book iv, chap. 3.)

33. By special order of Fuens-Zaldana, diaries of the autumn *entrada* of 1706 were kept by Ramírez and Ojuela. Durán was also ordered to keep a diary. All were to be sent to the Viceroy. Kino embodies Ramírez's and Ojuela's accounts in his history, but gives none of his own. Describing the view from Santa Clara, Ramírez says that while sea was visible as far as the eye could reach on the South, none was visible on the East, nor on the West as extending to the North or Northwest. On the contrary, what was plainly visible was the "Continuation of our land with that of the West, which was sand dunes and hillocks for more than 40, 50 or 60 leagues." (*Favores Celestiales*, part iv, lib. v, chap. 6.)

34. The most important of these decrees may be found in substance in Venegas, vol. ii, pp. 63, 139, 169; Translation, vol. i, pp. 272, 340, 369; translated excerpts, *Proceedings Mexican and American Claims Commission*,

Claim no. 493, p. 406. *Cédula* of 1719 inclosing one of 1716 (June 29), urging attention to earlier decrees; translated, *Proceedings Mexican and American Claims Commission*, p. 434. See also B. C., *Baja California Cédulas*, pp. 82, 98.

PIOUS FUND

35. Prior to 1716, the fund consisted of bequests, the capital of which was kept by the various donors under their own control, the interest being paid annually to the California Mission. But the sum for the support of one establishment having been lost by the failure of the donor in trust (Juan Bautista López), it was deemed needful that the moneys be invested in lands to be controlled by the Mission itself. Originally the Society of Jesus could not own temporalties, but upon petition of Salvatierra in 1717 it was given the power. Hereupon the Mission purchased an extensive tract from Captain Manuel Fernández de Azunio, but for what price is not known. It also loaned 54,000 *pesos* upon the security of the Jesuit College of San Ildefonso at Puebla.

Early in the eighteenth century, the Marqués de Villapuente had given to the California Mission the hacienda of Arroyozarco in the State of Mexico. In 1726 and 1735 the Marqués de Villapuente, the Marquesa de Torres de San Roda, and Doña Rosa de la Peña gave the hacienda San Pedro de Ybarra in the State of Guanajuato, together with lands in the Reyno de León (later Tamaulipas), called the hacienda San Agustín de los Amoles, and lands in the State of San Luis Potosí, called San Ignacio del Buey and San Francisco Xavier de la Baya. A further gift by Doña Josefa Paula de Argüelles comprised the haciendas of Maguey, Torreón Buey in Zacatecas, and of Cienéga del Pastor within the pueblos of Atotonilco el Alto y la Barca, whereof at the end of long litigation there was decreed to the California Mission the 4½ = 2–9 part of Cienéga in the State of Jalisco. (M. A., Arch. Gen., *Gobernación*, "Junta de Califs. 1824.")

According to Palou, the history of the Fund, and its condition in 1767 on the expulsion of the Jesuits, were as follows: —

LIST OF THE PIOUS WORKS FOUNDED BY VARIOUS PERSONS FOR THE
SPIRITUAL CONQUEST OF CALIFORNIA

Year		Pesos.
1698.	Don Juan Caballero founded the first mission, and for that purpose gave the sum of	10,000.00
1699.	The same founded the second mission	10,000.00
1700.	Don Nicolás Arteaga founded the third mission with the same amount	10,000.00
1702.	Various persons, through Father José Vidal, Jesuit, founded the fourth mission	7,000.00
1704.	The Marqués de Villapuente founded the fifth mission with the same amount	10,000.00
1709.	The same founded the sixth mission	10,000.00
1713.	The same founded the seventh mission	10,000.00

1718. His Excellency, Don Juan Ruiz de Velasco, founded the eighth mission — *Pesos* 10,000.00
1719. The Marqués de Villapuente founded the ninth mission — 10,000.00
1725. Father Juan María Luyando, Jesuit, founded the tenth mission — 10,000.00
1731. Doña María Rosa de la Peña endowed one of the missions through the Marqués de Villapuente — 10,000.00
1746. The Marqués de Villapuente founded the eleventh mission — 10,000.00
1747. Her Excellency Doña María de Borja, Duchess of Gandia, in her testament bequeathed for the missions of California (and it is shown that it was received) — 62,000.00

Total of Alms — 179,000.00

FUNDS AND PROPERTIES WHICH EXISTED AT THE TIME OF THE EXPULSION OF THE JESUIT FATHERS

In money which was found in the *procuraduría-general* of California at the time of the expulsion — *Pesos* 92,000.00
Goods found in the warehouse of said *procuraduría*, estimated by commercial men of Spain and Mexico — 27,255.06
Merchandise which was found in the warehouse of Loreto, according to the prices charged and for which it was sold — 79,377.03

Total amount of funds — 199,033.01
[198,632.09]

LOANS MADE BY THE PROCURADURÍA-GENERAL OF CALIFORNIA FROM THE FUNDS OF THE MISSIONS AS IS EVIDENCED BY THE RESPECTIVE DOCUMENTS

To the College of San Ildefonso of Puebla at three and one half per cent — *Pesos* 22,000.00
To the College of San Ignacio of Puebla with revenues of four per cent — 5,000.00
To the College of San Pedro y San Pablo of Mexico without indication of the percentage — 29,100.00
To the College of San Ildefonso of Puebla at three per cent — 23,000.00
To the College of San Gerónimo of Mexico at three per cent — 38,500.00
To the College of San Ildefonso of Puebla at three per cent — 9,000.00

Total investments — 126,600.00

GENERAL SUMMARY

Total of alms given — 179,000.00
Total of goods on hand — 199,033.01
[198,632.09]
Total invested or loaned — 126,600.00
Total amount of the Fund — 504,633.01
[504,232.09]

"Besides this capital there are the plantations called *Ibarra*, whose administrator told me that in ordinary years they produced twenty thousand dollars income clear, to which amount must be added the revenues from the haciendas of Arroyo-Sarco. Thus far the paper."

"From what is said I infer that at the expulsion of the Jesuit Fathers there existed only the said haciendas besides the goods and the investments, which amounted to 325,633 *pesos* and one *real*." (F. Palou, *Noticias*, tom. i, chap. 28, pp. 183–195.)

36. *Cédula* of 1703 (September 28); translated in full, *Proceedings Mexican and American Claims Commission*, Claim no. 493, p. 442.

37. Venegas, *Noticia*, vol. ii, p. 285.

38. *Ibid.*, p. 342; *Docs. para la Historia de Méj.*, série ii, tom. iv, pp. 26, 98.

39. Venegas, *Noticia*, vol. ii, p. 493; Translation, vol. ii, p. 158.

40. *Ibid.*, p. 502; Translation, vol. ii, p. 164. In translation the decree is much abbreviated. On Sept. 15, 1706, Lieutenant Manje wrote to Kino that he had already penned "a hundred sheets" advocating the establishment of a *villa* on the Colorado as an *escala y ante mural y refugio* for the Sobas, Pimas, Sobaipuris, Cocomoricopas, and Yumas, and for the reduction of the Moquis, Apaches, and nations of the north and northeast and northwest up to the Mar del Sur, and as a *refugio de las Navegantes de China*. (*Favores Celestiales*, part iv, book iv, chap. 3.)

41. *Noticia*, vol. iii, p. 140; Translation, vol. ii, p. 308. In 1765 Wenceslao Link (a Bohemian Jesuit) explored the northern peninsula well toward the Colorado. (*Diario*, 1766, B. C.)

42. *Noticia*, vol. iii, p. 1; Translation, vol. ii, p. 213.

43. Chihuahua, Arch. de Secretaría, Siglo xviii, leg. S.; Sedelmair, "Relación," 1746, *Doc. para la Hist. de Méj.*, série iii, tom. iv.

44. J. Baegert, *Nachrichten von der Amerikanischen Halbinsel California*, 1773.

45. P. Fages, *Informe del Estado de las Misiones de Baja California*, 1786 (B. C., *St. Pap. Miss. and Col.*, vol. i, p. 9). See also Viceroy to King, 1784 (M. A., Arch. Genl., *Historia*, 42; translated, *Proceedings Mexican and American Claims Commission*, p. 422, sec. 33).

46. J. Gálvez, *Informe* (Dec. 31, 1771), gives total population of the peninsula in 1769, Spaniards, Indians, and others, as 7888. Palou gives total registered population in 1772, " a large part wandering in the mountains," as 5074 in thirteen establishments.

47. Decree of Expulsion, Feb. 27, 1767; translated, *Proceedings Mexican and American Claims Commission*, p. 410.

CHAPTER V

REOCCUPATION OF MONTEREY, AND DISCOVERY OF THE BAY OF SAN FRANCISCO

HITHERTO the principal available sources for the Gálvez (Portolá) expedition have been the following: *Diario* of Portolá, early copy (B. C.) ; *Diario Histórico* of Pedro Fages, — an abbreviated French rendering of the original (*Annales des Voyages*, vol. ci); *Diario Histórico* of Miguel Costansó (Mexico, 1770), — Translations by William Revely (London, 1790), and by Charles F. Lummis (*Land of Sunshine*, 1901); *Noticias de la Nueva California*, by Francisco Palou (J. T. Doyle, 4 vols., San Francisco, 1874); *Diario* of Juan Crespi (Palou, *Noticias*, vol. ii), — translated as to portion San Diego to Monterey by Frank de Thoma (Los Ángeles *Times*, 1898); *Diario* of Junípero Serra (Edward E. Ayer Collection, Newberry Library, Chicago, holograph), — Translation by Charles F. Lummis (*Out West*); Letters of José de Gálvez to Fermín Francisco Lasuén and to Pedro Fages and Miguel Costansó, 1768 (B. C., *Archives of Santa Bárbara*, vol. i); *Instrucciones* of Gálvez to Vicente Vila and Pedro Fages (B. C., *Provincial State Papers*, vol. i); " Manifest " of the San Carlos (B. C., *Ibid.*); " Extracto de Noticias del Puerto de Monterey," Mexico, 1770 (Palou, *Noticias*, vol. ii), — translated (*Land of Sunshine*, 1901); *Informe General de Gálvez*, Dec. 31, 1771 (Mexico, 1867); Palou, *Vida de Serra* (Mexico, 1787); *Informe de Revilla Gigedo*, 1793 (M. A.), — Translation (*Land of Sunshine*, 1899); *Identification of Sir Francis Drake's Anchorage on the Coast of California in the Year 1579*, by George Davidson, California Historical Society Publication, pamphlet.

To the above there may now be added: *Instrucción que deberá observar el Capitán de Dragones, D. Gaspar de Portolá, en la expedición y viaje por tierra á los puertos de San Diego y Monterrey*, Cabo de San Lucas, 20 Febrero, 1769; *Instrucción que ha de tener presente Dⁿ Fernando de Rivera y Moncada para la proxima entrada por tierra á Monterrey*, Puerto de la Paz, 4 Abril, 1769 (S. A., Sevilla); *Diarios de los Viajes que el R. P. Fr. Juan Crespi y otros Misioneros del Colegio de San Fernando hicieron en la California, escritos por el mismo;* in six parts (each part by a separate missionary and with a prologue by Crespi), constituting the basis of Palou's *Noticias*, but with variations from the latter in substance and expression (Lenox Library, N. Y., Ramírez Coll.); Palou, *Noticias*, MS. copy, 2 vols. (Ayer Collection, Newberry Library); *Diario Histórico* of Pedro Fages (M. A., and Lenox Library, New York); *Diario del Viaje de Tierra hecho al Norte de la California*, by Miguel Costansó, San Diego, Feb. 7, 1770 (S. A., Madrid, and Sutro Library, San Francisco); *Diario de Navegación del Paquebot San Carlos . . . de la Paz al Puerto de San Diego*, by Vicente Vila (S. A., Madrid); *Relación*

Diaria de la Navegación del Paquebot San Carlos desde 11 de Enero al 1° de Mayo de 1769 á San Diego y Monterey, by Vicente Vila (S. A., Madrid); *Listas de Carga del Navio San Antonio, alias El Príncipe* (S. A., Sevilla); correspondence (during expedition) of Portolá, Fages, Costansó, Rivera y Moncada, and Crespi, with Viceroy Don Carlos Francisco de Croix (S. A., Sevilla, and M. A.); letter, Serra to Gálvez, Monterey, July 2, 1770 (S. A., Sevilla); general correspondence (preliminary to expedition) of Gálvez (35 letters) and of Viceroy Croix (M. A.); special correspondence of Rafael Verger, Guardian of the College of San Fernando, with *comisarios-generales* of the Indies (M. A., 15 letters, 1771–72), of four of which, dated June 30, Aug. 3, Aug. 27, and Aug. 28, 1771, originals are to be found in Boston Public Library. Of the Portolá diary and of the "Extracto de Noticias," the Spanish texts with translations have been published (1909) by the Academy of Pacific Coast History, vol. i, nos. 2 and 3, — Bancroft Library, Berkeley, California.

The later sources, besides contributing much of detail on all points, reveal for the first time the attitude of the College of San Fernando toward Gálvez and Alta California. (Specific citations below.)

1. A thousand Franciscans emigrated to Barbary at the close of the fifteenth century rather than submit to the rule of chastity. (H. C. Lea, *An Historical Sketch of Sacerdotal Celibacy in the Christian Church*, 1867, pp. 292–293; Mariana, *Historia de España*, vol. vi, p. 387.)

2. Sir A. Helps, *The Spanish Conquest in America*, 1900, vol. i, p. 179. "The Fathers [Jeronimite] asked the opinion of the official persons, and also of the Franciscans and Dominicans, touching the liberty of the Indians. It was very clear beforehand what the answers would be. The official persons and the Franciscans pronounced against the Indians, and the Dominicans in their favor." (*Ibid.* 359.) "There does not appear sufficient ground for the statement that the Franciscans were always opposed to the Dominicans on the question of the liberty of the Indian. At any rate, at this early period [1532] we find both Orders protesting in favor of the Indians." (*Ibid.*, vol. iii, p. 160, n. 1.)

3. Three Franciscans (Flemings) had reached Mexico as early as 1522. (Bancroft, *History of Mexico*, vol. ii, p. 160, etc.)

4. A "college" was a convent the inmates of which were trained for missionary work among the heathen. It differed from a convent *per se* in being independent of any other house or province. It possessed a "novitiate" (seminary) of its own for recruiting and instructing novices, a privilege accorded otherwise only to a province. The head of a college was called a guardian. He was elected (in an institution of full membership) by twelve councillors or voters, and the only officer to whom he was subject was a commissary-general in Spain, represented by a sub-commissary in Mexico or in one of the provinces. The conventual hierarchy was as follows: (1)

President (head of a group of two or more friars); (2) Guardian; (3) *Custodio* (director of a number of convents); (4) Provincial (head of a province, — a group of convents, usually not less than seven).

5. San Fernando, at first an *hospicio,* "home," was created a college on October 15, 1734, by a *cédula* issued by Philip V, in conformity with a Bull promulgated by Pope Innocent XI in 1682. The oldest Franciscan college in Mexico was that of Santa Cruz de Querétaro, founded in 1683. (Guardian Fray Rafael Verger to Manuel Lanz de Casafonda, *comisario-general de las Indias,* " Carta Segunda," par. 37, August 3, 1771, M. A., Museo Nacional, *Trasuntos.*) In 1771 the membership of San Fernando was as follows: Priests, 43; choristers, 7; laics (novices included), 22; lay brothers, 2 — 74 in all. ("Paper presented to Fourth Mexican Council," par. 17, August 26, 1771, by Fray Rafael Verger, *ut sup.*)

Because of the rumored differences between the Franciscans of Jalisco and Querétaro, an order had been procured from the Viceroy sending the Jaliscans to California and the Fernandinos with the Querétarans to Sonora. A vigorous protest from Palou, Crespi, Lasuén, and the other Fernandinos (four letters, Oct. 12–25, 1767, to the College of San Fernando) resulted in a resumption of the original plan. (M. A., Arch. Genl., *Documentos Relativos á las Misiones de Californias,* Qto i; Palou, *Noticias,* vol. i, p. 8, etc.)

6. Palou had been president of the Sierra Gorda missions. He was pronounced by Verger *mui capaz, verídico, y práctico en la reducción de Indios.* As for Serra, he was born at Petra, Mallorca, on November 24, 1713, and educated at the University of Mallorca, where later he became a professor of distinction, — *mui aplaudido en su empleo,* says Verger, *para su literatura y bellas prendas.* "But," continues the Guardian, "it will be necessary to moderate somewhat *su ardiente zelo.*" ("Carta Segunda," par. 1, M. A., Museo, *Trasuntos,* f. 128; Palou, *Vida de Serra,* p. 1.)

7. M. Ribero to Croix, March 23, 1768 (M. A., Arch. Genl., *Historia,* 14, f. 328).

8. Gálvez was born at Velez-Malaga in October, 1729. His parents were poor, but managed to send him to the University of Alcalá, where he graduated with the degree of doctor. He distinguished himself as an advocate, and, loving French society, made the acquaintance of one of the secretaries of the Marquis de Duras, the French ambassador. By the latter Gálvez was appointed advocate to the embassy, and in this capacity came to the notice of the Marqués de Grimaldi, who made him his private secretary. From this post the King (Charles III) advanced him to membership in the Council of the Indies. (*Biographie Universelle* (Michaud), Paris, 1856.)

9. *Plan para la Erección de un Govierno y Comandancia G^{ral} que comprehenda la Peninsula de Californias y las Provincias de Sinaloa, Sonora, y Nueva Viscaya,* Jan. 23, 1768 (M. A., Arch. Genl., *Provincias Internas,* 154; copy, Harvard Library, Sparks Collection, 98, with letter of approval

by the Archbishop of Mexico, Jan. 28, 1768, *Papeles Varios de America,* iii; translated, Appendix A of this volume).

10. *Los Rusos han hecho en varias veces diferentes tentativas para facilitarse una comunicación con la América, y ultimamente, lo han conseguido intentando la navegación por el Norte de la Mar del Sur. Se asegura que lo han logrado y que han llegado á tierra firme sin determinar en que grado, habiendo efectuado un desembarco en parage al parecer poblado de Salvages, con los quales pelearon con muerte de 300 Rusos.* Marqués de Grimaldi (First Secretary of State) to Croix, Jan. 23, 1768 (M. A., Arch. Genl., *Real Cédulas y Ordenes,* 92, f. 58). On Russian aggression, see also Costansó, *Diario Histórico;* translated, *Land of Sunshine,* vol. xiv, pp. 486–490.

The *junta* referred to in the Croix-Gálvez dispatch of Jan. 23, 1768, as having decided to send Gálvez to Sonora, Sinaloa, Nueva Vizcaya, and the Californias, was held in the City of Mexico on Jan. 21, 1768. Its determination was that *sobre este punto la nueva adquisizion de la rica peninsula de Californias, y los demas territorios que en la Sonora y Nueva Vizcaya poseian las Misiones de los regulares de la Compañia, es oy incomparablemente maior la conveniencia, y mucho mas urgente la nezesidad de que el Señor Visitador pase á las expresadas Provincias y arregle sus Pueblos, govierno y demas puntos que son indispensables,* etc., and that he *disponga su Viage á las zitadas Provincias de Californias, Sonora, y Nueva Vizcaya para mediados de Abril de este presente año, llevando la plena comision y ampleas facultades,* etc. (Harvard Library, Sparks Coll. 98, *Papeles Varios,* iii.) On Jan. 26, 1768, Viceroy Croix reported to the King that the *junta* had been held and that Gálvez had volunteered to go to the Californias and to the other Northern provinces. The Viceroy asked that the King "from his generous heart" condescend *aumentar al Visitador el sueldo.* (*Ibid.*) Croix to Julian de Arriaga, Minister of Marine and of the Indies, May 28, 1768, stating resolution to send an expedition to Monterey. (M. A., Arch. Genl., *Correspondencia de los Virreyes,* vol. xii, no. 376, f. 74, série ii (Croix), tom. ii.) Acknowledgment by Arriaga, Oct. 18, 1768, stating that "pending outcome of an expedition so important, the King would await with impatience news of the successive steps." (M. A., Arch. Genl., *R. Céd. y Ord.* 93, f. 163.)

As noted by Gálvez in his *Informe General* of 1771 (Dec. 31), the steps in the matter of the expedition to Monterey were the following: (1) An offer by the *visitador* in 1765 to go to Nueva Vizcaya and other provinces, in order to establish *poblaciones* for the raising of funds to maintain forces in Sonora in the perpetual struggle waged with the Indians; (2) a reply by Arriaga in 1767 (July 20), directing the calling of a *junta;* (3) a *junta* (1768, prior to March 2) at the capital, composed of the Archbishop and various ministers, approving Gálvez's offer, and indicating the peninsula of California as in need of visitation because of the recent expulsion of the Jesuits; (4) approval by the King in a royal order of Sept. 20, 1768; (5) urgent order by the King, Jan. 23, 1768, to Viceroy Croix, directing measures for defense of the California peninsula as against the Russians; (6) receipt of this order by Gálvez before his arrival at San Blas, whither, on April 9, he had set out from the capital, and where (Costansó, *Diario ;* translated, *Land of Sunshine*, vol. xiv, p. 489) he held a *junta* on May 16. Of the dispatches referred to by the *visitador*, only those of Jan. 23, 1768, and later, have been found in the Mexican Archives, and indeed it is they only that directly affected the Monterey expedition. (*Informe General de Gálvez*, Mexico, 1867; pp. 139–141.)

11. Letter to Serra from Santa Ana, July 12, 1768, announcing arrival *en el dia 5 del corriente.* (M. A., Museo, *Documentos Relativos á las Misiones de Californias*, Qto i.) The *visitador* set sail from San Blas on May 24 in the sloop Sinaloa. On the eighth day out, he was forced by contrary winds into a bay of Isabella Island, where he was held four days. On June 5, in a calm, the Sinaloa was rowed to the Tres Marías Islands, which for six days Gálvez carefully explored. Setting sail on the 13th, he was forced to Mazatlán. Here he remained until July 2, when, with a wind *fresco y favorable*, he started for the peninsula. (Croix to Arriaga, July 30, 1768, M. A., Arch. Genl., *Cor. de Virr.*, vol. xii, no. 515, f. 281, sér. ii (Croix), tom. ii.) As consorts of the Sinaloa from San Blas, were the brigantine Concepción and the bark Pisón. The Concepción reached Cerralvo Inlet on June 14, having lost sight of the Sinaloa and Pisón on the night of May 28. From the beach of *la enseñada de Cerralvo*, the cargo of the Concepción was transferred to Osio's hacienda, and from this beach, on June 19, Rivera y Moncada was notified of the hourly anticipated arrival of Gálvez. (M. A., Arch. Genl., *Californias*, 76.)

12. Portolá, in a report to Croix, of date Dec. 28, 1767, describes the peninsula as pure sand sown with thorns and thistles. On a journey from Santiago to La Pasión (ten long days), he had met with naught, *ni rancho, ni casa; ni aun el menor abrigo*, save the mining-camp of Osio. In this land, he continues, one need rather be *vaquero* than *soldado*. (M. A., Arch. Genl., *Californias*, 76, no. 1.)

13. On March 5, 1768, Portolá had been instructed by the Viceroy to intrust to the Franciscans in the peninsula only that which pertained to the *sagrada y espiritual* of the missions, and on April 9 he had reported having placed in the missions, as *administradores*, soldiers "that were very loyal" (M. A., Arch. Genl., *Californias*, 76, nos. 3, 10). Verger, writing to Casafonda on August 3, 1771, states (citing Palou) that the Spiritualties were intrusted to the Franciscans on April 9, 1768, and the Temporalties on August 12. Gálvez's own letters to Serra on the subject bear date Aug. 13. He says: "*Comisarios* are born to obey and not govern, except it may be their own mounts." (M. A., Museo, *Docs. Rel. á las Mis. de Califs.*, Qto i.) The *visitador* used the *omnimoda facultad* (which he held) from alarm at the waste practiced by the *administradores*, who, within six months of their appointment, had killed at one mission 600 cattle, at another 400, ·

and at another 300. (M. A., Museo, *Trasuntos*, "Carta Segunda," pars. 2, 3.)

14. Gálvez, writing on Oct. 31 from Santa Ana, speaks of the horror with which, on first "placing eyes upon the peninsula, and foot in it," he was inspired "by the universal ruin that impended." On Nov. 23, in a letter to Padre Basterra at Santa Gertrudis, he describes the natives as "wandering in the mountains like wild beasts seeking pasture," — beings for the redemption of whom settled habitations (*domicilios fixos*) are indispensable. "The total nakedness," he continues, "in which the men and women have lived, does not permit to be borne in them that modesty [*pudor*] which is the first incentive to every action and virtue in rational creatures. . . . It is needful that they be clothed, even though poorly. . . . In a word, *la California conquistada* must have no native not reduced *á Población y Civilidad*, and who is not fed and clothed!" Transfer of natives from the North, and land ownership: Letter, Gálvez to Serra, from Santa Ana, on Oct. 10, 1768 (M. A., Museo, *Docs. Rel. á las Mis. de Califs.*, Qto i); Gálvez to Lasuén, Nov. 23, 1768 (B. C., *Arch. Sta. Bárb.*, vol. i, pp. 22–28; Palou, *Noticias*, vol. i, pp. 25–29, 31, 55); Gálvez, Orders, Nov. 19 and 23, 1768 (*Informe General*, 1771); Bancroft, *North Mexican States and Texas*, vol. i, pp. 486–87, nn. 41, 42, 43.

15. Gálvez to Serra, Nov. 23, 1768 (M. A., Museo, *Docs. Rel. á las Mis. de Califs.*, Qto i).

16. Gálvez, *Decreto de Colonización en Baja California*, 1768 (B. C., *Prov. St. Pap.*, vol. i, pp. 61–66).

17. Palou, *Vida de Serra*, pp. 44, 261. In imitation of Saint Francis, Serra was wont to beat his shoulders with a chain; and, while holding aloft a crucifix in his left hand, to beat his breast with a stone. He also used fire.

18. Gálvez to Serra, Oct. 7, 1768, letter expressing wish that if not too severe a tax upon his energies, Serra might come to Santa Ana for a conference upon certain points which he holds pending. Same to Same, Oct. 22: Is as glad to hear that Serra will come as that the Lauretana, which had gone aground, is saved. (*Docs. Rel. á las Mis. de Califs.*, Qto i.)

19. San Carlos, 62 men, Crespi, *Diario* (Palou, *Noticias*, vol. ii, p. 13); "Manifest" of San Carlos (*Prov. St. Pap.*, vol. i, pp. 13–21).

San Antonio, 28 men, Costansó, *Diario Histórico;* Translation, *Land of Sunshine*, vol. xiv, p. 494.

First land division, 31 men, Crespi, *Diario* (Palou, *Noticias*, vol. ii, pp. 21, 40). (Indian auxiliaries), 42 men, Crespi to Guardian Juan Andrés, June 22, 1769 (M. A., Museo, *Docs. Rel. á las Mis. de Califs.*, Qto i).

Second land division, 19 men, Portolá to Viceroy, July 4, 1769 (M. A., Arch. Genl., *Californias*, 76; Palou, *Noticias*, vol. ii, p. 35). (Indian auxiliaries), 44 men, — making, for both divisions, a total of 226 men.

Says Mr. Zoeth S. Eldredge (*The March of Portolá*, p. 30): "Among the rank and file were men whose names are not less known: Pedro Amador, who gave his name to Amador County; Juan Bautista Alvarado, grandfather of Governor Alvarado; José Raimundo Carrillo, later *alférez* (lieutenant) and captain, comandante of the presidio of Monterey, of Santa Bárbara, and of San Diego, and founder of the great Carrillo family; José Antonio Yorba, sergeant of Catalonian volunteers, founder of the family of that name and grantee of the Rancho Santiago de Santa Ana; Pablo de Cota, José Ignacio Oliveras, José María Soberanes, and others."

20. M. A., Museo, *Docs. Rel. á las Mis. de Califs.*, Qto i.

21. *Ibid.*

22. *Ibid.*

23. *Ibid.*

24. Full list of articles taken from all the missions, attested by Palou, May 8, 1773 (M. A., Arch. Genl., *Prov. Int.* 211); summary by Bancroft (*History of California*, vol. i, p. 119, n. 9). In 1774 Francisco de Estavillo, *procurador-general* of the Dominicans for California, petitioned for a return of the *ornamentos* and *vasos sagrados* sent north by order of Gálvez; but the petition was denied by Fiscal Areche on the ground that the articles taken were either from an excess quantity in establishments yet existing, or from suppressed establishments. (M. A., Arch. Genl., *Prov. Int.* 211.)

On despoliation of the peninsula, see note 34, *post.* As to three Northern missions, Gálvez (M. A., Museo, *Docs. Rel. á las Mis. de Califs.*, Qto i). The plan at this juncture seems to have been for three establishments in what, later, was Alta California; and for two establishments auxiliary to these in the northern part of the peninsula. (Gálvez to Palou, Aug. 12, 1768, *Ibid.*)

25. As intimated, Gálvez named the intermediate mission San Buenaventura, because of the special favor with which that saint was regarded by Saint Francis. The story is that the latter, one day, meeting the Tuscan Giovanni de Fidanza, exclaimed, in prophetic vision of his future greatness, " O buona ventura"! — whence the appellation.

26. Gálvez to Palou, two letters, Oct. 7, 1768 (M. A., Museo, *Docs. Rel. á las Mis. de Califs.*, Qto i).

27. Gálvez to Serra, Dec. 28, 1768 (*Ibid.*).

28. " Manifest " of the San Carlos (B. C., *Prov. St. Pap.*, vol. i, pp. 13–21); Palou, *Noticias*, vol. ii, p. 13 ; Costansó, *Diario Histórico*, — Translation, *Land of Sunshine*, vol. xiv, pp. 490–491; Serra, *Diario*, — Translation, *Out West*, vol. xvi, p. 294.

29. M. A., Museo, *Docs. Rel. á las Mis. de Califs.*, Qto i. " On the 6th of January of this same year [1769], finding myself in the Port of La Paz, with his Eminence the Señor Inspector, I blessed the Packet named the San Carlos, saying the Mass aboard her, and blessed the standards; the Litany was sung, and other devotions to Our Lady. And his Eminence made a fervent exhortation with which he kindled the spirits of those who were to

go in that vessel to said Ports of San Diego and Monterey. These embarked on the 9th, at night, and on the 10th set sail." (Serra, *Diario;* Translation, *Out West,* vol. xvi, p. 294.)

30. M. A., Museo, *Docs. Rel. á las Mis. de Califs.,* Qto i.

31. Vila, *Diario de Navegación del Paquebot San Carlos* (S. A., Madrid, Dirección Hidrografía, *California, Historia y Viages,* t. i, caj. 7°, 63ª).

32. M. A., Museo, *Docs. Rel. á las Mis. de Califs.,* Qto i.

33. M. A., Museo, *Docs. Rel. á las Mis. de Califs.,* Qto i. Writing to Palou on Nov. 23, 1768, Gálvez asked prayers that (for the safety of the ships) the north winds might be put to sleep — *adormezca los Nortes.* (B. C., *Arch. de Sta. Bárb.,* vol. xi, p. 370.)

34. Palou, Jan. 7, 1772, list of mules and horses taken by Rivera y Moncada from the various missions of the peninsula, with Rivera's corrections (M. A., Arch. Genl., *Prov. Int.* 211). This list was made apropos of an order by Gálvez for a restoration of the animals. According to Bancroft (*North Mexican States and Texas,* vol. i, p. 491), Gálvez and Serra being in accord, there was no one to make objection to the despoiling of the peninsular missions for the benefit of those to be planted to the northward. On the contrary, on July 26, 1770, the *discretario* of the College of San Fernando addressed to Viceroy Croix a drastic criticism of the entire proceeding. Speaking of the spoliation wrought by Portolá's *administradores,* he said that it was great, but not nearly so great as that wrought by Gálvez for the Monterey expedition. Some 500 head of stock, in all, had been taken, and if not restored, the peninsular Indians could not be fed. (M. A., Museo, *Docs. Rel. á las Mis. de Califs.,* Qto ii). According to Serra, not a mule had been replaced up to April 22, 1773 (B. C., *Prov. St. Pap.,* vol. i, p. 91). It is the explanation of Palou that compensation was made by the government through the *almacén* (royal warehouse) at Loreto, and from the money left by the Jesuits (*Noticias,* vol. i, p. 232). Bitterly opposed as was the College of San Fernando to the spoliation by Gálvez, it yet dared not interfere in the matter even in restraint of its own sons Serra and Palou.

35. M. A., Museo, *Docs. Rel. á las Mis. de Califs.,* Qto i. Gálvez, in a letter to Serra of date March 28, 1769, makes mention of a *segunda or^n, positiva que dirigí al Capitán con la noticia del despacho del ultimo Paquebot desde el cabo.* (*Ibid.*)

36. Cáñizares, *pilotín* (master's mate) of the San Carlos, was detached for land duty

37. Portolá's birthplace was Balaguer, and his rank noble. He had seen service in Italy and Portugal. (Pub. Acad. Pacific Coast Hist., vol. i, no. 3, p. 6.)

38. J. Crespi, *Diario,* in Palou, *Noticias,* vol. ii, pp. 6–39; Crespi to Juan Andrés, Guard. San Fernando, San Diego, June 22, 1769 (M. A., Museo, *Docs. Rel. á las Mis. de Califs.,* Qto i); Portolá, *Diario* (B. C., Pinart, *Papeles Varios*); Portolá to Croix, San Diego, July 4, 1769 (M. A., Arch.

Genl., *Californias*, 76); M. Costansó, *Diario Histórico*, — Translation, *Land of Sunshine*, vol. xiv, pp. 490–491; Serra, *Diario*, — Translation, *Out West*, vol. xvi, p. 294; Fages and Costansó, Jan. 4, 1769 (M. A., Arch. Genl., *Californias*, 66).

39. Palou,*Vida de Serra*, p. 20. Padre Navarrete, who made the journey from Vera Cruz to the capital in 1646, wrote: "We passed through places infested with mosquitoes or gnats that sting cruelly." (Churchill, *Collection of Voyages*, vol. i, p. 208.)

40. M. A., Museo, *Docs. Rel. á las Mis. de Califs.*, Qto i.

41. The orders issued by Gálvez (March and April, 1769), covering the points indicated in the text, were nineteen in number. Rules were framed for compensation to be paid the Indians for their labor; for a distribution of house-lots (*solares*) and fields (*suertes*), and for a demarcation of commons (*ejidos*), — all to be recorded in a *Libro de Población*. It was provided (and herein a germ of conflict between State Sacerdotal and State Secular in the peninsula), that at Loreto the temporalties in charge of the padre (Palou) were to consist only of the Rancho San Juan and the *huerta* (garden) attached to the mission. Grain from the royal warehouse (*almacén*) was to be given to the mission in exchange for garden vegetables and garden fruit, and meat was to be supplied to the *jefe del Govierno* and royal commissary by the mission at a stipulated price. "Instruction to Felipe Neve" (addenda), 1774, no. 22 (M. A., Arch. Genl., *Prov. Int.* 166). By the College of San Fernando much of the foregoing, together with other portions of the policy of the *visitador* in the Californias, was disapproved. See this chapter, notes 24, 34, 78, 80, with citations.

42. Gálvez to Serra (two letters), La Paz, March 28, 1769 (M. A., Museo, *Docs. Rel. á las Mis. de Califs.*, Qto i). The parting words of Serra to Palou were pathetic: *Á Dios hasta Monterey, donde espero juntaremos, para trabajar en aquella Viña del Señor. Mucho me alegré de esto; pero mi despedida fué hasta la eternidad,* — Good-bye until Monterey, where I hope we shall meet to work together in the Lord's vineyard. At this I was much rejoiced, but my farewell was until eternity. (Palou, *Vida de Serra*, p. 68.)

43. Addenda to "Instructions to Felipe Neve," pars. 5, 13, 17 (M. A., Arch. Genl., *Prov. Int.* 166).

44. Crespi, *Diario*, Palou, *Noticias*, vol. ii, p. 26.

45. The selection of Joseph as patron saint was determined by the circumstance that prayers to him had been followed by relief from a locust plague. On September 15, 1768, the *visitador* had explained to Serra (in apology for not naming the Monterey presidio for Saint Joseph) that the latter would not be offended, as he was very humble, and devoted especially to poor artisans; and as already two churches were named for him in the peninsula. (M. A., Museo, *Docs. Rel. á las Mis. de Califs.*, Qto i.)

46. Vila, *Relación Diaria*, S. A., Madrid, Direc. Hid., *Costa No. de America*, t. i, pp. 276–282, C 2ª; Vila, *Diario de Navegación* [Log], *Ibid.*; California,

Historia y Viages, t. i, 7, 63ª. For the course of the San Carlos, see general map (pocket).

47. Serra, *Diario*, Ayer Coll., Newberry Library; Translation, *Out West*, vol. xvi.

48. Crespi, *Diario*, in Palou, *Noticias*, vol. ii, pp. 38–100; Portolá, *Diario* (B. C., Pinart, *Papeles Varios*); Costansó, *Diario Histórico*, — Translation, *Land of Sunshine*, vol. xiv. Says the latter (p. 494): "And this whole [sea] expedition, which had been composed of more than ninety men, saw itself reduced to only eight soldiers and as many marines in a state to attend to the safeguarding of the Barks, the working of the Launches, Custody of the Camp and service of the Sick." In his *Relación Diaria*, Vila states that up to March 29 there had died of his own crew sixteen men, and of the crew of the San Antonio nine. Of Fages's men six only were effective. Neither in the B. C. nor M. A. has anything been found relative to the number of the crew of the San Antonio. But it must have been approximately twenty-eight, taking the total of both ships at ninety.

49. M. A., Museo, *Docs. Rel. á las Mis. de Califs.*, Qto i.

50. M. A., Arch. Genl., *Californias*, 76.

51. "Instrucciones á Portolá y á Rivera y Moncada," Feb. 20 and April 4, 1769 (S. A., Sevilla, Audiencia de Guadalajara, est. 104, caj. 3, leg. 3); "Instrucciones á Vila" (B. C., *Prov. St. Pap.*, vol. i, pp. 22–31); "Instrucciones á Fages" (*Ibid.*, pp. 31–43); summary of foregoing instructions, Bancroft, *History of California*, vol. i, pp. 129, n. 7, 131, n. 11.

52. Portolá to Croix, San Diego, July 4, 1769 (M. A., Arch. Genl., *Californias*, 76); Croix to Portolá in approval, Aug. 12, 1769 (*Ibid.*); Crespi, *Diario* (Palou, *Noticias*, vol. ii, pp. 99, etc.).

53. Palou, *Noticias*, vol. ii, pp. 99, 248; *Vida de Serra*, p. 82.

54. The San José or Saint Joseph (*alias* el Descubridor) was dispatched from San Blas for La Paz, early in 1768, under Capitán and Piloto Don Domingo Antonio Calegari. (M. A., Arch. Genl., *Historia*, 329; Palou, *Noticias*, vol. ii, p. 33.)

55. Crespi, *Diario*, in Palou, *Noticias*, vol. ii, p. 252; R. Verger to Casafonda, "Carta Segunda" (M. A., Museo, *Trasuntos*, f. 128). Upon this occasion the blacksmith of the camp distinguished himself by his bravery, receiving a wound from an arrow. His name was Juan Joseph Chacón. (Fages to Gálvez, Feb. 8, 1770, M. A., Arch. Genl., *Californias*, 66.)

56. A copy may be found in the B. C.

57. Crespi, *Diario* (Palou, *Noticias*, vol. ii, pp. 100–175); Portolá, *Diario* (B. C., Pinart, *Papeles Varios*), — Spanish text, with translation, Publications Academy Pacific Coast History, vol. i, no. 3; Fages, *Diario* (M. A., Museo, *Docs. Rel. á las Mis. de Califs.* iv).

58. Costansó, *Diario Histórico*, Mexico, 1770; Translation, *Land of Sunshine*, vols. xiv, xv, 1901.

59. Fages: "All the country about San Gabriel Mission invites to oc-

cupation by families of Spaniards, among whom, with no prejudice to the mission, there might be allotted fertile lands with *sitios* suitable for every kind of livestock . . . there being begun in them [the settlers] hopes of a *población bien importante.*" (*Diario*, M. A., Museo, *Docs. Rel. á las Mis. de Califs.* iv.)

60. Costansó, *Diario* (S. A., Madrid, Direc. Hid., *Reino de Méjico*, t. i, 62ª, 141 á 209). As carefully worked out by Mr. Z. S. Eldredge, the route was as follows: July 24, Sierra San Onofre; 25, San Juan Capistrano, where Santa Catalina Island sighted; 28, Santa Ana River (Río Jesús de los Temblores); 30–31, San Gabriel Valley (San Miguel); Aug. 1, site of Los Ángeles (Río de Nuestra Señora de Los Ángeles de Porciúncula); 4–9, San Fernando Valley (Valle de Santa Catalina de las Encinas); 12, Santa Clara River, *via* Santa Susana Mountains; 14, San Buenaventura (la Asunción); 18, Santa Bárbara (Laguna de la Concepción); 28, Point Conception; 30, Santa Inéz River (Río de Santa Rosa); Sept. 1, Guadalupe Lake (Laguna Larga); 3–4, San Luis Cañon, Bald Knob (Point Buchón); San Luis Obispo; Morro Bay (Estero de San Serafín), *via* Cañada de los Osos; 13, Sierra de Santa Lucía; 16–20, San Caproforo Cañon — Mount Mars; 26, Salinas River (Río de San Elizarto), *via* Arroyo Seco (Cañada del Palo Caido, — Fallen Tree); 30, the Sea; Oct. 1, Point Pinos.

61. Portolá to Croix, San Diego, Feb. 11, 1770 (M. A., Arch. Genl., *Californias*, 76).

62. *Ibid.*

63. Crespi, *Diario*, in Palou, *Noticias*, vol. ii, p. 183; Translation, F. de Thoma, Los Ángeles *Times*, 1898. Of these trees Fages writes in his *Diario:* "Here are trees of girth so great that eight men placed side by side with extended arms are unable to embrace them."

64. *Ibid.*; Crespi to Guardian Juan Andrés, San Diego, Feb. 8, 1770, and to Gálvez, Feb. 9, 1770 (M. A., Museo, *Docs. Rel. á las Mis. de Califs.*, Qto ii, and Arch. Genl., *Californias*, 66); Portolá to Croix, San Diego, Feb. 11, 1770 (M. A., Arch. Genl., *Californias*, 76). On identity of the bay under Point Reyes with the San Francisco Bay of Cermeño, Palou, *Noticias*, vol. ii, pp. 198–208, vol. iv, pp. 221, 288–294. On the identity of the San Francisco Bay of Cermeño with Francis Drake's Bay, G. Davidson, *Identification of Sir Francis Drake's Anchorage* (Calif. Hist. Soc. Pub.), pamphlet; and *The Discovery of San Francisco Bay*, 1907. For route of Portolá, see general map (pocket).

65. Crespi, *Diario*, in Palou, *Noticias*, vol. ii, p. 200; Translation, F. de Thoma, Los Ángeles *Times*, 1898.

66. See note 65, chapter vi, Golden Gate.

67. Portolá to Croix, San Diego, Feb. 11, 1770 (M. A., Arch. Genl., *Californias*, 76); Crespi, *Diario*, in Palou, *Noticias*, vol. ii, p. 213; Same to Guardian Andrés and José de Gálvez, San Diego, Feb. 8 and 9, 1770 (M. A., Museo, *Docs. Rel. á las Mis. de Califs.*, Qto ii, and Arch. Genl., *Californias*, 66).

68. Portolá to Viceroy, Feb. 11, 1770 (M. A., Arch. Genl., *Californias*, 76). With regard to the number of sick or dead, at specific dates, the accounts conflict. In the text, reliance is placed upon the official letters of Portolá.

69. Portolá to Croix, Feb. 11, 1770, and "Noticia total de Grano y Arina," San Diego, Jan. 28, 1770 (M. A., Arch. Genl., *Californias*, 76); Costansó and Fages to Gálvez and Croix, five letters, San Diego, Feb. 3, 7, 1770 (M. A., Arch. Genl., *Californias*, 66). In one letter to Gálvez, Costansó and Fages mention "hot disputes" on this expedition — *contestaciones y disputas . . . agriarse el genio y humor de algunos de los altercantes*, etc. Writing to Gálvez from San Diego Feb. 8, 1770, Fages states that "there are left 60 men to be fed, including 4 padres and 8 seamen with Vila." From this force "28 men are to go to Velicatá to lighten the burden on the commissary." (*Ibid.*; Palou, *Noticias*, vol. ii, pp. 254–55, 257; *Vida de Serra*, pp. 90, 93–99.)

70. Portolá to Croix, San Diego, April 17, 1770 (M. A., Arch. Genl., *Californias*, 76).

71. Palou, *Noticias*, vol. ii, p. 264.

72. Portolá to Croix, Monterey, June 15, 1770, official report of occupation of the port, with attestation by Pedro Fages, Juan Pérez, and Miguel del Pino. (M. A., Arch. Genl., *Californias*, 76; Crespi, *Diario*, in Palou, *Noticias*, vol. ii, p. 269; Palou, *Vida de Serra*, p. 101, with letter by Serra describing ceremonies.)

73. J. Gálvez to Fages and Costansó, Cape San Lucas, Feb. 14, 1769 (B. C., *Prov. St. Pap.*, vol. i, p. 46); Serra to Gálvez, Monterey, July 2, 1770 (S. A., Sevilla, Aud. de Guad., est. 104, caj. 3, leg. 3); J. Velásquez, *Diario* (M. A., Arch. Genl., *Californias*, 76); Portolá to Croix, San Blas, Aug. 1, 1770, and Portolá to Croix, Guadalajara, Aug. 28, 1770 (*Ibid.*). In a letter of July 1, 1770, to Croix, Fages states that there remain at Monterey 12 volunteers, 6 cuirassiers, 5 seamen, and Prat the surgeon. (M. A., Arch. Genl., *Californias*, 66.)

74. "The corners of the principal front of the Cathedral are formed by two strong towers. . . . One [tower] has many celebrated bells, among them one weighing 100 *quintales*. . . . These bells are not rung except on occasions of joy and thanksgiving. . . . All the churches will answer this well-known chime immediately." (J. M. de San Vicente, *City of Mexico, its Cathedral and Palace*, Cádiz, — B. C., *Papeles Varios*, México, vol. v, no. 2; Palou, *Noticias*, vol. ii, pp. 269–282, vol. i, p. 101; *Vida de Serra*, pp. 104, 107–109.)

75. F. Trillo y Vermudez to Croix, San Blas, Oct. 17, 1769 (M. A., Arch. Genl., *Historia*, 329); Croix to the King, Dec. 20 and 31, 1769, — *visitador* persuaded to return to the capital (M. A., Arch. Genl., *Cor. de Virreyes*, vol. xv (serial vol. v), nos. 1259, 1260, fol. 50, 51); Falenback to Croix, Guadalajara, Aug. 23, 1769, — concerning *actividad y infatigable trabajo* of

Gálvez *in servicio de el Real y de el público*, etc. (M. A., Arch. Genl., *Historia*, 329).

76. M. A., Museo, *Docs. Rel. á las Mis. de Califs.*, Qto i.

77. *Ibid.*

78. *Ibid.*, vol. ii. The project of mission establishments, as far north as San Diego and Monterey, was at this juncture that of the government and of ardent individual missionaries, — the government to thwart Russia, and the missionaries to multiply conversions. As for the missionary colleges, they were for a conservative course. San Fernando was as bitter against the planting of establishments in Northern California as against the despoiling of the peninsula and the Gálvez rules for Loreto. Said Verger to Casafonda on June 30, 1771: "In no manner has this college approved the founding at one time so many and such missions. If missionaries have been sent, it has been perforce and because we have not been able to resist him that commands us with power absolute, admitting neither supplication nor argument. . . . Unless God our Master works with miracles and prodigies, a happy issue cannot be expected. ("Carta Primera," M. A., Museo, *Trasuntos*, f. 127.) It is declared (1) that Monterey is 790 leagues distant; (2) that navigation is perilous, and lives and ships would be lost; (3) that many soldiers would be needed; (4) that the Indians, as confessed by Serra, are great thieves; (5) that the Indian tongues are not understood; (6) that Indian docility, so much dwelt upon by Crespi and Serra, is a sham, as witness that attack on San Diego on August 15, 1769. ("Carta Segunda," M. A., Museo,, *Trasuntos*, f. 128, *passim.*) Commenting on the urgency of the *visitador's* letters, Verger, on August 3, 1771, thus addressed Casafonda: "Hardly had the [forty-five] padres reached this college, when the *visitador* and (in consequence) the Viceroy desired them to start for California. It was necessary to moderate this ardor, as already the padres had been ninety-nine days on the way from Spain, and half of them were ill and all debilitated." Furthermore, when of the forty-five "we would permit but thirty to go to the Californias, the *visitador* vented upon us the calumny, that we were excusing ourselves from the exercise of the ministry pertinent to a Seminary or College *de Propaganda Fide*, and this after the King had paid for the transportation of the missionaries hither." ("Carta Segunda," M. A., Museo, *Trasuntos*, f. 128, par. 38, 39.)

79. Gálvez to Serra, Sta. Ana, Oct. 10, 1768; and Gálvez, decree, La Paz, Nov. 19, 1768. The decree recites the discovery of various amounts of gold dust, and of gold and silver bullion, accumulated by the Jesuits, and not accounted for to the royal treasury as required by law. It recites, further, as fact, the maintenance of the missions by the *trabajo* (labor) and *sudor* (sweat) *de los miserables Indios*, at the same time that the Indians are neither fed nor clothed. Wherefore it is ordered that the gold and silver aforesaid (7650 *pesos*) be converted to the use of the Indians, and that *sínodos* (salaries) of padres, etc., be paid from the Pious Fund. (M. A., Museo,

Docs. Rel. á las Mis. de Califs., Qto i.) It is worthy of note that in effecting the Santa Expedición (and up to May 22, 1773) there was expended from the "Pious Fund," by order of the Viceroy, 136,184 *pesos*, 3 *tomines*, 9½ *granos*. (Viceroy to Arriaga, 27 Dec., 1774, — M. A., Arch. Genl., *Cor. de los Virreyes*, vol. lxii, no. 1681, sér. ii (Bucarely), vol. xlv.)

80. Croix to Palou, Nov. 12, 1770, three letters (M. A., Museo, *Docs. Rel. á las Mis. de Califs.*, Qto ii). The *sínodos* and foundation-fund assignments met with ridicule at San Fernando. It was stated to the Viceroy by the Discretario, that in the Sierra Gorda the *sínodos* were 300 and 450 *pesos*, according to the remoteness of the mission; and (" Carta Segunda," pars. 12, 13) it was pointed out by Verger to Casafonda that the Jesuits had been allowed 500 *pesos*, while to missionaries in Texas 450 were allowed. Strange that the *visitador*, who assumed the omnipotence of God, could do no better for California padres than 275 *pesos*. As for the 1000 *pesos* for founding a California mission (at Monterey, for example), the idea was worthy of laughter (*digna de risa*), and more a Don Quixote matter than a serious proposition. Monterey was 800 leagues from the capital, and thither must be taken implements for farming, — plough-shares, axes, hoes; a complete carpenter's outfit, saws, little and big, augers, adzes, planes, chisels, compasses, hammers; the tools of masons; cooking-utensils. A house, church, and granary would be necessary; and there must be livestock (not for a family but for a pueblo), — mules, horses, oxen. Then the Indians were to be taught to work, and at the same time instructed and fed, — all with 1000 *pesos!* "What solemn nonsense!"

In a caustic supplement to his " Carta Segunda," Verger notes that the projectors of the scheme for the conquest of California were actuated by a wish to be "honored for seeming great deeds, like a Hernán Cortéz." But so niggardly were they with supplies that three hens with their broods had been deemed sufficient for the three missions, San Antonio, San Gabriel, and San Buenaventura; and for the missions together, one rooster.

81. Serra and Fages, June 9, 1771, assignment of padres to San Antonio, San Gabriel, San Luis Obispo, San Carlos (M. A., Arch. Genl., *Californias*, 66). Founding of San Gabriel, Verger, *Informe* no. 4, 1772 (M. A., Museo, *Docs. Rel. á las Mis. de Califs.*, Qto ii) ; Palou, *Noticias*, vol. ii, p. 290; vol. iii, pp. 229–252.

CHAPTER VI

SAN FRANCISCO FOUNDED

NEW CHAPTER SOURCES: 1891. *Diarios* of Crespi and Peña, 1774; Letter of Serra to Bucarely, Sept. 9, 1774. (Publications of the Historical Society of Southern California, *Sutro Documents*, nos. 16, 18, 19, — Spanish texts with translations.)

1899. "Espedición y Registro de las Cercanías del Puerto de San Francisco," *Noticias* of Palou (manuscript translation by F. de Thoma, A. S. Macdonald Collection, Oakland, California).

1900. *Diario* of Garcés, 1775–76 (Translation by Dr. Elliott Coues, New York, *On the Trail of a Spanish Pioneer*); covers also the earlier *entradas* of Garcés, the still earlier *entradas* of Kino, and collateral matters.

1907–1909. *Diario* of Juan Bautista de Anza, 1774: one version, S. A., Sevilla; three versions, M. A.; one version, Ayer Coll., Newberry Library. Anza *diario*, 1775–76, M. A.; *Diario (borrador)* of Pedro Font, 1775–76, M. A. (manuscript translations, Zoeth S. Eldredge Collection, San Francisco) ; summary of Anza *diarios* by Z. S. Eldredge, *Journal of American History*, 1908–09.

1908–09. *Diario (borrador)* of Pedro Font, 1775–76 (Bancroft Library, Cowan Collection); *Diario* (complete) of Pedro Font, 1775–76 (John Carter Brown Library, Providence, R. I.; copy in Public Library, Los Ángeles, California).

1908–1910. Verger-Casafonda, and Verger-Vega, correspondence, 1771–72; dispatches of Bucarely to the King, 1770–76; Armona letters, 1770; Fages's *Diarios* of 1770 and 1772, Fages's letters of 1771, and Tulare report of 1773; Anza, Sr., correspondence, royal decree, etc., 1737–38; Anza, Jr., correspondence, 1772–76; Garcés's *Diario* of 1771, and correspondence of 1772–76; *Diario* of Juan Díaz, 1774; Costansó letters, 1772; Rivera y Moncada correspondence, 1773–76; Fuster on the affair of the neophyte Carlos, 1775; Escalante and Domínguez reports, 1776 (M. A.).

Facts and deductions: (1) Early application of the name San Francisco to the *estero* or present San Francisco Bay; (2) effort by Juan Bautista de Anza, Sr., to promote exploration westward, 1737–38; (3) outfitting and officering of first expedition of Juan Bautista de Anza, Jr.; (4) probable identification of San Carlos Pass (Z. S. Eldredge); (5) an expedition of Fages to San Francisco Bay, 1770; (6) Tulare Valley as seen by Fages, 1772. (Specific citations below.)

1. "Where I am on the Colorado, no troop of his Majesty has passed until to-day."

2. From Mexico on Sept. 15, 1771, Gálvez announced to Palou his im-

pending *viage á España,* and asked that there be procured for him some *perlas esquisitas* as a gift *á la Princesa, Nuestra Señora.* (M. A., Museo, *Docs. Rel. á las Mis. de Califs.,* Qto ii.)

3. Croix in 1783 was made Viceroy of Peru.

4. R. Verger to Viceroy Bucarely (Palou, *Noticias,* vol. i, p. 129).

5. Verger to Casafonda, " Carta Sexta," Jan. 23, 1772, stating that opposition to Dominicans was by Gálvez and Croix only, not by the Franciscan body. (M. A., Museo, *Trasuntos.*) At the same time it was not advisable to mingle the Orders in one college. (Same to same, Feb. 8, 1772, *Ibid.*)

6. M. A., Arch. Genl., *Real Céd. y Ord.* 96, f. 202; 97, f. 240; Verger to Comisario-General Manuel de la Vega, March 23, 1772, June 26, 1773 (M. A., Museo, *Trasuntos*).

7. Palou, *Noticias,* vol. i, p. 204, etc.

8. *Ibid.,* p. 259. A strong reason for admitting the Dominicans to California was that they might extend their occupation northeastward to the Gila-Colorado junction. Thus Bucarely in a letter to the King, October 27, 1772, expresses doubt whether it be wise to await the establishment of missions on the Colorado by the Dominicans before sending Anza thither, as a military expedition would be an obstacle to the conversion of the Gentiles. (M. A., Arch. Genl., *Cor. de Virreyes,* vol. xxxi, ser. ii (Bucarely), vol. xiv, no. 613, f. 35; *Ibid.,* June 26, 1774, vol. iv, serial vol. xxxviii, no. 1421, f. 1.) Cf. chapter vii of text, n. 52; chapter x, n. 10.

9. Armona had been appointed *Governador Yntendente y Comandante de Californias* in March or April, 1769. He had set forth from the capital for the peninsula on April 10, and had reached Loreto on June 12. Meanwhile Gálvez at Álamos, having been notified of the departure of Armona, had (June, 1769) written to Croix, stating that he had notified the Governor to visit him for instructions *viva voz,* and that it was his wish that the latter be granted a salary of 4000 *pesos* to enable him to live *con el lustre correspondiente* to his position (M. A., Arch. Genl., *Californias,* 67, nos. 5, 10, of no. 331). Reply had been made from Guadalajara, on July 4, that the total income for the peninsula was but 34,500 *pesos,* and that the cost of manning the presidio, packet-boats, etc., was 26,730 *pesos,* — a cost irrespective of the proposed salary for the Governor and of maintenance for the two *Reales* Sta. Ana and Loreto. (*Ibid.*) In 1770, June 19, Armona had written enthusiastically to Palou and Antonio López de Toledo (commissary) at Loreto, regarding supplies for San Diego; but by August of the same year he evidently had become disgusted with the narrow resources of his district. Thus on the 14th he had warned Serra to "go very slow" in his demands for guards for new establishments, as there were only 20 men at San Diego, and about the same at Monterey, without sufficient horses and *cuera.* The Indians now were "complacent" over their gifts, but so brutal and independent were they by nature, that it would not be long ere the Father-President "would have to offer to God the blood of arrows and the bitter-

ness of calumny." And the same day prediction had been freely made by the Governor to Palou that unless the peninsula were speedily succored there would supervene "a civil war a thousand times worse than that in Sonora" (M. A., Arch. Genl., *Californias*, 67, 76). On Nov. 12, 1770, Armona had been notified of the appointment of a successor, Felipe Barri. It is the comment of Verger on the retirement of Armona, that it was because he did not approve the decrees of Gálvez: *y este es un crimen lesae Majestatis*. ("Carta Segunda," M. A., Museo, *Trasuntos*.)

10. Letter Aug. 14, 1770.

11. States to Fages that 10 religious are being sent to erect four *doctrinas*, besides that of San Buenaventura, at fitting intervals between San Diego and Monterey, and that it is desired that as soon as possible he survey by land or sea the port of San Francisco, *y que no quede expuesto tan importante parage á ocupación ajena* (M. A., Arch. Genl., *Californias*, 66; B. C., *Prov. St. Pap.*, vol. i, p. 70). Apropos of the wish at the capital that the port of San Francisco be surveyed for a mission site, Fages on Nov. 21 set out from Monterey with 6 soldiers, and on the 26th came to the *cabeza* (head) *del Estero del Puerto de San Francisco*, hard by a river that held some *pozos* (pools) *de agua dulce*. On the 28th four soldiers explored further, and reported that "having gained a high hill, they had not been able to see the end of the *estero*, but had seen many cleft tracks left, it was thought, by *cíbolos* (bison)." They also had seen "*la Boca* (mouth) *del Estero* which they believed was that which entered by the *Bahía del Puerto de San Francisco*." On the 29th, "It was decided to return, as they could not (except by spending many days) pass to the other side *de la Punta de los Reyes*." (*Diario de Salida al Puerto de San Francisco*, 1770, M. A., Arch. Genl., *Cor. de Virreyes*, vol. xiv, ser. ii (Croix), vol. iv, no. 1176, f. 385; Letters, Fages to Croix, June 20, 1771, M. A., Arch. Genl., *Californias*, 66.)

On June 18, 1771, Serra, writing to Croix from San Carlos, announces the arrival on May 21 of the 10 religious, and acknowledges receipt of the *ornamento especial* sent by the Viceroy, which he has taken prompt occasion "to display [*lucir*] on the celebration of Corpus by the 12 priests now at the mission." Serra reports a failure as yet to found Santa Clara or San Francisco, because of Fages's insistence that there are not sufficient men for guards, and that the port of San Francisco must be fully surveyed. "But," he continues, "I wish first to see placed there the mission of my most beloved Padre Serafico, and, so far as I am concerned, this by the favor of God shall not be delayed." (*Ibid.*)

12. As for Rivera personally, he by July 3, 1770, had returned to San Diego, where he had remained till April 23, 1771. He then, by permission of the Viceroy, had retired to Loreto.

13. In one of his letters of June 20, 1771, Fages states to Croix that he has assigned 15 soldiers *de cuera* for the founding of San Buenaventura (M. A., Arch. Genl., *Californias*, 66). In a second letter to Croix he reports a dis-

cussion with Serra regarding the planting of a mission at San Francisco, but says that up to date he has not been able to effect anything *por faltarme soldados para la escolta;* as soon as he obtains soldiers, the Viceroy may be assured that he will found the mission. (*Ibid.*) On July 17, Fages reminds Croix that on Nov. 12, 1770, he had been promised 12 men from Guaymas, and that the men, recruited by Rivera in the peninsula, together with the escort at Velicatá, amount to about 21. As soon as these reach San Diego, he will found San Gabriel and San Buenaventura. Santa Clara shall come third. The day following (July 18), Fages announces the arrival of the 21 men, who bring word of the presence in the peninsula of the 12 from Guaymas. San Gabriel, San Buenaventura, and San Luis Obispo shall therefore be founded. (*Ibid.*) Barri's appointment was made known to Armona by a communication from the Viceroy, dated Nov. 12, 1770 (M. A., Arch. Genl., *Californias*, 76). On Oct. 24, 1771, Barri reported to the Viceroy that the troops available for both Californias were in all 82 cuirassiers, of whom 51 were at San Diego and Monterey, 12 at Velicatá, 9 at various other missions, and 10 at Loreto, ill and unarmed. To enable Fages to proceed with the work of founding missions in Alta California, and to enable Rivera to found the five establishments planned for the peninsula north of Santa María, there were needed 40 men additional. (M. A., Arch. Genl., *Californias*, 13. See also M. A., Arch. Genl., *Cor. de Virreyes*, ser. ii, vol. iv, no. 1176, f. 381.)

14. On July 22, 1772, Guardian Verger, in his fourth *Informe sobre las Misiones* to Viceroy Bucarely, makes relation in detail. The Indians, at first hostile, were led to throw down their bows and arrows by a likeness of the Holy Virgin which was shown them. They even assisted in the building of the mission houses. But soon Fages appeared, and, dismayed at the number of Gentiles crowding about, and the small guard with which to control them (10 men), gave orders for the admittance to the mission of only 4 or 5 Indians at a time. The padres had been admitting 40 or 50 at a time (unarmed), and the effect of the new order, when put in execution, was to anger the Indians, who, armed with clubs, rushed to the camp and began to plunder. For a time the mission was in a state of siege, but after some hostile interchanges the Indians offered peace. The declaration of Fages upon the whole affair was, that he could not now found San Buenaventura nor San Luis Obispo, because there was need of all his men to reinforce San Gabriel, San Antonio de Padua, and Carmelo, where he feared that already something might have happened. (M. A., Museo, *Docs. Rel. á las Mis. de Califs.*, Qto ii.)

15. *Vida de Serra*, pp. 58, 132–33, 146.

16. July 10, 1770, " Memorial of 15 points." No. 10 reads thus: "That neither the governor, nor royal commissary, be permitted to meddle in the temporalties intrusted by your Highness to the padres, since Antonio Josef López de Toledo was possessed of the idea that all there was in the

missions was at his disposal, and that *los Padres eran como subalternos suos.* (M. A., Museo, *Docs. Rel. á las Mis. de Calif.*, Qto ii; Palou, *Noticias*, vol. i, pp. 84–89.) Cf. chapter v, n. 41.

17. R. Verger to Viceroy Bucarely, Nov. 15, 1772: *Primer Informe ó Methodo nuebo de Misiones para su Gobierno espiritual y temporal.* Paragraph 19 states that, as early as 1719, Viceroy Baltasar de Zúñiga had decreed that the captains, governors, and other officers of the province of the Tejos (Texans) were to assist the padres of the colleges of Querétaro and Zacatecas by providing guards, and in every other way, as the padres should demand; and that in 1740 Viceroy Salazar had ordered the same thing under penalty of 200 *pesos.* Paragraph 5 states that in the Sierra Gorda, during the period of control of the temporalties by *caudillos, capitanes, y thenientes,* the Indians were made house-servants, *vaqueros,* etc., without pay, and that the secular officers appropriated the mission lands to their own uses, etc., with the result that the neophytes either fled to the hills or became *broncos* (morose) and discontented. The same was true of the peninsular California Indians under Portolá's *comisionados.* Paragraph 6: "No others than the missionaries are able to administer the temporalties and fill, in the name of his Majesty (whom God guard), the office of tutors and guardians of these new and helpless vassals. [Palou] writes that, unless the governor of the Californias [Barri] be given to understand that the government of the missions is exclusively for the padres, these establishments will be lost. 'The Governor and Fages,' he says, 'are already united and at one, intending to limit us to saying Mass and preaching.' If so, we may as well retire to our college, and the King be saved useless expense in seeking to spread the Catholic faith and to extend his dominion." Paragraph 7: "In the peninsula, Gálvez reserved only *causas de sangre* [causes of blood] to the Governor, and he gave the baton of local command to the Indian governors." In the Sierra Gorda, after the padres assumed the temporalties, "the Indians began to be tractable and docile. They were able to build churches of lime and stone, with arches adorned with their corresponding altars, *ornamentos,* and sacred vessels, — indeed to such perfection of civil life were they brought that, by the end of 1770, they were transferred to Archbishop Lorenzana, to be erected into curacies.

"There be some that scruple [*escrupulizan algunos*] that the religious interpose in the temporal affairs of the Indians, *y que los castiguen con azotes* [and that they punish them with stripes] when they absent themselves from the catechism and other services of the missions; . . . but in all this the missionaries do not proceed of their own authority, but *en nombre del Rey,* who makes of them tutors and guardians of the neophytes and Gentiles; hence vain is the fear that the royal jurisdiction will be prejudiced. (M. A., Museo, *Trasuntos.*) In 1771, in his "Carta Segunda," Verger had observed to Casafonda, that to some it doubtless seemed improper that the missionaries should control the temporalties of *Indios recién conquistados,* and that among objectors, at first, were the *visitador* and Viceroy. (*Ibid.*, f. 128.) See n. 18; see also chapter III, n. 25.

18. M. A., Arch. Genl., *Cor. de Virreyes*, vol. xl, ser. ii, vol. xxiii, no. 1019, f. 90; Palou, *Noticias*, vol. iii, pp. 35–66, par. 6, 8–9, 22, 26. In asking authority to transfer soldiers (par. 8), Serra alleged their *mal ejemplo, máxime en puntos de incontinencia*. Regarding reprehensible conduct of soldiers at San Gabriel, see Serra, "Representación de 21 de Mayo, 1773." They were wont, it seems, for their diversion to capture Indian women by use of the lasso. (*Cor. de Virreyes*, vol. and ser. *supra*, f. 158; B. C., *Prov. St. Pap.*, vol. i, p. 122; Palou, *Noticias*, vol. iii, p. 47; *Vida de Serra*, pp. 130–32.) Said Verger to Bucarely in his *Informe* of Nov. 15, 1772: "The padres do not assume to control the officers nor the soldiers, if the latter do not destroy by their ill living that which appertains to the apostolical preaching and paternal admonition of the former." "The tumults," says Father Luis Jayme of San Diego, "which have arisen in certain *rancherías* have been caused by the soldiers seizing the Indian women."

19. "Representación de 22 de Abril, 1773" (M. A., Arch. Genl., *Cor. de Virreyes*, vol. xl, ser. ii, vol. xxiii, no. 1019, f. 158; B. C., *Prov. St. Pap.*, vol. i, p. 91). "Representación de 13 de Marzo, 1773" (M. A., Arch. Genl., *Cor. de Virreyes*, vol. xl, ser. ii, vol. xxiii, no. 1019, f. 90; Palou, *Noticias*, vol. iii, p. 41, par. 5).

20. Palou, in an *Informe* to the College of San Fernando, Feb. 12, 1772, had dwelt on the right of the missionaries, *civilizar, educar, y corregir* the natives (Palou, *Noticias*, vol. i, p. 190), and the decision of the *junta* of May 9, 1773, was: *Se declaró así deberlo ejecutar en todo lo económico á que un padre de familia se maneja con el cuidado de su casa, educación y corrección de sus hijos*, etc. (*Ibid.*, vol. iii, p. 78). In his "Representación of March 13," par. 9, Serra had referred to the above as *costumbre inmemorial del reino desde su conquista* (*Ibid.*, pp. 47–48). The rule was indeed time-honored. Under Isabella and Charles V, the Indians were declared by law minors for life, — *no pueden tratar y contratar* (not competent to trade or contract) for more than five *pesos* (*Recopilación*, vi, tit. 10). This law was not abrogated till 1810. For instructions by Bucarely tending toward a modification of the power of State Sacerdotal, with respect to the Indians, see chapter VII of text, n. 21.

21. "Representación de 22 de Abril, 1773" (M. A., Arch. Genl., *Cor. de Virreyes*, vol. xl, sér. ii, vol. xxiii, no. 1019, f. 158). It is evident from the letter of Governor Armona to Palou and Toledo, June 19, 1770, that it was at first designed to forward supplies chiefly by land, establishing *una comunicación frecuente* between San Diego and Velicatá, *y á Monterey y puerto de San Francisco*. Serra's opposition to this was for the reason assigned; but it was also for a further reason. In journeying to and fro along the Santa Bárbara Channel, the soldiers were wont to debauch the native women. Said the Father-President: "It would be a miracle if so many Indian women,

as were to be encountered along this channel, did not corrupt the soldiers; and it would be equally a miracle if thus the Indian men were not converted from quietude and docility into tigers." (B. C., *Arch. Sta. Bárbara*, vol. i, p. 240; Palou, *Vida de Serra*, pp. 145, 152–153, 155.) The views of Serra were (later) shared by Garcés. On April 12, 1776, Garcés wrote: "Arrived at a *ranchería* [on the Channel] where the young women were in hiding on account of some experiences they had had on the passing of the soldiers." (*Diario*, E. Coues, *On the Trail of a Spanish Pioneer*, 1900, 2 vols., vol. i, p. 266.)

22. The plan of Echeveste made no provision for a lieutenant, but Ortega was made lieutenant and stationed at San Diego. (Palou, *Noticias*, vol. iii, p. 144.) Serra had asked that Ortega be made comandante to succeed Fages. (*Ibid.*, p. 43.)

23. Palou, *Noticias*, vol. iii, pp. 84–106. By a provision that payment to officers and men (governor and commissary excepted) be made in goods at an advance, in Lower California, of 100 per cent on original cost, and in Alta California of 150 per cent, a saving of 27,168 *pesos* was effected, which wrought a reduction in the total cost to the government. This total, according to Bancroft (*Hist. of California*, vol. i, pp. 211–214), was 90,476 *pesos*, and according to Revilla Gigedo (*Informe* of 1793; Translation, *Land of Sunshine*, vol. xi, p. 37), 92,476 *pesos*.

24. Anza, J. B., to Viceroy Juan Antonio (M. A., Arch. Genl., *Prov. Int.* 245).

25. Anza Sr.'s request was first referred to the Audiencia of Guadalajara, and on April 11, 1737, a report by Juan de Oliván Rebolledo (*oydor*) was returned, reciting: That in 1715 the Jesuit padre Agustín de Campos had written to the Viceroy Duque de Linares, asking that the *comisario-general* of the Franciscans consent to allow him to pass from Pimería Baja (under Jesuit control) to Pimería Alta (under Franciscan control), there to preach *la ley Santa de Dios* to the Indians of the Sierra Azul and kingdom of Moqui. Consent was refused, but later, the Bishop of Durango having been consulted by the King, there was issued (1732) a *cédula* sending forth to Pimería Alta three or four Jesuits, under escort of Juan Bautista de Anza, who at the same time was *á descubrir las tierras* (from Fronteras) *al Río Colorado* and to the Red Sea, and to determine whether California was an island. (M. A., Arch. Genl., *Historia*, 396.) The *junta* was to consult the Bishop of Durango and the prelate of the missions. (*Cédula* of 1738, *Ibid.*)

26. F. Garcés, *Diario*, August 8 to October 27, 1771 (M. A., Arch. Genl., *Historia*, 396); Juan D. Arricivita, *Crónica Seráfica y Apostólica del Colegio de Propaganda Fide de la Santa Cruz de Querétaro*, Mexico, 1792, chap. xvii, pp. 418–426, — translated in part, E. Coues, *Trail of a Spanish Pioneer*, vol. i, pp. 30–38.

27. Mr. James B. Ainza of San Francisco, who claims descent from Juan Bautista de Anza, states (San Mateo *Leader*, Oct., 1909) that his ancestor

was born at Arizpe in 1715, and was educated at the College of San Ildefonso, Mexico City.

28. Dr. H. E. Bolton, of Leland Stanford University, is engaged upon a study of this *entrada* of Garcés.

29. Anza to Bucarely, letter May 2, 1772 (M. A., Arch. Genl., *Historia*, 396).

30. M. Costansó to the Sr. Fiscal (Areche), Sept. 5, 1772. There were, said Costansó, three points to be considered: (1) The distance to be traversed; (2) the likelihood that the Pimas of the Gila and Colorado had news of the Monterey establishments; (3) the attainability and utility of communication with these establishments by way of Sonora. There would be difficulty in crossing the mountains, but passes used by the Indians no doubt existed. It was to be borne in mind that Northern California was poor in products, and that if succored from Loreto, it must, as far even as San Diego, be by a rough road (*áspero camino*) of 300 leagues; and if by sea from San Blas, over a course long and difficult, and in ships so small as not to be fitted to carry families for settling the land. If succored from Sonora, not only might every kind of grain and fruit be obtained, but this by a way not immoderate for length, and that would admit of the passage of families. (M. A., Arch. Genl., *Historia*, 396.)

31. The *fiscal* having on Oct. 12, 1772, reported favorably on Anza's project, Bucarely, on Oct. 13, called a *junta* for the 17th. By this body it was decided to ask the opinion of the Governor of Sonora. His reply (M. Santre to Bucarely) bore date Jan. 27, 1773. (*Ibid.*)

32. The influence of Serra in securing a determination of the matter is mentioned by Palou (*Noticias*, vol. iii, p. 155). Direct evidence of it is furnished by Arriaga in a dispatch to the Viceroy, dated March 9, 1774, which refers to a letter from Bucarely of date Sept. 26, 1773, wherein the latter had said that *haviendo oydo al Presidente de las Misiones de San Diego y Monterey, Fr. Junípero Serra, que apoyó el pensamiento de Anza, convocó V. E. á Junta de Guerra*, etc. (M. A., Arch. Genl., *Californias*, 72). At about the time of Serra's conferences with the Viceroy, Anza (March 7, 1773), replying to queries, wrote praising the padres as pioneers. A poor missionary on a poor horse was able to demonstrate that the Indians, if only well treated, were prone to be friendly. And he (Anza) had faith in Padre Garcés, whose reports regarding the Colorado River were most thorough of all. As to whether missions by the Dominicans on the further (California) side of the Colorado might be serviceable, he could not determine; but he thought that it might be necessary to erect missions on the Sonora side. If so, soldiers could be taken from the presidios San Miguel (Horcasitas) and Buenavista, which now were in a condition of tranquillity (M. A., Arch. Genl., *Historia*, 396). A little later (May 8), Garcés wrote to the Viceroy. He did not think Anza's expedition would be prejudicial to the Dominican missions, as they were far distant and among natives who were enemies to

the Yumas, through whose country Anza would pass. Communication, he thought, could be maintained by the existing presidios, Altar, San Miguel, and Buenavista. (*Ibid.*)

It is stated by Palou (*Noticias*, vol. iii, p. 154) that Anza had applied to Gálvez for permission to join the *Santa Expedición* of 1769 with a force from Tubac, but had been refused. In none of the correspondence in the Mexican Archives have I found allusion to such a request, save the following by Garcés in his letter of May 8: *Atendiendo tambien á que dicho capitán (segun me dijó) havía procurado hacer este gran servicio en tiempo de los Padres Jesuitas por cuio Visitador no tubó efecto*, etc.

33. J. B. Anza, *Diario de la Expedición que practicó por Tierra, el año de '74, el Teniente Coronel Don Juan Bautista de Anza á los Nuevos Establecimientos de la California* (M. A., Arch. Genl., *Historia*, 396); a careful rendering of the substance of the Diary by Zoeth S. Eldredge (*Journal of American History*, 1908–1909). On supplies, etc., at Altar, Anza to Bucarely, Jan. 18, 1774 (M. A., Arch. Genl., *Cor. de Virreyes*, vol. liv, sér. ii, vol. xxxvii, no. 1389). See also Palou, *Noticias*, vol. iii, pp. 152–160. For route, see general map (pocket).

34. Anza, *Diario;* F. Garcés, *Diario de la Entrada que se practicó á fin de abrir camino por los Ríos Gila y Colorado, para los Establecimientos de San Diego y Monterey* (M. A., Arch. Genl., *Historia*, 52; J. C. Arricivita, *Crónica Seráfica*, lib. iv, cap. i, pp. 450–56). Garcés says (Feb. 7) that he first met Palma on Aug. 24, 1771, on the occasion of his *entrada* of that year among the Yumas. The meeting is described in Garcés's Diary for 1771 (M. A., Arch. Genl., *Historia*, 396; Arricivita, *Crónica Seráfica*, *supra*).

35. Anza to Bucarely, Sitio de San Dionisio, Feb. 9, 1774. Díaz in 1540 had crossed the stream into the peninsula with royal troops. As to the crossing in 1774, Bernardo de Urrea to Bucarely, Altar, Feb. 22, and Governor Francisco Antonio Crespo to the same, Horcasitas, Feb. 25 (M. A., Arch. Genl., *Cor. de Virreyes*, vol. liv, sér. ii, vol. xxxvii, no. 1389).

Anza and Garcés both mention the striking scenery of the region (that of Fort Yuma). Pilot Knob and Chimney Rock are mentioned by Garcés as having been noted by him in 1771. Now (1774) they were named Cabeza del Gigante (Giant's Head) and la Campaña (the Bell), respectively. (Garcés, *Diario*, Feb. 9; Anza, *Diario*, Feb. 9.) In 1702, when in this locality on the way to the Quiquimas with Padre Gonzáles, Kino described "some very mighty rocks which seemed to have been made by hand with very great art."

36. From Santa Olaya, Anza, on Feb. 28, wrote to the Viceroy. He spoke of the *leguas de Medaños ó Arenales intrancitables* (impassable sand hills), to avoid which as much as possible he had descended the Colorado; of having left the poorest of his animals and seven of his own men with Palma; and of having no fear of the Cojats (M. A., Arch. Genl., *Cor. de Virreyes*, vol. lv, sér. ii, vol. xxxviii, no. 1421).

37. Anza, *Diario;* Garcés, *Diario*, Feb. 12. Of the Cajuenches, Garcés

says: *Esta nación tiene varios nombres : los Pimas la llaman Cojat, y á los que vivan en la sierra, llaman los de los Zapatos de mezcal ó, mas propriamente, Guarachas.* "But the Yumas call them Axagueches, and they say that this nation is the one that extends to San Diego."

38. Anza and Garcés, *Diarios.*

39. Anza, *Diario;* Garcés, *Diario;* Juan Díaz, *Diario en el viage para abrir camino de la Provincia de la Sonora á la California Septentrional y puerto de Monterey,* etc., 1774 (M. A., Arch. Genl., *Historia,* 396). Garcés points out that San Jacome had been abandoned, as he discovered later, because of a failure of water.

40. It has been shown by Mr. Zoeth S. Eldredge, in his rendering of Anza's Diary of 1774, that the statement by Bancroft (*History of California,* vol. i, p. 223) that Anza crossed by the San Gorgonio Pass (route of the Southern Pacific Railroad) is probably erroneous (*Journal of American History,* 1908).

41. Both Anza and Garcés wax enthusiastic over the beauty of the region about San Jacinto Lake. Nor were they unmindful of the mineral deposits of the country, for both mention a specimen of silver ore (*metal de plata*) which had been found (*Diarios,* March 16, 18).

As traced by Mr. Eldredge, the route of Anza was as follows: San Felipe River, Coyote Cañon, Horse Cañon, Vandeventer Flat, San Carlos Pass, Hemet Reservoir (Laguna del Príncipe), San Jacinto (San José) River, and San Jacinto Lake (Laguna de San Antonio de Bucareli). In June, 1910, the writer personally verified this route, and it corresponds closely with Anza's description of the route actually taken. San Carlos Pass to-day is a wild region of crags and boulders ("scrap-heap of the world," Font called it), covered thickly with live-oak, red-shank, sage-brush, willow and chimisal, and abounding in rattlesnakes. Vandeventer Flat lies at the foot of Santa Rosa Mountain, a peak of some 8000 feet; Lookout Mountain being considerably to the west of it. Hemet Valley is a long stretch of luxuriant pastures between parallel ridges of mountains, the easterly ridge containing the abandoned silver mine "Garnet Queen." Hemet Reservoir, much shrunken from Anza's Laguna del Príncipe (if such it be), supplies water by a pipe-line to the valley of the San Jacinto River, a stream dry in summer; and San Jacinto Lake (Anza's Laguna de Bucarely) is now locally known as Lake View. Of the gorge of the North Fork of the San Jacinto — a dashing cascaded stream — the Spaniards said not too much when they called it Cañada de Paraíso. For route, see general map (pocket).

42. No instrument for taking altitudes was carried on this expedition, and when San Gabriel was reached, and news received of the presence of the Santiago (with Serra on board) at San Diego, Padre Díaz went to the port to ascertain if an instrument might not be borrowed. An astrolabe was obtained at San Diego Mission, and Díaz, having been instructed in its use, awaited at San Gabriel the return of Anza from Monterey. Henceforth the altitudes were regularly taken (Anza, *Diario,* April 10, May 2, 27). A map

of the return route was made by Díaz, but it has not been found. See, further, Garcés to Viceroy Bucarely, April 27, 1774, "from the beautiful *Playa* of the Junction of the Rivers."

43. Anza, *Diario*. Garcés's Diary ends April 26, 1774, at the Gila-Colorado junction. From San Gabriel, April 10, Anza had written to Bucarely describing his journey to that point (M. A., Arch. Genl., *Cor. de Virreyes*, vol. lv, sér. ii, vol. xxxviii, no. 1421).

44. Palou, *Vida de Serra*, pp. 88–89.

45. P. Fages, *Salida que hizó el theniente de Voluntarios de Cataluña con seis soldados y un Harriero* (M. A., Arch. Genl., *Cor. de Virreyes*, Croix, 1770–71, vol. xiv, serial vol. iv, no. 1176). Printed in full as Appendix B.

P. Fages, *Diario* . . . *en Busca del Puerto de San Francisco*, March 20 to April 5, 1772. Besides Fages and Crespi, the expedition consisted of 14 soldiers and an Indian servant. On March 26, some very large animals were seen — bears and (from the description) mountain sheep. On the 27th, they saw the "great mouth of the *Estero de San Francisco paralelo á la Enseñada de la Punta de Reyes*, in front of which were *los siete farallones que, el Año de 1769, vimos quando acampamos serca á ella*. Within the *estero* there were seen (the standpoint was the Berkeley side of the bay) five islands, three of which formed a triangle opposite the mouth. On the 29th, San Pablo Bay (*una Baía Grande Redonda*) was observed, and on the 30th, *el Río Grande de Nuestro P. San Francisco* — the San Joaquín. (M. A., Arch. Genl., *Californias*, 66; J. Crespi, *Diario;* Palou, *Noticias*, vol. iii, p. 3; Crespi to Palou, May 21, 1772, Ayer Coll., Newberry Library, — translated, *Out West*, vol. xvi, p. 56.)

46. *que ya llamamos de S^n Fran^{co}.*

47. Costansó to Melchior de Paramas, secretary to Viceroy, Oct. 9, 1772 (Ayer Coll. ; translated, *Out West*, vol. xvi, pp. 58–59). Map reproduced in *Identification of Sir Francis Drake's Anchorage*, by George Davidson, appendix, no. 15, Pub. Calif. Hist. Soc., pamphlet. (See chart iv, chapter vi, of text.) Costansó's statement and map are at variance with Bancroft's assertions (*History of California*, vol. i, pp. 159, 232) that "it must be borne in mind that the inner bay was not named during this trip [that of Portolá in 1769], nor for some years later"; and (*Ibid.*, p. 245) that "from 1775 the newly found and grand bay bears the name San Francisco, which has before belonged to the little harbor under Point Reyes."

48. On hearing from the deer-hunters of the existence of the *brazo de mar ó estero*, Costansó had said: "We were more and more confirmed in our opinion that we were in the puerto de San Francisco and that this [the *estero*] was that spoken of by the *piloto* Cabrera Bueno in the following words: 'By the gorge [*barranca*] enters an *estero* of salt water without surf. Within we met friendly Indians and easily obtained fresh water and firewood.'" (*Diario*, S. A., Madrid, Direc. de Hid., *Reino de Méjico*, tom. i, C 2².)

49. The advisability of a speedy occupation of the shores of the *estero* had indeed been urged by Guardian Verger upon Comisario-General Casafonda shortly after the Fages-Crespi survey. Said Verger in a letter of date Dec. 22, 1772: "Cabrera Bueno locates the Port of San Francisco between Mussel Point and that of Reyes [rather a broad rendering of the Manila pilot's description]. What is to be seen between these two points is *una grande Enseñada*, and we judge that, upon the north side, it affords some protection from the northwest winds, which prevail in these seas almost the entire year, and at that protected spot would be called Puerto de San Francisco, as in the case of the port of Monterey. At the bottom of said *Enseñada* the land opens to the width of a league, and by this opening the sea enters, forming *un brazo ó estero*," etc. "In the named mouth, or opening, there is seen a *farallón* . . . and three Islands, but the entrance does not seem to be obstructed; and, from the fact of whales having entered, there seems to be some depth. . . . But," continues Verger, "if the entrance gives passage to ships, as is very probable, its occupation is highly necessary, for its shores abound in scrub-oak and live-oak for a shipyard. Moreover, the river that empties into the round bay is so copious that some of the explorers say the Ebro is not half so great. This indicates that it may rise in the interior sierras, and come from the East, joining with New Mexico. It also may approach the Colorado. . . . Great prejudice to the Crown of Spain must be feared should some foreign nation establish itself in this port." (M. A., Museo, *Trasuntos*.) The foregoing is Verger's " Carta Octava," to Casafonda, and the difference in tone between it and his " Carta Segunda," wherein the possibility of establishments in Northern California is ridiculed, is noteworthy.

In two dispatches, of dates June 26, and Nov. 26, 1774, the success of Anza was made known by the Viceroy to the King. The question of missions on the Colorado was broached, the importance of a continued good understanding with Palma emphasized, and the relative value of sea route and land routes to Monterey considered. (M. A., Arch. Genl., *Cor. de Virreyes*, vol. lv, sér. ii, vol. xxxviii, no. 1421; *Ibid.*, vol. xli, serial vol. xliv, no. 1609.)

50. Palou to College of San Fernando, April 22, 1774 (M. A., Museo, *Docs. Rel. á las Mis. de Califs.*, Qto ii).

51. Bucarely, Aug. 14, 1773 (M. A., Arch. Genl., *Misiones*, 13); *Instrucción al Comandante de San Diego y Monterey* (B. C., *Mayer MSS.* par. 18). Viceroy to Rivera y Moncada, Sept. 19, 1773; Rivera y Moncada to Viceroy, Oct. 12, 1773 (M. A., Arch. Genl., *Cor. de Virreyes*, vol. xxxi, sér. ii, vol. xiv, f. 143); Viceroy to King, May 27, 1774 (*Ibid.*, serial vol. xxxvii, vol. liv, no. 1389); Rivera y Moncada to Viceroy, June 16, Oct. 8, 1774 (M. A., Arch. Genl., *Californias*, 35). At the time of his appointment as comandante, Rivera had served thirty-two years, his term having begun in 1742.

52. M. A., Arch. Genl., *R. Céd. y Ord.* 104, f. 101.

53. Anza-Bucarely correspondence, and determinations of *junta* (M. A.; Arch. Genl., *Prov. Int.* 134); *Testimonio del expediente formado*, etc., *para la Segunda Expedición que deve hacer Don Juan Bautista de Anza, capitán del Presidio de San Ignacio de Tubac, desde él á Monterey*, etc. (*Ibid.*, *Californias*, 72). For the expedition the following were the estimates: (1) *Preparatory to assembling at Tubac:* 30 suits of clothing for men and women, — shirts, drawers, trousers, vests, skirts, capes, jackets, hose, boots, shoes, *rebozos*, sombreros; clothing for 90 boys and 90 girls; arms, — 20 fire-locks, 20 swords, 20 lances, 22 cuirasses, 20 cartridge-boxes with 14 charges, and 30 belts with the name "San Carlos de Monterey"; mounts for men, — 60 horses (two per man), 20 saddles, 20 pairs of spurs, 20 bridles, 20 pairs of cushions; mounts for women, — 60 mares, 30 saddles, 30 bridles; baggage, etc., — 20 mules, 20 outfittings for same, 30 shammy-skin bags; (2) *Seventy days' march to Monterey for 122 individuals:* 1 banner with the royal escutcheon, 11 camp-tents, tools, dishes, money-box with duplicate keys, registry-books; beef-cattle and other provisions, — 100 cows (one per day), flour, 6 boxes of chocolate, 3 demijohns of brandy, ham, sausages, and spices; a table for the comandante and for the saying of Mass; means of transport, — 4 relays of 132 mules, 100 outfittings for same, 20 drivers; provisions for the New Establishments, — 200 head of livestock (bulls and cows); articles for the Indians, — 6 boxes of beads, nearly all red (no black ones), tobacco, and (for Palma) 1 blue woolen cloak trimmed with gold braid, 1 waistcoat and pair of shammy-skin trousers, 2 shirts, 1 cap with escutcheon like that of the dragoons. *Signed :* Juan José de Echeveste, Dec. 5, 1774.

54. In his letters to the King of June 26, and Nov. 26, 1774 (note 49, *ante*), the Viceroy had spoken of the first expedition of Anza as a piece of good fortune reserved for the happy reign of "your Majesty"; for while the idea had been conceived by Anza the father, the execution had been left for Anza the son. Upon the latter, accordingly, it had been deemed fitting that the rank of lieutenant-colonel be conferred. The route to Monterey opened by Anza was styled *camino glorioso*, and the task achieved *prodigiosa operación*.

55. J. B. Anza, *Diario de la Ruta y Operaciones que yo, el Intrascripto Theniente Coronel y Capitán del Real Presidio de Tubac*, etc., *practicé segunda vez . . . á la California Septentrional . . . como consta de Superior Decreto de 24 de Nov. del Año de 1774*, etc. (M. A., Arch. Genl., *Historia*, 396); P. Font, *Diario, borrador* (M. A., Arch. Genl., *Historia*, 24); P. Font, *Diario*, complete (John Carter Brown Library); F. Garcés, *Diario* (M. A., Arch. Genl., *Historia*, 24), — Translation, E. Coues, *On the Trail of a Spanish Pioneer ;* Palou, *Noticias*, vol. iv, pp. 133–160.

56. Palou to Viceroy, Nov. 11, 1776 (M. A., Arch. Genl., *Prov. Int.* 23).

57. Anza, when within two days of San Gabriel on his first expedition, carved in the bark of a huge alder tree the symbol I H S. On the second

expedition, he carved beneath this symbol: *Año 1776 : Vinó la Expedición de San Francisco*. (Font, *Diario*, Jan. 2, 1776.) For route, see general map (pocket).

58. Anza, *Diario*, Jan. 1, 1776. The attack was one of determined ferocity. The few inmates of the mission — three soldiers, two padres (Jayme and Vicente Fuster), two blacksmiths, two boys (a son and nephew of Lieutenant Ortega), eleven in all — were awakened at about one o'clock at night by yells and commotion. Fuster and the men were driven from one cover to another, making a final stand in an adobe magazine, whence with musketry they kept their assailants at bay. As for Jayme, he was found dead in the dry bed of a creek, his body disfigured by blows. (Fuster to Serra, Nov. 28, 1775, M. A., Museo, *Docs. Rel. á las Mis. de Califs.*, Qto ii; J. F. Ortega, *Informe*, Nov. 30, 1775 (B. C.); Palou, *Noticias*, vol. iv, pp. 118–127.)

59. Fuster to Serra, Nov. 28, 1775 (M. A., Museo, *Docs. Rel. á las Mis. de Califs.*, Qto ii); F. F. Lasuén, to Guardian Pangua, Aug. 17, 1775 (*Ibid.*). Lasuén to Juan Prestamero, Jan. 28, 1776, telling of cessation of work on San Juan Capistrano at news of massacre, and of burying the bells of the proposed mission to save them. If work is not to be resumed, Lasuén wishes to retire to his college. (*Ibid.*)

60. Rivera y Moncada, writing to Padre Fuster, March 27, 1776, states that news of the San Diego affair was brought to him at Monterey on the evening of December 13, 1775, between seven and eight o'clock, by a squad of six soldiers commanded by Lieutenant Ortega. (M. A., Museo, *Docs. Rel. á las Mis. de Califs.*, Qto ii.)

61. Font, *Diario* (complete).

62. Anza, *Diario*, Jan., Feb., March, 1776; Palou, *Noticias*, vol. iv, p. 139, etc.

63. Palou, *Diario* (*Noticias*, vol. iii, p. 261); translated by Frank de Thoma, MS. 1899, Macdonald Coll. According to Palou, Rivera y Moncada on this occasion closely reconnoitred the estuary, pronouncing the mouth half a league wide, and stating that within was an island, and behind the island a very large bay of smooth water. Horses, Palou thought, if guided by skiffs, might be swum across the mouth of the estuary. Indeed, when seen near by, the mouth was only one quarter of a league in width. "Considering," he said, "that the cliff of the strait, or mouth, of the estuary of San Francisco is the extreme point of the land, and that up to the present day no Spaniard or any other Christian has set his foot upon it, it seemed proper to the commander and to me to plant the standard of the Holy Cross on its summit." Much notice, moreover, was taken of the redwoods. "In a *cañada* having a dense growth of timber, we came to a gigantic tree, the inside burned out, and the hollow trunk resembling a cave. One of the soldiers, mounted on horseback, rode into it, saying, 'Now I have a house if it should rain.'"

64. Palou, *Vida de Serra*, p. 202. The instructions were, that he *pasase*

al Puerto de San Francisco de ver si tenía entrada por la canal ó garganta que de tierra se había visto.

65. The name Golden Gate was originated by John C. Frémont. On his map of California and Oregon, published in 1848, the Greek form "Chrysopylæ" was used. In his *Geographical Memoir*, published at the same time, Frémont stated that Chrysopylæ (Golden Gate) had been applied to the entrance of San Francisco Bay for reasons (advantages of the bay for commerce) similar to those for which Chrysoceros (Golden Horn) had been applied to the harbor of Byzantium, now Constantinople. (30th Cong., 1st Sess., *Senate Docs., Mis.,* no. 143, p. 32.)

66. Log of the San Carlos (summary), report of Ayala, report of Cañizares, and map of the port of San Francisco from Archivo General de las Indias, Sevilla, edited by Z. S. Eldredge and E. J. Molera, *March of Portolá,* etc., San Francisco, 1909; Palou, *Noticias,* vol. iv, pp. 72–74, 102–103. Bucarely to King, Nov. 26, 1775, announces return of Ayala to San Blas, after having visited *el Puerto de San Francisco.* The diaries of Ayala and of his *piloto* Cañizares are highly commended for their information. By Cañizares and Juan Bautista Aguirre, the estuary was thoroughly explored, with the result that it was affirmed to be "not one port, but many with a single entrance." (M. A., Arch. Genl., *Cor. de Virreyes,* sér. i, vol. ii, no. 2032, f. 221.)

67. Palou, *Noticias,* vol. iv, pp. 100–102.

68. See chart v (Ayala), pp. 109–110 of text. Anza, *Diario.* Anza's first sight of the estuary was obtained on March 25, and it is worthy of note that he speaks of it as coming or extending from the Port of San Francisco, — *el Estero que sale del Puerto,* etc. According to Palou, Mission Bay received its name Los Dolores, from the circumstance that Aguirre had observed three Indians weeping on its shores. (*Noticias,* pp. 103, 142–43; but see Font, *Diario.*)

69. Anza, *Diario;* Font, *Diario;* Palou, *Noticias,* vol. iv, pp. 144–160.

70. For sketch, see text, p. 111.

71. Rivera, on March 27, had presented to Fuster a paper containing a formal statement of his reasons for his conduct in seizing Carlos. The paper was attested by Raphael de Pedro y Gil and Hermenegildo Sal. It charged Carlos, Carlos's brother Francisco, and another neophyte, Rafael, with having planned and brought about *la perdición, ruina, y destrucción* of the mission, and the deaths of Jayme and of the blacksmith and carpenter, — crimes for which right of asylum "could not be pleaded." Under Bulls by Popes Gregory XIV, Benedict XIII, Clement XII, and Benedict XIV, murderers, robbers, mutilators, forgers, heretics, traitors, etc., were denied the privilege of asylum. Besides, the place where Carlos had taken refuge was not a church but a storehouse (*almacén*). (M. A., Museo, *Docs. Rel. á las Mis. de Califs.,* Qto ii.) On April 3, Fuster wrote in great detail about the matter to Guardian Franco Pangua, of the College of San Fernando. Find-

ing Carlos in the church on March 27, he had informed Rivera, but, the case being one upon which he was in doubt, he had asked time to present it to the Bishop at Durango. This not being acceptable, he had consulted Lasuén and Amurrio (who were waiting to take charge of San Juan Capistrano). Rivera, pursuing the matter, had demanded a prompt answer. A paper had been given him, but he, declaring the whole affair an Indian trick, had run out a cannon and ordered the troop under arms. Fuster thereupon had rung the bell for prayer. Just as prayer was begun, Rivera had come with sword, staff, and a lighted candle. He had surrounded the building with soldiers, had entered with the candle in his hand, and with help from the soldiers had seized and bound Carlos. Thereupon he (Fuster) had called upon all to witness that, by decree of three Supreme Pontiffs, excommunication was *ipso facto* incurred by *los jueces seculares* who took from a church a refugee, without license from the Bishop. The Church of God, he had said, was not guarded after the manner of a castle. Rivera at the doorway had protested that "naught was intended by him against our Mother the Church." Fuster, then, in the presence of the *pobres Indios escandalizados,* had closed the church. (*Ibid.*) For his conduct, Rivera on May 13, at San Diego, offered to Fuster a bantering apology. His tempér, he said, was not stern, but, if crossed, it seemed so, —well, he relished jokes and a laugh. He was charged with having ordered his men to arms, but had not Cortés, upon a time, done this in the case of the Toltecs, saying, "It was a token of a *fiesta,* or holiday, for Spaniards to go armed"? (*Ibid.*)

As for Bucarely, he virtually was on the side of the padres, for on April 13, he had written to Serra that he had ordered Rivera to use measures of conciliation with the Indians. The words of the Viceroy were urgently commended to Rivera by Serra in a letter from San Diego, dated Oct. 5, 1776. The advice of the latter was to capture the leaders, assemble the Indians, explain the power of the King, then show mercy. "Thus will be exemplified the law which we enjoin upon them, to return good for ill and forgive their enemies." (M. A., Museo, *Docs. Rel. á las Mis. de Califs.*, Qto ii.) The outcome was a release of all prisoners (Carlos presumably included) in 1777, after the delivery to them of such a harangue as Serra had counseled. (B. C., *Prov. Rec.*, vol. i, p. 60.)

72. Anza, *Diario;* Font, *Diario.*

73. Garcés, *Diario,* translated by E. Coues; Garcés to Bucarely, Jan. 12, 1776, from Yuma, stating that he has been down the Colorado, having passed among the Cajuenches, Jallicuamais or Quiquimas, and Culapas, to the beaches of the sea, the waters whereof he has seen and enjoyed, especially in their flux and reflux. "All the nations await with joyful expectation the coming of the padres." (M. A., Arch. Genl., *Historia,* 52.)

74. The following is the description of the Tulare Valley by Fages: "The San Francisco [San Joaquín], which discharges into the estuary of that name, is more than 120 leagues in length by (in places) 15 or 20 in width, and it

winds through a plain which is a labyrinth of lagoons and tulares. The plain is thickly peopled, having many and large *rancherías ;* and it abounds in grain, deer, bear, geese, ducks, cranes, indeed every kind of animal, terrestrial and aërial. In the *rancherías,* in winter, the Indians live in large halls, the families separated from each other; and outside are their houses, spherical in form, where their grains and utensils are kept. The people are good-looking, excellently formed, frank and liberal. Theft does not seem to be practiced, and they use large stones for grinding. . . . The past year [1772], going in pursuit of deserters, I passed to the eastward of San Diego 50 leagues. Lack of water forced us to the Sierra, and we descended to the plain opposite to the mission of San Gabriel. We then followed the edge of the plain toward the north, about 25 leagues, to the pass of Buenavista. For most of the 25 leagues we traveled among date-palms; and to the east and south the land was more and more a land of palms, but seemed very scarce of water. Over all the plain we saw not a little smoke." (San Carlos, Nov. 27, 1773, M. A., Arch. Genl., *Californias,* 66.)

Fages's survey of the Tulares was from the vicinity of Buena Vista Lake. He describes the spot as seven leagues (18.41 miles) to the north of Buena-vista Pass (Tehachapi?). Most of his journey, however, was to the south of Tehachapi, and in the desert.

75. Palou, *Noticias*, vol. iii, pp. 41, 69, 78.

76. Crespo to Bucarely, Altar, Dec. 15, 1774 (M. A., Arch. Genl., *Historia,* 25). In an elaborate report to Bucarely, by Padre Díaz, from Ures on March 21, 1775, a route westward from New Mexico is advised, and the hope expressed that Crespo may be commissioned to explore it. (M.A., Arch. Genl., *Prov. Int.* 88.)

77. S. V. Escalante y F. A. Domínguez, "Diario . . . para descubrir el Camino desde . . . Santa Fé del Nuevo Mexico al de Monterey " (*Docs. para la Historia de Méjico*, sér. ii, tom. i, pp. 375–558); Coues, *Trail of a Spanish Pioneer*, vol. ii, p. 469; Bancroft, *History of Utah*, pp. 7–18.

S. V. Escalante to Pedro Fermín de Mendinueta (Governor of New Mexico), Guadalupe de Zuñi, Oct. 28, 1775, states that at the end of June, 1775, he made a tour of exploration toward Monterey, but not being able to cross the Río Grande de los Cominas (the Colorado), he for eight days examined the situation, defenses, water-supply, and means of subsistence of the Moqui pueblos. Forty-six leagues (120.98 miles) to the west of Zuñi he found seven pueblos distributed on three plateaus. On the first were Tanos (Teguas), 110 families; a new foundation by the Moquis of Gualpi, 15 families; and a third pueblo of 200 families. On the second plateau were the fourth pueblo (Mesaznabi), 50 families; the fifth (Xipaolabi), 14 families; and the sixth (Xongopabi), — better situated than any of the others, — 60 families. Two and one half leagues away lay the third plateau, and here was situated the pueblo (Oraibe), the best-constructed and best-known Moqui town in the Provincias Internas. It contained eleven sections with regular streets, and a population of about 800 families. On this third plateau were six great cisterns, in which, when it snowed or rained, quantities of water were gathered. To the east of Moqui were the Navajóes; to the west and northwest the Cominas; to the north the Iutas, with the Apaches of the Gila; and to the southwest the Mezcaleros, or, in Moqui speech, Ióchies and Tasabuez. The Moquis were much civilized, and diligent in weaving and cultivating the soil. They raised abundant harvests of maize, frixol, and chile, and grew some cotton. . . . The Moquis had proved obstinate and should be reduced by force. . . . They could be overcome by cutting them off from their watering places. . . . A presidio would be needed to keep them in subjection. Captain D. Francisco Antonio Crespo advised a Monterey connection *via* the Colorado, the Galchedunes, the Cominas, and Moqui, but this would be over an intolerable course. He (Escalante) would advise a course *via* the Iutas Payuchis, who, according to the map of the engineer Lafora, were in the same latitude as Monterey. [The Lafora map has been found in the Mexican Archives by Dr. H. E. Bolton.] (M. A., Arch. Genl., *Historia*, 25.)

Escalante y Domínguez to Governor Pedro Fermín de Mendinueta, Zuñi, Nov. 25, 1776. This communication states that the party of July 29, 1776, taking a course north-northwest, came at length to the Yutas, and afterwards to the Comanches Yamparicas and the great river which divides the Yuta and Comanche nations. Pressing further to the north and northeast, they attained latitude 41° 19', their highest point; then, passing the river, they kept west-southwest until, at 316 leagues from Sta. Fé, they reached the great valley and laguna of the Tympanogotzis, to which they gave the name of Nuestra de la Merced [Utah Lake]. "The valley," declares the two padres, "is bounded on the west by a *dilatada sierra* that runs to the northeast. It is so extensive and so fertile that there might be planted in it, and subsisted from it, a province like New Mexico." From Lake Merced the party set out in a southwesterly direction for Monterey; but having given largely of their provisions to the Yutas, and having encountered snow and cold almost intolerable, they (despite good fortune in killing two bison) turned backward from latitude 38° — by the Río Grande de Cojnina," for Moqui and Zuñi. The opinion is expressed that, to reach Monterey, from Lake Merced, would be a task easily accomplished even by a small party. (M. A., Arch. Genl., *Historia*, 52.) On the same date as the above, Domínguez wrote to the provincial of the Franciscans of New Mexico, Fray Isidro Murillo. Both communications stated that the Yutas and Comanches had heard naught of the Monterey settlements, and that at none of the Moqui pueblos were any willing to receive the Gospel. (*Ibid.*)

78. It will be remembered that as early as May 21, 1774, Garcés had been seeking to open communication with New Mexico, by means of a letter passed thither by the hands of the Moquis. What became of this letter we are not informed; but in 1776, having reached Moqui himself, he successfully dispatched thence a letter to the minister at Zuñi. (E. Coues, *Trail of a Spanish Pioneer*, vol. ii, p. 380, n. 17.) For route, see general map (pocket).

79. Garcés, *Diario;* Translation, E. Coues, vol. ii, p. 438.

80. Palou, *Noticias,* vol. iv, pp. 162–182. Fuster to Guardian Pangua, Sept. 29, 1776, — letter from San Gabriel describing arrival of the San Carlos and Príncipe at Monterey, June 3, 1776, and departure therefrom, on the 17th, of Anza's people for the founding of San Francisco. (Moraga, *Informe* of 1777, B. C.) For list of the founders see Appendix D.

81. Bucarely to King, Aug. 27, 1776. (M. A., Arch. Genl., *Cor. de Virreyes,* vol. lxxxii, sér. ii, vol. lxv, no. 2429.) From the affair of Carlos, it becomes apparent that the relation of State Secular to State Sacerdotal in Alta California was quite as strained under Rivera y Moncada as it had been under Fages. Indeed, the complaints of padres against Rivera were constant. See letters: Oct. 2, 1776, Lasuén to Pangua, on insolence of Rivera to padres, and insubordination of Ignacio Vallejo. (M. A., Museo, *Doc. Rel. á las Mis. de Califs.,* Qto ii.)

82. Palou, *Noticias,* vol. iv, secs. xiii, xxi; *Vida de Serra,* pp. 207–214, 224.

CHAPTER VII

THE PROVINCIAS INTERNAS

NEW CHAPTER SOURCES: Lacy-Grimaldi correspondence in full, 1773–74; Pérez, *Diario*, 1774 (M. A.); Crespi and Peña, *Diarios*, 1774, with translations in Sutro volume of Publications of the Historical Society of Southern California; Bucarely correspondence on Pérez expedition, 1774–76; settlers and ship's company, Santiago, 1774 ; Heceta, *Diario ;* Campa's account of discovery of Trinidad Bay, 1775 ; Bucarely correspondence on Heceta-Quadra expedition, 1774–76; Bucarely correspondence on Byng-Cook expeditions, 1776; on ships to be built at Lima, 1776, and on Arteaga expedition, 1779; Arteaga, Maurelle, and Quadra, *Diarios;* Bucarely on removal of Barri; Instructions to Neve, as governor of Alta California, Dec. 25, 1776 (M. A.); Instructions to Caballero de Croix, 1776 (Harvard University, Sparks Collection); Garcés, *Diario* (M. A.),—Translation, Coues, *On the Trail of a Spanish Pioneer;* Font, *Diario*, complete (John Carter Brown Library); Anza-Crespo-Díaz-Oconor correspondence, and Palma petition for Gila-Colorado presidios, 1775–76; Vicente de Mora, *Diario* of peninsular trip, 1774–75 (M. A.); Morfi's report to Bucarely, 1777 (Ayer Collection, Newberry Library); Barbastro and Neve on massacre by Yumas (M. A.); Croix, report to King, 1781 (S. A.); Letter, Serra to Bucarely, 1778; Report of Treasury Department on California, 1777 (M. A.). (Specific citations below.)

1. M. A., Arch. Genl., *R. Céd. y Ord.* 102, f. 168. Concerning the Laws of the Indies on navigating the Pacific, see chapter IX of text, n. 8.

2. Lacy to Grimaldi, Feb. 7, 1773 (*Ibid.*, 102, f. 178).

3. Lacy to Grimaldi, May 7 and 11, 1773 (M. A., Arch. Genl., *R. Céd. y Ord.* 103, f. 238; *Ibid., Historia*, 61, " Viajes y Descubrimientos," i; summary, B. C., Pinart *Papeles ;* Bancroft, *History of the Northwest Coast*, vol. i, p. 150, n. 20).

4. The maps presumably were G. H. Muller's, Amsterdam, 1766, and J. von Staehling's in *The New Northern Archipelago;* Translation from German edition, London, 1774. (Staehling map, Macdonald Coll., Oakland.) On Dec. 27, 1773, Viceroy Bucarely wrote to the King that hardly had there been time to make "a copy of the new map published in Russia this year, which, because it differed from that of 1758, it had seemed to him necessary for Pérez to take with him." (M. A., Arch. Genl., *Cor. de Virreyes*, ser. i, vol. ii, no. 1224, 60, f. 58.)

5. J. Pérez, *Diario* (M. A., Arch. Genl., *Historia*, 62) ; Pérez and Martínez, *Diario* (M. A., Arch. Genl., *Historia*, 61).

J. Pérez, "Relación del Viaje" (B. C., *Viajes al Norte* — copied from the Spanish Archives — no. 1; Bancroft, *History of the Northwest Coast*, vol. i,

p. 151, n. 23). Crespi, *Diario* (Palou, *Noticias*, vol. iii, p. 164); Peña and Crespi, *Diarios*, with translations (Sutro vol., Publications of the Historical Society of Southern California, p. 83 etc.). Bucarely to King, series of nine letters on Pérez expedition, July 27, 1773, to Sept. 28, 1774 (M. A., Arch. Genl., *Cor. de Virreyes*, sér. i, vol. xi, no. 1086, 57, f. 54 ; *Ibid.*, no. 1104, 58, f. 55; *Ibid.*, no. 1182, 59, f. 56; *Ibid.*, no. 1562, 80, f. 110; *Ibid.*, no. 1608, 94, f. 123; *Ibid.*, no. 1259, 62, f. 60; *Ibid.*, no. 1224, 60, f. 58; *Ibid.*, no. 1048, 56, f. 50; *Cor. de Virreyes*, 1774, vol. lviii, serial vol. xli, no. 1519, f. 1). *Instrucción que debe observar el Alférez* . . . *Juan Pérez*, Dec. 24, 1773 (M. A., Arch. Genl., *Historia*, 61, "Viajes y Descubrimientos," i). List of settlers and ship's company in detail, with two short notes by Serra to Bucarely, Jan. 7 and 27, 1774. (*Ibid.*)

6. Bucarely to King, reciting order of 24th of Aug., 1773 (M. A., Arch. Genl., *Cor. de Virreyes*, sér. i, vol. ii, no. 1182, 59, f. 56; *Ibid.*, no. 1608, 94, f. 123).

7. B. Heceta, *Diario* (M. A., Arch. Genl., *Historia*, 24, 324).

B. Heceta (B. C., *Viajes al Norte*, nos. 2, 3; Bancroft, *History of the Northwest Coast*, vol. i, p. 159, n. 36; Palou, *Noticias*, vol. iv, p. 75). Heceta, *Diario;* translation by Greenhow of part relating to discovery of the Columbia (*Oregon and California*, 1845, Appendix E). Miguel de la Campa to Guardian Pangua, Carmelo, Oct. 12, 1775, brief report of discovery of bay to which the name Trinidad was given (M. A., Museo, *Docs. Rel. á las Mis. de Califs.*, Qto ii).

8. Bucarely to King, series of eight letters on Heceta-Quadra expedition, Dec. 27, 1774, to Nov. 26, 1776 (M. A., Arch. Genl., *Cor. de Virreyes*, sér. i, vol. ii, no. 1815, 109, f. 189; *Ibid.*, no. 2032, 133, f. 221; *Ibid.*, no. 2033, 134, f. 223; *Ibid.*, no. 2034, 135, f. 224; *Ibid.*, no. 2073, 124, f. 231; *Ibid.*, no. 2031, 132, f. 220; *Cor. de Virreyes*, 1775, vol. lxv, serial vol. xlviii, no. 1752, f. 1; *Ibid.*, no. 1753). On March 27, 1775, Bucarely advises the King that three days out from San Blas the commander of the San Carlos, Miguel Manrique, had become insane, and that Ayala had been substituted in the command. On Dec. 27, 1775, Bucarely expresses the opinion that "if not wholly disproved by this voyage, it at least has been reduced to a very slender possibility that there leads westward any pass from Hudson's Bay." He furthermore approves a recommendation by Heceta that the port of Trinidad be fortified. On Nov. 26, 1776, Bucarely writes in the strongest terms of the courage and resourcefulness of Bodega y Quadra, and recommends him for promotion. In a letter of Aug. 27, 1775, the Viceroy reports the cost of Pérez's expedition as 15,455 *pesos*, and that of Heceta and Quadra as 11,215 *pesos*. (M. A., Arch. Genl., *Cor. de Virreyes*, Bucarely, 1775, vol. lxx, serial vol. liii, no. 1939, f. 8.)

9. Gálvez to Bucarely, Jan. 9, 1777 (M. A., Arch. Genl., *R. Céd. y Ord.* 110, f. 30).

10. By this time, fear of the English by way of a passage from Hudson's

Bay had practically ceased. Bucarely to King, Sept. 28, 1774 (M. A., Arch. Genl., *Cor. de Virreyes*, sér. i, vol. xi, no. 1562, 80, f. 110).

11. On March 23, 1776 (M. A., Arch. Genl., *R. Céd. y Ord.* 107, f. 198), the King had written to the Viceroy that Captain Cook, under pretext of restoring to the islands of Otaheyti an Indian taken thence on a previous voyage, was to visit the South Sea, but that his real object was to cruise for " our fleet, reconnoitre well the Ladrone Islands, and, passing thence to California, to open commerce with New Mexico and try to find the famous N.W. Passage, in order to gain the reward offered by the House of Commons." Against such attempts the *comandantes de la costa de California* were to be vigilant. Replying to the above on June 26, 1776, Bucarely reviewed the entire California situation: English voyages (from Anson's day) around Cape Horn; Byng's contemplated adventure *via* the North Pole; the proposed occupation of Trinidad Bay against Russia; the question of succor to the missions of Monterey by the San Blas transports or by the Anza route overland from Sonora. The conclusion was that the King should advise distinctly whether he (Bucarely) was to oppose Captain Cook " with force" from the moment he passed Cape Horn, or (the only thing really practicable) to withhold from him supplies and refreshment (M. A., Arch. Genl., *Cor. de Virreyes*, sér. i, vol. xii, no. 2296, 158, f. 21). Directions were sent to the Viceroy, Oct. 18, 1776, to proceed according to the provisions of the Laws of the Indies, whereby " there were to be admitted to California waters only the yearly Manila galleon and the San Blas transports," — a course which would involve the "detaining, seizing, and confiscating" of the interloping ships. (M. A., Arch. Genl., *R. Céd. y Ord.*, 109, f. 102; M. A., Arch. Genl., *Cor. de Virreyes*, no. 2534, 169, f. 41; *Ibid.*, vol. xiii, no. 2702, 187, f. 3; Captain J. Cook, A *Voyage to the Pacific Ocean*, 1785, 3 vols.; secret instructions, in vol. i, pp. xxxii–xxxv.)

12. Bucarely to King, Aug. 27, 1776, reports careening of the Santiago, and need of a vessel to go to Peru to carry the *visitador* for that viceroyalty. (M. A., Arch. Genl., *Cor. de Virreyes*, Bucarely, 1776, vol. lxxxii, serial vol. lxv, no. 2427, f. 5.) Bucarely to King, Sept. 26, 1776, suggests that the Viceroy at Lima (Peru) be instructed to build at Guayaquil two *fragatas* of twenty guns, drawing only twelve feet of water, for San Blas use. (*Ibid.*, vol. lxxxiii, serial vol. lxvi, no. 2507, f. 42.) Beginning Nov. 18, 1776, there was held at Tepic a *junta* of naval officers: Heceta, Quadra, Fernando Quirós, Diego Choquet de Islas, Ignacio Arteaga, Francisco Hijosa, Juan Manuel de Ayala, José de Cañizares, Francisco Antonio Maurelle, Francisco Álvarez Castro, and Juan Bautista de Aguirre. It was decided by this body of capable officers that the Santiago should proceed to Lima with the *visitador*, and that at Lima or Callao there should be constructed two ships fitted for northern explorations and effectively armed. (*Ibid.*, vol. lxxxvi, serial vol. lxix, no. lacking, f. 149.) On March 18, 1778, the King consented to a postponement of the expedition until 1779. (M. A., Arch. Genl., *R. Céd. y Ord.* 113, f. 251.)

13. Arteaga, Maurelle, and Quadra, *Diarios* (M. A., Arch. Genl., *Historia*, 63, 64); *Viajes al Norte*, nos. 4, 5, 6½ (B. C.); Bancroft, *History of the Northwest Coast*, vol. i, p. 173, n. 8. Bucarely to the King, Feb. 24, 1779, stating condition and outfit of the two vessels and fact of their sailing (M. A., Arch. Genl., *Cor. de Virreyes*, Bucarely, 1777, vol. cxvi, serial vol. xcix, no. 4261). Report of voyage, Viceroy Mayorga to the King, Dec. 27, 1779 (*Ibid., Cor. de Virreyes*, vol. cxxv, serial vol. iv, no. 187, f. 294; Palou, *Noticias*, vol. iv, p. 211).

14. Bancroft finds the name used in royal *cédulas*, as an official designation in 1712–13 (*History of North Mexican States and Texas*, vol. i, p. 636, n. 2).

15. In 1729 the number of presidios for New Spain was fixed at twenty — that of Santa Fé being the most remote. In 1766 the Marqués de Rubí inspected by royal order the presidios of Nueva Vizcaya, Sonora, Coahuila, and New Mexico. Of those constituting the New Mexico-Sonora [Arizona] group, Fronteras had been founded between 1680 and 1690, Terrente and Pitic in 1741, Horcasitas between 1746 and 1750, Tubac in 1752, and Altar in 1753–54. Of the Nueva Vizcaya-New Mexico group, Santa Fé had been founded in 1630, Janos between 1680 and 1690, and Paso del Norte in 1682. The two California presidios, Loreto and Cabo San Lucas, had been founded, the one in 1697 and the other in 1735.

16. M. A., Arch. Genl., *Prov. Int.* 154.

17. *Ibid.*

18. Beleña, *Recopilación de Leyes*, i, pt. iii, pp. 290–291. Location of capital confirmed by King, Feb. 12, 1782 [83]. (B. C., *Prov. St. Pap.*, vol. ii, p. 89; iii, p. 182.) On June 22, 1771, Viceroy Croix had written to Minister Arriaga that Arizpe would be a better location for the capital than Caborca. The latter had almost been destroyed by the Apaches. A *jefe superior* was needed in Sonora to aid the Californias, wherein the conquest had now been extended to Monterey. (Harvard Library, Sparks Coll. 98, *Papeles Varios de America*, iii.)

19. Cf. chapters iii of text, n. 26, and viii, n. 15.

20. B. C., *Documents for the History of Chihuahua*, p. 7. In 1794 the practices introduced by Croix were ordered by the King to be discontinued. (*Ibid.*, p. 14.)

Croix's instructions, which bore date, San Ildefonso, Aug. 22, 1776, were addressed to him as *Don Teodoro de Croix, Caballero del Orden Teutonico, Brigadier de mis Exércitos, segundo Teniente de la Compañía Flamenca de mis Rs Guardias de Corps, Governador y Comandante-General en gefe de las Provincias de Sinaloa, Sonora, Californias y Nueva Vizcaya*. It was stated that as early as 1752 it had been proposed to erect a *comandancia-general* for the interior provinces, and that in July, 1769, it had been resolved to do so. Besides the Californias and other provinces named by Gálvez, there were placed under Croix's command the *gobiernos subalternos* of Coahuila, Texas, and New Mexico, with their presidios, and all other presidios situated (under the *Reglamento para Presidios* of Sept. 10, 1772) *en el cordón ó Línea* from the Gulf of the Californias to the bay of Espiritu Santo [Texas, San Antonio River]. (H. E. Bolton, " Spanish Abandonment and Reoccupation of East Texas," *Quarterly of Texas State Hist. Assoc.*, vol. ix, no. 2.) The comandante-general was to be dependent directly upon the King and upon such orders as should reach him *por via reservada de Indias*, but he was to report all matters of consequence to the Viceroy, so that the latter might be informed and lend necessary aid. He was made superintendent of the *Real Hacienda* [Treasury] in the Provincias, and invested with the power of the *Patronato Real*. His capital was fixed at Arizpe in Sonora, as a point "near the frontier of that province, and central as between Nueva Vizcaya and the Californias," — a point, moreover, where he "straightway could be lodged *en la suntuosa casa* used by the *antiguos misioneros.*" He was ordered to establish a mint at his capital, and his salary was fixed at 20,000 *pesos* annually. He was to permit judicial appeals to the Audiencia of Guadalajara, but in matters military (*del fuero militar*) and of the *Real Hacienda* he was to act independently, reporting his acts to the King for approval. His personal guard was to consist of an officer and twenty men. In the interior provinces the missionaries were the principal *operarios* for winning the natives to the *Fé Católica*, and their requests should have prompt attention. It should be his especial care to establish, on the *línea de Presidios*, pueblos of Spaniards and of *Indios reducidos*, according to tit. 5, lib. 4, of the *Recopilación de Indias*.

With regard especially to Northern California, Croix was to be diligent in a high degree. He was to "conserve, foment and advance the *nuevas conquistas y Reducciones* effected [there], and also the presidios established in the ports of San Diego and Monterey." He was ordered to "visit and become acquainted with that province as soon as practicable." He was to take steps to assure communication by land between California and Sonora, availing himself of the *noticias, informes, y derroteros* of Don Juan Bautista de Anza. He was also to open communication between the presidio of Monterey and that of Santa Fé in New Mexico. Supplies and families of Spanish settlers for the Californias were to be brought from Sonora and Sinaloa. The naval and supply station of San Blas was to be maintained, and the Viceroy, as heretofore, was to send *memorias*. To the end of good government, the comandante-general was forbidden to accept gifts; and on his travels he was not to be received by pueblos or presidios with *fiestas* or other demonstrations, and his personal household was to be kept at a minimum. (Harvard Library, Sparks Coll. 98, *Papeles Varios de America*, iii.)

21. Instructions to Felipe de Neve, Sept. 30, 1774 (M. A., Arch. Genl., *Prov. Int.* 166, no. 22, par. 25). On Dec. 27, 1774, Bucarely stated to the King that the cause for the change of governors was *discordia . . . entre* [Barri] *y los P. P. Misioneros sobre puntos de jurisdicción* (M. A., Arch.

Genl., *Cor. de Virreyes*, Bucarely, 1774, vol. lxii, serial vol. xlv, no. 1643). The whole matter is set forth by Palou, *Noticias*, vol. iv, pp. 3 *et seq.*

The Barri-Mora conflict drew from the Viceroy an intimation that the power of the padres over the soldiery, and in other temporal respects, was limited. In his instructions to Neve, Bucarely stated that because of the privilege of chastising neophytes accorded to the padres on May 6 [9], 1773 (chapter VI of text, n. 20), it did not follow that the Governor was precluded from *la jurisdicción ordinaria . . . inseparable del empleo de gobernador.* Padres were not to use soldiers, without license of the Governor, except in an urgent and rare case. The power of dispatching boats pertained peculiarly to the Governor. (M. A., Arch. Genl., *Prov. Int.* 166, secs. 13, 14, 15.)

22. M. A., Arch. Genl., *Cor. de Virreyes*, Bucarely, 1776, vol. lxxxi, serial vol. lxiv, no. 2374; *Ibid.*, vol. lxxxii, serial vol. lxv, no. 2429; *Ibid.*, vol. lxxxvi, serial vol. lxix, no. 2636.

23. M. A., Arch. Genl., *Californias*, xiii, no. 32. Neve was to observe and enforce the instructions issued to Rivera y Moncada. In August, 1776, Bucarely had instructed Neve, on arriving at Monterey, to obtain supplies from the Gila and Colorado region, where in May and June there was abundant wheat, and in November and December, corn and beans. (B. C., *Prov. St. Pap.*, vol. i, p. 205.)

24. B. C., *Prov. Rec.*, vol. i, p. 66.

25. B. C., *Prov. St. Pap.*, vol. i, p. 252.

26. Neve to Bucarely, April 15, 1778 (B. C., *Prov. Rec.*, vol. i, p. 8, — translated by J. W. Dwinelle, *Colonial History of San Francisco*, 1863, Ad. v; Palou, *Noticias*, vol. iv, p. 203).

27. Croix to Rivera y Moncada, Arizpe, Dec. 27, 1779 (M. A., Arch. Genl., *Prov. Int.* 122; B. C., *Prov. St. Pap.*, vol. ii, p. 58).

28. Croix to Neve, Dec. 18, 1780 (B. C., *Prov. St. Pap.*, vol. ii, pp. 117–125); Croix to [King], about August, 1781, stating that he has sent to California 59 soldiers, 16 settlers, 65 women, and 89 children — 170 souls (S. A., Madrid, Dirección Hidrografía, *Virreinato de Méjico*, t. i, 9°, Doc. A. 3ª).

29. Neve to Croix, July 14, 1781 (B. C., *Prov. Rec.*, vol. ii, pp. 87–88).

30. *Recopilación de Leyes*, lib. iv, tit. v, ley vi. Towns may be founded by not less than thirty settlers who are to possess, each, a house, ten breeding cows, four oxen, or two oxen and two steers, one brood mare, one breeding sow, twenty breeding ewes of Castilian breed, six hens and one cock. . . . Such towns shall be granted, for occupancy, "four leagues of extent and territory in a square or prolonged form according to the character of the land, etc., with the condition that the limits of said territory shall be distant at least five leagues from any city, town, or village of Spaniards previously founded; and that there shall be no prejudice to any Indian town or private person"; translated, *Colonial History of San Francisco*, Ad. i.

31. *Instrucción para la Fundación de Los Ángeles*, 26 de Agosto, 1781 (B. C., *St. Pap. Miss. and Col.*, vol. i, p. 97; translated in part by Bancroft, *History of California*, vol. i, p. 345, n. 23).

32. B. C., *St. Pap. Miss. and Col.*, vol. i, pp. 105–119; Neve, *Reglamento y Instrucción*, 1781, sec. xiv; Arrillaga, *Recopilación*, 1828, 121–175, — Translation, C. F. Lummis, *Land of Sunshine*, 1897, vol. vi, nos. 2–6.

33. For explanatory definitions of the terms, *solares, suertes, ejidos*, etc., see Dwinelle, *Colonial History of San Francisco*, pp. 7–13.

34. Neve, *Reglamento*, sec. xiv, *supra*, n. 32. On *alcaldes*, etc., see text, chapter iii.

35. Los Ángeles, *padrón*, 1781, in Bancroft, *History of California*, vol. i, p. 345, n. 24.

36. B. C., *Prov. Rec.*, vol. iii, pp. 154–156; *St. Pap. Miss. and Col.*, vol. i, p. 30. Plat of town of San José (B. C., *St. Pap. Miss. and Col.*, vol. i, p. 243). Plats of Los Ángeles (*Prov. St. Pap.*, vol. iii, p. 55; *Prov. St. Pap.* (Benicia), vol. ii, p. 2; *St. Pap. Miss. and Col.*, vol. i, pp. 103, 307). Approval of design for founding Los Ángeles, Gálvez to Viceroy, Feb. 8, 1782 (M. A., Arch. Genl., *R. Cédulas*, 1782, 122, f. 55).

37. Serra to Bucarely, June 30, 1778 (Harvard Library, Sparks Coll. 98, *Papeles Varios de America*, v); Neve to Croix, Aug. 10, 1778 (B. C., *Prov. Rec.*, vol. i, p. 91); Neve to Fages, Sept. 7, 1782 (*Prov. St. Pap.*, vol. iii, p. 145).

38. At the time of the organization of the Provincias, there had been expressly reserved to the Viceroy the control of *memorias* (mission supplies), — a reservation construed by the missionaries as involving control of Mission, as distinguished from military, affairs (Bucarely to Neve, June 3, 1777). Concerning supplies and effects, Neve is not to communicate with the comandante-general, but with the Viceroy as heretofore (B. C., *Prov. Rec.*, vol. i, p. 66). In 1788 the Conde de Gálvez instructed Comandante-General Ugarte y Loyola that the latter had "full powers, though subordinate to the Viceroy, to whom he must report." The latter had "no part in financial administration. It was his business to fight and exterminate or subdue the wild Indians." (B. C., *Mayer MSS.*) On July 10, 1788, Viceroy Flórez wrote Governor Fages that it had been determined by the King himself that the superior government and not the comandante-general of the Provincias Internas was to pay the missionaries within the limits of the *comandancia*. (B. C., *Prov. St. Pap.*, vol. viii, p. 3.)

Facultad de Confirmar (B. C., *Arch. de Sta. Bárb.*, vol. xii, p. 270). What Serra was not willing to recognize was the fact that, in the case of the Provincias Internas, the *Patronato Real* had been attached to the *comandancia-general*; the *Patronato* itself being vested in the comandante-general, and the *vice-patronato* in each of the governors under him; and this not alone with regard to the secular clergy but also the regulars (cf. n. 21, *supra*).

39. Croix to Neve, July 19, 1779 (B. C., *Prov. St. Pap.*, vol. ii, p. 47; *St. Pap. Miss. and Col.*, vol. i, p. 28).

40. *Reglamento*, *supra*, n. 32. Approved by the King (M. A., Arch. Genl., *R. Cédulas*, 1781, 121, f. 266; *Ibid.*, 122, f. 55).

THE PROVINCIAS INTERNAS 433

41. Garcés, *Diario*, 1775–76; Translation, E. Coues, *On the Trail of a Spanish Pioneer*, vol. ii, p. 455; Anza to Bucarely, Mexico, Nov. 20, 1776 (M. A., Arch. Genl., *Prov. Int.* 23). Anza wrote: *La trasladación de los dos Presidios . . . á los Rios Colorado y Gila . . . son* [sic] *indispensables para sobstener y asegurar los Misiones.*

42. Pretensions and activity of the Dominicans: Vicente de Mora, *Diario*, 1774 (M. A., Arch. Genl., *Cor. de Virreyes*, vol. lv, sér. ii, vol. xxxviii, no. 1422, f. 7); Velásquez, *Diario*, 1775 (M. A., Arch. Genl., *Historia*, 52). Cf. chapter VI, n. 8; chapter X, n. 10.

43. J. Díaz, to Bucarely, San Miguel de los Ures, March 21, 1775 (M. A., Arch. Genl., *Prov. Int.* 88, no. 55). In this communication Garcés seems to have joined, but it is distinctively a Díaz production.

44. Crespo to Bucarely, Altar, Dec. 15, 1774 (M. A., Arch. Genl., *Historia*, 25, f. 252); Oconor to Crespo, Tubac, Nov. 25, 1774 (*Ibid.*); Oconor to Mendinueta, Sta. Fé, Nov. 9, 1775 (M. A., Arch. Genl., *Prov. Int.* 169).

45. *Ibid.*

46. B. C., *Reglamento para los Presidios*, etc., *Cédula de 10 de Septiembre de 1772*. Díaz to Bucarely, *supra*, n. 43. Bucarely to the King, letters, May 27, Oct. 27, 1775, reporting request by Díaz and Garcés to change location of presidios from sites as recommended by Inspector Marqués de Rubí. (M. A., Arch. Genl., *Prov. Int.* 23.) Approval by the King of request of padres, Feb. 14, 1776. (*Ibid.*) On objection by Anza, the presidio of Altar was not changed. Reporting on presidios in 1781, Comandante-General Croix digests the recommendations of all previous reports, and designates the following as a correct presidial line: —

San Miguel de Babispe	23 leagues	SO
Fronteras	29 "	O
Santa Cruz	25 "	NO
Nuevo de Buenavista	21 "	NO¼O
Tupson	26 "	NO
Total of the line	124 "	

— (S. A., Madrid, Direc. Hid., *Virreinato de Méjico*, t. i, 9°, Doc. A 3ª).

47. Rivalry much the same as later between the " Santa Fé " and the "Southern Pacific."

48. Morfi to Bucarely, *Informe*, 1777 (Ayer Collection, Newberry Library).

49. Bucarely to King, Aug. 27, 1776, announcing determination of Palma to accompany Anza to Mexico (M. A., Arch. Genl., *Cor. de Virreyes*, Bucarely, 1776, vol. lxxxii, serial vol. lxv, no. 2429, f. 10). Palma to Bucarely, Nov. 11, 1776, — a letter composed by Anza and signed by Palma with three X marks. This communication sets forth the life-history and creed of the Yuma chief, as interpreted by a Spanish mind. It is not so distinctively Indian as the autobiography of the Sac and Fox chief, Black Hawk, recorded

in 1833 by Antoine Le Claire, Indian agent at Rock Island, Ill., but it is not without interest. It states that its author reigns by right of descent, does not favor polygamy, and worships God, *criador de todos*, whom he calls *Duchi y Pá;* that he came to love Anza because the Spaniards were friends of his allies the Papagos; that Anza had from the first diligently instructed him in religion; that he had aided Anza in effecting a crossing of the Colorado, and that the latter thereupon had named him Salvador [Saviour] Palma, a name he had assumed instead of that given him in his own land, which was Olley-quotequiebe; that he had always kept faith with the Spaniards; that his people number 3000, and that he will be able to reduce neighboring vassal tribes to the Catholic faith and the royal dominion; finally, that he will keep open the way from Sonora and New Mexico to California (M. A., Arch. Genl., *Prov. Int.* 23, no. 7). On Palma's stay in Mexico City, see *Diario Curioso de México de D. José Gómez, Cabo de Alabarderos* (*Docs. para la Historia de México*, 1st ser., vol. i, Mexico, 1854, cited by Coues, *Trail of a Spanish Pioneer*, vol. ii, p. 503, n. 49).

50. M. A., Arch. Genl., *Prov. Int.* 23; *Ibid., R. Céd. y Ord.* 110, f. 193. In the dispatch of Feb. 14, 1777, the King (by Gálvez) gave orders that Palma's request for missions should be granted, after he had been sufficiently instructed "in our sacred religion." The matter of instruction had been dwelt upon in a report to Bucarely by the *fiscal*, dated Nov. 18, 1776, covering Palma's petition of Nov. 11 (M. A., Arch. Genl., *Prov. Int.* 23).

51. J. C. Arricivita, *Crónica Seráfica . . . del Colegio . . . de la Santa Cruz de Querétaro*, pp. 489 *et seq.*

52. It is stated by Croix in his report of 1781 that from 1745 to 1780 comandantes, inspectors, and padres, excepting Ugarte and Rocha, have favored the occupation of the Gila tributary San Pedro, and of the Gila itself. Nobody, however, has from actual personal examination been able to select just the right situations. "We, therefore," proceeds the report, "content ourselves with two pueblos of Spaniards among the Yumas, because these fortunate Indians have embraced [our] religion and vassalage voluntarily. We are postponing the reduction of the Pimas Gileños, of the Cocomaricopas, and of other nations, until such opportune time as God may appoint, and we are rectifying the Apache frontier by removing Horcasitas to Pitic, and by leaving Buenavista where it is." The report then continues: "It not being possible to transfer the [two] presidios to the Colorado, I determined to found two pueblos of Spaniards in the territory of the Yumas. For their security I destined a troop composed of a subaltern, a sergeant, two corporals, and eighteen men from each of the presidios, Altar, Horcasitas, and Buenavista, whose families, with twenty others, will constitute a population augmented by such Gentile Indians as may wish to join. I conferred the political and military command on Lieutenant D. Santiago Islas, and for the spiritual there were named the padres Fr. Francisco Garcés and Fr. Juan Díaz, with a *sínodo* of 400 *pesos* each. . . . The recruiting of families was

happily effected in Pimería Alta, and already they are at their destination with the troop and comandante. They were well received by the Yumas. The family of Captain Salvador Palma, with others of his nation, are now working with ardor in the formation of the pueblo. The troop and settlers have chosen an *habilitado-general*. . . . Doubtless results will be happy, for a union with the Spanish pueblos will foster the docility of the Indians, protect the communication with la Nueva California, render Sonora secure, and eventually New Mexico. These establishments, had the presidios been transferred, would have cost annually 18,998 *pesos*, 6 *reales ;* but as it is, they will cost only the subsistence of the settlers' families (47 *pesos* for each annually), a sum which as the families become self-supporting will be extinguished. . . . If the Yumas but keep loyal, the banks of the Colorado will soon be covered with fields, cattle, and towns of faithful vassals, whose resources, augmenting those of Sonora, will make for reciprocal defense; as also for the defense of the Californias, to whose jurisdiction [those towns] should belong, by reason of being on the further side of the river marking the limits of Sonora, and at a less distance from Monterey."

By the foregoing there were put in effect almost the exact recommendations of the Franciscan father, signing himself "The most unworthy minister of the Order St. Francis," whose " Brief Reflections " in favor of *custodias* are cited at length in chapter VIII of the text, note 9.

53. The news, as first carried to Croix, was that Rivera y Moncada had repulsed the Yuma attack. Says the comandante-general : "Moncada arrived happily at the Colorado, where he intended to winter. I am without other news than that the Apaches made an assault upon him of four hours without inflicting loss. The families of the settlers were already gone, and the expedition was beyond danger. In everything Rivera has conducted himself with his customary zeal, sexagenarian though he be." (S. A., Madrid, Direc. de Hid., *Virreinato de Méjico*, t. i, 9°, Doc. A 3ª.)

54. Arricivita, *Crónica Seráfica*, pp. 504–509. Dr. Elliott Coues, commenting on the massacre, says that he does not know where to find an exact parallel to it in Indian annals.

55. P. Font, *Diario*, complete (John Carter Brown Library); M. A., Arch. Genl., *Historia*, 24, — translated in part, Coues, *On the Trail of a Spanish Pioneer*, vol. i, p. 172, n. 15.

56. Arricivita, *Crónica Seráfica*, pp. 497–504: It is not to be overlooked that by his instructions (*ante*, n. 20) it was enjoined upon Croix to establish pueblo-missions, — missions composed of "Spaniards and of *Indios reducidos*."

57. Tubutama, Sept. 25, 1781 (M. A., Arch. Genl., *Historia*, 24, f. 66). The four murdered padres were buried in one coffin in the church at Tubutama.

58. Arricivita,*Crónica Seráfica*, etc., pp. 510 *et seq.* ; Council of War, report by Antonio Bonilla,· Arizpe, Sept. 10, 1781 (B. C., *St. Pap.* (Sacramento),

vol. vi, p. 124); Neve to Croix, Nov. 18, 1781 (*Prov. St. Pap.*, vol. ii, p. 69); Same to Same, March 10, 1782 (*Prov. Rec.*, vol. i, p. 76); Fages to Fray Agustín Morfi, Pitic, Feb. 12, 1782 (M. A., Arch. Genl., *Historia*, 24, f. 66); Examination of survivors of massacre (B. C., *Prov. St. Pap.*, vol. iii, pp. 319–32; Palou, *Noticias*, vol. iv, p. 228).

59. Correspondence, Neve-Croix (B. C., *Prov. St. Pap.*, vol. iii, pp. 236–39, 182–83, 185, 198–207; *Prov. Rec.*, vol. ii, pp. 47, 53, 57, 65–66; *Crónica Seráfica*, p. 514). The fact is strongly emphasized by Arricivita that the pueblo plan was contrary to the Laws of the Indies, because natives and Spaniards were permitted to dwell together.

60. June 3, 1777 (B. C., *Prov. Rec.*, vol. i, p. 70).

61. Neve . . . *al Comandante del Presidio de Sta. Bárbara* (B. C.).

62. Pangua-Mayorga Correspondence (B. C., *Arch. Sta. Bárb.*, vol. i, pp. 231–46; vi, 266–71). On Jan. 8, 1783, Guardian Pangua instructed President Serra not to consent to founding of presidio and missions on Sta. Bárbara Channel as by plan of Neve (B. C., *Arch. Sta. Bárb.*, vol. xii, p. 158). Presidio Sta. Bárbara founded: Neve to Croix, April 24, 1782 (B. C., *Prov. Rec.*, vol. ii, pp. 61–62); Serra, April 29, 1782 (*Arch. Sta. Bárb.*, vol. ix, pp. 293–94); Croix to Neve in approval, July 22, 1782 (*Prov. St. Pap.*, vol. iii, p. 232); Palou, *Noticias*, vol. iv, p. 235.

63. By the *Reglamento* of Neve there was prescribed for Alta California the following force: An *ayudante* (adjutant)-inspector, four *habilitados* (paymasters, chosen, one for each presidio by the company from its own subalterns), four lieutenants, six sergeants, sixteen corporals, 172 soldiers, a surgeon, and five master-mechanics.

As reported in 1777 for the use of Comandante-General Croix (M. A., Arch. Genl., *Californias*, 39), the California governmental establishment, under the *Reglamento* of Echeveste, was the following: —

ALTA CALIFORNIA

Monterey Presidio

Governor (4000 *pesos*), one sergeant, two corporals, two carpenters, two farriers, four muleteers, a storekeeper, 22 soldiers.

Monterey Missions

San Carlos, San Luis Obispo, and San Antonio de Padua, one corporal and five soldiers each.

San Diego Presidio

Lieutenant (700 *pesos*); thirteen officers and mechanics, with a commissary storekeeper and 47 soldiers.

BAJA CALIFORNIA

Loreto Presidio

Comandante (3000 *pesos*), lieutenant (500), *alférez* [sub-lieutenant], two sergeants, three corporals, a commissary, 39 soldiers.

San Diego Missions
San Diego de Alcalá and San Gabriel Arcángel, one corporal and five soldiers each.

San Francisco Presidio
Lieutenant (700 *pesos*), a sergeant, eight colonist families from Sonora, 29 soldiers.

Total of 166 officers and men, including eight heads of colonist families at San Francisco, at a cost of 63,222 *pesos*.

Total of 47 officers and men, at a cost of 31,287 *pesos*.

(Cf. estimated expenditures by Echeveste, chapter VI.)

64. In later years, when the pueblos had become degenerate, Governor Arrillaga wrote to Viceroy Iturrigaray, contending that the *gobernador* of Alta California had no political (civil) jurisdiction. "All," he said, "is military. It [the province] is composed of four presidios, three pueblos, and missions without *gente de razón*. In the latter the Indian who acts as governor, or *alcalde*, is subject *en lo civil* to the padre, and *en lo criminal* to the corporals [of the guard], by whom causes are remitted to this *superioridad*. The pueblos (little they merit the name) are composed of invalids and of a small number of citizens, who, though they have an *alcalde*, are ruled by the *gobernador* through a sergeant-*comisionado* who administers justice. Everything is done in a military way, and the *gobernador* intervenes in nothing except to refer some criminal proceeding to your Excellency. It is only with respect to the *Patronato Real* that a *gobernador* might exercise some authority, but there is so little occasion even for this that it does not deserve mention. If the *gobernador* should wish to act in civil matters, there is nobody with whom he could consult in seven hundred leagues. The presidial comandantes hold under their jurisdiction all the missions, and administer justice *militarmente* according to the *Reglamento*." (Loreto, Dec. 20, 1804, M. A., Arch. Genl., *Californias*, Segunda Parte, L. 18, no. 7102.)

The above was elicited by an order from the Viceroy directing Arrillaga to apply to the *Cámara de Indias* for authority as *jefe político*.

65. J. R. Robertson, *From Alcalde to Mayor*, MS. (Academy of Pacific Coast History, Bancroft Library, Berkeley, California.)

66. *Ayuntamientos* (town councils) were created in 1613 by Philip III (*Recopilación*, lib. iv, tit. 9, ley 10). They were at first popularly elective, but later were renewed by coöptation. Under the Spanish Constitution of 1812 — to be spoken of in chapter XII — *ayuntamientos* were permitted to pueblos of 1000 inhabitants. Small pueblos could unite or be joined to larger ones (Article 310).

67. Capital cases (other than those cognizable by court-martial) were, it would seem, referred by the Governor to the *Audiencia*.

CHAPTER VIII

STATE SECULAR *VS.* STATE SACERDOTAL

NEW CHAPTER SOURCES: Letters of Palou to Guardian Sancho of the College of San Fernando, and to José de Gálvez (Sept. and Nov. 1784), describing the last hours of Junípero Serra, — letters upon which Palou based in part his *Vida de Serra;* the *Intendencia,* its nature and history, as described by Viceroy Croix and by Gálvez (Ayer Coll., Newberry Library); plan of the *Custodia* by Bishop Reyes, and correspondence relative to putting the plan into effect, 1776, 1783, 1784; royal letter on the question of one padre at a mission (1784); Guardian Sancho on the conflict between the *Reglamento* and plan of the *Custodia,* 1785; Palou's letter (Alta California under Fages) to Manuel María Truxillo, 1787; proceedings of Doña Eulalia de Callis for divorce (1785), and Fages's letter thereon, 1787; the *Patronato Real* as discussed by Asesor Galindo Navarro, 1791. (M. A., except *Intendencia* dispatch.)

1. Palou to Guardian Juan Sancho, Sept. 7, 1784 (M. A., Museo, *Docs. Rel. á las Mis. de Califs.,* Qto iii); Same to Gálvez, Sept. 6, 1784 (*Ibid.*). On Sept. 13, 1784, Palou notifies Guardian Sancho of willingness to go to Madrid to oppose the transfer of the Alta California missions to the Dominicans, — missions "watered by the blood of Luis Jayme." The transfer (termed by Palou a second expulsion for the California Franciscans) was deemed a part of the plan of Bishop Reyes of Sonora, as related in text. So confident was Palou that a transfer would be effected that he instructed the padres in the South to make ready their inventories. (*Ibid.*) Reyes had advised the step in a letter to Comandante-General Neve, Dec. 13, 1783. (L. Sales, *Noticias de la Provincia de Californias,* 1794, pp. 71–75.)

2. Letter of Sept. 6, 1784, n. 1, *supra;* Palou, *Vida de Serra,* pp. 261–305. On Feb. 6, 1785, Guardian Sancho wrote to Palou acknowledging receipt of the news of Serra's death. (M. A., Museo, *Docs. Rel. á las Mis. de Califs.,* Qto iii.)

3. Manuel de la Vega (*comisario-general*) to Guardian Sancho, Oct. 20, 1784, stating that Palou, Oct. 5, has been granted permission by the King to retire to his college, but intimating that in the first instance applications for retirement should be made to him (M. A., Museo, *Docs. Rel. á las Mis. de Califs.,* 8vo i). The permission was forwarded to Monterey by the Audiencia of Mexico, Feb. 18, 1785 (M. A., Arch. Genl., *R. Audiencia, 1785,* 1, 136). Palou's departure was postponed, because if taken at once certain missions would be left *en solo ministro* (M. A., Museo, *Docs. Rel. á las Mis. de Califs.,* Qto iii).

4. Palou left Monterey about Dec. 7, 1785. He was heartily congratu-

lated on his retirement by Gálvez and by Fages (M. A., Museo, *Docs. Rel. á las Mis. de Califs.*, Qto iii). In his letter to Sancho, Sept. 13, 1784, he expresses a wish for a portrait of Serra and (in commemoration of Serra's last sacrament) that the posture be that of the Father-President "on his knees before the altar surrounded by Indians and by cuirassed soldiers, all bearing candles" (*Ibid.*). In his letter of Feb. 6, 1785, Sancho informs Palou that Serra's portrait is being painted at Verger's expense (*Ibid.*). The place of deposit and authenticity of various portraits of Serra are minutely discussed by Mr. George Watson Cole, *Missions and Mission Pictures*, Pub. Calif. Library Assoc., no. 11.

THE INTENDENCIA

5. The dispatch regarding *Intendencias* has not been found in the Mexican Archives. An intimation of its contents is made by Gálvez in the "joint dispatch" (M. A., Arch. Genl., *Prov. Int.* 154), and in his *Informe General* of Dec. 31, 1771, Mexico, 1867. Fortunately, however, the Ayer Collection (Newberry Library, Chicago) contains a complete copy of the missing paper. The instrument bears date Jan. 15, 1768 (eight days prior to the dispatch relative to a *comandancia-general*), and its main recitals are the following: At the beginning of the eighteenth century, Spain itself was the prey of "governors and subaltern judges, who, being temporary, regarded only their personal interest and enriched themselves at the expense of the state." This ruinous arrangement, uprooted at home by Philip V, obtains to-day in her rich and widespread dominions of America. Indeed, these dominions have "reached a point of decadence where they are menaced with total ruin, and it is necessary to apply the remedy which has cured the ills of the parent."

In "discharging his vast duties as captain-general, political governor, and general superintendent of the royal treasury, the Viceroy has hitherto possessed no other aid than that of the *alcaldes mayores.*" These officials "for the most part are regarded as tyrants, which in fact they are, for their term is but five years, and within it they seek to make themselves rich." In the principal localities there should be placed *Intendentes* as in Spain, men compensated by fixed salaries, thus ridding New Spain of more than 150 officials who each year filch from 500,000 to 600,000 *pesos*. This is the more necessary as the *alcaldes mayores* are accustomed to appoint lieutenants who pay to their superiors excessive annuities. The number of *Intendencias* should be eleven, — one, general in character, for the capital of Mexico, and the others for the provinces, all subject to the Viceroy. The *Intendencias de Provincia* should be located one in each of the localities — Puebla, Oaxaca, Mérida or Campeche, Valladolid de Michoacán, Guanaxuato, San Luis Potosí, Guadalaxara, Durango, Sonora, and Californias. For the *Intendentes* of Guadalaxara, Durango, Sonora, and Californias, the salaries should be 8000 *pesos;* for those of the remaining localities, 6000 *pesos;* and for the *Inten-*

dente-General, 12,000 *pesos*. Besides *Intendentes*, "there should exist in the various capitals *corregidores*, or political governors, as in Spain, with power to name *subdelegados* in the more considerable pueblos." "The two *Intendencias* of Sonora y Californias, which, together with that of Durango, are to be immediately subject to a *comandancia-general*, as proposed in a separate report, will produce copious additions to the royal treasury by the incomparable wealth of these great provinces. Under an authorized *comandancia*, the *Intendencias* last named will curtail the considerable expenses now incident to their eight presidios, and will render it possible to convert the missions into curacies."

The foregoing dispatch was approved on January 16, 1768, by the Bishop of Puebla, and on the 21st by the Archbishop of Mexico. The latter said: "The main subsistence of the *alcaldes mayores* is derived from the *repartimientos* of clothing, mules, and other commodities which they make (they and their lieutenants) to the Indians at a high price. . . . These *repartimientos* were necessary at the beginning of the conquest, but now the Indians weave their own clothing and raise their own livestock. . . . In Spain, an *alcalde mayor* ordinarily is an educated man; here, not. . . . In Spain, recourse to superiors is easy; here, it is a matter of 100 or 200 leagues to the Royal Audiencias. In Spain, peace and order prevail in the pueblos, etc.; here, it is constantly necessary to appeal to the strong hand."

On March 29, 1778, there was created by order of the Minister for the Indies (José de Gálvez) the *Intendencia* of Buenos Ayres, the first *Intendencia* in the two Americas. The order reads : *Consiguientemente y haviendo manifestado la esperiencia, las ventajas q, ha conseguido la Real Hacienda en la mejor Administración de las rentas y Trop^s en la seguridad y subcistencias con el Establecim^{to} de las Yntendencias en los reyños de Castilla, y lo mismo con la que se halla establecida en la Ysla de Cuba, se ha servido el Rey crear una Yntendencia de Exército y R^l Hac^{da} para el nuevo Virreynato de Buenos Ayres, con el importante objecto de ponerse en sus devidos valores las rentas de todas sus Provincias y Territorios, y de fomentar sus Poblaciones, Agricultura y Comercio, á nombre de S. M. para este Empleo al Yntendente D^n Manuel Frez que lo fué en la expedición Militar destinado á la América Meridional.*

So far as North America was concerned, the plan of *Intendencias* was not put in operation till 1786, when, by a decree (*orden*) dated Sept. 4, *Intendentes* were placed in "Mexico [City], Puebla, Vera Cruz, Mérida, Oaxaca, Valladolid, Guanajuato, San Luis Potosí, Guadalaxara, Zacatecas, and (for Sonora and Sinaloa) Durango and Arizpe." None was appointed for the Californias.

6. Feb. 22, 1769, "The reduction of the natives *en policía* [to civil status] is a thing so important as to admit neither of excuse nor delay." (M. A., Museo, *Docs. Rel. á las Mis. de Califs.*, Qto i.)

7. M. A., Museo, *Docs. Rel. á las Mis. de Califs.*, Qto ii.

8. *Informe*, no. 4 (M. A., Museo, *Trasuntos*).

9. M. A., Arch. Genl., *Misiones*, 14. In support of his plan of the *Custodia*, — a plan the complement (ecclesiastically) of the *Intendencia* system of secular control, — Reyes was successful in marshaling a powerful *junta*, headed by the Franciscan *comisario-general* of the Indies, Manuel de la Vega. The conclusive argument for the plan was the great distance between missions and their colleges or provincials, and the varying sets of rules governing missions.

THE CUSTODIA

Much light is shed upon the *Custodia* by the following interesting paper, which, though without date, evidently was written some time in 1779, and is signed "The most unworthy minister of the Order of Saint Francis ": —

"The history of the Indies shows a rapid spiritual and temporal conquest by the Spaniards during the first twenty years. Since this epoch there has been little advance, and now we are unable to support our pueblos and *provincias internas*. Yet we are not to think that the valor, zeal, and spirit of Spaniards have failed. We simply have changed our method. Formerly the missionaries entered the country of the Indians, formed *villas* and *pueblos unidos*. Fifty or one hundred families cultivated the soil, worked the mines, and bred livestock. The missionaries established themselves along with the Spaniards, built small convents where they observed their sacred law, lived in community, and at opportune times visited the mountains, prevailing upon the Indians by exhortation to become reduced to pueblos and to the *doctrina*. As the towns grew and the Indians became converted, more missionaries were obtained. In this way were established all the cities, *villas*, pueblos, and convents of New Spain.

"At the beginning of the past century [seventeenth], there was established the existing government of missions and presidios. The first of these in New Spain was the *Villa* of Sinaloa, founded in 1611. Its missionaries and soldiers were the first that opened the royal exchequer to cover *sínodos* [salaries] and *situados* [allowances]. They altered the fixed plan of our ancestors and started the abuses and errors now practiced. The missionaries became convinced that to reduce the Indians to pueblos, and to convert them, it was needful to assist them in all temporal respects. Thus the missionaries became charged with the obligation of feeding, clothing, and housing the Indians. It was at the beginning of the last century that there was introduced the abuse of furnishing to the Indians pick-axes, axes, hoes, etc., for building houses and cultivating the soil; and it is to be noted that from this epoch expenses have vastly increased, and that we have lost whole provinces, with many ancient towns, notably in Texas, Coahuila, Nueva Vizcaya, Nuevo México, and Sonora.

"In the provinces named we come upon ruins of Spanish and Indian pueblos. If we ask of the missionaries the cause of these ruins, of the decadence of the missions, of the repugnance of the Gentiles to gather in *doctrinas*, and of the innumerable apostates fugitive in the mountains, they attribute all to the natural inconstancy of the Indians and their impatience of subordination and labor. But it is my conviction, after many years' experience in missions, that the true causes are the following: (1) The confiding to a single missionary of two, three, or more widely separated pueblos, with the result that the Indians fail of instruction in religion and in Christian obligations, becoming in some cases worse than Gentiles; (2) the exempting of the Indians from tithes, whereby there is imposed upon the missionary the burden of countless personal community services; also the punishing of Indians with lashes for small faults, which in the case of the old and married produces shame and *saxza* of mind, so that at times the victims die of chagrin and melancholy, or desert to the mountains, or, if women, are rejected by their husbands; (3) the confiding (upon secularization) of a large district to a single curate, with the result of much apostasy, as upon the four rivers, Sinaloa, Fuerte, Mayo, and Hiaqui, and in the Sierra Gorda; (4) the levying of contributions by curates; (5) the maintaining of dispersed ranchos of Spaniards, mulattoes, and other castes, who by their isolation become a prey to Gentile Indians; (6) the keeping of lands in common, whence it results that the most powerful appropriate them in order to form haciendas fifteen, twenty, and thirty leagues in extent; (7) unlimited authority on the part of *alcaldes mayores;* lack in Spanish pueblos of subordinate judicial officers; helplessness in Indian pueblos on the part of ordinary *alcaldes* against the *alcaldes mayores;* (8) failure to observe the printed *Reglamento de Presidios* requiring the presidios to be so aligned as to protect the frontier of the internal provinces.

"All of the above evils may be corrected under the plan of four Franciscan *custodias* resolved upon by the supreme government; but the following safeguards should be instituted: (1) The *comisario-general* of the Indies should choose the first *custodios* and missionaries, but by and with the advice of Padre Reyes; (2) a *junta* of the most distinguished subjects of the Provincias should be assembled to fix the limits of *custodia* districts, assigning to each a portion of the infidel frontier.

"It is especially necessary to give attention to California, where the missions [those of Baja California] are almost entirely ruined. Navigation and commerce with the four rivers and missions of the coasts of Cinaloa, Ostimuri, Pimería Alta and Baja should be encouraged, as these provinces are near the interior [gulf] coast of California, and extend well toward the Colorado River. The *Custodia* of California should place missionaries in the pueblos nearest the sea in the aforesaid provinces, so that small boats may be built and mutual succor given. In this way, in time, there would be occupied the islands, María, Tiburón, and others. . . . In all the Provincias there are no schools for the instruction of the youth. It should be ordered that in every *hospicio* there be at once placed primary teachers, and later teachers of a grade more advanced. Uniformity among missionaries should be enforced to the extent that they wear robes of the same color, length, and cut, and there should be adopted a uniform set of ordinances. . . . In all the Provincias the Indians should retain their natural liberty without obligation to perform community labor, or render personal service to missionaries or secular judges. . . . There should be put in effect the instruction of Visitador-General Gálvez, that lands be granted to the Indians in severalty — one irrigated plot and one range plot; and that, without prejudice to the Indians, the same favor be granted to Spaniards, mulattoes, and the other castes. To the padre missionary there should belong only the *huerta* [garden] of the mission; all the mountains and uncultivated lands remaining the common property of the pueblos. The Indians should be compelled to assemble in pueblos of fifty or more families, as likewise the Spaniards, mulattoes, and other castes, thus lessening the danger of Gentile raids. In every pueblo of fifty families there should reside one missionary priest; in every pueblo of a hundred families, two missionary priests; and so forth. In all frontier pueblos and missions there should reside two missionary priests of experience and proved fidelity, and to these there should be given liberal alms. The Indians should pay tithes, but all brotherhoods and almoners, even though of the mendicant orders, should be prohibited. In every mission there should be elected annually two *alcaldes*, two *regidores*, and a *síndico-procurador*. In pueblos where Spaniards and Indians live together, the offices should be divided, but the *síndico-procurador* should be a Spaniard. Inasmuch as large settlements of Spaniards have ever been the safeguard of our American colonies, and the means of controlling the fickleness of the natives, let there be conceded by his Majesty the privileges of one or two cities and of four or six *villas* in the provinces of California, Sonora, Nueva Vizcaya, and Nuevo México. The foregoing suggestions having been observed, the *milicia* could be so handled as to afford a good defense, even though all the presidios were suppressed, establishments which (besides being useless as now distributed) are a burden on the royal treasury of a million and more than 200,000 *pesos* annually." (S. A., Madrid, Bib. Nac. MS., no. 2550.)

10. M. A.,Arch. Genl., *Misiones*, 14. The protest (Sec. 24) points out that the *Custodia* plan as advocated by Reyes squarely contradicts statements of the prelate made in his *Informe* of 1772.

11. Reyes's plea for *custodias* was sent to Gálvez on Sept. 9, 1776. On May 20, 1782, there was issued a royal decree establishing the system. On Feb. 11, 1783, the protest by the colleges was signed. The reply of the Bishop bore date June 20, 1783, and on Jan. 14, 1784, the protest was disallowed under the *rúbrica* of Gálvez (M. A.,Arch. Genl., *Misiones*, 14). In 1783 (Jan. 8), Guardian Pangua instructed Serra (should he receive orders to establish the *Custodia* in Alta California) to temporize; and on Feb. 3, Pangua addressed a letter to Guardian Pérez of Santa Cruz (Querétaro) and one to the

Guardian of the Guadalupe College (Zacatecas) couched in terms afterward employed in the protest. In 1785 (April 12), Guardian Sancho instructed Lasuén (president of the Monterey establishments) that there remained naught to be done but, *punto en boca* [stitch in lip], to obey the royal orders (B. C., *Arch. Sta. Bárb.*, vol. xii, pp. 158, 200, 214–15). Meantime in Sonora Bishop Reyes found himself thwarted. On July 24, 1784, he wrote to Neve (comandante-general after Croix) that upon him, "in whom, for the Provincias Internas, there resided *todas las Vice-Regias Facultades*, it depended to establish and confirm the *Custodia*, already erected, of San Carlos de Sonora." "License, it was reported, had been given for many *religiosos* to withdraw from their missions, and if they withdrew, the *Custodia* must perish from *insubsistencia.*" This letter on Oct. 1 was followed by one to the Viceroy, stating that Neve had just died. The Viceroy in 1785 addressed to each of the colleges — San Fernando, Santa Cruz, and Guadalupe — an injunction of obedience, an injunction reflected in the *punto en boca* order of Pangua to Lasuén (M. A., Arch. Genl., *Mis.* 14). As late as 1787 (March 20), a royal *cédula* required missionaries for the California establishments to be taken from Michoacán if they could not be supplied by the College of San Fernando (B. C., *Arch. Sta. Bárb.*, vol. x, p. 287). In 1784 (Nov. 9) Palou had sent to Bishop Reyes a plan of the Californias, showing by the sparseness of population, the vastness of the distance, and the roughness of the roads, how impossible it would be to collect there in support of the *Custodia una tortilla de limosna.* (M. A., Museo, *Docs. Rel. á las Mis. de Califs.*, Qto iii.) The *Custodia* in Sonora, J. D. Arricivita, *Crónica Seráfica*, pp. 564–75.

12. M. A., Museo, *Docs. Rel. á las Mis. de Califs.*, Qto ii; B. C., *Arch. Sta. Bárb.*, vol. x, p. 99. Lasuén makes the point that by the same laws appealed to by Neve, *alcalde* elections are required to take place *en presencia de los curas* [secular priests], and that the missionaries do not presume to be such. In other words, it is not contemplated by the Laws of the Indies that neophytes will be competent to choose *alcaldes* until they have so far progressed as to be free of missionary jurisdiction. On Dec. 9, 1782, Fages instructed Palou that the Indians at his mission must, on Jan. 1, 1783, proceed to an election of *alcaldes.* (B. C., *Prov. Rec.*, vol. iii, pp. 71, 170.)

13. Neve to Fages, Sept. 7, 1782, "Instrucción" (B. C., *Prov. St. Pap.*, vol. iii, p. 127; *St. Pap. Sac.*, vol. i, p. 72). Stopping of the galleon at San Francisco or Monterey, see chapter x.

14. Fages to Palou, Jan. 2, 1787. Official communications may be franked but not *correspondencia* by the padres *entre sí.* (*Ibid.*)

15. Croix to Mayorga, Sept. 27, 1781 (M. A., Arch. Genl., *Californias*, 33). Communication emphasizes point that departure of padres without a government license, and unlicensed change of padres from one station to another, are acts contravening the *Patronato Real.* Replies by Serra to letters from Croix covering same point, April 26 and 28, 1782. The Father-President argues that the *Patronato Real*, in the matters mentioned, applies not to

missions, but to *beneficios eclesiásticos formales y formados como son los curatos.* (*Ibid.*, 2, Segunda Parte.)

16. Yet what were the padres to do? Their work as missionaries often compelled them to pay visits to distant *rancherías*, absenting themselves for a night. Moreover, the mission herds and flocks (nearly 13,000 head) made *vaqueros* necessary. If soldiers might not be used as escorts, nor even dispatched as messengers, and if *vaqueros* there were none, neophytes must be employed instead, — contrary as the practice was to the law of 1568, which forbade Indians to ride, save by special license of a governor. Lasuén to Croix, Oct. 20, 1787. (M. A., Arch. Genl., *Californias*, 12.)

17. This rule was laid down by Neve in his instructions to Soler, July 12, 1782. It provided that absconders should be tempted back by promises communicated to them by other Indians that they would not be punished. "On kind treatment depended the good order of the peninsula" (B. C., *Prov. St. Pap.*, vol. iii, p. 113, secs. 33 and 34). Neve's own instructions from the Viceroy (chapter VII of text, n. 21) were to same effect. Fages thereon, letter to J. A. Romeu, Feb. 26, 1791 (*Ibid.*, vol. x, p. 151, par. 8).

18. Dec. 7, 1785 (B. C., *Prov. Rec.*, vol. iii, p. 60).

19. The government (wrote Father Cambón of San Francisco, early in 1783) favored not the padres, who prior to the coming of Neve had freely visited the presidios in all weathers to hear confessions and say Mass. Why, therefore, should the padres favor the government? And, the summer preceding, Father Lasuén had written to the Guardian of San Fernando: "The same author of the *Reglamento* who would consign an uncompanioned padre, surrounded by Gentiles and attended by neophytes little reliable, to illness without succor, and death without the sacraments, this same Felipe de Neve has just now been accorded a personal adjutant [Nicolás Soler] at a salary of 2000 *pesos*. Adjutants I am bound to suppose necessary, but what I cannot understand is, how there is to be ascribed to a king, so provident and liberal for the temporal good of his possessions, a conception so narrow and limited for their spiritual good; the latter good being, in the royal mind, the principal one, and the former the accessory." (July 8, 1782, M. A., Museo, *Docs. Rel. á las Mis. de Califs.*, Qto ii.)

20. In a letter from Madrid to the College of San Fernando, dated Feb. 12, 1784, it is stated by Antonio Ventura de Taranco that the King has received the complaint of the padres that the order (by Neve) reducing the quota at a mission contravened the royal *cédulas* of Nov. 3, 1744, Dec. 4, 1747, and Sept. 10, 1772, and that he would take the matter under consideration (M. A., Museo, *Docs. Rel. á las Mis. de Califs.*, Qto iii). That the order was reactionary is plain. It was a settled policy that missionaries should not be solitary. Bishop Reyes, in his plea for the *Custodia*, argued that by the plan of the Mission (as carried out in Sonora) establishments had but one padre, whereas by the *Custodia* plan there would be an *hospicio* with many padres. Writing on August 20, 1785, Guardian Sancho points

out that at the same time the *Reglamento* required one padre in California, the *estatutos* for the *Custodia* (par. 6, no. 3) required *que ningún Misionero pueda vivir solo en las Misiones ó nuevas conversiones.* (M. A., Museo, *Docs. Rel. á las Mis. de Califs.*, Qto ii.)

21. Palou speaks of having seen the *Reglamento* in September, 1784. Guardian Sancho names December as the month of promulgation in the Californias.

22. *Expediente formado sobre resiprocas quexas del Governador Don Pedro Fages y Religiosos de aquellas Misiones, 1787.* (M. A., Arch. Genl., *Californias*, 12.)

23. *Ibid.*

24. Discussing the *Patronato Real,* Lasuén observed (as had Serra) that it was largely without pertinence in frontier regions like the Californias. Still the padres did not dispute the Governor's authority as *vice-patrono.* Apropos of the *Patronato,* Comandante-General Pedro de Nava in 1791 (Oct. 11) issued to the College of San Fernando elaborate instructions, prepared by Asesor [Solicitor-General] Galindo Navarro. The document traces the history of the power (chapter iii of the text, n. 26), citing specifically the *Recopilación,* ley 1, tit. 2, lib. 1; ley 1, tit. 6, lib. 1. *Curatos* and *doctrinas* (villages of converts) are first considered, and then missions. The latter, it is stated, are conducted by *religiosos que se destinan á tierras y paises de infieles y gentiles, antigua ó nuevemente descubiertos con el santo fin de predicar el Evangelio, instruir en el Doctrina Christiana, reducir á pueblos, y convertir á Nuestra Santa Fé Católica á sus naturales y habitantes.* These are the true missions treated of in leyes 36, 37, and 38 (lib. i, tit. 6). When missions in *nuevos descubrimientos* are to be erected, the following is the course to be pursued: (1) The governor of the province and the *ordinario* (bishop) are to be consulted, and the number and qualifications of padres are to be specified; (2) removals of padres by provincials are to be made only for just and necessary causes; and (3) viceroys, *audiencias, justicias,* archbishops and bishops are to help and honor mission undertakings. But (it is stated) a great abuse, *antiguo y contrario á las citadas leyes,* prevails in the Provincias Internas. More than a century has elapsed since missions there became *verdaderas doctrinas y beneficios curados,* subject to leyes 24 and 41, tit. 6, lib. 1, of the *Recopilación,* yet they continue to be classed as *nuevas conversiones.* It is only in Nueva California that true missions now exist. (M. A., Museo, *Docs. Rel. á las Califs.*, Qto iii.)

25. Goycochea (comandante at Santa Bárbara) to Fages, Nov. 19, 1786 (B. C., *Prov. St. Pap.,* vol. vi, p. 57); Fages to Vicente Félix (*Prov. St. Pap.,* vol. vii, p. 145). Visiting of *rancherías,* except by license, forbidden. Indian women at pueblos not to be allowed in houses. Punishment of an Indian to be conducted in presence of the head man of his *ranchería,* and to consist of fifteen or twenty lashes applied humanely. Whites to be punished for misdemeanors against Indians. It is significant that while at the pueblos a

comisionado was needed to oversee Spanish *alcaldes*, such oversight by the padres in the case of Indian *alcaldes* was (at first) not permitted. On necessity for *comisionados*, Fages to Romeu, Feb. 26, 1791 (*Ibid.*, vol. x, p. 151, pars. 5, 6, of doc.).

26. B. C., *Arch. Sta. Bárb.*, vol. viii, pp. 133–34; xii, pp. 24–25.

27. B. C., *Prov. St. Pap.*, vol. vi, pp. 51, 58; vii, pp. 43, 58–59. Fages to Palou, Jan. 2, 1787, describes the founding of Sta. Bárbara Mission as effected Dec. 16. (M. A., Museo, *Docs. Rel. á las Mis. de Califs.*, Qto iii. See *Prov. Rec.*, vol. i, pp. 192–93; *Prov. St. Pap.*, vol. vi, pp. 112–13.) Six new missionaries had arrived from Spain. Writing on June 22, 1787, to the Guardian of San Fernando, the Secretary-General for the Indies said that until the appointment of a successor to José de Gálvez, who had died at Aranjuez on the night of June 17, passes to missionaries could not be given. (M. A., Museo, *Docs. Rel. á las Mis. de Califs.*, Qto iii.)

28. B. C., *Prov. St. Pap.*, vol. v, p. 9.

29. M. A., Museo, *Docs. Rel. á las Mis. de Califs.*, Qto iii.

30. Correspondence, Fages, Ugarte y Loyola, Revilla Gigedo, 1789–1790. Fages's letter asking to be relieved bore date Dec. 4, 1789. Romeu appointed May 18, 1790. (M. A., Arch. Genl., *Californias*, 70; B. C., *Prov. St. Pap.* (Benicia), vol. i, pp. 8–10. See also *Prov. St. Pap.*, vol. ix, pp. 308, 346–47; x, pp. 139, 144–45.)

31. B. C., *Prov. St. Pap.* (Benicia), vol. i, pp. 8–10; x, pp. 150–51.

32. B. C., *Prov. Rec.*, vol. iii, pp. 127, 144; ii, pp. 105–06, 111; *Prov. St. Pap.*, vol. v, pp. 254–55.

33. *Instancia de Doña Eulalia Callis, muger de Don Pedro Fages, governador de Californias, sobre que se le oyga en justicia y redima de la opresion que padece, 1785.* (M. A., Arch. Genl., *Prov. Int.* 120.)

34. M. A., Museo, *Docs. Rel. á las Mis. de Califs.*, Qto iii.

CHAPTER IX

DOMESTIC EQUILIBRIUM

New Chapter Sources: *Informe*, J. B. Matute to comandante at San Blas, Nov. 7, 1793, covering expedition by sea to the port of Bodega; *informe* by Pedro Callejas, Guardian of San Fernando, Oct. 23, 1797, on provision of *Reglamento* reducing quota of padres at missions; letter, R. Verger, Guardian of San Fernando, to M. L. Casafonda, Comisario-General of the Indies, June 30, 1771, stating that the missions of the peninsula never would become pueblos; *expediente* on the charges preferred by Padre Antonio de la Concepción — a collection containing (besides documents hitherto available) Borica's *informe*, Dec. 31, 1798, and *Resumen y Notas de los estados de Misiones*, July 8, 1797; Lasuén's request for Concepción's deportation, Aug. 19, 1797; Borica's reply, Dec. 13, 1797; Buenaventura Sitjar's letter to Lasuén, Jan. 31, 1799, describing Concepción's conduct at San Miguel; *informe* by Miguel Lull, Guardian of San Fernando, Oct. 9, 1799; *informes* by padres at Purísima and San Buenaventura, 1800, and by R. Carrillo, comandante at Santa Bárbara, 1802; letter by Guardian and *discretos* of San Fernando to Viceroy, March 23, 1805; letters of *fiscal* to College of San Fernando and to Governor Arrillaga, April 19, 1805; medical report and orders for Concepción's return to Spain, 1801–1805. (M. A.) Mention should also be made of documents in the Spanish Archives pertaining to the Nootka Sound affair. See *The Nootka Sound Controversy*, W. R. Manning, Washington, 1905. (Specific citations below.)

1. Order dated Nov. 23–24, 1792, carried into effect 1793 (*Instrucciones de los Virreyes*, secs. 291–293).

2. Captain J. Cook, *A Voyage to the Pacific*, 3 vols., vol. ii, pp. 295–96, vol. iii, pp. 434–35.

3. W. Coxe, *Russian Discoveries*, pp. 209, 210, 234–35, 248.

4. R. Greenhow, *Oregon and California*, chap. 7; H. H. Bancroft, *Northwest Coast*, vol. i, chap. 6.

5. Comte de la Pérouse, *Voyage autour du Monde*, Paris, 1798, 4 vols., vol. ii, pp. 309–317. Captain Cook regarded the fur trade as of problematical outcome even for England, unless an interoceanic passage were discovered.

6. M. A., Arch. Genl., *Historia*, 396.

7. S. A., Arch. Gen. de Indias, Sevilla, 90–3–18, cited in *The Nootka Sound Controversy*, W. R. Manning.

8. W. R. Manning, *The Nootka Sound Controversy*, chap. 13. See also Greenhow, pp. 191, 210; Bancroft, *Northwest Coast*, vol. i, chap. 7; Conde de Revilla Gigedo, *Informe*, April, 1793, — Translation, *Land of Sunshine*, vol. xi, p. 168.

Assertion by Spain of exclusive sovereignty in the Pacific: Laws of Philip II, based on grant by Pope Alexander VI and successors. By these laws all intercourse with foreigners, except by express permission, was forbidden under penalty of death and confiscation. Said Antonio de Morga in his *Sucesos*, 1609: "The crown and sceptre of Spain have extended themselves wherever the sun sheds its light, from its rising to its setting, with the glory and splendor of their power and majesty " (B. and R., *Philippine Islands*, vol. xv, p. 37). In accordance with this idea, the Manila galleon, upon reaching that part of the North Pacific where direction was changed to the south, was said to have entered the "Gulf of New Spain." Said Montesclaros, Viceroy of Peru, addressing the King in 1612: "They [the Dutch] content themselves with going in the Pacific where they are received, and with receiving what they are given, without caring much whether others enter that district, while your Majesty desires, as is right, to be absolute and sole ruler, and to shut the gate to all who do not enter under the name and title of vassals." (*Ibid.*, xvii, p. 228.) In 1692 a strong royal order was issued against foreigners in the Pacific. (Manning, p. 357.) In 1788, when the American ship Columbia entered the Pacific, she stopped at a port in the island of Juan Fernández. Here she was permitted to refit and continue her voyage to Nootka Sound. For granting the permission the governor of the islands (Blas Gonzáles) was cashiered by the Captain-General of Chile, who in turn was sustained by the Viceroy of Peru. (Manning, pp. 309–10.) In point of usage and treaties, Spain's pretension as to the Pacific was strong — treaties of 1670 and 1783. (*Ibid.*, p. 358; also Pizarro y Mangino, *Compendio Histórico*, etc., *para excluir á todas las Naciones de la Navegación de las Mares de Indias*, etc., Ayer Coll., Newberry Library.) "The Nootka Convention," observes Dr. Manning, "was the first express renunciation of Spain's ancient claim to exclusive sovereignty over the American shores of the Pacific Ocean and the South Seas." (*The Nootka Sound Controversy*, p. 462.)

9. W. R. Manning, *The Nootka Sound Controversy*, p. 442.

10. *Ibid.*, pp. 442–45; Flórez-Revilla-Gigedo correspondence, Aug. 27–Sept. 30, 1789 (M. A., Arch. Genl., *Historia*, 65); Same, with full correspondence on seizure of British vessels (S. A., as cited by Manning in *The Nootka Sound Controversy*, chap. 6). See also H. H. Bancroft, *Northwest Coast*, vol. i, chap. 7.

Martínez's diary for 1789 has been lost. Bancroft (*Northwest Coast*, vol. i, p. 212) reports it not found; and Manning (p. 342, n. *a*) reports it missing from S. A. at Sevilla. There exists in the M. A. a letter from Martínez to Flórez, dated Dec. 6, 1789, reporting his arrival at San Blas *en devido cumplimiento de la Sup^{or} Orden de V. E. de 25 de Febrero*. Revilla Gigedo was surprised at the return of Martínez, but later (Feb. 26, 1790) it came to his knowledge that on October 13, 1789, an order for Martínez's transfer to Spain had been issued from Madrid, because of failure to provide support for his family. (M. A., Arch. Genl., *Historia*, 65.)

11. Fidalgo and Elisa, B. C., *Viajes al Norte de Californias*, nos. 8, 10, 7; M. A., Arch. Genl., *Historia*, 68, 69, 71; Malaspina, M. A., Arch. Genl., *Historia*, 397; J. Caamaño . . . "á comprobar la Relación de Fonte," M. A., Arch. Genl., *Historia*, 69, 71.

12. G. Vancouver, *A Voyage of Discovery to the North Pacific Ocean . . . in the years 1790–95*, 3 vols., 1798, vol. i, p. 388; Greenhow, *Oregon and California*, pp. 239–46; Revilla Gigedo, *Informe*, April, 1793, — Translation, *Land of Sunshine*, vol. xi, pp. 168–73.

13. Revilla Gigedo, *Informe*, April, 1793; Translation, *Land of Sunshine*, vol. xi, p. 169. The instructions from Spain were that the boundary line between California and the free territory on the north be fixed at 48°, Nootka being divided between Spain and England.

14. Bancroft, *Northwest Coast*, vol. i, pp. 302–303; Manning, *The Nootka Sound Controversy*, pp. 467–71.

15. Basadre y Vega to Viceroy Gálvez, Dec. 20, 1786 (M. A., Arch. Genl., *Historia*, 396).

16. Pérouse, *Voyage autour du Monde*, tom. ii, pp. 288–89.

17. B. C., *Prov. St. Pap. Mil.* (Benicia), vol. xx, p. 3; *St. Pap.* (Sacramento), vol. i, p. 115; vol. v, p. 6.

18. Arrillaga to Viceroy, acknowledging receipt of instructions, July 16, 1793 (B. C., *Prov. St. Pap. Mil.* (Benicia), vol. xix, pp. 1–2).

19. *Ibid.*

20. Arrillaga to Viceroy, Aug. 20, 1793: mentions instructions to occupy Bodega, as of date March 30, and reports as to land expedition thither (B. C., *Prov. St. Pap.*, vol. xxi, p. 113). J. B. Matute to comandante at San Blas, Nov. 7, 1793: full report of expedition by sea (M. A., Arch. Genl., *Historia*, 71). Interest attaches to this report as covering facts upon which Bancroft found no information. Bodega project abandoned, Viceroy to Arrillaga, June 9, 1794. (*Ibid.* See also B. C., *Prov. St. Pap.*, vol. xi, p. 175.)

21. Borica to Francisco Joaquín Valdéz (B. C., *Prov. St. Pap.*, vol. xxi, p. 198). Other letters (May 16, 17, 21, and June 15, 1794) to his brother-in-law, to his mother-in-law, Doña Juniata, to Arrillaga, and to Valdéz. To Arrillaga he is very jocose, describing the *habilitado* at Loreto as what he himself would be as prior of Santo Domingo, and observing that his "jewel of a treasurer has gone on sprees which interfere with work." (*Ibid.*, pp. 201–205.)

22. Borica to Antonio Cordero (*Ibid.*, p. 209). Other letters, — to Manuel de Cárcaba, "My Lord Fox," Savino de la Pedruzea, Antonio Grajera, to his sister (Bernarda), and to Francisco Hijosa, — Nov. 13, 1794 to Sept. 13, 1795. From Cárcaba he asks five or six pairs of gloves, — buckskin, chamois, rabbit-skin, — as at Monterey it is quite cold. To the same he expresses hope that they both may be made generals when the Prince of Asturias marries. To Hijosa he sends seal-skins for gifts to Cárcaba and Lanza. (*Ibid.*, pp. 210–228.)

23. In 1776 (Oct. 23), Bucarely, pursuant to instructions (chapter vii of text, nn. 11, 12) had ordered Neve to see that Captain Cook's vessels were refused admission to California ports (B. C., *Prov. St. Pap.*, vol. i, p. 213). In 1780 (Aug. 25) Croix had advised Neve of the supposed approach of a part of Admiral Hughes's fleet to the South Sea, with the object of destroying commerce and ransacking the meridional coasts of the Spanish dominions, etc. (*Ibid.*, vol. ii, p. 112.) In 1789 (May 13) Fages had warned Argüello, at San Francisco, to capture the Columbia with "skill and caution" should she appear (B. C., *Miss. and Col.*, vol. i, pp. 53–54). The Columbia and her commander were as courteously treated by Martínez at Nootka as they had been by Gonzáles at the Juan Fernández Islands. (Letters of Martínez, (M. A., Arch. Genl., *Historia*, 65.)

24. Stringent orders by Viceroy to Arrillaga, August, 1793, to expel foreign ships from California ports "without pretext or excuse," save in most urgent cases of distress (B. C., *Prov. St. Pap.*, vol. xi, p. 96). In 1795 orders were issued by Borica that all ships which approached California ports under Spanish colors were on landing to be searched, in order to determine whether Spanish or not. (*Ibid.*, vol. xiii, p. 16; vol. xiv, p. 29.)

25. Viceroy Miguel José de Azanza to Borica, Dec. 21, 1799, Feb. 8, 1800, regarding Kamtchatka. (B. C., *Prov. St. Pap.* (Sacramento), vol. ix, p. 54; *Prov. Rec.*, vol. x, p. 5.) Fear of the United States was not a new emotion in Spain. In 1783 the Conde de Aranda (just returned from signing, at Paris, the treaty preliminary to the recognition by Great Britain of American independence) had proposed an independent Mexico and Peru as an offset to independent America, — a land which otherwise might be expected to encroach on New Spain. Furthermore, in 1787 there had arrived at Vera Cruz, as viceroy of Mexico, Manuel Antonio Flórez, vice-admiral of the royal navy, and on Dec. 23, 1788, Flórez, citing the Nootka voyages of the Columbia, had thus written to his government: "We ought not to be surprised that the English colonies of America, being now an independent Republic, should carry out the design of finding a safe port on the Pacific and of attempting to sustain it by crossing the immense country of the continent above our possessions of Texas, New Mexico, and California." (Flórez to Valdéz, S. A., Arch. Genl. de Indias, Sevilla, 90–3–18, cited by Manning.)

26. Costansó, *Informe*, Oct. 17, 1794 (B. C., Pinart Collection, *Papeles Varios*, p. 193). On July 25, 1795, Viceroy Branciforte advised Borica of the sending of aid sufficient to man the three batteries at San Francisco, Monterey, and San Diego. (B. C., *Prov. St. Pap.*, vol. xiii, p. 51.)

27. The total military force of Alta California after 1796–97 was 280 men of the presidial companies, and 90 Catalan volunteers and artillerymen. In 1794, Costansó placed the total at 218. In 1795, Branciforte placed it at 225. Arrillaga desired 271, and Borica 335 men. Córdoba sent to Mexico plans for fortifications (Córdoba, *Informe*, 1796). Borica to Viceroy (B. C., *St. Pap.* (Sacramento), vol. iv, pp. 56–57).

28. Plan of Pitic (B. C., *Miss. and Col.*, vol. i, p. 343; translated, J. W. Dwinelle, *The Colonial History of San Francisco*, 1863, Add. no. vii). Commentary on Plan of Pitic (*Ibid.*, pp. 30–33).

29. *Informe*, May 11, 1796 (B. C., *Arch. Sta. Bárb.*, vol. ii, p. 73).

30. *Informe*, May 14, 1796 (M. A., Museo, *Docs. Rel. á las Mis. de Califs.*, Qto ii; B. C., *Arch. Sta. Bárb.*, vol. ii, p. 42).

31. B. C., *St. Pap.*, vol. xiii, p. 183.

32. Córdoba to Borica, July 20, 1796 (B. C., *Miss. and Col.*, vol. i, p. 576).

33. Branciforte to Borica, instructions as to founding of *villa*, Jan. 25, 1797 (B. C., *Miss. and Col.*, vol. i, p. 78). List of colonists, Jan. 23, 1797 (B. C., *Prov. St. Pap.*, vol. xv, p. 223).

34. Instructions, Borica to Moraga, July 17, 1797 (B. C., *Miss. and Col.*, vol. i, p. 360).

35. Borica to *comisionado* at Branciforte, Jan. 25, Oct. 29, Dec. 5, 1798 (B. C., *Arch. Sta. Cruz*, p. 71; *Prov. St. Pap.*, vol. xxi, p. 50). Borica to *alcalde* of San José, March 27, April 8, 1799; same to *comisionado* of San José, April 20, 1799 (B. C., *Prov. Rec.*, vol. iv, pp. 291, 293, 294).

36. B. C., *Prov. Rec.*, vol. iv, p. 56; *Prov. St. Pap.*, vol. xxi, p. 271.

37. B. C., *Prov. Rec.*, vol. vi, p. 55; *Prov. St. Pap.*, vol. xvii, p. 19.

38. M. A., Arch. Genl., *Prov. Int. 5*, exped. 11.

39. Branciforte to Guardian of San Fernando, Aug. 19, 1796, stating that it would be impracticable to conform to the *Reglamento* with respect to foundations toward the east, as there were no fit lands, and it would not be prudent to expose missionaries or guard to the *genio feroz* of the Gentiles there. (M. A., Museo, *Docs. Rel. á las Mis. de Califs.*, Qto iii.)

40. POPULATION OF ALTA CALIFORNIA

	A. D. 1783	A. D. 1790	A. D. 1795	A. D. 1797	A. D. 1800
Neophytes	4027	7353			13,500
Spaniards		970		1200	1200
Neophytes and Spaniards				11,226	12,921

— (B. C., *St. Pap. Mis.*, vol. i, p. 5; M. A., Arch. Genl., *Californias*, 74.)

According to figures submitted by Borica on July 24, 1797, the total of Spaniards was 832; of Indians, 11,060; of *mestizos*, 464; of mixed color, 385; of slaves, 1. The grand total of population was 12,748 (M. A., Arch. Genl., *Californias*, 74). At the end of 1804 the grand total of neophytes was reported as 19,099 (M. A., *Docs. Rel. á las Mis. de Califs.*, Qto i).

In 1800, the total livestock was 187,000 head: 88,000 sheep, 74,000 cattle, 24,000 horses, 1000 mules, etc.

41. On Sept. 10, 1790, Fages computed as needful for the instruction of neophytes in each of the presidial districts of Alta California: 2 carpenters, 2 smiths, 1 armorer, 1 mason, 1 weaver, 1 master-mechanic, 1 tanner, 1 stone-cutter, 1 tailor, 1 potter. In 1790 there were the following craftsmen

in Los Ángeles: 3 ploughmen, 1 builder, 1 tailor, 2 shoemakers, 1 master-mechanic, 1 smith, 1 *jomateros*, 6 herdsmen, 2 muleteers, 7 pickmen. In 1790 in Alta California as a whole there were: 2 silversmiths, 5 miners, 38 ploughmen, 19 owners of ranchos, 2 master-mechanics or builders, 5 carpenters, 3 smiths, 6 tailors, 2 masons, 8 shoemakers, 1 doctor, 123 herdsmen and muleteers. In 1797, Borica reported the principal branch of mission industry to be the weaving of woolen cloth. At San Luis Obispo, San Gabriel, San Francisco, and San Juan Capistrano some cotton cloth was woven, but as the raw material must be obtained from San Blas, it was difficult to continue the work. At all the missions hides were cured and deer-skins collected. Some Indians of San Carlos were being taught carpentry and masonry. At San Francisco two or three were being taught blacksmithing, and at Santa Clara, tanning. There was a mill at San Luis Obispo and another at Santa Cruz. (*Resumen y Notas de los Estados de Misiones*, July 8, 1897, — M. A., Arch. Genl., *Prov. Int.* 216.)

42. Borica to Father José Lorente, Feb. 1, 1795: Guards will be furnished to padres, even though forbidden by orders, strictly construed (B. C., *Prov. St. Pap.*, vol. xxi); Branciforte to Guardian of San Fernando, Nov. 7, 1795 (M. A., Museo, *Docs. Rel. á las Mis. de Califs.*, Qto iii).

43. Borica to Lasuén, Sept. 22, 1796 (B. C., *Prov. Rec.*, vol. vi, p. 173). Borica to same, Dec. 2, 1796 (*Ibid.*, p. 178). Lasuén to padres from Soledad to San Diego, circular directing elections *pro forma* and as a means merely for neophyte enlightenment for the future. "There can be no regular civil government as by Laws of Indies till the missions become pueblos or *doctrinas.*" (B. C., *Arch. Sta. Bárb.*, vol. xi, p. 138.) Viceroy to Lasuén, Dec. 20, 1797, calls attention to requirement of *Reglamento* as to *alcaldes*, and explains that elections are for the political advancement of Indians as contemplated by law 20, tit. i, lib. vi of the *Recopilación*. (*Ibid.*, vol. x, p. 90.) Cf. chapter viii of text, nn. 6, 12, 24.

44. As stated in chapter viii, note 20, the provision of the *Reglamento* for reducing the quota of padres from two to one at a mission was contravened by the royal order of May 20, 1782, approving the *estatutos* of Comisario-General Manuel de la Vega, which provided that *ningún Misionero pueda recidir, ni vivir solo en los Pueblos, Misiones y nuevas conversiones.* On Feb. 3, 1797, Branciforte wrote to the Guardian of San Fernando, stating that he could not find the *cédula* in his *secretaría de cámara*, and asking for a copy. On Oct. 23, 1797, a full exposition of the law was made by the Guardian (Pedro Callejas). He showed that by law 24, 7, part 1 (?) of the *Recopilación*, it was decreed that no religious ought to be allowed to die alone in *villa* or *castillo*, or to be placed alone in a parochial church, but with brethren, so that he might be aided "to contend with the world, the flesh, and the devil." In confirmation of the old law there were *cédulas* by Felipe V and Fernando VI, of dates Nov. 13, 1744, and Dec. 4, 1747. (M. A., Museo, *Docs. Rel. á las Mis. de Califs.*, Qto iii.)

As for chaplain duty at the presidios (an old question), reports to Borica by the comandantes of the four presidios show that it was reasonably well performed everywhere save at San Francisco. (M. A., Arch. Genl., *Californias*, 12.)

45. June 30, 1771 (M. A., Museo, *Trasuntos*).

46. To Pedro de Alberni, August 3, 1796 (B. C., *Prov. St. Pap. Mil.* (Benicia), vol. xxiv, pp. 7-8).

The backward condition mentioned to Alberni was ascribed by Borica to four distinct causes: (1) Loss of freedom, the Indians being a race unable to endure subjection of any kind, industrial or political; (2) insufficient food, the missions not raising enough grain; (3) filth of body and abodes; (4) corralling of Indian girls and women at night in straitened and ill-ventilated quarters, — *monjas*, so-called, or nunneries. The Governor had inspected some at a time when they were empty, and "so pestiferous were they that he had not been able to endure them for a single minute." Indian mortality was great. From 1769 to 1797, baptisms had been 21,653 and deaths 10,437. If gain was to be made, the Indians must be given more freedom, fed on warm meals, punished more moderately, compelled to bathe often, and to keep their huts clean. The girls and women must be provided at night with spacious quarters. There soon would be no Indians on the existing plan of treatment. (*Resumen y Notas de los Estados de Misiones*, July 8, 1897, — M. A., Arch. Genl., *Prov. Int.* 216.) Replying to Borica, Lasuén asserted that the mission Indians were fatter and better than the Gentiles. The *monjas* were kept as clean and well ventilated as possible, and it was not the inmates that died, but those that betook themselves to the mountains. (Lasuén to Guardian of San Fernando, Nov. 12, 1800, June 19, 1801, — *Ibid.*, secs. 27, 28, 31.)

The object of the *monjas*, it may be explained, was the preservation of morality. As for Indian mortality at this period, the following table was submitted in 1796 for the period 1792-96: —

At San Francisco,	15.75 per cent
Sta. Clara,	12.62
Sta. Cruz,	11.75
San Carlos,	7.87
La Soledad,	6.83
San Antonio,	4.12
San Luis Obispo,	5.50
La Purísima,	5.50
Sta. Bárbara,	8.45
San Buenaventura,	7.50
San Gabriel,	6.87
San Juan Capistrano,	5.75
San Diego,	6.25

In Europe the mortality (in villages) was stated to be 2.5 per cent; and in towns of moderate size, 4 per cent. In Spain as a whole it was a little over 3 per cent. (B. C., *Misiones*, i.)

47. On Sept. 27, 1793, Guardian Pangua of San Fernando reported to Viceroy Revilla Gigedo that the Alta California missions were in no condition to be secularized. "These new Christians," he said, "like tender plants not yet well rooted, easily wither, reverting to their old Gentile liberty and indolent savage life." He even remarked that the Sierra Gorda establishments had deteriorated since secularization (M. A., Arch. Genl., *Prov. Int.* 5). On Dec. 27, 1793, the Viceroy wrote to the government at Madrid: "I am not well satisfied with the missions that have been secularized, nor will I take this step [Secularization], unless success is assured. *Clérigos* [curates] can do no more than *religiosos* [friars]." (B. C., *Miss. and Col.*, vol. i, p. 25, sec. 423.)

48. In 1785, 1788, and 1791, Fages had complained of punishment of neophytes by various padres. (B. C., *Prov. Rec.*, vol. iii, pp. 51, 67; *Prov. St. Pap.*, vol. x, p. 167.)

49. M. A., Museo, *Trasuntos*. Serra cites also the example of San Francisco Solano in Peru, who, though gifted by God with the power of taming the ferocity of the most barbarous by his presence and sweet words, nevertheless corrected disobedience even on the part of *alcaldes* by the lash. (B. C., *Arch. Sta. Bárb.*, vol. x, p. 99.)

50. Neve, instructions to his successor, Sept. 7, 1782. For cattle-stealing he has been compelled to punish both neophytes and Gentiles, by eight or ten days in the stocks, or twenty or twenty-five lashes (B. C., *Prov. St. Pap.* (Sacramento), vol. i, p. 72). Borica to Padre Mariano Apolinario, Sept. 26, 1796 (B. C., *Prov. Rec.*, vol. vi, p. 174 *et seq.*). In 1787, Fages had ordered fifteen or twenty lashes for cattle-stealing (*Prov. St. Pap.*, vol. vii, p. 145). Gasol, Guardian of San Fernando, forbade more than twenty-five lashes for neophytes. (B. C., *Patentes Eclesiásticas*, part ii, sec. 8.)

51. B. C., *Prov. St. Pap.*, vol. xiii, p. 147. Borica to Lasuén, Sept. 15 and Oct. 3, 1796 (B. C., *Prov. Rec.*, vol. vi, pp. 172, 176). For securing the return of runaways, the padres at San Francisco were in the habit of sending out neophyte bands. Against this practice Borica issued orders to Alberni (B. C., *Prov. St. Pap.*, vol. xxiv, p. 8; *Prov. Rec.*, vol. v, p. 91). On July 1, 1798, Borica wrote to the Viceroy that since October, 1796, the rigor with which the Indians of San Francisco had been treated had ceased. "I do not attribute," he said, "the merit of this change to myself. . . . The true author is Father José María Fernández." (B. C., *Prov. Rec.*, vol. vi, p. 97.)

52. Grajera, comandante at San Diego, was ill; his report was sent in 1799.

53. The history of Father Concepción, as above set forth, is based upon the complete *expediente* in the Mexican Archives, entitled "Expediente

^{sre} denuncia que hizó el Padre Ant. de la Concep^{n} acerca de los Desordenes de las Misiones de Californias y mal trato q en ella se da á los neofitos" (Arch. Genl., *Prov. Int.* 216). The document entitled "La restitución á España del Misionero Fr. Antonia de la Concepción pr causa de sus enfermedades" has also been used. (M. A., Arch. Genl., *Californias*, 59.) Bancroft lacked many of the documents contained in the *expediente*. He lacked also the document pertaining to the restitution.

54. See chapter x, n. 10, where the matter is considered in connection with Arrillaga.

55. On the subject of secular education under Borica, see Bancroft, *History of California*, vol. i, pp. 642–644, and notes. In 1796, Salazar urged that instruction in *primeras letras* be given in all the missions.

56. The separation was effected August 29, 1804.

CHAPTER X

THE PROBLEM OF SUBSISTENCE

NEW CHAPTER SOURCES: B. C., Russian-American Series, MS. (Translation by Ivan Petróff) reëxamined; Mary Graham, *Our Centennial* — "Concepción Argüello," San Francisco, 1876; *The Mercury Case*, original manuscript, — Los Ángeles Public Library. (Specific citations below.)

1. Fages to Croix, June 26, 1772. States non-arrival of ship at Monterey, and scarcity. Reports having given orders for the formation of two parties to kill bears and that already some thirty have been killed. Replying to above on Oct. 14, Croix complains of lack of information concerning presidio and missions; alludes to suspicion of their abandonment; asks regarding discovery of port of San Francisco. (M. A., Arch. Genl., *Californias*, 66.)

2. May 21, 1772, Ayer Coll.; Translation, *Out West*, vol. xvi, p. 56.

3. Nov. 26, 1773 (M. A., Museo, *Docs. Rel. á las Mis. de Califs.*, Qto ii). A cause of failure by transports to reach Monterey, and sometimes San Diego, was the conviction, then strong in Mexico, that these points could better be reached overland from the peninsula (chapter VI, n. 21). On Dec. 2, 1772, the Viceroy reprimanded Fages for allowing the San Antonio to protract her voyage to Monterey. Her cargo should have been sent by land (B. C., *Prov. St. Pap.*, vol. i, p. 77). But in 1774, when Serra went north in the Santiago, the Viceroy became vexed that Pérez was induced to stop at San Diego. (M. A., Arch. Genl., *Cor. de Virreyes*, sér. ii, 38/55, no. 1421; *Ibid.*, Bucarely, 1774, 41/58, no. 1519.)

4. Cf. chapter IX, n. 8, 24. Arrillaga on Spain's attitude toward commerce: "Trade has been entirely neglected by us, but now the government is beginning to open its eyes with regard to these [California] ports. . . . The class of people engaged in [trade] is now so much respected that the King, in opposition to the rules of the Court, has given to many of them the title of *marqués*, which has never happened in Spain before. Yet when it was wished to advance our [California] trade, some private persons, who had from olden times been sending an occasional galleon from Manila to Acapulco, protested against it as an infringement upon their rights. . . . The Manilans ship on their galleon some Chinese goods. . . . We do business with some Mexicans, who, with the help of the two men-of-war annually dispatched along our coasts from San Blas, send us some goods at excessive prices, and we have to pay the *piasters* in advance in order to obtain the following year the necessaries of life." (N. P. Rezánoff to Russian Minister of Commerce, New Archangel, June 17, 1806.) See P. Tikhmeneff, *Historical Review of the Russian-American Company*, St. Petersburg, 1861 (B. C., Translation, Ivan Petróff), part ii, pp. 828–832.

5. M. A., Arch. Genl., *Cor. de Virreyes*, Bucarely, Sept. 26, 1774; *Ibid.*, 1774, 41/58, no. 1519; *Ibid.*, 1776, 67/84, no. 2542.

6. Neve to Fages, Sept.7, 1782, par. 17 (B. C., *Prov. St. Pap.* (Sacramento), vol. i, p. 72); Fages to Romeu, Feb. 26, 1791, par. 16 (B. C., *Prov. St. Pap.*, vol. x, p. 151). Prior to 1801 the stopping of the galleon at San Francisco or Monterey seems to have been dispensed with. (See Tagle's petition as cited at p. 189 of text, and Arrillaga as quoted in n. 4, *supra*.)

7. Viceroy to King, Oct. 27, 1785, inclosing *expediente* on advisability of concession and recommending it. (*Cor. de Virreyes*, Conde de Gálvez, 1785, 1, 138, no. 250.) Fages to Romeu, Feb. 26, 1791, pars. 16, 17, 18, on evils of free commerce (B. C., *Prov. St. Pap.*, vol. x, p. 151). See Bancroft, *History of California*, vol. i, p. 625, n. 2.

8. May 24, 1797 (B. C., *Prov. St. Pap.* (Sacramento), vol. ix, p. 22); Nov. 16, 1797 (B. C., *Prov. Rec.*, vol. vi, p. 61).

9. Beltrán, *Informe*, March 7, 1796 (B. C., *Prov. St. Pap.*, vol. xiv, p. 140). Borica to Viceroy, Sept. 11, 1796. It was the recommendation of the latter that Alta California be defined to extend from San Diego Presidio to that of San Francisco, "the last point that we can possess with exclusive dominion on the Northwest Coast, according to the agreement with the Court of London made in the year 1790" (B. C., *Prov. St. Pap.* (Sacramento), vol. iv, p. 49). Viceroy Iturrigaray to Governor of Californias, Aug. 29, 1804, citing royal order concerning division (B. C., *Prov. St. Pap.*, vol. xviii, p. 175; *Instrucciones de los Virreyes*, Mexico, 1867, secs. 290, 291, 293). The dividing line was declared coincident with "the stream and *ranchería* of Rosario at Barrabas."

10. From 1781 (year of the massacre on the Colorado) to 1796, the question of a Sonora-California or New Mexico-California connection had been given but little attention. In 1785 a proposal by Fages to open communication with New Mexico was forbidden by Viceroy Conde de Gálvez, on the ground of Indian hostility (B. C., *Mayer MSS.*, no. 8; *Prov. St. Pap.*, vol. xviii, p. 34). But in 1796, Aug. 20, Viceroy Branciforte wrote to Governor Borica, favoring a new attempt to found a mission on the Colorado, as suggested by the latter (B. C., *Prov. St. Pap.* (Sacramento), vol. v, p. 27), and on Sept. 11, 1796, Borica revived the plan (cf. chapter vi, n. 8; chapter vii, n. 52), whereby the Dominicans of the peninsula were to push on to the river. Let them (he said) occupy Tucsón with a view to a connection between California and New Mexico (*Ibid.*, vol. iv, p. 49). On Oct. 5, 1796, Borica wrote to the Viceroy as per the present chapter, and it was this letter that drew forth objection from Lasuén (B. C., *Arch. Sta. Bárb.*, vol. x, p. 73 *et seq.*).

Meanwhile (June, 1796), Arrillaga, lieutenant-governor of the Californias at Loreto, had begun (in the interest of the Dominicans) a survey of the peninsula to the northeast. Already there had been established the Dominican missions S^{mo} Rosario, San Pedro, Santo Domingo, San Vicente,

Santo Tomás, and San Miguel, the last only a day's journey south of San Diego; and Arrillaga's tour was for determining the practicability of a mission and presidio near the gulf on the northeast. It resulted in the founding (Nov. 12, 1797) of the mission Santa Catarina, and in a recommendation for the founding of a presidio of one hundred men either at Santa Olaya or at the mouth of the Colorado (B. C., *Prov. St. Pap.*, vol. xvi, p. 136). On Dec. 22, 1797, Borica sent Arrillaga's recommendation to the Viceroy, but advised conciliation of the Indians in order to remove the hostile feeling engendered in 1781 (B. C., *Prov. Rec.*, vol. vi, p. 65).

Pedro de Nava's *informe* bore date Chihuahua, July 20, 1801. It reviewed the communications of Borica and Arrillaga, stating objections. A New Mexico-California connection was desirable for California but not urgent. New Mexicans might be harmed by trading westward. At present Chihuahua fully met all needs, and Indians were too warlike. The *gente de razón* reported idle by Concha were required to repopulate the four abandoned pueblos on the Camino Real between Paso del Norte and Santa Fé. (B. C., *Prov. St. Pap.*, vol. xviii, p. 34.)

11. Borica in his report on commerce alludes to "the cattle ranches of Monterey, San Diego, and the newly established one in San Francisco, which are administered on the King's account."

12. Revilla Gigedo, *Informe sobre las Islas de la Mesa ó Sanduich*, Dec. 27, 1789 (M. A., Arch. Genl., *Cor. de Virreyes*, Revilla Gigedo, 1789, no. 199).

13. Jan. 28, 1797 (B. C., *Arch. Sta. Bárb.*, vol. vi, p. 185). Gálvez had said: "The idea came to me of proposing to H. M. that he order a fraternity to be founded under his immediate and supreme protection, with the jurisdiction and title of *Propaganda Fide*," etc. (*Informe*, 1771, Mexico, 1867, p. 147).

14. April 7, 1801 (B. C., *Prov. St. Pap.*, vol. xviii, p. 107). Colonial projects other than those mentioned in the text were not lacking. In 1792, Alejandro Jordán proposed to found a colony in California to supply San Blas with products, but the offer was declined by the King in 1794, for the reason that free trade by the transports would be sufficient. (Arrillaga to Viceroy, Nov. 8, 1792, etc.; Bancroft, *History of California*, vol. i, p. 503, n. 8.)

15. The leading authorities are R. Greenhow, *Oregon and California*, Boston, 1844; W. Sturgis, "Northwest Fur Trade," Hunt's *Mercantile Magazine*, vol. xiv; Russian-American Series (MS., in B. C.), translated from the Russian by Ivan Petróff; Bancroft, *History of the Northwest Coast*, vol. i, chaps. 10, 11; Same, *History of Alaska*, chap. 11.

16. As carried on under Vicente Basadre for the Spanish Government (cf. chapter IX, n. 5), the otter-skin trade was in the hands exclusively of the padres and Indians. (Fages, *Bando*, Aug. 29, 1786, — B. C., *Prov. St. Pap.*, vol. vi, p. 140; *Arch. Sta. Bárb.*, vol. i, p. 283; vol. x, p. 8; Fages, *Bando*,

Sept. 15 and 20, 1787, — B. C., *Arch. Sta. Bárb.*, vol. xii, p. 3; *Prov. Rec.*, vol. i, p. 35.) In 1788, Father Cambón welcomed the decrees of Fages as giving to the neophytes opportunity to trade and barter in merchandise of their own land — something hitherto monopolized by the soldiery (M. A., Museo, *Docs. Rel. á las Mis. de Californias*, Qto iii). In 1790, when the trade as a government monopoly ceased, the padres were deprived of a market, save as they were able to sell a few skins through the medium of the transports, or save as they sold them to American smuggling vessels. In Jan., 1791, the Guardian of San Fernando gave orders that skins were to be sent to Mexico, and Lasuén's instructions to the padres were to send them so packed that the college *síndico* "alone should know what was being sent" (B. C., *Arch. Sta. Bárb.*, vol. ix, p. 314). In 1805, the Russians thought of California as a source of bread-supply, and also, perhaps, of furs, "if not with permission of the Viceroy, at least in a private manner with the missionaries. . . . The missionaries, as far as known, were the chief agents in the contraband trade." (Tikhmeneff, *Historical Review of the Russian-American Company*, St. Petersburg, 1861, in B. C.; Translation (MS.), Ivan Petróff.) In 1806, José Gasol, Guardian of San Fernando, warned the Alta California padres not to provoke the accusation that " some of their number were trading with foreigners." (B. C., *Patentes Eclesiásticas*, p. 3.)

17. M. Rodríguez, *Informe*, April 10, 1803 (B. C., *Prov. St. Pap.*, vol. xviii, p. 252). R. J. Cleveland, *A Narrative of Voyages*, etc., 2 vols., 1842, vol. i, pp. 210–16.

18. Tikhmeneff, *Historical Review of the Russian-American Company*, St. Petersburg, 1861 (B. C.); Translation, Ivan Petróff, part ii, p. 766, etc.

19. K. Khlebnikoff, *Alexander Baránoff*, St. Petersburg, 1835 (B. C.); Translation, Ivan Petróff.

20. Tikhmeneff, part ii, p. 710. Rezánoff's instructions to Schwostoff, says Tikhmeneff, were to go to the south end of Saghalien Island, destroy the Japanese settlements, making prisoners of all the able-bodied men, especially the mechanics and tradesmen. The old and sick were to be set at liberty, never to visit Saghalien again, except to trade with the Russians. Schwostoff was to gather all the Japanese idols and a few priests, to be sent to an island in Sitka Bay, called Japanese Island to this day. . . . No reply by the Czar was made to Rezánoff's letter (quoted in text), and the Chamberlain tried to revoke his orders to Schwostoff, but the latter insisted on carrying them out. With the Juno, tended by the Awos under Davidoff, he went to Aniva [?], burned villages, destroyed Japanese vessels, appropriating cargoes and carrying on piracy for a whole summer to "coax" the Japanese into friendship. The vessels returned to Okhotsk, where the goods were seized and men arrested. (*Ibid.*, part i, pp. 176–78.)

21. Tikhmeneff, part ii, p. 766, etc. It is noteworthy that it was Rezánoff's opinion that the Russian missionaries (of whom there were a number

in the Northwest) might with profit imitate the Jesuits of Paraguay, "entering into the extensive views of the government."

22. Tikhmeneff, part ii, p. 769, etc.

23. Tikhmeneff, part ii, p. 799.

24. Tikhmeneff, part ii, pp. 801–828.

25. G. H. Langsdorff, *Voyages*, London, 1814, vol. ii, p. 153.

26. Langsdorff notes that the padres were "much pleased" with the following articles exhibited from the stores on board the Juno: linen cloths, Russian ticking, English woolen cloth. Articles inquired for were: tools for mechanical trades, implements for husbandry, household utensils, shears for shearing sheep, axes, large saws for sawing-out planks, iron cooking-vessels, casks, bottles, glasses, fine pocket- and neck-handkerchiefs, leather, particularly calf-skins, and sole-leather. (*Ibid.*, p. 173.) The ladies at the presidio inquired, he says, for cotton and muslin, shawls, striped ribands, etc. (*Ibid.*, p. 174.)

27. Tikhmeneff, part ii, pp. 808–28.

28. Langsdorff, part ii, p. 217. "The whole family of Argüello and several other friends and acquaintances had collected themselves at the fort, and wafted us an adieu with their hats and pocket-handkerchiefs."

29. *Ibid.*, pp. 183, 385.

30. Mary Graham, *Our Centennial*, San Francisco, 1876.

31. Tikhmeneff, part ii, pp. 808–28. Apropos of Chinese laborers, it is interesting to note that in 1788, Meares shipped, by the Iphigenia, Chinese smiths and carpenters to Nootka Sound, "because of their reputed hardiness, industry, and ingenuity, simple manner of life, and low wages. . . . If hereafter," Meares records, "trading-posts should be established on the American coast, a colony of these men would be a very important acquisition." (W. R. Manning, *The Nootka Sound Controversy*, p. 289.)

32. Rezánoff intended first to establish a settlement on the Strait of Juan de Fuca at Port Discovery; then settlements at Havre de Grey and on the Columbia River. "The advantageous position of the port of San Francisco was sure to attract the commerce of all nations" (Tikhmeneff, pt. i, p. 175). In 1813, Viceroy Calleja claimed a recognition by Russia (*vide* treaty, 8th of July, 1812) of Juan de Fuca Strait as the northern limit of Alta California (B. C., *Prov. St. Pap.*, vol. xix, p. 33).

33. Bancroft, *History of California*, vol. ii, pp. 298–99, and notes.

34. B. C., *Prov. St. Pap.* (Sacramento), vol. v, p. 59.

35. B. C., *Prov. St. Pap.*, vol. xix, p. 14.

36. *Ibid.*, p. 73. Arrillaga to Viceroy, Jan. 2, 1806, reporting statement by "Don José Ocain" that an individual from Philadelphia had asked Congress for 40,000 men with whom to take possession of New Spain. (B. C., *Prov. Rec.*, vol. ix, p. 70.)

37. *The Mercury Case*, MS., Los Ángeles Public Library.

38. The private rancho is considered in chapter xvi.

39. B. C., *Prov. Rec.*, vol. i, pp. 173, 181.

40. B. C., *Arch. Sta. Bárb.*, vol. vi, p. 35. Macario de Castro to Arrillaga, San José, March 24 and June 5, 1805, on necessity of killing mares (B. C., *Prov. St. Pap.*, vol. xix, p. 77). Petition of Russian-American Company stating that immense herds of wild cattle and horses range as far north as the Columbia River, and that an annual slaughter of 10,000 to 30,000 head has been ordered. (Potechin, *Selenie Ross*, 2, 3; Langsdorff, *Voyages*, vol. ii, p. 170.)

41. B. C., *Prov. St. Pap. Mil.* (Benicia), vol. xxxiii, p. 19. Depredations in 1801 (B. C., *Prov. Rec.*, vol. xi, p. 159).

42. B. C., *Arch. Sta. Bárb.*, vol. xii, p. 89.

43. Lasuén to Guardian of San Fernando, June 16, 1802: cites failure on the Colorado; makes mention of preference by Santa Bárbara Channel Indians for the Mission plan, when "some years ago" given a choice between it and *ranchería* plan (M. A., Museo, *Docs. Rel. á las Mis. de Califs.*, Qto iii).

44. M. A., Arch. Genl., *Californias*, 41; *Cor. de Virreyes* (Azanza, 1800), sér. ii, 8/199, no. 806; B. C., *Prov. Rec.*, vol. ix, p. 86.

45. Arrillaga to Viceroy, *Informe*, July 15, 1806 (*Prov. Rec.*, vol. ix, p. 86).

46. B. C., *Prov. St. Pap.*, vol. xix, p. 343.

47. Bancroft, *History of California*, vol. ii, p. 162, n. 8. On transfer of corporal and soldier, B. C., *Arch. Arzobispado*, vol. ii, p. 6. On one occasion the Governor asserted himself roundly, to wit, when in 1810 Guardian Gasol empowered a padre to take a judicial declaration (B. C., Gasol, *Patentes*, 1806; *Prov. Rec.*, vol. xii, p. 102).

48. The need of education was recognized (*Informe*, note 45, *ante*).

49. B. C., Santa Inés, *Lib. de Misión*, p. 3; *Arch. Sta. Bárb.*, vol. viii, p. 151; *Prov. St. Pap.*, vol. xviii, p. 359.

CHAPTER XI

THE PROBLEM OF SUBSISTENCE (*continued*)

1. Sola to Viceroy, July 3, 1816, acknowledging receipt of news of the insurgent ships from Don Bernardo Bonavía, comandante-general of the Provincias Internas. Annexed to Bonavía's letter were communications from Paita, stating that there had reached that port a ship of the Royal Philippine Company (the San Fernando) with news of " an insurgent expedition from Buenos Ayres commanded by General Braun of the Anglo-American nation. It was the object of these *piratas infames* to harry all the coast and then take refuge in the United States." (M. A., Arch. Genl., *Prov. Int.* 23.)

2. B. C., *Arch. Arzob.*, vol. iii, part i, p. 55; *Prov. St. Pap.*, vol. xx, pp. 104, 111; *Arch. Sta. Bárb.*, vol. xii, p. 358.

3. B. C., *Arch. Arzob.*, vol. iii, part ii, pp. 2–24, 41. Writing to Guerra on Dec. 11, 1818, Padre Luis Martínez of San Luis Obispo ventured upon some jocose counsel. " Remember," he said, " the tactics of the Galicians. In the front rank they placed women, and when the French, who always paid homage to women, advanced, they [the French] quickly abandoned warfare for gallantry. If you wish to conquer the insurgents, you must do the same." (B. C., Guerra, *Docs. para la Historia de Calif.*, vol. iii, p. 9.)

4. Sola, *Informe*, Dec. 12, 1818; Bustamente, *Historical Picture*, vol. v, p. 62; Payéras, *Informe*, 1817–18 (B. C., *Arch. Sta. Bárb.*, vol. xii, p. 100); Gonzáles, *Experiences*, p. 6. Joseph Chapman, an American impressed by Bouchard at the Sandwich Islands, deserted at Monterey, and became an early foreign settler in California. (Cf. chapter xiv, n. 28.)

5. Antonio Ripoll to Governor Sola. The taste for war inspired in Padre Ripoll by the insurgent demonstration induced the padre to undertake a systematic organization of the neophytes of the mission of Santa Bárbara. In 1820 (April 29) he wrote thus to Sola. Noticing that the Indians were filled with enthusiasm to defend their " king, their country, and their religion," he was forming a company of 100 men — *compañia de Urbanos Realistas de Santa Bárbara*. Their arms were to be good bows and arrows. Besides, he was forming a company of axemen (*macheteros*), fifty strong, and a squadron of lancers, thirty strong. "Thus will the insolent insurgents or pirates, who shall venture to attack us, be warned." (B. C., *Arch. Arzob.*, vol. iv, part i, p. 17.)

6. B. C., *Arch. Sta. Bárb.*, vol. vi, p. 215.

7. B. C., *Prov. Rec.*, vol. ix, p. 161. The Lima ships came again in 1817.

8. B. C., *Prov. St. Pap.*, vol. xix, pp. 341, 344; vol. xx, pp. 103, 148; Sola to Viceroy, July 3, 1816 (M. A., Arch. Genl., *Prov. Int.* 23, no. 52).

9. B. C., *Prov. St. Pap.*, vol. xx, p. 168. Wilcox (known to the Spaniards as Don Santiago) wooed Concepción with the plea that by marrying him she would win a convert to the Catholic faith. The lady's reply was: "I did think something of saving his soul, but his Divine Majesty took from me the foolish fear of its loss, for I remembered that Concepción was not necessary to him if his conscience was sincere. . . . The poor fellow, I pity him and am grateful to him," etc. (B. C., Guerra, *Docs. para la Historia de Calif.*, vol. vi, p. 132.)

10. B. C., *Arch. Sta. Bárb.*, vol. iii, p. 104.

11. B. C., *Prov. Rec.*, vol. ix, p. 116. In 1801, Dec. 12, the King had granted to New California the privilege of naming a delegate from the presidios. (*Ibid.*, p. 13.)

12. M. A., Arch. Genl., *Prov. Int.* 23, no. 1.

13. *Ibid.*

14. B. C., *Prov. St. Pap.*, vol. xix, p. 33.

15. B. C., *Conferencia celebrada en el Presidio de San Francisco*, etc., October, 1816.

16. B. C., *Prov. St. Pap.*, vol. xx, p. 5; vol. xxii, p. 28.

17. B. C., Vallejo, *Historia de California*, vol. iv, p. 209.

18. B. C., P. Tikhmeneff, *Historical Review of the Russian-American Company*, part i, p. 221.

19. B. C., Sarría, *Informe*, Nov., 1817, p. 73; *Libro de Misión*, p. 5. See *Arch. Sta. Bárb.*, vol. iii, p. 142; vol. iv, p. 157; vol. xii, p. 125; Payéras, memorandum, *Docs. para la Hist. de Calif.*, vol. iv, p. 344.

20. B. C., *Arch. Arzob.*, vol. iii, part ii, pp. 90, 96. Payéras made protest against any commingling of the Cholos with the Indians.

21. B. C., *Prov. St. Pap.*, vol. xviii, pp. 200, 202.

22. E. Tapis, to Arrillaga, March 1, 1805. "The story goes that after a fit of frenzy the woman said that Chupu had appeared, assuring her that the Gentiles and Christians would perish of the epidemic, if they did not offer Chupu alms, and did not bathe their heads with a certain water. The news of the revelation flew throughout the huts of the mission at midnight, and nearly all of the neophytes, including the *alcalde*, went to the woman's house to offer beads and seeds, and to witness renunciation by the Christians. Though the tale was spread throughout the Channel *rancherías* and into the mountains, the missionaries remained ignorant of it, for Chupu had said that whoever should tell the padres would die immediately. But after three days a neophyte woman, casting aside fear, related the whole story. If the frenzied woman had added to her tale that, for the epidemic to cease, it was necessary to kill the padres, the two soldiers of the guard, the *alcaldes* and others, as much credit would have been given to this as to the first part of her account." (B. C., *Arch. Sta. Bárb.*, vol. vi, p. 32.)

23. Tapis to Arrillaga, Feb. 21, 1805. "The guards of the seventeen missions are reduced to two or three each. The missions, excepting Santa Inés,

which is entitled to ten men, can have, each, but six men, including the corporal. (B. C., *Arch. Sta. Bárb.*, vol. xii, p. 75.)

24. P. Muñoz, *Diario de la Expedición hecha por Don Gabriel Moraga á los Nuevos Descubrimientos del Tular*, Sept. 21 to Nov. 2, 1806 (B. C., *Arch. Sta. Bárb.*, vol. iv, p. 27). "We found, after having traveled five leagues, the *Río de los Santos Reyes*, which had been discovered in the previous year, 1805."

25. B. C., E. Tapis, *Informe*, 1805-06, p. 81.

26. The trial of the cook (Nazarío by name) makes an interesting record. The crime was not denied. Nazarío confessed, and his words were taken down. He was angry, he said, with the padre because on Dec. 15 he had given him fifty lashes, and on the night of the same day twenty-four lashes, on the morning of the 16th twenty-seven lashes, and on the afternoon of the 16th twenty-five lashes. "I was so tormented with the many lashings that I received that, as I could take no other revenge, I resolved on the night of the 16th to put poison in the padre's soup to see if I and the other Indians of the mission could not thus be delivered. This padre is unbearable. Sometimes I did not save food for the family of the sergeant, either because there was n't enough, or I forgot. For the omission I was given fifty lashes. When I was being punished, and he did not do it himself, he would get some servant to sing *merienda, merienda* [food, food]. None of the mission Indians like him, much less the Gentiles." The prosecutor in summing up said: "It is proved by the culprit's declaration that in two days he received more than two hundred lashes and this without serious cause." His sentence was eight months' detention at the San Diego Presidio. (B. C., *Prov. St. Pap.* (Benicia), vol. xlix, p. 4.)

27. B. C., *Arch. Obispado: Monterey y Los Ángeles*, p. 86; *Arch. Sta. Bárb.*, vol. xii, p. 93. Quintana was accused of inflicting cruel punishments. It was alleged by the Indians that he had ordered an iron strap made with which to punish for fornication and theft. Sola defended the padre against these charges. (B. C., *Prov. Rec.*, vol. ix, p. 139.)

In 1877 Mr. Bancroft obtained from an Indian, Lorenzo Asisara, the story of the Quintana murder as related to Asisara by the latter's father, a neophyte of Santa Cruz. Quintana, it would seem, was seized, gagged, and strangled. Fear of his iron strap was intense. (J. D. Amador, *Memorias*, p. 58.)

28. B. C., *Arch. Sta. Bárb.*, vol. xii, p. 101.

29. B. C., *Arch. Sta. Bárb.*, vol. vi, p. 102.

30. B. C., Guerra, *Docs. para la Hist. de Calif.*, vol. v, p. 31. And yet again, Payéras, Petition to Sola, Sept. 17, 1819: "Apostates are increasing and the haughty and wandering spirit is growing astonishingly. . . . The cause of this is that expeditions have ceased. . . . The missions can be attacked, when least expected, by strong bodies composed of Christians and Gentiles, who with the greatest insolence deride the soldiers and challenge them to fight." (B. C., *Arch. Arzob.*, vol. iii, part ii, p. 90.)

31. By 1820, State Secular was indebted to the missionaries in the sum of 400,000 *pesos*. Sola to Sarría, May 29, 1821 (B. C., *Prov. St. Pap.* (Sacramento), vol. xviii, p. 44).

The *Comisario-Prefecto* was the immediate local representative of the *Comisario-General* of the Indies in Madrid. The appointment for Alta California would seem to have followed upon Borica's suggestion that the presidents of missions be made subject to local prelates or inspectors. Regarding the threatened excommunication, see B. C., *Protesta de los Padres contra Gabelas*, 1817, by Sarría, Amorós, Durán, Viader, and Marquínez.

32. B. C., *Decreto de las Cortes de 13 de Septiembre de 1813;* Translations, Jones, *Land Report*, no. 8; Dwinelle, *Colonial History of San Francisco*, 39.

33. B. C., Gasol, *Patentes*, 1806, sec. 10. At the same time the padres were warned not to employ female servants, but to depend entirely on men or boys.

34. B. C., *Arch. Sta. Bárb.*, vol. vi, p. 63. In 1820, Guardian Baldomero López wrote to the president of the missions: "To such a height has rumor mounted in this capital [Mexico] that the missionaries of Alta California are said to go about in vehicles of two wheels and carriages of four wheels. . . . I do not doubt it will be said that the poor missionary fathers of New California do not suffer the hardships which they proclaim, but enjoy themselves to an extent such that they ride in carts and carriages, a thing becoming the rich and powerful but not the poor."

35. The petition was preceded by a letter to the Viceroy, from Sola, of date August 21, 1816, representing need for padres (M. A., Arch. Genl., *Historia*, 287). Protest by Payéras (B. C., *Arch. Arzob.*, vol. iv, part i, p. 25).

36. *Expediente . . . la primera Junta de California, celebrada ante el Exmo Sor Virrey Don Juan Ruiz de Apodaca, en 5 de Julio de 1817* (M. A., Arch. Genl., *Gobernación*, "Indios Barbaros," 1).

37. B. C., *Arch. Sta. Bárb.*, vol. iii, p. 219.

38. B. C., *Arch. Arzob.*, vol. iv, part i, p. 66. *Cédulas Reales* (1818), 218; (1820) 223 (M. A., Arch. Genl.).

39. B. C., *Arch. Arzob.*, vol. iv, part i, p. 68.

40. *Ibid.*, p. 23. On July 16, 1821, Payéras assured the Bishop of Sonora that it was the wish of the Alta California missionaries to fulfill the requirements of Article 3 of the Decree of 1813, and "dedicate themselves to spreading religion in places yet unreduced" — places, so far as Alta California was concerned, lying east and north of the existing mission chain (*Ibid.*, p. 73). On Aug. 25, José María Estudillo of San Diego wrote to Sola, expressing the opinion that the Decree of 1813 would not be carried out in Alta California, because of the peculiar condition of the missions there (B. C., *Prov. St. Pap.*, vol. xx, p. 291).

41. Arrillaga, *Informe*, 1806 (B. C., *Prov. Rec.*, vol. ix, p. 86); Sola,

Informe, 1817 (B. C., *Prov. Rec.*, vol. viii, p. 155); Sola, *Tour of Inspection*, 1818 (B. C., *Prov. Rec.*, vol. viii, p. 176).

42. The death-rate of 1820 was 42 per cent of the population as a whole. In 1810 it had been 45 per cent of the original population plus baptisms.

43. Sola, 1817, 1818, note 41, *ante*. Sola sought to enforce the Spanish laws against selling or giving wine to the Indians. These laws were given by Philip III, 1594; Philip IV, 1637. (*Recopilación*, law 36, lib. 6, tit. 1; also law 7, lib. 6, tit. 13, B. C., *Arch. Sta. Bárb.*, vol. vi, p. 104.)

CHAPTER XII

THE RIGHTS OF MAN

New Chapter Sources: Iturbide correspondence, including instructions to Agustín Fernández de San Vicente ; *diario*, Captain José Romero — Colorado expedition; instructions from Mexico to establish a fort and military colony on Carmelite Bay (M. A.). (For chart of Secularization movement, see pocket.)

1. Plan of Iguala and Treaty of Córdova, summarized by Bancroft, *History of Mexico*, vol. iv, pp. 710, 728.

2. Oct. 22, 1821 (M. A., Arch. Genl., *Prov. Int.* 23).

3. Dec. 10, 1821 (*Ibid.*).

4. Gonzalo Ulloa, Jan. 10, 1822 (*Ibid.*).

5. Iturbide correspondence, 1822, nos. 1–55. "Junta de Califs.," 1822–31 (M. A., Arch. Genl., *Gobernación;* M. A., Arch. Genl., *Prov. Int.* 23, exped. no. 5).

6. *Ibid.* ; Treaty with Spain (1819) for the acquisition of the Floridas (W. McDonald, *Select Documents*, 1776–1861).

7. *Ibid.*

8. *Ibid.*

9. *Acta celebrada en la capital de la Nueva California*, Payéras to College of San Fernando, April 14, 1822; Sola to Minister of Relations, April 13, 1822. The letter reached Mexico, July 20 (M. A., Arch. Genl., *Californias*, 45; *Sec. de Gob.*, nos. 319, 320).

10. April 17 (B. C., *Prov. St. Pap.* (Sacramento), vol. xviii, p. 4; M. A., note 9, *supra*).

11. Sola to José de la Guerra y Noriega, Oct. 9 (B. C., *Prov. Rec.*, vol. xi, p. 78). Payéras to the padres, Oct. 9 (B. C., *Arch. Sta. Bárb.*, vol. ix, p. 106). Already in 1821 (June 18) Payéras had written to his college that he intended to take "the most intelligent and useful Indians and form with them two pueblos; or to add them to the pueblos established by the whites " (B. C., *Arch. Sta. Bárbara*, vol. iii, p. 190).

Citizenship for the Indian, including the franchise, was a Spanish (Secular) idea of long standing. (*Recopilación de Leyes de las Indias*, lib. vi, tit. iii, ley 15.) The minority of the Indian in respect to contracts, etc., was abolished by the Cortes in 1810. (Cf. text, chapter vi, n. 20.)

12. B. C., Arch. Genl., *Misiones*, vol. i, p. 520.

13. B. C., as cited by Bancroft, *History of California*, vol. ii, p. 494.

14. Federation was a popular idea. On Aug. 7 the *diputación* of Arizpe had invited Alta California to become one of a union, to consist of Nueva

Vizcaya, New Mexico, and the Californias. A like invitation had also come from Cajaca and Jalisco.

15. M. A., Arch. Genl., *Gobernación*, 1826, *Indiferente*, leg. 7; translated by Bancroft, *History of California*, vol. ii, p. 511, n. 2 ; main provisions, *vide* Secularization Chart (pocket).

16. Representation was based upon population (one *diputado* for each 40,000 to 80,000), but each state and territory was allowed a *diputado* regardless of population (B. C., *Constitución Federal de los Estados Unidos Méxicanos*, Mexico, 1828, tom. i, tit. ii, art. 5; tit. iii, art. 11). So far at least as executive functions were concerned, the *Actas Constitutivas* had apparently designed the two Californias, together with Colima, to be one political unit (*Acta Constitutiva*, art. 7). A separate *jefe político* for Lower California was not provided until March, 1830, when Captain Mariano Monterde was named. (B. C., *Superior Gov. St. Pap.*, vol. vi, pp. 6, 7.)

17. Colonization: B. C., *Ordenes y Decretos de la Soberana Junta Provisional Gubernativa*, vol. iii, p. 64, — translated, Dwinelle, *Colonial History of San Francisco*, 1863, Add. xii, xiv; Wheeler, *Land Titles*, pp. 7–9; summaries, Bancroft, *History of California*, vol. ii, p. 516, n. 8; vol. iii, p. 34, n. 7. The law took its inception from a recommendation by the Regency, Nov. 26, 1821 (M. A., Arch. Genl., *Fomento, Col. y Ter. Baldíos*, leg. 1, exped. 1). Naturalization: *Vide* T. Hittell, *History of California*, vol. ii, p. 100; M. A., Arch. Genl., *Fomento, Col. y Ter. Baldíos*, leg. 4, exp. 117. Cf. J. R. Robertson, *From Alcalde to Mayor* (B. C. MS.).

18. M. A., Arch. Genl., *Gobernación*, 1826, *Indiferente*, leg. 7; *Californias*, 18, exped. 25. Herrera, *Causa contra el comisario sub-principal de Californias*, 1827 (B. C., *Dept. St. Pap. Mil.* (Benicia), vol. lxxiii, pp. 62 *et seq.*).

19. *Proceso contra Joaquín Solís y Otros*, 1829 (B. C., *Dept. St. Pap. Mil.* (Benicia), vol. lxxii, pp. 25 *et seq.*, and vol. lxxv, p. 13).

20. F. W. Beechey, *Narrative of a Voyage to the Pacific*, etc., 1825–28, 2 vols., London, 1831.

21. The Federal Constitution of 1824 prescribed no form of internal representative government for the territories. Echeandía, therefore (under the Spanish Constitution of 1812 as interpreted by Sola), ordered an election of five provincial electors — one from each presidial district, and one from Los Ángeles — to choose a territorial *diputación* (legislature) of six *vocales* and a president, and a delegate to Congress. In 1828 the Governor gave orders that the election of *vocales* and delegate should thereafter be by an electoral body chosen as follows: (1) Municipal electors were to be chosen in each presidio and pueblo by the vote of all citizens over eighteen years of age, — 9 for Monterey, 8 for San Francisco, 7 each for Santa Bárbara and Los Ángeles, 5 for San José, and 3 for San Diego; (2) by the municipal electors there were to be chosen six *partido* electors (one for each presidial and pueblo district), and by these there was to be chosen, first, a delegate, and next *vocales* (Echeandía, *Bando sobre Elecciones*, 1828, July 30,

B. C., *Legislative Rec.*, vol. 1, p. 104). These regulations Echeandía pronounced in conformity with Article 16 of the Federal Constitution, and an order of the government of July 19, 1824.

22. A. Duhaut-Cilly, *Voyage autour du Monde*, 1826–29, Paris, 1835; Italian edition, Turin, 1841, 2 vols.

23. As early as September, 1822, orders for a survey westward from Tuçón to the peninsula had, at the solicitation of Sola, been issued by Lieutenant-Colonel Antonio Narbona, comandante in Sonora.

24. Narbona's instructions to Romero contemplated the selection of a presidio site at the mouth of the Colorado; the gathering of skulls and skins of animals; of skulls of Gentile Indians; of minerals, etc. The Casa Grande was to be visited, and it was to be ascertained whether the North Americans had established relations with the natives. (*Informe* (Narbona), with Romero's diary and Romero's and Caballero's letters, M. A., Arch. Genl., *Relaciones*, vol. i, Carpt[a] no. 189.)

25. M. A., Arch. Genl., *Fomento, Baldíos*, leg. 2, exped. 52.

26. B. C., Mexico, *Mem. Relaciones*, 1823, pp. 31–33 (Bancroft's translation).

27. B. C., *Junta de Fomento de Californias*, Mexico, 1827.

28. B. C., *Arch. Arzob.*, vol. iv[2], p. 6.

29. B. C., Ripoll to Sarría, May 5, 1824 (*Arch. Arzob.*, vol. iv[2], p. 95).

30. Sarría to Argüello, April 14, 1825; explanation that oath to the Constitution would be a violation of oath of allegiance to the Spanish King (B. C., *Arch. Arzob.*, vol. iii[2], p. 127). Order for arrest of Sarría, Mexico, June 29, 1825 (B. C., *Sup. Gov. St. Pap.*, vol. iii, p. 4). Oath as taken or refused by each padre, 1826 (M. A., Arch. Genl., *Californias*, " Misiones," 18, exped. 24). In California there was strong opposition to expulsion of the padres. The *ayuntamientos* of San José and Monterey petitioned the Mexican Government against it.

31. Echeandía to Minister of Relations, Jan. 29, 1828: reports flight of Ripoll and Altimíra on Jan. 25, and asks whether, in order to avoid another like scandal, he shall not grant license of departure to such other padres as have refused to swear to the Constitution. The Minister of Justice, March 19, 1828, recommends that, in view of arrangements already made by the College of Zacatecas to supply missionaries to Alta California, and in view of the law for the expulsion of Spaniards, the incorrigibles be given license to depart. The Harbinger will be seized at whatever Mexican port she may stop. As she is an Anglo-American vessel, representation will be made to the United States (M. A., Arch. Genl., *Californias*, " Misiones," 18, exped. 26).

32. With regard to Ripoll and Altimíra, see A. Ord, *Ocurrencias en California* (B. C.). With regard to Martínez, see Ord, and E. de la Torre, *Reminscencias* (B. C.). See also *Proceso contra Solís* (*ante*, n. 19), Sarría, *Defensa del Padre Luis Martínez*, 1830 (B. C.), and Martínez, *Letters to*

José de la Guerra (B. C., Guerra, *Docs. para la Historia de Calif.*, vol. iii, pp. 12, 13).

33. Echeandía, April 28, 1826 (B. C., *Dept. St. Pap.*, vol. i, p. 130); Same, emancipation decree, July 25, 1826 (B. C., *Arch. Arzob.*, vol. v, p. 104; M. A., Arch. Genl., *Californias*, "Misiones," 18, exped. 24; summary by Bancroft, *History of California*, vol. iii, pp. 102–03).

34. Secularization plan, 1829–30 (B. C., *Leg. Rec.*, vol. i, p. 135; summary by Bancroft, *History of California*, vol. iii, p. 302, n. 2). Education was to be a fundamental feature. See Secularization Chart (pocket).

35. *Decreto de Secularización*, Jan. 6, 1831 (B. C., *Arch. Sta. Bárbara*, vol. ix, p. 420; summary by Bancroft, *History of California*, vol. iii, p. 305, n. 6). Supplementary *Reglamento*, Nov. 18, 1832 (B. C., *Miss. and Col.*, vol. ii, p. 63; summary by Bancroft, *History of California*, vol. iii, p. 314, n. 23).

36. On Oct. 17, 1829 (in accordance with a decree of Aug. 29), the first *asesor* (solicitor-general) for Alta California was appointed, in the person of the *licenciado*, Rafael Gómez of Jalisco. The position was resigned by Gómez in 1834, and Cosme Peña was named (M. A., Arch. Genl., *Justicia*, 104). Cf. chapter xiv, on California judicial system under Mexican régime.

On Oct. 6, 1829, Echeandía reported the arrival at Monterey of "Don Abel Stearns with four others, and one woman, bearing a passport from the supreme government."

37. First steps toward resistance: Pío Pico, *Narración Histórica*, p. 24 (B. C.); summary by Bancroft, *History of California*, vol. iii, p. 200, n. 36; *Pronunciamiento* (translated by Bancroft, *Ibid.*, p. 202, n. 39); Victoria to Mexico, dispatches (L. Alamán, *Sucesos de California*, 1831, B. C., *Sup. Gov. St. Pap.*, vol. viii, p. 13).

38. Pío Pico, *Historia de California*, pp. 35–40 (B. C.); J. Ávila, *Notas*, pp. 11–15 (B. C.).

39. M. Vallejo and S. Argüello, *Expediente vs. Victoria*, Feb. 17, 1832 (B. C., *Leg. Rec.*, vol. i, p. 298).

40. M. A., Arch. Genl., *Californias*, "Misiones," 44, exped. 8. See also Bancroft, *History of California*, vol. ii, pp. 496–506, and notes.

CHAPTER XIII

FEDERALISM AND CENTRALISM

1. B. C., *Vallejo Docs.*, vol. i, no. 241, p. 10.

2. B. C., *Vallejo Docs.*, vol. i, no. 286.

3. He had served throughout the war for independence, and in May, 1824, had asked to be empowered to reduce to civilization the Gentiles who dwelt upon both banks of the Río Colorado. It had been his design to plant a colony to serve as a barrier against the "ambitious schemes of the barbarous Russians," and the "silent encroachments of the people of the Estados Unidos del Norte." But his backer in the undertaking, Don John Ytale [Hale?], who was to bring a thousand families from Ireland, had failed him, and the design had come to naught. (M. A., Arch. Genl., *Gobernación, Fomento de Californias*, 1824. See also Bancroft, *History of California*, vol. iii, p. 234, n. 23. Cf. McNamara project, chapter xv of text.)

4. M. A., Arch. Genl., *Gobernación, Fomento de Californias*, 1833.

5. B. C., *Sup. Gov. St. Pap.*, vol. viii, p. 32.

6. [Figueroa to Vallejo, June 24, 1835:]

"*Very Private.*

"The frontier, on the northern side of the bay of San Francisco, and Sacramento River, may, from its topographical situation, be somewhat difficult to colonize; but this government trusts that for the honor of the National Government, and your own proper interest in the social order, you will not let escape an opportunity to deserve the premium to which all men aspire, — *Posthumous Fame.*

"This territorial government knows and is persuaded of all that you have informed it respecting the danger to which this frontier is exposed on account of our *Neighbors of the North*, and it recommends that the Mexican population be always greater than that of the foreign, who in virtue of colonization should solicit lands in that precious portion of the territory trusted to you by the government, for which it again charges you to give titles only to those who *may prove they merit them*, bearing in mind the importance of the port of Bodega, and Cape Mendocíno, which points are necessary for the preservation of the national welfare.

"The government omits recommending the secrecy that this note requires, which you will reveal only in the last extremity ; and it has confidence that you will labor with assiduity in an object so sacred, in which are concerned the general good and the peculiar welfare of the territory in which you were born. This is warranted by the prudence, patriotism, and good faith of which you have given so many proofs, and by your offering again to give proof of them to the government. God and Liberty."

— (California *Star*, March 13, 1847.)

7. M. A., Arch. Genl., *Gobernación, Jefes Políticos*, 1833; *Ibid.*, *Colonización*, exped. 120; Figueroa, "Manifesto" (B. C., *Leg. Rec.*, vol. iii, p. 190; Translation, *Missions of California*, Zamorano, 1835, p. 63).

8. Arrillaga, *Recopilación*, 1833, pp. 19, 311; translated in part, Bancroft, *History of California*, vol. iii, p. 337.

9. B. C., *St. Pap. Miss. and Col.*, vol. ii, p. 270; translated, *Hartman's Brief*, ex. no. 4 ; Jones, *Report on Land Titles ;* summary by Bancroft, *History of California*, vol. iii, p. 273, n. 5.

10. M. A., Arch. Genl., *Fomento de Californias*, leg. 6, exped. 162; B. C., *Dept. St. Pap. Mil.* (Benicia), vol. lxxxviii, p. 11.

11. Figueroa, "Manifesto" (Translation), p. 20.

12. B. C., *Arch. Los Ángeles*, vol. iv, p. 155 ; translated by Bancroft, *History of California*, vol. iii, p. 282, n. 17. See also Figueroa, "Manifesto" (Translation), pp. 64, 66, 75.

13. Figueroa, *Informe*, April 11, 1835 (M. A., Arch. Genl., *Fomento de Californias, Colonización*, exped. 161; *Justicia*, 150).

14. Echeandía had spread among the neophytes the idea that he had come as a liberator. At San Miguel, San Luis Obispo, San Juan Capistrano, San Fernando, and San Buenaventura, the Indians were assembled and addressed by representatives of the Governor. At San Buenaventura they were told to ignore the padre if necessary, and also the guard, and to apply for liberation to the comandante of the presidio of Santa Bárbara (B. C., *Docs. para la Historia de California*, vol. iv, p. 789). In 1828, Oct. 20, the Governor wrote to Mexico that the neophytes at most of the missions were clamoring to be formed into pueblos (B. C., *St. Pap.* (Sacramento), vol. x, p. 39). At all events, they became highly uneasy, abusing the *alcalde* at Los Ángeles, and refusing at San Luis Rey and San Juan Capistrano to work in the fields (B. C., *Dept. Rec.*, vol. v, p. 44; Beechey, *Voyage*, vol. ii, pp. 12, 320; Ord, *Ocurrencias*, p. 52). Yet so habituated to wardship were the Indians that often they refused to be swayed by the appeals of the Governor's agents (B. C., *Dept. St. Pap.*, vol. iii, p. 3; *Dept. Rec.*, vol. ix, p. 85; Alvarado, *Historia de California*, vol. iii, p. 6).

Flogging, discontinued by Echeandía, was revived by the Zacatecans (B. C., *Vallejo Docs.*, vol. ii, nos. 41, 52, 142; *Dept. St. Pap.* (Benicia), vol. ii, p. 12). But García Diego, the prefect, was opposed to flogging. ("Carta Pastoral," July 4, *Arch. Arzob.*, vol. v, part i, pp. 80, 82).

15. B. C., *Vallejo Docs.*, vol. xxxi, no. 28; summary by Bancroft, *History of California*, vol. iii, p. 328, n. 50.

16. Figueroa to Mexican Government, Oct. 5, stating that the neophytes of San Juan Capistrano were more civilized than other neophytes, and that he should emancipate them all (B. C., *St. Pap. Miss. and Col.*, vol. ii, p. 72). Reports on San Juan, San Diego, and San Luis Rey (B. C., *Vallejo Docs.*, vol. xxxi, nos. 36, 37, 38).

17. B. C., *St. Pap. Miss. and Col.*, vol. ii, p. 253, — translated, *Hartman's*

Brief, ex. 2; Dwinelle, *Colonial History of San Francisco,* Add. 3, — summary by Bancroft, *History of California,* vol. iii, p. 342, n. 4.

18. Arrillaga, *Recopilación,* 1835, p. 189.

19. M. A., Arch. Genl., *Gobernación,* "Congreso Genl.," leg. 12.

20. Alvarado to Vallejo, "Carta Confidencial," Nov. 7, 1836 (B. C.,*Vallejo Docs.,* vol. iii, no. 262); *Honolulu Gazette,* Dec. 2, 1837, — impartial as to Isaac Graham.

21. "Plan de Independencia" for California, Nov. 7, 1836 (B. C., *Bandini Docs.,* no. 41; summary by Bancroft, *History of California,* vol. iii, p. 470, n. 28).

22. J. Castro, *Decretos,* Dec. 7 and 9, 1836, nos. 5, 7, 8, 9 (B. C.).

23. B. C., *Arch. Los Ángeles,* vol. i, p. 106; vol. iv, p. 238.

24. "Plan de Independencia," *supra,* n. 21. Alvarado later confessed to a design to place Alta California under foreign protection. (Alvarado, *Historia de California,* vol. iii, pp. 199, 205, B. C. ; Vallejo, *Historia de California,* vol. iii, p. 245 B. C., Cf. text, chapter xv.)

25. *Plan de Gobierno,* Sta. Bárbara, April 11, 1837; summary by Bancroft, *History of California,* vol. iii, p. 507, n. 47.

26. B. C., *Vallejo Docs.,* vol. iv, no. 276; translated by Bancroft, *History of California,* vol. iii, p. 529, n. 24.

27. "Tratado de Las Flores," April 23, 1838 (B. C., *Vallejo Docs.,* vol. xxxii, no. 130; translated by Bancroft, *Hist. of Calif.,* vol. iii, p. 562, n. 36).

28. Like California wars in general, this war had been bloodless. So much impressed with the humor of this circumstance was Lieutenant Juan Rocha, of the Los Ángeles force, that he is said to have observed that in future he should take with him his barber to bleed him, as thus only would blood ever be seen.

A plot to assassinate Alvarado when in Los Ángeles in 1837 was disclosed to him by a woman, heavily veiled, whom the Governor believed to be Doña Concepción, the erstwhile fiancée of Rezánoff.

29. Prefectures: Arrillaga, *Recopilación,* 1837, p. 202; translated, F. Hall, *History of San José,* 1871, p. 489.

30. Arrillaga, *Recopilación,* 1835, p. 583; translated, *Hartman's Brief,* ex. 6; Halleck, *Report on Land Titles,* p. 154.

31. B. C., *Arch. Sta. Bárb.,* vol. x, p. 205; translated by Dwinelle, *Colonial History of San Francisco,* Add. xxxvii; summary by Bancroft, *History of California,* vol. iv, p. 55, n. 21.

32. *Instrucciones;* translated, Halleck, *Report on Land Titles,* p. 156; summary by Bancroft, *History of California,* vol. iv, p. 56, n. 23.

33. B. C., *Vallejo Docs.,* vol. xxxiii, p. 30; translated by Dwinelle, *Colonial History of San Francisco,* Add. xxxix; summary by Bancroft, *History of California,* vol. iv, p. 59, n. 28.

34. Dissolution of pueblo at San Juan Capistrano and gradual extinction of pueblos Las Flores, San Dieguito, and San Pascual. (Bancroft, *History of California,* vol. iii, p. 626; vol. iv, pp. 196, 625, with citations.)

CHAPTER XIV

ANGLO-AMERICANS

NEW CHAPTER SOURCES: Castro letters and diplomatic correspondence in Isaac Graham affair; protest by Viceroy Iturrigaray against occupation by Americans of the region at the mouth of the Columbia River; Vallejo list of the Bartleson-Bidwell Company, Castro-Alvarado letter to Mexican Minister of Relations, 1844; *informes* with regard to Pious Fund, 1793, 1823; Arrángoiz correspondence relative to "Anglo-Americans." (M. A.) (Specific citations below.)

1. M. A., Arch. Genl., *Justicia*, 1, 1840. Castro to Alvarado, April 8, 1840; Alvarado to Minister of Interior, April 22, 1840 (B. C., *Dept. Rec.*, vol. xi, p. 67).

2. Vallejo to Minister of War, Dec. 11, 1841: gives white population of Alta California as 6000, Indians 15,000 (M. A., *Californias*, 1841, leg. 2).

3. Bancroft (*History of California*, vol. iv, p. 5, n. 4) states that no explanation is anywhere given of the manner in which Garner's confession was obtained. Castro in his letter of April 8 (not cited by Bancroft) says: *Habiendo comparecido le hice entender que el Gobierno tenia fundados avisos de la intentona de varios estrangeros que maquinavan una desastrosa revolución y que ya se tomban medidas muy energicas para aprehender á los malvados. Sobresaltado de temor, el dicho individuo me contestó al momento dicendo: "que si se le ofrecia seguridad de su vida y de sus propriedades descubriría esta funcion y los cabecillas de ella." Le aseguré de mil maneras esto, infundiendole confianza, y declaró que los cazadores G^{rl} Graham y Alverto Morris y otros heran los principales caudillos.*

On the arrests, see Bancroft, pp. 11–15 and notes. Castro, in a letter to Alvarado of April 15 (not cited by Bancroft), quotes a letter from José M. Covarrubias, captain of auxiliaries, stating that the latter on the 7th went to the pueblo de Alvarado, arrested the foreigners there, dispatched a force over the Sierra de Sanfrancisquito, which arrested " Juan Copinger" and his companions, and was now sending a party to the port of San Francisco to make arrests, and would send a force to the Contracosta of San Pablo and valley of San José.

4. Bancroft (*History of California*, vol. iv, p. 18) gives a list of 47 names. An official list, certified at Monterey on April 22 by Juan Miguel Ctnzar, gives 46 names, and of these only 23 are found in Bancroft's list. It would appear that the other 23 were names of men from the South who were substituted for 23 apprehended in the North. (M. A., Arch. Genl., *Californias*, 1840.)

5. The course of events at Tepic was as follows: (1) Delivery by Castro of

letter from Vallejo, of date April 25, 1840 (also perhaps of Alvarado's letter of April 22, cited *supra*), charging prisoners with *conspirando contra la integridad del Territorio de la República;* (2) letter by T. J. Farnham, May 22, to Eustace Barron, British vice-consul, and José M. Castaños, American vice-consul at Tepic, alleging causeless arrest and inhuman treatment, — the letter being accompanied by a declaration of seventeen American citizens of Los Ángeles, dated April 29, that the prisoners were innocent; (3) letter by British and American vice-consuls, of date May 22, to M. C. Negrete, comandante of the canton, conveying complaint of prisoners; (4) representation, May 22, by twenty-three of the prisoners (English) to the British minister in Mexico, Richard Pakenham; (5) letter from British minister, June 3, to the Mexican Minister of Relations, asking serious attention to the case of the prisoners, as the British Government would require such attention; (6) letters from British vice-consul, June 13, accusing Castro of having sought to make Alta California independent of Mexico in 1836, and stating that of the prisoners twenty-five [*sic*] were English, and twenty-three American; also stating that prisoners were being fed at cost of himself and the American vice-consul; (7) letter from British minister reiterating demands, — to which reply, June 23, that until trial of the imprisoned, guilt or innocence could not be predicated. On June 11, twenty-three of the prisoners (English) made affidavits as to their arrest and treatment. Of these affidavits that by Albert F. Morris is the most striking. Affiant states that on reaching Monterey after his arrest he was taken to the Governor's house; that there soldiers were drawn up in two files, between which he was made to walk in the train of people bearing crucifixes; that a chair was brought, and that, being seated therein, a priest said prayers over him, preparatory, as he was given to understand, to his death, and that this fate, he believes, would have befallen him had not the arrival of Farnham caused a diversion (M. A., Arch. Genl., *Justicia*, 1). Thomas J. Farnham, whose efforts for the prisoners were unceasing, was the author of several books of travel, one of which, accompanied by a biographical sketch, is printed by Mr. R. G. Thwaites in vol. xxviii of his *Early Western Travels*. Mr. Farnham, who died in 1848 in San Francisco, left a son, Mr. Charles Haight Farnham, who became a friend of Francis Parkman; and wrote the *Life of Parkman* for the standard edition of the latter's works.

6. See Bancroft, *History of California*, vol. iv, pp. 30–41, and notes.

7. B. C., Sutter, *Personal Reminiscences;* Same, "Petition to Congress," 39th Cong., 1st Sess., *Sen. Misc. Docs.* 38; Alvarado, *Historia de California*, pp. 206 *et seq.* (B. C.)

8. P. Kostromitinof to Alvarado, Oct. 29, 1840: "The Emperor of all the Russias having consented to the abandonment of the establishment of Ross," etc., Kostromitinof announces himself empowered to negotiate details (M. A., Arch. Genl., *Californias*, 1840).

9. Bancroft, *History of California*, vol. iv, chap. 6.

10. Viceroy Iturrigaray, January 20, 1807, wrote thus to the Spanish Government: "The Marquis de Casa Yrujo, minister plenipotentiary of his Majesty to the United States of America, has informed me that the party sent by that government three years ago to explore the course of the Misury to the South Sea, reached the coast in the month of November, 1805, after having traversed by land a distance of 340 miles from the banks of the said Misury. Having turned to embark on a river called Kooskooskee, they descended it to the river last-named, and explored the Pacific Ocean at the river's mouth. Although this discovery, made in the territories of the King our master, without his permission, brings no present advantages to the American Government, it is the opinion of the marquis that it will offer advantages in the future, because in the lands about the sources of the Misury there are found furs abundant and of good quality which may easily be exported by merchants of those states (merchants whose sagacity is proverbial) to the Philippine Islands from the Kooskooskee and Columbia rivers. In order by timely action to prevent this, the same marquis thinks it would be wise to form an establishment at the mouth of the last of the two rivers named, with suitable defenses and absolute prohibition of entrance to any American or foreigner of other nationality, making the fruit of this discovery our own, with the object (not difficult in time of peace) that the Philippine Mercantile Company shall organize there a trade with the tribes of Judah." (M. A., *Cor. de Virreyes*, Yturrigaray, 23/225.)

11. For routes of Smith, Patties, and Walker, see general map (pocket).

12. John Bidwell, "The first Emigrant Train to California," *Century Magazine*, vol. xix, pp. 106 *et seq.* See general map (pocket).

13. The apprehensions of Alta California at this period are comprehensively set forth by José Castro in a letter to the President of the Mexican Republic, dated August 13, 1840; Castro then being in Mexico, whither he had gone to convey the Grahamites. The letter states that such is the number of foreigners clandestinely in the country that they could seize control if so disposed, and that they do in fact incite the Indians (an allusion to horse-stealing operations, considered *post*); that such is the emigration to Oregon, by way of the Columbia, that fears are entertained that this frontier may prove the basis of a new movement to be concerted between the emigrants without and the adventurers within; that it is the custom of the North United States to increase its possessions (as in the case of Texas) by selling land to emigrants from all Europe, professing the while to be keeping within its limit of 37° [*sic*]; that by its trappers the North illegally conducts the otter and beaver trade; that by its ships it illegally conducts the whale fishery; that in the course of their peregrinations the Americans rob, insult, and commit excesses, and that demands for redress should be made to the Cabinet at Washington; that Alta California is on the verge of shipwreck; that the port of San Francisco excites the admira-

tion and envy of European nations, and that the Anglo-American Commercial Company (that exists in the Sandwich Islands) has, in conjunction with the settlers on the Columbia, already projected a railway; that when the Spanish Cortes was considering the question of Mexican independence, the Russian minister had said that if there was exacted indemnification from Mexico, he was authorized to purchase Alta California up to 37° as a granary for Russia ; that even to-day the Russians hold Ross; that Mexican colonies should be planted toward the Columbia.

14. M. A., Arch. Genl., *Californias*, 1841, leg. 2; B. C., *Vallejo Docs.*, vol. x, 332.

15. M. A., *Californias*, 67.

16. *Ibid.*, 61. Bancroft prints a list of the Bartleson-Bidwell Company. It agrees with a list made by Vallejo, excepting that on Vallejo's list there appears the name U. W. Davison, — a name not given by Bancroft. (M. A., Arch. Genl., *Californias*, 1841.)

17. *Ibid.*, 64; *United States Exploring Expedition, 1838–1842*, Philadelphia, 1844–58, 20 vols.; vol. v, on California.

18. *Ibid.*, 68.

19. A change was vigorously opposed by Alvarado, who sent Manuel Castañares to Mexico to work against it. (Bancroft, *History of California*, vol. iv, chap. 11.) Alvarado minimized the danger from foreigners.

20. Message of President of United States to House of Representatives, on conduct of Jones, Feb. 22, 1843 (27th Cong., 3d Sess., *House Ex. Doc.* 166; M. A., Arch. Genl., *Californias*, 1842). Full correspondence, Micheltorena with Mexican Government, letters, Alvarado to Micheltorena, nos. 8, 9, 10, Oct. 19, 20, 21, announcing capitulation; Articles of Capitulation, Oct. 19; proclamation to the inhabitants of the two Californias, Oct. 19; letters, Jones to Micheltorena, announcing "later accounts from Mexico which induce me to believe that amicable relations have been restored between the two nations," Oct. 21, Nov. 1 (M. A., Arch. Genl., *Operaciones Militares*, leg. 2, frac. 1).

Letters, J. N. Almonte (Mexican minister to the United States) to Mexican Government: Letter of March 20, expressing opinion that United States was striving to gain time, so as to avoid necessity of punishing Commodore Jones, and that Mexico should insist on punishment; March 25, asking bill of items as basis of demand for indemnification; April 28, mentions rumor circulated by an officer in the United States squadron that Jones's coach (at San Pedro) was drawn by Mexican soldiers, — item appeared in *National Intelligencer;* letter, F. de Arrángoiz, Mexican consul at New Orleans, Feb. 12, 1843, announcing that Jones had been superseded by Commodore Dallas (M. A., Arch. Genl., *Internacional*, 1843 and 1847).

21. T. ap Catesby Jones, narrative printed in *Southern Vineyard*, Los Ángeles, May 22, 1858 (B. C.).

22. M. A., Arch. Genl., *Relaciones, Reseñas Políticas*, 1841–42; Dispatches, "Californias," nos. 4, 129, 183, 265, 374; replies, nos. 31, 73, 85. In a dispatch by the consul (no. 348, Dec. 1, 1842) it is reported that rumors of an agreement to cede California to the United States in payment of the Mexican debt are current.

23. The order is declared to be based on power given the President under the law of Feb. 22, 1832 (M. A., Arch. Genl., *Californias*, 1843). "About this order and the motive which prompted it," Bancroft says, "there is a mystery that I am unable to penetrate " (*History of California*, vol. iv, p. 380). The dispatches of Arrángoiz would seem to make all clear as to motive.

24. The order was sent also to the governors of Sonora, Sinaloa, Jalisco, and Coahuila, and receipt acknowledged. Almonte's dispatch (the basis for a repetition of the order) was accompanied by a letter written by a friend detailing a conversation with "a Mr. Pearce of Missouri," who said that Americans, being unable to enter California without passports, would go in great numbers to Oregon and "settle *sobre la línea* [on the line]." They would take, Almonte thought, their slaves with them.

25. Letters, Waddy Thompson, United States minister to Mexico, to Mexican Minister of Relations, Dec. 22, 30, 31, 1843, with reply of Minister of Relations, Jan. 3, 1844. (M. A., Arch. Genl., *Californias*, 1843, 1844.)

26. No acknowledgment of receipt of the order by Micheltorena is to be found.

27. See general map (pocket).

28. See general map (pocket). Gilroy was the first foreigner to settle permanently in California. He was a Scotch sailor, left at Monterey in 1814. His true name was John Cameron.

29. See general map (pocket).

30. See general map (pocket).

31. See general map (pocket). The course and distances of the Oregon Trail are set forth generally in Emerson Hough's *The Way to the West*, 1903, pp. 287 *et seq.*, and in R. Parrish's *The Great Plains*, 1907, chap. 5. But see H. M. Chittenden, *The American Fur Trade of the Far West*, 1902, map and text; and for detailed notation of localities, R. G. Thwaites's *Early Western Travels*, 1905, vol. xxx (Palmer's "Journal "), vol. xxvii (De Smet's "Letters").

32. See general map (pocket). T. J. Farnham, "Travels" (*Early Western Travels*, vol. xxviii, p. 113, and notes); J. Bidwell, "First Emigrant Train to California," *Century Magazine*, vol. xix, pp. 106 *et seq.*; Bancroft, *History of California*, vol. iv, chaps. 10, 16, 24.

33. Letter to Minister of War, Feb. 23, 1843 (M. A., Arch. Genl., *Californias*, 1843).

34. B. C., A. F. Coronel, *Cosas de Calif.*, p. 53; J. B. Alvarado, *Historia de California*, vol. v, p. 40; E. de la Torre, *Reminiscencias*, p. 106, relating the outraging in public plaza by the Cholos of an intoxicated Indian woman.

35. J. B. Alvarado and J. Castro, to President Santa Anna, May 30, 1845. Micheltorena's soldiers as jail-birds and vagabonds are accused of committing "immoralities, robberies, and murders." Condition of the department outlined. Justice ill administered by reason of long time consumed in appeals to courts of final resort in Mexico. Court of final resort should be the Tribunal of the department itself (M. A., Arch. Genl., *Gobernación*, 1845, *Indiferente*, leg. 29½). Treaty, Dec. 1, 1844 (B. C., *Guerra Docs.*, vol. i, p. 39; summary by Bancroft, *History of California*, vol. iv, p. 470, n. 20).

36. J. A. Sutter, *Personal Reminiscences*, p. 77 (B. C.); Same, *Diary*, p. 5; *Micheltorena-Sutter Correspondence*, Dec. 23, 1844, *La Minerva*, May 29, 1845 (B. C.).

37. Alvarado and Castro, *Exposición contra Micheltorena*, Jan. 29, 1845 (B. C., *Leg. Rec.*, vol. iv, p. 294).

38. B. C., *Leg. Rec.*, vol. iv, p. 32.

39. B. D. Wilson, *Observations on Early Days*, p. 46; Pío Pico, *Historia de Calif.*, p. 112 ; Alvarado, *Historia de Calif.*, vol. v, p. 66; Wiggins, *Reminiscences*, p. 8; Davis, *Glimpses of the Past*, p. 117 (B. C.); Treaty (B. C., *Arch. de San José*, vol. i, p. 5; summary by Bancroft, *History of California*, vol. iv, p. 509).

40. M. Castañares: Letters to Minister of Relations, August to September, 1844, January to March, 1845 (M. A., Arch. Genl., *Gobernación*, 1844, 1845, *Indiferente*, leg. 27).

41. On May 30, 1845, José Castro petitioned President Herrera for the appointment of José María Castañares as governor. Ignoring the petition, but replying to the Alvarado-Castro letter of same date, the Mexican Government deduced a series of conclusions: That it was needful to name for governor a native or a citizen of Alta California; to settle the question of the location of the capital; to give final appellate authority to the local court; to reinforce the presidios and to improve communication. All these matters were to be referred to Híjar and Andrés Castillero as a commission for establishing in Alta California public tranquillity (M. A., Arch. Genl., *Gobernación*, 1845, *Indiferente*, leg. 29½). Instructions to Híjar (B. C., *Dept. St. Pap.* (Benicia), vol. iii, p. 72). On May 9, 1845, Colonel Don Ignacio Iniestra was notified of his appointment as comandante-general and inspector of the Californias. Elaborate correspondence regarding enlistments and supplies (M. A., Arch. Genl., *Operaciones Militares*, leg. 7, frac. 1).

42. On January 18, 1845, the Mexican Government had issued a decree subjecting Alta California to Article 134 of section 17 of the *Bases Orgánicas*, which permitted the President to appoint a governor without awaiting or heeding a list of candidates. (*Méx. Col. de Leyes*, Palacio, 1844–46, p. 81.)

43. Conjectured by Bancroft that the recognition was part of price to the South for consenting to deportation of Micheltorena. The law of 1835, fixing the capital at Los Ángeles, had been bitterly resented. On April 22,

1840, Alvarado had submitted an elaborate plea prepared by the Departmental *Junta* for a restoration of the capital to Monterey (M. A., Arch. Genl., *Justicia*, 183, no. 13). On Aug. 2, 1844, Castañares offered a plea that the capital should be located wherever, for the time being, circumstances might dictate, it being remembered that the North was where invasion threatened.

44. Arrillaga, *Recopilación*, 1836, p. 107; *Proc. Mex. and Am. Claims Commission*, Claim no. 493, — Transcript (Washington, 1902), pp. 20, 469.

45. Appointment, arrival in California, etc., Robinson, *Life in California*, p. 195; Sir G. Simpson, *Narrative of a Journey Round the World*, London, 1847, 2 vols., vol. i, p. 388.

46. Micheltorena, decree of restoration (B. C., *St. Pap. Miss. and Col.*, vol. ii, p. 392; translated by Bancroft, *History of California*, vol. iv, p. 369, n. 1). Before quitting Mexico, the Bishop had obtained concessions as follows: Mission houses to be restored to padres; padres to remain at posts until curates appointed; authority to plant new missions; authority to found a missionary college and a female seminary, to locate an episcopal palace at San Diego, and to open a road to Sonora. (Translation, *Hartman's Brief*, ex. 10; summary by Bancroft, *History of California*, vol. iv, p. 334, n. 10.)

47. Arrillaga, *Decretos y Ordenes*, 1830, vol. i, p. 334; vol. ii, p. 150; Translation, Santa Anna decree (accompanied by Spanish text), *Mex. and Am. Claims Commission*, Claim no. 493, — Transcript, p. 38.

48. On June 12, 1793, the following statement as to the condition of the Pious Fund was rendered to Viceroy Revilla Gigedo: —

PIOUS FUND

(Continued from Chapter iv, n. 35)

	Pesos
Cash on hand belonging to the Fund on the 16th of November...	4,473.84

Amounts invested on interest and by whom owing	Pesos	
The College of San Gregório at 3 per cent	38,500.00	
The Marquis of Aguazo and Count of Álamo at 3 per cent	20,000.00	
Nicolás de la Puente at 3 per cent	20,000.00	
Pedro Cadrecha at 3 per cent	6,000.00	
The Marquis of Guardiola at 3 per cent	50,000.00	
José Manuel Reyes at 3 per cent.	42,000,00	176,500.00

Real estate		
The hacienda of Arroyo Zarco (as appraised in the year 1768 for the real estate, cattle, and grain) at the end of December, 1781, including the value of the dam and house	300,715.47	
The hacienda of San Pedro de Ybarra y Rieyerera, San Francisco Xavier, according to the appraisement made in 1768, as to the property and at the end of 1781 for the cattle and grain	174,843.34	
The haciendas of San Agustín de los Amores, San Ygnacio del Buey y Huasteca, by the same appraisements, stock and for the goats introduced in 1791	172,404.84	647,963.65
Total amount of the Fund		828,937.49

The yearly income of the said fund, taking the average of five years...

Pesos
55,177.38

Expenses of the missions

34 Dominican Missionaries in charge of 17 missions at 350 *pesos* each, and 250 *pesos* for the dotation of Alampara at the Presidio of Loreto.. 12,150.00

13 Missions of the Fernandinos at 800 *pesos* each................. 10,400.00   22,550.00

Other expenses

Advances made to the haciendas on an average of one year with another...................................... 23,000.00

Aid toward the general expenses............................ 1,000.00

Rent of Guapango....................................... 150.00   24,150.00

Total... 46,700.00

Comparison

Yearly income... 55,173.37

Yearly expenses... 46,700.00

Balance... 8,473.37

— (*Mexican and American Claims Commission*, Claim no. 493; Transcript, p. 433.)

By the above it appears that at the end of 1792 the Fund was in excellent condition, its total being 828,937 *pesos*, from which there was derived an average annual income of 55,177 *pesos*, — an excess over expenditure of 8473 *pesos*. In 1805, however, the haciendas had become deteriorated, and schemes of promotion were broached, with the alternative of selling the haciendas. Then in 1811 there befell the devastation of the war for independence and a suspension of payment of missionary stipends. During the years 1819–23 the annual income was 13,730 *pesos*, 5665 *pesos*, 737 *pesos*, (no income), and 138 *pesos*.

In 1836 (as noted in the text) the administration of the Fund, which, since the expulsion of the Jesuits, had been in the hands, first of the Spanish, and next, of the Mexican Government, was given to the first bishop of Alta California. In 1842 it again was assumed by the state, the haciendas being sold and the government pledging itself to pay on the proceeds 6 per cent interest from the tobacco revenue. The Bishop of Alta California protested against resumption of state control, and on April 3, 1845, such of the properties as remained unsold (an inconsiderable portion) were restored to him. (Translation of restoration decree, *Mex. and Am. Claims Commission*, Claim no. 493, — Transcript, p. 581; résumé of history of Pious Fund, *Ibid.*, p. 374; *Colección de Leyes y Decretos desde 1° de Enero*, 1834, Edición del Constitucional, no. 20, Mexico, 1851, pp. 100–101; Spanish text of the Bishop's protest, *Mex. and Am. Claims Commission*, Claim no. 493, — Transcript, p. 359.) Cf. *History of the Pious Fund of California*, by John V. Doyle, Papers, California Historical Society, vol. i, part i, 1887.

49. B. C., *Leg. Rec.*, vol. iv, pp. 20, 25; translated, *Hartman's Brief*, ex. 15.

50. Decree, May 28, 1845 (B. C., *Leg. Rec.*, vol. iv, p. 63); Decree, Oct. 28, 1845 (Pico, *Reglamento*) ; translated, *Hartman's Brief*, exs. 17, 18.

51. On sales, see United States *vs.* Workman (U. S. Sup. Court Reps.), 1 Wall. 745. Decree, March 30, 1846 (B. C., *Leg. Rec.*, vol. iv, p. 336; *Hartman's Brief*, ex. 23). For conveyances, see Hartman (Spanish and English). Translation of decree of March 30, 1846 (Bancroft, *History of California*, vol. v, p. 559, no. 5). List of sales (*Ibid.*, p. 561, n. 8). Order of Mexican Government (Montesdeoca order) against interference with Micheltorena's order for restoration of missions to padres (B. C., *St. Pap. Miss. and Col.*, vol. ii, p. 404; translated, Bancroft, vol. v, p. 560, n. 6). In the so-called Mission Cases, decided in the U. S. District Courts for California, in 1859, it was contended (1) that it was not within the power of local authorities to *sell* the public lands, — they could only make grants; and (2) that the grants (so-called) did not conform to the requirements of law. The decision (which was against the validity of the sales so far as they included the mission buildings and gardens) was placed upon the ground that the Montesdeoca order was still valid.

52. Figueroa, Oct. 15, 1833, elections — only *emancipados* to vote; neophytes are not citizens (B. C., *Dept. St. Pap.* (Ángeles), vol. xi, p. 12). The ideas of San Vicente, emphasized by Echeandía, regarding neophyte citizenship and right to the ballot, were thus modified.

On September 30, 1849, the *alcalde* of San Juan Bautista reported the decline of that mission pueblo, urging changes (B. C., *Unbound Docs.*, p. 183), cited by Robertson, *From Alcalde to Mayor* (MS.). By a decree of Pío Pico (1846) the following are recognized as pueblos: Los Ángeles, Santa Bárbara, San José, Monterey, San Diego, San Francisco, Branciforte, Sonoma, San Juan Bautista, San Juan Capistrano, San Luis Obispo. (Robertson, *supra.*)

53. On condition and appearance of Alta California presidial settlements, see F. W. Beechey, *A Voyage to the Pacific*, London, 1831; R. H. Dana, *Two Years Before the Mast*, New York, 1840; Sir E. Belcher, *Narrative of a Voyage Round the World*, London, 1843; A. du Petit Thouars, *Voyage autour du Monde*, Paris, 1840.

54. Municipal government in Monterey was instituted about 1820, when an *alcalde* was chosen. Beginning with 1827 there was chosen an *ayuntamiento*, or town council, composed of an *alcalde*, two *regidores*, and a *síndico*. At Santa Bárbara the first *ayuntamiento* was elected by order of Echeandía in 1826 (*Dept. St. Pap.*, vol. i, pp. 189–90); but during the Zamorano-Echeandía contest the town was declared by the *diputación* as yet embryonic, and in 1833 Figueroa essayed to perfect its organization. The result was a vote in 1834 by the *diputación* to create an *ayuntamiento*, with *alcalde*, four *regidores*, and *síndico* (*Dept. St. Pap. Mil.* (Benicia), vol. lxxvi, pp. 6–9; *Leg. Rec.*, vol. ii, pp. 51–68, 188–89). At San Francisco the establishment of municipal rule was due directly to Figueroa. On Nov. 3,

1834, the *diputación* voted to create an *ayuntamiento*, with *alcalde*, two *regidores*, and *síndico*, to reside at the presidio and assume the political and judicial functions formerly exercised by the comandante. Judicial administration, as carried on in Alta California prior to 1824, is well indicated in Argüello's *Plan de Gobierno*. Thus, Title IV of the Plan, Art. 1: "For Civil Cases in towns [pueblos] there shall be three resorts [*instancias*], 1st, to *alcalde;* 2d, to comandante; 3d, to governor. Civilians at presidios will apply first to comandante; secondly and finally, to governor. Art. 2: Criminal cases will be tried by a court-martial, whose sentence will be executed without appeal" (*Leg. Rec.*, vol. i, pp. 17–19; translated by Bancroft, *History of California*, vol. ii, p. 511, n. 2). In 1835 (Jan. 12) petitions for land grants were directed to the *alcalde*, "since San Diego is no longer a presidio"; and on Feb. 5 the comandante referred to the *alcalde* petitions for lands, as involving an exercise of powers no longer his (*Arch. S. Diego*, pp. 32 and 35).

55. Echeandía to Minister of Justice, June 25, 1829: reports misdemeanors as determined by *alcaldes*, and more serious causes as referred first to presidial comandantes and then to governor, who consults *asesor-general* of Sonora, from whom matter may go to Minister of War in Mexico (B. C., *Dept. Rec.*, vol. vii, p. 21). Alta California subject to Circuit Court of Sinaloa (B. C., *St. Pap.* (Sacramento), vol. xix, p. 47). It was at Echeandía's request that an *asesoría* for Alta California was established (*vide* chapter XII, n. 36).

56. Victoria to Minister of Justice, Sept. 21, 1831 (M. A., Arch. Genl., *Justicia*, 130).

57. Law of 1837 regarding judiciary (May 22), translated, Hall, *History of San José*, p. 518. During 1839 and 1841 complaints of the failure to organize courts of first instance (courts of record superior to *alcalde* or justice courts) were emphatic. Alvarado to Minister of Interior, March 9, 1839, transmitting report of departmental commission (M. A., Arch. Genl., *Justicia*, 207). In these complaints San José was prominent (*Ibid*).

58. The abolition was the result of a *Junta Consultiva y Económica*, Oct., 1843. The restoration (July 4, 5, 1845) was effected by dividing Alta California into two prefectures as before, but the *partidos* were altered. In the first prefecture (that of Los Ángeles), extending from San Luis Obispo southward, there were three *partidos* — Los Ángeles, Santa Bárbara, and San Diego. In the second prefecture (that of Monterey), extending from San Miguel northward, there were two, — Monterey and Yerba Buena. Moreover, there was to be but one prefect (at Monterey), while *ayuntamientos* were permitted only to Monterey and Los Ángeles. In the remaining *partidos*, affairs were to be managed by a council consisting of a justice of the peace and two citizens under the presidency of a sub-prefect. (B. C., *Leg. Rec.*, vol. iv, p. 79; *Dept. St. Pap.* (San José), vol. v, p. 98.)

59. J. Gregg, *Commerce of the Prairies*, New York, 1845; republished by

Mr. R. G. Thwaites, *Early Western Travels*, vol. xix; Chittenden, *American Fur Trade*, vol. ii, p. 504.

60. J. J. Warner, *Reminiscences*, Pub. Hist. Soc. South. Calif., vol. vii, p. 189.

61. Bancroft, *History of California*, vol. iii, pp. 386, 395, and notes; vol. iv, p. 74, and notes. J. O. Pattie, *Personal Narrative*, Cincinnati, 1831, republished by Thwaites, *Early Western Travels*, vol. xviii. See general map (pocket).

62. B. C., *Dept. St. Pap.* (Ángeles), vol. iv, p. 99.

63. B. C., *Dept. St. Pap.*, vol. vi, pp. 169, 171.

64. "When Jackson's party came from New Mexico to California in 1831," writes Mr. J. J. Warner, "there could not be found in either Tucsón or Altar — although they were both military posts and towns of considerable population — a man who had ever been over the route from those towns to California by the way of the Colorado River, or even to that river, to serve as a guide, . . . and the trail from Tucsón to the Gila River at the Pima villages was too little used and obscure to be easily followed, and from those villages down the Gila River to the Colorado River, and from thence to within less than a hundred miles of San Diego, there was no trail, not even an Indian path." (Pub. Hist. Soc. South. Calif., vol. vii, p. 188.)

CHAPTER XV

WAR WITH THE UNITED STATES

NEW CHAPTER SOURCES: Official letters, Sir George Simpson to Governor of Hudson's Bay Company; consular letters, James A. Forbes (Monterey), and Barron-Aberdeen official correspondence (B. A.); letters of Anthony Butler to President Andrew Jackson, and Thompson-Webster correspondence (A. A.); *Diary of James K. Polk,* Chicago, 1910; official correspondence of Thomas O. Larkin, reëxamined (B. C.); instructions of Secretary George Bancroft to Commodore John D. Sloat (*Nation*), instructions of Bancroft to Commodore Robert F. Stockton (A. A., Navy), and letters and statements of John C. Frémont (*Century Magazine*); Larkin, Sutter, Richardson letters, citations and excerpts by W. R. Kelsey, *The United States Consulate in California,* Pub. Acad. of Pacific Coast History, Berkeley,1910; official letters, Admiral Sir George Seymour (B. A.); Gillespie-Flóres Articles of Capitulation and correspondence, and official reports of Flóres (M. A.); *Diary,* R. C. Duvall of U. S. SS. Savannah; *Californian,* 1846–47 (reëxamined); San Francisco *Star,* 1847. (Specific citations below.)

1. Prudencia Higuera of Martínez, who in 1840, as a child, lived near San Pablo, and whose male relatives exchanged with American captains hides for cloth, axes, shoes, fish-lines, and grindstones, says: "My brother had traded some deer-skins for a gun and four tooth-brushes, the first ones I had ever seen. I remember that we children rubbed them on our teeth till the blood came, and then concluded that after all we liked best the bits of pounded willow-root that we had used for brushes before. After the ships sailed, my mother and sisters began to cut out new dresses, which the Indian women sewed. On one of mine mother put some big brass buttons about an inch across, with eagles on them. How proud I was! I used to rub them hard every day to make them shine, using the tooth-brush and some of the powdered egg-shell, that my sisters and all the Spanish ladies kept in a box to put on their faces on great occasions. Then our neighbors, who were ten or fifteen miles away, came to see all the things we had bought. One of the Moragas heard that we had the grindstones, and sent and bought them with two fine horses. [A] girl offered me a beautiful black colt for six of my buttons, but I continued for a long time to think more of these buttons than of anything else I possessed." (*Century Magazine,* vol. xix, p. 192.)

2. *Missionary Herald,* Boston, 1844. Concerning the American missionaries, Sir George Simpson wrote in 1842: "They [the Sandwich Islanders] are too much under the influence of the Calvinist Missionary Society in the United States . . . and they [the missionaries] have had sufficient in-

fluence to get one of their own number, a narrow-minded, illiterate American [William Richards] installed as Prime Minister or principal Councillor of the King."

3. In 1847 the *Star* gives the population of San Francisco as, whites 375, Indians 34, Sandwich Islanders 40, negroes 10.

4. Same journal states, Sept. 4, 1847, that prior to April, 1847, there were in San Francisco 22 shanties, 31 frame dwellings, 26 adobes, — in all, 79 structures. On Nov. 16, 1846, Larkin observed to Samuel J. Hastings: "It [Monterey] will not increase fast. It will, I think, be a good, moral, gentle town. . . . Yerba Buena, and other places in and about San Francisco, will be the busy, bustling, uproarious places."

5. J. Douglas, *Journal* (B. C.).

6. B. A., Public Record Office, America, 388 (*American Historical Review*, vol. xiv, no. 1, "Documents," Joseph Schafer). But on Nov. 25, 1841, Simpson had written: "Any title the Russian-American Company could give us would be of no avail unless backed by a force of 80 to 100 men. . . . Under these circumstances, I made . . . no offer, nor did I encourage the hope of our becoming purchasers." (*Ibid.*, 399.)

7. B. A., F. O., Mexico, 136 (*American Historical Review*, vol. xiv, no. 4, "English Interest in the Annexation of California," Ephraim D. Adams).

8. *Ibid.*, Barron to Aberdeen, Sept. 9 and Oct. 19, 1843; and Barron to Aberdeen, Jan. 20, 1844 (F. O., Mexico, 179).

9. *Ibid.*, Aberdeen to Barron (F. O., Mexico, 179).

10. *Ibid.*, Aberdeen to Elliott (F. O., Texas, 20); E. D. Adams, *British Interest and Activities in Texas*, Johns Hopkins Press, 1910.

11. Eugène Duflot de Mofras, *Exploration de l'Oregon, des Californies*, etc., Paris, 1844.

12. J. B. Alvarado, *Historia de California*, vol. iii, p. 203. The author here states that in 1827 he had been in negotiation with Don Diego Forbes regarding a protectorate, but that he is glad nothing came of it, because, "I do not think it possible that under the dominion of aristocratic England we could have made the great and admirable progress we have made under the banner that the immortal Abraham Lincoln caused to wave triumphantly over the proud city of Richmond."

13. F. W. Beechey, *Narrative of a Voyage to the Pacific*, 1825–28, 2 vols., London, 1831.

14. B. W. Morrell, *Narrative of Four Voyages*, New York, 1832, p. 210.

15. Butler to Forsyth, June 9, 1835 (24th Cong., 1st Sess., *House Ex. Doc.* 256); Butler to Forsyth, June 17, 1835 (A. A., State); J. S. Reeves, *American Diplomacy under Tyler and Polk*, Johns Hopkins Press, 1907, pp. 69–74.

16. Thompson to Webster, April 29, 1842 (A. A., State); Webster to Thompson, June 27, 1842 (*Letters of Daniel Webster*, Van Tyne, p. 269; Reeves, *American Diplomacy*, pp. 100–103). As early as April 25, 1842, Webster had intimated to Lord Ashburton, then negotiating the Treaty

of Washington, that the United States might yield something in the Oregon matter for the sake of acquiring California (B. A., F. O., America, 379). It is interesting to note that in 1843, Forbes suggested to Barron that Great Britain exchange Oregon for California (*Ibid.*, F. O., 179); and that on August 4 and 14, 1844, Larkin suggested that England be granted eight degrees north of the Columbia River, in exchange for eight degrees of California south of the 42d parallel. A tripartite treaty between Great Britain, Mexico, and the United States was favored by Webster (Niles, *Register*, vol. lxx, p. 257; Tyler, *Letters and Times*, vol. ii, pp. 260–62, vol. iii, p. 206; J. Schouler, *History of the United States*, vol. iv, p. 447). See R. W. Kelsey, *The United States Consulate in California*, p. 49 (Pub. Acad. Pacific Coast History, vol. i, no. 5).

17. Everett to Calhoun, March 28, 1845 (A. A., State).

18. J. K. Polk, *Diary*, Sept. 17, 1845; Reeves, *American Diplomacy*, p. 275.

19. Buchanan to Larkin (*The United States Consulate in California*).

20. Larkin, *Official Correspondence*, July 20, 1846 (B. C.), states that the general (Castro) put a paper in his (the consul's) hands, containing a plan for declaring California independent in 1847 or 1848. The general asked if after so many revolutions he "would find repose and receive a benefit." As early as April 23, 1846, Larkin had told Castro that "by adjusting circumstances he could secure to himself and his friends fame and honor, permanent employ and pay." (*Ibid.*)

21. R. W. Kelsey, *The United States Consulate in California*, chap. 7. T. O. Larkin, *Off. Cor.*, April 17, 1846 (B. C.).

22. The contention of Mr. Reeves, that "the Mexican War was not the result of the annexation of Texas," is broad; but his remark (*American Diplomacy*, p. 90), that Von Holst's *Constitutional History of the United States* (valuable as it is) is little else than a paraphrase of the *Diary* of John Quincy Adams, is not unenlightening.

23. Of Frémont's personal appearance, Professor Josiah Royce writes in the *Atlantic Monthly* for October, 1890: "The charming and courtly manner, the deep and thoughtful eyes, the gracious and self-possessed demeanor," etc.

24. "Report of Exploring Expedition to the Rocky Mountains in the year 1842, and to Oregon and California in the years 1843–44" (28th Cong., 2d Sess., *Sen. Doc.* 174).

25. "Geographical Memoir upon Upper California," 1848 (30th Cong., 1st Sess., *Sen. Doc.* 148).

26. Niles, *Register*, vol. lxxi, p. 188.

27. *Ibid.*, and S. F. *Alta*, June 15, 1866.

28. Kelsey points out (*The United States Consulate in California*, pp. 96–97) that it is not improbable that Frémont was on his way to Santa Bárbara for supplies, as he had arranged for supplies to be delivered at that

point. Frémont himself (*Century Magazine*, vol. xix, p. 921) says: "The Salinas Valley lay outside of the more occupied parts of the country, and I was on my way to a pass opening into the San Joaquín Valley at the head of a western branch of the Salinas River." But see Vice-Consul Forbes to Consul Barron, Jan. 26, 1846 (B. A., F. O., Mexico, 176).

29. M. A., Secretaría de Fomento, *Colonización y Terrenos Baldíos*, leg. 7, ex. 221.

30. *Sawyer Documents* (B. C.).

31. *Ibid.*

32. On Nov. 5, 1845, Sutter wrote to Larkin: "I wish you had not been so much engaged that you could not come up here to assist your respectable countrymen . . . if it would be not in your power, or in the power of a Man of War to protect them, *I will do it*. The snow is on top of the mountains, their animals are worn out . . . they could not leave the country [under orders of expulsion] before the next month of May or June." (*Off. Cor.*) On July 8, 1846, Larkin wrote to Sloat: "From April to June the foreigners in the Sacramento Valley were continually harassed by verbal reports and written proclamations that they must leave California." John Bidwell states that, so far as he knew, there was no disquiet among the settlers, but on this point the testimony of Larkin, who, besides being entirely friendly to the Californians, was taking official cognizance of their conduct, is clearly the best evidence.

FRÉMONT AND SECRETARY BANCROFT

33. Mrs. Frémont (Jessie Benton) contends (*Century Magazine*, vol. xix, p. 923, n. 2) that the instructions to Larkin from the Secretary of State differed from those to Commodore Sloat, the latter instructions being the ones by which Frémont was governed. But an examination of the navy files has brought to light the Bancroft dispatch to Sloat. It bears date Oct. 14, 1846, three days prior to the dispatch to Larkin. "You will communicate," it says, "frequently with our consul at Monterey, and will ascertain as exactly as you can the nature of designs of the English and French in that region, the temper of the inhabitants, their disposition toward the United States, and their relation toward the central governments of Mexico. You will do everything that is proper to conciliate toward our country the most friendly regard of the people of California." (*Nation*, vol. lii, no. 1351.) Many years later (Sept. 3, 1886) Mr. Bancroft (not having before him what he had written in 1846, and depending on memory) wrote to Frémont from Newport, R. I.: "It was made known to you on the authority of the Secretary of the Navy that a great object of the President was to obtain California. If I had been in your place, I should have considered myself bound to do what I saw I could to promote the purpose of the President. You were alone; no Secretary of War to appeal to; he was thousands of miles off; and yet it was officially made known to you that

your country was at war; and it was so made known expressly to guide your conduct," etc. As pointed out by Professor Josiah Royce (*Nation*, *supra*), not only was Frémont without *official* information that his "country was at war," — he was without any information of it.

34. A curious forecast of the course of the settlers in seizing the horses is contained in a letter from William A. Richardson to Larkin, as early as Dec. 19, 1845. He says: "I arrived here [Santa Clara] last night; everything is in a very disorderly state; they are fortifying in San José; . . . you will hear very soon of a general turn-out; if the party goes over to the north to pass over horses as they say, we shall be ready to oppose them and give them a warm reception if required." (Cited by Kelsey, *The United States Consulate in California*, p. 51, no. 12.)

35. *Bear Flag Papers* (B. C.).

36. M. A., Arch. Genl., *Internacional*, 1842 and 1847; *Mem. de Relaciones*, 1846, Prefectura del 2 Distrito del Dep. de Califs. On June 18, Manuel Castro wrote to the Mexican Minister of Relations: "This prefecture has been informed that this treacherous crime has been committed with the privity or by the order of the [herein-mentioned] Frenot [Frémont], who has camped in Sutter's establishment; also with that of the captain of the U. S. warship Portsmouth, anchored in the port of San Francisco, because the said ship has helped the invaders of Sonoma with a boat-load of provisions."

37. The flag (constructed by William L. Todd of Illinois) was five feet long and nearly a yard wide. Along the lower edge was a stripe of red flannel. In the upper left-hand corner was a red star, five-pointed and fifteen inches in diameter. Facing the star was a bear. Beneath the star and bear was the emblem "California Republic." This flag, which was preserved in the hall of the California Pioneers in San Francisco, was destroyed by the earthquake-fire of 1906. For the Ide proclamation, etc., see Bancroft, *History of California*, vol. x, pp. 150–160.

38. "I had anticipated," wrote Larkin on July 20, 1846, "the pleasure of following up the plans partially laid down in the dispatch to this office of Oct. 17, 1845, and of bringing them to a conclusion in the latter part of 1847 through the will and voice of the Californians." And on Jan. 14, 1847, he wrote: "It has been my object for some years to bring the Californians to look on our countrymen as their best friends. . . . The sudden rising of the party on the Sacramento under the Bear Flag, taking California property to a large amount, and other acts, completely frustrated all hopes I had of the friendship of the natives to my countrymen." (*Off. Cor.*, B. C.)

CONDUCT AND MOTIVES OF JOHN C. FRÉMONT

39. Whether or not Frémont, in furthering the "Bear Flag revolt," was guided by official instructions brought to him by Gillespie, has been much discussed.

(1) No instructions are to be found in the Navy Department. Personal examination of the secret records of the Department was made by the editor of the *Century Magazine* in 1891. (See vol. xix of the *Century*, p. 928.)

(2) The papers brought by Gillespie were: (*a*) letters of introduction to Larkin and Frémont; (*b*) duplicate of Buchanan's dispatch to Larkin creating him confidential agent (destroyed and contents committed to memory); (*c*) letters to Frémont from Senator Thomas H. Benton. (30th Cong., 1st Sess., *House Report*, 817, pp. 12, 13; *Senate Rep.* 75, pp. 373–74; *Century Magazine*, vol. xix, p. 922.)

(3) Frémont in his *Memoirs* (Chicago, 1887, p. 520), and in the last word penned by him relative to his connection with the Bear Party (*Century Magazine*, vol. xix, p. 917), claims to have been guided not by instructions from the responsible head of a department, but by personal and intimate knowledge of the wishes and designs of the government, obtained, first, from Senator Benton, second, from the Benton letters brought by Gillespie, and third, from Gillespie himself. He says (*Century Magazine*, vol. xix, p. 922): "Lieutenant Gillespie brought a letter of introduction from the Secretary of State, Mr. Buchanan, and letters and papers from Senator Benton and family. The letter from the Secretary of State was directed to me in my private or citizen capacity, and though seeming nothing beyond an introduction, it accredited the bearer, and in connection with circumstances and place of delivery it indicated a purpose in sending it. From the letter I learned nothing, but it was intelligibly explained to me by my previous knowledge, by the letter from Senator Benton, and by communications from Lieutenant Gillespie. . . . The letter of Senator Benton, while apparently one only of friendship and family details, was a trumpet giving no uncertain note. Read by the light of many conversations and discussions with himself and other governing men in Washington, it clearly made me know that I was required by the government to find out any foreign schemes in relation to California, and to counteract them so far as was in my power. His letters made me know distinctly that at last the time had come when England must not get a foothold, that we *must be first.* I was to *act* discreetly but positively."

So far as the foregoing is concerned, Frémont, in countenancing and aiding the Bear Party, acted on his own responsibility, but under a strong conviction of duty; one inspired by communications (from persons identified with the government) that war with Mexico was imminent (if not already declared), and that at the first breath of war the government was determined to seize California.

But the foregoing is not all with which we have to reckon. Frémont, besides being unprovided with instructions to interfere in California affairs, possessed what virtually were instructions to the contrary. On June 16, two days after the capture of Sonoma, he wrote to Lieutenant Montgomery:

"The nature of my instructions [as topographical engineer] and the peaceful nature of our operations do not contemplate any active hostility on my part even in the event of war between the two countries [Mexico and the United States]; and therefore, although I am resolved to take such *active* and precautionary measures as I shall judge necessary for our safety, I am not authorized to ask from you any other than such assistance as, without incurring yourself unusual responsibility, you would feel at liberty to afford me." And not only so. On Gillespie's arrival, the dispatch to Larkin (creating the latter confidential agent and directing a policy of conciliation) was communicated to Frémont. In 1884, in a conversation with Professor Josiah Royce (*Atlantic Monthly*, vol. lxvi, p. 556), Frémont, forgetful that it was the dispatch to Larkin which he had seen, denied the existence of any such document, and claimed that he himself had received a dispatch from Secretary Buchanan of a different tenor. But a copy of the dispatch to Larkin being shown to him, and it appearing (*National Intelligencer*, Nov. 12, 1846) that on May 24, 1846, he had written to Senator Benton that though expecting word from Buchanan he had "received nothing," Frémont in 1891 (*Century Magazine*, vol. xix, p. 922) admitted that the dispatch to Larkin was after all what had been communicated to him by Gillespie. His words are: "This officer [Gillespie] informed me also that he was directed by the Secretary of State to acquaint me with his instructions to the consular agent, Mr. Larkin." In furthering the Bear Flag Revolt, then, Frémont, by the documents and by his own admission, was consciously disregarding the official plans of the government.

How far, in view of everything, such disregard of official plans was morally culpable, the reader will decide. To some it will be indubitable that Frémont could not have done as he did without being actuated by unworthy personal motives. To others it will be just as indubitable that in doing as he did his motives were of the best. It is his own explanation (given in vindication of himself in 1891) that "this idea [of conciliation embodied in the instructions to Larkin] was no longer practicable, as war was inevitable and immediate; moreover, it was in conflict with our own [unofficial and inferential] instructions. We dropped this idea from our minds, but falling on others less informed, it came dangerously near losing us California."

40. B. A., F. O., Mexico, 196 (*American Historical Review*, vol. xiv, no. 4, p. 754).

41. To Minister Charles Bankhead, late in 1844, and again to H. M. Consul Mackintosh, in July, 1845, McNamara proposed to plant a colony in California, and submitted to the President of Mexico a request for a grant of lands. The region within which the grant was desired was defined as between the Cosumnes River on the north, the extremity of the Tulares on the south, the San Joaquín River on the west, and the Sierra Nevada on the east. The colony was to consist of 2000 Irish families, and its objects were to "advance the cause of Catholicism," and to check "further usurp-

ations on the part of an irreligious and anti-Catholic nation [the United States]." Mexico favored the plan. Pico and the California Assembly accepted it with modifications, and on July 4 a grant was signed. No attempt was ever made to secure recognition of it. On the part of Great Britain the matter was ignored, although Bankhead reported to Aberdeen, May 3 and July 30, 1845. (B. A., F. O., Mexico, 185, no. 52; 186, no. 74.) Frémont, "California Claims" (30th Cong., 1st Sess., *Senate Rep.* 75), contains documents with translations.

42. Admiral Sir George Seymour, to Minister Bankhead in Mexico, June 13, 1846: "Having, however, detached the Juno last month with instructions to Captain Blake, if the inhabitants of California declared their independence of Mexico, to endeavor to induce their leaders not to place themselves under the control or subjection of any foreign power, I think it my duty to call at Monterey to ascertain if the inhabitants should have come to any resolution which will facilitate the maintenance of their independence." (B. A., F. O., Mexico, 197, Bankhead's no. 91; Admiralty-Secretary, In-Letters, no. 5561, — *American Historical Review*, vol. xiv, no. 4, p. 758.)

43. 29th Cong., 2d Sess., *H. Ex. Doc.* 4, p. 640, etc.

44. Seymour had "called at Monterey" pursuant to his intention as announced in his dispatch to Bankhead (note 42, *supra*). His object, therefore, was to ascertain whether "the inhabitants [had] come to any resolution which [would] facilitate the maintenance of their independence." Finding Sloat in possession, he stated that his object was a mere stop on his way to the Sandwich Islands (B. A., F. O., Mexico, 198).

45. 31st Cong., 1st Sess., *H. Ex. Doc.* 1. Commodore Stockton's orders from the Navy Department (never before published) appear in this volume as Appendix E.

46. M. A., Arch. Genl., *Operaciones Militares*, 1846, frac. 1, leg. 13.

R. F. Stockton, "Report of Operations on the Coast of the Pacific" (31st Cong., 1st Sess., *H. Ex. Doc.* 1, Military and Naval Operations, 30th Cong., 2d Sess., *Sen. Ex. Doc.* 31).

47. B. D. Wilson, *Observations on Early Days in California;* S. C. Foster, *Ángeles*, 1847–49; Lugo, *Vida de un Ranchero* (B. C.).

GILLESPIE-FLÓRES ARTICLES OF CAPITULATION

48. Articles of Capitulation (translation): "(1) Captain Gillespie will retire from the plaza of Los Ángeles with all his force within the time necessary to prepare his march to the port of San Pedro; remaining in said port the time indispensable for arranging everything essential to embarkation; under word of honor not to protract the time. (2) He will quit said plaza with all the honors of war, taking his private and personal property. (3) He will take the artillery mounted in this plaza with the customary quantity of ammunition, leaving said artillery in the port of San Pedro, at

the time of embarkation, in charge of an officer of the Mexican forces. (4) All the other stores and effects (property of the United States) shall be delivered by inventory to a Mexican official. (5) All arms taken by the United States forces shall be promptly restored to their owners. (6) Prisoners shall be exchanged grade for grade, and such as by the continuance of hostilities are taken hereafter shall be treated according to the laws of war between civilized nations. (7) All the property and persons of all the foreigners of each nation shall be respected, and no account shall be made of their past conduct.

"Additional. The term fixed for evacuation of the plaza shall be nine o'clock of the morning of the thirtieth instant.

"Further. The forces of Captain Gillespie, in passing to the port of San Pedro, shall not be molested in any manner by the Mexican forces; the intention being that an observation corps shall march at the distance of a league from them.

"Further. The horses and other transportation (taken by Captain Gillespie's forces), that may not belong to any individual under the command of the captain, shall be delivered to the commissioner on the part of the commander of the Mexican forces that shall be named to receive them after arrival at San Pedro.

"These articles and additions have been accepted by said Commissioners of both belligerent forces, giving their word of honor that they be faithfully observed: In testimony whereof they affix their signatures . . . José Mª SEGURA (Rúbrica), T. Cor^l y Cap^n; LEONARDO COTA (Rúbrica), Ten^{te} de Auxiliares; EDWARD GILCHRIST (Rúbrica), Surgeon California Battalion; NATHANIEL M. PRYOR (Rúbrica), Lieutenant. These stipulations approved: JOSÉ M. FLÓRES, Commander in Chief of the Mexican forces: Approved, ARCH. H. GILLESPIE, Capt. and Military Commandant."

CORRESPONDENCE BETWEEN FLÓRES AND GILLESPIE, OCT. 2-6, 1843

(Summary): Gillespie to Flóres, San Pedro, Oct. 2: Denies violation of any article of capitulation; states that no commissioner from Flóres has arrived to receive public property; horses loaned as transports have been returned and paid for; arms of particular individuals are to be delivered at time of embarkation; gratified that Flóres "appreciates the high sense of honor of Dr. Gilchrist, as it is quite impossible for an American officer to violate his pledged word of honor in the slightest degree." Same to same, Oct. 3: denies bad faith; "no more time has been employed at this point than is absolutely necessary for the safety of the force under my command at sea." Same to Same, Oct. 3: Embarkation will take place as soon as the ship is ready to receive the troops. Flóres to Gillespie, Palo Verde, Oct. 4: Charges Gillespie with repairing his artillery and erecting intrenchments, and asks: "Do these things belong to preparations necessary for departure? Is this the conduct of troops under capitulation? Ought I to remain a cold spectator of those acts militating against the security of the forces I command?" Gillespie is then informed that his embarkation must be effected "within two hours of this very day." Gillespie to Flóres, Oct. 4: "Although the preparations of the vessel to receive the force under my command are not concluded, I find myself obliged to give way to your pressing demands, and embark the troops, which will take place by sunrise to-morrow morning." (M. A., *Operaciones Militares*, 1846, frac. 1, leg. 13.) See also Flóres to Mexican Government. (*Ibid.*)

49. March, 1847, Los Ángeles to Monterey and back, 800 miles in eight days.

50. On Oct. 5, at a banquet at Yerba Buena, Stockton delivered a speech. "A few nights," he said, "after my arrival [at Monterey] from the south, I was aroused by a courier bringing sad intelligence. Two hundred mounted armed men had made an attack upon our little band in the city [of Los Ángeles], etc. Yes, fellow citizens, those very men who refused the offer of a fair fight under every advantage of numbers, being almost two to one, . . . went like cowards, like miscreants, like assassins in the darkness of midnight, and fell upon our little band of brothers who were left for their protection, etc. We go this time to punish as well as to conquer. . . . Cheer up, then, and let no man think there's danger. What if there be 10,000 men of Sonora! Who cares?" (*Californian*, Oct. 24, 1846.)

51. S. W. Kearny, Reports (30th Cong., 1st Sess., *Sen. Ex. Doc.* 1, p. 513); W. H. Emory, "Notes of a Military Reconnoissance" (30th Cong., 1st Sess., *H. Ex. Doc.* 41, p. 55); P. St. G. Cooke, "Journal of March of Mormon Battalion" (30th Cong., Special Sess., 1849, *Sen. Doc.* 2).

52. W. F. Swasey, *The Early Days and Men of California*, Oakland, 1891, pp. 76, 141; Frémont, *Memoirs*, p. 599.

53. On November 7 the *Californian* had remarked: "We now have some hopes that the Californians will give us an example of their bravery by coming to an open and honorable engagement, instead of making a rush and then flying to the bush to hide themselves for a month or two."

54. R. F. Stockton, Report to Secretary of the Navy (30th Cong., 2d Sess., *Sen. Ex. Doc.* 31); Emory, "Military Reconnoissance." Larkin was regarded as the author of the conflict with the United States. As a prisoner, he was at Natividad, where "a Californian, seeing a relative shot, called out, 'This man caused it all,' and, coming full speed toward him, leveled his gun." Larkin escaped by backing his horse behind that of a Californian. There was talk of sending Larkin to Sonora, but the Californian officers feared that they in turn might be sent "round the Horn" by Stockton. Larkin says: "Altogether there were 900 men in arms on the California side, every man with good horses and a lance, most of them with swords, pistols, rifles, and carbines; with all their countrymen to aid; a perfect knowledge of every hill and valley; and an utter contempt for foreign infantry, especially seamen; yet they did not succeed." ("Journal," *Californian*, Feb. 27, 1847.)

CHAPTER XVI

MISSION, PRESIDIO, PUEBLO, AND PRIVATE RANCHO'

1. "ALTHOUGH the mission buildings differ widely in treatment and detail, there is a general family resemblance, as if they had been designed by a single mind ; usually the façade of a central romanesque pedimented gable with pilasters supporting the pediment; with a square tower or belfry pierced with romanesque windows flanking each side, the arched entrance in the centre being usually surmounted by a square projecting cornice. Sometimes one of the towers has been omitted, as at Santa Inéz; sometimes partly missing, as at San Luis Rey, or wholly missing, as at San Gabriel, where the entire façade has been destroyed." (William L. Judson, Pub. Hist. Soc. South. Calif., vol. vii, p. 117.)

2. *Primer Informe ó Methodo Nuebo de Mision para su Gobierno Espiritual y Temporal,* R. Verger (Guardian of San Fernando) to Viceroy Bucarely, Nov. 15, 1772 (M. A., Museo, *Trasuntos*). A detailed account of mission routine in the establishments of Sonora, Nueva Vizcaya y Nueva México (S. A., Madrid, Bib. Nac. MS., no. 2550). See also Doña Eulalia Pérez, *Una Vieja y sus Recuerdos* (B. C.); Estevány de la Torre, *Reminiscensias* (B. C.).

3. "The native instruments of California were a flute of elder wood or deer's horn and the wooden rattle [clap-stick]." In 1811 President Tapis thus described the native music and dance: [At San Antonio] "they still preserve a flute which is played like the *dulce*. It is entirely open from top to bottom, and is five palms in length. Others are not more than about three palms. It produces eight tones [*puntos*] perfectly. They play various tunes [*tocatas*], nearly all in one measure, most of them merry. These flutes have eleven [*sic*] stops; some more, and some less. They have another musical instrument, a string instrument, which consists of a wooden bow to which a string of sinew is bound, producing a note. They use no other instruments. In singing they raise and lower the voice to seconds, thirds, fourths, fifths, and octaves. They never sing in parts, except that when many sing together some go an octave higher than the rest. Of their songs most are merry, but some are somewhat *mistes* in parts. In all these songs they do not make any statement [*proposición*], but only use fluent words, naming birds, places of their country, and so on." [At San Carlos] "they use a split stick like a distaff which serves them to beat the measure for their songs, which, whether happy or sad, are all in the same tone [*tonada*]. For instance, they sing as follows to the lively tunes, in which they mention their seeds or their asanas: '*Bellota-a-a, bellota; mucha semilla-a-a, mucha semilla.*' If the song is one of vengeance ór bad wishes, which is very often, and from which many fights result, they sing and dance to the same time, speaking ill of that

nation with which they are on bad terms, thus: '*Manco-o-o, manco*,' or other words or defects which they know concerning the nation or person which they are comparing [*contrapuesta*]." [At Santa Cruz] "their dances are most insipid. They gather in a circle and without moving from the spot bend their bodies. They move their feet and make many contortions to the sound of their disagreeable voices, with which they do not form articulate words." ("A Mission Record of the California Indians, from a manuscript in the Bancroft Library": Univ. of Calif. Pubs. in Am. Arch. and Eth., vol. viii, no. 1.)

4. Says Tapis: "What is truly noteworthy is the admirable time and imperturbable gravity kept by those who sing and dance. . . . In Spanish they sing perfectly and learn easily all that is taught them. They sing a chorus or a mass, even though containing solo parts. They, both men and women, have clear and sonorous voices and an ear for music." (*Ibid.*, from portions omitted by Kroeber.)

5. For plans of presidios at Monterey and San Francisco, see chapter XVI of text, pp. 338, 346.

6. "Usage here allows [even] a mother to chastise her son, so long as he remains unmarried and lives at home, whatever may be his age, and regards a blow inflicted on a parent as a high offense. I sent for the culprit [who had struck his mother]; laid his crime before him, for which he seemed to care but little; and ordered him to take off his jacket. . . . Then putting a *reata* into the hands of his mother, whom Nature had endowed with strong arms, directed her to flog him. Every cut of the *reata* made the fellow jump from the floor. Twelve lashes were enough; the mother did her duty, and, as I had done mine, the parties were dismissed." (W. Colton, *Three Years in California*, 1850.)

7. W. A. Streeter, *Recollections of Santa Bárbara* (B. C.).

8. E. Pérez, *Recuerdos* (B. C.); José del Carmen Lugo, *Vida de un Ranchero* (B. C.).

9. W. H. Davis, *Sixty Years in California*, San Francisco, 1889.

10. *Three Years in California.*

11. J. B. Alvarado, a child of six years, was present on the occasion. His description (possibly somewhat colored by time) is the one used.

12. Manuel Torres, *Peripecias de Vida California* (B. C.).

13. *Mayer MSS.*, no. 18 (B. C.).

14. G. Navarro, *al Com^{te} G^{rl} relati^{vo}, á la distribución de tierras á los Pobladores de California*, Oct. 27, 1785 (B. C., *St. Pap. Miss. and Col.*, vol. i, p. 323). Navarro describes the tenure of the private rancho as a *merced* [license] *y concesión*, and the *pastos de aprovecham^{to}* should, he states, be in common, as prescribed for Hispaniola in *Recopilación*, lib. iv, tit. xvii, ley 5 (*Ibid.*).

15. By 1790 there were in California nineteen private ranchos (Borica, chapter IX of text, n. 41). By 1823 there were not to exceed twenty, to wit:

SANTA BÁRBARA DISTRICT

San Rafael (to Verdugo).
Los Nietos (Sta. Gertrudis) to Nieto.
Portezuelo (to Verdugo).
Simí (San José de García y) to Pico.
Refugio (to Ortega).
San Pedro (to Domínguez).
Conejo (Altagracia) to Polanco.
Santiago de Santa Ana (to Yorba).
Vírgines (to Ortega).
Félix.
San Antonio (to Lugo).
Sauzal Redondo (to Ávila) 1822.

MONTEREY DISTRICT

Pájaro (to Castro).
Potrero (Familia Sagrada) to
Torre, 1822.
Buenavista (to Soberanes).

SAN FRANCISCO DISTRICT

San Isidro (to Ortega).
San Antonio (to Peralta).
Las Ánimas (to Castro).
Tularcitas (to Higuera).
Llano del Abrevadero (to Higuera) 1822.

In 1907, the General Land Office of the United States Government issued under the direction of I. P. Berthrong, a land-grant map of the State of California, showing the location of Spanish and Mexican grants to the number of 553.

16. Concerning the Vallejo house at Sonoma, Torres says: "I found the *patio* full of servants of both sexes, but in the group the women prevailed. . . . I asked the General's wife in what so many Indians were occupied. 'Each one of my children, boy or girl,' she said, 'has a servant who has no other duty than to care for him or her. I have two servants for myself. Four or five grind the corn for the tortillas, for here we entertain so many guests that three grinders are not enough. Six or seven serve in the kitchen. Five or six are constantly busy washing the clothes of the children and servants. And nearly a dozen are required to attend to the sewing and spinning. As a rule, the Indians are not inclined to learn more than one duty. She who is taught cooking will not hear to washing clothes; and a good washerwoman considers herself insulted if she is compelled to sew or spin. All our servants are very clever. They have no fixed pay; we give them all they need. If sick, we care for them; when their children are born, we act as godparents, and we give their children instruction.'"

17. Sets of instructions for the *juez de campo* are preserved in B. C., *Arch. Sta. Cruz*, p. 94, and *Arch. Monterey County*, vol. ii, pp. 17, 56.

18. The description is by Lieutenant Joseph Warren Revere of the United States Navy. Regarding horses he was an expert, having, as he says, "mounted the noblest of the race in the stables of Mohammed Ali, Viceroy of Egypt, as well as those belonging to other potentates in Syria, Egypt, and Barbary, besides choice specimens of the Persian stock in British India." (*A Tour of Duty in California*, New York and Boston, 1849.)

19. The old Spanish serenades, once sung everywhere in California, are rapidly disappearing. Mr. Charles F. Lummis is doing much to preserve them by phonographic record. Already the Southwest Museum has

500 cylinders of his procuring. Mr. Lummis says: "A poor old washerwoman, proud of her race, was a perfect bonanza of the early California songs; while a rich young matron, a famous toast, equally cherishes this her inheritance. A blind Mexican lad has been one of the stanch props of the work ; and several brave young women, who could ill afford the sacrifice of time, have contributed to science far more in proportion than does many a rich 'patron.' The most extraordinary achievement has been that of Miss Manuela C. García, of Los Ángeles, who has sung the records of no less than 150 songs, with the full words! Few can do that in any language, from sheer memory. Doña Adalaida Kemp, of Ventura, comes next with sixty-four records. Credit and gratitude belong also, in generous measure, to the Misses Luisa and Rosa Villa, Don Rosendo Uruchurtu, Mrs. Tulita Wilcox Miner, Don Francisco Amate, and many others." (*Third Bulletin*, The Southwest Society of the Archæological Institute of America, p. 59.) In illustration of the Spanish-California serenade, the *Bulletin* prints the following: —

Serenade

La Noche Está Serena

La noche está serena, tranquilo el aquilón;
  Tu dulce centinela te guarda el corazón.
Y en alas de los céfiros, quevagan por doquier
  Volando van mis súplicas, á tí, bella mujer,
  Volando van mis súplicas, á tí, bella mujer.

De un corazón que te ama, recibe el tierno amor;
  No aumentes mas la llama, piedad á un trobador.
Y si te mueve á lastima mi eterno padecer,
  Como te amo, amame, bellísima mujer!
  Como te amo, amame, bellísima mujer!

[So still and calm the night is,
  The very wind 's asleep;
Thy heart's so tender sentinel
  His watch and ward doth keep.
And on the wings of zephyrs soft
  That wander how they will,
To thee, oh woman fair, to thee)
  My prayers go fluttering still. }   (*Bis.*)

Oh take the heart's love to thy heart
  Of one that doth adore!
Have pity — add not to the flame
  That burns thy troubadour!
And if compassion stir thy breast
  For my eternal woe,
Oh, as I love thee, loveliest)
  Of women, love me so!] }   (*Bis.*)

20. *Crusoe's Island*, etc., New York, 1864, p. 183.
21. M. A., Museo, *Docs. Rel. á las Mis. de Califs.*, Qto iii.

22. Says Guadalupe Vallejo: "One of the customs which we always observed at the wedding was to wind a silken tasseled string or a silken sash, fringed with gold, about the necks of the bride and groom, binding them together as they knelt before the altar. . . . A charming custom among the middle and lower classes was the making of the satin shoes by the groom for the bride. A few weeks before the wedding he asked his betrothed for a measurement of her foot, and made the shoes with his own hands; the groomsman brought them to her on the wedding-day." (*Century Magazine*, vol. xix, p. 189.)

23. "As late as 1870 we find mention of the officer who, next to the *alcalde*, embodied the life of the early Spanish and Mexican civilization: —

"'The municipal law of California contains proof of [Spanish] influences. Tribunals of conciliation, community property, separate property of the wife, domestic relations, descents and distribution, trespass on land, proceedings in action, may be mentioned as examples. . . . To California is granted the distinguished privilege of uniting in her jurisprudence the common law of England and the civil law of Rome, each the product of a great civilization.'" (John J. Boyce of Santa Bárbara, in address before San Francisco Bar Association, Jan. 12, 1895.)

"The memory of the Spanish origins was preserved also in the number of legal questions that were brought up in courts and engaged attention for many years. Most prominent among these questions was that of the titles to the pueblo lots, which arose out of the *alcalde* grants of the transition period. The Spanish local institutions came to have a real significance to the people of the places where these contests occurred. San Francisco was the centre of the controversy, and for many years the titles were indefinite. Never did the welfare of so many people depend on the decision of a judicial tribunal as to the legal existence of a pueblo at that place." (J. R. Robertson, *From Alcalde to Mayor*, MS., B. C.)

APPENDIX

APPENDIX A

PLAN FOR THE ERECTION OF A GOVERNMENT AND GENERAL COMMANDANCY

Which includes the Peninsula of Californias and the Provinces of Sinaloa, Sonora, and Nueva Viscaya

[Archivo General of Mexico, *Provincias Internas*, 154. This important document (here published for the first time) is the joint work of Visitador José de Gálvez and Viceroy Marqués de Croix. It bears date January 23, 1768. The translation is by Miss Emma Helen Blair, of Madison, Wisconsin.]

If, since the glorious Conquest which the great Hernan Cortes made of the broad Domains which come under the name of Nueva España, effort had been made by his Successors in this Government to Second and to carry out the lofty designs of that Hero, the Light of the Gospel and the supremacy of the August Kings of España would have reached even to the utmost Bounds, not yet known, of this immense Continent. But as the spirit of activity and of Conquest was extinguished with the life of that inimitable Man, with his death came to an end the rapid advances which he accomplished in this new World; and at last we have not even maintained and conserved the possession which we enjoyed, in undisturbed tranquillity, of the richest territories on the Frontiers of Sonora and Nueva Viscaya.

The more immediate (and perhaps the exact) causes of this failure, and of the veritable ruin which has befallen the unfortunate inhabitants of those Provinces, with grave injury to the State, are, in reality, the utter neglect with which they have been regarded at Mexico in these latter years; the considerable distance at which they are situated, more than Six Hundred Leagues, from this Capital; and the pressing Crowd of more immediate business and cares which engross the entire attention of any Viceroy of Nueva España. For, as he is not supplied with

Subordinates to assist him, it is not possible for him to make active provision, or for the influence of his authority to be felt, at the remote confines of an almost boundless Empire.

This practical knowledge which the present Viceroy has been acquiring, with no less discomfort than hardship, and the favorable opportunity afforded to him by the present expedition to Sonora, have made him reflect very seriously on the means which may be most suitable and efficacious for reëstablishing this great Monarchy in its earlier prosperity, and to put the distant Provinces into condition for maintaining themselves with Vigor, and for enlarging the [Spanish] domination — extending at the same time the Catholic Faith, in acknowledgment and reward for which God is allotting to the Crown of España the Richest Empires of the Universe.

With the view, then, of establishing in the uncultivated Provinces of this [new] world good order and Justice, and the opulence which is natural for them if they are placed under proper management, he proposes, and sends to the Viceroy by this post, another and separate Plan for Intendancies, in imitation of those which exist in the Metropolitan Province. And to the end that Our Sovereign the King may secure the important advantages of quickly aggrandizing the Rich Frontiers of this Empire, he has come to an agreement with the Visitador-General to develop the idea of a General Commandancy, suitably empowered, which shall comprehend under its exclusive administration the aforesaid Provinces of Sonora, Sinaloa, Nueva Viscaya, and the Peninsula of Californias. That region will now begin to recognize the Spanish Power, and to repay part of the great amount that it has cost the Crown and the Nation since its discovery and the foundation of the first Jesuit Missions.

What has most contributed to this idea — which the Viceroy and the Visitador regard as very serviceable, and its execution as quite indispensable — is the previously planned decision which has been reached in Council, and fully approved, that the Visitador shall go to establish Settlements in the said Provinces, and organize the Government of the latter with full powers and Commission from the Viceroy. The object of this action is to facilitate and hasten the erection of such Government and Commandancy upon the footing which is proposed in this Plan, since obstacles can never arise between two faithful Servants of the King who, Moving toward the same end, with upright intentions, always agree in their discussions and unite their efforts, with mutual concessions.

In view of these facts, and with the further incentive of having seen a project which was laid before the Lords Ministers of Madrid in December, 1760, for the creation of a Viceroyalty independent from that of Mexico, and including all the Provinces situated in the great district under the jurisdiction of the Audiencia of Guadalaxara, the Viceroy and the Visitador have concluded that it will be much more advantageous and less expensive to establish an authorized Government and General Commandancy in the three frontier Provinces. For [such a Government], possessing all the powers necessary to maintain them free from the invasions of the Barbarians, and gradually to extend their boundaries, will render them of use to their Sovereign Master; and it will be responsible only to the Chief who represents him in these Domains, and subordinate to him only so far as to report Affairs to him and to request his aid when that may be necessary.

In this manner will be avoided the difficulties, always odious, which usually arise over jurisdiction or limits between coördinate officials when they have similar duties; and by surrendering to the Commandancy of the Frontier Provinces the entire authority — which is indispensable in regions so far distant, in order not to cause failure in opportunities and in the most important projects — the exceedingly important object will be attained of furnishing life and movement to regions so extensive, fruitful and rich by Nature, which can in a few years form a New Empire, equal or even superior to this one of Mexico.

Nor are these advantages and utilities, although great, the only ones which the proposed new Government will yield; for as soon as the activity of a Commandant with authority and energy is felt, many dangers can be averted which now threaten us, by way of the South Sea, from certain foreign Powers who now have an opportunity and the most eager desire to establish some Colony at the Port of Monterrey, or at some other of the many harbors which have already been discovered on the western Coasts of this new World.

In this report is purposely omitted extended discussion of the continual attempts by which France and England have striven, for some two centuries, to find a passage from the Northern to the Southern Sea — especially by their Colonies in this North America — and of the exertions that the Russians are making, through the Sea of Tartary, to penetrate into our Indias. This is partly because Field-Marshal Don Antonio Ricardos departed from here the year before, with the purpose of presenting an elaborate Memorial on these facts, which are more easy to verify in Europe; and partly because the Prime Minister of España knows very well that the English — who now, as a result of the last War, are Masters of Canada and a great part of Luciana [Louisiana] — will spare no expense, diligence, or hardship to push forward the discoveries which the French made through those Colonies, a new Viceroyalty. It has seemed proper to put forth this idea clearly, for the reasons above explained, as well as to avoid so great expenses, when the same results can be obtained by means of the Commandancy which is proposed in this Plan.

Nor is it reckoned expedient that the new Governor and Commander-in-Chief establish his residence in the City of Durango, the Capital of Nueva Viscaya, as was proposed in the year 1760 — not only because that Town is very distant from Sonora, and much farther from the Californias, which at the present time need an active and continual promotion; but because (from the necessity of stationing an Intendant in Durango, if the Separate Plan which is sent be approved), the establishment which is therein proposed would be in any event less advantageous [at Durango]. For the Governors who have hitherto administered Nueva Viscaya have all (excepting the present one) lived in the Town of San Felipe de Chihuahua, which is the Frontier settlement and a very important Mining Centre, where the presence of a Governor who can defend it is certainly needed.

In this connection, likewise, [it may be noted] that for the present the Audiencia of Guadalaxara remains in that Capital, where it was established, with the object of avoiding the great expenses which would assuredly be caused by its transfer; and if in the course of time (which must make known the benefits that the General Commandancy will produce) it shall seem expedient, as it may, to locate the Superior Tribunal of Nueva Galicia, or to erect another, in the Capital which is to be established in Sonora, it would be very easy to carry out that plan then at little expense, and with the knowledge which experience furnishes in all human affairs.

What is judged to be certainly indispensable, and to be immediately effected, is the erection of a central Settlement on the confines of Sonora — either on the shore of the Gila River, or very near it (arrangements being meanwhile made to set up the Government at the Mission of Caborca, as being the station most advanced toward the Frontier), or else at the junction of that River and the Colorado. Then, the Capital of the New Government being located at almost equal distances from the Californias and Nueva Viscaya, its Chief with his administrative measures can proceed to either Province with the same ease — and indeed he ought to travel through them and visit all places, in order that by examining them with his own eyes, and gaining specific knowledge from being actually in the field, he may be enabled to shape his course with good judgment.

No less necessary and useful will be a Mint, which ought to be erected in that same Capital of Sonora, in order that Commerce may have free course, to the benefit of the public and of the Royal Treasury; and that the poor Vassals who have settled in those remote regions may not be under the painful necessity of transporting all the Gold and Silver to Mexico. [This they have done], with only damages and great expenses which utterly ruin them, or, when not so heavy, deprive them of the profits which the richness of the Ores would allow them if they could sell those metals in the same Region where they dig and Smelt them. And, lest it be feared that the establishment of a Mint in that Province would cause notable diminution in the Output of the Mint at Mexico, that of Sonora could be restricted to the coining of only a Million *pesos* each year; for that sum would be sufficient at present to supply that province with Money and to give a like share to the Californias and Nueva Viscaya — where, in truth, through the lack of Money, the King is suffering a great diminution in his Imposts, and the inhabitants intolerable grievances.

In the Capital which should be founded, a Bishop's See also ought to be erected, setting aside for the support of this New Dignity the Province of Sonora, also Sinaloa (which belongs to the Bishopric of Durango, and is at the considerable distance of more than Two Hundred and Fifty leagues), and the Peninsula of Californias. Although the last-named, as is claimed, is included in the Diocese of Guadalaxara, neither the reverend Bishops nor their Visitadors ever possessed any acquaintance with it; and consequently neither is the See of Nueva Galicia injured by the separation of Californias, nor is the loss which that of Durango will actually experience by cutting off from it Sonora and Sinaloa worthy of consideration, for in those territories there are very few Curates and the tithes are almost nothing. But these will very soon be increased, with the Government and General Commandancy in the undeveloped territories which are assigned to the new Bishopric.

It would be idle to enumerate the great [advantages] which the Bishop's See that is proposed in the Metropolis of Sonora would confer on Religion and the state; for the ardent zeal and Apostolic ministry of a Diocesan Prelate would immensely advance the conversion of the Heathen, hastening their reduction by influences near at hand, and conquering many souls for the Creator, at the same pace with which new Domains are acquired for the Sovereign who is His Immediate Vicar in the world. And it is certain that in no part of America are there so fine opportunities and so abundant a harvest as in the confines of Sonora and in the Missions of Californias; for the Tribes of Indians are exceedingly numerous, and their natural disposition renders them most easily persuaded of the infallible truth of the Catholic faith.

In view of these just considerations, the erection of the new See should not be considered a burden, even though it might be necessary at the beginning to assist the Prelate and his limited Church with some revenue from the Royal Treasury; for such pension would not continue long, when we consider the natural fertility of those lands — which, placed under cultivation, will yield the most abundant produce — and just as certainly would the Royal Estate be repaid [for this outlay] and even much more, on account of the richness of the Mines in those Provinces, which are well understood and known by all.

As to what is proper for the General Commandant, it is proposed that he should be independent of the Audiencia and President of Guadalaxara; and it would be necessary to confer on him the salary of twenty thousand *pesos*, in order that he may have barely means on which to live with any [suitable] display in those remote regions, and to meet the expenses of his journeys from one Province to another, without its being necessary for him to avail himself of the [extra] imposts, [now] condemned, which have been tolerated in the Indias, and which have brought them into the melancholy decadence which they are suffering up to the present time. If perchance this salary, and those of the three Intendants who in another Plan are proposed by the Californias, Sonora, and Durango, shall seem excessive, it will be easy to make it evident by experience that the Treasury will be well indemnified for the amount of all these expenses. For after the second year from the establishment of these positions the amount allotted to them certainly cannot reach even the tenth part of the increase which will appear in one branch of revenue alone, the fifths of the Silver and the Gold which may be dug and smelted in Sonora and Californias. To this must be added the revenue from the Pearls; from that fishery, although it might be very abundant on the Coasts of that Peninsula, nothing has been thus far produced to the Royal Treasury.

The greatest saving of expense which should be reckoned upon to the benefit of His Majesty is in the very large expense-accounts [*situados*] of the many Garrisons [*Presidios*] which exist in the Californias, Sonora, and Nueva Viscaya; for, as the profitable idea of establishing Settlements on the Frontiers of these Provinces has for its aim to guard them from the invasions of the Infidel Indians, it will result in liberation from the useless and insupportable burden of so many Garrisons, which, as events prove, are of little or no use. For, although six of these are maintained in the Province of Sonora alone, it is more often invaded and more devastated, than the others — because those Garrisons are, in effect, really Rancherías, and chiefly serve to enrich the Captains and their outfitters.

It is true that, in order to garrison the Capital that is projected in Sonora and to guard the chain of Settlements on the Frontiers (which should be quasi-Military), two Companies of Dragoons and three of Mountain Fusileers, each of a hundred men, will be needed; but nothing is easier than to fill out this force by adding fifty recruits to the two [companies?] who have gone on the Sonora expedition. Taking for granted that the expense of these Veteran Bodies hardly reaches the third part of that which is caused at present by the Garrisons, it is clear that the Royal Treasury, thus coming out with much profit, would be able to pay the salaries of the Commandancy and intendancies; and the Frontiers of the three Provinces would be really shielded from the incursions of the Barbarians. For the new Towns, protected by the Squads into which the Fusileer Companies should be divided, could immediately be put into condition to defend their respective territories, and in time to aid in extending the [Spanish] domination — in view of which, and with these obligations, the Colonists must be established in the new Settlements, giving to each one the Arms necessary for his defense.

With the five Companies of Veteran Infantry and Cavalry, the Militia which the new Towns ought to form, and those who may be recruited in the Town of San Felipe de Chihuahua and its vicinity, it is estimated that the new General Commandant will be able for the present to maintain the defense of the Provinces embraced in his Government. If afterward he shall need, as is probable, larger forces for the expeditions which he will find expedient to send out for the purpose of advancing the Conversions and discoveries, it should not be difficult to increase the troops, either regular or provincial, when experience makes known the great benefits which are promised by this useful establishment in Provinces which are undoubtedly more abundant and rich in mineral products than any others that have been discovered in this Northern America.

Recently news has come that [the English have gone] as far as the Lake of Bois, from which issues the deep-flowing River of the West, directing its course, as discovered, toward the Sea of that name; and if it empties therein, or reaches the South Sea, or is (as may be the case) the famous Colorado River, which forms the Gulf of Californias, there is no doubt, in whichever of these alternatives, that we already have the English very near to our Settlements in New Mexico, and not very distant from the Western Coast of this Continent of America.

Moreover, the Prime Minister of our Court knows, from the voyages and memoirs that are published in Europe, that the Russians have been gaining an intimate knowledge of the navigation of the Sea of Tartary; and that they are, according to very credible and well-grounded statements, carrying on the Fur Trade on a Continent or Island which, it is estimated, lies at the distance of only eight hundred leagues from the Western Coast of Californias, which runs as far as Capes Mendocino and Blanco.

But, while the attempts of Russia and England need not revive at this time all the suspicions and anxieties that Spain manifested in former days (especially after the Reign of Felipe Second) for discovering and gaining possession, by way of the South Sea, of the alleged passage which the other Nations were seeking by way of the North Sea, it is indubitable that since the year 1749 [sic] — in which Admiral Anson came to the Western Coast of this Kingdom, as far as the entrance to the Port of Acapulco — the English and the Dutch (who afterward brought their ships from Eastern India within sight of Cape San Lucas and the Coasts of New Galicia) have acquired a very detailed knowledge of the Ports and Bays which we hold on the South

Coast, especially in the Peninsula of Californias. With all this no one can regard it as impossible or even very difficult for one of those two Nations or for the Moscovites to establish, when that is least expected, a Colony at the Port of Monterrey, where they would have all desirable facilities and conveniences; and that thus we should come to see our North America invaded and exploited by way of the South Sea as it has been by that of the North.

In these circumstances, it seems as if worldly prudence may counsel, and even carry into effect, that we should take proper precautions in time, putting into practice whatever measures may be feasible to avert the dangers that threaten us. And, as at present the Peninsula of Californias is free from obstruction, it follows that we should and easily could — its population being increased by the aid of the free Commerce which ought to be carried on between that territory and this Kingdom — transport a Colony to the Port of Monterrey with the same vessels that we now have in the South Sea, which have been built for the use of the Sonora expedition. It only remains to establish in this Province the General Commandancy, which very soon can promote and facilitate the Settlement of Monterrey, and of other points on the Western Coast of the same Californias — where there are good Harbors, and the soil is more fertile and productive than that of the North Shore.

A Chief who is on the ground and energetic will secure considerable extensions to the Frontiers of Sonora and Nueva Viscaya, unless he is insufficiently provided with the funds that are necessary in order that the establishment of his Government may produce the utilities and advantages that ought to be expected. These are set forth at length in the project, already cited, which was presented to the Court in the year 1760, with the aim of securing the erection [of such a Government]. If the decision be reached that it is more expedient to maintain on the Frontiers of Chihuahua an Official, subordinate to the Governor, for the defense of that Mining Centre, a suitable person for that employ is Captain Don Lope de Cuellar, who was appointed by the Viceroy in fulfillment of the instructions addressed to him for the

expulsion of the regulars belonging to the Company [of Jesus].
As that measure would do away with the office of *corregidor* that
was established in that Town, which enjoys very considerable
imposts, from the fund that they produce can be drawn the Salary of two thousand *pesos*, which of course will be an addition to
his pay sufficient to maintain the said Governor. At the same
time he ought to look after the affairs of the Royal Treasury,
with rank as Deputy of the Intendant of Nueva Viscaya — who
must reside in the Capital City of Durango, and be, like the Intendants of Sonora and Californias, directly subordinate to the
General Commandant of the three Provinces, since that Chief
is responsible for rendering account to the Viceroy of Nueva
España of whatever enterprises he may undertake, and of all
occurrences worthy of note in the region under his command.

An examination of this plan will make evident at first view
that in it are discussed only the principal points and designs of
the idea, and that its sole aim, with nothing else in view, is to
promote the public Interests of the King and the State in an
establishment which, besides the urgent necessity of effecting
it, carries the special recommendation that it will be very advantageous in a short time; for, from now on, the Foundations of
the Work are going to be laid with Solidity, Integrity, and Zeal.

At Mexico, the twenty-third of January, [in the year] One
Thousand, Seven Hundred, and Sixty-Eight.

DON JOSÉ DE GÁLVEZ.

To THE MARQUÉS DE CROIX.

APPENDIX B

EXPEDITION WHICH WAS MADE BY DON PEDRO FAGES, LIEUTENANT OF THE CATALONIAN VOLUNTEERS, WITH SIX SOLDIERS AND A MULETEER

[Archives of Mexico. Cor. Vir., Sér. iii, T N 4/14, 1176, f. 385 (*Sc.* 385–389). A. Gen. y Púb., Croix, 1770–71, 4/14, copy no. 2. This document (here published for the first time) is a diary kept by Lieutenant Fages on a tour of exploration made by him to San Francisco Bay in 1770. The translation is by Miss Emma Helen Blair, of Madison, Wisconsin]

November 21, 1770. We set out from Monterrey about 11 o'clock, and immediately went around the head of a large inlet, and took a N. E. course. After a march of three leagues, we halted on the other side of the River Carmelo, a name which was given to it by mistake at the first exploration of Monterrey. All day we traveled through somewhat rolling country, part of it good soil, part sandy.

November 22. We set out early in the morning, crossed the flats of the aforesaid River, and at four leagues distance we entered the Arroyo, in which no water flowed; it was thickly set with Alders, Live-oaks, and other Trees which we could not identify. We saw many paths made by bears, which we knew by the locks of their hair; only the path which we followed [showed the tracks] of Heathens. We went forward through this Arroyo about a league, and, following in the same direction on the slope of a hill, ascended to the top of it, from which we descried at some distance a spacious Valley; this was four leagues broad in some places, and ran from N.W. to S.E. We descended by the slope of a hill, and after going one eighth of a league came to a narrow Valley which ran from N.E. to S.W., in which we made our camp. It contained a small Arroyo with water, which ended

not far away among its own scanty sands; its breadth was 200
Varas, and it received the name la Cañadita ["the little brook"].
This day's march was five leagues. [On the left-hand margin
is written: "To la Cañadita, 5 leagues"; on the right-hand margin, "From Monterrey, 8 leagues."]

November 23. We left the Camp at la Cañadita, and after
marching half a league reached the large Valley which we saw
from the top of the Hill; we crossed it, which cost us three leagues.
We saw on the way many herds of Wild Pigs [*Berrendos*], and
some of these numbered more than 50; we also saw many Geese,
of which we killed four. The Soil of this Valley was very good.
From this place we crossed a small valley abounding in patches
of reeds, which at the right-hand side had a Pool of fresh water.
Very soon afterward we had to cross an Arroyo in which Alders
grew thickly, and this one had a large Pool of fresh water. After
that, we made our way through a gap in the Mountain range
that lay before us; it was overgrown with Oaks, and had many
Freshwater Pools, which at the edges were thickly fringed with
reeds [*tule*]. At a little distance from them we halted, in the bend
of a Hill at the foot of which ran a tiny Rivulet, which hardly
supplied drink for our Animals. This day's march was four
leagues, in a N.E. Direction.

In the evening of this day a reconnoissance was made in the
direction of the N.E., for the distance of some two leagues,
climbing up a very rocky Hill; from the top of this was seen an
immense number of Ridges which stretched directly across our
course, which obliged us to retrace our steps. This place was
called los Berrendos. [On the left margin: "To the Pools, 4
leagues"; on the right margin, "From Monterrey, 12 leagues."]

November 24. We left this Camp, and, returning on our path
for the distance of a league, which we had marched on the preceding day, we took a N.W. direction, through the Valley which
we had crossed the day before, on the right-hand side along
the foot of the Hills which shut it in, leaving on the left hand
many patches of reeds. We crossed many bear-trails, and at the
end of them was a very large Pond. At the upper end of this
was a Ranchería of Heathens, in which we saw about fifty Souls.

Two of these Heathens were going with two little Rafts to hunt
Ducks in the Pond. With all the efforts that we made, we could
not succeed in pacifying them; the only result was, that they
uttered loud cries, and two of them hastened over the plain to
notify of our passage two very large Rancherías which stood in
the middle of it, within our view. In consequence, the people
rushed out to gaze on us, at a distance, and were lost in admiration at seeing a soldier, as he marched, kill nine Geese with three
shots. We continued our journey, and when we had completed
a five leagues' march, we halted on a rising ground close to the
same Valley, between two little Springs [*Ojitos*] of excellent
water. Camp of los Ojitos. [On the left margin: "To the Camp
of los Ojitos, 5 leagues"; on the right margin, "From Monterrey, 17 leagues."]

November 25. We set out from the Camp of los Ojitos and
crossed some Hills, not very high, which stood close to the Camp,
and went toward the same Valley, to the N.W. All this day's
March was over level Ground, of good soil, with many Oaks
and some Live-oaks. On the right hand we left an Arroyo which
came out of the Ridge, thickly set with Alders, but containing
no water. The Ridge which we were leaving to the right was
very bare, having many outcroppings of Ore Rock [*Panino*]
which showed various sorts of lustre; and some of the Soldiers
said that it seemed to have traces of Metals, for which reason
I gave orders that some pieces of it be collected. This day we
advanced about five leagues; we came to a halt under a Hill on
the right hand, which formed a slender Rivulet [*Arroyto*] of excellent water, enough for us and the Animals. [On the left margin: "To the Camp at el Arroyto, 5 leagues"; on the right margin:
"From Monterrey, 22 leagues."]

November 26. We started very early in the morning, and continued to follow the same Valley, although now its course was
deflected toward the N.N.W. We proceeded some four leagues,
over ground thickly set with Oaks, Live-oaks, and other Trees
which we could not identify. On the way we descried a very
large Ranchería of mountain Heathens, and when we undertook
to go near it the people took to flight; nevertheless, we were able

to pacify them with the many trinkets that we offered them, and induced them to accept some strings of Glass Beads, and Ribbons. We saw likewise two other Rancherías, but small ones, and some columns of smoke on each side of the Valley. Four Heathens followed us until we made halt at the head of the *Estero* of the Port of San Francisco, alongside a river, [in a place] which had some Pools of excellent fresh water. [On the left margin: "To the Estero of San Francisco, 4 leagues"; on the right margin, "From Monterrey, 26 leagues."]

November 27. We set out in the early morning, crossing the Valley in a N.E. direction, which cost us about two leagues. We went around the heads of many inlets which branch from the large one, and took a Northerly direction; and after going one league we had to pass an Arroyo abounding in Alders and other Trees, which had no water. Near this was a lake of excellent fresh water, the circumference of which was fringed with reeds, rushes, and many grassy places — among which were abundance of Geese, and we succeeded in killing seven of them. We saw close by the Lake many Heathens, of friendly and pleasant manner, to whom we presented some strings of Glass Beads; they returned the favor by giving us some Feathers, and Geese stuffed with Grass, which they use [as decoys] in order to catch enormous numbers of these Birds. At three leagues from this place we passed an Arroyo with considerable water, well covered with Alders, Laurels, and other Trees which we did not recognize, and halted in a level spot close by.

The entire March of this day was six leagues; the Soil was very good, and full of cracks, which made crosses in more than one sense of the word. We passed two Rivulets of very good water, and we marched all Day, leaving at the right hand some Hills — not very high, of good Soil, and here and there the Slopes dotted with many Laurels.

November 28. Four Soldiers went out to explore the Country, and at night they came back, saying that they had gone about seven leagues toward the North. They said that the land was very good, and level; that they had climbed to the top of a Hill, but had not been able to discern the end of an inlet which lay before them and communicated with the one which was at our left hand. They had seen many tracks of cloven feet, which they believed to be those of Mexican Bulls [*Zibolos: i. e.*, buffaloes]; also that close to the Hills which they left at the right hand were some little springs of Water, and that they had crossed two little streams like it. They added that they had seen the mouth of the *estero* which they believed was the one which had its entrance through the Bay of the Port of San Francisco — which I made certain by having viewed it.

November 29. On this day we determined to return to our starting-point, on seeing that it was impossible for us to pass over to the other side of the Punta de los Reyes without wasting many days' time, also because of the anxiety that I felt about the Camp, the Farm-work, and the care of the Cattle. Retracing the march that we had made on the 27th, we halted in the same place [as then], without anything new occurring. This day's march was the same [as before], six leagues. As we passed along our way, near a little brook about 20 Heathens came out to see us; and some of the women began to entertain us with Dancing and many gestures of joy. One of the Women made us a quite long harangue. We gave them some large Beads, and they returned the compliment with some Feather ornaments. We saw on this day the smoke from many fires.

November 30. We set out at an early hour from the Head of the Inlet, and marched four leagues. We passed along the edge of a small Ranchería, in which there were four Women and three Infants; they were frightened, and gave us two stuffed Geese. We halted at the same place which we occupied and from which we set out on the 26th.

December 1. When we started the Sun was already high, because we had lost some Animals; but we encountered them along the road on which we were returning. This day we marched five leagues, the same as on November 25.

December 2. Early in the morning we set out, in a S.E. direction, and marched five leagues without the least incident. The Land was the same as on November 25; and we halted about half a league from the place where the little springs were, on the Monterrey side, at some little Pools in a small Arroyo.

December 3. We began our march an hour after the Sun rose, because we had lost two Animals, but we found them after we had gone a league. We crossed the Valley, leaving at the left hand the ranchería, Pond, and reedy ground, and at the right the [smaller] rancherías that we had seen on November 24; and they even seemed to us much larger [than before]. After going five leagues we reached the Camp of la Cañadita, at which we came to a halt and pitched our Camp.

December 4. We started early in the morning, climbing up the slope which we had descended on the 22d of November, and went toward the Arroyo, which we crossed on the same day, crossing the flats in it, where we saw many flocks of Geese. We came to the river, which we crossed at the same place as before; and after marching eight leagues we arrived at this Royal Presidio of San Carlos at Monterrey, where we found that nothing new had occurred. This expedition was made in the service of His Majesty, with the object of reconnoitring the country as far as the Port of San Francisco.

PEDRO FAGES.

APPENDIX C

GOVERNORS OF THE CALIFORNIAS

(Spanish Régime 1767–1804)

(Dates of service in the case of each governor are from assumption to surrender of office.)

Gaspar de Portolá,
November 30, 1767, to July 9, 1770.

From May 21, 1769, Portolá's position was in fact that of Comandante-militar for Alta California. From July 9, 1770, to May 25, 1774, the position of Comandante was filled by Pedro Fages; and from May 25, 1774, to February, 1777, by Fernando Rivera y Moncada.

Matías de Armona,
June 12, 1769, to November 9, 1770.

After Armona's appointment, but prior to his arrival on June 12, 1769, Diego (?) González served as lieutenant-governor. From June 24, 1769, to June 13, 1770, Armona was absent in Sonora, and Juan Gutiérrez served as lieutenant, or acting, governor, to October 3, 1769, when he was succeeded by Antonio López de Toledo, who served until June 13, 1770. From November 9, 1770 (date of Armona's retirement) the acting governor was Bernardino Moreno.

Felipe Barri,
March ——, 1770, to March 4, 1775.

Felipe de Neve,
March 4, 1775, to July 12, 1782.

In February, 1777, Neve took up his residence at Monterey in Alta California, and Rivera y Moncada went south to assume the lieutenant-governorship at Loreto. The acting lieutenant-governor, pending Rivera's arrival, was Joaquín Cañete.

APPENDIX 521

Pedro Fages,
July 12, 1782, to April 16, 1791.

On July 18, 1781, Rivera y Moncada was killed on the Colorado, and Joaquín Cañete served as lieutenant-governor till late in November, 1783, when he was succeeded by José Joaquín de Arrillaga.

Antonio Romeu,
April 16, 1791, to April 9, 1792.

José Joaquín de Arrillaga,
April 9, 1792, to May 14, 1794.

During this period, Arrillaga was lieutenant-governor and Comandante of Lower California, and governor of the Californias *ad interim*.

Diego de Borica,
May 14, 1794, to March 8, 1800.

José Joaquín de Arrillaga,
March 8, 1800, to November 16, 1804.

Until March 11, 1802, when he died, Pedro de Alberni, who outlived Arrillaga, was Comandante-militar for Alta California.

GOVERNORS OF ALTA CALIFORNIA
(Spanish Régime 1804–1821)

(The decree making Alta California a separate province bore date August 29, 1804, and reached Arrillaga November 16.)

José Joaquín de Arrillaga,
November 16, 1804, to July 24, 1814.

José Darío Argüello,
July 24, 1814, to August 30, 1815.

Governor *ad interim*.

Pablo Vicente de Sola,
August 30, 1815, to November 10, 1822.

GOVERNORS OF ALTA CALIFORNIA
(Mexican Régime 1821–1847)

Luis Antonio Argüello,
November 10, 1822, to November ——, 1825.

Until April 2, 1823, Argüello's authority was derived from the Spanish Regency. After that date until November 17 it was derived from Iturbide as Agustín I. After November 17 it was derived from the *Congreso Constituyente* [National Congress]. In March, 1823, Iturbide named Naval Captain Bonifacio de Tosta governor of Alta California.

José María Echeandía,
November ——, 1825, to January
31, 1831.

In 1824 José Miñón was appointed
governor of Alta California, but
he declined the office.

Manuel Victoria,
January 31, 1831, to December 6,
1831.

Antonia García was first appointed as Echeandía's successor,
but the appointment was revoked.

José María Echeandía,
November 6, 1831, to January 14,
1833.

De facto *Jefe político* and *jefe
militar* in the district south of, but
not including, Santa Bárbara.

Pío Pico,
January 27 to February 16, 1832.

Jefe político by appointment of
the Diputación.

Agustín V. Zamorano,
February 1, 1832, to January 14,
1833.

De facto *Jefe militar* in the district
north of and including Santa Bárbara.

José Figueroa,
January 14, 1833, to September
29, 1835.

Early in 1833 Figueroa asked to
be relieved of office. On July 16th,
1833, José María Híjar was appointed *jefe político*, but the appointment was revoked by President Santa Anna on July 25. On
July 18, 1834, Figueroa withdrew
his request to be relieved.

José Castro,
September 29, 1835, to January 2,
1836.

From October 8, 1835, to January 1, 1836, the position of *jefe
militar* was held by Nicolás Gutiérrez.

Nicolás Gutiérrez,
January 2 to May 3, 1836.

Mariano Chico,
May 3 to August 1, 1836.

Nicolás Gutiérrez,
August 1 to November 5, 1836.

José Castro,
November 5 to December 7, 1836.

Castro was *jefe militar* until November 29, when he was succeeded by Mariano Guadalupe
Vallejo.

Juan Bautista Alvarado,
December 7, 1836, to December 31,
1842.

Manuel Micheltorena,
December 31, 1842, to February 22,
1845.

Pío Pico,
February 22, 1845, to August 10,
1846.

José María Flóres,
October 31, 1846, to January 11,
1847.

Andrés Pico,
January 11 to January 13, 1847.

Until August 7, 1839, Alvarado was governor *ad interim.* On June 6, 1837, Carlos Carrillo was appointed governor, and on December 6, he assumed office at Los Ángeles, but he was arrested and deposed by Alvarado on May 20, 1838.

By the departmental junta Pío Pico was declared governor *ad interim* on February 15, 1845.

José Castro was *jefe militar* for same period.

APPENDIX D

THE SPANISH FOUNDERS OF SAN FRANCISCO

[From the diary of Fray Pedro Font, A. D. 1776, and here printed (it is believed) for the first time. Original document is in the John Carter Brown Library at Providence, R. I.]

SERGEANT, soldiers, and settlers, with their respective families, whom — by order of his Excellency the Viceroy — Don Juan Bautista de Anza, lieutenant-colonel of cavalry and captain of the Royal Presidio of Tubac, in the province of Sonora, has conducted to the presidio of Monterey in Northern California, for the purpose of turning them over to their comandante, Don Fernando de Rivera y Moncada.

Presidio Soldiers

1. Lieutenant Don Joseph Joachín Moraga came without wife and family because of the illness of his wife, whom he left in Terrente where he lives.

1. Sergeant Juan Pablo Grijalva and his wife María Dolores.

Valencia.
Children:
María Josepha,
5. María del Carmen,
Claudio.

Domingo Alviso
and his wife,
María Angela Chumasero.
Children:
6. Francisco Xavier,
Juan Ignacio,
María Loreto.

Valero Mesa,
and his wife,
María Leonor Barboa.

Rosalia Samora,
wife of Salvador Manuel.

Ygnacio Linares,
and his wife,
Gertrudis Rivas.
6. Children:
José Ramón,
Salvador Ygnacio,
María Gertrudis,
María Juliana.

Justo Roverto,
and his wife,
María Loreto Delfina.
4. Children:
Joseph Antonio,
Joseph Matias.

8. Children:
Joseph Joachín,
Joseph Ignacio,
Joseph Dolores.
Joseph Antonio,
Juan,
María Manuela.

Ramón Bajórquez,
and his wife,
María Francisca Rovero.
4. Children:
María Gertrudis,
María Michaela.

Carlos Gallegos,
2.   and his wife,
María Josepha Espinosa.

Juan Antonio Amézquita,
and his wife,
Juana Goana.
Children:
Salvador Manuel,
8. María Josepha,
María Dolores,
María Matilde,
María de los Reyes.

Antonio Quiterio Aceves,
and his wife,
María Feliciana Cortés.
Children:
8. Joseph Cipriano,
Juan Gregorio,
Juan Pablo,
Joseph Antonio,
María Petra,
María Gertrudis.

Phelipe Santiago Tapia,
and his wife,
Juan María Cárdenas.
11. Children:
Joseph Bartolomé,
Juan Joseph,
Joseph Cristóval,
Joseph Francisco,
Joseph Victor,

Gabriel Peralta,
and his wife,
Francisca Manuela Valenzuela.
6. Children:
Juan Joseph,
Luis María,
Pedro,
Gertrudis.

Soldiers (Recruits)
Juan Athanasio Vázquez,
and his wife,
Gertrudis Castelo.
Children:
Josepha Tiburcio,
6. Joseph Antonio,
Pedro Joseph,
María Antonio Bajórquez,
wife of Joseph Tiburcio.

Joseph Antonio García,
and his wife,
Petronila Josepha.
7. Children:
Joseph Vicente,
Joseph Francisco,
Juan Guillermo,
María Graciana,
María Josepha.

Lasa Ortiz.
Children:
4. Juan Francisco,
María Francisca.

Ygnacio Soto,
and his wife,
Bárbara Espinosa.
4. Children:
Joseph Antonio,
María Francisca.

Pablo Pinto,
Francisca Xaviera Ruelas.
Children:
6. Juan María,
Joseph Marcelo,
Juana Santos,
Juana.

María Rosa,
María Antonio,
María Manuela,
María Ysidora.

Ygnacia María Gutiérrez,
 and his wife,
Ana María Ossuna.
5. Children:
María de los Santos,
María Petra,
Diego Pascual.

Agustín Valenzuela,
 and his wife,
3. Petra Ygnacia Ochoa.
Children:
María Zeferina.

Luis Joachín Álvarez de Acenedo,
 and his wife,
María Nico.
5. Children:
Francisca María,
Ygnacio María,
María Gertrudis.

Sebastián Antonio López,
 and his wife,
Phelipa Neri.
5. Children:
Sebastián,
María Thomasa,
María Justa.

Juan Francisco Vernal,
 and his wife,
María Soto.
Children:
9. Joseph Dionisio,
Joseph Joachín,
Joseph Apolinario,
Juan Francisco,
Thomás Januario,
Ana María,
María Theresa.

Juan Salvio Pacheco,
 and his wife,
María Carmen del Valle.

Joseph Antonio Sotélo,
 and his wife,
3. Peralta.
Children:
Ramón.

Pedro Bajórquez,
 and his wife,
3. María Francesca de Lara.
Children:
María Agustina.

Santiago de la Cruz Pico,
 and his wife,
María Jacinta Bostida.
Children:
8. Joseph María,
Joseph Dolores,
Joseph Patricio,
Francisco Javier,
María Antonia Thomasa.

Joseph Manuel Valencia,
 and his wife,
María de la Luz Muñoz.

María Encarnación.
María Martina.
Vicente Félix (widower).
 (His wife died on the way,
 on the 24th of November at
 dawn.)
Children:
Joseph Francisco,
Joseph Dorotheo,
Joseph de Jesús,
Joseph Antonio Capistrano,
María Loreto,
María Antonia,
María Manuela.

Casimiro Varela,
1. Marida de Juana,
Santos Pinto.

1. Ygnasio Anastasio Higuera —
 husband of Michaela Bajórquez.

7. Children:
Miguel,
Francisco.

Joseph Antonio Sánchez,
   and his wife,
María Dolores Morales.
Children:
5. Joseph Antonio,
María Josepha,
Ygnacio Cárdenas
   (his adopted son).

Joachín Ysidro Castro,
   and his wife,
María Martina Botiller.
Children:
Ygnacio Clemente,
11. Joseph Mariano,
Francisco,
Francisco Antonio,
Carlos Antonio,
Ana Josepha.

Nicolás Galindo,
   and his wife,
3. Theresa Pinto.
Children:
Juan Venancio.

Pedro Pérez de la Puente,
Marcos Villela,
3. Dn. Francisco Muñoz.
   (The three are unmarried.)

Christóval Sandoval,
1.   and his wife,
Dolores Ontiveros.

Feliciana Arballa,
   (widow),
3. María Thomasa Gutiérrez,
María Eustaquia.
   (The three are unmarried.)

Bartholomé.
María Gertrudis.
Bárbara.

Manuel Ramírez Arrellano,
   and his wife,
4. María Agueda López de Aro.
Children:
Mariano Mathias Vega
   (his adopted son).

Settlers who were not Soldiers
Joseph Manuel Gonzáles,
   and his wife,
María Michaela Ruez.
Children:
6. Juan Joseph,
Ramón,
Francisco,
María Gregoria.

Nicolás Antonio Berrélleza,
2. María Ysabel Berrelleza.
   (Brother and sister, and unmarried.)

According to this list, there were 193 persons. I do not know if it be complete or lacks some name, since I was not permitted to be informed; yet I was so far favored as to be allowed to see the list, which I copied.

APPENDIX E

SEALED ORDERS ISSUED TO COMMODORE ROBERT F. STOCKTON IN 1845

[These orders have never before appeared in print. The author is indebted for them to the courtesy of the U. S. Navy Department.]

S. O. NAVY DEPARTMENT,
October 17, 1845.

Commodore R. F. Stockton,
Comdg. U. S. S. Congress,
Norfolk, Va.

COMMODORE, — So soon as the U. S. frigate, of which you have volunteered to take the command, shall be in all respects ready for sea, and you shall have received Messrs. Ten Eyck and Terrell, the Commissioner and Consul to the Sandwich Islands, you will proceed directly to the Pacific, touching at such ports as you may think proper.

On reaching the Pacific, you will by letter, as often as occasion offers, inform Commodore Sloat of your approach, and will, in the mean time, make the best of your way to the Sandwich Islands.

You will there land Messrs. Ten Eyck and Terrell at the place of their destination. During your presence at the Islands, you will do all in your power to cherish, on the part of their government, good feelings towards the United States. You may find there United States stores of which you will avail yourself.

Having done this duty at the Sandwich Islands, you will next proceed with all dispatch to perform the special duty assigned you by the sealed instructions which you are not to open till you pass the Capes of Virginia.

You will communicate to all the officers under your command the order of this Department that no one be concerned in a duel.

Commending you and your ship's company to the protection of Divine Providence, and wishing you all a pleasant cruise and a safe return to your country and friends, I am,

Very respectfully,
GEORGE BANCROFT.

NAVY DEPARTMENT, Octo. 17, 1845.

SEALED ORDERS,
not to be opened till the U. S. Frigate " CONGRESS"
shall be without the Capes of Virginia.

Commodore R. F. Stockton,
    Commanding U. S. Frigate "CONGRESS."

SIR: So soon as the U. S. Frigate "CONGRESS," under your command, shall be in all respects ready for Sea, you will proceed directly to the Pacific, touching at such ports on your way as you may think necessary. You will find Commodore Sloat as soon as possible and report to him as forming part of the squadron under his command. The dispatches for Commodore Sloat, herewith forwarded to you, you will deliver so soon as you have opportunity.

When you have finished your duties at the Sandwich Islands, you will sail directly for Monterey, and in person, or by a perfectly trustworthy hand, deliver the enclosed letter to our Consul at that place. You will confer with the Consul, gain all the information you can on Mexican affairs and do all in your power to conciliate the good feeling of the people of that place towards the United States. On leaving Monterey, you will join the squadron of Commodore Sloat.

Commending you and your ship's company to the protection of Divine Providence, and wishing you all a pleasant cruise and a safe return to your country and your friends, I am,

                    Very respectfully,
                            GEORGE BANCROFT.

INDEX

INDEX

𝕿𝖍𝖊 𝕽𝖎𝖛𝖊𝖗𝖘𝖎𝖉𝖊 𝕻𝖗𝖊𝖘𝖘

CAMBRIDGE . MASSACHUSETTS

U . S . A